Human-Computer Interaction Series

Human-Computer Interaction is a multidisciplinary field focused on human aspects of the development of computer technology. As computer-based technology becomes increasingly pervasive – not just in developed countries, but worldwide – the need to take a human-centered approach in the design and development of this technology becomes ever more important. For roughly 30 years now, researchers and practitioners in computational and behavioral sciences have worked to identify theory and practice that influences the direction of these technologies, and this diverse work makes up the field of human-computer inter-action. Broadly speaking, it includes the study of what technology might be able to do for people and how people might interact with the technology.

In this series, we present work which advances the science and technology of developing systems which are both effective and satisfying for people in a wide variety of contexts. The human-computer interaction series will focus on theoretical perspectives (such as formal approaches drawn from a variety of behavioral sciences), practical approaches (such as the techniques for effectively integrating user needs in system development), and social issues (such as the determinants of utility, usability and acceptability).

Author guidelines: www.springer.com/authors/book+authors > Author Guidelines

For further volumes:
http://www.springer.com/series/6033

Panos Markopoulos · Boris de Ruyter ·
Wendy Mackay
Editors

Awareness Systems

Advances in Theory, Methodology,
and Design

 Springer

Editors
Assoc. Prof. Panos Markopoulos
Eindhoven Univ. of Techn.
Dept. Industrial Design
Den Dolech 2
5612 AZ Eindhoven
The Netherlands
p.markopoulos@tue.nl

Boris de Ruyter
Philips Research Laboratories
Prof. Holstlaan 4
5656 AA Eindhoven
The Netherlands
boris.de.ruyter@philips.com

Wendy Mackay
Universite Paris Sud
INRIA
490 Batiment
91045 Orsay Cedex
France
mackay@lri.fr

ISSN 1571-5035
ISBN 978-1-4471-2285-2   ISBN 978-1-84882-477-5 eBook
DOI 10.1007/978-1-84882-477-5
Springer Dordrecht Heidelberg London New York

British Library Cataloguing in Publication Data
A catalogue record for this book is available from the British Library

Printed on acid-free paper

Springer is part of Springer Science+Business Media (www.springer.com)

Preface

1 About Awareness and Awareness Systems

As people engage in ordinary activities, they maintain *awareness* of others around them, which amounts to *an understanding regarding what others do, where they are, or what they say*. This understanding can help people in making inferences regarding intentions, actions or even emotions of others and provides a context for their shared activities and social interactions. Awareness of others extends to people not in the immediate vicinity but of whom one can have an understanding of whereabouts and current activities, within some time frame, e.g., knowing the whereabouts of a friend or their state of mind after a recent meeting or thanks to a recent communication.

Awareness systems can be broadly defined as *systems intended to help people construct and maintain awareness of each others' activities, context or status, even when the participants are not co-located.* Supporting awareness can bring about important, if subtle, benefits, such as increasing the effectiveness of collaborative work, fostering social relationships and improving the general well-being of individuals. The work described in this volume addresses these themes, making explicit the nature of these benefits and how they are attained through the design and use of awareness systems.

Importantly the definitions above focus on awareness of people rather than on systems and their environment. This can be contrasted to the concept of *situation awareness* as this has been studied extensively in the field of human factors. Situation awareness can be understood as "knowing what is going on" or more precisely "the perception of the elements in the environment within a volume of time and space, the comprehension of their meaning and the projection of their status in the near future." (Endsley and Garland, 2000, p. 5) A more generic definition of situation awareness is provided by Sarter and Woods (1991) as "the accessibility of a comprehensive and coherent situation representation which is continuously being updated in accordance with the results of recurrent situation assessments."

Both these definitions of situation awareness assume an objective reality, an actual situation that the individual concerned has to understand in order to operate successfully. The accuracy of this understanding is paramount for ensuring successful performance. Some notion of completeness with respect to a bounded task domain is implicitly assumed to be meaningful and desirable. The design of systems to support situation awareness can then be reframed as choosing the appropriate representations, appropriate abstractions and aggregations of information to overcome limitations of human perception and cognition.

In the context of cooperative work, the classic notion of situation awareness can be applied to describe awareness of actions and context of others, through which individuals align and integrate interdependent activities: "the up-to-the minute knowledge of other people's activities that is required for an individual to coordinate and complete their part of a group task" (see Gutwin and Greenberg, 2002). Taking this perspective, awareness pertains to knowledge of others and phenomena that are not tangential or external to the task (Schmidt, 2002).

This book takes a broader perspective on awareness that examines the social interactions between individuals and groups. In this context, awareness takes a different meaning and can serve a different purpose. Individuals may seek awareness for their own sake, as a means for understanding their own self, reflecting on relations with others or simply as a means for engaging with their social network. At work they may seek awareness of the social context, giving rise to informal and serendipitous interactions (Dourish and Bly, 1992) and knowledge sharing. At leisure they may seek the formation and strengthening of social ties (Markopoulos et al., 2005) or provide affective support to each other (Romero et al., 2007).

Contrary to the assumptions underlying the notion of situation awareness, accuracy and completeness of awareness is not the golden standard to strive for. Full knowledge of activities of others is usually not at all desirable, with people preferring to control the flow of information from others (Palen and Dourish, 2003) or preferring to cooperatively agree on setting limits to this awareness in order to facilitate social processes and allow equivocation and politeness (Aoki and Woodruff, 2005).

The discussion on awareness in this volume highlights a number of issues that become important when awareness is considered in the context of social interactions: how individuals assign meaning to information provided by others, how they selectively attend to this information, how intentions are assigned to information provided to others and how the awareness that results is associated with benefits and costs for individuals.

Apart from a narrower focus on the object of awareness, a major departure from the theme of situation awareness concerns the granularity and purpose of awareness. Whereas situation awareness typically concerns the time frame of a particular task or a mission, this volume considers a much more variable time frame that may even extend to weeks or months.

Another departure from the concept of situation awareness concerns its purpose. While situation awareness considers that the purpose of awareness is to support a task typically involving some decision, in the present context, awareness is often an end in itself that provides affective benefits, e.g., staying in touch, feeling connected or lowering the barriers for serendipitous social interactions between individuals. The same awareness information may be used and appropriated by individuals to address different purposes: to coordinate a shared activity, to appraise a social relation or even to reflect on one's self and one's relations with others.

Current awareness systems have been deeply influenced by the *media spaces* of the late 1980s, which supported sustained audio/video links among remote coworkers and emphasized the importance of awareness for maintaining social coherence; see Bly et al. (1993) for an excellent review of this literature. At the time computer-supported cooperative work systems were usually measured in terms of productivity, the benefits of awareness proved difficult to operationalize (Gross et al., 2005). As a result, awareness systems were sometimes criticized as having marginal benefit (Schmidt, 2002) and were largely ignored for a decade.

However, the prevalence of the World Wide Web and significantly cheaper consumer electronics has led to a resurgence of interest in awareness systems, both as research prototypes and as commercial applications. No longer expensive and difficult to install or maintain awareness systems have moved from the office into domestic and health-care environments and are starting to appear on mobile devices as well.

Today, many of the functions that appeared in early research prototypes have reached the general public: instant messaging and mobile phones provide awareness cues about others who are currently online and Internet-connected photo frames and robots permit users to display awareness information, either from broadcasts such as the weather or from members of one's social network. As this technology becomes more affordable, with greater quality and diversity, awareness systems offer tremendous potential for innovation, with a wide range of forms and contexts for transforming the space around us.

The research culture has changed as well, making it easier to justify systems in terms of their support for maintaining informal social relationships, both in the home and the office, and valuing systems that move beyond simple collaboration. For example, Putman (2000) defines the creation of social capital as an important feature of social organization and argues that systems should support social relations, including the norms, networks and trust that facilitate cooperation and co-ordination for mutual benefit. We adopt a correspondingly broad interpretation of awareness and a more inclusive consideration of potential benefits.

2 About This Volume

The pragmatic and broad definition presented in the previous paragraph was adopted recognizing that a bewildering variety of practices, application domains, and systems are associated with the terms awareness and awareness systems.

Awareness systems vary greatly, applying different strategies for collecting, communicating and displaying information and serving diverse purposes. Awareness research is often characterized along specific axes such as the location or the context of use of awareness systems, e.g., at work, at home, and on the move, or time/duration over which awareness is built up ranging from momentary pauses to months-long connections. Some awareness systems are utilitarian, designed to support awareness during specified collaborative work tasks. Others act as a decorative, informal background for daily activities. Some awareness systems incorporate rich media, using video and audio to provide interaction that approaches face-to-face communication. Others value simplicity and privacy, providing aesthetic communication appliances that exchange minimal or abstracted information or convey simple meanings such as "I'm thinking of you". Some systems are assumed to be "always on" rather than to be activated in the context of a specific task, allowing participants to pay attention or not as they engage in other activities. Others provide short-term awareness in the context of separate, primary activities. The level of synchrony may also vary; some systems require simultaneous awareness, whereas others reflect activity patterns over time that may be consulted at leisure. Levels of interaction among participants range from providing implicit awareness through simple capture of ongoing activities to demanding conscious and focused action from the participants, even to the extent of making this very fact communicable as a token of appreciation to the other party.

The diversity described above was noted already by Schmidt (2002), who commented that awareness has become an elastic concept used to describe anything from the moment-to-moment aligning and integration of activities of cooperating actors to messaging applications. In his introduction to the special issue on Awareness Systems of the *CSCW Journal*, he went on to criticize some of the assumptions and paradoxical arguments that have been either explicitly or implicitly adopted by researchers in the field, e.g., that awareness can be achieved without attention, that there are somehow fundamental divides between intentional and explicit coordination and implicit practices.

Many of the concerns raised by Schmidt persevere today, as the field has grown even further in size and diversity, and some of the themes originally discovered in the context of cooperative work are magnified when transposed in the domain of leisure or everyday social interactions. Overloading terminology seems to remain prevalent and may even be unavoidable, as awareness is recognized as an important concept in different domains. On the other hand, several researchers have responded to Schmidt's call for conceptual clarity, developing a range of specialized and focused theoretical works that can guide the design of awareness systems, help explain the phenomenon of awareness in its various manifestations and guide the design and evaluation of awareness systems.

This volume captures the state of the art regarding such developments; it was designed to put together works that help look beyond point solutions, that can provide a theoretical underpinning for design and development work and systematize evaluation practices. Starting from a related workshop on Awareness Systems, which was held as part of the ACM CHI conference in 2005, and following the publication of a dedicated special issue by the HCI journal by early 2007, a call for chapters was issued to put together a more comprehensive collection of works that could be used as a source material for master students and researchers working in this field.

3 Organization of Material in This Volume

The chapters in this volume are organized in four parts as follows:

3.1 Part I: Introduction to the Topic of Awareness

Part I starts with an historical overview of awareness research in computer-supported cooperative work (CSCW) over the past 20 years, by **Markus Rittenbruch** and **Gregor Mcewan**. Covering topics such as the conceptualization of the notion of awareness, prototypes illustrating approaches to providing awareness, models and extensions of awareness. This chapter provides a thorough introduction to the field of awareness research that is highly commendable for research students in this field.

Whereas the first chapter takes a more historical perspective and focuses upon cooperative work, Chapter 2 by **Markopoulos** focuses on awareness systems used for informal social communication. It provides a brief overview of related works, describing the related design space and identifying eight interaction design challenges that designers of social awareness systems are called to resolve.

Chapter 3 by **Greenberg, Neustaedter** and **Elliot** describes the notion of interpersonal awareness and discusses how home inhabitants achieve awareness of each other by exchanging information. They then consider how different locations lend meaning to the information displays within them as people make use of different timings, ownership and awareness relating to these locations.

3.2 Part II: Theoretical Perspectives

This part presents several studies that propose some theoretical underpinning to the design of awareness systems. First **Eggen** and **Mensvoort** discuss a range of concepts that play an important role in designing awareness displays: different levels of awareness, transitions between these levels, use of multiple modalities, and aesthetic quality of information displays. The chapter discusses three design concepts: "Home Radio", "Data Fountain" and "Birds Whispering", concluding with a philosophical look at our future where information decoration becomes our next nature and the responsibilities this brings upon interaction designers.

Oulasvirta discusses the interpretation of awareness cues by individuals through social cognitive processes. The chapter reviews relevant factors, such as pre-knowledge of the person and of the situation, the task at hand, available cues, the abstractness of cues, and the order of processing the cues. Evidence is gathered from two sources: field trials with awareness systems and experimental research on social cognition. The chapter concludes with a discussion on design implications.

Metaxas and **Markopoulos** present a development of the spatial model of focus and nimbus model by Benford. Their model makes salient the social interaction issues relating to awareness systems, and that allows to reason about social interaction issues surrounding the use of awareness systems, such as reciprocity, accountability, equivocation, deception, which are relevant for enabling users to protect their privacy and to manage how they present themselves to others.

Vetere, Smith and **Gibbs** discuss the notion of phatic interaction, i.e. communication between individuals pertains to how a communicative connection is maintained rather than how to convey information as such. By asking "What phatic exchanges should the awareness system support?" instead of "What information should the awareness system convey?" the authors advocate reorienting our design focus to seriously consider the extent to which awareness systems contribute to feelings of awareness and ongoing connectedness between people.

Privacy challenges in Awareness Systems are discussed thoroughly by **Patil** and **Kobsa**. They discuss the nature of privacy concerns surrounding awareness systems and their use, along with various principles and techniques for addressing them. They argue that meeting the challenges posed by privacy concerns holistically requires that designers consider them in every phase, from conception to deployment.

Romero and **Markopoulos** introduce the Privacy Grounding Model, an application of Common Ground Theory, to describe how interpersonal privacy is cooperatively managed by individuals over communication media.

Kainulainen, Turunen and **Hakulinen** describe the use of auditory displays for supporting group and peripheral awareness. In particular, it focuses on the use of speech and non-speech audio for presenting awareness information, the range of interaction techniques they can offer, and how they can be used to support awareness in different settings.

3.3 Part III: Applications

The collection of papers in this part aims to portray the diversity of applications that are described as awareness systems and the scope of the relevant design space. Also, shared concerns and practices amongst the different application domains emerge illustrating some of the trade-offs discussed in the earlier chapters.

Cohen and **Fernando** discuss narrowcasting: the deliberate filtering of multiple duplex information streams. Narrowcasting addresses the need to control the transmission from multiple sources to sinks which arises in current multimodal and multi-user systems. A set of narrowcasting operations based on a first-order logic formalization of the focus–nimbus model have been implemented in a range of applications that are described.

Ibanez, Serrano and **Garcia** describe Emotinet, a flexible and extensible framework for the development of social awareness systems. Emotinet was initially designed and developed to facilitate our explorations on how to augment a person's work environment with information which enables to feel the presence of intimate companions.

The chapter by **Tran, Yang** and **Raikundalia** presents an investigation into mechanisms to enhance awareness support in text-based, computer-mediated communication (TCMC). It describes the design and evaluation of two prototypes: Relaxed Instant Messenger (RIM), a sequential interface with an adaptive threaded interface to enhance users' awareness of turn-taking and conversational coherence, and Conversational Dock (ConDock), which uses a focus and context visualization technique to support awareness of multiple conversations.

Morris explores the potential of social network feedback displays. Visualizing data on remote and face-to-face interaction were gathered by wireless sensor networks, these displays were designed to raise awareness of social connectedness as a dynamic and controllable aspect of well-being. This chapter reviews the psychological rationale for these applications and highlights some reactions of participants to the displays.

A popular scenario of using context-sensing technology for monitoring the well-being of a lone elderly is explored by **Metaxas, Metin, Schneider, Markopoulos** and **de Ruyter**. The *Daily Activities Diarist* illustrates the potential and the pitfalls associated with systems of this ilk, especially when inferences regarding user activity need to be made. The authors make the case for narrative presentation of awareness information and for "seamful" design of awareness systems.

Rittenbruch, Mansfield and **Viller** discuss the notion of intentional enrichment: the process of actively engaging actors in the awareness process by enabling them to add meaning to seemingly disjoint activities. They discuss the challenges of designing such systems and some experiences from the design of anybiff application. The chapter concludes with implications for extending current awareness and instant messaging tools.

The last two chapters of this part focus on how awareness displays can be embedded in their physical and social context. **Cheverst, Dix, Fitton, Graham** and **Rouncefield** describe not only a 27-month-long deployment of the Hermes messaging system at the University of Lancaster but also two other messaging systems they developed: SPAM and Hermes@Home. The chapter can help designers understand the various dimensions of situatedness for situated messaging systems and how these dimensions can be exploited to arrive upon appropriate designs.

3.4 Part IV: Evaluation

This final part presents three chapters illustrating different approaches towards the evaluation of awareness systems.

Sellen, Taylor, Kaye, Brown and **Izadi** describe an exemplary field trial of the Whereabouts Clock they developed. This is a "domestic" awareness system that displays the location of family members deliberately coarse-grained categories (HOME, WORK, SCHOOL or ELSEWHERE). The results show that awareness of others through the Clock supports not only family communication and coordination but also more emotive aspects of family life, such as reassurance, connectedness, identity, and social touch.

Matthews, Hsieh and **Mankoff** present a collection of design of evaluation knowledge relevant to peripheral displays. In particular, we discuss peripheral display design implications, evaluation criteria, formative evaluation methods, summative lab methods, and summative field methods. As an example a case study is presented where lab and field evaluations of the same two email peripheral displays were carried out using a variety of methods. The case study highlights the different data yielded by and the pros and cons of each method.

Finally, turning to quantitative methods, **IJsselsteijn**, **van Baren**, **Markopoulos**, **Romero**, and **de Ruyter** present ABC questionnaire, an instrument developed for the quantitative measurement of the affective costs and benefits relating to the use of awareness systems to connect individuals or groups. The chapter focuses on the discussion of the concepts underlying the instrument and on instructing interested readers how to use it.

4 Conclusion

As editors we hope that this volume is useful to its readers. In collecting the chapters for this book we have aimed to

- provide a theoretical and methodological underpinning for the design of awareness systems;
- provide a reflective account of the field, tracking progress from past visions to current trends and future challenges;
- put together a representative collection of design concepts in the area.

Some of the chapters are of a distinctly theoretical nature; we hope that designers can find them a useful resource when considering awareness systems. The chapters collected illustrate also some of the contemporary concerns for this vibrant research field: privacy, understanding and using situatedness of the display, communicating intentionality, peripherality of displays, etc.

Given the size of this field and the rapid rate of progress, the collection of works presented here cannot be considered comprehensive. However, to our view, the volume packages a coherent collection of related works in a volume, can be a valuable guide and introduction to interested students and designers and a thorough introduction to researchers starting in this field.

Eindhoven, The Netherlands   Panos Markopoulos
Eindhoven, The Netherlands   Boris De Ruyter
Orsay Cedex, France   Wendy Mackay

References

Aoki P.M., Woodruff A., Making Space for Stories: Ambiguity in the Design of Personal Communication Systems. In Proceedings CHI 2005, ACM Press, New York, 181–190.

Bly S.A., Harrison S.R., Irwin S. (January 1993) Media spaces: Bringing people together in a video, audio, and computing environment. Communications of the ACM 36(1), 28–46.

Dourish P., Bly S. (1992) Portholes: Supporting awareness in a distributed work group. Proceedings CHI'92, ACM Press, New York, 541–547.

Endsley M.R., Garland D.J. (2000) Situation Awareness Analysis and Measurement. Lawrence Erlbaum Associates, London.

Gross T., Stary C., Totter A. (2005) User-centered awareness in computer-supported cooperative work systems: Structured embedding of findings from social sciences. International Journal of Human–Computer Interaction, 18(3), 323–360.

Gutwin C., Greenberg S. (2002) The effects of workspace awareness support on the usability of real-time distributed groupware. ACM Transactions on Computer–Human Interaction, 6(2), 243–281.

Markopoulos P., IJsselsteijn, W., Huijnen C., de Ruyter B. (2005) Sharing experiences through awareness systems in the home. Interacting with Computers, 17(5), Elsevier, 506–521.

Palen L., Dourish P. (2003) Unpacking "privacy" for a networked world. In Proceedings CHI'03. ACM, New York, 129–136.

Putman R.D. (2000) Bowling Alone: The Collapse and Revival of American Community. Simon and Schuster, New York.

Romero N., Markopoulos P., van Baren J, de Ruyter B., IJsselsteijn W., Farshchian B. (2007) Connecting the family with awareness systems. Personal and Ubiquitous Computing, 11(4), Springer, 299–312.

Sarter N.B., Woods D.D. (1991) Situation awareness: A critical but ill defined phenomenon. International Journal of Aviation Psychology, 1, 45–57.

Schmidt K. (2002) The problem with awareness. Computer Supported Cooperative Work, 11: 285–298.

Contents

Contributors

Barry Brown UC San Diego, Dept. of Communications, San Diego CA, USA, Barry.AT.Brown@acm.org

Keith Cheverst Department of Computing, Infolab, Lancaster University, Lancaster, Lancashire, UK, kc@comp.lancs.ac.uk

Michael Cohen Spatial Media Group, University of Aizu, Japan, mcohen@u-aizu.ac.jp

Boris de Ruyter Philips Research Laboratories, Prof. Holstlaan 4, 5656 AA Eindhoven, The Netherlands

Terry Dishongh Digital Health Group, Intel Corporation, terry.dishongh@intel.com

Alan Dix Department of Computing, Infolab, Lancaster University, Lancaster, Lancashire, UK, dixa@comp.lancs.ac.uk

Berry Eggen Department of Industrial Design, Eindhoven University of Technology, The Netherlands, j.h.eggen@tue.nl

Kathryn Elliot Rounding SMART Technologies, Calgary, Alberta, Canada, krounding@smarttech.com

Owen Noel Newton Fernando Mixed Reality Lab., National University of Singapore, Singapore, newtonfernando@mixedrealitylab.org

Dan Fitton Department of Computing, Infolab, Lancaster University, Lancaster, Lancashire, UK

David García University Pompeu Fabra, Barcelona, Spain, david.garcian@upf.edu

Martin Gibbs Department of Information Systems, University of Melbourne, Parkville, Victoria 3010, Australia, martin.gibbs@unimelb.edu.au

Connor Graham Department of Computing, Infolab, Lancaster University, Lancaster, Lancashire, UK, cgraham@unimelb.edu.au

Saul Greenberg University of Calgary, Calgary, Canada, saul.greenberg@ucalgary.ca

Jaakko Hakulinen Speech-Based and Pervasive Interaction Group, TAUCHI, Department of Computer Sciences, University of Tampere, FIN-33014, Finland, jaakko.hakulinen@cs.uta.fi

Gary Hsieh Carnegie Mellon University, 5000 Forbes Avenue, Pittsburgh, PA 15213, USA, garyh@cs.cmu.edu

Jesús Ibáñez Department of Technology, University Pompeu Fabra, Barcelona, Spain, jesus.ibanez@upf.edu

Wijnand IJsselsteijn Eindhoven University of Technology, Department of Industrial Engineering & Innovation Sciences, Den Dolech 2, 5612 AZ Eindhoven, Eindhoven, The Netherlands, W.A.IJsselsteijn@tue.nl

Shahram Izadi UC San Diego, Department of Communications, San Diego CA, USA, Barry.AT.Brown@acm.org

Anssi Kainulainen Speech-Based and Pervasive Interaction Group, TAUCHI, Department of Computer Sciences, University of Tampere, FIN-33014, Finland, Anssi.Kainulainen@cs.uta.fi

Joseph 'Jofish' Kaye Nokia Research Center, jofish@jofish.com

Alfred Kobsa Department of Informatics, University of California, Irvine, CA, USA, kobsa@uci.edu

Jay Lundell Digital Health Group, Intel Corporation, jay.lundell@intel.com

Jennifer Mankoff Carnegie Mellon University, 5000 Forbes Avenue, Pittsburgh, PA 15213, USA, jmankoff@cs.cmu.edu

Tim Mansfield Queensland University of Technology, GPO Box 2434, Brisbane QLD 4001, Australia, tim.mansfield@qut.edu.au

Panos Markopoulos Department of Industrial Design, Eindhoven University of Technology, Den Dolech 2, 5612 AZ Eindhoven, The Netherlands, p.markopoulos@ tue.nl

Tara Matthews IBM Research, Almaden Research Center, 650 Harry Road, San Jose, CA 95123, USA, tlmatthe@us.ibm.com

Gregor McEwan NICTA and HxI Initiative, Locked Bag 9013, Alexandria NSW 1435, Australia, gregor.mcewan@nicta.com.au

Georgios Metaxas Eindhoven University of Technology, The Netherlands, margaret.morris@intel.com

Barbaros Metin USI Program, Eindhoven University of Technology, Den Dolech 2, 5612 AZ Eindhoven, The Netherlands, b.metin@tue.nl

Margaret E. Morris Digital Health Group, Intel Corporation, margaret.morris@intel.com

Brad Needham Digital Health Group, Intel Corporation, brad.needham@intel.com

Carman Neustaedter Kodak Research Labs, Rochester, NY, USA,
carman.neustaedter@kodak.com

Antti Oulasvirta Helsinki Institute for Information Technology HIIT and
University of California, Berkeley, CA, USA, aoulasvirta@acm.org

Sameer Patil Department of Informatics, University of California, Irvine, CA,
USA, patil@uci.edu

Gitesh K. Raikundalia School of Computer Science and Mathematics, Victoria
University, Melbourne City, 8001, Australia, Gitesh.Raikundalia@vu.edu.au

Markus Rittenbruch NICTA and HxI Initiative, Locked Bag 9013, Alexandria
NSW 1435, Australia, markus.rittenbruch@nicta.com.au

Natalia Romero Eindhoven University of Technology, The Netherlands

Mark Rouncefield Department of Computing, Infolab, Lancaster University,
Lancaster, Lancashire, UK

Jutta Schneider USI Program, Eindhoven University of Technology,
Den Dolech 2, 5612 AZ Eindhoven, The Netherlands, j.m.schneider@tue.nl

Abigail Sellen Microsoft Research, 7JJ Thomson Ave., Cambridge, UK,
CB3 OFB, asellen@microsoft.com

Oscar Serrano University Pompeu Fabra, Barcelona, Spain,
oscar.serrano@upf.edu

Jeremy Smith Department of Information Systems, University of Melbourne,
Victoria, Australia

Alex S. Taylor Microsoft Research Cambridge, Cambridge, UK,
ast@microsoft.com

Minh Hong Tran Faculty of Information and Communication Technologies, Swinburne University of Technology, Hawthorn, VC 3122, Australia,
mtran@ict.swin.edu.au

Markku Turunen Speech-Based and Pervasive Interaction Group, TAUCHI,
Department of Computer Sciences, University of Tampere, FIN-33014, Finland,
markku.turunen@cs.uta.fi

Joy van Baren Elsevier, The Netherlands

Koert van Mensvoort Department of Industrial Design, Eindhoven University of Technology, Den Dolech 2, 5612 AZ Eindhoven, The Netherlands,
K.M.v.Mensvoort@tue.nl

Frank Vetere Department of Information Systems, University of Melbourne, Australia, f.vetere@unimelb.edu.au

Stephen Viller School of Information Technology and Electrical Engineering, University of Queensland, Brisbane, QLD 4072, Australia, viller@itee.uq.edu.au

Yun Yang Faculty of Information and Communication Technologies, Swinburne University of Technology, Hawthorn, VC 3122, Australia, yyang@ict.swin.edu.au

Part I
Awareness in Context

Chapter 1
An Historical Reflection of Awareness in Collaboration

Markus Rittenbruch and Gregor McEwan

Abstract　Mutual awareness has been a focus point of research in Human–Computer Interaction (HCI) and Computer-Supported Cooperative Work (CSCW) since the early 1990s. At its essence, mutual awareness refers to a fundamental quality of collaborative work, the ability of co-workers to perceive each others' activities and expressions and relate them to a joint context. In this chapter, we explore the history of awareness concepts by analysing existing literature in order to identify trends, research questions, research approaches and classification schemes throughout different stages of research into awareness. We have adopted a historical angle in the hope that it will allow us to show how awareness research has progressed over time. We document this development using three different phases: *(1) Early exploration of awareness* (approximately 1990–1994), *(2) Diversification and research prototypes* (approximately 1995–1999) and *(3) Extended models and specialisation* (approximately 2000–now). While these phases are to some extent arbitrary and overlapping, they allow us to highlight differences in research focus at the time and understand research in context.

1.1 Introduction

Awareness and awareness systems for collaboration have been a focus point of research in Human–Computer Interaction (HCI) since the mid-1980s. The early years of research were primarily about discovering that awareness was important for collaboration, mostly through field studies and the growing use of network communication. While in the last few years awareness concepts have grown increasingly complex, knowledge of what awareness in collaboration actually means has not progressed at the same pace. Early dichotomy-based classifications, such as synchronous vs. asynchronous or social vs. task awareness, fail to accurately

M. Rittenbruch (✉)
NICTA and HxI Initiative, Australia; Locked Bag 9013, Alexandria NSW, 1435, Australia
e-mail: markus.rittenbruch@nicta.com.au

P. Markopoulos et al. (eds.), *Awareness Systems*, Human-Computer Interaction Series, DOI 10.1007/978-1-84882-477-5_1, © Springer-Verlag London Limited 2009

describe the complexity of awareness research in Computer-Supported Cooperative Work (CSCW) today. In this chapter we will initially take a look at the history of awareness in collaboration by analysing existing literature in order to identify research questions, research approaches and classification schemes throughout different stages of research into awareness. We use this review to extract the characteristics and trends of awareness research over the last 20 years, and provide a picture of how CSCW's knowledge of awareness has progressed and changed.

Why another survey? Surprisingly, despite the popularity of awareness research in HCI and CSCW, the existing research has rarely been summarised in a structured manner. Schmidt (2002) delivers an eloquent critique of awareness research, in which he is concerned with the notion and understanding of the phenomenon of awareness in collaboration, and he points out that our knowledge is far from complete. Gross et al. (2005) provide a comprehensive analysis of awareness approaches, but their main focus is on the terminology used to describe concepts in CSCW and social science research fields. We follow a more pragmatic approach by focussing on what researchers have achieved in awareness research and how this knowledge has been used by designers of awareness systems. In particular we want to find out what tools are available to describe, conceptualise, design and implement awareness in collaborative work and how these tools have evolved over time. We believe that this approach will help researchers understand awareness research, and that it will be of value in developing and addressing new research into awareness.

We approach the development of awareness knowledge from an historical angle and show how understanding of awareness, awareness concepts and models and awareness prototypes progressed through different stages, increasing in complexity and differentiation. Section 1.2 covers roughly the years 1986–1994, revisiting the origins of awareness research in HCI and CSCW, including the exploration of the phenomenon of awareness through field studies and early prototypes (e.g. Bowers 1994; Dourish and Bellotti 1992; Dourish and Bly 1992; Heath and Luff 1991). Section 1.3 covers roughly the period 1995–1999, when awareness concepts and models were developed and increasingly differentiated. We analyse a multitude of intersecting terminologies that are used to specify certain types of awareness, for instance the common distinction between task-based, formal activities from informal, social activities (Tollmar et al. 1996; Prinz 1999). In Section 1.4, covering roughly the years from 2000 to 2006 and early 2007, we show how awareness research has developed and diversified (e.g. Simone and Bandini 2002; Boyle and Greenberg 2005), how awareness research expanded into other domains (e.g. Mynatt et al. 2001; Neustaedter and Brush 2006) and in general how it moved out of the distributed office environment.

This chapter concludes in Section 1.5, by taking a look back at all the topics covered in our historical survey and reflecting on the larger trends that have occurred over the last 20 years of collaboration awareness research. We finish this last section with some speculation as to where these trends might go next and the open research that remains.

1.2 Early Exploration of Awareness

In this section, we explore the early concepts of awareness in the field of CSCW. This early work shows how researchers began to realise that there was more to collaboration than simply direct interaction between people and with shared objects. Successful collaboration is a complex social activity with many subtle peripheral and non-verbal cues between people and around artefacts – in short, it depends on awareness.

While there were earlier technologies that, with the benefit of hindsight, could be considered to provide awareness information (for example, e-mail and the UNIX "who" command), we concern ourselves here with work that formed the basis for rich CSCW research streams about supporting awareness in its various forms. We begin by discussing some workspace studies that made clear the complexity of collaboration activities and demonstrated the need for awareness support. We follow by discussing early media space research, that started from a practical basis of connecting people and discovering what happened. We then provide an overview of some concepts that were in their infancy but proved very important to later research – event-based awareness and the COMIC spatial model of awareness.

1.2.1 Workplace Studies

The workplace studies described below provided real-world justification for awareness research. They showed how awareness was a vital part of collaborative activity, whether it was high intensity, real-time collaboration, as in a London underground control room (Heath and Luff 1991) or constant, peripheral awareness that led to collaborative scientific publications (Kraut et al. 1988). The third work that we present below, Harper et al.'s (1989) air traffic control study, provided an early and firm illustration of the real-world complexities of awareness interactions. Each of these bodies of work has continued to be extremely influential in awareness research and are still referenced strongly today.

1.2.1.1 London Underground

Heath and Luff's (1991) study of collaboration and coordination inside a London underground railway control room is one of the primary works in identifying the phenomenon of awareness and its relevance in collaborative work. Even though they never mention awareness explicitly, their ethnomethodologically informed analysis provides a picture of how awareness forms the basis of real world, tightly coupled collaboration.

The original motivation for the study was fairly specialised. Heath and Luff's wanted to perform a workplace study in a technological setting, thus providing greater relevance to the *Computer* part of CSCW. Their original goal was to use the study as the basis for design of a system, and their paper reports success in this goal. However, the great contributions of their work to future researchers are the direct findings in their workplace observation study.

The study was an ethnographic observation of a London underground railway control room. There were two people working in the control room, the divisional information assistant (DIA), who made public announcements to passengers and communicated with station managers, and the line controller, who coordinated the running of the railway. These two sit at a semi-circular display and "use a range of devices similar to the technologies being developed in CSCW; they use audio and video channels of communication, a shared display, various keypads and monitors" (Heath and Luff 1991). The railway service was also coordinated through the use of a paper timetable. Heath and Luff observed and recorded how these two people coordinated their activities to keep the trains running and passengers informed in the face of minor train delays, absentees, breakdowns and other unexpected disruptions.

Their observations provide insight into how people work together in highly inter-dependent, real-time situations. They observed how the two actors would surrepti-tiously monitor the other's activities in order to inform their own actions, modifying what they were doing to incorporate new information from the other, even though there was no explicit communication. Thus, when the controller told someone to hold up a train, the DIA would make a passenger announcement about the delay simply because he overheard the phone call. The actors also deliberately modified their behaviour to assist the other in monitoring, by doing such things as talking themselves through their task so the other could overhear. Also, because they were monitoring both the local environment and their co-worker, they were able to take over each other's tasks when the other was overloaded.

In awareness terms, though Heath and Luff do not use the term "awareness", the controller and DIA maintained awareness of each other and their environment and they intentionally structured their activities to assist the other in being aware of them and the relevant environmental events.

1.2.1.2 Patterns of Scientific Collaboration

In 1988, Kraut et al. (Kraut et al. 1988) published a workplace study clearly demonstrating the importance of physical proximity for collaboration. They showed that the reason for this was that co-located colleagues had more opportunities for frequent, high-quality informal communication. This work is the basis for much research later into informal interaction and the awareness requirements for support-ing it.

They studied a group of 93 psychology academics in multiple departments that had written at least two internal reports recently, with at least one of the reports hav-ing a co-author. There were 4278 unique collaboration pairings in the group. These were then correlated with the physical proximity of the offices of the collaborators. Their results were that over 80% of collaborations were with people on the same floor and that being on different floors reduced collaboration to the same extent as being in different buildings. Even after correcting for the fact that people in proximal offices are likely to have similar research interests, there was still a significant effect from proximity.

Kraut et al. concluded from these results, as well as past studies and interviews, that "What appears to be important ... is the opportunity for unconstrained interaction that proximity provides". Communication that is frequent, high quality, usually unplanned and low cost has a great impact on the likelihood and longevity of collaboration. It is important to note that this type of communication is not just a requirement of sustaining or supporting existing collaboration, but of getting the collaboration going in the first place. People who are around each other and communicate frequently, regardless of work-related content, are more familiar with each other.

In addition, as they spend more time together, they are more likely to discover common points of interest that lead into collaboration. It is in referring to this behaviour that Kraut et al. make their only explicit reference to awareness in this paper. They state that *"increased awareness of the attributes of one's neighbors allows one to choose partners judiciously"*.

Despite the paucity of direct mentions of awareness in this paper, it still informed a large body of awareness research. The study motivated support for unplanned casual interactions, which was the basis of media space research (e.g. Buxton and Moran 1990; Mantei et al. 1991; Dourish and Bly 1992; Fish et al. 1992), and also sparked a rich stream of research in informal awareness (see the section on Informal Awareness). The tie to media spaces was encouraged by Kraut et al. (1988) as they explicitly mention media spaces as a possible technical solution to the distance problem. Other early media space work started to investigate awareness as a requirement for informal interaction. More detail about media spaces follows this section.

1.2.1.3 Air Traffic Control

This early field study of air traffic control by Harper et al. (1989) was important for two reasons. First, it documented the complex awareness and interaction practices of a highly integrated group in a high-pressure situation. Second, the study demonstrated clearly the dangers of ignoring these complex practices when introducing technology support.

The study was situated in an air traffic control room. Small teams of controllers were responsible for geographical sectors, through which planes would fly. They would direct the planes to make sure they maintained sensible courses and avoided other planes. At the boundaries of the sectors, controllers would have to hand off planes under their control to other controllers. As there were usually large numbers of planes, the situation was high pressure – there were a large number of tasks to perform with high stakes.

Awareness of the current task for an individual controller was supported by paper flight strips, which described important details about each plane. These were printed by an automated system and delivered to the relevant controller by assistants. As the controllers worked they would annotate the flight strips with important updates and flag any issues. The annotations and positions of the flight strips allowed any of the team to see the status of the flight zone at a glance. Agreements between sector teams about how to hand off planes between sectors would also be annotated on the flight strips. The flight strips were the central artefacts for mediating awareness and collaboration.

The introduction of technology to this collaboration was initially a failure because it failed to take into account the complex interaction that went on in the team. For example, the deployed system removed the collaborative benefits of the flight strips in providing awareness to the team and supporting the cross-team communication.

The study was an important motivating case for future awareness, and CSCW, research as it showed how the design of a technical system was sensitive to the complex work practices of the group it was supporting.

1.2.1.4 Workplace Studies Summary

The three workplace studies listed here are often referenced as motivation for collaborative awareness research, right up to the present day (e.g. Boyle and Greenberg 2005; Rittenbruch et al. 2007).

Next, we discuss early media spaces and how they started to support and investigate various types of awareness.

1.2.2 Early Media Spaces

Media Spaces use always-on, or at least always-available, video and audio channels to connect distance-separated locations or sites. The sites are usually common areas or individual workspaces, and the media space allows individuals or small groups to communicate from each location. Media spaces enable distance-separated people to feel as if they were all in the same area. After 1988, this motivation became more grounded by the scientific collaboration report by Kraut et al. (1988).

Early research into video media spaces can be seen as exploring and identifying the important elements of spatial proximity and how these could be captured by media spaces. Most of this early media space research concerned just informal interaction, but researchers at the European office of Xerox PARC (EuroPARC) also had the idea that awareness was a fundamental requirement for informal interaction.

1.2.2.1 The First Media Space

The first media space in HCI research[1] was created at Xerox PARC in the mid-1980s (Stults 1986). Stults reports that he was motivated by seeing that some of

---

[1]The first media space by the definition here was actually a public art installation called "Hole-In-Space"; Galloway and Rabinowitz (1980) Hole-in-Space. Mobile image videotape. Santa Monica,

his colleagues, whose offices opened onto the hallway, were unable to receive the community benefits of having offices adjoining the commons area. The lab also had a lot of audiovisual equipment that was used for videoconferencing and video-phone research. The equipment was sitting idle when nobody was in a call, and so they decided to just leave the audiovisual links on all the time and "build an elec-tronic space to serve much of the role that the common area serves" (Stults 1986). The media space allowed participants to communicate informally and be aware of opportunities to interact with others.

The first media space setup used analog video and audio feeds from each of four offices, the common area in Palo Alto and the common area in Portland. Each of these locations had a monitor display and a remote display. All the remote displays were synchronised showing the same thing and the switch was in the Palo Alto common area.

While this report predates the explicit mention of awareness, Stults comments on the value of maintaining "background contact" with others while engaged in indi-vidual work, having "discussions that spanned two offices" and the significance of being able to "move fluidly from one use to the other" (Stults 1986). These comments strongly foreshadow the later media space research on awareness, casual interaction and the transition between them.

This system continued to be developed at Xerox PARC in both the Palo Alto and Portland sites and was used to provide facilities for awareness and social interaction between their common areas, as well as means for collaboration and meeting in teams spread over the sites. Bly et al. (1993) provide an excellent review of this media space development and their experiences of using it every day. The article also contains an excellent discussion and reflection on media spaces in general, and is an excellent starting point for reading on media spaces.

1.2.2.2 Second Generation Media Spaces

During the early 1990s, media spaces were a popular topic in CSCW research. A variety of media space implementations and evaluations were published (e.g. Bux-ton and Moran 1990; Fish et al. 1990; Borning and Travers 1991; Mantei et al. 1991; Dourish and Bly 1992; Fish et al. 1992; Gaver et al. 1992). All of these systems took inspiration from the first media spaces implemented at Xerox PARC (Stults 1986; as well as successors) and were motivated by the Kraut et al. (1988) study on pat-terns of scientific collaboration. As with the collaboration study, the media space investigations were concerned with informal interactions rather than awareness and in most cases awareness was not mentioned explicitly.

However, one group realised that awareness was an important precursor for infor-mal interaction. In 1991, media space-related publications from EuroPARC started to contain discussions about how awareness of others was necessary to prompt

Calif., 1980. http://www.ecafe.com/getty/HIS/ but it was not supporting collaboration and did not have much influence on awareness research in CSCW.

casual interactions (Borning and Travers 1991; Gaver 1991; Dourish and Bly 1992; Gaver et al. 1992). These publications used many different terms for the particular type of awareness that prompted casual interactions, such as general awareness, casual awareness, shared awareness, unobtrusive awareness, distributed awareness and passive awareness. Despite the range of descriptive terms, the concept was entirely consistent – to support informal interactions, people need to be aware of others' presence, activities and availability.

Each of these aspects of awareness – presence, activity and availability – are used to motivate features in the EuroPARC systems. Polyscope and Vrooms (Borning and Travers 1991) and Portholes (Dourish and Bly 1992) all offer a grid of always-on video of offices and common rooms. RAVE (Gaver et al. 1992) offers an always-on view of a common area, a *glance* feature to view a selected office node and an *office share* feature to create a persistent audio/video connection to another office node. Portholes is an interesting example as it demonstrates that low-resolution, infrequently updated images still provide enough awareness to support informal interactions and a feeling of connection. Of course other media space implementations provide awareness as well, simply by having always-on video links, though in these cases the motivation is usually that always-on video provides lightweight facilities to engage in informal interaction.

At this point it is worth saying a few words about privacy in these early systems. While we do not want to offer a complete review of privacy research, awareness and privacy are very intertwined topics so we will mention privacy briefly. There is a trade-off and a tension between privacy and awareness – more awareness means more opportunities for privacy violations, yet more privacy means less awareness and missing chances for valuable serendipitous interactions. The developers of media spaces were very aware of the potential privacy problems of having always-on video and audio links and dealt with it in a number of ways. Most media spaces enforced reciprocity or at least symmetry (Alice has the capability to see the same information about Bob as Bob can see about Alice, but she can choose not to use that capability) (Borning and Travers 1991), although hardware limitations restricted how much that could be done, as it is usually possible to be out of view of the camera while still viewing the display. In some cases where the media space connected common areas, such as VideoWindow (Fish et al. 1990), the area was considered public and so explicit controls were not provided there. In media spaces that connected office spaces, there were usually explicit controls to temporarily turn off the "always-on" facilities and to refuse direct connections. Borning and Travers (1991) and Gaver et al. (1992) provide good discussions of privacy in media spaces, breaking it down into elements such as control, knowledge, symmetry, intention and avoiding unnecessary intrusions.

1.2.2.3 Media Spaces Summary

Media spaces in these early days were seen as a direct method of, at least partially, replacing the need for physical proximity. After these early systems, however, the perception seemed to change slightly so that they were seen as a component of distributed awareness and collaboration. In research after 1994, media spaces are most often seen as part of a system that incorporates video and audio but also with many more channels of communication (e.g. Mansfield et al. 1997b; Greenberg and Rounding 2001; McEwan and Greenberg 2005). Over time the concept of a media space seems to be migrating to cover these new systems.

Next we talk about the initial forays into the world of event-based awareness, which prompted a great deal of research, especially in the late 1990s.

1.2.3 Event-Based Awareness

Event-based awareness is, at its simplest level and as the name suggests, concerned with providing people with awareness of what is going on around them, as expressed by discrete events. The real strength in this early investigation of awareness came in giving more control to the recipient of information.

The first of the event-based awareness systems was the Khronika system (Lövstrand 1991), which notified people of high-level events such as seminars, social outings and weather.

The important idea in Khronika was in decoupling the sender and receiver. In contrast to message-sending models, such as e-mail, where the sender specifies the receiver(s), Khronika allowed the sender of information to simply post information events to the server, without any concern about who should receive it (although there was an option to restrict the possible set of recipients if needed). Receivers of information would specify general rules (which would later be known as subscriptions) about what kind of information they were interested in and how and when they wanted to receive it. As Lövstrand explains:

> Thus, if user A enters a seminar event for 14:00 on Friday and user B has a daemon looking for seminars with a 15 minute warning, B's daemon will trigger and schedule a notification for 13:45 the same day (Lövstrand 1991).

This model removes the need for the sender to know who wants to receive the information they are sending, reducing the risk of missing someone important or sending people irrelevant information. It also gives the receiver more control over what kind of information they receive and allows them to monitor for information they may not have known existed.

Gaver (1991) used Khronika to implement a prototype sound notification system to explore his new notion of general awareness (mentioned earlier in Section 1.2.2.2). Sounds, such as low conversation or of water boiling in a kettle, enabled awareness of meetings or informal gatherings. This awareness led to informal interactions, which in turn lead to collaboration (previously discussed in Section 1.2.1.2).

Event-based awareness, as pioneered by Khronika, is partly an infrastructure mechanism for delivering different types of awareness information. However, the important conceptual contribution is in decoupling the senders from the receivers. This gave power to the recipients that they did not otherwise have in a directed message model. We will see this concept used later in future awareness research.

Later streams of research also look at how to also provide control to the sender of information.

1.2.4 Awareness in a Spatial Metaphor

Many CSCW systems employ a spatial metaphor, leveraging participants' natural knowledge about using physical space to facilitate virtual collaboration. Awareness systems are no exception, and early spatially based awareness models started with the COMIC[2] awareness model.

Benford and Fahlen (1993) created the COMIC awareness model for application to any environment that can be mapped to a spatial metaphor. Their primary application was within an immersive 3D world. The model consists of six components: *medium, aura, focus, nimbus, awareness* and *adaptors*.

- *Medium* is the collaborative environment. It defines how information is propagated. For example, in the physical world, we can hear people behind other objects and we can see for large distances in uninterrupted lines. In virtual worlds, communication is often text based and a text message may be clear throughout a room but completely invisible outside.
- *Aura* is a boundary around each entity (person or object), defining their possible range of interaction. For example, in the virtual world a person may not be able to interact outside the current room.
- *Focus* is a person's area of attention. They can direct their focus to control what they perceive. For example, a person is only visually aware of what they are looking at – visual focus is directional and blocked by walls.
- *Nimbus* describes the area of effect of the information that an entity provides. For example, a person cannot be seen from outside a room – their visual nimbus only extends to the walls.
- *Awareness* is a function of both focus and nimbus. If a person is within an object's nimbus then they may be partially aware of it, if the object is within their focus then they are fully aware of it and able to interact. The exact relationship of focus, nimbus and awareness is defined by the medium. For example, a person in the same room looking at another would be very aware of them, while when they look away they are only partially aware of them.
- *Adaptors* are modifiers on focus and nimbus. For example, a telescope increases the range of visual focus, and a megaphone increases auditory nimbus.

This model is interesting in its decoupling of the provider of information and the recipient of information, in a similar way to Khronika's event-based awareness. The

---

[2]The Computer-based Mechanisms of Interaction in Cooperative Work (COMIC) project was a multi-site multidisciplinary European research project investigating the basic principles, techniques and theories to support CSCW systems, and ran from September 1992 to August 1995.

primary conceptual difference here is that there is control given to the provider as well as the recipient – the provider controls their nimbus, or the information they are sending, and the recipient controls their focus, or how they pay attention to information around them. While this idea is based around a spatial model – Benford and Fahlen's main example is in a Virtual Reality System – later refinements generalised it to other settings (discussed later in Section 1.3.2.2).

1.2.5 Early Exploration of Awareness Summary

In this section, we explore the early concepts of awareness in the field of CSCW. This early work shows how researchers began to realise that there was more to collaboration than simply direct interaction between people and with shared objects. Successful collaboration is a complex social activity with many subtle peripheral and non-verbal cues between people and around artefacts – in short, it depends on awareness.

While there were earlier technologies that, with the benefit of hindsight, could be considered to provide awareness information (for example, e-mail and the UNIX "who" command), we concern ourselves here with work that formed the basis for rich CSCW research streams about supporting awareness in its various forms. We begin by discussing some workspace studies that made clear the complexity of collaboration activities and demonstrated the need for awareness support. We follow by discussing early media space research that started from a practical basis of connecting people and discovering what happened. We then provide an overview of some concepts that were in their infancy but proved very important to later research – event-based awareness and the COMIC spatial model of awareness.

1.3 Diversification and Research Prototypes

The time period from about 1995 to 1999 was the most active phase in awareness research, with many research groups dedicating themselves to awareness research and producing a wealth of publications. During this period a whole range of new concepts and terminologies were introduced to awareness research. Rodden (1996) introduced the nimbus–focus model which was based on the COMIC spatial model (Benford and Fahlen 1993). A large number of often highly related notions of awareness were introduced, such as social awareness (Tollmar et al. 1996), workspace awareness (Gutwin and Greenberg 1995b; Gutwin 1997) and contextual awareness (Mark et al. 1997) to name just a few. The appearance of these notions and concepts highlights the need to understand different facets of awareness as well as a trend towards greater specialisation. We will start this section by revisiting the more prominent notions and concepts in their respective research context.

Because this period was so active, we cannot hope to capture all of the research related to awareness. However, there are a smaller number of general trends in awareness research that characterise the period. In this section we will describe these trends, starting with the theoretical and moving to the concrete, and briefly discuss some representative research examples within each trend. The sections proceed as follows:

- "The Social Context of Awareness" summarises concepts that place awareness in the larger sociological context of interaction.
- "Awareness Frameworks and Models" provides examples which show a strong research trend in creating models and classification schemes for awareness.
- "Collaborative Environments" describes how theoretical principles and infrastructure were used in the creation of collaboration environments.
- "Physical Display of Awareness" looks at applications for presenting awareness information outside of these comprehensive collaboration environments.
- "Infrastructure" describes the important work in building infrastructure to support awareness, primarily through event distribution architectures.

1.3.1 The Social Context of Awareness

In this section we identify an important research stream that sought to place awareness within the larger social activity and context. The fundamental principle is that people do things other than be aware of each other, and awareness fits into that larger context.

The two examples of this type of research differ a lot in their approach. The first group of work is about the possible negative consequences of providing awareness information. When awareness information is provided inappropriately, the providers may have their privacy infringed, and receivers of the information may be interrupted unnecessarily or receive information they are uncomfortable with.

The second approach, the locales framework, places awareness within the larger social structure and interactions of a person or group.

We differentiate this type of research from the models and classifications described later (see Section 1.3.2) as they take an inward view of describing awareness itself, rather than positioning it in a larger context.

1.3.1.1 Awareness, Privacy and Interruption

Privacy and interruption were issues raised in the early explorations of media spaces (see Section 1.2.2) and many of the prototypes had features to maintain privacy and minimise interruption while still providing awareness information. These features centred on methods for establishing connections and ensuring reciprocity. In the late 1990s, research began to appear specifically about the trade-off between awareness and privacy. The techniques for achieving balance in the trade-off focussed on transforming the display of awareness information to hide sensitive details and to make it "quieter" to avoid distracting interruptions.

Hudson and Smith (1996) were the first to clearly state the trade-off between awareness and privacy. They focused on the problem specifically within media spaces. Their proposed solution was to transform the video or audio feed so it removed potentially privacy violating details while still providing enough information for awareness of activity and presence. For example, one of their prototypes subtly displays image differences over a standard background frame so that the viewer, rather than see full video of a person, would see blocky shadows moving across the still image of the room.

The AROMA system (Pedersen and Sokoler 1997) took the transformation idea even further by fully abstracting awareness information. The abstraction allows presentation of the useful components of the information, e.g. presence, without also presenting privacy violating information, e.g. still wearing pyjamas while working at home. While the framework was generic, potentially incorporating a large number of abstract displays using display, sound, mechanical and other types of devices, their prototype made use of a drifting cloud animation, a mechanical toy merry-go-round, a sea shore soundscape, and temperature of a handrest surface. These abstract representations were linked to various indications of activity, such as how many people were around.

This work is strongly related to ambient displays (see Section 1.3.4) and seems to have arisen in parallel from different motivations.

1.3.1.2   The Locales Framework

The locales framework draws upon Anselm Strauss's (2003) Theory of Action to inform the design of CSCW systems. The intention of the framework was to act as a bridge between the rich social and technical streams of research in CSCW by providing a common vocabulary for communication between the theoretical and the technical. However, the most important contribution is in its amalgamation of most of the existing theoretical knowledge in CSCW at the time. We spend some time discussing the various aspects of the locales framework here because it relates awareness to the context of general CSCW theory of the time.

The locales framework was published in many contexts over a period of many years, with a first appearance in 1995 (Fitzpatrick et al. 1995). This first version of the locales framework was closely tied to the WORLDS collaborative environment (discussed in Section 1.3.3.2). We offer a simplified overview of this first version in Fig. 1.1. There are three primary entities of concern: *people*, *sites* and *means*. *Social worlds*, *locales* and *trajectories* describe the interactions of these primary entities.

People organise themselves into *social worlds*, defined by the framework as a group with a common purpose or primary activity. *Sites* are the places where the social worlds perform their activities. The *means* are artefacts used by people within the sites to support the activities. *Locales* describe the relationship between sites and means in use by social worlds. This means that the locale is different if a different social world uses the same site and means, or if the same social world starts using a different site and means. For example, while social worlds 3 and 4 share the same

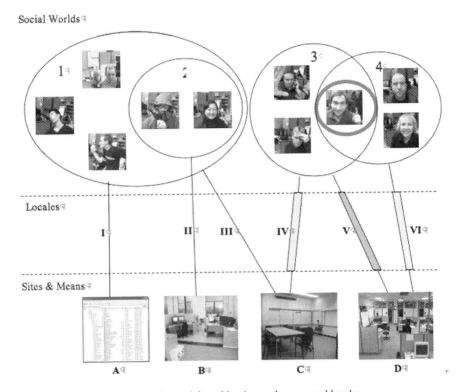

Social Worlds

Locales

Sites & Means

Fig. 1.1 The locales framework – social worlds, sites and means and locales

site and means (seminar room D), the different uses of the room create two distinct locales, labelled V and VI in the figure. *Trajectories* describe how social worlds, sites and means, and locales evolve over time.

For example, Fig. 1.1 shows four social worlds across the top row, labelled 1, 2, 3 and 4. These four social worlds are related to each other through the people that belong to them, i.e. social world 1 is a superset of social world 2. The figure also shows four sites, labelled A, B, C and D. A is a virtual site – a shared filesystem, and B through D are physical – two different work rooms (B and D) and a seminar room (C). Each of these sites also contains many means, e.g. the virtual files in A, and the tables and whiteboards in C.

The next locales framework publication (Fitzpatrick et al. 1996) while still based on the same principles of social worlds, locales, interaction and trajectory changed the structure of the ideas considerably. The framework was now composed of five aspects: locale foundations, mutuality, individual views, interaction trajectories and civic structures.

Locale foundations describe the aspect of social worlds and the locales that they use. Social worlds typically use many different locales when engaging in their activities and this aspect relates to their basic structure.

A major contribution described in Locale foundations is the concept of *centres and peripheries* in contrast to the more usual *boundaries*. Each social world has a centre defined by the collective purpose of the social world. Each person's relationship to the social world is represented as a distance from the centre rather than the binary "on" or "off" which is part of the rooms metaphor used by many groupware systems. For example, at an instant in time a group may be planning an event. Those very close to the centre may be involved in detailed organisation. Another person, who may just attend the event, is somewhat more removed. Yet another may skip this particular event, so they are closer to the periphery of the group, at least for the moment. In real-world situations such as these, boundaries are made only if required; in practice people can fluidly adjust their "membership" from centre to periphery as a consequence of their interests and their actions. Of course, some social worlds have explicit rules, membership lists and duties that define people's roles and what they do, but even these have varying participation levels.

Mutuality incorporates the issues of *presence, awareness, capability* and *choice*. Presence is the information that an entity makes available about itself, and entities have capabilities for perception of this information. Within those capabilities, the entities can make choices about how much they perceive of others' presence. The combination of the presence information and the perception choices determines awareness between entities. Note how similar these concepts are to focus and nimbus in the spatial model (Benford and Fahlen 1993) introduced in section 1.2.4. The locales framework authors acknowledge this work but note that the framework abstracts from the spatial requirement. It is even closer to the generalised model of awareness (Rodden 1996) that will be introduced shortly (Section 1.3.2.2). Explicit reference to Rodden (1996) does not occur until 1998; however, there appears to be parallel development during this time.

Individual Views. As an individual engages in work, he/she is rarely involved in a single task to the exclusion of all others. There are two important aspects to be considered; a *view* on one social world, and an individual's *viewset* across multiple social worlds. A view is how an individual sees a single social world (the people and the locales), and it is dependent on the level of engagement with the centre of that world. A viewset incorporates the individual's views of all the social worlds with which they are engaged, e.g. when juggling work and family tasks. The viewset will change continually without fully switching out of any of the tasks.

Interaction Trajectories describe how all five aspects of the locales framework change over time. Locales will be set up, used so that the sites and artefacts are modified, and eventually discarded. Individual views and viewsets will constantly change as their focus changes and their relationships to others changes.

Civic Structure describes the relevant outside influences on a social world. No social world operates in isolation. Members are involved in multiple worlds at once. For example, the many social worlds within an organisation (or social group) overlap and influence one another.

The final version of the locales framework (Fitzpatrick et al. 1998a; Fitzpatrick 2003) focused on using the framework as a tool for constructing, understanding and bridging the sociological and the technical. The framework helps to understand the sociological relations of a context as well as the holistic technical view, and as a list of all the things to consider in analysis and design of a CSCW system.

The locales framework is unique in its coverage. The component aspects were also revolutionary – especially those of locales, centres and individual viewsets. The contribution to awareness is in showing how awareness fits into a larger context.

Unfortunately the locales framework did not make a huge impact on CSCW design. The related work was mostly in the WORLDS and Orbit systems (described in Section 1.3.3) and in some analysis work on the Elvin notification system (described in Section 1.3.5), all of which were within the same group. We believe that this is due firstly to the complexity of the theory's relationship to design, making it hard to use it directly, and secondly to its descriptive rather than prescriptive nature.

1.3.1.3 Social Context Summary

The results of the two social context research areas we have discussed here differed greatly. The work on privacy and interruption left open questions and room for more investigation and models to be developed (see Section 1.4.1.4). The locales framework prompted different uses, as a guide for design of tools such as Orbit and Community Bar (McEwan and Greenberg 2005), and also as a way of describing the social positioning of tools and practices (Fitzpatrick et al. 1999; Fitzpatrick 2003).

In the next section we go on to talk about work, specifically about awareness itself rather than the social interaction framework around it.

1.3.2 Awareness Frameworks and Models

While HCI researchers had realised the importance of awareness in supporting collaboration, the question remained how awareness support could be represented at a conceptual level. Early implementations like media spaces implemented awareness support in a fashion that was very closely modelled on reality. However, if awareness support was to be realised beyond direct audio–video links, researchers needed to understand more details of awareness, such as how people gain mutual aware-

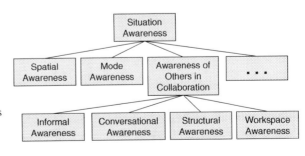

Fig. 1.2 Situation awareness and subtypes (Gutwin 1997, p. 20)

ness of work practices and the types of information that are required to create that awareness.

In this section, we discuss representative samples of awareness models and frameworks. This includes some of the major conceptual awareness models, Gutwin's workspace awareness model (1997), Rodden's model of awareness (1996) and the event pipeline model produced by Fuchs and his colleagues (1996).

1.3.2.1   Workspace Awareness

In 1995 Carl Gutwin and Saul Greenberg published the first version of their influential workspace awareness framework[3]. The framework was targeted at supporting awareness for small distributed teams using real-time synchronous shared workspace groupware (Gutwin and Greenberg 1995b; Gutwin et al. 1995)[4]. They define *workspace awareness* as: "The collection of up-to-the-moment knowledge a person uses to capture another's interaction with the workspace" (Gutwin and Greenberg 1996).

While the original publications in 1995 were not linked to situation awareness, Gutwin extended the model in his PhD dissertation (1997) to include this concept. Gutwin saw workspace awareness as a specialisation of situation awareness. Situation awareness had emerged from psychological concepts and phenomena observed in military aviation (Gilson 1995). Adams et al. defined situation awareness as "the up-to-the minute cognizance required to operate or maintain a system" (Adams et al. 1995). Situation awareness describes single-person activities (perception, comprehension and prediction), and is primarily concerned with interaction with complex technical environments (aircraft, power plants, etc.). Gutwin used situation awareness as a framing concept for awareness and decomposed it hierarchically to position his own workspace awareness work. In doing so he also named and positioned other types of awareness that had appeared in CSCW research.

Spatial and mode awareness are specialisations of situation awareness. Spatial awareness is the ability of a pilot to understand his location in an airspace (Fracker 1989). Mode awareness is "the ability of a supervisor to track and to anticipate the behaviour of [mode-based] automated systems" (Sarter and Woods 1995).

Gutwin contrasted these single-user types of awareness with *awareness of others in collaboration*, which he then breaks down further into four different concepts. *Informal awareness* deals with the presence and availability of people (Who is around?; Are they available for collaboration?, etc.) (e.g. Dourish and Bellotti 1992). Other authors commonly refer to this type of awareness as presence awareness or

---

[3] A later summary of the framework was also published in 2002. Gutwin and Greenberg (2002) A Descriptive Framework of Workspace Awareness for Real-Time Groupware. Comput Support Coop Work 11: 411–446, however, it did not extend the basic notions of the concept. It is preferable as a reference and is the definitive version of the work.

[4] An early version of the concept was also published under the term *group awareness*. Gutwin and Greenberg (1995a) Support for Group Awareness in Real Time Desktop Conferences. In: Proceedings of the 2nd New Zealand Computer Science Research Students Conference.

social awareness (e.g. Tollmar et al. 1996; Prinz 1999). *Conversational awareness* comprises awareness of utterances as well as awareness of facial expressions, gestures and other forms of non-verbal communication. *Structural awareness* refersto the structure of the working process including organisational settings like rules of interacting, power and status relationships as well as roles of persons within the working process. While not the main contribution of the dissertation, this collection of terms and partial taxonomy has had its influence on later work, for example, the term "informal awareness" has become semi-standard (e.g. Boyle and Greenberg 2005; Greenberg and Rounding 2001; McEwan and Greenberg 2005).

The workspace awareness framework itself consists of three parts, the type of information that makes up workspace awareness, the mechanisms people use to gather information and the ways people use workspace awareness information in collaboration. With regard to awareness information, Gutwin and Greenberg rely on five questions to describe awareness information: who, what, where, when and how. Based on those categories they define specific questions targeted at analysing awareness in shared workspaces. For instance, in the "who" category the authors specify such questions as: "Is anyone in the workspace?" and "Who was here, and when?".

Gutwin and Greenberg's work stands out from other awareness work at the time as it offers a comprehensive model that addresses awareness from a conceptual rather than a technological angle. The framework allows designers to systematically analyse and describe interactions in shared workspaces.

1.3.2.2 The Focus/Nimbus Model of Awareness

In 1996, Rodden published a generalised version of the spatial COMIC model of awareness (Benford and Fahlen 1993). He generalised the model by reducing the concepts to the generic set of focus, nimbus and awareness. Medium, aura and adaptors are now considered to be part of the specific applications of the general model. He also refined the concepts of focus, nimbus and awareness to be object based rather than space based, thus extending the application of the model to contexts that cannot be easily mapped to a spatial metaphor.

In Rodden's generalised model, focus and nimbus are recast in terms of set theory. In the spatial model they are specified as a volume in the space, and awareness is calculated as a function by the degree of volume overlap. In the new object-based model, focus and nimbus are each sets of objects and awareness is calculated as a function of the set intersection. The benefit of the object-based method is that there no longer has to be a mapping of the application to some concept of volume, allowing the model to be used much more generically to model awareness in any collaborative application. To summarise one of Rodden's examples, in a workflow application a person's nimbus would be the set of tasks already completed, while their focus would, most of the time, be the set of tasks they were just about to do next.

The value of this model is that, like the original spatial model, it makes a distinction between the sender's control of the information they provide and the recipient's control of their attention to perceiving information. It also provides a framework for modelling how the interactions of sender's information and recipient's attention combine to result in the recipient having awareness of the sender.

Although regarded as influential, the model was not widely adopted beyond the original scale of work on collaborative virtual environments (Sandor et al. 1997) until later. McEwan and Greenberg (2005) implemented an awareness system, Community Bar, that gives user explicit control over the nimbus and focus settings.

1.3.2.3   Event Pipeline Model

The event pipeline model extended the concept introduced by Khronika (Lövstrand 1991) of decoupling senders and receivers of discrete awareness events. The extensions were an important development and captured the fundamental concepts for event-based awareness research in CSCW.

Starting in 1995, Fuchs and his colleagues published a number of studies on a generic event distribution model. The work was first published as part of the GroupDesk model (Fuchs et al. 1995). Building on the notions developed in GroupDesk, Fuchs then developed the PoliAwaC system as part of the PoliTeam project (Fuchs et al. 1996). The model underlying PoliAwaC introduced a number of innovations. As we discussed earlier, Khronika was the first system to introduce the notion of event-based awareness with the decoupling of senders and receivers. The work described here takes the event-based awareness further by adding a number of concepts that give individual users greater control over the event distribution process. The model, here referred to as the event pipeline[5] model, is summarised in Fig. 1.3.

The model is based on the persistent storage of events in a database. User actions, which manipulate system objects, like documents, generate that are recorded and stored in an *event database*. The recorded events are made available for other users through notification mechanisms at the user interface.

Privacy filters let senders select an appropriate level of privacy. All outgoing events that are based on a user's action are matched against individual privacy filter. On the receiver side the model contains interest filters, which let receivers select which notifications they want to receive, and when and how they want to receive them. The filters were introduced with the aim of reducing the large flow of information that event-based systems produce. In addition to these individual filters the model also introduced a global filter that allowed for organisation-wide policies to be reflected in the event distribution model, as well as the notion of conflict resolution between participating parties (Pfeifer and Wulf 1995).

The aim in the 1996 publication (Fuchs et al. 1996) was to apply the model in the context of PoliTeam, a research project that was concerned with supporting the col-

---

[5]The model was never consistently named. The original paper written in German refers to it as *Ereignissdienst* (event service). Rather than using this generic term we will use the term "event pipeline" which was coined by one of Fuch's co-authors, Volker Wulf. Fuchs himself published the AREA model which has a much broader scope.

Fig. 1.3 The event pipeline model (Fuchs et al. 1996)[6]

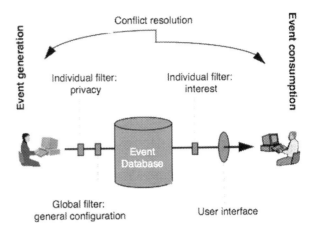

laboration between government departments situated in Bonn and Berlin (Klöckner et al. 1995). The pipeline model itself is described more comprehensively in Fuch's dissertation (Fuchs 1997). Fuch's dissertation is also the foundation for the AREA model described in Section 1.3.5.

1.3.3 Collaborative Environments

So far in this section we have discussed theoretical approaches to awareness to inform design. In this section we discuss collaborative applications.

In the second half of the 1990s, there was a trend to build complete environments that would manage all of the collaborative interactions for a group. These environments would contain access to all of the shared resources for the group and provide awareness of people's presence in the environment and their activities around the shared resources. Rather than being single collaborative applications, they would provide access to a range of applications and group them by task environment.

The common organising metaphor was room based, where users entered a room for a particular context or task, and moved into a different room when working on a different task. An interesting variation on the usual room metaphor was the Orbit system, which was based on the locales framework and supported the concept of individual viewsets containing views of multiple locales simultaneously.

1.3.3.1 DIVA, GroupDesk and PoliAwaC

From about 1995 onwards researchers at GMD[7] explored aspects of awareness through a succession of prototypes, DIVA (Sohlenkamp and Chwelos 1994),

---

[6]Translated by the authors.

[7]GMD is the *Gesellschaft für Mathematik und Datenverarbeitung* (Society for Mathematics and Information technology), now a part of the Fraunhofer Society.

GroupDesk (Fuchs et al. 1995), PoliAwaC (Fuchs et al. 1996) and BSCW (Bentley et al. 1995; Prinz 1999). Many of those prototypes were applied in the context of the PoliTeam project to support communication between government departments in Germany.

The research undertaken at GMD was characterised by a number of commonalities. First, all prototypes were built on the notion of shared workspaces, and implemented both asynchronous and synchronous aspects of awareness. Second, the design of the system and the underlying awareness concepts were tightly coupled. All prototypes, with the exception of DIVA, utilised an object-oriented notion to describe the system as well as the awareness concept. And third, most of these systems were based on the event pipeline architecture (Fuchs et al. 1996) (see Section 1.3.2.3). We will look at some of these systems and their impact on awareness research in more detail.

These systems were highly relevant for the development of awareness research. They introduced notions that lead to an understanding of asynchronous awareness mechanisms such as notification, event generation, event distribution and notification subscription. Below we discuss each of the prototypes in turn.

DIVA was an early groupware prototype that was based on the virtual office metaphor (Sohlenkamp and Chwelos 1994). The system used a simple abstraction of an office environment consisting of people, rooms, desks and documents. Rooms were shared workspaces that contained representations of people, desks and documents and provided an audio–video link between participants. Rooms allowed participants to control different levels of access and visibility, with the interaction closely tied to imitating real-world interactions. For instance, users could only be present in one room at a time and in order to work closely with another user they would locate themselves around the same desk. DIVA combined a number of groupware services including shared editors (text editors, drawing tools, music editors, etc.) as well as support for synchronous and asynchronous awareness.

The system implemented many innovative awareness features including privacy support and access control. DIVA showed presence and virtual location by placing icons of users in rooms. Rooms had three access settings, providing varying amounts of awareness information to those outside the room. In addition, users could disable the audio–video link temporarily while in a room in order to receive phone calls. Another interesting privacy feature was "private conversations". Users could initiate private conversations by dragging their icon so that it overlapped with the icon of another user. During a private conversation other members of the room could still overhear the conversation but at a reduced volume.

The literal composition of workspaces allowed users to gain awareness about who was working with whom on which documents. A "catch-up" mechanism was used to replay changes made to shared documents: "DIVA ... provides a uniform mechanism for catch-up ... based on the replay of saved history. Changes made by others are replayed with animation so that they may be viewed exactly as if the user had been there watching them being made, except that the replay may be sped up" (Sohlenkamp and Chwelos 1994).

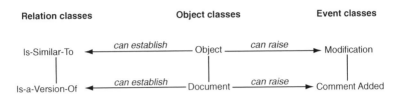

Fig. 1.4 GroupDesk model, class relationships (Fuchs et al. 1995)

After DIVA, in 1995 Fuchs et al. introduced their event distribution model (also referred to as the GroupDesk model, shown in Fig. 1.5). The model becomes the starting point for a series of prototypes, namely, GroupDesk (Fuchs et al. 1995), PoliAwaC (Fuchs et al. 1996; Fuchs 1997), AREA (Fuchs 1999) and had influenced the design of BSCW (Bentley et al. 1995; Prinz 1999) and NESSIE (Prinz 1999).

The GroupDesk model (shown in Fig. 1.4) used an object-oriented approach to model the awareness mechanism. It consisted of two major components, a model of the working environment, which described actors, artefacts, their relationships as well as events, and a model of awareness, which described "work situations", "interest contexts", "event distribution" and "event notification". The object-oriented approach allowed the authors to represent specific kinds of working situations based on a general relationship between objects, events and relations.

The model contained three concepts: objects, relations and events. Objects represented any entity that was modelled by the system (e.g. documents, folders, representations of departments). Objects representing users were referred to separately as actors. Relations linked objects to each other and actors. Events were divided into two types. Modification events represented user-initiated changes of objects within

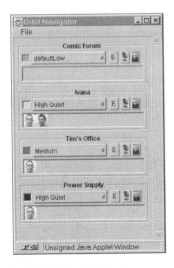
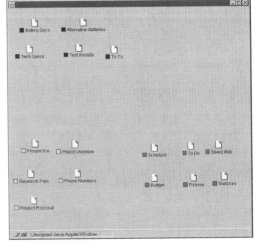

Fig. 1.5 Orbit–Gold interface

the system, e.g. editing of a document. Activity events described synchronous activities, e.g. presence in a workspace.

The main innovation of the GroupDesk model was the level of control it provided for event distribution and notification based on user preferences. Up to that date users had little control over which awareness information they were interested in and how the awareness information was displayed. The GroupDesk model introduced subscription mechanisms that allowed users to define "interest contexts". These subscriptions specified the type of objects, relationships and events. The model also introduced the idea that event notification could occur on different levels of intensity, from urgent and highly disruptive to peripheral and ambient.

The first GroupDesk prototype was just a simple shared workspace system built to evaluate aspects of the event model and lacked an implementation of the event subscription mechanisms described in the model. Later prototypes from the group, such as PoliAwaC (Fuchs et al. 1996; Fuchs 1997), implemented the concepts in the model more completely.

1.3.3.2 WORLDS and Orbit

The WORLDS (Tolone et al. 1995) and Orbit systems (Mansfield et al. 1997a; Mansfield et al. 1997b) are worth discussing here as they are the only systems of this time to explicitly implement the concepts of the locales framework. Both systems were built in conjunction with the development of the locales framework and so reflected the framework principles and helped to refine the theory. WORLDS reflected the early versions of the locales framework, emphasising social worlds and different locales for different tasks, while Orbit incorporated the later concepts of individual views and viewsets.

WORLDS provided a very "room-like" view of locales and the relations between them. The interface showed a single locale at a time, with the tools and artefacts for the locale displayed within it. A number of functions supported moving between locales, including user bookmark lists of favourite locales, "portals" to locales that could be placed in other locales and home locales for users.

Awareness of others was provided through media space components (i.e. audio and video links), to all locale members, opened when entering a locale. Workspace awareness was at the artefact level, where shared documents would be marked with change events, similar to other similar collaborative environments such as DIVA (Sohlenkamp and Chwelos 1994).

In contrast, Orbit provided a view of locales that was much closer to the final version of the locales framework. A user was able to see and interact with all their locales at the same time, and they could dynamically adjust their view on each locale to reflect its pertinence to their current task. This design feature was a marked departure from the collaborative environments of the time and has been seen infrequently since.

The Orbit interface is shown in Fig. 1.5. It consisted of two windows: the navigator (left) and the workspace (right). The navigator listed the locales and showed presence information of other people in those locales. The workspace showed documents that the user was interested in, selected from all of their locales. Documents were linked to locales through colour, e.g. the "Power Supply" locale is marked black, and all its documents are also marked with a black colour chip (Power Supply documents are all in the top left corner of the workspace). Orbit also provided text chat through integration with the Tickertape tool (Fitzpatrick et al. 1998b), as well as audio and video links with other people.

The importance of these two systems lies in their theoretical foundations and in their concept of awareness that, although only in a very simple manner, contrasted with the prevailing event-based model. The transition from theory to design and implementation is a challenge that continues to face CSCW, and the relationship between the locales framework and WORLDS/Orbit is one of the few examples of such a transition. In regards to the underlying model of awareness, Orbit was more closely aligned with thefocus/ nimbus model of awareness than the event-based models, even though the nimbus was adjusted to equal the focus, enforcing reciprocity.

1.3.3.3 Collaborative Environments Summary

Collaborative environments were usually developed in tandem with theory and the environments that we have discussed here were the implementation side of the theoretical models and frameworks discussed in the previous section. WORLDS and Orbit informed and were informed by the development of the locales framework, while the GMD prototypes were developed along with the event pipeline model. Other systems also explored theoretical concepts, such as the TeamRooms prototype (Roseman and Greenberg 1996) which was an exploration of the "rooms" metaphor and also incorporated early ideas from what would become the workspace awareness framework.

1.3.4 Physical Display of Awareness

An important and influential concept for the presentation of awareness information began to gather research attention. The use of physical devices for interaction with digital artefacts was being driven by the increased interest in ubiquitous computing, and in the late 1990s this trend started to incorporate awareness. We look at two important example publications illustrating ambient display of awareness and conveying awareness of loved ones. Both of these publications were influential and foreshadowed much future research.

Ishii and Ullmer (1997) introduced their seminal work on tangible computing. They describe tangible computing in three concepts: "*interactive surfaces; ... coupling ... with graspable physical objects; and ambient media for background awareness*". They present a number of examples of ambient media in the paper as well, such as the ambientROOM, which incorporates ambient light, shadow, sound, airflow and water flow.

Ambient awareness displays provide information in a format that encourages peripheral awareness, which occurs when we are aware of some information without focussing our attention on it. An illustrative example from Ishii and Ullmer is the way people are aware of the weather outside the window without concentrating on it. When there is an interesting change in the information, such as when a storm appears, our attention is drawn to it and we consciously focus on the information. Ishii and Ullmer built an ambient display that projected ripples on the ceiling, and varied the frequency of ripples dependent on weather activity outside.

The principle was also observed in the media spaces work, where the value of peripheral displays of colleagues was noted by Bly et al. (1993). Similar to the peripheral media spaces, ambient displays show awareness information in a non-intrusive manner so that users can concentrate on their main task, but also allow interruption for interesting events.

There are other, earlier implementations of ambient awareness devices in the past, such as Gaver's EAR system (Gaver 1991) and Jerimijenko's Dangling String (Weiser and Brown 1995). However, this earlier work did not seem to capture the imagination of researchers as much as Ishii and Ullmer's, perhaps because of its "packaging" in the larger framework of tangible computing. The important concepts from this work were non-intrusive display of awareness information, capturing attention at interesting events and allowing the user to transition from the peripheral display into a detailed and interactive representation of the information.

Strong and Gaver's (1996) Feather, Scent and Shaker prototypes offer an interesting contrast to the predominantly workplace-oriented awareness research seen up to this point. Their target was to support awareness in intimate, personal relationships where companionship, mood and emotion were the important factors rather than an explicit transfer of information. As such, the prototypes were sensual and abstract. The emphasis on intimate relationships in personal life was an important driver for the later trend in awareness in home environments (see Section 1.4.2.1).

1.3.5 Infrastructure

During this time period it was becoming clear that while research prototypes were providing valuable insight into the design and implementation of awareness systems, there was a distinct lack of awareness infrastructures that would allow groupware designers to build systems quickly. Infrastructure systems were needed to allow for awareness information to be easily shared and so enable designers to concentrate on presentation and interaction. In addition, the focus on collaboration environments proved limiting when it came to collecting awareness events from applications outside the groupware environment.

Awareness infrastructure took the form of event distribution architectures. Systems such as AREA (Fuchs 1999) and NESSIE (Prinz 1999) introduced the notion of a generic infrastructure and cross-application awareness. However, they did not provide a general accessible service that other groupware developers could build on. During the same time the use of notification services to support awareness was being explored (Ramduny et al. 1998).

In this section we discuss three examples of event distribution infrastructure. AREA supports both synchronous and asynchronous notifications and incorporates the event pipeline model concepts of privacy and interest. NESSIE also implements the event pipeline model but has a greater focus on sources of awareness event information and output modalities for notification. Elvin (Segall and Arnold 1997) is one of the most successful notification services, which is independent of that work and implemented event distribution on a lower level. By providing a generic infrastructure, all of those systems enable awareness events to be shared amongst applications.

1.3.5.1 Area

The emergence of event-based awareness systems posed additional challenges to the design of awareness systems. In general, event-based systems generate a large number of events, making it necessary to allow recipients of awareness information to subscribe to relevant information and influence the types of notification they receive.

The AREA framework (Fuchs 1999) is a result of research on event notification models undertaken by Fuchs and his colleagues over a number of years. While the original ideas for event notification were discussed in the GroupDesk system (Fuchs et al. 1995), Fuchs extended the model as part of his PhD work (Fuchs 1997).

AREA is defined as both a semantic model as well as a groupware infrastructure component. The semantic model is based on the notions of event distribution, user-defined interests and privacy specification. Privacy and interest specifications can be seen as implementations of the privacy and interest filters featured in the event pipeline model (Fuchs et al. 1996).

1.3.5.2 NESSIE

The NESSIE system (Prinz 1999) was one of the first groupware architectures to allow handling of events created by other applications or generated by sensors. The NESSIE model used "sensors" and "indicators" to gather events and distribute event notifications. Sensors could be physical sensors installed in people's offices as well as macros in programs like Microsoft Word that delivered information about changes in documents. Indicators allowed targeted event notifications. Furthermore, users had access to a configuration interface that allowed them to individually combine the sensors and indicators they wanted to use for a given situation.

NESSIE supported the use of ambient displays for awareness information. For example, the *activity-balloon* ambient device (Fig. 1.6, bottom left), small tower with a balloon on top indicated virtual presence by blowing up the balloon when a remote person was present. In addition NESSIE supported the virtual 3D interfaces "SmallView" and "Theater of Work" (Fig. 1.6, projected display) to provide a virtual world for distributed interactions (Prinz and Gross 2001).

Fig. 1.6 Ambient and 3D
interfaces in NESSIE[8]

1.3.5.3 Elvin

Elvin (Segall and Arnold 1997) was not created specifically for awareness events,
but rather as generic event infrastructure. Despite not being built for the purpose of
awareness, Elvin gained exposure to the collaborative research community through
its use in a number of collaborative awareness tools. It was used in the Tickertape application (Parsowith et al. 1998) and it was used to pass awareness events
in the Orbit system (see Section 1.3.3.2). It also served as the foundation technology for awareness within an organisational setting, ranging from within small teams
to across organisational structures with many event sources and presentation interfaces, as reported by Fitzpatrick et al. (1999).

The strength of Elvin is in its content-based subscription and routing of notifications. Producers of information can send out unstructured information about
events, and consumers subscribe by specifying something about the information
content they want to receive. For example, if Alice is interested in awareness, she
can subscribe to every event that includes the word "awareness" anywhere in its
content, so that she can see chat messages discussing awareness, meetings concerning awareness, code changes to awareness prototypes, and anything else about
awareness. In practice this means that (a) producers of information do not have
to worry about who, if anyone, is interested in the notifications they are sending

---

[8]From http://www.ercim.org/publication/Ercim_News/enw42/prinz.html.

and (b) consumers can subscribe based on free-form ideas of interesting message content.

The idea of decoupling producers of notifications from the consumers of the information was used earlier in the Khronika system (see earlier Section 1.2.3), but in Khronika there was a specific structure to events and consumers had to subscribe based on the fields in the structure. Elvin does not impose any structure and consumers are free to subscribe to any part of the notification content.

1.3.6 Summary of Diversification and Research Prototypes

This period could be characterised as the golden age of awareness research as it was the period with the most research directed primarily on awareness. During this time the major thrust of research was in developing models and theories to capture how awareness worked and how it was part of collaborative activity. Alongside the theories, comprehensive collaborative environments were developed to test and provide feedback for the theoretical aspects.

In the next section we will see that awareness becomes more of an application component. Development of comprehensive theories starts to dwindle and collaborative environments are replaced by suites of supporting applications that integrate with individual work. To replace these research directions we see an emphasis on extending awareness to other groups of people in different domains.

1.4 Summary of Extended Models and Specialisation

The time period covered in this section is characterised by a number of research trends. Each of these trends is driven by a need to understand awareness in a broader context. First we can see an increasing specialisation of existing awareness models. While the previous time period was concerned with understanding and conceptualising awareness support, the current research period is concerned with addressing issues like support for context information or the relationship between privacy and awareness in more detail (Section 1.4.1.4). Second, awareness research is increasingly penetrating new domains as researchers start to look outside the workplace. Domestic and medical settings are two domains that stand out in this context. Third, we can see a trend where technical developments have opened up new avenues for awareness research. In particular, the increasing popularity of instant messaging has led to the widespread distribution of tools that support awareness of availability and have been extended in various ways to support other types of awareness. Last but not least, we also see the emergence of requirements for new awareness concepts that cover different types of group configurations which go beyond standard distributed settings. The introduction of tabletop devices, for example, has highlighted an increased need for technological support for co-located work on a large shared screen. Notions of proximity and group building in ubiquitous computing and new types of collaboration, such as mixed presence collaboration, have posed new opportunities and challenges to awareness research.

1.4.1 Models and Diversifying Types of Awareness

While the time period between 1995 and 2000 was undoubtedly the most active when it comes to producing concepts and implementations of awareness, work on awareness concepts and models still continues in the current time period. In many cases this work can be characterised as an extension of existing models. For instance, the event notification infrastructure (ENI) (Gross and Prinz 2003 Prinz and Gross 2004) adds an additional layer of modelling to the existing NESSIE (Prinz 1999; Simone and Bandini 2002) model. By comparison, Simone and Bandini's (2002) reaction–diffusion metaphor takes an existing model from a different domain and applies it to HCI research.

At the same time, many researchers started to fill in the details of particular types of awareness, rather than the issue of how awareness worked in general. Their approach was to look at supporting a particular type of awareness.

In addition, work on the relationship of privacy and awareness continued and started to untangle the confusing mess of concepts involved in the word "privacy".

1.4.1.1 ENI

Event notification infrastructure (ENI) (Gross and Prinz 2003 Prinz and Gross 2004) is conceptually based on prior awareness research undertaken at GMD (Fuchs et al. 1995; Fuchs 1999; Prinz 1999). ENI extends the NESSIE awareness model (Prinz 1999) and integrates the notion of "contexts" into the model. Context information includes locations, artefacts and applications and other information, which is linked to a specific context. ENI adds this information to existing event information in an awareness system.

The model contains three fundamental steps. First, the model tries to determine in which context a user is currently working. The authors suggest a context mapping mechanism that maps events gathered from sensor information against rules saved in a context database. Second, the model identifies the context of the user who is receiving the notification. The authors are less specific about how to achieve this context mapping. In their prototypical implementation (Prinz and Gross 2004), the working context is derived from the selection of shared workspaces. Third, the model checks which notification information that the user wants to receive (user preferences).

The ENI model tries to improve awareness support by gathering additional information and allowing users to receive awareness information in a more context-specific manner. However, the context mapping mechanisms underlying this concept is highly complex. It is unclear who performs this mapping and how inter-individual differences between users can be addressed. The authors refer to this issue as future research.

1.4.1.2 Reaction–Diffusion Model

The reaction–diffusion model of awareness (Simone and Bandini 2002) is a model based on a spatial metaphor. It owes a lot of its origins to the COMIC spatial model (Benford and Fahlén 1993; Rodden 1996; see also earlier Sections 1.2.4 and 1.3.2.2) but extends it with the motivating idea that awareness is a complex phenomenon and so needs a complex metaphor to describe it. They propose the metaphor of reaction and diffusion, common in many other fields such as biology, chemistry and physics.

The common fundamental principle in reaction and diffusion metaphors is that there are many entities in an environment, which move around in the environment and react when they come into contact with each other. For example, in a biological setting there may be zebras on a grassy plain. Each of the entities has a *state*, in our example most of the zebras have a healthy state but there are a few with a virus. The entities move around, or *diffuse*, and come into contact with each other. When they come into contact, they possibly undergo a *reaction*, which changes their state. To take our zebra example again, when an infected zebra comes into contact with a healthy one, there is a possibility of a reaction that changes the healthy zebra to the state of being infected. Contact is defined in terms of each entity having multiple *fields*, roughly equivalent to nimbus, and *sensitivity functions*, roughly equivalent to focus.

There are four types of rules to be determined for applying the metaphor to a particular setting:

1. *Field diffusion rules* define the different possible types of fields along with their area of effect and how they propagate through the environment.
2. *Trigger rules* define how the fields affect sensitive entities.
3. *Transport rules* when entities' positions are changed by fields.
4. *Reaction rules* define how an entity's state is changed by a field.

The reaction–diffusion model of awareness differs from the earlier spatial models mostly in its complexity, which means it can provide more detailed and complex descriptions and explanations of the formal interactions of awareness information. The extra detail helps ease applying the theory to design of a system.

1.4.1.3 Types of Awareness

While not counting as full models of awareness by any stretch, there was work that addressed specific types of awareness and so served to fill the classification space without defining an awareness classification taxonomy. Two example types of awareness are intentionally enriched awareness and informal awareness.

Intentionally enriched awareness (Rittenbruch 2002; Rittenbruch et al. 2007) is based on the observation that many awareness concepts assign a passive role to the person whose actions are being observed. This approach directly contradicts research that shows that people in real-life collaborative situations are often actively involved in providing invaluable information which helps others to understand their actions in context (Heath et al. 2002; Schmidt 2002). Intentionally enriched awareness acknowledges this fact and provides people with means and mechanisms to enrich awareness information by deliberately adding contextual information. One of the main challenges of this approach is to provide the right balance between additional workload and perceived benefit for the individual. See the chapter on intentionally enriched awareness in this book for a more comprehensive conceptual discussion of this approach. Intentionally enriched awareness is discussed in more detail in Chapter 19.

Informal awareness is the now reasonably stable term for the awareness effects observed primarily through media space research that have been labelled peripheral awareness and general awareness amongst other terms. This is a background awareness of work colleagues, incorporating knowledge of presence, activity and availability. Informal awareness is the foundation for casual interaction, which in turn proves to be vital for supporting ongoing collaboration.

Some research into media spaces continued, such as the deployment of a VideoWindow (Fish et al. 1990) called vKitchen at Microsoft (Jancke et al. 2001). Most research into this phenomenon in recent years has taken the approach of how to design informal applications that support and enhance the informal awareness and casual interaction capabilities of small groups of collaborators. A large part of the motivation for the approach has been studies of Instant Messenger (e.g. Nardi et al. 2000), which show that the simple clients provide a great benefit in informal awareness information and simple transitions to casual interaction. With this motivation, amongst others, prototypes supporting rich multimedia awareness and interaction have been developed, such as the Notification Collage (Greenberg and Rounding 2001) and the Community Bar (McEwan and Greenberg 2005). While these systems provided rich presence and availability information with various multimedia communication channels, activity awareness was minimal. Tee et al. (2006) extended this work to provide extra activity awareness through sharing of screen snapshots.

There are of course many other terms for types of awareness around, but listing them all is beyond the scope of this chapter. Gross et al. (2005) provide an excellent coverage of all the different definitions that have been used.

1.4.1.4   Privacy Continued

Privacy research continued from the work discussed earlier in Section 1.3.1.1. Some research was into trying to ameliorate the privacy invasiveness of media spaces, taking the approach of removing privacy violating details while retaining enough information for awareness (e.g. Junestrand et al. 2001). However, Neustaedter et al. (2006b) showed that at least blur filtration failed to achieve the required balance.

Previous literature on privacy was of a "bottom-up" nature, focussing on the issues arising in technical systems such as media spaces. Palen and Dourish (2003) were the first to address this issue by developing a model of privacy based on the work of social psychologist Irwin Altman (Altman 1975; Altman 1977). The contribution in this important work was to frame privacy as a boundary regulation process. This highlighted the fact that people did not simply want both privacy and awareness all the time in competition with each other, but instead carefully regulated information flow on a moment by moment basis.

Perhaps the most comprehensive description of privacy to come out of this time period comes from Boyle and Greenberg (2005), who draw both upon a wide variety of fields such as anthropology, architecture, law and sociology, and also upon the technical reports of media space privacy issues. Using both theoretical and technical approaches grounded the principles in real details while at the same time providing a framework to relate issues and gain an overall understanding of privacy regulation.

1.4.1.5 Summary of Models and Diversifying Types

The work in this section has all been a continuation of work in earlier years: ENI is a direct continuation of the GMD event-based awareness research; the reaction–diffusion model is a continuation of other spatial models of awareness; privacy research dates right back to the days of early media space development; and the diversifying types of awareness research are in the tradition of workspace awareness. The main purpose of this section has been to show that these strong streams of awareness research did not suddenly end in the year 2000.

The next section discusses a trend that has a more recent beginning, where awareness research starts to move out of the workplace.

1.4.2 Awareness in Different Domains

In the two earlier time periods we have considered so far, 1986–1994 and 1995–1999, the focus has predominantly been on supporting awareness in an office environment. There has been an assumption that users are in the workplace and using a standard personal computer. In recent years, however, we have seen an increasing amount of research that applies awareness to other domains. These domains are numerous, including home living, healthcare in homes and in hospitals, education, gaming, industrial workplaces, art installations and many others. Fundamental to this research is the concept that new domains mean new awareness behaviour and new requirements for awareness support. Perhaps this is the reason for so much domain-driven research – it is insufficient to simply apply what is known about awareness in the office, so the particular properties of the domain need to be understood before support can be provided.

In this section we use the domestic domain as an illustrative example. While there are many other domains driving awareness research of different types, space does not permit a full discussion. Other domains that are receiving a great deal of awareness research attention include health, both home care (e.g. Pinelle and Gutwin 2002; Palen and Aaløkke 2006) and hospital based (e.g. Bardram et al. 2006; Munkvold et al. 2006), education (e.g. Ganoe et al. 2003) and games (e.g. Dyck et al. 2003; Brown and Bell 2004).

1.4.2.1 Domestic Awareness

While research on applying CSCW to the home environment dates from the late 1990 s (e.g. Hindus 1999; Hughes et al. 1998; Junestrand and Tollmar 1999), this early work focussed either on the home as a site for work or on directed communication mechanisms. It was not until after 2000 that awareness in the home was addressed explicitly.

As noted by Strong and Gaver (1996) (see also Section 1.3.4), awareness in personal relationships has a different character to workplace awareness. In personal and intimate relationships, such as those found in a home environment, the goal is for an emotional connection and feelings of intimacy (Gaver and Martin 2000). The information conveyed is usually of a general form about health, activity, environment, relationships and events, and must show trends and patterns (Mynatt et al. 2001).

The home environment also differs greatly in character from the workplace. The home is often thought of as a sanctuary, where everything is intensely personalised to provide a restful, soothing environment. Home-based awareness devices must be simple and aesthetically compatible with the personal environment (Hindus et al. 2001). Home activities are also different than the workplace, being less task focussed and comprised of more seemingly mundane activities such as coordinating schedules (Edwards and Grinter 2001). Furthermore, people often have strong emotional ties to objects within the home, and purely functional objects are often neglected, requiring an awareness device to have strong meaning attached to it (Tollmar and Persson 2002). Successful prototypes of home awareness devices incorporated the above principles – they were intimate, simple, aesthetically pleasing and emotionally meaningful.

Most early (early in this context means around 2000–2002) prototypes were severely limited in their utility due to technical constraints concerning networking or sensing. The constraints meant that any deployment was very small. Extensive field trials have only started appearing recently, such as the digital family portrait study (Rowan and Mynatt 2005), where the technology was the result of detailed participatory design some years before (Mynatt et al. 2001). The field study was successful in providing a feeling of "peace of mind" amongst distributed family members. Another recent field study, also testing the result of an extensive participatory design (Neustaedter and Brush 2006), was the study of the LINC home calendar system (Neustaedter et al. 2007). LINC was designed to support family activity awareness and the resulting coordination activities.

Recent years have also produced more detailed work on the overall properties of domestic awareness. Neustaedter et al. (2006a) investigated the different groups of people with whom people want to remain in contact and what kinds of information needed to be maintained about members of each group. They found that the relevant groupings of contacts were home inhabitants, intimate socials and extended socials. Elliot et al. (2005) and Crabtree et al. (2003) investigated the contextual properties of location for awareness in the home, showing that where and when devices are deployed is a vital factor for their usefulness and uptake.

1.4.2.2 Summary of Awareness in Different Domains

The example of the domestic domain demonstrates an important lesson. Each domain context is fundamentally different in its requirements. While the emphasis is still on people and so the mechanical aspects of how awareness works are the same (possibly indicating that the general models of awareness are still applicable), people have different expectations and behaviour in the workplace, in the home and at play. Any intervention of awareness-supporting technology needs to reflect that.

1.4.3 Technology Driven Awareness Research

Over the last few years a number of new interaction technologies have led to new opportunities for awareness research. First and foremost the emergence of instant messaging (IM) has led to the widespread distribution of tools that support the awareness of availability. While instant messaging became popular in the late 1990s, HCI research only recently discovered its potential for supporting collaboration and awareness between co-workers (Nardi et al. 2000; Herbsleb et al. 2002; Isaacs et al. 2002; Voida et al. 2002), as well as its use in non-work-related communities (Grinter and Palen 2002).

The majority of instant messaging clients are built around the notion of buddy lists. In the simplest case a user can see whether his "buddies" are available or not available for a chat. In addition to basic availability many instant messaging clients also support more extended status messages either by providing standard status messages (e.g. in ICQ "Available", "Away", "Do not disturb", etc.) or allowing custom messages through free-form text (e.g. iChat). Status messages have become a focus of research as they allow users to relay awareness information which extend the original focus on availability. Smale and Greenberg (Smale and Greenberg 2005) have investigated how the name field in an instant messaging client is used to broadcast personal information to other members of a group. They identified a rich set of communication practices used to communicate different aspects of a person's work or personal context to others. Other research has focussed on the enhancement of existing IM capabilities by adding dedicated awareness functionality (Tran et al. 2005).

Another major technology influence, this time hardware based, has been the proliferation of mobile devices. People are frequently in meetings, moving between locations or on travel away from their usual office (Bellotti and Bly 1996). Awareness is still important in these situations, and research into supplying awareness in a mobile situation was begun early in this latest time period (Tang et al. 2001). In this situation, information about location and "nearness" and the appropriate methods for contacting people become more important.

1.4.4 Group Configuration

The awareness research in earlier time periods that we have reported in this chapter has predominantly focussed on a particular group configuration. This configuration involves individuals, each with their own single-user computer. While this is a common group setup, in recent years we have seen a variety of other configurations being investigated. These alternative configurations are common situations in work and other contexts.

1.4.4.1 Semi-Public

Semi-public displays are large displays that are placed in the common areas of a workplace, such as the kitchen area or in hallways. The displays are not fully public, as they are not available to the general populace, but they are not completely private either. The role of these displays is to enhance the awareness information that the group already has of each other (Huang and Mynatt 2003).

Semi-public displays have been used for many different purposes since the coining of the term in 2003 (Huang and Mynatt 2003). For example, specialised versions of Instant Messenger (Huang et al. 2004), posting and sharing multimedia information (Churchill et al. 2004) and presence displays (Terrell and McCrickard 2006).

1.4.4.2 Co-Located

Co-located collaboration research is concerned with situations where the group is all together and working on the same task at the same time. Interestingly, many of the early studies that guided distributed awareness research studied co-located participants to see the important factors that needed to be transferred to the distributed case (e.g. see Section 1.2.1, Gutwin 2002). Co-located collaboration research is based on the realisation that, while some awareness issues are simplified by all the collaborators being in the same place at the same time, there are some unique issues in supporting this domain.

From a low-level technical perspective, there is the issue of supporting multiple people interacting with a single display simultaneously. Solutions for this problem are known as single display groupware (SDG) (Tse and Greenberg 2004; Hutterer and Thomas 2007).

One frequent scenario for co-located collaboration involves the group members positioned around a horizontal tabletop display and all interacting simultaneously with equal participation. Such a display has to support the behaviour of people normally using a table surface, including collaboration cues such as orientation (Kruger et al. 2003) and territoriality (Scott et al. 2004). An extension to this domain is looking at the use of upright displays to augment the tabletop display (Wigdor et al. 2006).

There are different common co-located settings that can be imagined. For example, in an educational setting, there are distinct power structure roles of teacher and student. At this time there are even commercial movements into this domain (http://education.smarttech.com). There are also synchronous co-located situations in the hospital domain (e.g. Wilson et al. 2006).

1.4.4.3 Partially Distributed

Partially distributed groups are composed of a co-located core group, consisting of two or more people, and a number of distributed, "satellite" individuals. This configuration is not currently the focus of much work, and the studies that have been conducted seem to be from a single research group (Bos et al. 2006).

The main property of these groups is a bias towards collaborating with co-located collaborators. In competitive trading situations where the resources are with the co-located group, this is a disadvantage to the distributed members. However, if resources are with distributed members then the co-located members' bias can place the advantage with the distributed individuals (Bos et al. 2006).

1.4.4.4 Mixed Presence

Mixed presence groups consist of a mixture of co-located and distributed, with multiple distributed sites and multiple people at each site. This means that all group members have co-located and distributed collaborators.

While there has not been a great deal of work so far concerning mixed presence groups, one primary issue has been identified. Presence disparity (Tang et al. 2005; Tang et al. 2006) is the bias that group members have for interacting with co-located collaborators over the distributed collaborators. The group then effectively dissolves into a bunch of co-located subgroups. However, Tang et al. (2006) and Epps and Close (2007) suggest that the effects can be reduced, or even overcome, by increasing the presence cues for the remote participants.

Sometimes there are other boundaries reinforcing the divisions of location as well. When the connection is between normally self-contained teams at each site, the collaboration difficulties increase (Mark et al. 2003).

1.4.4.5 Summary of Group Configuration

Research of various group configurations can be seen as part of the general diversification of collaboration research. It seems to be of the same trend as the move into different domains. The community has come to a point where awareness knowledge can be applied to domains outside the office and to groups that are not just made up of distributed individuals. The broadening of application contexts is important for much the same reasons as the move to different domains – real collaborating groups are often in these situations. These groups need appropriate awareness support.

1.4.5 Summary of Extended Models and Specification

In this section we have seen two dominant research trends. The first is a continuation of open research from our last rough time period (1995–1999), with some even predating that and extending back to the first time period (1986–1994). This trend includes such things as modelling awareness and investigating the relationship of awareness to privacy. However, even this long-term research has not resulted in awareness being a "solved problem". One of the most interesting open areas, in our opinion, is the gap between theory and design. There are very few examples of trying to use theory directly for design, and even fewer successful cases.

The second strong trend that we have highlighted is the opening up of awareness research to new contexts. This has been driven by new domains, new group configurations and popular technology use. These newer avenues of research have very few solutions and have asked many new questions, as applying awareness to a new domain is not simply a case of transferring results from the workplace.

1.5 Trends and Conclusions

Awareness is a topic that lies at the very core of CSCW research. Reflecting on more than 20 years of awareness research, we have identified a number of general research trends. These trends do not exist in isolation but are linked to the general development of the research in HCI and CSCW. We believe that our review of awareness has identified the driving research questions in the area and provided an overview of how the body of knowledge has grown and matured.

Unlike Schmidt's (2002) critique of awareness, our main objective was not a critical reflection of shortcomings of existing research but rather to provide an overview that takes into account the contextual research trends during different time periods. We have also attempted to show how different streams of awareness research relate to each other. The benefits that we see in such an approach are twofold. First, this chapter should enable researchers to get familiar with the development of awareness research over time and understand awareness approaches in context. Second, we believe that understanding research trends and thrusts are a valuable resource in determining and addressing new challenges. In each of the rough time periods that we have discussed, 1986–1994, 1995–1999 and 2000–2007, we have identified key characteristics and trends of the research into collaborative awareness.

The first time period (1986–1994) was characterised by the realisation that awareness is a vital factor in collaboration. Inspired by field studies, the original research goal was to understand and describe the concept of awareness and to answer the question of how awareness could be applied to distributed work. Both the realisation of importance and the resulting investigation arose in parallel through field studies, such as Heath and Luff's (1991) London underground study and Kraut et al.'s (1988) scientific collaboration study, and also through practical use of available technology, such as the media space work.

During the second time period (1995–1999), these initial concepts were extended through research undertaken in two major research thrusts. First, the conceptual understanding of awareness matured through theoretical work, such as the nimbus–focus model (Rodden 1996) and frameworks that enabled software designers to integrate awareness as part of their system design. Gutwin's workspace awareness framework (Gutwin 1997) stands out in this context as one of the most comprehensive frameworks on awareness for small teams. Other researches, such as

GroupDesk (Fuchs et al. 1995), AREA (Fuchs 1999) and NESSIE (Prinz 1999) put a stronger emphasis on system design and added important knowledge about implementing event-based awareness. Second, there was a move towards collaboration environments that incorporated awareness features. This was in line with a general trend in CSCW during that time, away from single functionality systems like shared editors, towards environments which were intended to be a single system for collaborating. A large number of these systems were based on the shared workspace metaphor. DIVA, with its very literal implementation of the shared office metaphor, is probably the earliest example (Sohlenkamp and Chwelos 1994). Many other systems that we have covered here are based on the collaborative environments approach including Orbit (Mansfield et al. 1997b), PoliAwAC (Fuchs 1997) and TeamRooms (Roseman and Greenberg 1996).

During the third time period (2000–2007), there was an emergence of a number of additional research trends. Research on awareness models continued to some extent, but became increasingly more specialised. For example, Simone and Bandini's (2002) work on the reaction–diffusion metaphor can be seen as a continuation of theoretical work in the tradition of models like the nimbus–focus model (Rodden 1996). Prinz and Gross's ENI model (Gross and Prinz 2003 Prinz and Gross 2004) addresses questions of integrating additional contextual information and deducting context from sensed information. The concept of intentionally enriched awareness (Rittenbruch et al. 2007) critiques the notion of a "passive actor" and extends event-based awareness mechanisms by integrating information deliberately provided by users. In addition to work on models, we can see the increased application of existing concepts to inform the design of awareness prototypes. The design of the Community Bar system (McEwan and Greenberg 2005) for instance is based on nimbus–focus model as well as the locales framework (Fitzpatrick 2003).

With regard to the design and application of awareness systems, two major trends have emerged. First, groupware designers are moving away from comprehensive virtual environments and are focussing on more targeted solutions. Interoperability between different services is becoming increasingly important. This development is driven by a number of technical trends. Different interfaces such as mobile devices and digital tabletops as well as research fields such as ubiquitous computing have caused a paradigm shift and have required a redefinition of the notions of awareness.

Second, we have observed a shift away from the workplace office as the main domain for awareness research. A number of awareness concepts and systems have recently targeted other domains, most notably health and domestic domains (see Section 1.4.2), and have expanded the notion of the types of groups that can be supported beyond distributed individuals in offices (see Section 1.4.4). This development is congruent with an increased understanding of CSCW as a research field that targets a wide range of domains which include the home, health, education and many other areas, work and non-work related.

Overall, our survey shows that there are a wealth of models, designs and field studies to draw from when considering new research avenues in awareness. Many of the current research trends we discussed during the most recent time period are portals to new research challenges. The most prominent of these is in applying awareness to domain-specific applications. This area of study is still in its early days and there are many domains offering rich opportunities for research. Another area already discussed, mixed presence collaboration, also has considerable room for future research on awareness.

As this chapter has progressed, an evolution in the way researchers approach awareness has become apparent. In the older research, awareness was treated as an independent concern. This treatment was more apparent in the theoretical work, but even in the systems that had other functionality, there was a sense of "this is the awareness part", "this is the communication part" and so on. This was a natural and effective strategy when awareness was a new area of research. However, more recent work treats awareness as a concept tightly integrated with other concepts such as communication or sharing. The focus is on how to support people in context rather than about awareness specifically.

This approach to awareness has implications for future research. One of these is in the area of evaluation. Each of the systems that we have discussed in this chapter has been evaluated to varying levels of thoroughness. While the systems have been evaluated, there is little in the way of direct measures of awareness itself. One example approach is the ABC-Q measure used in the ASTRA system (Romero et al. 2007) used in the domestic domain.

Awareness in collaboration is far from a solved problem and there will be many open research challenges for a long time still. We are actively engaging in some of the open research discussed above in our own research program and we see other researchers starting to tackle these issues, as well as many others we have not mentioned. We look forward to seeing how research in the field of collaborative awareness develops.

References

Adams M, Tenney Y, Pew R (1995) Situation awareness and the cognitive management of complex systems. Human Factors 37(1): 85–104

Altman I (1975) Environment and Social Behavior: Privacy, Personal Space, Territory and Crowding. Brooks/Cole Pub. Co., Inc., Monterey, CA

Altman I (1977) Privacy regulation: Culturally universal or culturally specific? Journal of Social Issues 33(3): 66–84

Bardram JE, Hansen TR, Soegaard M (2006) AwareMedia: a shared interactive display supporting social, temporal, and spatial awareness in surgery. In: Proceedings of the 20th anniversary Conference on Computer Supported Cooperative Work (CSCW '06). ACM Press: 109–118

Bellotti V, Bly S (1996) Walking away from the desktop computer: distributed collaboration and mobility in a product design team. In: Proceedings of the Conference on Computer Supported Cooperative Work (CSCW '96). ACM Press: 209–218

Benford S, Fahlen L (1993) A Spatial Model of Interaction in Large Virtual Environments. In: Proceedings of the Third European Conference on CSCW (ECSCW'93). Kluwer: 109–124

Bentley R, Horstmann T, Sikkel K et al. (1995) Supporting collaborative information sharing with the World-Wide Web: The BSCW Shared Workspace system. In: Proceedings of the 4th International World Wide Web Conference (WWW'95): 63–74

Bly S, Harrison S, Irwin S (1993) Media spaces: Bringing people together in a video, audio, and computing environment. Communication of the ACM 3(1): 28–47

Borning A, Travers M (1991) Two approaches to casual interaction over computer and video networks. In: Proceedings of the Conference on Human Factors in Computing Systems (CHI '91). ACM Press: 13–19

Bos N, Olson JS, Nan N et al. (2006) Collocation bindness in partially distributed groups: is there a downside to being collocated? In: Proceedings of the Conference on Human Factors in Computing Systems (CHI '06). ACM Press: 1313–1321

Bowers J (1994) The work to make a network work: studying CSCW in action. In: Transcending Boundaries, CSCW '94. Proceedings of the Conference on Computer Supported Cooperative Work. ACM, New York, NY, USA: 287–298.

Boyle M, Greenberg S (2005) The language of privacy: Learning from video media space analysis and design. ACM Transactions on Computer-Hum Interaction 12(2): 328–370

Brown B, Bell M (2004) CSCW at play: 'there' as a collaborative virtual environment. In: Proceedings of the Conference on Computer Supported Cooperative Work (CSCW '04). ACM Press: 350–359

Buxton W, Moran T (1990) EuroPARC's Integrated Interactive Intermedia Facility (IIIF): Early experiences. In: Proceedings of the Conference on Multi-user Interface and Applications: 11–34

Churchill EF, Nelson L, Denoue L et al. (2004) Sharing multimedia content with interactive public displays: a case study. In: Proceedings of the Conference on Designing interactive systems (DIS '04). ACM Press: 7–16

Crabtree A, Rodden T, Hemmings T et al. (2003) Finding a place for Ubicomp in the home. In: Proceedings of the Fifth International Conference on Ubiquitous Computing (Ubicomp '03). Springer Verlag: 208–226

Dourish P, Bellotti V (1992) Awareness and coordination in shared workspaces. In: Proceedings of the Conference on Computer Supported Cooperative Work (CSCW '92). ACM Press: 107–114

Dourish P, Bly S (1992) Portholes: supporting awareness in a distributed work group. In: Proceedings of the Conference on Human Factors in Computing Systems (CHI '92). ACM Press: 541–547

Dyck J, Pinelle D, Brown B et al. (2003) Learning from games: HCI design innovations in entertainment software. In: Proceedings of the Graphics Interface (GI '03): 237–246

Edwards K, Grinter R, E. (2001) At home with Ubiquitous computing: Seven challenges. In: Proceedings of the Conference on Ubiquitous Computing (Ubicomp '01). Springer Verlag: 256–272

Elliot K, Neustaedter C, Greenberg S (2005) Time, ownership and awareness: the value of contextual locations in the home. In: Proceedings of the 7th International Conference on Ubiquitous Computing (Ubicomp '05). Springer Verlag: 251–268

Epps J, Close B (2007) A study of co-worker awareness in remote collaboration over a shared application. In: Proceedings of the Conference on Human Factors in Computing Systems (CHI '07), Extended Abstracts: 2363

Fish RS, Kraut RE, Chalfonte BI (1990) The videowindows system in informal communications. In: Proceedings of the Conference on Computer Supported Cooperative Work (CSCW '90): 1–11

Fish RS, Kraut RE, Root RW et al. (1992) Evaluating video as a technology for informal communication. In: Proceedings of the Conference on Human Factors in Computing Systems (CHI '92): 37–48

Fitzpatrick G (2003) The Locales Framework: Understanding and Designing for Wicked Problems. Kluwer Academic Publishers, Dordrecht, Boston, London

Fitzpatrick G, Kaplan S, Mansfield T (1996) Physical spaces, virtual places and social worlds: A study of work in the virtual. In: Proceedings of the Computer Supported Cooperative Work (CSCW '96). ACM Press: 334–343

Fitzpatrick G, Kaplan S, Mansfield T (1998a) Applying the locales framework to understanding and designing. In: Proceedings of the Proceedings Australasian Computer Human Interaction Conference (OzCHI'98). IEEE: 122–129

Fitzpatrick G, Mansfield T, Kaplan S et al. (1999) Augmenting the workaday world with Elvin. In: Proceedings of the Sixth European Conference on Computer-Supported Cooperative Work (ECSCW '99). Kluwer Academic Publishers: 431–450

Fitzpatrick G, Parsowith S, Segall B et al. (1998b) Tickertape: awareness in a single line. In: Proceedings of the Conference on Human factors in computing systems (CHI '98). ACM Press: 281–282

Fitzpatrick G, Tolone WJ, Kaplan SM (1995) Work, locales and distributed social worlds. In: Proceedings of the Fourth European Conference on Computer-Supported Cooperative Work (ECSCW '95). Kluwer Academic Publishers: 1–16

Fracker M (1989) Attention allocation in situation awareness. In: Proceedings of the Human Factors Society 33rd Annual Meeting: 1396–1400

Fuchs L (1997) Situationsorientierte Unterstützung von Gruppenwahrnehmung in CSCW-Systemen. Dissertation: Universität Gesamthochschule Essen

Fuchs L (1999) AREA: A cross-application notification service for groupware. In: Proceedings of the Sixth European Conference on Computer Supported Cooperative Work (ECSCW'99). Kluwer Academic: 61–80

Fuchs L, Pankoke-Babatz U, Prinz W (1995) Supporting cooperative awareness with local event mechanism: The group desk system. In: Proceedings of the Fourth European Conference on Computer Supported Cooperative Work (ECSCW'95). Kluwer Academic Publishers: 247–262

Fuchs L, Sohlenkamp M, Genau A et al. (1996) Tranzparenz in kooperativen Prozessen: Der Ereigisdienst in POLITeam. In: Proceedings of the Deutsche Computer Supported Cooperative Work (DCSCW '96): 3–16

Galloway K, Rabinowitz S (1980) Hole-in-Space. Mobile image videotape. Santa Monica, Calif., 1980. http://www.ecafe.com/getty/HIS

Ganoe CH, Somervell JP, Neale DC et al. (2003) Classroom BRIDGE: Using collaborative public and desktop timelines to support activity awareness. In: Proceedings of the 16th annual ACM symposium on User Interface Software and Technology (UIST '03). ACM Press: 21–30

Gaver B, Martin H (2000) Alternatives: exploring information appliances through conceptual design proposals. In: Proceedings of the Conference on Human Factors in Computing Systems (CHI '00). ACM Press

Gaver W, Moran T, MacLean A et al. (1992) Realizing a video environment: EuroPARC's RAVE system. In: Proceedings of the Conference on Human Factors in Computing Systems (CHI '92). ACM Press: 27–35

Gaver WW (1991) Sound support for collaboration. In: Proceedings of the Second European Conference on Computer-Supported Collaborative Work (ECSCW '91). Kluwer, Dordrecht: 293–308

Gilson RD (1995) Special issue on Situation Awareness. Hum Factors 37(1): 3–4

Greenberg S, Rounding M (2001) The Notification Collage: posting information to public and personal displays. In: Proceedings of the Conference on Human Factors in Computing Systems (CHI '01). ACM Press: 514–521

Grinter RE, Palen L (2002) Instant messaging in teen life. In: Proceedings of the Conference on Computer Supported Cooperative Work (CSCW '02). ACM Press: 21–30

Gross T, Prinz W (2003) Awareness in context: A light-weight approach. In: Proceedings of the Eight European Conference on Computer-Supported Cooperative Work (ECSCW'03). Kluwer Academic Publishers: 295–314

Gross T, Stary C, Totte A (2005) User-centered awareness in computer-supported cooperative work-systems: structured embedding of findings from social sciences. International Journal of Human-Computer Interaction 18(3): 323–360

Gutwin C (1997) Workspace Awareness in Real-Time Distributed Groupware. Calgary, Alberta Canada: University of Calgary

Gutwin C, Greenberg S (1995a) Support for Group Awareness in Real Time Desktop Conferences. In: Proceedings of the 2nd New Zealand Computer Science Research Students Conference

Gutwin C, Greenberg S (1995b) Workspace Awareness in Real-Time Distributed Groupware. Calgary, Alberta Canada, Department of Computer Science, University of Calgary. http://grouplab.cpsc.ucalgary.ca/papers/1995.html

Gutwin C, Greenberg S (1996) Workspace awareness for groupware. In: Proceedings of the Human Factors in Computing Systems (CHI' 96). ACM Press: 208–209

Gutwin C, Greenberg S (2002) A descriptive framework of workspace awareness for real-time groupware. Comput Support Coop Work 11: 411–446

Gutwin C, Stark G, Greenberg S (1995) Support for workspace awareness in educational groupware. In: Proceedings of the Conference on Computer Supported Collaborative Learning (CSCL '95). LEA Press: 147–156

Harper R, Hughes J, Shapiro D (1989) Working in harmony: an examination of computer technology in air traffic control. In: Proceedings of the First European Conference on Computer Supported Co-operative Work (ECSCW '89). Kluwer Academic: 77–87

Heath C, Luff P (1991) Collaborative activity and technological design: task coordination in London underground control rooms. In: Proceedings of the Second European Conference on Computer-Supported Cooperative Work (ECSCW '91). Kluwer Academic Publishers: 65–80

Heath C, Svensson MS, Hindmarsh J et al. (2002) Configuring awareness. Computer Support Cooperative Work 11(3–4): 317–347

Herbsleb JD, Atkins DL, Boyer DG et al. (2002) Introducing instant messaging and chat in the workplace. In: Proceedings of the Conference on Human Factors in Computing Systems (CHI '02). ACM Press: 171–178

Hindus D (1999) The Importance of Homes in Technology. In: N. Streitz, J. Siegel, V. Hartkopf, and S. Konomi, (Eds.) Cooperative Buildings - Integrating Information, Organizations, and Architecture. *Proceedings of the. Second International Workshop on Cooperative Buildings (CoBuild'99), Pittsburgh, U.S.A., October 1-2, 1999. Lecture Notes in Computer Science 1670.* 199–1207. Springer: Heidelberg.

Hindus D, Mainwaring SD, Nicole L et al. (2001) Casablanca: designing social communication devices for the home. In: Proceedings of the Conference on Human Factors in Computing Systems (CHI '01). ACM Press

Huang EM, Mynatt ED (2003) Semi-public displays for small, co-located groups. In: Proceedings of the Conference on Human Factors in Computing Systems (CHI '03). ACM Press: 49–56

Huang EM, Russell DM, Sue AE (2004) IM here: public instant messaging on large, shared displays for workgroup interactions. In: Proceedings of the Conference on Human Factors in Computing Systems (CHI '04). ACM Press: 279–286

Hudson S, Smith I (1996) Techniques for addressing fundamental privacy and disruption trade-offs in awareness support systems. In: Proceedings of the Conference on Computer Supported Cooperative Work (CSCW '96). ACM Press: 248–257

Hughes JA, O'Brien J and Rodden T (1998) Understanding Technology in Domestic Environments: Lessons for Cooperative Buildings. In: N. A. Streitz, S. Konomi, and H. J. Burkhardt, (Eds.) *Proceedings of the First international Workshop on Cooperative Buildings, integrating information, Organization, and Architecture Lecture Notes In Computer Science,* vol. 1370. Springer-Verlag, London, 248–261.

Hutterer P, Thomas BH (2007) Groupware support in the windowing system. In: Proceedings of the Eight Australasian Conference on User Interface (AUIC '07). Australian Computer Society, Inc: 39–46

Isaacs E, Walendowski A, Whittaker S et al. (2002) The character, functions, and styles of instant messaging in the workplace. In: Proceedings of the Conference on Computer Supported Cooperative Work (CSWC '02). ACM Press: 11–20

Ishii H, Ullmer B (1997) Tangible bits: towards seamless interfaces between people, bits and atoms. In: Proceedings of the Conference on Human Factors in Computing Systems (CHI '97). ACM Press: 234–241

Jancke G, Venolia GD, Grudin J et al. (2001) Linking public spaces: technical and social issues. In: Proceedings of the Conference on Human Factors in Computing Systems (CHI '01). ACM Press: 530–537

Junestrand S, Keijer U, Tollmar K (2001) Private and public digital domestic spaces. International Journal of Human-Computer Studies 54(5): 753–778

Junestrand S and Tollmar K (1999). Video Mediated Communication for Domestic Environment, architectural and technological design. In: N. Streiz, J. Siegel, V. Hartkopf, and S. Konomi, (Eds.) *Cooperative Buildings, Integrating Information, Organizations and Architecture, Proceedings, Lecture Notes in Computer Science, 1670, 177–190.* Springer, Heidelberg, Germany.

Klöckner K, Mambrey P, Sohlenkamp M et al. (1995) Bridging the Gap between Bonn and Berlin for and with the users. In: Proceedings of the European Conference on Computer Supported Cooperative Work (ECSCW'95). ACM Press: 17–31

Kraut R, Egido C, Galegher J (1988) Patterns of contact and communication in scientific research collaboration. In: Proceedings of the Conference on Computer-supported cooperative work (CSCW '88). ACM Press: 1–12

Kruger R, Carpendale S, Scott S, D. et al. (2003) How people use orientation on tables: comprehension, coordination and communication. In: Proceedings of the Conference on Supporting Group Work (GROUP '03). ACM Press: 369–378

Lövstrand L (1991) Being Selectively Aware with the Khronika System. In: Proceedings of the Conference on European Computer Supported Cooperative Work (ECSCW'91). Kluwer Academic Publishers: 265–277

Mansfield T, Kaplan S, Fitzpatrick G et al. (1997a) Evolving Orbit : a progress report on building locales. In: Proceedings of the Conference on Supporting Group Work (Group '97). ACM Press: 241–250

Mansfield T, Kaplan S, Phelps T et al. (1997b) Orbit – supporting social worlds. In: Proceedings of the Fifth European Conference on Computer Supported Cooperative Work (ECSCW' 97). Kluwer Academic Publishers: 13–14

Mantei MM, Baecker RM, Sellen AJ et al. (1991) Experiences in the use of a media space. In: Proceedings of the Conference on Human Factors in Computing Systems (CHI '91). ACM Press: 203–208

Mark G, Abrams S, Nassif N (2003) Group-to-group distance collaboration: examining the space between. In: Proceedings of the Eighth European Conference on Computer-Supported Cooperative Work (ECSCW '03). Springer Verlag: 99–118

Mark G, Fuchs L, Sohlenkamp M (1997) Supporting groupware conventions through contextual awareness. In: Proceedings of the Fifth European Conference on Computer Supported Work (ECSCW '97). Kluwer Academic Publishers: 253–268

McEwan G, Greenberg S (2005) Supporting social worlds with the community bar. In: Proceedings of the Conference on Supporting Group Work (GROUP '05). ACM Press: 21–30

Munkvold G, Ellingsen G, Koksvik H (2006) Formalizing work: reallocating redundancy. In: Proceedings of the 20th anniversary Conference on Computer Supported Cooperative Work (CSCW '06). ACM Press

Mynatt ED, Rowan J, Craighill S et al. (2001) Digital family portraits: supporting peace of mind for extended family members. In: Proceedings of the Conference on Human Factors in Computing Systems (CHI '01). ACM Press: 333–340

Nardi BA, Whittaker S, Bradner E (2000) Interaction and outeraction: instant messaging in action. In: Proceedings of the Conference on Computer Supported Cooperative Work (CSCW '00). ACM Press: 79–88

Neustaedter C, Brush AJ, Greenberg S (2007) A digital family calendar in the home: Lessons from field trials of LINC. In: Proceedings of the Graphics Interface (GI '07). ACM Press: 199–206

Neustaedter C, Brush AJB (2006) "LINC-ing" the family: the participatory design of an inkable family calendar. In: Proceedings of the Conference on Human Factors in Computing Systems (CHI '06). ACM Press: 141–150

Neustaedter C, Elliot K, Greenberg S (2006a) Interpersonal awareness in the domestic realm. In: Proceedings of the 20th Australasian Computer-Human Interaction Conference (OzCHI '06). ACM Press: 15–22

Neustaedter C, Greenberg S, Boyle M (2006b) Blur filtration fails to preserve privacy for home-based video conferencing. ACM Transactions on Computer-Human Interaction 13(1): 1–36

Palen L, Aaløkke S (2006) Of pill boxes and piano benches: "home-made" methods for managing medication. In: Proceedings of the 20th anniversary Conference on Computer Supported Cooperative Work (CSCW '06). ACM Press: 79–88

Palen L, Dourish P (2003) Unpacking "privacy" for a networked world. In: Proceedings of the Conference on Human Factors in Computing Systems (CHI '03). ACM Press: 519–523

Parsowith S, Fitzpatrick G, Kaplan S et al. (1998) Tickertape: notification and communication in a single line. In: Proceedings of the 3rd Asia Pacific Computer Human Interaction (APCHI '98). IEEE Computer Society, Los Alamitos, CA, USA: 139–44

Pedersen ER, Sokoler T (1997) AROMA: abstract representation of presence supporting mutual awareness. In: Proceedings of the Conference on Human Factors in Computing Systems (CHI '97). ACM Press: 51–58

Pfeifer A, Wulf V (1995) Negotiability as a strategy for conflict management. In: Proceedings of the International Workshop on Concurrent/Simultaneous Engineering Frameworks and Applications: 333–343

Pinelle D, Gutwin C (2002) Groupware walkthrough: adding context to groupware usability evaluation. In: Proceedings of the Conference on Human Factors in Computing Systems (CHI '02). ACM Press: 455–462

Prinz W (1999) NESSIE: An Awareness Environment for Cooperative Settings. In: Proceedings of the Sixth European Conference on Computer-Supported Cooperative Work (ECSCW '99). Kluwer Academic Publishers: 391–410

Prinz W, Gross T (2001) Ubiquitous awareness of cooperative activities in a theatre of work. In: Proceedings of the Fachtagung Arbeitsplatzcomputer: Pervasive Ubiquitous Computing (APC '01). VDE Publisher: 135–144

Prinz W, Gross T (2004) Modelling shared contexts in cooperative environments: Concept, implementation and evaluation. Computer Supported Cooperative Work 13(3–4): 283–303

Ramduny D, Dix A, Rodden T (1998) Exploring the design space for notification servers. In: Proceedings of the Conference on Computer Supported Cooperative Work (CSCW'98). ACM Press: 227–235

Rittenbruch M (2002) Atmosphere: a framework for contextual awareness. International Journal of Human-Computer Interaction 14(2): 159–180

Rittenbruch M, Viller S, Mansfield T (2007) Announcing activity: Design and evaluation of an intentionally enriched awareness service. Human-Computer Interaction 22(1&2): 137–171

Rodden T (1996) Populating the application: A model of awareness for cooperative applications. In: Proceedings of the Conference on Computer Supported Cooperative Work (CSCW '96). ACM Press: 87–96

Romero N, Markopoulos P, Van Baren J et al. (2007) Connecting the family with awareness systems. Personal Ubiquitous Computing 11(4): 299–312

Roseman M, Greenberg S (1996) TeamRooms: Network Places for Collaboration. In: Proceedings of the Conference on Computer Supported Cooperative Work (CSCW '96): 325–333

Rowan J, Mynatt ED (2005) Digital family portrait field trial: Support for aging in place. In: Proceedings of the Conference on Human Factors in Computing Systems (CHI '05). ACM Press: 521–530

Sandor O, Bogdan C, Bowers J (1997) Aether: An awareness engine for CSCW. In: Proceedings of the Fifth European Conference on Computer Supported Cooperative Work (ECSCW '97). Kluwer Academic Publisher: 221–236

Sarter N, Woods D (1995) How in the world did we ever get into that mode? Mode error and awareness in supervisory control. Human Factors 37(1): 5–19

Schmidt K (2002) The problem with 'awareness'. Computer Supported Cooperative Work 11(3–4): 285–298

Scott SD, Sheelagh M, Carpendale MST et al. (2004) Territoriality in collaborative tabletop workspaces. In: Proceedings of the Conference on Computer Supported Cooperative Work (CSCW '04). ACM Press: 294–303

Segall B, Arnold D (1997) Elvin has left the building: A publish/subscribe notification service with quenching. In: Proceedings of the Australian UNIX and Open Systems User Group Conf. (AUUG '97): 243–255

Simone C, Bandini S (2002) Integrating Awareness in Cooperative Applications through the Reaction-Diffusion Metaphor. Computer Supported Cooperative Work 11(3–4): 495–530

Smale S, Greenberg S (2005) Broadcasting information via display names in instant messaging. In: Proceedings of the Conference on Supporting Group Work (GROUP'05). ACM Press: 89–98

Sohlenkamp M, Chwelos G (1994) Integrating communication, cooperation, and awareness: The DIVA virtual office environment. In: Proceedings of the Conference on Computer Supported Cooperative Work (CSCW '94). ACM Press: 331–342

Strauss A (2003) Continual Permutations of Action. Aldine De Gruyter, New York

Strong R, Gaver B (1996) Feather, scent and shaker: Supporting simple intimacy. In: Proceedings of the Conference on Computer Supported Cooperative Work (CSCW '96), Videos, Demonstrations, and Short Papers. ACM Press: 29–30

Stults R (1986) Media Space. XEROX Parc Technical Report, XEROX Parc Technical Report

Tang A, Boyle M, Greenberg S (2005) Understanding and mitigating display and presence disparity in mixed presence groupware. Journal of Research and Practice in Information Technology 37(2): 71–88

Tang A, Neustaedter C, Greenberg S (2006) VideoArms: Embodiments for mixed presence groupware. In: Proceedings of the 20th BCS-HCI British HCI Group Conference (HCI '06). Springer Verlag: 85–102

Tang JC, Yankelovich N, Begole J et al. (2001) ConNexus to awarenex: extending awareness to mobile users. In: Proceedings of the Conference on Human Factors in Computing Systems (CHI '01). ACM Press

Tee K, Greenberg S, Gutwin C (2006) Providing artifact awareness to a distributed group through screen sharing. In: Proceedings of the 20th anniversary Conference on Computer Supported Cooperative Work (CSCW '06). ACM Press: 99–108

Terrell GB, McCrickard DS (2006) Enlightening a co-located community with a semi-public notification system. In: Proceedings of the 20th anniversary Conference on Computer Supported Cooperative Work (CSCW '06). ACM Press: 21–24

Tollmar K, Persson J (2002) Understanding remote presence. In: Proceedings of the Second Nordic Conference on Human-Computer Interaction (NordCHI '02). ACM Press: 41–50

Tollmar K, Sandor O, Schömer A (1996) Supporting social awareness @work – design and experience. In: Proceedings of the Conference on Computer Supported Cooperative Work (CSCW '06). ACM Press: 298–307

Tolone W, Kaplan S, Fitzpatrick G (1995) Specifying dynamic support for collaborative work within WORLDS. In: Proceedings of the Conference on Organizational Computer Systems (COOCS '95). ACM Press: 55–65

Tran MH, Yang Y, Raikundalia GK (2005) Supporting awareness in instant messaging: An empirical study and mechanism design. In: Proceedings of the Australasian Computer-Human Interaction Conference (OzCHI '05). Computer-Human Interaction Special Interest Group (CHISIG) of Australia: 1–10

Tse E, Greenberg S (2004) Rapidly prototyping single display groupware through the SDGToolkit. In: Proceedings of the Fifth Australasian Computer-Human Interaction Conference (OzCHI '04). Australian Computer Society, Inc.: 101–110

Voida A, Newsletter WC, Mynatt ED (2002) When conventions collide: the tensions of instant messaging attributed. In: Proceedings of the Conference on Human Factors in Computing Systems (CHI '02). ACM Press: 187–194

Weiser M, Brown JS (1995) Designing calm technology. PowerGrid Journal 1.01

Wigdor D, Shen C, Forlines C et al. (2006) Table-centric interactive spaces for real-time collaboration: solutions, evaluation, and application scenarios. In: Proceedings of the Conference on Collaboration Technologies (CollaTech '06). Information Processing Society of Japan: 9–15

Wilson S, Galliers J, Fone J (2006) Not all sharing is equal: the impact of a large display on small group collaborative work. In: Proceedings of the 20th anniversary Conference on Computer Supported Cooperative Work (CSCW '06). ACM Press: 25–28

Chapter 2
A Design Framework for Awareness Systems

Panos Markopoulos

2.1 Introduction

This chapter discusses the design of awareness systems, whose main function is a social one, namely, to support social communication, mediated social interactions and eventually relationships of the individuals they connect. We focus especially on connecting friends and family rather than on systems used in the context of collaborative work. Readers interested in this latter kind of applications are referred to the design frameworks by Ginelle and Gutwin (2005) and Gutwin and Greenberg (2002). Below, we outline the relevant design space and the corresponding challenges for the design of awareness systems. The challenges pertain to social aspects of interaction design rather than the technological challenges relating to such systems. As such, they are inspired by Jonathan Grudin's exposition of design challenges for the domain of groupware applications (Grudin, 1994).

Considered at a high level of abstraction, the systems discussed here are examples of groupware since they support informal processes within a group of individuals. To an extent, some of Grudin's eight challenges apply also to this domain; however, there are important differences between groupware intended to support cooperative work processes and the class of systems considered here, which leads to a different and more specialized set of issues that need to be considered by designers. These differences are illustrated by considering the benefits awareness systems are intended to provide in the domain of informal, social communication.

2.2 Awareness Systems for Supporting Social Relations and Needs

A common denominator for research in this field is the ambition to go beyond means for rich and efficient information exchange and onto supporting sustained

P. Markopoulos (✉)
Department of Industrial Design, Eindhoven University of Technology, Den Dolech 2,
The Netherlands
e-mail: p.markopoulos@tue.nl

P. Markopoulos et al. (eds), *Awareness Systems*, Human-Computer Interaction Series, DOI 10.1007/978-1-84882-477-5_2, © Springer-Verlag London Limited 2009

and almost effortless communication between individuals or groups. Such sustained communication, it is hoped, will enable users over time to build up and maintain an understanding of the activities of each other. Awareness of others, can directly address social and affective needs, or, less ambitiously, act as a trigger and frame of reference for communication through other media (Romero et al., 2007a) that are better suited for addressing these needs.

Compared to groupware, the class of systems discussed here does not assume that users engage in shared tasks or work on shared documents/products. Consequently, optimizing performance of shared tasks is not a central concern for users and designers alike. Awareness information can be quite general and unrelated to users' own activities and purposes, but still useful in the context of their interpersonal interactions and social activities.

Interest in this field is young, but growing rapidly. Inspiring for later work has been some design-driven research into supporting 'intimacy at a distance' by Gaver and his colleagues. For example, the concepts of the 'feather, scent and shaker' (Strong and Gaver, 1996) or the concepts developed as part of the Presence project (Gaver and Hooker, 2001) have inspired researchers to explore ways in which computer-mediated communication systems could address social, affective or even playful interpersonal interactions. The Casablanca project (Hindus et al., 2001) proposed two classic concepts of simple and lightweight means for connecting households: The 'Intentional Presence Lamp' through which remote individuals can signal their presence at home to each other, and the 'Scan Board' which enables two households to share an electronic writing surface. Since then, a multitude of related design concepts has followed, each exploring different settings and proposing various means for connecting closely related people.

Works, like the AROMA project (Pedersen and Sokoler, 1997) and the Digital Family Portrait (Mynatt et al., 2001) focused on *'peripheral awareness'*, advocating that awareness should be achieved with minimal cognitive effort. Emphasizing on the benefits awareness systems can provide rather than on how user's perceive awareness information leads Liechti and Ichikawa (2000) to define the concept of *affective awareness* as 'the general sense of being in touch with someone's friends and family'.

Awareness can concern a variety of issues that are relevant in the context of social interactions. It can concern anything from awareness of simple facts or events, such as presence at a fixed location, all the way to a rich and nuanced understanding of another person's daily activities, 'projects' that occupy them, their hopes and tribulations, successes and failures and so on. There is a large collection of similar, derived or related conceptions of interpersonal awareness that can be achieved through technology. Concepts presented in research literature often overlap. An attempt to operationalize such definitions and propose a measurement instrument is presented by IJsselsteijn et al. (Chapter 20).

Design explorations in this field, theoretical analyses and empirical works are helping build up a body of knowledge for how the design of these systems can influence the usage patterns that we should expect to emerge. The sections that follow attempt to distil and compile some of this knowledge in a way that can guide the design of awareness systems designed for social and leisure use. First though, we take a sceptical stance questioning whether awareness needs are a technology in search of a problem or whether they target actual human needs.

2.3 Do Awareness Systems Represent a Technology Push?

In setting out to design awareness systems, it is wise to ask some fundamental and potentially nagging questions: Does anybody need awareness systems? Do they address an actual need or are they yet another technology push?

It is not unusual, that a user study at the outset of a design project will survey a target user group regarding the potential acceptance of a planned technological innovation. All too often, informants may respond with complete certainty that they have all the technology they need and react negatively to any new technology offering. Reaching such an apparent impasse may be disheartening but often means that more effort should be invested on understanding user needs. Needs develop from people's usage of existing technologies (see Carroll and Rosson, 1992 for a related argument), so it cannot be assumed that an ultimate equilibrium state has been reached where people's needs have been met conclusively. Designers need to dig deeper, understanding how current technologies are used and appropriated and eventually to identify or even predict needs that will emerge together with newly available technologies and emerging social trends.

Framing awareness needs in terms of usage patterns and emerging trends should not be taken to suggest that these are a temporary side effect of existing technological developments, or a phenomenon incidental to the contemporary technological and societal context. This is far from being the case. For centuries people have used all available means to construct and maintain awareness, and current technologies are also employed to serve this purpose.

The implication of this argument is that human needs served by awareness are fundamental and timeless. In contrast, the concrete design challenge for any particular awareness system is defined ephemerally and in relation to an extant set of norms, technologies, communication patterns and rituals that support awareness. By focusing our attention on 'awareness systems' we are looking to step up the frequency, detail and automation of sharing awareness information in comparison to currently conventional forms of communication, like phone, mail or text messaging systems.

To illustrate the point we discuss how awareness systems can help meet human needs, which we describe at a fundamental and generic level. More specifically, social needs are discussed here in terms of a high-level categorization (Kenrick et al., 2004), which identifies the following basic human social need as generic across individuals and societal norms:

Affiliating with others and establishing social ties
Understanding ourselves and others by obtaining social information or feedback for our actions.

Gaining and maintaining status, presenting ourselves positively, supporting self-esteem.

Protecting ourselves and those we value, caring for our family and social group.

Attracting and retaining mates, finding and keeping partners.

In the following paragraphs we review some works on awareness systems and relate them to such high-level goals that motivate human social behaviour.

2.3.1 Affiliation with Others

Awareness systems have been proposed as ways of establishing new ties, e.g. finding like-minded individuals or people in a similar context, discovering common interests and ties to people in one's own organization. For example, systems have been designed for a work context with the aim to encourage serendipitous information sharing by coworkers or to enhance their social interactions, see, for example, Dourish et al. (1996) and Rittenbruch et al. (2007). The 'pixel kissing' concept developed by the project FLIRT (Bell et al., 2000) proposed matching commuters to strangers having similar travel patterns.

An even larger number of concepts aim to preserve and strengthen existing ties by supporting informal communication, chatting or affective communication. *Social connectedness* has emerged as one of the most central motives related to the use of awareness systems. It can be defined broadly as an assessment made by individuals regarding their emotional distance from others, and pertains to an important dimension of the general and fundamental human need to belong. There is by now some evidence that awareness systems can support social connectedness with closely related individuals. Romero et al. (2007a) showed how increasing awareness by sharing small daily life experiences through the ASTRA system (see Fig. 2.1) could have a measurable impact on social connectedness between household with family ties after 1 week of use. An experiment on the use of domestic media spaces to connect remote friends watching the same broadcast television programme (Markopoulos et al., 2005b) provided evidence that group attraction between remote friends increases as a result of having a peripheral awareness display of other group members.

2.3.2 Obtaining Social Information and Self-Presentation

Sharing and learning information about others is a basic social need for people. A clear manifestation of this is smalltalk and gossip, a common use of telephony. Sharing trivia or simply sharing social information is supported directly by systems like ASTRA (Romero et al., 2007a) or 'Anybiff' (Rittenbruch et al., 2007). The exchange of daily trivia through ASTRA also supports the need on the one hand to learn about others and on the other to achieve self-appropriation. This usage pattern

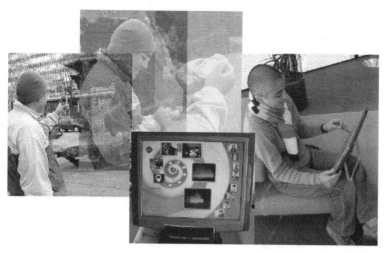

Fig. 2.1 The ASTRA system (Romero et al., 2007a) supports communication between members of different households. While on the move, individuals can send snaps or written notes to the related households. On the home device, notes in the form of a 'postcard' appear on a time line spiral visible for all the family. These 'postcards' can trigger communication, as they can be discussed during a phone call or simply browsed 'offline'

of self-expression and presentation through an awareness system has been found also during the field deployment of the Whereabouts clock by Sellen et al. (2006), see also Chapter 18.

Similar usage patterns were also found by the InterLiving project (Hutchinson et al., 2003) that developed simple monofunctional but flexible appliances ('technology probes') to support intrafamily communication. Their 'MessageProbe' enabled members of a distributed family to communicate by posting digital Post-It notes. Their 'VideoProbe' helped capture and share impromptu images among members of a distributed family. Trials involving a total of five families in three countries and extending up to 6 weeks with some of them showed how playful interaction was a preferred use of the system providing a way to express oneself using the system as a stage.

2.3.3 Attracting and Retaining Mates

While not explicitly discussed under the header of awareness systems there has been a lot of interest in services enabling strangers with similar interests or activity patterns to meet, or conversely, to support emotional communication. Considering the large number of related design proposals there has been little research in studying the deployment of such systems for the purposes of evaluating how well they support this human motive.

A much bigger range of design prototypes have been reported for supporting intimate relationships and intimacy over a distance. Following the early works by Gaver described above, design concepts such as Hug over a Distance (Vetere et al., 2005) and Physical Minimal Intimate objects (Kaye et al., 2005) explore ways to enable and enhance affective communication between remote partners.

2.3.4 Protecting Ourselves and Those We Value

Awareness systems have been designed to inform about the well-being of loved ones, for example to ensure their well-being. The Digital Family Portrait (Mynatt et al., 2001; Rowan and Mynatt 2005) is a classic example of a system designed to serve this human need. Another example is the Daily Activities Diarist (Metaxas et al., 2007, and Chapter 15) that provides an automatically updated record of daily life activities of a senior relative and displays it at the home of their children or other intimate socials.

Awareness systems of this ilk support a twofold aim: awareness of the state of the elderly can enable faster assistance to them when this is needed, and for the rest of the time, can provide peace of mind to the family and to the seniors themselves. This claim has been supported empirically by several studies. An early study based on simulating the data collection of the system was reported by (Consolvo et al., 2004) concerning the CareNet Display. This is a decorative 'ambient' display that helps local members of an elder's care network provide her day-to-day care. Users are presented with an overview of the medication, outings, meals, activities, mood, falls and calendar of the remote elderly person. Four elderly and their care network totalling 13 people participated in a 3-week-long study; this study concluded that the display had an overall positive effect on the stress levels of the care network of the elderly and that it raised awareness about the elder's daily life. Similarly positive results have been reported by Rowan and Mynatt (2005) regarding the evaluation of the Digital Family Portrait, by Metaxas et al. (2007) and Chapter 15, regarding the Daily Activities Diarist system, and, more recently, regarding the evaluation of Aurama, another picture frame based awareness system relying on sensor technology and displaying long-term trends relating to the well-being of the elderly person (Dadlani et al., 2008).

2.3.5 Conclusion

In this section we have linked the benefits that awareness systems are aimed at providing to social needs of humans discussed at a very fundamental level. It would be unconventional and probably unwise to base design decisions upon such a fundamental consideration of human behaviour. In the context of a design project, needs specific to a target user group and a targeted social and technical context can be much more operationally defined, e.g. expressing affection, sharing stories, reassuring oneself, coordinating actions with others.

In summary, the need for awareness of others is deeply ingrained in our social nature as human beings and it is not ephemeral or specific to our technological era. In the context of a specific design project, it is useful to understand what the super-ordinate social needs are that shape emerging communication patterns. Drawing such links explicitly can be fruitful when we borrow methods of inquiry from social psychology to evaluate the resulting patterns of behaviour that arise (see Chapters 18–20 regarding the evaluation of awareness systems).

2.4 The Design Space of Social Awareness Systems

This section presents a few dimensions along which awareness systems can be characterized. Classifications of awareness systems have been proposed in the past, see, for example, Gross et al. (2005) for an extensive classification of earlier research. The aim here is not to provide a comprehensive scheme for classifying awareness systems as many of the choices discussed are not exclusive to each other. Rather we hope to make explicit some of the fundamental decisions that are involved in the design of awareness systems.

McCrickard et al. (2003) discuss what they call 'notification systems', systems that aim to 'deliver current, valued information through a variety of platforms and modes in an efficient and effective manner'. They introduce three parameters to describe the priorities for the designers of such systems, regarding their support for interruption, reaction and comprehension. Following that model the systems discussed here aim for a relatively low level of interruption (claiming attention from another primary task to the notification), low or relatively low reaction (rapid and accurate response to the notification) and, finally, variable comprehension (remembering and making sense of the information they convey at a later time). Considering the display of awareness information, the class of systems discussed here correspond roughly to the categories of ambient media and secondary displays as these are discussed by McCrickard et al. (2003).

Pousman and Stasko (2006) examine the design space of ambient information displays, distinguishing the dimensions of *information capacity*, *notification level* (a dimension ranging from calm/peripheral to attention demanding), *representational fidelity* (that can be indexical, iconic or symbolic) and *aesthetic emphasis*. These dimensions are also relevant in the present context, though our discussion has a more general scope. The concepts of notification level and representational fidelity are retained for the specific context of social awareness systems.

The dimensions discussed in this section are the following:

Awareness of place versus awareness of people
Precision
Accuracy
Notification level
Input automation

Private versus shared nature of awareness displays
Level of user control

2.4.1 Awareness of People or Places?

Awareness is often tied to a specific place where members of a community or group work, live or pass by. For example, media spaces provide sustained audio–video links between fixed locations in a building, e.g. rooms, corridors. Another example is that of environments augmented with sensing capabilities for awareness purposes (e.g. the Digital family portrait and the Diarist systems mentioned above).

Designers need to address the private or public nature of the places connected by an awareness system, taking into account the degree of control individuals can or should have regarding the capture and dissemination of awareness information. Crucially, the knowledge receivers of this information have of the place concerned and how human activity unfolds inside it needs to be considered; familiarity with the space and its use can help users interpret displayed patterns of activity. Helping people at one location understand the context and the manner in which information about them is presented at another is an important challenge: individuals need to adapt their presentation for this remote context. Providing suitable cues for users regarding the context in which information about them is presented is part of the design challenge for these systems, but it can also become a useful resource for users who can capitalize on the situatedness of the display in conveying intentions and nuanced meanings, as is discussed by Cheverst et al. (see Chapter 17).

Alternatively, awareness information can be tied to an individual, e.g. when information about him/her is obtained through mobile services; it can also be tied to a group of connected individuals, forming one's social network or a community. For example, one can find out about other individuals whether they are busy, available for communication or not. In such cases, awareness information pertains to a large proportion of a person's daily life and activities. Depending on the technology used for capturing context can, potentially, impinge on the privacy of others. Consider for example using portable devices to create audio–video links between mobile individuals. Whereas a room geared with such equipment can be clearly related with warnings to people entering it, who can also choose whether to do so, portable and always on audio–video capture equipment can be a threat to the privacy of individuals a person interacts with or who simply happen to be close by.

2.4.2 Precision

We can distinguish awareness systems with respect to their precision and accuracy. Figure 2.2 illustrates how awareness information regarding children at school was presented to parents on their PC at home and at work during a recent investigation (Khan and Markopoulos, 2007). We shall use this example to explain the concepts introduced in this section.

Awareness information consisted of two parts: presence and activity. Children participating in the study carried a Bluetooth headset which was detected by a desktop computer at their class. This device gave real time information regarding their presence in the classroom. When the Bluetooth headset would be detected in range of the classroom computer, a colourful icon would be presented floating on the desktop of the remote parent. A grey icon would indicate the child was out of range. The text line below the image showed the planned (not actual) activity of the child according to the school's week schedule.

Precision can be understood in terms of the granularity of the awareness information and how rich a communication channel it is. For example, in Fig. 2.2, the icon indicating whether the child is in the class or not carries one bit of information that is a coarse grain indicator of the location of the child. The Whereabouts clock (Sellen et al., 2006, see also Chapter 18) conveys two bits of information for location awareness, distinguishing between four locations: at home, at work, at school and 'other'. In the Diarist system, the top level view represented a choice of six locations, while the blog and the narrative represented increasing levels of detail. In media spaces, a blurred image offers less precision over the full video image, see, for example, Markopoulos et al. (2005a).

Designers may opt for low precision to protect the user privacy. However, it is often the case that more precise information is needed. In the evaluation of the awareness system of Fig. 2.2 parents reported needing more detailed awareness, e.g. whether their child is alone, who the child interacts with (see Khan and Markopoulos, 2007). In this case, they required higher precision (more information, giving more detail). Other parents who preferred to know whether the child was out of bounds of the school, an issue more relevant to their concerns. Going out of bounds would be a reason for concern. In a flexible system users may prefer to vary the precision of the information about them as a means for managing their own awareness and privacy needs.

Precision can also be applied to characterize affective communication. A messaging system may convey one bit of information that may be interpreted as 'I am thinking of you' (as in Kaye et al., 2005 or Strong and Gaver, 1996) or may be tied

Child's device is detected   Child's device is not detected   There is a technical problem

Fig. 2.2 An awareness system for parent regarding their children at school (Khan and Markopoulos, 2007). The awareness display is a graphical widget for a Windows platform that 'floats' over any other window on the PC. It displays (**a**) whether a child is in the vicinity of the class and (**b**) the scheduled activity of the child at school

to richer information like texting or pictures, as, for example, in the ASTRA system (Romero et al., 2007a).

Precision thus relates directly by the amount of information conveyed. It corresponds to the dimension of 'information capacity' according to Pousman and Stasko (2006) or, more generally, the richness of the communication medium used.

Apart from varying the amount of information conveyed about a person, place or community precision can vary with regards to how much this information is abstracted. We discuss two different types of abstraction as these were identified by Pedersen and Sokoler (1997).

Connecting places through audio and video links, sending pictures, all involve transferring concrete, un-interpreted information. *Feature degradation* allows for reducing detail, e.g. showing people as silhouettes only (see Markopoulos et al., 2005a) which can be less privacy threatening compared to full video. *Feature abstraction*, can involve interpretation of the information presented, e.g. when image processing would be used to infer whether someone is in a room or not. This abstraction can be effected both at the capture side, i.e. the side of the person(s) or places we aim to support awareness of, as well the presentation side, where information is presented.

Feature degradation and feature abstraction are often combined. Abstracting information at the capture side amounts to context sensing and interpretation. Compared to removing detail at the side of the receiver this approach reduces the privacy risk for users by capturing only necessary information. For example, if the system should let users know that their elderly parent has a visitor at home, it is not necessary to identify this person. The challenge for designers using interpretation of the information (or filtering in any case) at the capture side is to let people entering this space know the exact content and nature of information the system captures and shares with others.

At the display side, presenting interpreted information can offer the advantage of economy and ease of use. It is not always straight forward to make inferences from raw data at a level comparable to that of humans viewing a visualization of this data, see, for example, Begole and Tang (2007). Controlling the abstraction level of information presented may allow users to manage the amount of information presented to them and how obtrusive that information can be. A rare example where users can control feature degradation at both the presentation and the capture sides is the Community Bar, developed by G. McEwan (Romero et al., 2007b).

2.4.3 Accuracy

Accuracy refers to the correctness or reliability of the information presented. Especially interesting is whether the information presented helps users reach the right inferences regarding the individuals they wish to be aware of.

Accuracy may be compromised as a result of technical constraints or simply by the way information collection is implemented. For example, in Fig. 2.2, children's scheduled activities are reasonably precise and rich descriptions but they are described as scheduled by the school a week in advance. As such, they may not be accurate, e.g. because some activity runs late, or a teacher falls ill.

Accuracy may also be manipulated by users deliberately. The need to allow deception in its various forms has been underlined by Price et al. (2005) as an essential means for people to protect their privacy. People can manage their accessibility to others, how they present themselves to others or how to share information by varying the accuracy (but also the precision) of the information they present. This may not be just for self-serving purposes; it may often be a means to save face for the other party avoiding unnecessary misunderstandings or other social costs; see the argument for supporting equivocation in such systems by Aoki and Woodruff (2005).

As is often the case, accuracy trades off with precision. Users and designers alike face this trade-off – given an increase the precision of awareness information they may prefer the ability to modify its accuracy.

Unlike awareness for supporting cooperation or situation awareness as this discussed in the Human Factors literature maximum accuracy is not the golden standard to strive for in the domain of social awareness systems. Designers need to be thoughtful and parsimonious in detail and quantity of awareness information and should more often than not provide control to users over the accuracy of the information shared.

On the other hand, providing users with full control over the accuracy of awareness information may work against the purpose of the system. For example, systems supporting health awareness are often intended to provide support, protection and reassurance for some distant individual. In these cases, they can only succeed to do so if they provide accurate and up-to-date information. If the person concerned could prevent the system from sharing some kinds of information, e.g. an elderly not showing that he does not feel well to prevent others from worrying and to avoid disturbing them, then the system provides little added value to any of its users.

Awareness information may also deteriorate in quality because of technical reasons. For example, a network failure, a sensor running out of battery, etc. In cases where erroneous information is shown the benefits of an awareness system are cancelled out. For example, in the field trial of the Diarist a technical failure leads one user to be quite worried, as it was showing that her father was out all night.

2.4.4 Notification Level

This dimension concerns the presentation side of an awareness system. It has been discussed by McCrickard et al. as the *interruption dimension*, and a more refined description has been provided by Matthews et al. (2004). We adopt here the classification by Pousman and Stasko that distinguishes five levels of notification:

User poll (the user has to explicitly invoke the presentation of the awareness information)
Change blind (changes are not noticeable on a display that the user can consult at will)
Make aware (changes are noticeable but do not draw attention)
Interrupt (user is interrupted but can ignore the display)
Demand attention (have to be attended to, e.g. a modal dialogue box)

Depending on the nature of the user activity supported, the importance and the criticality of the information presented through an awareness system, the designer may choose between a peripheral display, i.e. one that is non-disruptive and that meshes in the environment of the user or a display that is intended to interrupt and attract attention to itself (for a theoretically based analysis of peripheral displays, see Matthews et al. (2007))

Most of the systems discussed here fall into the low to middle range of the notification level dimension (user poll and change blind). However, it may be that some specific information items need to be presented more conspicuously to the users, e.g. when the information presented is life or safety critical.

2.4.5 Input Automation: Explicit Versus Implicit Input

An awareness system can assemble the information it presents through explicit input by its users or implicitly by sensing, logging and interpreting their activity (that is not assumed to be related to the use of the awareness system); see Abowd and Mynatt (2000). In the context of awareness systems, this distinction concerns how the user controls an awareness application: what information is captured about a place or a person, who is it shared with and how information is displayed; see Fig. 2.3.

Consider some examples featuring increasing levels of control by their users:

The Digital Family Portrait and the Diarist mentioned already capture a specific set of parameters regarding the activity of a senior person living alone. Neither this person nor their relatives can choose how this information is presented.

InfoCanvas (Miller and Stasko, 2001) allows users to tie specific information to interactive artefacts that are able to display it.

Social networking applications (e.g. setting your status at home or not, sending a message, or updating a blog), let users control which information to share and to adjust their presentation to the intended audience and context.

ASTRA (Romero et al., 2007a) is a completely manual system, where the users create and share pictures and notes.

People are extremely skilled at making such adaptations, and a technological system can go very wrong when it attempts to substitute user explicit input. Subtleties of language are hard to reproduce, timing, accuracy of information, precision, empathy with the audience; each of these aspects is one way in which people demonstrate their social skills, when communicating unaided by a system.

Fig. 2.3 The Photomirror application for creating awareness for members of the same household who follow different routines. The mirror is placed in the hallway of a home. A computer display was placed behind a highly translucent mirror. The camera on the top of the frame supports implicit input; it captures still pictures when it detects motion. The detachable camera at the bottom of the frame supports explicit input. Users can pick it up and create 30ʹ video clips. All media is placed on a time-ordered grid. Gradually all information fades away, and the system becomes a mirror. The information is very imprecise and non-persistent in order to avoid privacy problems. (See Markopoulos et al., 2005a)

Social skills of this kind are an essential component of human intelligence and one that current automated systems are far from being able to emulate or substitute.

There are advantages to implicit input. An obvious one is that they save effort for their users, who when having to update the system with information may forget to do so or may make errors. Automated systems offer the possibility of scaling up usage and connectivity, they can capture information that can be tedious for humans to capture interactively or that only makes sense if there is some reliable capture mechanism, e.g. for health monitoring an indication that someone's heart rate is within safe bounds or not, or for a dementia patients whose location is tracked by the system.

A limitation of automated sensing systems is that they do not help convey *intentionality*. Sending a regular and automated log of activities of one's holidays will be less appreciated than a personally addressed and well-timed message (see Romero et al., 2007a). To give an example from a different domain, sending an invitation for coffee to a colleague is warmer and more inviting than an automatically generated announcement that you are having a coffee break. Intentionality can be expressed in the content, the timing of the message, and also, by considering the environment in which it will be displayed.

2.4.6 Private Versus Shared Nature of Awareness Displays

A large range of awareness systems rely on public displays. These can be large screens that are situated at places where they can be noticed at opportune moments, they can be physical decorative artefacts that can be viewed from a distance. Corridors, coffee corners are popular choices for placing such displays in the workplace. The mantelpiece or the fridge might be preferred in the household. Awareness displays can be intended for private use, such as a 'sidebar' on a computer monitor, or a buddy list for an instant messenger or a contact list for a mobile phone.

Designers have to resolve what information is relevant to users and what is an appropriate way to present the 'trickle' of information that an awareness system presents in a way that can be perceived by the user, without being disruptive. For example, having information displayed as a screen saver on a mobile phone would also mean that most often it is out of sight (the phone could be either in their pocket or simply it could be too small to notice).

The choice can be very simple when the purpose of the awareness system has been settled: Is it intended to support a group or to support an individual? Should it be used specifically at one location or independently of location? A halfway solution is to support a public display that while viewed by many can be understood by intended users only, e.g. ones who occupy a place regularly and have learnt to interpret abstract and perhaps personally meaningful display patterns.

2.4.7 Level of User Control

This dimension concerns the kind of control offered by awareness systems, focusing especially at the level of controlling information flow:

On–off: Many systems offer no other control to their user than an on–off switch. Typically an awareness system consists in a specific information capture and an information display component, which are connected over a network. The designer chooses the mapping and the user is only able to activate or deactivate the system. As most systems presented so far are essentially research prototypes, this is the only degree of control allowed to their users.

Publish/subscribe: A more flexible mechanism involves offering specific awareness information sources to the connected community, while individuals wishing to view this information can subscribe to this information.

Filtering existing flows of information: Assuming that individuals wish to control the flow of information from them to others and vice versa, the system could allow the users to modify the precision or even the accuracy of the information presented or shared about them.

Full control of information flows: A more flexible system would open up control of what information is captured, the precision and accuracy offered at each side, the connections between different nodes in a network and even the degree to which the preferences of users regarding the flow of information are observable to others (see Chapter 6 regarding the focus–nimbus model).

The options listed provide an increasing level of control and flexibility to their users; these bring along increased workload and complexity. Empirical evaluations reported in the literature have concerned mostly very simple systems, with minimal flexibility. Such evaluations have demonstrated the potential of awareness systems and documented a range of usage patterns for them. Surveys of people's needs and field trials seem to support the need for more control over their privacy but it is not clear whether the extra effort required to operate such systems can justify the extra benefits they provide over simpler solutions.

2.5 Challenges for the Design of Awareness Systems

This section discusses some challenges that need to be addressed for the design of awareness systems supporting social communication. In a brief form they are as follows:

- Minimize procedural effort
- Support transitions to other media
- Designing agency in awareness systems
- Reciprocity, equity of costs and benefits
- Balancing accountability and autonomy
- Designing beautiful seams (seamful design)
- Data proportionality

2.5.1 Minimize Procedural Effort

Minimizing the effort required to operate any interactive device is a general ambition for the field of interaction design. Applying this general principle to a particular design context is in most cases straightforward, as the effort is understood with respect to a specific task that needs to be accomplished. In the case of awareness systems though, the notion of effort has to be unpacked.

In the context of awareness systems and interpersonal communication in general, it is useful to distinguish between the 'procedural' effort that one needs to expend in order to operate a system (e.g. starting up, logging in, navigating menus) and the effort put to attend personally to an individual (sender or recipient of information). It seems that procedural effort is not appreciated by any of the connected individuals (in their role of sender or recipient), so this should be minimized. Personal effort allows for expressiveness, which is valued as an element of communication, (Romero et al., 2007a) so it should be supported. For example, a scheduled message for wishing 'happy birthday' to friends and relatives will not be appreciated (when recognized as such) compared to one where the sender put personal effort in constructing and sending the message.

Another issue that is less clearly understood is how much effort individuals are willing to expend on connecting to different members of their social network. It is clear, that this is not uniform and also may change according to time and context. Consider, for example, a system showing one's availability for interruptions during working hours and suppose the designer wishes to add the possibility of indicating the appropriate moment to call. An application that requires the user to switch from the current activity to providing input to the awareness system will cause a major disruption of his/her work. Further, the sender will be aware that attending the request disrupts attention from the current task and will be hesitant to initiate such an interruption.

Keeping effort low refers both to input and output. Effort can be kept low by requiring very little effort for feeding information to the system (and one's social network) or even doing so automatically, with the help of context sensing. At the display side, minimizing effort may mean having very clearly understandable, non-disruptive displays that are very selective regarding the amount of information they present. When larger information is presented or when more effort is needed to interpret the information, the effort expended should be meaningful in the context of the social interaction between the individuals concerned.

A case where meaningful effort is deliberately encouraged while procedural effort is low is informative art (Redström et al., 2000), where deeper reflection and a longer period of viewing might be required to decipher it. Similarly, the Home Radio discussed by Eggen and Mensvoort (Chapter 4) presents patterns of activity that only become meaningful after some period of time and when concerning intimately related individuals.

2.5.2 Support Transitions to Other Media

Next to the communication of information itself, communicating parties invest a lot of effort on managing the process of the communication. This activity has been described as outeraction (Nardi et al., 2000) and it can constitute an important use of awareness information, e.g. helping individuals while initiating conversations, managing a conversation thread. While many research prototypes consider awareness system in isolation, which allows for a focused evaluation, it is necessary to consider these in their wider context of use as one of the many available channels of communication between individuals, playing a complementary role to other media.

The ASTRA system was designed with outeraction in mind: trying to trigger phone calls or e-mails. In general, knowledge about other people, their activities, context, or thoughts can provide the trigger or even the pretext for communication. In some cases it may simply help individuals to recognize an opportune moment to communicate or to choose the appropriate communication medium; indeed a recent survey of awareness needs for young working couples with children (Khan and Markopoulos, 2007) found availability for contact is one of the most wanted pieces of awareness information. The most common example of providing this type of awareness are popular 'buddy lists' of instant messaging applications, which help find out when members of one's social network are on line in order to enter into communication with them. Going further, knowing if someone is watching the same broadcast sport event may be a trigger for a telephone call, or knowing your partner is busy at a meeting can help choose the right time for the phone call.

2.5.3 Designing Agency in Awareness Systems

As argued by Heath et al. (2002) people support awareness-building by 'configuring' their behaviour for their intended audience. This configuration may amount to ensuring that one has the attention of one's audience and that the audience understand information presented to them. It can also mean that one may self-sensor avoiding to act in some ways when observed.

A communication pattern that has been observed in a few cases, e.g. the Inter-Living project as mentioned earlier, the trials of ASTRA but also the Photomirror (Markopoulos et al., 2005a) was how users hijacked the application provided to use it as a stage to be creative and perform to other users. In the first case, they started creating funny staged pictures on a theme and on the second they started performing to the camera. While this is not the purpose of awareness systems it can be both the way users choose to appropriate a system and also a vehicle for designers to encourage and support awareness.

When information is collected and presented automatically it does not carry the explicit intent by the sender. Expressions of intentionality require flexible communication means, e.g. text, photos, that allow users to mould the message content and form to their needs. On the contrary, awareness systems that only capture and convey one type of information in a specific way (e.g. a presence lamp, or even systems like the scent and feather discussed earlier as proposals for emotional communication) do not provide sufficient flexibility to express intentions. Simple messaging systems such as AnyBiff (Rittenbruch et al., 2007) (also in Chapter 16), support this usage pattern in an effective and lightweight manner.

People will use their knowledge (if any) of where the information is presented and to whom in order to adapt the content and the form of their message. This topic is discussed extensively in Chapter 17. This derives from two motivations of people: to present themselves appropriately and to minimize effort. For example, if you address a message to colleagues who will read it at the common room you can easily refer to their whereabouts or that they know you are not present.

The above examples favour the need to add expressiveness and to allow the user to maintain initiative in capturing, conveying information and 'configuring' awareness in the sense introduced by Heath et al. (2002). Leaving the initiative to the user can be a valuable aspect of an awareness system.

On the other hand, as discussed earlier, there are cases where awareness can be valued exactly because it is not created automatically and does not represent the agency of its users. For example, a system that displays well being information regarding a lone elderly without his/her intervention or control can provide higher levels of reassurance to his/her children without the elder having to worry that he/she is seen as grumbling or putting a burden upon the latter.

2.5.4 Reciprocity, Equity of Costs and Benefits

Considered as a form of groupware, awareness systems need also to provide equity between those shouldering the costs and those enjoying benefits. Equity does not necessarily amount to perfect equality, but needs to fit the social relation between the individuals concerned.

Parents may not mind spending effort to be informed of their young children's whereabouts. An elderly adult may be prepared to put some effort into providing an adult child or a grandchild with awareness information in order to be involved in their life (and vice versa) and enhance their feelings of connectedness.

Further to the effort involved in providing information to a system or to consuming information, costs can refer to loss of privacy, expectations that are unmet and obligations created when another person is aware of your whereabouts or vice versa. Benefits as discussed above can refer to connectedness, peace of mind, etc.

As a general heuristic for supporting personal privacy designers could choose to minimize information flow asymmetry, see Jiang et al. (2002). When information flow is completely unidirectional, awareness systems run the risk of being perceived as monitoring systems. Monitoring systems can be useful, e.g. to support health applications, or situations where the social relationship between the connected individuals is already unbalanced and their respective roles justify one monitoring the other. In other cases, the asymmetry may create problems, e.g. when one actor can be observed via a video camera while the other cannot. Minimizing information flow asymmetry can be a good way of protecting user privacy and letting users resolve privacy issues in their own way.

Reciprocity does not mean that the same information needs to be provided to each other. Considering the example of awareness systems for the elderly, several of the studies discussed have shown that the elderly are happy to know daily routine activities and events of the life of their children. They are less interested to know their eating and sleeping patterns, to monitor their health in detail, etc., which are more important for the children to know about their elderly parents. Reciprocity in this case would mean providing a two-way flow of information, with different content but ideally with commensurate costs and benefits for both parties.

2.5.5 Balancing Accountability and Autonomy

One of Grudin's eight challenges for groupware design is to enable social norms to apply also to social interactions through the system. Following a similar line of thought Erickson et al. (2002) introduced the concept of *social translucence* that is one of the most important considerations in designing an awareness system and one that distinguishes between an awareness system and a monitoring system.

A socially translucent system, following Erickson et al. allows communicators to be aware of each other, but also to observe what the other party is aware of. This awareness of the other person's awareness, they argue, can make individuals accountable to each other, enabling the application of social norms and the emergence of behaviours common in our daily social contact. On the other hand, awareness is now possible through an increasing proportion of our daily life. Sustained awareness and translucence with an ever increasing proportion of our social network, over more contexts, locations and times can be undesirable and it can violate social norms, create obligations and expectations that individuals are not prepared to meet.

The notions of plausible deniability, deviance, ambiguity or deception have been discussed by different authors precisely to describe the need of individuals to avoid this accountability, to apply social norms of equivocation to avoid difficult social situations and diffuse these obligations; see Fig. 2.4. See Aoki and Woodruff (2005) for an excellent discussion. Field testing of awareness systems has shown often a deviant behaviour: users intentionally not announcing their presence, switching off their system so that they can remain invisible to them or to other parties, or avoiding to input information regarding their activities and whereabouts. For example, in a recent experiment (Janse et al., 2007) where we compared a variant of the 'intentional presence lamp' and a presence lamp that operates through sensing the proximity of a user by RFID tags, users did not mind whether presence detection was automated or not, but in both cases found ways to control when their presence should not be known (e.g. by leaving their RFID token in a car, or by deciding not to announce their presence at home until they had settled in their homes). In general, users seemed to need a simple and direct control by which to suspend all information communication about them.

Fig. 2.4 This concept prototype by L. Hurkx (Graduation project, TU/e, Department of Industrial Design, 2006) allows an elder living alone announce her interest to go for a walk with her neighbour and friend. When she places the clogs on their base, the figures on the tile surface will appear. At the other side her friend may notice this non-obtrusive invitation, but does not have to decline. The system was designed to relax the feelings of obligation and the loss of face when one party would decline. It uses ambiguity and the lack of persistence of the display (which fades out) to provide plausible deniability that would be hard to provide with other means of communication or with a face-to-face invitation

Balancing the tension between translucence and ambiguity requires parsimony in how much information is conveyed and the provision of appropriate controls for users to allow them to dynamically adapt to different contexts of use. This is not a trivial design challenge. Chapter 9 discusses the Privacy Grounding Model, a theoretically motivated model for how interpersonal privacy is coordinated in mediated communication. Following this model, lightweight means of interaction that can operate without interfering with the main function of an awareness system need to be created that will allow users to cooperatively ground mutual privacy borders in order to address this tension.

2.5.6 Designing Beautiful Seams (Seamful Design)

Unless in very simple cases, one cannot assume that awareness information presented is reliable. Erroneous information or system behaviour can arise because of malfunction of context sensing technology or a problem in the network, etc. While one can hope that technology improvements can reduce these problems, another source of erroneous information is harder to prevent. In cases where context sensing is involved for capturing awareness information, it is typical that heuristics are applied relating what information is sensed by technical means and what inferences need to be drawn. For example, in buddy lists the online status is often related to availability. In the Diarist (Metaxas et al., 2007) when pressure sensors detect weight on more than one armchairs of the living room presence of a second person in the house is assumed or presence of a house occupant was detected when a Wi-Fi signal emitted by a mote would be received. It is only very likely that some of these heuristics will cease to hold as the situations in which such systems are deployed change unpredictably.

Seamful design (Chalmers and Galani, 2004) is an approach to designing ubiquitous computing systems that allows users to expose technological 'seams', i.e. aspects of the underlying technological infrastructure that explain and disambiguate the operation of the system at a surface level. In the case of awareness systems, designers can choose to expose the 'seams' of an awareness system, i.e. its internal workings which at first sight are irrelevant for the user but which may need to be inspected when things go wrong. For example, in the awareness system for the school shown above, it was decided to offer a different graphical presentation for the cases where technical problems prevent the awareness display from being refreshed versus the cases where the child is not detected in range. In the case of Diarist, a detailed narrative explained the basis on which inferences were drawn regarding the presence or activity of the elderly person concerned.

2.5.7 Data Proportionality

As sensing technology and video capture technology become cheaper, it is only too tempting to introduce automatic capture of awareness information, given the advantages mentioned above. It is important though for designers to remain critical with respect to introducing such privacy threatening technologies. Implicit input should be used only to such an extent that the benefits it provides outweigh the potential loss of control and privacy (Markopoulos et al., 2005a).

For example, if the affective benefits relating to a presence lamp application are only slight compared to announcing presence based on an explicit interaction (flicking a switch), one should probably question the value of doing this automatically. If increasing the confidence with which such information can be automatically extracted, one would combine different streams of data, e.g. video images from the location in question, audio and sensor data, the sensing might improve but the privacy risks for individuals would be excessive for the simple function of announcing presence at home.

The concept of data proportionality has its origins in legislation regarding fair information practices. It was developed by Iachello and Abowd (2005) as a framework for structuring decisions about privacy while designing ubiquitous computing systems. Achieving data proportionality is not trivial, but considering this issue helps designers be explicit about judgements and trade-offs regarding the privacy threats awareness systems may bring about.

2.6 Conclusion

This chapter has discussed awareness systems for social communication purposes like connecting friends and family.

First, it summarized a growing body of empirical research showing that related benefits are experienced by users of awareness systems. The collection of works reviewed was organized in terms of fundamental social goals of humans making the point that awareness systems address actual and real needs and are not an ephemeral trend that results from a technology push.

The design space of awareness systems was sketched out in terms of seven dimensions. It has a broader scope than the classification of Ambient Information Displays by Pousman and Stasko (2006) in that it addresses not just the presentation of awareness information but also the way information is captured and disseminated (who gets to know what). Issues such as aesthetics or the semantics of graphical representations (which were important considerations for Pousman and Stasko) are less of a concern in the present context, and were not dealt with.

Compared to the classification by Gross et al. (2005), the classification presented here concerns awareness systems for social use rather than cooperative work. Further, we have focused not on categorizing different conceptions of awareness and system properties but on characterizing a design space along choices that concern the designers of awareness systems.

Eight challenges for the design of these systems have been discussed. Apart from their number they are very different to the challenges discussed by Grudin (1994) that concerned groupware. The two sets of challenges overlap regarding the potential disparity of costs and benefits from such a system. Most of Grudin's challenges do not apply when considering the social use of awareness systems. Consider, for example, his challenge of reaching a critical mass of users (prisoner's dilemma). A system may be valuable even supporting a one-to-one awareness if the relation is valuable enough and there exists a shared motivation to connect with each other. The challenges discussed in this chapter can be at some level considered as specializing Grudin's challenge on 'supporting existing social practices', though in our case these refer to informal social relations rather than work-oriented interactions.

Acknowledgements This work is supported by the European Community under the 'Information Society Technologies' Programme, FP6, project ASTRA IST 29266.

References

Abowd, G. D. and Mynatt, E. D. (2000). Charting past, present, and future research in ubiquitous computing. ACM Trans. Comput.-Hum. Interact. 7, 1 (Mar. 2000), 29–58.

Aoki, P. M. and Woodruff, A. (2005). Making space for stories: ambiguity in the design of personal communication systems. Proceedings CHI '05. ACM Press, New York, NY, 181–190.

Begole, J. and Tang, J. C. (2007). Incorporating human and machine interpretation of unavailability and rhythm awareness into the design of collaborative applications. Human-Computer Interaction 22 (1–2): 7–45.

Bell, D., Hooker, B., and Raby, F. (2000). FLIRT: Social services for the urban context.

Carroll, J. M. and Rosson, M. (1992). Getting around the task-artifact cycle: how to make claims and design by scenario. ACM Trans. Inf. Syst. 10, 2 (Apr. 1992), 181–212.

Chalmers, M. and Galani, A. (2004). Seamful interweaving: heterogeneity in the theory and design of interactive systems. Proceedings DIS 2004, 243–252.

Consolvo, S., Roessler, P., and Shelton, B. E. (2004). The CareNet display: lessons learned from an in home evaluation of an ambient display. Proceedings UbiComp '04, 1–17.

Dadlani, P., Sinitsyn, A., Fontijn, W., and Markopoulos, P. (2008). Aurama: supporting connectedness between elderly and their children with long-term trend awareness of wellbeing. Proceedings 7th Workshop on Social Intelligence Design, December 2008, Puerto-Rico.

Dourish, P., Adler, A., Bellotti, V., and Henderson, A. (1996). Your place or mine? Learning from long-term use of audio-video communication. CSCW Journal 5(1), 33–62.

Erickson, T., Halverson, C., Kellogg, W. A., Laff, M., and Wolf, T. (2002). Social translucence: designing social infrastructures that make collective activity visible. Communications of the ACM 45, 4 (Apr. 2002), 40–44.

Gaver, W. and Hooker, B. (2001). The Presence Project. London, RCA: CRD Publishing.

Ginelle, D. and Gutwin, C. (2005). A Groupware Design Framework for Loosely Coupled Workgroups, Proceedings ECSCW 2005, Springer, 65–82.

Gross, T., Stary, C., and Totter A. (2005). User-centered awareness in computer-supported cooperative work systems: structured embedding of findings from social sciences. International Journal of Human-Computer Interaction 18(3), 323–360.

Grudin, J. (1994). Groupware and social dynamics: eight challenges for developers. Communications of the ACM 37, 1 (Jan. 1994), 92–105.

Gutwin, C. and Greenberg, S. (2002). A descriptive framework of workspace awareness for realtime groupware. Computer Supported Cooperative Work 11, 3 (Nov. 2002), 411–446.

Heath, C., Svensson, M. S., Hindmarsh, J., Luff, P., and vom Lehn, D. (2002). Configuring awareness. Computer Supported Cooperatuve Work 11, 3 (Nov. 2002), 317–347.

Hindus, D., Mainwaring, S. D., Leduc, N., Hagström, A. E., and Bayley, O. (2001). Casablanca: designing social communication devices for the home. Proceedings CHI '01. ACM, New York, 325–332.

Hutchinson, H., Mackay, W., Westerlund, B., Bederson, B. B., Druin, A., Plaisant, C., Beaudouin-Lafon, M., Conversy, S., Evans, H., Hansen, H., Roussel, N., and Eiderbäck, B. (2003). Technology probes: inspiring design for and with families. Proceedings CHI '03. ACM, New York, 17–24.

Iachello, G. and Abowd, G.D., (2005). Privacy and proportionality: adapting legal evaluation techniques to inform design in ubiquitous computing. Proceedings CHI 2005, 91–100.

Janse, M. D., Vink, P., Soute, I., and Boland, H. (2007). Perceived Privacy in Ambient Intelligent Environments. First International Workshop on Combining Context with Trust, Security and Privacy. Moncton, New Brunswick, Canada, July 30, 2007.

Jiang, X., Hong, J. I., and Landay, J. A. (2002). Approximate information flows: socially-based modeling of privacy in ubiquitous computing. Proceedings of the 4th International Conference on Ubiquitous Computing, Göteborg, Sweden, September 29 – October 01, 2002. G. Borriello and L. E. Holmquist, (Eds.) LNCS, vol. 2498. Springer-Verlag, London, 176–193.

Kaye, J., Levitt, M. K., Nevins, J., Golden, J., and Schmidt, V. (2005). Communicating intimacy one bit at a time. Proceedings CHI '05. ACM Press, New York, 1529–1532.

Khan, J.V. and Markopoulos, P. (2007). On the role of awareness systems for supporting parent involvement in young children's schooling, Proceedings HOIT 2007, Kluwer.

Kenrick, D. T., Cialdini, R. B., and Neuberg, S. L. (2004). Social Psychology: Unraveling the Mystery. Allyn and Bacon.

Liechti O. and Ichikawa, T. (2000). A digital photography framework supporting social interaction and affective awareness. Personal and Ubiquitous Computing, Springer, 4, (1).

Markopoulos, P., Bongers, B., van Alphen, E., Dekker, J., van Dijk, W., Messemaker, S., van Poppel, J., van der Vlist, B., Volman, D., and van Wanrooij, G. (2005a). The PhotoMirror appliance: affective awareness in the hallway. Personal and Ubiquitous Computing, 10 (2–3), 128–135.

Markopoulos, P., IJsselsteijn, W., Huijnen, C., and de Ruyter, B. (2005b). Sharing experiences through awareness systems in the home. Interacting with Computers, 17, 5, Elsevier, 506–521.

Matthews, T., Dey, A. K., Mankoff, J., Carter, S., and Rattenbury, T. (2004). A toolkit for managing user attention in peripheral displays. Proceedings UIST '04. ACM, New York, 247–256.

Matthews, T., Rattenbury, T., and Carter, S. (2007). Defining, designing, and evaluating peripheral displays: an analysis using Activity Theory. Human-Computer Interaction, 22 (1), Laurence Erlbaum, 221–261.

McCrickard, D. S., Chewar, C. M., Somervell, J. P., and Ndiwalana, A. (2003). A model for notification systems evaluation—assessing user goals for multitasking activity. ACM Trans. Computer-Human Interaction, 10, 4, 312–338.

Metaxas, G., Metin, B., Schneider, J., Markopoulos, P., and De Ruyter, B. (2007). Daily activities diarist: supporting aging in place with semantically enriched narratives, INTERACT 2007, Springer, LNCS 4663: 390–403.

Miller, T. and Stasko, J. (2001). The InfoCanvas: information conveyance through personalized, expressive art. Extended Abstracts CHI '01. ACM Press, 305–306.

Mynatt, E. D., Rowan, J., Craighill, S., and Jacobs, A. (2001). Digital family portraits: supporting peace of mind for extended family members. Proceedings CHI '01. ACM Press, New York, 333–340.

Nardi, B. A., Whittaker, S., and Bradner, E. (2000). Interaction and outeraction: instant messaging in action. Proceedings CSCW '00. ACM Press, New York, 79–88.

Pedersen, E. R., and Sokoler, T. (1997). AROMA: abstract representation of presence supporting mutual awareness. Proceedings CHI'97, 51–58.

Pousman, Z. and Stasko, J. (2006). A taxonomy of ambient information systems: four patterns of design. Proceedings AVI '06. ACM, New York, 67–74.

Price, B., Adam, K., and Nuseibeh, B. (2005). Keeping ubiquitous computing to yourself: a practical model for user control of privacy, International Journal of Human-Computer Studies, 63 (1–2), Elsevier, 228–253.

Redström, J., Skog, T., and Hallnäs, L. (2000). Informative art: using amplified artworks as information displays. ProceedingsDARE '00. ACM, New York, 103–114.

Rittenbruch, M., Viller, S., and Mansfield, T. (2007). Announcing activity: design and evaluation of an intentionally enriched awareness service. Human-Computer Interaction, 22 (1), Laurence Erlbaum.

Romero, N., Markopoulos, P., Baren van, J., Ruyter de, B., IJsselsteijn , W., and Farshchian, B. (2007a). Connecting the family with awareness systems. Personal and Ubiquitous Computing, Springer-London, 299–312.

Romero, N., McEwan, G., and Greenberg, S. (2007b). A field study of community bar: (mis)-matches between theory and practice. Proceedings GROUP '07, 89–98.

Rowan, J. and Mynatt, E. D. (2005). Digital family portrait field trial: Support for aging in place. Proceedings CHI '05. ACM, New York, 521–530.

Sellen, A., Eardley, R., Izadi, S., and Harper, R. (2006). The whereabouts clock: early testing of a situated awareness device. CHI '06 Extended Abstracts, ACM Press, New York, 1307–1312.

Strong, R. and Gaver, W. W. (1996). Feather, scent, and shaker: supporting simple intimacy. Proceedings of CSCW'96, Nov. 16–20, Boston, New York: ACM Press.

Vetere, F., Gibbs, M. R., Kjeldskov, J., Howard, S., Mueller, F., Pedell, S., Mecoles, K., and Bunyan, M. (2005). Mediating intimacy: designing technologies to support strong-tie relationships. ProceedingsCHI '05, 471–480.

Chapter 3
Awareness in the Home: The Nuances of Relationships, Domestic Coordination and Communication

Saul Greenberg, Carman Neustaedter, and Kathryn Elliot

3.1 Introduction

Computing has changed dramatically over the last decade. While some changes arose from technological advances, the most profound effects are in *how* technologies are used by everyday people for activities other than task-oriented work. Computers are now central to new ways of engaging in play, interpersonal and small group communication, community interaction, entertainment, personal creativity dissemination, personal publication, and so on. We are particularly interested in *domestic computing*, where technology mediates how families and other inhabitants interact within the context of the home. While domestic computing can incorporate many things, we focus in this chapter on the role awareness plays in domestic coordination and communication.

As we will see, the home has its own special attributes. The behaviors, actions, and interactions of people within the home are quite different than its workplace counterparts (e.g., see Whittaker et al., 1994 for awareness in the workspace). The opportunities to "improve" home life via technology intervention are also murkier. The home is a well-oiled machine, where people have developed many social practices that enable fluid and flexible interactions and coordination. Because it works so well, it is not always obvious if and how technology can be designed to improve how people go about their daily home life.

In this context, we need to understand the key role that awareness plays in the home. Similar to the work settings described in other chapters in this book, we believe that awareness is the "glue" that makes home life work. Yet awareness in the home is very different from awareness at work. This chapter explains some of these differences by summarizing and reflecting on our current understanding of awareness in the home. Our explanation is formed from the combination of existing theories, other people's studies of domestic culture, lessons learned from technol-

S. Greenberg (✉)
University of Calgary, Calgary, Canada
e-mail: saul.greenberg@ucalgary.ca

P. Markopoulos et al. (eds.), *Awareness Systems*, Human-Computer Interaction Series,
DOI 10.1007/978-1-84882-477-5_3, © Springer-Verlag London Limited 2009

ogy design, and our own semi-structured contextual interviews of 10 households (see Elliot et al., 2005; Neustaedter et al., 2006; Elliot, 2006; Neustaedter, 2007 for methodological details).

We begin by defining *interpersonal awareness* (Section 3.2), which considers the spectrum of relationships that people have with others both within and outside the home. Specifically, interpersonal awareness is defined as the awareness information and mechanisms necessary to satisfy people's real need and desire to know about each other (Neustaedter et al., 2006; Neustaedter, 2007). As we will see, differing relationships implies different needs for interpersonal awareness. We then focus on communication information in the home (Section 3.3), where we explicate how *contextual locations* mediates this communication (Section 3.4) through the interplay of *time,ownership*, and *awareness* (Section 3.5) (Elliot et al., 2005; Elliot, 2006).

3.2 Interpersonal Awareness

Home inhabitants naturally maintain some semblance of awareness of their family members and friends (Mynatt et al., 2001; Tollmar and Persson, 2002; Beech et al., 2004). For example, parents often need to be aware of their children's extracurricular schedules to coordinate rides, or a spouse may plan dinner depending on when their partner may be home (Neustaedter et al., 2006). We also know that this awareness extends beyond immediate home members to include others such as friends and the extended family (Grinter and Palen, 2002; Mynatt et al., 2001). Friends may want to know about another's schedule to plan a night out. Families need to know the well being of an elderly parent who lives elsewhere (Mynatt et al., 2001).

We use the term *awareness* here as this is how prior work studying domestic culture has characterized the types of knowledge we have just described. However, awareness is a widely used (and sometimes considered overused) term that encompasses many different situations (Schmidt, 2002). We have further classified awareness in the domestic realm as *interpersonal awareness* because the existing research shows that awareness in the domestic realm is focused on existing interpersonal relationships between people. The means by which these relationships are formed and maintained is described in detail in the disciplines of sociology and social psychology (e.g., Smith and Williamson, 1977).

Our interest lies in understanding how interpersonal awareness is acquired and used between individuals with established relationships, where all have a real need and desire to know about each other. As we will see, awareness cannot be described as a single generic entity. It must consider the people involved, their relationships, and whether they live together. We previously described such a model of interpersonal awareness (Neustaedter et al., 2006; Neustaedter, 2007), and this forms our basis for how we think about the interpersonal awareness space in domestic environments. In the next section, we outline the spectrum of people within one's social network for whom interpersonal awareness is desired. Subsequently, we describe the information that is maintained and its uses across this spectrum, and the techniques people use to maintain the awareness. Illustrative examples are drawn from our own contextual studies.

3.2.1 Social Groupings for Awareness

Our model explicates three groups of social contacts in the domestic setting: *home inhabitants*, *intimate socials*, and *extended socials*. These three groups are best viewed as broad clusters defining a spectrum of relationships vs. strictly bounded groups. Figure 3.1 provides a preview of results to come. We now describe each group in detail. Here we tend to use the words need and desire interchangeably. This is because we have found that, as it relates to interpersonal awareness, desires often strongly relate to what one perceives to be needs.

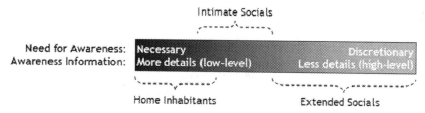

Fig. 3.1 The range of awareness needs for three social clusters

3.2.1.1 Home Inhabitants

Home inhabitants contain those people with whom one lives: significant others, family members, and roommates (Fig. 3.1, left end of spectrum). The number of home inhabitants will naturally vary based on the household, though commonly this ranges from one to six people. Almost all participants in our contextual study—which primarily contained families and roommates who were close friends—said they had a strong need to maintain a daily awareness of their home inhabitants.

3.2.1.2 Intimate Socials

Intimate socials contain those people with whom one has a close personal relationship, but does not live with. This group generally consists of one to six people. People still have a strong desire for awareness of those in this group (Fig. 3.1, middle of spectrum). For example, one of our participants maintained a close relationship with her mother, desiring awareness on a weekly basis. Other example intimate socials reported by our participants included significant others that they were not living with, immediate family members (e.g., parents, siblings), and close friends; only a few reported work colleagues as fitting this category. Other studies also found that people typically have a strong need for awareness of elderly parents (Mynatt et al.,

2001) along with children who have recently moved away from "home" (Tollmar and Persson, 2002).

While proximity is important for determining who is an intimate social, it is not the only dominant factor. About two-thirds of our participants had intimate socials in the same city as they lived. About half had people from a different city but within the country, and about one-quarter had people from a different and faraway country.

Most participants said their main reason for desiring an awareness of intimate socials was because she/he was close to them as she/he was considered family. A strong need to maintain awareness of an intimate social does not necessarily imply a frequent need. While nearly all participants had intimate socials for whom they desire a near-daily awareness, over one-third of the participants had intimate socials for whom they desired only weekly awareness. Thus, we emphasize that it is not the frequency of awareness that defines an intimate social but the strength of a person's need for that awareness.

3.2.1.3 Extended Socials

Extended socials also contain the family and friends of interest to a particular person. However, the relationship is much more casual and the desire for awareness is more discretionary (Fig. 3.1, right end of spectrum). All our participants had friends who were extended socials. About two-thirds had coworkers/teachers, two-fifths had siblings, and about two-thirds had other relatives. Most participants had fewer than 20 extended socials, though some had much larger groups. We found that the frequency of desired awareness is highly dependent on the individual. We also found that people share their more significant life changes instead of smaller details with extended socials (specific instances of this are described in the next section). While nearly all participants wanted more frequent awareness of their extended socials, they found it difficult to maintain because of scheduling difficulties, distance separation, or the time limitations. This suggests that a natural trade-off exists between acquiring an awareness of more individuals vs. distractions, interruptions, and feelings of information overload; people may not actually want an awareness of more people in practice.

3.2.2 Interpersonal Awareness Information

We found the interpersonal awareness information that people like to maintain for their family and friends generalizes to knowledge of one's context at varying levels of detail depending on the individual and her interpersonal relations. People want to know this information in order to coordinate, promote feelings of connectedness or comfort, or simply to have shared personal knowledge. This information typically falls into three interrelated categories: location, activity, and status. These categories largely parallel existing definitions of context (Dey, 2001), yet they contain subtleties specific to interpersonal awareness and, most important, they differ between our three social groups.

3.2.2.1 Awareness of Location

Imagine asking a family member or friend the question, "Where are you going?" You would likely expect different answers depending on who you asked just like you would share different information based on who asked you. This is precisely what we found. For home inhabitants, people want to know detailed location information: day-to-day or sometimes even moment-to-moment knowledge of the specific whereabouts of a cohabitant along with an understanding of where one plans to be. For example, one working mother from our study liked to know if her teenage son was at a friend's house after school or if he had gone straight home providing her with a feeling of comfort. Sometimes only a general understanding of locations is needed: for another mother in our study, knowing that someone has gone out to run errands, but not necessarily knowing which errands, is enough information. This kind of knowledge helps them coordinate household plans like dinner times. For many people, location information translates into knowing one's presence at a particular location (Tollmar and Persson, 2002). For example, a married couple with no children in our study both liked to know that the other is somewhere in their home simply because the knowledge is comforting.

For intimate socials, people want similar location details but at a lesser level of detail, typically daily or every few days, and often this awareness is of past locations or upcoming ones. For a teenaged person in our study, this meant knowing what her close friends had planned for the weekend so she could coordinate activities with them. Adult children may desire to know whether their elderly parents are at home, have left home, or, in serious cases, are at the hospital (Mynatt et al., 2001), again creating comfort.

For extended socials, people want to know even less details about location or may not even care about one's location except in special circumstances. Normally this involves knowing what city or area an extended social resides in or their location of work. For example, one participant told us she was often curious to know where her extended socials currently work.

3.2.2.2 Awareness of Activity

Now imagine asking a social contact, "What are you doing?" Again, you would expect a variety of answers depending on the person and their relationship to you. For home inhabitants, people want to know about their daily activities along with their upcoming plans. This includes knowing specifics about one's schedule of work/school and social activities. Work details generally include knowing the days and times that one is working, rather than knowledge of work appointments and meetings. For example, one wife liked to know what specific projects her husband was working on (though not the fine details of the projects) and what days he had to work. Social activities typically include knowing the activity's day/time, the type of activity (e.g., watching a movie at the theater, visiting a friend), and the other people involved in it (e.g., which friends vs. just strangers). As one would expect, we found parents were typically much more aware of the activities of younger children, and less so for older teenagers. Households must coordinate their day-to-day plans (Ling, 2000) and it is often necessary for cohabitants to schedule their activities and events based on the activities of each other. For example, two parents of children aged 14 and 16, commented that they need to know their children's schedules in order to coordinate rides to various activities. Other researchers report similar findings (Beech et al., 2004; Neustaedter et al., 2009).

For intimate socials, people want details about past or upcoming social or work activities, rather than knowledge of current activities. For example, a mother from our study wanted to know what her girlfriends had been up to last week and if anything "major" happened at her job simply to maintain a level of shared personal knowledge. Intimate socials also use activity awareness to coordinate but to a lesser extent than home inhabitants. For example, two teenagers in our study wanted to know the availability of their friends, so they can "hangout" with them. Detailed current knowledge of the availability of one's intimate socials was generally only desired by teenagers or significant others who did not live together, e.g., fiancés, girl/boyfriends. In the case of one graduate student living at his parents' home, awareness of his fiancée was much more like awareness of his cohabitants because of the close relationship with her.

For extended socials, people want to know activity information at an even higher level still. This typically equates to knowing major events or life changes, e.g., changing jobs, moving to a different city, getting married, having children. Awareness of activities of extended socials most often provides feelings of connectedness or comfort. For example, in the case of an aging elderly parent, knowing she is active can provide a sense of comfort that she has not fallen or is sick in bed (Mynatt et al., 2001). Activity awareness was generally only used by extended socials for coordination at a macro level, e.g., planning visits or holidays to see these people.

3.2.2.3 Awareness of Status

Now imagine asking a social contact, "How are you doing?" The answers would again vary where we have found they will often relate to one's location or activity as people almost always have feelings or attitudes associated with events or situations in their lives. For home inhabitants, status involves knowing how one feels about most aspects of their lives in addition to knowing how healthy one is and knowing about personal relationships (e.g., who is dating whom). Parents have a strong desire to make sure that things are going well for their children and, as providers, to ensure they have what they need. One mother in our study was concerned daily about how her children are feeling because she wanted to provide emotional support when needed. Often this will involve knowing how they are feeling about school, such as whether a test result went well or if they are feeling overwhelmed with homework. Significant others share similar information about their lives, which can also make them feel more connected to one another (Gaver, 2002).

For intimate socials, the same status information is desired but typically about only a selection of activities or health information. This often equates to knowledge about a shared interest or outing, a particular relationship, or a health problem. For example, a daughter recently moved out of town to go to college. The daughter and mother talk on the phone at least once a week and often their discussions will surround the daughter's latest boyfriend. A married couple was often quite concerned about the health and well being of one of their parents who recently suffered a stroke. They try to talk to her every few days to ensure she is still feeling fine where this knowledge is used to monitor and assist.

For extended socials, most people primarily want to know status information about health changes. Extended socials are much less intimate and feelings are not typically shared, at least not in great detail. In some cases, knowledge of status can even translate into a lack of comfort or worry if "bad news" is found out about a social contact, e.g., a relative is ill.

3.2.3 Techniques for Maintaining Awareness

The third aspect of interpersonal awareness that we describe is *techniques for maintaining awareness:* the methods people use to acquire and maintain interpersonal awareness. We found that interpersonal awareness is typically maintained using one or more of the following techniques: *visual cues from domestic artifacts,* and *direct* or *mediated interaction.* These techniques are not hierarchical in nature; rather, each technique offers contexts for which it is particularly well suited and each comes with its own limitations.

3.2.3.1 Visual Cues from Domestic Artifacts

Households are displays where people leave imprints of their lives and activities throughout the home (Hindus et al., 2001; Taylor and Swan, 2005). Here home inhabitants receive awareness information from the presence or absence of particular domestic artifacts from routine locations (Elliot et al., 2005). Often these cues are noticed as background activities requiring little thought or active attention. For example, a college student living at home explained to us how when arriving home he would automatically check, without much thought, whose cars were at home as he entered the garage. This information led him to quickly understand which family members were around. His father similarly commented that he could tell if his sons had gone out mountain biking (a common activity) by peering into the garage to see if the bicycles were gone. Other participants we interviewed used similar strategies with items like keys or wallets left in routine locations. Related research has pointed out that the *status* of domestic artifacts also provides *location* awareness. For example, the status of a light (on/off) can often indicate the presence and location of household members: if the light is on, likely someone is in that room (Tollmar and Persson, 2002). Naturally, inference errors can occur when gathering awareness through these types of visual cues, yet despite this, people still rely heavily on cues presented by domestic artifacts for maintaining awareness of home inhabitants. Further depth analysis of the use of domestic artifacts for awareness is described later in this chapter.

3.2.3.2 Direct and Mediated Interaction

When people are co-located with their social contacts in and around the home, they naturally converse and share awareness information through face-to-face interaction (Hindus et al., 2001; Tollmar and Persson, 2002). Simple conversations as people go about their home activities can provide awareness. For example, many of the mothers we interviewed talked about checking the family calendar in the evening or morning and then discussing its contents with family members to bring people "up to date" on family activities. Significant others have even been found to streamline their conversations to develop short-hand interactions involving brief instructions, which are generally only understood by family members (Ling, 2000).

The use of face-to-face interaction declines for intimate socials as they are not collocated as often as home inhabitants. Face-to-face interactions with intimate socials typically occur during social outings or shared activities. While people are together, like home inhabitants, they will discuss their activities which in turn provide an awareness and shared understanding.

Extended socials often have few opportunities for awareness gathering through face-to-face interaction because they are seen on a much less frequent basis, (e.g., visits to faraway family). We did find though that face-to-face communication allowed people to learn indirectly about extended socials. For example, children may learn about the health of a grandparent by talking with their mother after she has visited the grandparent. There are, of course, exceptions to these general cases: sometimes contacts are seen frequently, yet few details are shared because of the nature of the relationship (e.g., carpools).

Mediated interaction is vital for providing social contacts with awareness information when they are not collocated. Even in the case of home inhabitants, they are not always home at the same time (e.g., someone is at work) making it impossible to gather awareness through face-to-face interaction. In this case of *time separation*, mediated interaction is crucial. Nearly all participants from our study used some form of handwritten notes to provide awareness information for their home inhabitants, most often because it was very simple to do. Here individuals write a note to a cohabitant or the entire household using media like sticky notes, message pads, scraps of paper, the family calendar, or whiteboards (Elliot et al., 2005). The most crucial aspect of leaving notes that we found was the *location* of the note itself. Households typically have well-established routines for locations (Crabtree et al., 2003) where they can help determine who a note is for (Elliot et al., 2005). For example, one mother described a situation where she wanted her teenage son to see an important note when he arrived home from school. She stuck it on the television because she knew that watching TV was one of the first things he did when arriving home. We will return the role of locations and routines later in this chapter.

Technologies like telephones, e-mail, and instant messaging (IM) are used by individuals to maintain an awareness of their social contacts, this time for all social groupings. Here mediated interaction is used to overcome challenges of *distance separation*. We found people almost always choose the technology that is both easy for them to use and likely to reach their social contacts. Telephones and mobile phones were convenient for reaching contacts at work or while mobile. Information would be exchanged much like in face-to-face situations. We found that middle-aged adults favor the telephone because new technologies seem "foreign" or daunting to them. Yet many found other technologies like e-mail very useful especially for contacts overseas when phone rates become expensive. Other non-technologies like letters (for postal mail) fulfill similar purposes yet only one person reported using these.

Heavy computer users would routinely use e-mail or IM to exchange information. People enjoyed using e-mail as it allowed them to share awareness information asynchronously (also found by Tollmar and Persson, 2002). For one mother, sending an e-mail to her son from work to home was easier than trying to catch him on the phone because he may not have arrived home yet, or he could be at a friend's house. Our participants told us that IM provides near synchronous conversations when both parties were around, but when not, provided an easy way to leave an asynchronous message for another. One young common-law couple said they both have an IM client running on their computers when at work. This provides them with a very quick and easy communication channel to make plans or update the other on their day's activities. Many teenagers we interviewed like using IM because of its near synchronous nature, with some reporting that IM allowed them to have multiple simultaneous conversations with different people. Others have reported similar findings (Grinter and Palen, 2002).

In summary, awareness must be considered within the quite broad context of the home setting. We have shown that there is a whole spectrum of relationships. Each has different needs for interpersonal awareness, and each has different methods for maintaining it. Table 3.1 summarizes this range of needs and methods. This suggests that a spectrum of design solutions is needed to address interpersonal awareness needs: we cannot simply migrate awareness technologies from the workplace into the home.

3.3 Communication Information in the Home

For the remainder of this chapter, we focus on home inhabitants. Our goal here is to understand how households and individuals currently handle communication information in the home: what communication information is present and manipulated by inhabitants, and the role meta-data about each message plays in how it is handled (Elliot et al., 2005; Elliot, 2006). As with the previous section, this explication is formed from the combination of existing theories, studies of domestic culture, lessons learned from technology design, and our own semi-structured contextual interviews of households (Elliot et al., 2005; Elliot, 2006).

We asked all members of each household to show us what communication information they used, and where this information was located in the home. We found

Table 3.1 The characteristics, needs, and awareness patterns of each social group

	Social grouping characteristics	Frequency of awareness	Awareness information	Techniques for gathering awareness
Home inhabitants	Household members/families; Small groups of one to six people	Frequent updates, moment-to-moment or daily	Detailed information about activity, location, and status	Visual cues from domestic artifacts Face-to-face and mediated interaction
			About the past, present, and upcoming events	
Intimate socials	Close personal contacts; Small groups of one to six people	Some what frequent updates, daily to weekly	Detailed information about activity, location, and status	Face-to-face and mediated interaction
			About the past and upcoming events	
Extended socials	Extended family and friends; Large groups of usually fewer than 20 people, but sometimes larger	Infrequent updates, weekly to monthly or even less frequent	Non-detailed information about activity, location, and status	Fewer opportunities for face-to-face interaction; mostly mediated interaction
			About the past and upcoming events	

that people would naturally provide a four part answer when generally asked about a specific piece of communication information:

1. *What is it?* What is this information about? What is it related to?
2. *Whose is it?* Who needs to pay attention to it? Should I pay attention to it? Is it mine? Who else needs to see it?
3. *What needs to be done with it?* What actions need to be taken?
4. *When do I/others need to interact with it?* Is it urgent? At what point of time will I/others need to interact with this information?

In analyzing our data, we saw many similarities in the kinds of communication information present in the home, in spite of the diversity of the homes, their layouts, and the people within them. We found five categories of communication information in the home distinguished in terms of how the information was used or its intended purpose, as described below.

3.3.1 Reminders and Alerts

Reminders and alerts are intended or used as a memory trigger, e.g., to-do lists, reminder notes or e-mails, instant messages, or warning tags. We saw three subtypes of this information: *reminders* that remind people about things they know but may forget, *to-do* lists that contain a list of things that must be done, and *alerts* that remind or inform people of critical information. This category is highly time sensitive. The goal of messages in this category is to convey information at the right time, whether this time is related to the urgency of the message (e.g., a reminder to call the shop right away, since it closes early), or to its relevancy (e.g., remembering to return a DVD on your way to work, or remembering what errands you need to run on the way home). Another example is a mother who wanted to remind her son that he is to put dinner in the oven when he arrives home from school. She placed this note on the son's computer monitor because there is some urgency to it illustrated in (Fig. 3.2a).

Fig. 3.2 Examples of information types

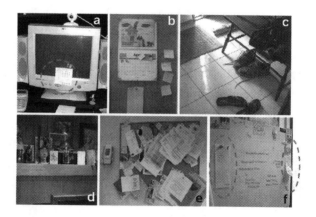

3.3.2 Awareness and Scheduling

Awareness and scheduling was the second most common type of communication information and entails much of the information we described in Section 3.2 of this chapter. To briefly recap, *awareness information* is used to maintain an understanding of the presence and activities of household members, e.g., this information is used to know who is currently at home. *Scheduling information* includes items such as one's calendar activities or time schedule, e.g., what time someone will be returning to the house. Both awareness and schedule information involve knowing details about the day-to-day routines of household members. While awareness and scheduling information is not as time sensitive as reminders and alerts, it is critical to the smooth functioning and micro-coordination of the household and the comfort of its inhabitants. Its goal is to provide people with knowledge of the whereabouts and activities of others. For example, we saw that this information is particularly important for families with children, where parents need to coordinate who drives the children to their various activities. A more mundane example is knowing or deciding when dinner will be served. While some of this information is left explicitly (e.g., as a note in a central common location such as the kitchen table), other times it is left implicitly through routine actions and gathered peripherally (e.g., the presence or absence of cars or shoes, as illustrated in Fig. 3.2c). Other examples include a family calendar (Fig. 3.2b), where events for members of the household (such as a ride schedule) are explicitly written down so that they are not missed or forgotten.

3.3.3 Visual Displays

Visual displays are to be shared or admired. Examples include the display of birthday cards on the hall table, postcards on the fridge door, awards on the wall, children's artwork on the fridge, or funny comics in the computer room. These are all pieces of infrequently updated information that the family wishes to display in a public location, where it attracts the attention and comments of both household members and guests. Figure 3.2d illustrates a mantle in a family room containing pictures, birthday cards, awards and medals, as well as children's artwork and souvenirs. These are all pieces of infrequently updated information that the family wishes to display in a public location, where it attracts the attention and comments of both household members and guests.

3.3.4 Notices

Notices provide household members with information about activities or contacts outside the home. Thus, the defining characteristic of a notice is that it comes from something or someone outside the home. The most common example of this category is phone messages. Notices also include newsletters, forms or notices from school, letters, etc. For example, a family may have a bulletin board littered with these types of notices (Fig. 3.2e). This information may be very time sensitive (e.g., a school notice that needs to be signed right away, or an urgent phone message) or not at all (e.g., the latest church bulletin). This information keeps the family aware of what is happening with their outside activities and contacts. As with visual displays, this category of information is often shared between home members and publicly displayed; however, its content is more practical and more frequently updated.

3.3.5 Resource Coordination

Resource coordination includes any information used to manage the sharing of a common resource. For example, resource coordination items may include contact information, financial data, charts for sharing chores, bills to be split among

roommates, or notes on food that is not to be eaten by others. Items from this category are less common, but still present in every home from our contextual studies.
One example we saw describes how two roommates coordinate the sharing of gro-
ceries: on the left of their fridge door was a shopping list; on the right side were
receipts for the recent grocery purchases (Fig. 3.2f).

In summary, understanding the types of communication information that people
display and use in their homes is the first step to knowing how to handle a particular
piece of information, i.e., *What is it?* We will see that this is not enough: other
factors come into play to help people understand information and how it should be
handled, as described below.

3.4 Contextual Locations

Every household we looked at had a set of key locations (places) that inhabitants
used for displaying, interacting, organizing, and coping with communication information. We found that these places within the home are more than they initially
seem to be. No matter what the answers were to what is it, who is it for, when do
they need it or what needs to be done for a given piece of information, when we
asked people "How do you know?" they would almost always reply with some variation of "Well, because it is on the fridge" or "...in the doorway" or "...on her
placemat". People use placement to filter and manage communication information
in their homes.

These places provide household members with important meta-data about the
communication information located there. This meta-data includes *time* information, *ownership* information, and *awareness* information. Places are what enable
people to answer our guiding questions for each message: whose is it, what needs
to be done with it, and when do I/others need to interact with it. In this way, space
is interwoven not only with action (Rodden et al., 2004), but also with this rich context and meta-data about the messages placed there. We call these places *Contextual
Locations*, since they provide the information in them with context, and therefore
richer meaning.

We first describe how places for information are initially selected. We then
describe the ways these chosen contextual locations afford time, ownership, and
awareness to the information placed there.

3.4.1 Location Placement in the Home

We consider contextual locations to include any place where communication information is placed. These could be static (e.g., the kitchen table) or dynamic (e.g., a
day planner carried in a purse). In our study, the number of distinct communication
information locations per household appears to be determined by two separate factors. The first is the house size: we found that the larger the home, the more locations
present. The second factor is the number of independent adults in the household. The

presence of children does increase the number of locations, but not as significantly as the presence of another adult. However, couples tended to have fewer locations than two unmarried friends or roommates, because they typically had very entwined lives. The number and placement of these locations is part of the home ecology, where it is a shared household understanding that develops over time. To illustrate, one participant household contained a group of roommates who had been living together for only a few weeks. While each had a good understanding of places for their individual information, the shared locations were not yet well formed or understood. Insufficient time had passed for meaning and use of these locations to evolve.

Through their everyday routines, households implicitly select locations in order to provide answers to the four information questions. These locations develop social meaning over time, and become a strong shared language in the home. People rely on their knowledge of home routines (their own and those of others) as well as the placement of main traffic paths and common areas to find suitable places for information.

3.4.2 Pathways and Routines

Information locations tend to group themselves along pathways through the house (Crabtree and Rodden, 2004), for instance the path from the front door to the kitchen. Since these are routes most of the household will pass through over the course of the day, they are chosen as places to leave the information people need to or want to see. Part of this is derived from familiarity, where people know the routines of other household members—what they do when they come home, where they go, where they leave things like keys or purses—and use this knowledge in deciding where to leave messages. As Tolmie et al. (2002) found "Routines are resources for action, and knowledge of others' routines can be resources for interaction."

In one of our households, the teenage son enters through the front door, passes through the kitchen, and then goes down to the basement. Parents leave notes for him on the kitchen counter since he has to pass by it on his way to the basement stairs. Knowledge of his routine, as well as the pathway he takes from the entrance way to the basement, meant that this was the logical place for this information. Households use their knowledge of routines and pathways to select information placement.

Once these locations are established, however, they themselves become an element in daily routines. For example, many of our participants would describe locations they would explicitly check for information as part of their routine upon arriving home. These would include locations such as the answering machine or the kitchen table. Information locations may create or establish new routines.

3.4.3 Constellations

Areas also tend to be grouped. One communication area will normally cause other ones to form nearby, since it is often convenient to have different kinds of communication information in close proximity. We call these location groupings *constellations*, since they consist of many unique locations linked by common activities or subjects. For example, if the kitchen counter is used to organize coupons and flyers, other locations such as the family grocery list will usually be nearby. Constellations are most often present in common, frequently visited areas of the house, such as the kitchen, family room, entrance way, etc.

In addition, communication media and technology such as phones and computers also attract communication information. Since this technology is less portable, information typically comes to them. Since locations group together as we described above, constellations will often form around these areas. For example, for obvious reasons phone messages usually go next to the phone (when the phone is tethered). Calendars are also often near the phone, so that people can check their schedules when making plans with others (Neustaedter et al., 2009). Other types of information, such as school newsletters, are needed near the calendar as they augment its information (Neustaedter et al., 2009). This creates an information constellation around the phone. Information locations tend to group themselves so that other relevant information and useful technology is nearby.

3.4.4 Location Attributes and Proximity

The attributes of a location affect both how suitable it is for information display and the kinds of information left or placed there. For instance, it would make very little sense to organize school handouts by pinning them up on the wall in the bedroom. Information would not be at hand when it is needed, and important events or letters might get missed. It is much more likely that these handouts will be stacked in piles on the kitchen counter, because it is flat, and they can be moved around easily. As a common, frequently visited place, the kitchen counter is a location where everyone who needs this information can get at it.

There is also the issue of relevance—information related to something needs to be near it, so the media will be chosen to adapt to the location, as discussed earlier. Phone messages will often be left on sticky notes near the wall phone; shopping lists on the fridge will be magnetic, etc. Places in the home will be repurposed as information locations to meet people's need for organization.

3.4.5 Visibility vs. Practicality

The fitness of a location for communication often dominates other seemingly more practical factors. For example, it may be more practical to put new information in a location that has the space for it instead of an already heavily used information-crowded location. But this is not done. For example, there may be ample space in the basement for school handouts or church newsletters, but because the basement is not a commonly frequented place, information might be missed. Instead, it is added to the already busy central bulletin board. While it takes up much needed space, competes for attention, and gets in the way, it is more easily accessed. A second example would be placing a DVD that needs to be returned to a DVD-rental store on the first stair leading down to the entryway as all household members will see it (and perhaps trip over it) as they go by, even though it might be less hazardous to leave it by the TV. Location has such great value in terms of providing organization and relevance that it overrides more practical considerations.

3.5 Time, Ownership, and Awareness

The above attributes and groupings described how people choose locations to communicate with members of their household; these locations become part of the household's shared language. Next, we will see how choice of location adds valuable information to messages placed there as meta-data regarding time, ownership, and awareness.

3.5.1 Time

One primary way locations add information is in timing, where time attributes—urgency, relevance, when it needs to be seen or used, the dynamics of the information—are all conveyed by the location in which the information is placed. This helps people answer the question when do I/others need to interact with this information.

3.5.1.1 Urgency and Relevance

There is a definite correlation between location choice, and when information will be needed or when it should be seen. One of the most frequently stated reasons for location choice by our participants was the need for the information to be seen at a certain time. This time could be when one eats breakfast, or leaves the house in the morning, or sits down to watch TV. People use their knowledge of the routines of themselves and others to know where to put information so that it is seen in a timely way.

Household members use this knowledge to convey urgency in a message, to make sure information is at hand when needed and to provide a type of priority system for themselves and others. For example, messages from a mother to her teenage son were usually left near the computer upstairs (Fig. 3.2a), where the mother knew it would be seen at some point. However, she would place urgent notes on the TV screen instead, as she knew her son would surely see it as soon as he returned home, since the first thing he does after school is watch TV.

This information also works for recipients of information. Household members know when there may be messages for them at certain locations. For instance, upon

Fig. 3.3 Envelopes placed
with keys

arriving home from school or work, people typically have a set of places they will check either implicitly or explicitly for information. If there is nothing in these locations, they assume there is nothing they need to address.

Figure 3.3 reveals another example where the placement of information is very frequently used to create timely reminders. Here, household members may leave things that need to be mailed with one person's wallet and keys (e.g., a letter tucked by a wife into her husband's wallet), which in turn is a part of a key rack constellation, so that it is seen when he picks up his keys to leave in the morning. This type of reminder, done by leaving things where they will be noticed at the right time, was common to all households. Thus, locations provide a vital means for people to convey time-related relevance and urgency.

3.5.1.2 Information Dynamics

We also found that information will change location over time as its dynamics change. This includes relevance to other messages, whether or not actions associated with that information have been taken, whether the message is still useful, and its temporality (e.g., is it a new message or an old one).

We saw that as information becomes less relevant or is dealt with, it is often moved to a new location. For example, when bills first arrive in the home, they are usually sorted and left for the person who pays them. This person will then open them, and move them to a second location, for example, the computer, in order to remember to pay them online. Once the bills have been paid, they are moved to a third location for storage, a filing cabinet, for example. This is true of much information that moves through the home—postcards and pictures may be placed in one location until everyone has looked at them, then in another place *for* long-term storage or display.

For example, in one household, members left phone messages as sticky notes on the outside of a cupboard door above the main household phone (Fig. 3.4a). After dealing with a message, the member may throw it out. However, if the member needs

Fig. 3.4 Information dynamics

to keep the message, e.g., contact information that one does not wish to lose, it may be placed on the inside of the cupboard door for a kind of longer term common archive (Fig. 3.4b). The household knows that messages on the inside of the door are there for storage, while those on the outside still need to be dealt with. In this way, locations provide a sense of the dynamics of the information.

3.5.2 Ownership

One of the most important and most pervasive ways in which we saw location used was to implicitly or explicitly attach ownership to information. Not all information within the home is relevant to all members, so households use locations to define who information belongs to. This allows people to not only manage complexity, but to answer the questions whose information is this and what needs to be done with it.

3.5.2.1 Spaces

Each location within the home has an owner—this could be either the person who the space explicitly belongs to (e.g., a child's bedroom) or an implicit owner (e.g., mom always works in that spot at the kitchen table, so it has become her spot). The knowledge of who a space belongs to is used to not only decide where to leave messages, but also gives family members an understanding of which messages belong to them, and which information they are expected to act upon. Ownership of the space implies ownership of the information and responsibility for it.

Fig. 3.5 Spatial ownership

We found four main subtypes of location ownership within homes: public spaces, public subset spaces, personal spaces, and private spaces. *Public spaces* are those owned by everyone in the home. For example, the main house phone or the fridge door is usually considered public spaces, and messages affixed to them or near them may be for anyone. Everyone can see the fridge door (Fig. 3.5a), place items on it, and interact with those items.

Public subset spaces are those that are public, but only to a subset of household members. Couples within a household of other roommates or parents in a family home typically have public subset spaces: spaces that are public and shared by them, but that do not belong to others in the home. For example, consider the desk in Fig. 3.5b shared by parents in one of our participant homes. The parents leave a shared calendar for each other to see and use on the desk, but they know that their two adult sons do not look at, write on, or otherwise interact with it. The sons know that this calendar is just for their parents because it is located in their parents' space. However, if they have events that they want their parents to note, they may leave a note for them next to the calendar.

The other two types of spaces belong to individuals, where information within them are understood to be for the owner only. The first type is *personal spaces*: publicly visible spaces intended for only one individual. These could be the door to a bedroom, a placemat at the kitchen table, etc. Other members of the house will leave information in these places for the owner, and the owner will leave information there for themselves. For example, one person had a "personal placemat" that contained items placed there by that person for their own use (Fig. 3.5c). Yet because it is publicly accessible, others may leave things there for this person to see and act upon.

The final type is *private spaces*, intended for only one individual and not publicly visible or usable by others: day timers (Fig. 3.5d), purses, bedroom bulletin boards, etc. Information left in a private space by its owner are usually personal reminders, personal scheduling, and contact information. Its owner typically does not expect others to see information in these locations.

Knowing who the space belongs to gives household members a quick way to understand whether or not the information located there is something they should pay attention to. It also helps them decide where to leave information that others need to be aware of or take action on. Spatial ownership (implicit or explicit) indicates or implies information ownership or information action responsibility.

Spatial ownership may also vary by time or activity. For instance, O'Brien et al. (1999) found that users of a technology would often "own" or control the space around it. For example, someone watching TV in the living room temporarily controls that space, and may displace other activities taking place in that room, such as a noisy board game, or someone wishing to study. We found that if this shift in ownership is routine, information placement may become a part of it. We saw our earlier example of a mother leaving an urgent note for her son on the screen because she knows that he will watch TV soon after he gets home from school. He owns the TV space at this specific time, so notes needing to be seen at that time and pertaining to him will be left there. He also knows that notes stuck on the TV screen at this time are his. Spatial ownership may have routine variations based on time and activity.

3.5.2.2 Visibility and Privacy

We also found that the visibility of the different locations within the home implies not only information ownership but also the privacy level of the message. Information that household members do not need or necessarily want others to see will be placed in locations that are less visible and therefore more private. Information to be shared with others (e.g., awards, pictures, messages to all) is put in the highly visible and publicly accessible locations. Household members use this in order to protect their own privacy and to protect that of others when it is needed. For example, a husband may leave a message for his wife from the doctor tucked in her purse, rather than on the kitchen table where their houseguest may see it. They use this knowledge to know when information has been placed somewhere for sharing, or when this information is more personal and sensitive. The visibility of the location of a piece of information implies its privacy level.

3.5.2.3 Actions

The location of a piece of information implicitly attaches intended or expected actions to it. Often information is placed in a certain location so that a member of the household will know they are expected to do something with it (also observed by Crabtree and Rodden (2004). Using previously mentioned examples, this may be a letter to be mailed placed by car keys, or a stack of bills to be paid placed by the computer.

Seeing a message in a certain location lets people know what they are expected to do with it. This may be a simple reminder to oneself, as in the example of a person putting a DVD to be returned by the door, so they can see it as they leave and infer that it is ready to be returned. This is one direct way space is interwoven with action, as in Crabtree et al.'s coordinate displays (Crabtree et al., 2003; Crabtree and Rodden, 2004).

Location ownership indicates responsibility for these actions. People will place information for others in locations that "belong" to that person as a request for action. For example, a child may place a school notice for their parent to sign on the parent's desk. Personal reminders are often left in personal or even private locations. Action triggers placed in public areas, such as the DVD return example above, can be taken care of by any household member. The location of information implies intended actions and responsibility for those actions.

3.5.3 Awareness

Finally, locations include meta-data for communication information by providing awareness information for family members. Awareness information for home inhabitants is very important to people for scheduling, coordination, and comfort (Neustaedter et al., 2006).

3.5.3.1 Presence

The presence or absence of an object from its routine location provides information, especially awareness information. For instance, many of our participants mentioned knowing whether or not someone was home by the presence or absence of their cars in the garage or on the street. What shoes were in the entryway or what keys were on the key rack were also frequently cited as a way of knowing who was around, including whether or not guests were there.

For example, one of the participant households evolved a particularly rich system for handling awareness information. Each member of the household would wear different colored slippers while in the main floor of the house, as it was tiled and cold on bare feet. These slippers would be left in the main entryway when the wearer was not in (Fig. 3.6a), or at the foot of the stairs when they were upstairs in the carpeted area of the home (Fig. 3.6b). In this way, family members always knew who was home, and their general location in the house. Thus, the presence of an object in a routine location can provide information to household members.

3.5.3.2 Monitoring

The above assignment of actions through locations combined with the information gathered through the presence or absence of artifacts also works as a form of internal monitoring. Household members know whether others have completed their tasks because they can see what information is present in which locations. This is discussed by several previous authors, e.g., Harper et al. (2001); Hindus et al. (2001); Tolmie et al. (2002). Harper et al. (2001) calls this workflow control or workflow management. While the home is definitely not as work oriented as the office, there are still jobs that must be done to keep the household running smoothly. One example is a wife seeing that her husband has not paid the bills yet since they are still in a pile on the corner of the desk, instead of being filed. She knows he has been busy, so she takes on the job of paying them herself. He then knows she has done this because the bills have been moved. A second example (Harper et al., 2001)

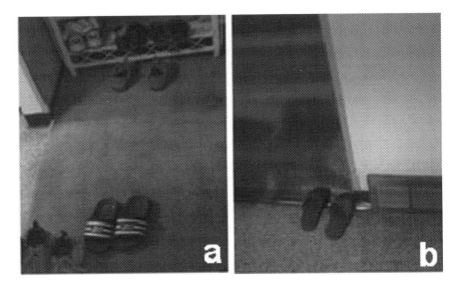

Fig. 3.6 Slippers show presence and location

is parents placing their teenager's cell phone bill in the doorway to his bedroom to make sure he sees it. Once they know he has been home and has therefore seen it, they can then ask if he has paid it—he has become accountable for it because they know he has seen it. Household members use locations to monitor and help each other.

3.6 Conclusion

This chapter is just a first attempt at explicating the nuances of awareness in the home. We defined the notion of interpersonal awareness, where the differing relationships that people have with others both within and outside the home imply different awareness needs. We then narrowed in on communication information between home inhabitants within the home, where we considered how the home mediates communication through contextual locations and its interplay with time, ownership, and awareness.

This description of awareness in the home can be used in many ways. First, it provides a framework that lets us analyze existing technologies to understand why they succeed or where they fail at providing awareness for family and friends. In Neustaedter et al. (2006) and Neustaedter (2007), we show how such an analysis can be applied to awareness appliances and instant messaging systems. Second, it provides a framework supporting requirements analysis and design. In particular, the model lets designers ask questions about exactly what social relationships are being supported, what the particular awareness needs are, and what affordances of the home exist and should be exploited as part of the design. An example of how this is done is described in our analysis of the family calendar as a coordination and awareness medium (Neustaedter 2007, 2009), and the subsequent design of the LINC family calendaring system (Neustaeder and Brush, 2006). Another example is the development of the StickySpots messaging system (Elliot et al., 2007), which exploits contextual locations to embed technology in the social practices of the home. Third, the framework can be used to compare and contrast awareness needs of different contexts. For example, Neustaedter et al. contrasted the differences between awareness in the workplace vs. awareness in the home, where they explain why one could not simply take what is known about workplace and apply it to the home setting (Neustaedter et al., 2006).

Of course, much is left to do. There are many subtleties and immense variations in home life. Many factors come into play that will influence the awareness needs of a particular home: the social relationships of people within it, the relationships these people have to those outside the home, the socioeconomics of home inhabitants, the physical properties of the actual home, the artifacts and furnishings within it, and so on. Our work is just a beginning.

Acknowledgment   Research was partially funded by the NSERC Nectar Research Network, and by the NSERC/iCORE/SMART Industrial Chair in Interactive Technologies. This chapter combines work previously reported in Elliot et al. (2005) and Neustaedter et al. (2006).

References

Beech, S., Geelhoed, E., Murphy, R., Parker, J., Sellen, A., and Shaw, K., The Lifestyles of Working Parents, Report HPL-2003-88R1, HP Labs (2004).

Crabtree, A., Hemmings, T., and Mariani, J. Informing the Development of Calendar Systems for Domestic Use. *Proc. ECSCW'03,* Helsinki, Finland, (2003).

Crabtree, A. and Rodden, T. Domestic Routines and Design for the Home. *Computer Supported Cooperative Work,* Vol. 7. Kluwer, 191–220, (2004).

Crabtree, A., Rodden, T., Hemmings, T., and Benford S. Finding a Place for UbiComp in the Home. *Proc. Ubicomp'03.* Springer-Verlag (2003), 208–226.

Dey, A., Understanding and Using Context, *Personal and Ubiquitous Computing,* Vol. 5(1), (2001).

Elliot, K. Contextual Locations in the Home, MSc Thesis, *Department of Computer Science, University of Calgary,* Calgary, Alberta, December (2006).

Elliot, K., Neustaedter, C., and Greenberg, S. StickySpots: Using Location to Embed Technology in the Social Practices of the Home. *Proc. 1st Int'l Conference on Tangible and Embedded Interaction – TEI'07,* Feb 15–17. (2007).

Elliot, K., Neustaedter, C., and Greenberg, S. Time, Ownership and Awareness: The Value of Contextual Locations in the Home. In Beigl, M., Intille, S., Rekimoto, J. and Tokuda, H. (Eds.) *Ubicomp 2005: Ubiquitous Computing, 7th International Conference on Ubiquitous Computing,* 251–268, Springer, (2005).

Gaver, B., Provocative Awareness, *Journal of CSCW,* Vol. 11(3) (2002), pp. 475–493.

Grinter, R.E., and Palen, L., Instant Messaging in Teen Life, *Proc. ACM CSCW'02,* ACM Press, 21–30 (2002).

Harper, R., Evergeti, V., Hamill, L. and Strain, J. Paper-Mail in the Home of the 21st Century. *Proc. Okios Conf Digital Tech. in Home Environments.* (2001).

Hindus, D., Mainwaring, S.D., Leduc, N., Hagström, A.E., and Bayley, O., Casablanca: Designing Social Communication Devices for the Home. *Proc ACM CHI'01,* ACM Press, 325–332, (2001).

Kraut, R., Egido, C., and Galegher, J., Patterns of Contact and Communication in Scientific Observation, *Proc. CSCW'88*, ACM Press, 1–12 (1988).

Ling, R., Direct and Mediated Interaction in the Maintenance of Social Relationships, *Home Informatics and Telematics: Information, Technology and Society*, Kluwer, 61–86 (2000).

Mynatt, E., Rowan, J., Jacobs, A., Craighill, S., Digital Family Portraits: Supporting Peace of Mind for Extended Family Members, *Proc. ACM CHI'01*, ACM Press, 333–340, (2001).

Neustaedter, C. Domestic Awareness and the Role of Family Calendars, PhD Dissertation, *Department of Computer Science, University of Calgary*, Calgary, Alberta, February (2007).

Neustaeder, C. and Brush, A.J. "LINC-ing" the Family: The Participatory Design of an Inkable Family Calendar, *Proc. ACM CHI 2006,* ACM Press, 141–150, (2006).

Neustaedter, C., Brush, A.J., and Greenberg, S. "The Calendar is Crucial": Coordination and Awareness through the Family Calendar. *ACM Trans. Computer Human Interaction (TOCHI)*, ACM Press. (2009).

Neustaedter, C., Elliot, K., and Greenberg, S. Interpersonal Awareness in the Domestic Realm. *Proc. OZCHI.*, Sydney, Australia, (2006).

O'Brien, J., Rodden, T., Rouncefield, M., and Hughes, J. At Home with the Technology: An Ethno. Study of a Set-Top-Box Trial. *ACM TOCHI* Vol. 6(3), 282–308, (1999).

Rodden, T., Crabtree, A., et al. Between the Dazzle of a New Building and its Eventual Corpse: Assembling the Ubiquitous Home. *Proc. ACM DIS'04*, 71–80, (2004).

Schmidt, K. The Problem with 'Awareness', *Computer Supported Cooperative Work*, Vol. 11, Kluwer, 285–298, (2002).

Smith, D. and Williamson, L. *Interpersonal Communication: Roles, Rules, Strategies, and Games*, Wm. C. Brown Publishers (1977).

Taylor, A. and Swan, L. Artful Systems in the Home, *Proc. ACM CHI'05*, ACM Press, 641–50, (2005).

Tollmar, K. and Persson, J. Understanding Remote Presence, *Proc. NordiCHI'02*, ACM Press, 41–49, (2002).

Tolmie, P., Pycock, J., Diggins, T., MacLean, A., and Karsenty, A. Unremarkable Computing. *Proc. ACM CHI'02*, ACM Press, 399–406, (2002).

Whittaker, S., Frohlich, D., and Daly-Jones, O. Informal Workplace Communication, *Proc. ACM CHI '94*, ACM Press, 131–137, (1994).

Part II
Theoretical Perspectives

Chapter 4
Making Sense of What Is Going on 'Around': Designing Environmental Awareness Information Displays

Berry Eggen and Koert Van Mensvoort

4.1 Introduction

Picture this: it is 40,000 years ago, and you are an early *Homo sapiens*. You are standing on the savannah. Look around you. What do you see? No billboards, no traffic signs, no logos, and no text. You might see grassland, some trees, or a bank of clouds in the distance. You are in a kind of vast, unspoilt nature reserve. Are you feeling wonderfully relaxed yet? Don't be mistaken. Unlike the woodland parks where you sometimes go walking of a Sunday, this is not a recreational environment. This is where you live. You must survive here, and the environment is full of information that helps you to do so. An animal you are going to hunt has left tracks in the sand. Are the berries on that tree edible or poisonous? And that birdsong: Does it mean there's going to be a storm and winter is on its way? Or are the silly birds just singing for their own enjoyment? You can't be sure: you have to interpret it all. And you are good at that. So good, that you have succeeded in surviving in this environment.

Let's return to the 21st century. You are an average Western human being. You are looking at a spreadsheet or a word document on a computer screen, trying to figure out what's going on. It is said that we live in an age of information. Although it is unclear what exactly this means, many of us suffer from wrist, back, and neck pain. All of us, then, have been born into a world full of abstract technologies and systems. We are forced to adapt to them in order to survive. Berries, grassland, birds, and clouds have long since ceased to be the things we need to read in order to survive. Insofar as these elements still exist in our environment, they have taken on a recreational role. Instead, we live in a world of screens. We use these flat rectangular objects to inform ourselves about the state of our world. We use screens to check our e-mail, screens to monitor safety on the streets, and screens to follow fashion. Our scientists use screens to explore the outer limits of the universe and to descend

B. Eggen (✉)
Department of Industrial Design, Eindhoven University of Technology, The Netherlands
e-mail: j.h.eggen@tue.nl

P. Markopoulos et al. (eds.), *Awareness Systems*, Human-Computer Interaction Series,
DOI 10.1007/978-1-84882-477-5_4, © Springer-Verlag London Limited 2009

into the structures of our genes. A painful truth: many of us spend more time with computer monitors than with our own friends and families.

In this chapter we discuss the design of awareness information displays. More specifically, we focus on the challenges and possibilities for the design of awareness systems that aim to seamlessly merge with the physical, social, and cultural context of everyday life in order to inform people without overburdening them. The million dollar question is: How do we integrate all those indispensable information streams into our environment? The design of Calm Technology, as formulated by Weiser and Brown (1996), forms an important 'leitmotiv' for most of the research-through-design projects presented in this chapter.

The chapter starts with an overview of related work, i.e., projects addressing the presentation of, and interaction with, awareness information in the environment. Relevant work by Dourish and Bly (1992), Strong and Gaver (1996), Hindus et al. (2001), Mynatt et al. (2001), and others, will be reviewed.

Next, based on the literature and on our own reflections of Calm Technology, we introduce a number of key concepts that, in our view, play an important role in the interaction design of environmental awareness information displays. Topics that will be addressed include the different levels of awareness that need to be supported by any awareness system interaction style and more specifically the smooth transitions between these levels. The combination of different output modalities, like, for example, sound and lighting, into effective audio—visual information renderings that integrate with the environmental characteristics is another topic of interest. A third topic concerns the esthetic qualities of the information renderings that will decorate people's habitat. In view of the tension between 'signal' and 'noise,' information decoration is not only about esthetics but can also be considered a means to make the environmental 'noise' acceptable.

The main part of the chapter will consist of the presentation and discussion of three design research projects that illustrate the practical application of the key concepts for interaction design of awareness systems.

The 'Home Radio' project was developed to support family members staying in touch with their home, extending the home experience beyond the boundaries of the physical home. This project was presented in 2003 at the Home Oriented Information Technologies (HOIT) conference, but, unfortunately, the accepted refereed paper was never properly published. We will re-use parts of this paper in this chapter.

The 'Data Fountain' and the 'Birds Whispering' projects were carried out at the Department of Industrial Design of the Eindhoven University of Technology. Both projects explore the possibilities of making use of architectural space by decorating it with awareness information. The 'Data Fountain' project uses a real-life fountain to display dynamic information structures extracted from the Internet. Within the 'Birds Whispering' project audio-only renderings of a colony of birds were designed and implemented in an actual office space. Birds can roam the office space and react to the presence and behavior of office workers.

At the end of the chapter we will go over the main lessons learned in the projects and review and generalize these findings in relation to the key concepts of interaction design of environmental awareness information displays that were introduced in the first part of the chapter. We conclude by taking a philosophical look at a future in which our information-decorated environment has become next nature. It is part of the responsibility of interaction designers of future awareness systems to ensure that people can make sense of what is going on 'around.'

4.2 Related Work

As mentioned earlier, our vision is strongly influenced by the ubiquitous computing paradigm (Weiser, 1991). Early on, Weiser and Brown (1996), the founders of this 'third wave' of computing, have introduced the need for what they call Calm Technology. Most devices based on computer technology, like handhelds, mobile phones, and PCs in all sorts and sizes, currently behave in ways which makes it difficult for people to ignore their presence in daily life. As human attention already seems to have become a scarce resource today, the ubiquitous computing scenario in which computers will be everywhere in our environment could easily lead to situations that would be totally unacceptable to people. This danger was actually confirmed in earlier family studies on people's home experience where people worried about an increasing 'information overload' and stated that 'freedom from choice, i.e., freedom of not having to choose or act' should be guaranteed in their home of the future (Eggen et al., 2003).

Weiser and Brown (1996) propose how ubiquitous computing systems should engage people's attention: 'Calm Technology engages both the center and the periphery of our attention, and in fact moves back and forth between the two' (p. 3). The periphery is informing without overburdening because people can attune to information without explicitly attending to it. Weiser and Brown further state: 'The result of calm technology is to put us at home, in a familiar place. When our periphery is functioning well we are tuned into what is happening around us, and so also to what is going to happen, and what has just happened' (Weiser and Brown,1996, p. 3). The quality of the periphery to induce a subjective feeling of knowing what is going on 'around' us is served as an important source of inspiration for the projects presented here.

The importance of providing informal awareness to support casual interaction has been addressed in research on media spaces for distributed work groups. Various modalities have been used to present information that supports general awareness of the daily work environments of remote coworkers. Dourish and Bly (1992), for example, displayed periodic video snapshots of selected offices and common areas at remote sites on a person's computer screen to support shared awareness. Greenberg and Kuzuoka (2000) and Lock et al. (2000) have used physical objects, so-called tangibles, to capture and present a remote person's activities. Audio-only media spaces have been studied by Gaver et al. (1991) and Ackerman et al. (1997). These studies all deal with the problem of how to display information about remote site activities in such a way that the risk to distract people from their main work task is minimal. By using audio or physical objects as alternative communication channels for rendering awareness information, the visual communication channel can be relieved and remain fully allocated to primary computer screen-based office tasks.

Building on the office-related research on awareness displays, a number of studies have been reported in literature that try to apply and extend knowledge available for the workplace to awareness issues relevant for the home domain. These studies differ with respect to the user needs they aim to support. Go et al. (2000) have proposed the concept of Familyware to support the shared feeling of connection between people and their extended family including close friends. People use physical everyday objects to intentionally send simple messages to their loved ones. Mynatt et al. (2001) use a Digital Photo Frame to display qualitative information about the daily activities and well-being of elderly people providing their extended family peace of mind. Hindus et al. (2001) investigated how media spaces could be brought into homes and home life to support social communication between extended family members. Besides physical objects, they also used audio-only and multimodal awareness representations to mediate shared presence. Finally, Tollmar and Persson (2002) developed a light sculpture to support remote presence for distributed family members.

The studies mentioned above share a number of similarities. They all aim to display information at the receiver's site in an unobtrusive way to ensure that a person's ongoing activities are not interrupted. Often tangible objects are used to mediate social communication between extended family members, with the exception of Hindus et al. (2001) who, in addition, studied audio-only mediated presence. In most cases, the design of the tangible objects is inspired by the work of Ishii and his colleagues on tangible interaction (Ishii and Ullmer, 1997; Ishii et al., 1998; Dahley et al., 1998) and the esthetic objects designed by Strong and Gaver (1996) to support intimacy at a distance. Except for the Familyware tools that require a person to explicitly take initiative in sending a simple message to a loved one, all other applications feature an 'always-on' display of awareness information. But even in this case, the monitoring of remote activities has to be intentionally turned on or off. Most studies mention the importance of taking the sender's privacy into account. However, little is said about user requirements that might be important at the receiver's site. Hindus et al. (2001) report that people expect that social communication devices respect privacy and that they should not create new obligations. 'Users already feel increasingly obliged to keep in touch, and can see added communication as extra responsibilities' (Hindus et al., 2001, p. 331). Similar remarks with respect to existing and future communication devices were made by the families that participated in our investigations on the home experience (Eggen et al., 2003).

Recently, a number of commercial awareness systems have entered the market. An example of a commercially available awareness system is the Nabaztag (2007), an Internet-enabled multimodal bunny (Fig. 4.1). The bunny can adjust the light in its belly, or move its ears to communicate visually, but it can also play audio messages. Furthermore the user can move its ears to communicate with the rabbit or send a message to a paired rabbit at another location. Nabaztag can connect up

Fig. 4.1 Nabaztag, the
Internet-enabled smart rabbit

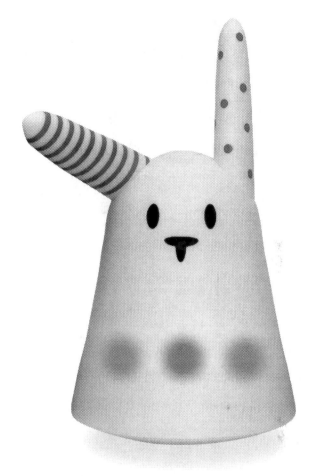

to a local wireless network and can be used as an alarm clock, weather beacon, traffic, and stock news/alerts. It can also accept and notify on incoming messages via Web, e-mail, SMS, phone, and spoken messages. It can be useful, for instance, if you're waiting for an important e-mail or phone call, you can go about your business and spend some time with family instead of being glued in front of the computer. When your call or message comes in, the bunny will visually alert you. Furthermore there's the ability to create and program your own content and events. You can create your own Nabcast channels and broadcast them to other rabbits. There's an API for programming and interfacing with other applications.

Ambient Devices is a company that, based on technology developed at Ishii's 'Tangible Bits' research group at the MIT Media Lab, has launched a number of awareness products that offer consumers access to digital information (Ambient Devices, 2007). Devices like, for example, the Ambient Orb and the Ambient

Fig. 4.2 The Ambient Orb and the Ambient Umbrella of Ambient Devices

Umbrella are part of a bigger system solution that includes a service delivery infrastructure (Fig. 4.2). The Ambient Orb is a frosted-glass ball that glows different colors to display real-time stock market trends, traffic congestion, pollen forecasts, or any other ambient information channel: weather, wind speed, pollen, traffic congestion, energy pricing, and more (Ambient Devices, 2007). The handle of the Ambient Umbrella glows if rain is forecast, reminding its owner. One's actual decision to take it might be influenced by the frequency the handle pulses.

In the next section we discuss, based on the related work presented above, a number of key concepts we consider of particular interest for the design of environmental awareness displays.

4.3 Key Concepts

4.3.1 Smooth Transitions Between Levels of Awareness

In natural situations the availability of information is often very smoothly regulated. Consider the weather as an example. During the day you are more or less aware of the state of the weather. Before you go out you explicitly decide whether or not you need an umbrella. Implicitly, you already knew whether the umbrella question was relevant. Imagine that you were completely unaware of the weather and had to check a Web site to find out if you need an umbrella when you leave your house. Sounds absurd? Still, this is the model in which information is often presented to us. The Ambient Umbrella of Ambient Devices (Fig. 4.2) provides an interesting alternative to this problem although the spatial accessibility of the ambient information might be restricted depending on the physical location of the umbrella. Its location might be perfect if the umbrella (stand) cannot be perceptually missed while going away. In case the umbrella is out of sight, however, ambient information is lacking and explicit action needs to be planned to check the umbrella handle in order not to get soaked. Information designers are usually inclined to place the message at the center of our field of attention (to make sure it comes across). Did no one ever tell them it can be considered impolite to always come straight to the point? We humans have evolved precisely to attend to information at the edges of our field of attention, and when necessary transfer it to the center ourselves. Some data should be continuously available in the environment – not in the center, but rather at the border of one's attention focus. When designing ambient awareness systems it is crucial to be attentive to the different possible levels of awareness and the transitions between them.

4.3.2 Combination of Different Output Modalities

The rectangular flat screen is the default and predictable choice for an information display, while other solutions can be cheaper, more elegant, or more effective. Depending on the environmental circumstances and the required level of awareness other information displays than the ubiquitous flat screen should be designed based on alternative output modalities: (indirect) lighting, sound, gesture, touch, or even odor. Having combinations of different output modalities can support transitions between different levels of awareness. Also, different output modalities can be combined into coherent dynamic behavior patterns of tangible objects (e.g., Nabaztag). The mapping between information and modalities can be organized in a sequential or parallel way (Coutaz et al., 2005).

4.3.3 Context is Content

We believe 'context' plays an important and often underestimated role in human communication and cognition. As an example, let's consider the following situation. Suppose a man and a woman are having a love affair. They go out together, are having a nice time and after a while he uses the three words: I love you. This terse sentence touches on a truckload of associations: Shakespeare, Casanova, Titanic, and soap operas. 'What do you mean?' strictly speaking could be her only valid reply. It's amazing that she still understands what he says. She deduces his romantic intentions from the way he touches her and the look in his eyes. The place they are in and the memories of their earlier experiences. In fact: from everything except his words. For these words are so full of meaning that they've become totally meaningless. This example shows how context can determine content. Implicit information plays a bigger role then we are often aware of.

Now then, what happens if we start looking at every pattern in our environment as a possible information carrier? Look around you, wherever you are. Try to recognize all of the forms and patterns in the spacesuch as the flowered wallpaper, the humming of the air conditioning, the fish in the aquarium, and a shadow on the wall. Do you realize how few of the patterns in our environment are being used as information carriers? Information overload? What information overload? The so-called information society has barely scratched the surface of our human bandwidth. We see enormous opportunities for situated information appliances that are tightly integrated within their context. While currently information carriers are usually developed as such and randomly put inside an existing environment, we should move toward integrating them with the environmental characteristics. Our environment was previously made up of objects; now it consists of information. When architects design buildings, they will have to consider to what degree those buildings function as information carriers. (If they neglect this, they run the risk of LED screens being attached to the buildings in due course.)

4.3.4 Information Decoration

Besides the fact that we can learn a lot from old nature, where information is present in a well-integrated way, we think we can learn from the decorative world. For centuries, people have been utilizing decorative patterns, indoors and out, with the aim of improving and giving an identity to the atmosphere around them. We believe environmental information designers can learn from the world of decoration. The primary goal is not information but esthetics. Information decoration means seeking a balance between esthetic and informational quality. Of course this is not always appropriate; some messages (such as fire alarms) are too urgent to work subtly into the wallpaper and must be brought to attention unambiguously. But even in the preamble of a potential disaster is the level of urgency gradually building up over time. This increasing urgency could be 'calmly' presented in the environment in order to set optimal conditions for vigorous human action to control the damage or even prevent the accident from happening. Information decoration lends itself primarily to the kind of data we wish to have available at all times but to be able to ignore: the online status of my friends, the traffic update, the weather forecast, and the number of unread messages in my inbox.

We want to emphasize that information decoration should go further than just making data look better: it requires a genuinely different information model. Traditional information theory usually advises against things like ambiguity and repetition. In information decoration, these factors play an influential role, because ambiguity and repetition are classic esthetic means of achieving interesting images. The big advantage of information decoration is that if it's not informative, it's still decorative. That's more than you can say for most contemporary carriers. Information decoration is not only about esthetics but can also be considered a means to make the environmental 'noise' acceptable.

A simple example of information decoration is depicted in Fig. 4.3. In addition to its default explicit digital time display, this cooking timer has a 'information decoration' modus in which the passing of time is displayed implicitly through the number of blocks piled at the bottom. In this mode it resembles a sandglass with a natural 'analogue' appearance (Amadana, 2007).

Fig. 4.3 A typist's work
environment

4.4 Case 1: Home Radio

I have completely lost time while writing the paper. But over the last couple of minutes, the feeling that now it is really time to quit writing and leave for home can no longer be ignored. Subconsciously, I know dinner preparations back home are in full swing. Right on time, the changing office atmosphere, once again, has gently but effectively interrupted a satisfying flow experience. Family, here I come! Am I hungry!

The Home Radio concept was developed to support family members staying in touch with their home, extending the home experience beyond the boundaries of the physical house. The focus is on families that still live together sharing one physical house. The need to stay in touch for these families may differ from the needs of extended families, i.e., families that no longer share the same house. An ethnomethodological study on people's home experience showed, in line with Hindus et al. (2001), that family members are first of all concerned with other members of the household (Eggen et al., 2003). Together they form a small and intimate community that uses communication technology, not only to express personal intentions and emotions, but also to convey presence and concern (Tollmar et al., 2000). Communication needs with respect to the extended family can be very different. Mynatt et al.(2001), for example, developed the 'Digital Family Portrait' concept that provides awareness of the daily life of senior adults, addressing the desire of extended family members to keep their parents safe. In this section, we describe the two design cycles that led to the Home Radio concept.

4.4.1 First Design Cycle: Sound Solutions

The scope we set for the first design cycle was to find an adequate process for acoustically representing people, objects, and activities in the home, and to explore if the home feeling could be remotely experienced by using the auditory modality.

4.4.1.1 Design Rationale

Based on the earlier mentioned home studies (Eggen et al., 2003), we set the following high-level goals for the first design cycle:

- The information should be presented in the background, creating a reassuring feeling that everything at home is fine.
- The information provided should only be in the foreground when it is meaningful and appropriate. The system should not interrupt and distract attention from other activities unless there is a good reason to do so.
- The system should support smooth transitions from subliminal awareness (background) to direct interaction (foreground), to avoid messages that unnecessarily attract attention by their sudden appearance instead of their inherent priority.
- People should have control over how the system deals with privacy, both at the sender's and the receiver's site, to avoid that too much detail or a certain category of messages leads to undesired exposure or monitoring of people and their activities.

4.4.1.2 Main Findings

During the first iteration cycle of the Home Radio project, we encountered many design issues for which ready-made solutions were not available. Small-scale sound design activities and informal pilot tests were applied to explore the possibilities for using sound to design a system that supports family members to stay in touch with the emotional and intimate qualities of home life while being away from it. We gained a deeper insight into the problems that have to be dealt with when designing such a system and we were able to refine some of the requirements for future realizations of the Home Radio concept.

The main findings of the first design cycle in which we explored audio-only solutions can be summarized as follows:

- Modeling home life is complex. The first design cycle clearly established the need for a home information model that describes people, home objects and activities and their relationships. This kind of information is considered crucial for the successful development of meaningful representations of home life that can be remotely experienced by members of a household.
- Special attention is required for the level of detail that needs to be encoded in the audio stream. Preferably, different levels of representation should be supported, including an interaction model that enables people to listen to details (zoom in), or ignore details and listen to the overall situation (zoom out).
- The event-to-sound mapping should not be too explicit. Users should always be in control of the system to prevent overexposure and privacy conflicts.
- Sound is a volatile communication medium. Capturing or replaying of information to get a better overview of current or past events is not supported in an 'always-on' scenario. Multimodal information displays (including sound) could overcome this drawback.

4.4.2 Second Design Cycle: Home Radio

Based on the lessons learned in the first design cycle, we added the following goals to our original list of design goals for the second design cycle:

- The audio-only design space should be expanded by including other interaction modalities.
- The interaction environment should be taken explicitly into account in the design of the output of the system.

4.4.2.1 Exploration of the Design Space

The design space was opened up by relaxing the audio-only constraint. To systematically explore this space we decided to follow a scenario-based design approach. Initially, a total of 19 scenarios were developed covering a wide range of design solutions. These scenarios describe user–system interaction behavior in a specific context of use with a focus on communication and interaction.

The scenarios featuring the different design concepts were systematically evaluated and weighed against 25 criteria. These criteria were derived from the requirements for the Home Radio system mentioned earlier and from user, business, and research criteria used in the Home Experience study (Eggen et al., 2003). The criteria were grouped according to the following themes: integration in the cultural and physical environment, supporting personalization, design principles for intelligent environments, and feasibility. Systematic analysis of the scenarios enabled us to identify the strong aspects of the various design proposals. It also helped us to specify aspects that needed special attention during the design of the final concept.

In-depth discussions about what exactly should be communicated through these concepts and how this relates to the privacy of the members of the household led to the following line of thought. By asking people what they want to know about their home while being away from it, we realized we had been focusing on the house as a medium. By reconsidering the house as a physical structure, we realized that this structure is not static at all, but that it becomes alive when people are present in it. For example, water and gas start to flow through pipes, electricity and data streams run through cables when activities take place. These utility streams can be considered the veins of the 'modern' home. They partly behave autonomously, as is the case for energy consumption caused by equipment in standby mode, or by heating systems that are automatically controlled by thermostats. But in many cases, the utility streams are caused by inhabitants interacting with objects or involved in activities, for example, when taking a shower, or opening a fridge. This insight that home activities can be traced in terms of fluctuations of the utility streams and the notion that the signatures of these fluctuations can be used in defining an activity, became the guiding principle of the next phase of the project where design solutions had to be generated.

4.4.2.2 Generation of Design Solutions

Before the actual design of the final Home Radio demonstrator started, we further explored the utility streams concept through the analysis of a 'day-in-the-life-of-...' scenario. A newly written scenario featured the fictional 'Rodenburg' family and focused on different members of the household: one family member at home, creating the stream and another person at work, experiencing the stream. The story describes events such as watching television, leaving home, taking a shower, etc. Special attention was paid toward key events where communication between the home and its inhabitants was particularly valued. We also looked at the effect of these events on the utility streams.

From this exercise we concluded that utility streams indeed create patterns that people can use to extract meaningful information about home activities. The abstract representation of this information shows great promise with respect to meeting the privacy requirements that were stated for the Home Radio concept. It was also noted that the home life involves many rituals. These rituals give rise to recurrent patterns of activities. After sometime these patterns will be subconsciously perceived by the user of the system and become part of the periphery.

One of the concepts, which used moving images on a wall, and was nicknamed the 'Rotating Lantern,' seemed to best support the utility streams concept. The output of the system consists of audio and video projection. The composition of this output is determined by the number and intensity of the utility streams. Also the environment in which the output is presented is considered important for the communication and interaction.

Audio. The audio part of the interface consists of three categories. The first category consists of four characteristic sounds that each relate to a specific stream: bongo-like sounds for electricity, bell-like sounds for communication, string-like sounds for gas, and water-like sounds for water. The volume of each of these sound streams relates to the intensity of the corresponding utility stream. Interaction with the system has no effect on these sounds. The second category consists of sounds which are heard when a new activity appears in the interface. These signaling sounds are gentle chimes. Finally, the third category is a sound which acts as feedback on interaction with the system. This sound is heard as long as someone is 'zoomed' in on a specific activity. The sound resembles wood-chuck rhythms.

Video. Within the projection, activities are graphically visualized as blocks, the color relating to the nature of the stream: yellow for electricity, green for communication, red for gas, and blue for water. The size of a block relates to the intensity of the corresponding utility stream. The blocks enter and leave the canvas at certain moments in time. When blocks are entering or leaving the stage the other blocks will shrink or grow in size to find their balance. When a block enters the canvas the other blocks are pushed to the right or pushed downward. The latest additions are always situated in the top left corner of the canvas, thereby creating a time line. On top of the blocks highly transparent images are seen which gives the squares a kind of texture. The transparent image can be seen more clearly by selecting a block, thus slowly making the image less transparent. An impression of the wall projection is shown in (the background of) Fig. 4.4.

Fig. 4.4   Home Radio — video projections of utility streams

Environment. The system is projected in an architectural space. When projected on the ceiling above a desk, light reflected from the ceiling causes a 'blended' color glow on the desk and its surroundings. Together with the sound this creates an ambient information display.

Interaction. Different states are distinguished that describe the way a user interacts with the system. These states range from ambient communication/ interaction to direct communication/interaction.

1. *Ambient.* In the first state, the system is present all the time but very much in the background. The user is doing activities and the system is used to enhance the environment (context of use) in an atmospheric way (much like the way we play a CD or adjust lighting in a room). It is an ambience which surrounds us. In this state the sound and light are present but not obtrusive. It sets a scene to pleasantly work in. But this system is not just a system to create an ambience; it is also capable of sending information to the user. The user knows that this stream is related to events that happen somewhere else, and is therefore aware of meaning in the sound/light. This may be a learning process in which a person expects certain sounds/colors on certain times. She 'knows' the normal behavior of the system, and therefore also recognizes differences from the usual. The system is in its most ambient state and the user can experience this as pleasurable without wanting to know more. Feelings of the user can be that she likes the ambience and that she feels that things are happening. Her home is alive, and fluctuations are subconsciously perceived.

2. *Attentive.* The user enters a second state when she is intrigued by something that triggered her in the first state. It can also be that the user is just curious

and wants to be entertained. It should be noted that when a user is adapted to the system, information can enter the user on a subconscious level; someone just reacts without knowing why. The information presented in this state is still abstract but more structured. The activities can be distinguished from each other, and processes can be monitored more closely. If in the first state she noticed that some activity was dominant, she can now see if it was just one element, several elements, or even which activity exactly. But still there is a possibility that she does not understand the information or that she recognizes something that deviates from the 'usual' is out of proportions. Then she should be able to enter an even more specific level, namely the third state.

3. *Interactive*. The third state provides the maximum level of information the system can give about the streams. It is exact information which has lost its ambient character. This part of the system is only reached when a user has a direct interaction with the system. This interaction should be fun and natural and a user would like to do this even when she is not triggered specifically but just want to play around. The means of interaction and the specific information given have not yet been defined in the system. In the current demonstrator this is done by selecting a block with a pointing device. In future realizations, we would like to explore direct interaction through speech or gesture.

An artist impression of the three different states is shown in Fig. 4.5.

4.4.2.3 Evaluation and Main Findings

The Rodenburg scenario was re-used as an evaluative tool. A part of the scenario was refined and used to drive the demonstrator. A 'real-time' experience was simulated based on a fictional hour of activities. The demonstrator was subjected to an informal appraisal involving a small number of user interface experts. Below we discuss some of the remarks made and issues raised by the experts.

The experts thought the audio—visual representation showed great potential with respect to its ability to present information in the background. The combination of visual projections in the environment and the subtle sounds that signaled the start of new streams entering the display scored were believed to facilitate smooth transitions from background awareness to the attentive and interactive states. The experts found it difficult to assess whether the current implementation could create a reassuring feeling that everything at home is fine. To answer this question the system should not only be assessed for a longer period of time, but it should also be installed in the physical, social, and cultural context of a real home.

The utility streams idea was judged attractive and novel. In particular, this concept scored high with respect to possibilities to properly deal with privacy. Privacy of the sender seems to be guaranteed, but also at the receiver's site there seems to be a number of advantages. It is very difficult, if not impossible, for people who do not belong to the household to interpret the changing audio and visual representation. Correct interpretation can only be achieved if the patterns of home life of that family are known and learned.

Fig. 4.5 Home Radio – interaction states: ambient (l); attentive (r); interactive (b)

People can interact with the system in an implicit or explicit way. In the current system, the implicit way of interaction has been studied. At the sender's site, the inhabitant carries out her own activities and the system taps into the traces the activities leave in the utility streams. Would people find this too much of an intrusion? Would they prefer to interact with the system in an explicit way? If this is the case then she actively interacts with the system and the issue shifts from 'privacy' to 'personal expression.'

The visualization part of the interface could have been more dynamic. In the current system all new activities start from the top left. Although this creates a time line it might look a bit boring. Other solutions can be found like surfacing from the middle and letting other blocks get pushed in all directions. The system, then, only moves when there are fade-in and fade-outs. This may not be realistic because the streams themselves are not constant but have their own fluctuations, thus having effect on the interface.

Overall, the user interface experts were positive and thought the current demonstrator complied to a large extent with the requirements that were defined at the start of the project.

4.5 Case 2: Data Fountain

> In the morning paper, I can read the weather report as well as the stock quotes. But when I look out of my window I only get a weather update and no stock exchange info. Could someone please fix this bug in my environmental system? Thanks.

Fountains are charming phenomena. You find them on squares, in gardens, or even indoors on tabletops. Usually a fountain is placed in a space for esthetic reasons. Despite of the fact that they are artificially made, people associate fountains with a sense of naturalness. We find this intriguing. A fountain is perceived as a source of quietude, not stress. People experience a fountain as a pleasant object in their environment. This quality makes it a suitable object for 'calm' technology. The goal of the Data Fountain project is to rethink fountains as information displays. Of course fountains that vary their spouting pattern already exist. The water ballet is well known. But always, an emotional value of some sort (often music) is translated into the emotional value of the fountain. The notion of displaying 'explicit' information onto the fountain is new. The esthetic value of the fountain display is a huge benefit in information design. Its presence won't bother people who are not interested in the data; information decoration instead of information push.

We equipped fountains with a control that can vary the height of the water jet (see Fig. 4.6). Through an Ethernet connection and a frequency modulator the fountain pumps are controlled. The fountain will function as a calm display. It can display the latest traffic news, remote weather conditions, train departure times, the amount of people waiting in line at a post office, etc. Or, depending on the context in which the fountain is placed, more personal data like the amount of e-mail in your inbox or the distance between yourself and your lover.

4.5.1 Mapping Money Currency Rates to Water Jets

Our Data Fountain was connected to real-time money currency rates on the Internet. It is refreshed every 5 s. This mobile fountain measures 5×4×3 meters. The relation between money and water is evident. On our Data Fountain we display the Yen, Euro, and Dollar (¥€$). Currency rates are closely interconnected; their interdependence is visible in water. The design of the casing was kept as minimal as possible. The water is the thing to look at and listen to.

It was our goal to display a general 'feeling' of the relation between the different currencies in the water jets. The currency exchange rates are available with a four digit precision (0.0000). Within this short time span, the currency rates alteration is generally very small or zero. The larger changes in the currency rates are a result

Fig. 4.6 Data Fountain, money currency rates displayed with an Internet-enabled water fountain

of many microfluctuations that happen over time. Through a short user survey we learned the perceived strength of a monetary value is derived from both the long-term relation between the currencies and daily fluctuations (see Fig. 4.7). At first we tried a linear mapping of the currency rates onto the fountain jets. Due to their smallness, the microfluctuations became invisible. The result was a fountain that changed slowly over a few days time. This didn't satisfy us, so we decided to try a more sensitive mapping. Now the microfluctuations were visible but took precedence over the long-term development. This resulted in a very noisy and seemingly randomly moving fountain. We wanted to display both the long-term development, as well as microfluctuations to control the height of the fountains. In the final design the basic level of the fountains is derived from the longer term development of the currency rates. This basic level changes slowly over time. In addition to that we exaggerate the microfluctuations with temporary 'jumps' and 'drops' of the water jets. The jumps and drops generate the lively expression of the real-time trading taking place. For instance, if the dollar rises on a certain day, the dollar jet will make many upward jumps throughout the day. This is perceived as an optimistic (rising) dollar.

4.5.2 Rethink Fountains as Information Displays

When we see a fountain in public space, we always wonder what its spraying pattern tells us. Usually fountains are just standing there being decorative. Perhaps in

Fig. 4.7 Data with natural phenomena, like for instance the weather, usually explicit as well as implicit data are available. For abstract cultural data, like for instance financial information, the implicit data is missing!

Fig. 4.8 During the project we considered various ways to present the currency rates information, among them the data plant

the future, it will be considered rude to place a fountain in public space that has nothing to say. The information displayed on the fountain will become part of a discussion about the design of public space. The context plays an important role in the communicational value; a fountain in front of a metro station will probably means something different than a fountain in front of a stock exchange.

4.6 Case 3: Birds Whispering

Sometimes I can hear the birds whistling in my office. Normally you don't hear them, but if you listen carefully, you do. They give me a cozy feeling that makes me want to take a break from work and go for a walk to the coffee machine. I know some of my colleges are there, because they are represented by the birds. One bird for each person. Good chance we will have some informal chitchat, down the hall.

In this project bird sounds are used to communicate information about people and places. The sounds of birds function as a calm information display that represents the presence of certain people in a certain space. When you are outdoors, in a garden or in the woods or even within cities, you continuously hear the sounds of birds whistling. To us, these bird sounds are meaningless; the information is meant for birds only. But has it been always like that? Forty thousand years ago people might have suspected hidden messages about the future, the weather of something magical within the sounds of birds. Evolution equipped us with lots of subtle sensibilities to gather information from our environment. In this project we made the birds' whispering meaningful again.

4.6.1 Representing the Presence of People Through Bird Sounds

The goal of the project was to create a subtle indoor soundscape that was pleasant to have around, but also informative in relation to the presence of people in the space. The project was conducted inside one of the office gardens at the TU/e Industrial Design faculty. The goal was to create a virtual colony of birds inside the office space that would react to the movement and activities of people in the space.

4.6.2 Noise vs. Silence

Sound has a possible (both positive and negative) influence on our function. Because we receive signals from our surroundings our level of activation increases (physiological arousal). In a space where there are no external stimuli at all, such as sound, air current, sufficient light, smells, or changes of it, we will feel stifled or musty. At this moment we become insufficiently irritated and our level of activation is low. This possible negative influences our performance level. The faster fatigue of people who are hard of hearing originates beside other factors also. Sound can irritate us also and can become an annoying experience. It will act then as a stressor.

Psychologically it is interesting that the sound of one's own drilling machine arouses less irritation than that of the neighbors even though it's louder. People are not used to silence at all; there are sounds and noise everywhere. Even when people define a specific place as silent, there will be always some background sounds such as the wind, a fan somewhere in the distance, or some other rustle.

4.6.3 Sound Design

The choice for bird sounds was made at an early stage of the project. After considering different types of more abstract soundscapes, we easily converged to the use of bird sounds. Although we were a bit concerned that the user group would perceive the bird sounds as kitsch, it turned out they appreciated them as long as they were lively and non-repetitive and kept in the background. To meet this requirement a system was build to generate dynamic and complex bird whistling from snippets of bird sounds.

We investigated different methods to generate the birds, and there are basically two approaches:

- The birdsong can be synthesized using a program like MATLAB or a regular synthesizer, or, alternatively,
- They can be sampled and filtered to remove the background noise.

The big advantage of synthesizing over sampling is that the sound is created with absolutely no noise and acoustics. The sound won't need any cleaning and sounds like it is produced inside the very speaker. A disadvantage, though, is that subtle effects which real birds can add to their sounds, like their own 'timbre,' are very difficult to reproduce with formulas and buttons. An extreme example is the sound of a crow: this is simply impossible to create without sounding at least a bit fake. We concluded that only birds that 'peep' and have basic songs can be synthesized convincingly. Exact copies of the songs of, for example, a Goldcrest are still nearly impossible to make. The birds we synthesized turned out more like imaginary birds, based on real ones. This is no problem though, as they still sound like the real thing; people didn't notice that a particular birdsong that is being generated does not really exist as long as it sounds convincing.

With only birds that peep and make simple songs, the soundscape becomes very monotonous. So 'back up' our synthesized birds, we wanted to add some really familiar birds in the form of samples. We also added sampled songbirds to increase the variety of sounds. We noticed that although a sample can sound a bit unclean when carefully auditioned, the samples really don't sound bad when they are put into the composition of birds. And because there was no other way to add more complex birds, we decided to use both synthesized and sampled sounds in our soundscape.

Especially for the songbirds, we had to make some sort of algorithm that plays the different sounds the bird can make, but doesn't sound like it's constantly repeating.

The way we did it was by breaking up the birdsong or sound into small segments in such a way that they could all be played in random order. Say you have a birdsong with four segments. If you just play it you will have one variation. If you split it up and randomize the order of the segments every time it is played, you suddenly have 24!

The birds that we chose all live in the Netherlands. We didn't want the workspace to turn into a rainforest or any exotic habitat: the birds should all be familiar so that they conform to our everyday experience of being outside.

4.6.4 Scenarios

Another important design decision dealt with the relation between the birds and the people. Various scenarios were considered. In an early scenario, which was not implemented, the idea was to have the bird sounds represent absent people. The main function of this concept is that the emptiness created by an absent colleague will be filled up, so that a team of coworkers always is 'complete.' Every person has got his own sound, and if that sound is played then the rest of the team will know who's absent in the group because they will recognize the type of the bird. In this concept every person would have a sound which represents his character. Absent colleagues would be able to communicate through the birds, for instance when working at home. A possible disadvantage of this system is that the bird sounds can irritate the present persons in the group. The team members do know whether someone is absent or not, so they probably don't need sounds to hear that. But on the other hand, the sounds might be a nice way to fill the silence.

A second concept was the 'Utility Bird' scenario, in which the soundscape is used to convey information about the tools, appliances, and resources relevant for the workspace: the printer, meeting rooms, coffee machine, elevator, and toilets. This system is very functional, and therefore the information is relevant because it provides information about your workspace. If you understand the system and it doesn't matter in which state of understanding you are, you can get a lot of information out of it; you are able to know if it had sense to go to a meeting room because you are able to hear if it is occupied or not. The same for the printer; it is useless to print a file if you know that there are 100 pages of printing in line with you. What is very important is to understand that the information is definitely not in the foreground, and so it will never force itself. We think it positive that this 'Utility Bird' scenario has a learning curve. If you work on a place for a longer while, you will probably just know where all the bird songs are coming from, without anybody telling you: 'if you hear a swallow singing, the lift is being used.' We don't want to tell people what the birds are telling, they would have to find out by themselves. The exciting thing about this concept is that one bonds with the system because everyday it is better understood.

A third concept, which we fully implemented, was the idea of the bird colony as an autonomous entity, with a natural tendency to move to the quiet places in

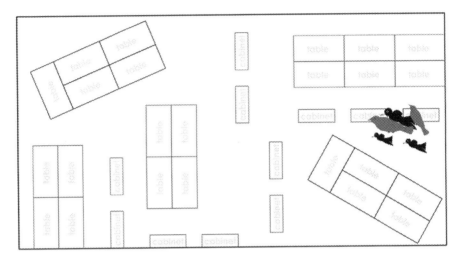

Fig. 4.9a The birds are just flying around in the workspace

the office space. This was realized with a system consisting of eight speakers and eight microphones. Using Max MSP the sound levels of the eight locations in the room were continuously measured. The virtual birds could move between speakers and did so depending on the sound volume measured at the location of the speaker. Once people would move into an area and started conversations or made other kinds of sounds, the birds would find their way into a quieter area of the office space. The final result was a subtle soundscape of bird sounds that emphasized quiet locations in the office space to the inhabitants (Figs. 4.9a, b and c).

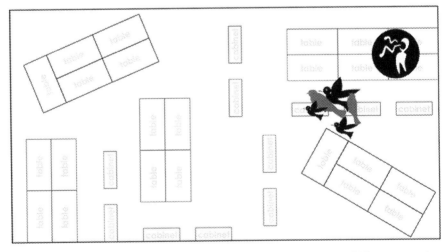

Fig. 4.9b ... until they get disturbed. When people are talking loudly, they will fly away to a place where it is quieter

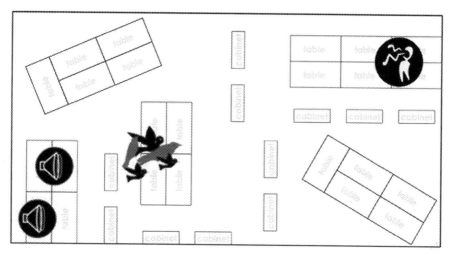

Fig. 4.9c   And if someone turns on music this place, the birds will search for another place. The birds will always fly to the quietest place

4.7 Discussion and Conclusions

It is said that we live in an information age; that is, we face big challenges concerning information management. Evidently, the manner in which information is made available is not optimally matched to human perception, or more precisely, human bandwidth. Today, duplication of data has become extraordinarily simple; it is high time we adjust its presentation to suit human beings' needs, abilities, and desires.

In this chapter we explored alternative ways of designing environmental awareness information displays. We introduced a number of key concepts that play a role in the design of environmental awareness information displays:

- the different levels of awareness that need to be supported by any awareness system interaction style and more specifically the smooth transitions between these levels,
- the combination of different output modalities, like, for example, sound and lighting, into effective audio–visual information renderings that integrate with the environmental characteristics, and
- the esthetic qualities of the information renderings that will decorate people's habitat.

Different levels of awareness and smooth transitions between these levels were explicitly addressed and designed in the Home Radio project. The combination of different output modalities into effective audio–visual information renderings that integrate with the environmental characteristics were realized in the Home Radio (sound and lighting) and the Data Fountain (visual and auditory information) projects. A focus on esthetic qualities steered the design of the information renderings of the Data Fountain and Birds Whispering projects. Also, in these projects, the characteristics of the real-world environment in which the designed artifacts are ultimately supposed to come into existence determined the final information renderings to a large extent. In these projects we explicitly faced the challenge to design a balance between pure information and esthetics. Where traditional information theory usually advises against ambiguity and repetition (redundancy), we learned these factors play an influential role in information decoration. This finding is in line with what is known in the arts where ambiguity and repetition are classic esthetic means of achieving interesting images.

Today, we still live in a world of screens. They were originally found only in offices, but nowadays the screen virus has spread to shops, squares, and railway stations — more or less all public space is filled with them. According to Dutch government guidelines, a screen worker may spend a maximum of 6 hours a day working at a monitor. It is unclear to what degree they took into account exposure to garish LED screens on the street when this rule was formulated. Personally, it gives us a dreadful feeling when after a long day of computer work, on our way home or during a night out, we are once again forced to look at a screen hanging randomly in public space. The really brutal thing about screens is that they seldom enter into a relationship with their environment. Some new TVs, though, might form an exception, as they have ambient lights (for instance, on the back of the screen) controlled by the image on the screen (Diederiks et al., 2004). In general, however, screens are isolated, draining elements that do nothing but try to seize our undivided attention and turn our environment into a Swiss cheese of realities (screens are even more obtrusive than, say, posters, which stand still and have a light intensity linked to their environment). Perhaps you would expect us to start arguing now for screen-free environment. But that is not what we set out to do. Despite our criticism on the contemporary 'screen virus,' the merging of virtual and physical spaces is an inevitable development, and we should welcome it. After all, remaining seated in front of the computer, stiff from RSI, is no alternative. If we are charitable, we can look at the contemporary screen virus as a transitional phase — a growing pain, if you will, of the information age. Tiling our environment with screens is an extremely literal, and on top of that rather unimaginative, way to introduce virtuality into the physical world: simply piling it on where seamless integration was what was wanted.

Although they are made to inform us, all too often the busy flickering noisy screens are also a source of distraction. They demand our attention, thus creating a nervous and restless environment. Is this the future of our environment as an information carrier — feeling as if you're being pounced on by a lion at every street corner? No thank you. 'Attention' is the scarcest resource in the information age. We like to sustain the claim by Weiser and Brown (1996) that the periphery can and should be used to calmly inform us without overburdening. There is still sufficient space at the edges of our field of attention; let us utilize our human bandwidth sensibly.

Before human cultural progress went in full swing, the environment was our interface and evolution equipped us with the capability to read our environment for vital information. Today, the phenomena of old nature — clouds, wind, trees, birds, etc. – are no longer crucial for our survival. We've long left the savannah and have become dependent on abstract and complex data that is habitually presented to us in ways that force us to adjust to the world of systems. Technology is getting so omnipresent up to the level that it is becoming our next nature (Mensvoort, 2006). As a result of ambient intelligence, our environment becomes the interface, again. It is part of the responsibility of interaction designers of future awareness systems to make sure that in this next nature people can make sense of what is going on 'around' them. In old nature the availability of information is often very smoothly regulated. We believe this can be a source of inspiration in designing these systems, but wish to stress this should specifically be searched in the pragmatic functioning of the older natural phenomena (just mimicking the first appearance will only lead to the frustration of the fake, the less powerful derivative). In our design research we have experimented with different materializations. We conclude that being inspired by old nature does not necessarily mean that the new design will have the same appearance as the source of inspiration. No plastic flowers please! We want new wallpaper. We want new furniture. We want a houseplant that has something to say. New media may lead to new types of perceptions that did not exist before, but nonetheless feel natural. Paving stones that show us the way. Trains that blush before they take off. When autumn comes, the street will be littered with flyers.

Acknowledgments   The authors like to thank Marco Rozendaal and Othmar Schimmel who were part of the Home Radio project. Also all students of the Department of Industrial Design of the Eindhoven University of Technology who were involved in the Data Fountain and Birds Whispering projects are thanked for their contributions.

References

Ackerman, M., Hindus, D., Mainwaring, S.D. and Starr, B. (1997). Hanging on the 'Wire: A Field Study of an Audio-only Media Space. ACM Transactions on Computer Human Interaction 4, 39–66.

Amadana (2007). http://en.amadana.com/product/mt123/mt123.html (retrieved May 2007).

Ambient Devices (2007). http://www.ambientdevices.com (retrieved May 2007).

Coutaz, J., Nigay, L. and Salber, D. (1995). Multimodality from the User and System Perspectives. ERCIM Workshop 'Towards User Interfaces for All: Current Efforts and Future trends', 30 – 31 October 1995, ICS-FORTH, Heraklion, Crete, Greece.

Dahley, A., Wisneski, C. and Ishii, H. (1998). Water Lamp and Pinwheels: Ambient Projection of Digital Information into Architectural Space. Proceedings of the ACM CHI'98 Conference on Human Factors in Computing Systems, 269–270.

Diederiks, E.M.A., Meinders, E.R., Van Lier, E., Peter, R.H., Eggen, J.H. and Van Kuijk, J.I. (2004). Method and System for Controlling an Ambient Light and Lighting Unit. Patent WO2004006570.

Dourish, P. and Bly, S. (1992). Portholes: Supporting Awareness in a Distributed Work Group. Proceedings of the ACM CSCW'92 Conference on Computer Supported Cooperative Work, 541–547.

Eggen, B., Hollemans, G. and Sluis, R. van de (2003). Exploring and Enhancing the Home Experience. Journal on Cognition, Technology and Work, Springer-Verlag, London Ltd. 5, 44–54.

Gaver, W.W., Smith, R.B. and O'Shea, T. (1991). Effective Sounds in Complex Systems: The ARKola Simulation. Proceedings of the ACM CHI'91 Conference on Human Factors in Computing Systems, 85–90.

Greenberg, S. and Kuzuoka, H. (2000). Using Digital but Physical Surrogates to Mediate Aware-ness, Communication and Privacy, in Media Spaces. Personal Technologies 4, 1–17.

Go, K., Carroll, J. and Imamiya, A. (2000). Familyware: Communicating with Someone You Love. Proceedings of the IFIP HOIT 2000 Conference on Home Oriented Informatics and Telematics.

Hindus, D., Mainwaring, S.D., Leduc, N., Hagstrom, A.E. and Bayley, O. (2001). Casablanca: Designing Social Communication Devices for the Home. Proceedings of the ACM CHI'01 Conference on Human Factors in Computing Systems, 325–332.

Ishii, H. and Ullmer, B. (1997). Tangible Bits: Towards Seamless Interfaces Between People, Bits and Atoms. Proceedings of the ACM CHI'97 Conference on Human Factors in Computing Systems, 234–241.

Ishii, H., Wisneski, C., Brave, S., Dahley, A., Gorbet, M., Ullmer, B. and Yarin, P. (1998). Ambient-ROOM: Integrating Ambient Media with Architectural Space. Proceedings of the ACM CHI'97 Conference on Human Factors in Computing Systems, 173–174.

Lock, S., Allanson, J. and Phillips, P. (2000). User-Driven Design of a Tangible Awareness Landscape. Proceedings of the ACM DIS'00 Conference on Designing Interactive Systems, 434–440.

Mensvoort, K. van. (2006) Exploring Next Nature: Nature Changes Along With Us. In Seltman, G., Lippert, W. (Editors). Entry Paradise, New Design Worlds, Birkhauser, ISBN: 3764376961.

Mynatt, E.D., Rowan, J., Jacobs, A. and Craighill, S. (2001). Digital Family Portraits: Supporting Peace of Mind for Extended Family Members. Proceedings of the ACM CHI'01 Conference on Human Factors in Computing Systems, 173–174.

Nabaztag (2007). http://www.nabaztag.com/ (retrieved May 2007).

Strong, B. and Gaver, B. (1996). Feather, Scent and Shaker: Supporting Simple Intimacy. Proceed-ings of the ACM CSCW'96 Conference on Computer Supported Cooperative Work, 29–30.

Tollmar, K., Junestrand, S. and Torgny, O. (2000). Virtually Living Together. A Design Framework for New Communication Media. Proceedings of the ACM DIS'00 Conference on Designing Interactive Systems, 83–90.

Tollmar, K. and Persson, J. (2002). Understanding Remote Presence. NordiCHI, 41–49.

Weiser, M. (1991). The Computer for the Twenty-first Century, Scientific American 265, 94–104.

Weiser, M. and Brown, J.S. (1996). The Coming Age of Calm Technology. PowerGrid Journal v 1.01. http://www.teco.edu/lehre/ubiq/ubiq2000-1/calmtechnology.htm

Chapter 5
Social Inference Through Technology

Antti Oulasvirta

5.1 Introduction

Awareness cues are computer-mediated, real-time indicators of people's undertakings, whereabouts, and intentions. Already in the mid-1970s, UNIX users could use commands such as "finger" and "talk" to find out who was online and to chat. The small icons in instant messaging (IM) applications that indicate coconversants' presence in the discussion space are the successors of "finger" output. Similar indicators can be found in online communities, media-sharing services, Internet relay chat (IRC), and location-based messaging applications. But presence and availability indicators are only the tip of the iceberg. Technological progress has enabled richer, more accurate, and more intimate indicators. For example, there are mobile services that allow friends to query and follow each other's locations. Remote monitoring systems developed for health care allow relatives and doctors to assess the wellbeing of homebound patients (see, e.g., Tang and Venables 2000). But users also utilize cues that have not been deliberately designed for this purpose. For example, online gamers pay attention to other characters' behavior to infer what the other players are like "in real life." There is a common denominator underlying these examples: shared activities rely on the technology's representation of the remote person. The other human being is not physically present but present only through a narrow technological channel.

There are, roughly speaking, three ways to conceptualize how awareness cues influence human action. First, one can argue that an awareness cue, such as "Antti is away from the keyboard," is associated with one dominant interpretation—for example, an availability inference like "Antti is not available for chat." In other words, the content of a cue (more or less) *determines* the interpretations it can reliably serve. Just as the buttons of a dialog box determine the possible uses, awareness cues are interface elements tied to certain functions and designers decide these

A. Oulasvirta (✉)
Helsinki Institute for Information Technology HIIT and University of California,
Berkeley, CA, USA
e-mail: aoulasvirta@acm.org

P. Markopoulos et al. (eds.), *Awareness Systems*, Human-Computer Interaction Series,
DOI 10.1007/978-1-84882-477-5_5, © Springer-Verlag London Limited 2009

functions. Thus, designers design the uses of the system and there is little flexibility on the users' part. Second, according to one reading of situated action theory (Suchman 1987), human action is best understood in terms of how it makes use of contextual circumstances. Human action is poorly explainable in terms of fixed mental capacities or preprogrammed action plans. Awareness cues are a natural part of these circumstances, of the context. Cues therefore feature in human action as *situational resources*, one source among many. As "the situation" is the arbiter of how humans act, any given cue is in principle infinitely "flexible." A priori, designers have little or no control over how the system will be used. Designers must study the contexts of use if they are to understand in which situations cues can be utilized as resources and in which not.

These two views represent two extremes of a sort of determinism: either the cue determines its use or the user's situation does. Between these two extremes is a third view, which places the locus not to the cue or to the context but to the human mind. There must be some logic in and limitations on making sense of a cue, and this logic must be sensitive to the situation at hand. We know from our everyday experience, and from research, that we sometimes succeed in our interpretations and can go beyond the literal meaning of a given piece of information, and we also know that sometimes our interpretations go wrong. What explains these two different outcomes? Moreover, given the *same* description of events, people can identify action at different *levels* (Vallacher and Wegner 1985). For example, the action of throwing of a brick can be identified at the lower level of picking up the brick and throwing it or at the higher level of a robbery or a misdemeanor. Proper explanations of "awareness" require answers to these questions.

This chapter puts forward a particular approach to the problem: a "translation" of Social Cognition research[1]—traditionally focused on face-to-face situations—to a setting where the cues are not "direct" or "natural" but essentially mediated by technology. Social Cognition has its roots with classic European thinkers like Wundt, Le Bon, and Durkheim and with later Gestalt psychologists such as Lewin and Koffka, who theorized about the relationship between the psychological and the social. The birth of Social Cognition as a scientific field coincided with the cognitive revolution that puts forward an antithesis to behaviorism's nonacceptance of the inclusion of mental or cultural elements in scientific explanations of human behavior. The foundational question of Social Cognition is that of the (mental) processing and storage of social information. Under this umbrella, modern Social Cognition has studied attitudes, attributions, categories, prototypes, and other representations, as well as group dynamics, social identity, and many other themes, and many of the concepts have gained status within folk psychology. Generally speaking, Social Cognition subscribes to methodological individualism, which treats "the social" as *factors* in the analysis of an individual. Present-day Social Cognition is

---

[1] To avoid confusions, let us distinguish between social cognition as the scientific enterprise and as the mental process. In this chapter, "Social Cognition" refers to the former and "social cognition" to the latter.

divided, roughly, into two schools: the American school, adhering to the experimental method and methodological individualism, and the continental European school, which is more philosophically oriented and opposes some of the presumptions of the American school. This chapter adheres to the American, "mainstream" version of Social Cognition as presented in textbooks like those of Fiske and Taylor (1991) and Moskowitz (2004).

According to this view, an awareness cue is devoid of meaning. An awareness cue is the end result of a long chain of material causation influenced by a remote person —"the inferree." Although awareness cues can be essential ingredients in social inference, they by no means dictate its outcome. The social cognitive account of this problem covers not only the negative side of human cognition—the errors, illusions, and biases inherent in social inference—but also the positive side—those factors that are essential to our ability to make sense of the world and go beyond the literal meaning of cues. Social Cognition provides an explanation concerning how social inference both constitutes and is constituted by action and intentions.

The approach maintains that individual acts of interpretation are the basis of a user's "being aware" of another human—that is, so-called awareness. The atom of awareness is an individual act of *inference*, which encompasses both the processing of cues and its outcome. Inferences partially rely on technologically produced cues, which, in comparison to face-to-face situations, are relatively incomplete and uncertain. Technologically produced cues can be augmented with additional "unnatural" elements that are not found in face-to-face situations. Bearing in mind the fundamental limitations of the human cognitive system, one must find it surprising that reasonable inferences can be drawn at all from such cues. According to the findings of Social Cognition, people do not thoroughly evaluate all available information, as is implied by normative theories of rationality, but apply shortcuts and simple rules to overcome these limitations. These rules draw heavily from prior knowledge about the other person and are sensitive to perceived frequencies of events. Pre-knowledge and inferential shortcuts together enable "jumping to conclusions" quickly, and they enable arriving at interpretations that go beyond the literal meaning of the cue. The downside is that biases and errors are bound to occur, and effort is needed to turn aside or override routinely produced interpretations.

The goal of this chapter is to outline a social cognitive view of awareness research and to review the underlying premises. In particular, we look at how the relationship of the cue, the cognition, and the context is constructed. Several key questions about the nature of awareness will be addressed. To provide illustrations of what this approach implies for design and engineering practices, examples from studies of mobile awareness will be analyzed.

This chapter by no means constitutes the first application of social psychological research to the study of awareness systems. One influential framework has been that of Gutwin and Greenberg (2002), who borrowed Neisser's notion of schema and Endsley's (1995) notion of situation awareness to explain workspace awareness. Another influential piece of work, although carried out in a different application domain, has been the analysis of *social cues* in e-mail by Sproull and Kiesler (1986). The work in this chapter was precipitated by the regrettable fact that, despite such endeavors, social cognitive approaches have generally failed to secure a position that would reflect the depth and breadth of work done in the parent field. Another problem has been that social psychological approaches have been confined to certain narrow areas of application and the more general questions of social inference through technology have not been addressed holistically and systematically. Unfortunately, the majority of research on awareness systems remains technology-driven and scientific progress is accomplished mainly by trial and error. This hampers the accumulation of empirical findings and construction of theories. Consequently, awareness, as a scientific concept, has come to mean almost everything and therefore nothing (Gross et al. 2005; see also Rittenbrush and McEwan, Chapter 1). That said, the goal of this chapter is first and foremost to start rebuilding the bridges between Social Cognition and awareness technologies by updating the general theoretical framework. It is generally a reasonable strategy to attempt to replace concepts stemming from common sense with more accurate scientific concepts. Therefore, this work involves revisiting a few of the basic notions in earlier literature.

5.2 Projections of the Social

This section analyzes the notion of an awareness cue. An awareness cue (hereafter referred to simply as a cue) is essentially any signal or symbol or mark in the user interface—typically textual, graphical, or auditory—the content of which is produced (or influenced), in real time, by the actions or properties of a remote person. Computationally, a cue is produced by gathering data from hardware or software sensors and applying computational transformations, then transmitting the outcome and presenting it in some human-understandable way. All awareness cues together in the user interface constitute what is called here its *projection* of a remote person.

It makes sense to define awareness cues in this way, somewhat narrowly, when they are to be analyzed via Social Cognition's theories. The criterion that they are *automatic* makes sense, because, as soon as *user*-created messages and signals are included, the uses of awareness systems become dominated by social *interactive* phenomena like self-presentation, performances, discourse, and coordinations. It makes sense to narrow awareness cues to live cues as opposed to, for example, histories and trajectories of past events. The Social Cognition approach is by no means limited to real-time cues, but adding time as a factor would complicate the analysis. For the purposes of this work, we deliberately apply a narrow scope. Finally, if awareness cues ought to be analyzed through social cognitive theories, it makes sense to focus on cues related to other people, as opposed to location-centered, object-centered, or document-centered cues. Many well-known findings of Social Cognition are instances of more general principles of cognition, yet it makes sense to restrict the scope of the approach for the sake of simplicity. It cannot be presumed that inferences of nonliving entities are governed by the same tendencies. Despite this admittedly narrow definition, awareness cues defined like this are truly ubiquitous. Basically, all automatic and real-time sources of information that people appropriate to apprehend the undertakings of a remote person can be analyzed as awareness cues. If a piece of information that was *not* originally designed to be an awareness cue is in fact utilized as such, it must be analyzed accordingly. The domain of social inference through technology is therefore broader than the domain of awareness technologies.

In this section, we discuss two important topics: (1) the ontological status of a cue and (2) *limits* to what a cue can be.

5.2.1 Anatomy of a Cue

It would be a fallacy to postulate that cues are meaningful because "meaning" was designed or imbued "in" them. Let us consider an example at a very concrete level. Awareness cues essentially consist of changes in the transparencies of R-, G-, and B-type liquid crystals that we call "pixels" on a display. The immediate causes of changes are controlled by the computer according to some programmed logic. This logic links the changes produced to changes in sensor data registered by the program. Thus, an icon we see on the display is the product of a long chain of material transformations and causations, the effective source of which is a change in the material state of an object that we call a sensor. Now, to the extent that this state was influenced by a human being—for example, by his or her Bluetooth device introducing a detectable pattern in the proximate electromagnetic radiation field—the cue can be said to be materially caused by the behavior of that person.

Cues are essentially material objects that can be perceived and interpreted by a human. The meaning-giving process starts with the individual's perception of the cue.

5.2.2 Limitations of All Intermediaries

In fact, everything we perceive of the outside world is mediated in one way or another. For example, my "seeing" of green leaves from the window is the outcome of a chain of causation that commenced from the scattering of 510-nm-wavelength photons from the surface of leaves. There is no substantiated reason to claim that the injection of a technological intermediary in the chain would *have to* transform the outcome to something "unnatural," given that it does not distort the outcome in any way that is noticeable to the human observer. This argument has a radical implication: Technology can, in principle, mediate perception and action in a natural and perfect way.

As we know, perfect mediation is impossible, because of fundamental limitations of the mediating capacity of technological intermediaries:

1. *The noise problem*: Technological sensing of the world, as any sensing, is prone to errors and noise. This may mean something as simple as lag or something as devastating as one of the sensors being cut off totally.

2. *The augmentation problem:* Technological sensing is not only incomplete but can also at times fabricate, embellish, and confabulate details. This is not solely a matter of errors in sensor-based measurement. For example, the literal meaning of a location cue is that a particular mobile device, the one that senses it, is in a particular location. Nevertheless, the interpretation that awareness applications are an attempt to convey is that the *person* (the owner of the device) is in that location. Anybody who uses more than one phone or does not always carry his or her phone knows that this assumption is problematic.

3. *The keyhole problem*: The projection is inherently limited in scope and misses some aspects of the to-be-presented situation, which at some point may be important. In such a situation, the user must "move the keyhole"—proactively make the missing information perceivable, which may not always be possible.

A resulting empirical question is how users learn to cope with the implications of these limitations (for an interesting discussion of ways to exploit these problems for the benefit of the user, see Chalmers and Galani 2004).

5.2.3 Can the Social be Projected?

If we forget the quest for perfect cues, the cues must simplify and abstract the remote state of affairs in order to be of practical value. This, in essence, involves *replacing* a stream of data with simpler data or some human-recognizable symbol or label. This brings about a problem that is here called

4. *the symbolization problem*: Can computers adequately—that is, in a human-approvable manner—give labels to states of affairs outside its "skin"?

An abstraction inherently omits information. For example, district labels attached to GSM cell IDs are abstractions of electrical changes in the receiver device. A consequent problem for the user is that high-fidelity abstractions are needed in some situations, while in others these might be unnecessarily detailed. For example, Weilenmann (2003) has studied the location-telling practices of people, reaching the conclusion that it is impossible to find one generic method to operationalize location in awareness systems.

There may be an even more serious problem, one posed by computers' limits in "understanding" human activities (Dreyfus 1992; Searle 1980). It is fundamentally difficult to program a computer to recognize *social events*—for instance, something as mundane as a person *inviting* another person or that a "game" is going on. There is no one pattern in language, turn-taking, gaze, posture, or other overt behavior that could be preprogrammed into an infallible "invitation recognition machine." Even if a very large number of different styles of invitation were "hard-wired" into the computer, or learned by means of supervised learning from a data set, the machine would still perform only very locally, devoid of more fundamental understanding of those social practices where invitations are defined. The source of this problem is that understanding sociocultural meanings of human actions requires active *participation* in the culture within which those actions occur. For example, through social learning with their parents, infants learn perspective-taking, the ability to simulate the intentions and reactions of another human being, and this ability is central not only for social interaction but also for many complex cognitive feats (Tomasello et al., 2005). On account of being excluded from the interactive practices, the computer cannot achieve the level of an adept human member of that culture. Unable to learn concepts by grounding them to bodily and social interaction, the computer is doomed to function as the Chinese room of Searle (1980), translating meaningless symbols into other symbols, never truly understanding the activity.

The moral is that the limits of awareness systems may be in cues that represent aspiration to represent phenomena that are constituted in or by social interaction. Unfortunately, many of the automatic cues people would *want* to include in their awareness systems—like interruptibility, availability, activity, and place—are examples of such cues.

5.3 Inferring a Projection

Despite the aforementioned limitations, users can in certain circumstances arrive at high-level interpretations from lower level cues and vice versa. This section discusses how this is possible. It first presents a definition of social inference adopted from the literature. We then investigate some of the key phenomena, involving (1) the use of pre-knowledge, (2) the temporal order of processing, and (3) the use of inferential rules and heuristics. We finally turn to criticisms that can be raised against this kind of mentalist explanation. The purpose is not to summarize findings in the field of Social Cognition; rather, the aim is to offer a cursory overview of some of the key analytical concepts.

5.3.1 Elements of Social Inference

The locus of the meaning of a cue is the intrapsychic process of inference. Generally speaking, an *inference* has three components: (a) a set of premises; (b) a conclusion; and (c) rules, principles, templates, or procedures that connect the premises to the conclusion in a reasonable manner (Hastie 1983). Hence, the analysis of social inference involves both (1) the process and (2) its outcome. This definition is pragmatic as well; designers need to know not only how a certain awareness cue was used but also how the interface was processed for arrival at a given conclusion.

Social inference is a special case of inference wherein the conclusion concerns another person or a group of people. Social inference is so fundamental to all social interaction that the topic has gained much ground in today's Social Cognition literature. Causality attributions, attitudes, schemas that influence the process, memory for information about other people, heuristics, and biases are among the key topics. In the discussion that follows, we provide one interpretation of these theories, a theoretical cross-section from pre-knowledge to heuristics.

5.3.2 The Cognitive Miser

Cognitive psychology has revealed fundamental limitations to inference. These limitations are so pervasive that Fiske and Taylor (1991) call people "cognitive misers." Table 5.1 presents their view of what social inference entails and how each phase in the process is compromised by potential biases. Three cognitive processes take the foreground in interpreting *technological* projections of people (adopted and modified from Fiske and Taylor, 1991):

1. *Schemas.* Schemas are cognitive structures that represent knowledge about a concept or a type of stimulus, including its attributes and the relations among those attributes (Hastie 1983). They facilitate top-down, conceptually driven, processes. They are concerned with the general case, abstract generic knowledge that holds across many particular instances. They store knowledge at a molar level rather than including all of the individual experiences in their "raw form." For example, an inferrer may know, on reading an alarm profile cue, that the inferree is in a classroom, because students are supposed to keep audio alarms silent during classes. Perhaps the most well-known subtype of schemas is the *script*, a schema that organizes temporal and causal dependencies in a social event such as going to a restaurant (Schank and Abelson 1977). Research has amassed findings about the contents, conditions, and effects of schema use. It has identified factors relating to goals; social identity; whether role or trait schemas are used first; how visual and physical cues trigger schemas; and the effects of

Table 5.1 The standard model of social inference paraphrased from Fiske and Taylor (1991, p. 348): Inferential processes and potential sources of bias

Phases of inference process	Potential sources of bias
1. Gathering information	Drawing on preexisting theories, especially ones that are salient and/or held with confidence
2. Sampling information	Drawing on preexisting theories; using extreme cases, small samples, or biased samples; ignoring sample data altogether in favor of cases
3. Selecting what information to use	Inability to combine joint probabilities; inability to distinguish diagnostic from nondiagnostic information; inability to correct for regression artifacts
4. Integrating information	Irregular or improper weighing of cues; use of the wrong cues; use of too few cues; irregular application of a decision rule

mood, accessibility, power, and salience. Importantly, the way in which cues are presented can affect the activation of relevant schemas and vice versa. A cue can activate a schema, and an active schema can guide the selection and processing of cues.

2. *Person memory.* Person memory entails the encoding processes, representations, and access of memories involving other people. Person memories contain information about the appearance, behavior, and traits of another person. Several categories of explanatory models have arisen, ranging from associative network models to procedural memory, exemplar models, and parallel distributed processing, each organized either by person or by group. Again, how cues are presented can affect the encoding and reactivation of person memories, and vice versa: the active person memories can guide the selection and processing of cues. Users have been found to use both person-specific knowledge and general schematic knowledge when inferring mobile awareness cues (Oulasvirta et al. 2007).

3. *Heuristics*: People often use heuristics or shortcuts that reduce complex problem solving to more simple judgment operations. Four well-known heuristics are (1) the representativeness heuristic, (2) the availability heuristic, (3) the simulation heuristic, and (4) anchoring and adjustment (Tversky and Kahneman 1974). Without heuristics, the inference process would often be unmanageable. We will discuss how the way cues are presented in the interface may affect the use of heuristics.

Despite the fact that the description of social cognitive mechanisms is framed in terms of judgment errors, there are many *virtues* achieved by using heuristics:

- *Familiarity*: the ability to transform a problem into a more familiar form, in relation to which previous knowledge can be applied.
- *Selectivity*: the ability to sift the relevant from the irrelevant.
- *Anticipation*: the ability to utilize knowledge of event structures and frequencies for anticipating future events.
- *Situational sensitivity*: the ability to take into account situation-specific knowledge (e.g., schemas) and person-specific knowledge (e.g., person memories) in one's interpretation. On the one hand, coherence of action over time can be reached only if a new situation does not arbitrarily change a well-known course of action. On the other hand, one must be sensitive to the unique features of the situation at hand. If preconceptions dictate the inference, the cues will have no informative value and they will be useless.
- *Rapidity*: the ability to process information rapidly enough to accommodate the moment-to-moment demands of social interactions.

We return to these virtues later in this section and in Section 5.5.

5.3.3 The Mediated "Social" as an Intrapsychic Process

Of the many questions these arguments have raised but left unanswered, let us answer one that is more philosophical.

On the surface, the social cognitive approach may look harmless. It may seem merely *adding* to preexisting conceptions of awareness the individual's mind, seated somewhere "between" the user interface and the subsequent action. However, there is an ontological payload with deep implications.

Social Cognition, as a field, is generally regarded as holding an intrapsychic model of "the social." That is, other humans are treated as *factors and content* of cognitive processing, but another human is never the sole or direct cause of behavior. However, the social cognitive approach is not an utterly mentalist view of the mind, because the psychological construction of reality is itself heavily affected by "the social" outside the mind, in turn, because the relevant representations and inferential skills have been learned from interaction with comembers of the culture (Augoustinos and Walker 1995).

Awareness, from this perspective, is the *outcome* of inferential processing, and this outcome is in the mental realm. Awareness is essentially a mental representation, or a belief state, that concerns somebody else's current situation. Awareness exists, ontologically speaking, primarily as a mind's construction rather than as a practice or an activity. This does not mean that the activities wherein inferences take place are not important, as they evidently are. However, it does imply that it would be a fallacy to hold action (or practice) and inference (or awareness) to be tantamount to each other. Neither are the two analytically inseparable (see Schmidt 2002).

On the surface, this characterization resembles the influential definition of awareness put forth by Gutwin et al. (1996). Following Endsley's (1995) notion of situation awareness, they defined awareness as the collection of knowledge a person holds about another person. Similarly, Dourish and Bly (1992) characterized awareness as "*knowing* who is around, what activities are occurring, who is talking with whom" (p. 541, emphasis added). The model of awareness proposed by Gutwin and Greenberg (2002) follows Neisser's (1976) perception—schema—action cycle. In that model, environment modifies knowledge schemas, which in turn direct exploration and affect the sampling of the environment.

The present framework and that of Gutwin and Greenberg (2002) disagree on the question of "where" the meaning of a cue lies. An engineer might claim that the meaning of a cue has been predetermined by the engineer or the designer. In their framework, Gutwin and Greenberg treat awareness cues as if there were a *mapping* from an "awareness widget" to a set of inferences. They categorize awareness cues into three classes—identity, location, and action. They further claim that users can accurately predict the other's actions and intentions *if* the cue shows the other's body and movement in real time. By contrast, the present framework posits that the range of potential inferences of a cue is much broader, although not unlimited or arbitrary. This is particularly salient in the context of mobile awareness, where the processing goals and settings are more diverse and unpredictable than in the groupware settings that Gutwin and Greenberg studied.

Consider Table 5.2. The table is based on interviews of three user groups who used a mobile awareness system (see Fig. 5.1) for a longer period of time. The

Table 5.2 Inferences of a location cue in three different user groups (Oulasvirta et al. 2007). Self-reports from posttrial interviews (the location cue was implemented as a district label for frequently visited GSM cells, district labels being fetched from a teleoperator's database)

	Family (N = 4)	Entrepreneurs (N = 5)	Schoolmates (N = 6)
Inferences	Home, school, work	Home, school, particular room, particular restaurant, proximity/distance from self, attendance at a class, the next place, availability for communication, availability for face-to-face meetings	Home, school, floor in a building, particular room, being on the move, being with friends, being in a public space, preferred communication channel, availability for communication, availability for face-to-face meetings

table collects their self-reports on inferences of the *location* cue. These inferences were collected through the cue-based narrative interview method, as reported in Oulasvirta et al. (2007). The extent of inferences that can be based on a single cue, such as location, is quite an indisputable evidence against the claim that cues prescribe the user's inference, although a cue certainly contributes to this process by constraining the space of meaningful and valid inferences. The mind's inference process is a necessary condition for a cue to achieve personal meaning to the user. Inferences are not products of a deterministic process but conditioned by epistemic skills and the processing goals in the pursuit of which they are produced.

5.4 The Psychology of Action

The question of how action shapes and is shaped by inference should be a central topic in social cognitive analysis of awareness. In 1992, Dourish and Bellotti defined awareness as something that "provides context" for one's own "activity" (p. 107). Social inferences are embedded in the continuous construction and management of social relationships. We know the key inferences of a few social activities. For example, inferences central to *collaborative* tasks include the copresence, visibility, audibility, cotemporality, simultaneity, sequentiality, reviewability, and revisability of action (Fussell et al. 2005). Within psychology, the relevant area of inquiry is called the psychology of action (Gollwitzer and Bargh 1996).

Three elements jointly influence which kind of action can be based on the cues, as well as the will to continue with a chosen course of action (following Covington, 2005):

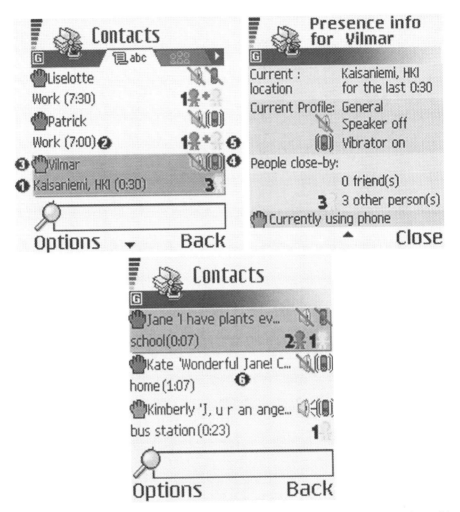

Fig. 5.1 (**a**) The standard ContextContacts integrated with the contact book of a mobile phone, (**b**) a detailed view for a selected contact, and (**c**) a version with the free-text cue. Callouts for cues: (1) district (automatic label for a GSM cell ID) or place (user-defined label), (2) duration of stay cue in hh:mm format, (3) phone manipulation (gray hand = no use for over 15 min, red hand = recent use), (4) alarm profile (audio/vibra and on/off), (5) number of people or friends in the vicinity (yellow/green person icons displayed according to the presence of unknown/recognized Bluetooth phones), and (6) free-text cue

1. The kinds of goals that the user brings to the inference situation.
2. The motivating properties of these goals.
3. The relevant reward structures.

   Again, the purpose of this chapter is not to lay out a theory but to illustrate opportunities that modern psychology can furnish for research. These opportunities go beyond those of Neisser's 1976 model utilized by Gutwin and Greenberg (2002). Importantly, modern theories may explain why awareness cues are appropriated differently in different settings and by different users.

5.4.1 Goals and Motivations

One argument in modern psychology is that there are basic needs shared by all humans that are individually translated into motivations, which in turn are situationally translated into goals for action. In other words, the inference process is "sandwiched" between motivations and goals.

According to Deci and Ryan's (2000) influential theory, competence, autonomy, and relatedness are the three basic psychological needs shared by all humans (see Oulasvirta and Blom 2008 for a more thorough treatment of the topic). Let us take one of these under closer scrutiny.

Relatedness is the need to establish close emotional bonds and attachments with other people. It reflects the desire to be emotionally connected to and interpersonally involved in warm relationships (Reeve 2001). Deci and Ryan (2000) describe it as the desire to feel connected with other people through loving and caring and also being loved and cared for. Awareness features that help to convey emotions, feelings, and intentions to other people may support the need for relatedness. They may provide possibilities for people to please others and gain their approval. For example, users of online multiplayer games have appropriated their aliases to show group (clan) affiliation to others.

The need for relatedness is ultimately translated into *goals* that regulate action in concrete situations where awareness cues are utilized. One conceptualization of these goals is that through them users can approach awareness cues in the pursuit of certain influence on other people or with a more exploratory mindset. It is known that *active* perceivers, immersed in the interactions that they seek to interpret, who can affect the objects of their perception, have different motivations and information-processing goals than do passive perceivers, who cannot affect the objects of their perceptions (Jones and Nisbett 1971). Active perceivers in general "concentrate primarily on the relation between their influencing behaviors and the responsive behaviors of their target and ignore other important sources of information relevant to social inference" (Gilbert et al. 1987, p. 861).

In Oulasvirta et al.'s (2007) study of a mobile awareness system, the distinction between active and passive perception is made clear. The cues (see Fig. 5.1) were used for tasks like coordinating decisions on mobility and calling—for example, whether the other person concerned is approaching the meeting point; if the other person is close; and whether he or she is interruptible, likely to answer the telephone and available, etc. For such task-driven interpretations, the timeliness, accuracy, and reliability of cues are of crucial importance.

However, many users also mentioned feeling of *companionship* as the main benefit of using the system, a use rather different from task-oriented ones. Users expressed feelings of presence, closeness, affection, communality, and connectedness as being mediated by mobile awareness cues. Oulasvirta et al. (2007) argued that this manifests a less task-oriented processing goal and involves more holistic reading of cues. The cues were used for staying in touch and for gaining reassurance about the well-being of others (e.g., to know whether others had arrived home safely)—in other words, benefits that can be plausibly inferred to be relevant in terms of the basic need for relatedness. Moreover, there were instances of the users *tracking* each other and looking at awareness cues for a long time. This resembles "awareness moments" reported in the use of IM (Nardi et al. 2000). Moreover, there were a few reports evidencing that extraneous effort was put into keeping the phone close to oneself just to maintain a connection to others. Repeatedly, looking at cues may associatively prime the related person memory and thus increase the probability that it "pops into mind" and is actually acted upon (Bargh and Ferguson 2000). This may constitute a feeling of "awareness" that continues even in the absence of the cues themselves. In exploratory processing, the aim is in constructing a more holistic representation of the other so that he or she can be felt as "present."

5.4.2 Perception, Action, and Feedback

The arena of motivational dynamics is shaped and modulated by cognitive processes of two kinds: perceptions and expectations. The outcome achieved is evaluated and the process may restart at a later time with new expectations, motivations, and perceptions. The following mental events may take place when one is using the cues to make a decision to call a friend:

1. Expectations: for example, believing that a friend is interruptible on his or her lunch hour.
2. Inference: inferring from the cues that there is an opportunity to call the friend.
3. Action: placing a call but failing to reach the callee.
4. Evaluation of feedback: judging whether the chosen time was wrong.
5. Updating of expectations and restarting from step 1 at a later time.

One psychological event that bridges goal-setting and the user interface is *forethought*. Future-directed plans are rarely specified in full detail at the outset, because anticipation of situation details is difficult. Therefore, through the exercise of what Bandura (2001) calls forethought, people motivate themselves and guide their actions in anticipation of future events. Via representation of future states in the present, a foreseeable future is converted into current drivers and regulators of behavior.

An interesting hypothesis is that forethought plays a particularly vital role in the initial stages of learning an awareness system. The outcomes of action alternatives are envisioned and utilized as a basis for selecting one's action. However, utility mispredictions can surface, stemming from biased retrospective evaluations and from

misguided theories of the future. Because action based on incorrectly predicted utility can lead to mismatch of expectations and achievements, and thus discourage the
user from using the system, it is essential that attention be paid to designing the
cues so as to minimize the possibility of such mismatches. The other component
in expectations is cost. Cost can be conceptualized in terms of the negative aspects
of engaging in the task, such as fear of failure, or the lost opportunities resulting
from making one choice rather than another. In practical circumstances, when one
is deciding on whether to act upon an inference or not, cost could mean, for example, time, effort, or money. A possible implication of design is that, if forethought is
to be supported, awareness cues should be descriptive (Antti is busy writing a paper)
instead of prescriptive (Don't call), because cues of the latter type provide poorer
means for imagining alternative outcomes for actions.

The lesson is that inference of cues links to action through interplay of expectations that motivate action, actions that produce effects, and effects that are evaluated
as feedback.

5.5 Examples From Mobile Awareness Systems

The body of research studying social inference through technology is tremendous in volume, at least when interpreted in the broadest sense of the notion.
However, the efforts are distributed across several topics, covering a broad
range—like videoconferencing, telepresence, social behavior in online communities, awareness, and remote collaboration. This unfortunate "balkanization" is not
merely symptomatic of applied Social Cognition; it characterizes almost all applied
psychology that examines Human-Computer Interaction (Carroll 1997). Consequently, the foundations of inference through technology have not been thought out
systematically.

The following examples are from a particular application domain, mobile awareness. They come from studies that have not concentrated solely on the evaluation of
applications but explored more fundamental questions of social inference of awareness cues.

The awareness system studied is ContextContacts, one of many systems of its
type (Bardram and Hansen 2003; Burak and Sharon 2003; Holmquist et al. 1999;
Isaacs et al. 2002; Marmasse et al. 2004; Milewski and Smith 2000; Tang et al.
2001). The interface is presented in Fig. 5.1. The driving idea in the system's design
was to integrate awareness cues into the contact book of a mobile phone, thus transforming it into a group-oriented venue in which the presence and undertakings of
other members can be easily viewed and acted upon.

Controlled laboratory studies (e.g., the work of Oulasvirta et al. 2005) have been
conducted concomitant with A—B intervention trials in the field (Oulasvirta et
al. 2007). These studies examined (1) pre-knowledge, (2) task orientation, and (3)
selectivity. The results are, by and large, aligned with the predictions of Social Cognition research.

5.5.1 Effects of Pre-Knowledge

The earlier paper (Oulasvirta et al. 2005) reported a set of experiments that was conducted to find out how background knowledge about another person features in the inference process. Simulacra of real mobile awareness cues were used.

In the first experiment, 10 participants were presented with five different cues adopted from ContextContacts (district, district with duration of stay, current alarm profile, whether the phone has been in use in the past 2 minutes, and whether the person is in the company of six or more people), one at a time. The participants were asked to list *as many situations as possible in which a given person could realistically be, given that information.* There were two conditions in which such enumeration was carried out: (1) the person is unknown and (2) the person is known, a coworker we named and with whom everybody was at least familiar. The idea behind this manipulation was to assess the effect of background knowledge by comparing inferences for a known and unknown person. The participants were also asked to place an imaginary monetary bet to represent confidence in their guess. In studies of decision-making, this is commonly used as an intrasubject metric for perceived value.

The results (shown in Figs. 5.2 and 5.3) support the hypotheses of Social Cognition:

1. In general, pre-knowledge helps one to make more *elaborate* inferences.
2. However, pre-knowledge works only when the cue is familiar. In the set of five cues we studied, two cues, "duration of stay" and "number of people present," did not see a benefit from pre-knowledge.
3. Inferrers think that they can make more accurate inferences when they can utilize their pre-knowledge about the person.
4. Inferrers also draw *more* inferences when they can utilize pre-knowledge.

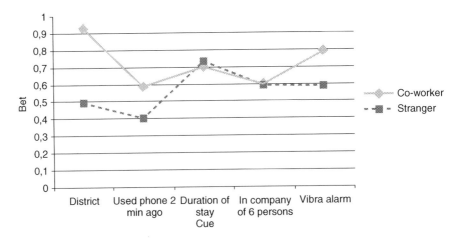

Fig. 5.2 The effect of pre-knowledge on the certainty felt about an inference

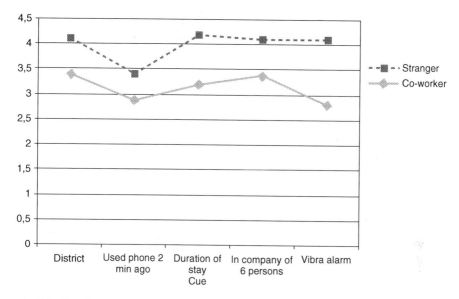

Fig. 5.3 The effect of pre-knowledge on the number of inferences (activities mentioned)

The main thrust of these findings is that pre-knowledge is necessary for interpretive flexibility.

A related question is *what kind* of pre-knowledge is useful. This question can be studied only in a situation where the inferrers have developed inferential skills with the particular set of cues involved. In a field trial of ContextContacts (Oulasvirta et al. 2007), both person-specific memories and more general types of knowledge, schemas, were identified as being utilized in the interpretation of cues:

1. *Person-specific knowledge*, similar to person memories, of the other person's current activity. One participant, for example, said that if the phone is not in silent mode but she knows that the person is at school, then she knows when to call because she knows when the breaks start and end. Known regularities of the movement patterns of a person also helped to augment, and at times overcome, the low granularity of the district cue in the system. For example, the information that two schoolmates always "hung out" together after school in a certain place was utilized. Patterns of alarm profile switching were also employed.
2. Schematic, *general knowledge* concerning typical activities for the time of day was utilized often. Social knowledge (e.g., that phones should be silent during classes) was also utilized to explain the alarm profiles observed. Moreover, semantic knowledge of an area was used to draw conclusions as to possible activities when another was seen in an unexpected or unusual location.

The key point from these findings is that the availability of specific and general pre-knowledge constrains the range of inferences possible for a cue. Novel cues most likely require more practice before becoming useful. However, if general and person-specific memories can be directly applied, this can be avoided, as Fig. 5.2 indicates.

5.5.2 Selective Processing of Cues and Transfer

In the second laboratory experiment reported in the 2005 paper by Oulasvirta et al., we studied whether the *order* in which cues are processed affects interpretation. If order affects outcomes, as the anchoring heuristic suggests (Tversky and Kahneman 1974), the user interface should guide users to process the best anchors first.

In the study, 10 participants were asked to make interpretations based on *pairs* of cues. An anchor was presented first—for example, the current district of another person—and an inference of the other person's current undertaking was committed to paper. Then, another cue was presented, and the participant was asked whether this *additional* information would *change or augment* the original inference. The results are presented in Table 5.3.

The results are symptomatic of *anchoring*: for some pairs. Dramatically different inferences were reported, and subjective utilities ascribed, when the order of presentation was reversed. Consider the case where "Turnover of BT devices in range" (e.g., "20 devices recently") is the anchor for the phone manipulation cue: the perceived utility was 0.34. By comparison, when the order was reversed and the phone manipulation cue presented first, the perceived utility doubled to 0.74.

These findings are backed up by users' self-reports in the field study of Oulasvirta et al. (2007). In that study, the users reported using heuristic-like cue-to-inference mappings when using the system. Consider the following excerpt:

> I've often had situations when I check—for example, during a school day—whether a friend is available or not. In practice, I check whether the phone is silent or not. You cannot call a person with no [audio] alarm. [The respondent was an entrepreneur.]

However, inference based on a single cue was not always achievable. The following quote illustrates *anchoring* on the "hand cue:"

> The hand was mostly white, but it did give more hope when it was red. At the point when you call, I do not often look at whether it's red or not. The only thing is that when there's no audio or tactile alarm, there's no hope of reaching the other person if the hand is white. But if it is a red hand, you usually thought that he or she might notice your call. [The respondent was an entrepreneur.]

In addition to the hand cue, the district cue was a dominant anchor, while the Bluetooth-based cues were predominantly used as secondary cues:

> When I haven't been able to participate in some group work, I've been looking [at the yellow person] to see when they are leaving. Then the place thing [district] has been used. And then how many people there are, and my friend Julia is visible as a yellow guy. Nina is usually also there but there are no traces of her; she's not visible as a yellow guy. [The respondent was a student.]

Table 5.3 Utility attributions with interference based on one cue ("Bet" Column) and two cues ("Utility" columns)

Anchors	Bet	Utility of additional cues							
		District	Alarm profile	Number of BT devices on range	Duration of stay	Phone manipulation	Turnover of BT devices on range	Predicted district with ETA	No. of unread messages or unanswered calls
District	0,63	–	0,66	0,66	0,88	0,55	0,71	0,83	0,51
Alarm profile	0,73	0,58	–	0,81	0,82	0,67	0,83	0,86	0,56
Number of BT devices on range	0,48	0,64	0,53	–	0,64	0,39	0,56	0,77	0,51
Duration of stay	0,52	0,53	0,51	0,65	–	0,40	0,54	0,97	0,43
Phone manipulation	0,48	0,77	0,62	0,66	0,71	–	0,74	0,83	0,62
Turnover of BT devices on range	0,70	0,85	0,59	0,50	0,75	0,34	–	0,56	0,45
Predicted district with ETA	0,75	0,68	0,42	0,50	0,64	0,31	0,83	–	0,49
No. of unread messages or unanswered calls	0,68	0,70	0,58	0,88	0,78	0,72	0,66	0,66	–

Without these rapid and effortless, yet effective, means for selecting cues, users would easily become overwhelmed with "information overload." Selection appeared to be natural to the users; only one expressed difficulties, complaining about "symbols starting to flash in your eyes."

We also learned that this kind of selection can be very rapid. We measured what we dubbed the "pre-called delay": the time for which users keep a contact highlighted in the contact list before pressing the "place call" button. This is indicative of their reading of the cues. Most probably this time is spent in assessing whether the person is going to be available. When we compared cue-augmented contacts to unaugmented contacts, a substantial difference was observed; when there are no cues for a contact, 60% of calls are placed within less than 1 second after moving the selector on top of the contact. When the cues *are* present, 60% of the time the users pause for 1—3 seconds before placing the call. This is tentative evidence for the usefulness of integrating mobile awareness cues with communication functionality.

One explanation for the apparent fluency in selection is that interpretations were facilitated by the *transfer* of interpretation skills. The users had already used time of day as an implicit cue long before this trial, for example, in their daily decisions of when to call a person. Transfer is a good candidate to explain the fluent use of the hand cue as well, because of its resemblance to availability cues in IM. Similarly, locations are related at the beginning of phone calls, particularly in mobile coordination (Laurier 2001), which may have provided a source of transfer for the district cue. From this perspective, the case of Bluetooth cues is interesting, because, whereas one group found almost no uses for it, another developed an inferential skill for its use. They reported multiple interpretations of those cues, but only toward the end of the trial. Learning of interpretation skills may help to reconcile the dilemma involving the known limitations of the cognitive machinery versus the skilled worker's ability to use tacit cues innovatively (Heath and Luff 1992; Schmidt 2002).

5.6 Conclusions

Computer-mediated indicators related to remote people feature so commonly in contemporary information and communication technologies, not only in awareness systems, that the question of how they are interpreted and acted on lies at the heart of one of the most significant developments in the history of personal computing: the transformation in common thought of the personal computer from a tool for an individual into a tool for social interaction. The stakes are high—if it is found that no fundamental limitation to awareness cues exists, they can ultimately serve as artificial proxies for humans, perfectly replicating the companionship and presence of other human beings. On the other hand, if theoretical or practical limitations do exist, it is important to chart what they are.

   The quest for an answer is fueled by the ongoing "ubiquitous computing" revolution, which will soon warrant more imaginative and pervasive forms of awareness. However, attempts to find a conceptual basis for developing these systems have been disappointing. According to Schmidt (2002) and Gross et al. (2005), the term "awareness" has not been used consistently among researchers and its very definition is problematic (see also the historical review offered by Rittenbrush and McEwan, Chapter 1). Flavors of awareness, such as "general awareness," "collaboration awareness," "peripheral awareness," "background awareness," "passive awareness," reciprocal awareness," "mutual awareness," and "workspace awareness," are seen frequently in the literature. From the Social Cognition perspective, a likely explanation for this dispersion is that attributes of activity—as in *collaboration* awareness—have been confounded with attributes of cognitive processing—as in *peripheral* awareness. The boundaries among technology, human, and action have become blurred. Omitting social inference from the analysis may have led to the untenable conclusion that awareness can be almost anything.

   The field has also suffered from romanticizing of users' abilities. For example, Schmidt (2002) and Heath and Luff (1992) admire users' "highly active and highly skilled" ways of constructing awareness in everyday cooperative settings. Schmidt (2002) concludes his influential editorial as follows: "From a cognitivist point of view, the very notion that an actor is able to pick up and relate to occurrences beyond the scope of his or her line of action and without interrupting that line of action is difficult if not outright impossible to fathom" (p. 293). In light of the present approach, expert interpretation of technological projections can be explained by cognitive skills that allow the inferrer to anticipate, select, filter, elaborate upon, and enrich the cues. This approach may help to explain why novices are unable to reproduce the feat and why even skilled users sometimes fail to achieve meaningful and actionable interpretations. The Social Cognition approach to awareness calls for empirical searching for explanations, not mystification of users' abilities.

   To conclude, the social cognitive approach appears auspicious. It helps us to see essential connections between user interfaces and human action, it brings in a wealth of findings from a field that has studied analogous problems for decades, it opens a plethora of new questions for study, and it can sensitize designers to design issues that were previously not even noted. To produce research hypotheses, one can simply take any empirical finding from a textbook in Social Cognition—typically of the form "Cognitive event C organizes the processing of social setting S so as to make behavior B more probable," and replace "social setting S" with "technology-mediated cue of social situation S." Some of the key concepts in Social Cognition, such as attitudes, attribution, social judgment, prototypes, group dynamics, and social identity, will become amenable to investigation in awareness research through this kind of translation. Integrative research into this topic will reveal the limitations and capabilities of technological projections of people. Designers should be aware, however, that the way argumentation works within the Social Cognition approach is not from design to inference but vice versa: one must understand the principles and conditions of social inference in order to understand how to best support it.

Acknowledgments   The author wishes to express gratitude to Sampsa Hyysalo, Giulio Jacucci, Esko Kurvinen, Kari Kuutti, Jaakko Lehikoinen, Esko Lehtonen, Panos Markopoulos, Miikka Miettinen, Mika Raento, Mikko Salminen, and Sakari Tamminen for valuable feedback. Esko Lehtonen produced the figures in Section 5.5. This work has been funded by the 6th Framework Research Programme of the EU, through the projects PASION (FP-2004-IST-4-27654) and IPCity (FP-2004-IST-4-27571), as well as by the Academy of Finland project ContextCues.

References

Augoustinos, D. and Walker, D. (1995), *Social Cognition: An Integrated Introduction*. Sage Publications Inc.

Bandura, A. (2001). Social cognitive theory: An agentic perspective. *Annual Review of Psychology, 52* (1), 1—26.

Bardram, J.E. and Hansen, T.R. (2003). The AWARE architecture: supporting context-mediated social awareness in mobile cooperation. In *Proceedings of CSCW'03*, ACM Press, New York, pp. 192—201.

Bargh, J.A. and Ferguson, M.J. (2000). Beyond behaviorism: on the automaticity of higher mental processes. *Psychological Bulletin, 126* (6), 925—945.

Burak, A. and Sharon, T. (2003). Analyzing usage of location based services. In Proceedings of CHI'03, ACM Press, New York, pp. 970—971.

Carroll, J.M. (1997). Human-Computer Interaction: Psychology as a Science of Design. *Annual Review of Psychology, 48,* 61–83.

Chalmers, M. and Galani, A. (2004). Seamful interweaving: heterogeneity in the theory and design of interactive systems. In *Proceedings of DIS'04*, ACM Press, New York, pp. 243—252.

Dourish, P. and Bellotti, V. (1992). Awareness and coordination in shared workspaces. In *Proceedings of CSCW'92*, ACM Press, New York, pp. 107—144.

Dourish, P. and Bly, S. (1992). Portholes: Supporting awareness in a distributed work group. In *Proceedings of CHI'92*, ACM Press, New York, pp. 541—547.

Deci, E.L. and Ryan, R.M. (2000). The "What" and "Why" of goal pursuits: Human needs and the self-determination of behavior. *Psychological Inquiry, 11* (4), 227—268.

Dreyfus, H. (1992), *What Computers Still Can't Do: A Critique of Artificial Reason*. MIT Press, Cambridge, MA.

Endsley, M. (1995), Toward a theory of situation awareness in dynamic systems, *Human Factors, 37* (1), 32—64.

Fiske, S. and Taylor, S.E. (1991). *Social Cognition.* McGraw-Hill, New York.

Fussell, S.R., Kraut, R.E., Gergle, D., and Setlock, L.D. (2005). Visual cues as evidence of others' minds in collaborative physical tasks. In B.F. Malle and S.D. Hodges (Eds.), *Other Minds: How Humans Bridge the Divide Between the Self and Others*, The Guilford Press, New York, NY, pp. 91—105.

Gilbert, D.T., Pelham, B.W., and Jones, E.E. (1987). Influence and interface: what the active perceiver overlooks. *Journal of Personality and Social Psychology, 52* (5), 861—870.

Gollwitzer, P.M. and Bargh, J.A. (1996). The Psychology of Action: Linking Cognition and Motivation to Behavior. New York, NY: Guilgord Press.

Gross, T., Stary, C., and Totter, A. (2005). User-centered awareness in computer-supported cooperative work-systems: Structured embedding of findings from social sciences. *International Journal of Human-Computer Interaction, 18* (3), 323—360.

Gutwin, C., Greenberg, S., and Roseman, M. (1996). Workspace awareness support with radar views. In *Proceedings of CHI'96*, ACM Press, New York, pp. 208—209.

Gutwin, C. and Greenberg, S. (2002). A descriptive framework of workspace awareness for real-time groupware. *Computer Supported Cooperative Work (CSCW), 11,* (3), 411—446.

Hastie, R. (1983). Social inference. *Annual Review of Psychology, 34* (1), 511—542.

Heath, C. and Luff, P. (1992). *Technology in Action.* Cambridge University Press, UK.

Holmquist, L.E., Falk, J., and Wigström, J. (1999). Supporting group awareness with interpersonal awareness devices. *Personal Technologies, 3* (1/2).

Isaacs, E., Walendowski, A. and Ranganthan, D. (2002). Hubbub: A sound-enhanced mobile instant messenger that supports awareness and opportunistic interactions. In *Proceedings of CHI '02*, ACM Press, New York, pp. 179—186.

Jones, E. E. and Nisbett, R. E. (1972). The actor and the observer: divergent perceptions of the causes of behavior. In E. E. Jones, D. Kanouse, H. H. Kelley, R. E. Nisbett, S. Valins, and B.INTtie;Weiner (Eds.), *Attribution: Perceiving the Causes of Behavior.* General Learning Press, Morristown, NJ, pp. 79—94.

Laurier, E. (2001). Why people say where they are during mobile phone calls. Environment and Planning D: Society and Space, *19* (4), 485—504.

Marmasse, N., Schmandt, C., and Spectre, D. (2004). WatchMe: Communication and awareness between members of a closely-knit group. In *Proceedings of UbiComp 2004*, Springer, pp. 214—231.

Milewski, A.E., and Smith, T.M. (2000). Providing presence cues to telephone users. In *Proceedings of CSCW'00*, ACM Press, New York.

Moskowitz, G.B. (2004). *Social Cognition: Understanding Self and Others.* The Guilford Press, New York.

Nardi, B., Whittaker, S., and Bradner, E. (2000). Interaction and outeraction: Instant messaging in action. In *Proceedings of CSCW'00*, ACM Press, New York, pp. 79—88.

Neisser, U. (1976), *Cognition and Reality: Principles and Implications of Cognitive Psychology.* WH Freeman, New York.

Oulasvirta, A. and Blom, J. (2008). Motivations in personalisation behavior. *Interacting with Computers, 20* (1), 1—16.

Oulasvirta, A., Raento, M., and Tiitta, S. (2005). ContextContacts: Re-designing smart phone's contact book to support mobile awareness and collaboration. In *Proceedings of Mobile HCI 2005*, ACM Press, New York, pp. 167—174.

Oulasvirta, A., Petit, R., Raento, M., and Tiitta, S. (2007). Interpreting and acting upon mobile awareness cues. *Human-Computer Interaction, 22* (1), 97—135.

Reeve, J. (2001). *Understanding Motivation and Emotion.* Harcourt College, Orlando, FL.

Schank, R. and Abelson, R. (1977), *Scripts, Plans, Goals and Understanding: An Inquiry Into Human Knowledge Structures.* Halsted Press division of Wiley [distributor].

Schmidt, K. (2002). The problem with "awareness": Introductory remarks on "awareness in CSCW". *Computer Supported Cooperative Work, 11* (3—4), 285—298

Searle, J. (1980). Minds, brains, and programs. *Behavioral and Brain Sciences, 3* (3), 417—457.

Sproull, L. and Kiesler, S. (1986). Reducing social context cues: Electronic mail in organizational communications. *Management Science, 32* (11), 1492—1512.

Suchman, L. (1987). *Plans and Situated Action: The Problem of Human—Machine Communication.* Cambridge University Press, Cambridge.

Tang, P. and Venables, T. (2000). Smart homes and telecare for independent living. *Journal of Telemedicine and Telecare, 6* (1), 8—14.

Tang, J.C., Yankelovich, N., Begole, J., Van Kleek, M., Li, F., and Bhalodia, J. (2001). ConNexus to Awarenex: extending awareness to mobile users. In *Proceedings of CHI'01*, ACM Press, New York, pp. 221—228.

Tomasello, M., Carpenter, M., Call, J., Behne, T., and Moll, H. (2005). Understanding and sharing intentions: The origins of cultural cognition. *Behavioral and Brain Sciences 28*(5), 675—691.

Tversky, A. and Kahneman, D. (1974). Judgment under uncertainty: Heuristics and biases. *Science, 185*, 3—20.

Vallacher, R. and Wegner, D. (1985). *A Theory of Action Identification.* Lawrence Erlbaum, Hillsdale, NJ.

Weilenmann, A. (2003). I can't talk now, I'm in a fitting room: formuling availability and location in mobile phone conversations. *Environment and Planning, 35* (9), 1589—1605.

Chapter 6
Abstractions of Awareness: Aware of What?

Georgios Metaxas and Panos Markopoulos

6.1 Introduction

This chapter presents *FN-AAR*, an abstract model of awareness systems. The purpose of the model is to capture in a concise and abstract form essential aspects of awareness systems, many of which have been discussed in design essays or in the context of evaluating specific design solutions.

The FN-AAR model is described using concepts from simple set theory expressed in the standard Z notation (Spivey, 1992). Z is a formal specification language based on first-order logic and Zermelo-Fraenkel set theory that has become an ISO standard (ISO/IEC, 13568:2002). Its syntax and semantics are based on classical mathematics and allow the abstract specification of systems in a model-oriented way. Apart from its mathematical toolkit for common operations on sets and numbers, Z specifications use elements such as axiomatic definitions and schemas also.

Contrary to many formal system specifications expressed in mathematical notations like Z, it is not suggested that abstract models like the one presented should be used as the blueprint of an implementation. The model we present is silent about development and implementation, aiming to provide a tool for thought and for reasoning about the design space of awareness systems. Rather we aim that the model should be a useful point of reference for researchers in the domain of awareness systems or students wishing to get deeper into this area. Designers of awareness systems may find it useful to consider the range of relationships between information artefacts connecting individuals and groups and in doing so make related design choices more explicit.

A benefit of such an abstract model is that it helps make explicit the similarities and the critical differences between awareness system concepts that proliferate in related literature. Despite their great number and diversity, awareness systems cluster around a few basic themes, e.g. conveying simple presence information at a particular location, sustained audio–video links between places, serendipitous

G. Metaxas (✉)
Eindhoven University of Technology, The Netherlands
e-mail: margaret.morris@intel.com

P. Markopoulos et al. (eds.), *Awareness Systems*, Human-Computer Interaction Series, DOI 10.1007/978-1-84882-477-5_6, © Springer-Verlag London Limited 2009

discovery of information about others, like communicating to someone that you think about him/her and supporting flexibility and the conjoint creation of meaning between communicating individuals. Many of these concepts are discussed in other chapters of this book in terms specific to the applications discussed. While there are often crucial differences between the specific systems discussed in terms of which information is captured, how it is displayed, interpreted and used in context, there is also a significant overlap between these concepts that can become explicit only if such systems are described in some relatively abstract terms.

Next to representation, reasoning is also an important benefit of abstract models. Theoretical discussions motivating the design of such systems gravitate towards the phenomena surrounding the social aspects of using awareness. For example, T. Erickson et al. (2002) have introduced the concept of *social translucence* that encapsulates issues of inter-subjectivity between users. Other authors discuss *privacy* and ways in which users of communication systems might manage their accessibility to other individuals or services (Boyle and Greenberg, 2005; Hong and Landay, 2004; Blaine et al., 2005; Iachello et al., 2005). This chapter illustrates how the abstract model supports the expression of relevant properties of awareness systems and reasoning about them. Crucially, the precision of the modelling approach allows the reader to draw links between these different notions that have remained hazy and elusive in earlier literature.

6.2 Related Works

An early influential model in the domain of awareness systems is the "event propagation model" by Fuchs et al. (1995) and Sohlenkamp et al. (1997). This model identifies three basic information processing functions that an awareness system has to support: capturing information regarding a particular individual, group or location, disseminating it and displaying it to the intended receivers. The model of Fuchs proposes the representation of the environment as a semantic network, where awareness about changes and activities in the system is supported by the generation and distribution of events in the semantic network. The propagation of events from a source to a sink is filtered by individual outgoing filters, such as privacy filters, at the source (event generation) side, and individual incoming filters (interest filters), at the event consumption (sink) side (Fig. 6.1).

The event propagation model can be useful as an abstract reference model for the implementation of awareness systems, though it was not aimed at, and it does not allow further reasoning regarding the nature of information captured and how it is transformed through each of the functional components it identifies.

In a similar direction, (Simone and Bandini, 2002) propose a model based on a "reaction–diffusion" metaphor. The model is based on the notions of *space* and *fields*. *Space* is populated by entities, and it is used to evaluate when entities come in contact and to express how fields propagate in the space. *Fields* are the means by which awareness information is brought in and propagated in the space and influences the entities able to perceive it. The model contains concepts to express

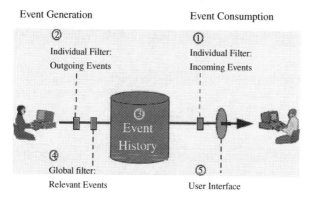

Fig. 6.1 The event propagation model (figure adapted from (Sohlenkamp et al., 1997))

the emission and the reception of the fields by the various entities populating the space. The mechanisms governing the *emission* and the *reception* of fields provide the capability of modulating *awareness* on the side of the emitter as well as of the receiver.

Probably the most influential conception of awareness that abstracts away from the information-flow aspects and focuses on the communicational aspects of awareness is the *focus–nimbus* model. Benford et al. (1993, 1995; Benford and Fahlen, 1993) introduced the notions of nimbus and focus in a spatial model of group interaction in order to address mutual levels of awareness within a virtual environment.

- *Focus* represents a sub-space within which a person focuses their attention. The more an object is within your focus, the more aware you are of it.
- *Nimbus,* on the other hand, represents a sub-space across which a person makes their activity available to others. The more an object is within your nimbus, the more aware it is of you.

Based on these notions, Benford et al. define a "measure of awareness" as a functional composition of *focus* and *nimbus* quantifiers; this measure answers the question: "In a given room, how aware is entity i of entity j via medium k?", i.e.

$$Level \ of Awareness : A_{kij}(f_{ik}, n_{jk}) : \mathbb{R}^2 \to \mathbb{R}$$

This function evaluates to a measure of awareness of a given entity i to another j based on values of the focus of entity i on $j (f_{ik})$ and the nimbus of entity $j (n_{jk})$ at i.

Rodden (1996) rendered the focus–nimbus model in graph theoretic terms extending its application to a wider range of cooperative applications, beyond the boundaries of spatial applications. The principal aim of their model is to allow reasoning about potential awareness among users, in terms reflecting on the "likelihood" of actions by one user being noticed by another. Rodden abstracts away from

Fig. 6.2 Some of the discrete
awareness modes (4 out of 16
arrangements)

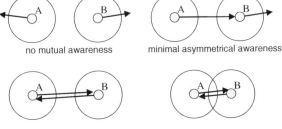

no mutual awareness   minimal asymmetrical awareness

minimal mutual awareness   fully reciprocal mutual awareness

the spatial approach by linking users to the presence space by nimbus and focus functions, i.e. functions that relate users with objects that are characterizing user's nimbi and foci. By estimating the awareness overlap for two users, one can evaluate the strength of awareness between two users, either from a continuous or a discrete point of view. This estimation depends on the existence of metric functions for focus and nimbus; however, these functions will have to be application specific and the subject of empirical validation (Rodden, 1996).

In Fig. 6.2, we can see some of the different modes of awareness that can pertain among two users when we consider a discrete representation of awareness (see Chapter 11 for more examples).

The focus–nimbus model has provided the conceptual foundation for several applications, e.g. the multi-modal streaming interface discussed in Chapter 11 and also in other works (see, for example, Fuchs et al., 1995).These interpretations of Rodden's model illustrate the face validity of the model and its practical relevance. On the other hand, they are application specific and are not intended for reasoning regarding user-relevant properties of mediated interaction. Examples of such properties concern privacy, translucence, etc.

The abstract model described in the remainder of this chapter is based on the focus–nimbus model. It provides the foundation for describing mathematically the design space of awareness systems in terms of the content exchanged and elementary user behaviours pertaining to sharing information about themselves or perceiving information about others. In the following sections we will make an overview of that model and examine several notions and properties related to the communicative perspective of awareness systems, such as social translucency, symmetry and intentionality in awareness systems. In order to support such reasoning the model needs to address the question "*What* are the entities aware of regarding each other?" rather than "*How much* aware are two entities about each other?"

This approach responds to Schmidt's reflection on the concept of awareness (Schmidt, 2002) where he criticized the endemic lack of conceptual clarity for the research domain of awareness systems. Noting the contradictory uses of the term awareness, he argued that dichotomies between attention and peripheral awareness, active and passive awareness, explicit and tacit, etc. are misleading. Rather he argued that awareness should be described in reference to activities, practices or phenomena or object that a person is made aware of.

6.3 Model Overview

The model discussed here describes *what* the entities are aware of regarding each other in a particular *situation*. For that, the original focus–nimbus model is extended and populated with several notions such as *entities, aspects, attributes, resources and observable items*. Before we proceed to formal definitions, let us introduce these notions with the help of a simple scenario:

> John and Anna are seniors living alone; sometimes they invite each other for a walk. They like to do this easily and without putting social pressure on each other so recently, they installed a system that helps them convey their wish for a walk. When they feel like walking, they can flick a switch concealed in a decorative object in their living room; the system indicates their intentions to the other side by lighting a small lamp in a visible position in the living room.

Entities are representations of actors, communities and other agents (possibly artificial) within an awareness system. The actors of the above scenario (i.e. *John* and *Anna*) are represented in an awareness system with the corresponding entities.

Aspects are characteristics that refer to an entity's state. An aspect can be conceived as a complement to the phrase "I want to be aware of your . . .". In the above scenario "John wants to be aware of Anna's wish for a walk"; thus, the phrase "wish for a walk" is an aspect, i.e. a characteristic of *Anna's* state that may be shared with *John*. The notion of an aspect is broad and loose enough to encompass terms like "location", "activity", "aspirations", or even "focus" and "nimbus".

Attributes are placeholders for the information exchanged between *entities*. An attribute can be thought of as a potential answer to the request "Tell me something about your 'X aspect'". In our scenario, an answer to *John's* request "Anna tell me something about your 'wish for walk'" could be "My 'wish for walk' is moderate"; thus, the answer "My 'wish for walk' is moderate" is an attribute, binding the value "moderate" to the aspect "wish for walk".

In any situation an entity makes its state available to other entities using one or more attributes. Awareness though is dynamic. One's *nimbus* is populated with *attribute providers*, i.e. functions that return those attributes that one makes available to other entities in a specific situation.

A *resource* is a binding of an *aspect* with a way of displaying one or more attributes about this aspect. In any situation an entity might employ one or more resources in order to be able to perceive certain aspects of other entities. Roughly speaking a *resource* is a statement such as "I shall display the attributes you provide to me about your . . . by . . .". In our example, "John plans to display the attributes that Anna provides to him about her *wish for walk* by *turning the lamp either on or off*".

One's *focus* is populated with *resource providers*, i.e. functions that return one's resources that are engaged to display information about other entities in a specific situation.

An *observable item* is the result of displaying some attributes about an aspect using a *resource*. Roughly speaking an *observable item* contains the answer to the question "How are these attributes displayed to you?". In our scenario, a possible answer to the question "How is 'moderate wish for walk' displayed to you?'" could be "by dimming the light on my desk".

The negotiation of the reciprocal *foci* and *nimbi* of two entities in a given situation (i.e. the corresponding "produced" *attributes* and *resources*) is a function that returns the *observable items* that are displayed to the two entities about each other's states, effectively characterizing their reciprocal awareness.

In the above scenario, *John* indicates his wish to go for a walk to *Anna* using the *walk switch*. We can consider that *John's* nimbus contains an *attribute provider* that returns (in any situation) an attribute about *John's* wish for walk based on the state of the *walk switch*. On the other hand, *Anna* can check *John's* wish for walk by glancing at the corresponding *lamp*. Systemwise we can consider that *Anna's focus* is expressed via a resource that switches the lamp on/off depending on *John's wish for walk*.

Needless to say that neither the *walk switch* nor the *lamp* implies necessarily that Johns does actually wish to walk (he may forget to push the switch); nor do they imply that Anna will necessarily notice the lamp. We can imagine that *Anna* can unplug the lamp or even "assign" it to another person. So *Anna* can become aware of *John's* mood for walk by manipulating her *focus*. Similarly, we can imagine that *John* could choose not to let *Anna* know about the state of the *walk switch*, thus, *John* lets *Anna* become aware of his mood for walk by manipulating his *nimbus*.

In the following sections we will walk through the formal definitions of the notions introduced above.

6.3.1 Observable Items and Awareness

Imagine a situation where "John is sitting on his sofa reading a magazine. Nearby, on his desk the 'walk lamp' illuminates indicating that Anna feels like going for a walk."

In the above situation the illuminating lamp is an *Observable Item* that indicates to *John* whether *Anna* wants to go for a walk. Notice here that the term *observable* neither implies that *John* sees the lamp nor means that *he* perceives it as an indication for Anna's wish to go for a walk. It only instructs that the lamp is available for observation and that it is possible for *John* to perceive. *John's* lamp may be switched on whether he is looking at it or not.

Another useful remark is that the term *observable* does not imply a visual display. The information carried by an observable item may be revealed in any perceivable modality (auditory, visual, tactile, etc.).

Building on the above example, the model asserts that in any situation there is a set of observable *items* that a given entity can observe. The set of observable items that are available to an entity characterize its awareness of other entities' situation and activities. More specifically, in the context of an awareness system we can consider that an entity i becomes aware of the state of entity j through an awareness-characteristic function a_{ij}, which under a given situation r returns the set of observable by entity i items that present information regarding entity j:

$$\forall i, j : Entity; \ a_{ij} : RealSituation \ \rightarrow \ \mathbb{F} \ ObservableItem;$$

The exact semantics of a_{ij} will be shaped out as we advance in the notions of focus and nimbus. For convenience, we use $a^r{}_{ij}$ to denote $a_{ij}\ (r)$.

As a simple example of *ObservableItem*, consider the following function:

$$lightIllumination : Lamp \ \times \ Voltage \ \rightarrow \ ObservableItem;$$

We do not need to define the function *lightIllumination* in detail but one can imagine that this function returns the effect of applying the specified voltage on a lamp source. For example *lightIllumination (lamp1, 240 V)* represents an observable item that originates from applying *240Volts* on *lamp1*.

In the aforementioned scenario we can state that

$$a^r_{John, \ Anna} \ = \ \{lightIllumination(lamp\ 1, 240V\ )\}$$

i.e. the *awareness* of *John* about *Anna* in a situation(*r*) is a set that includes one observable item that indicates Anna's wish to walk by illuminating *lamp1*.

Note that it would be more appropriate to say "potential awareness", since we have not modelled whether John perceives and correctly interprets the display. For brevity, we use instead the term "awareness" and we imply a corresponding interpretation for statements such as "John is aware of Anna's wish for a walk". In cases where we wish to emphasize the focus of attention in terms of perception and cognition of the actors, we shall be referring to their *physical (inherent) focus*.

6.3.2 Attributes, Attribute Providers and Nimbus

In order to address the question "What is an entity x aware of regarding entity y?" we have to address also the question "What is entity y exposing to entity x?".

To commence we consider that in any situation an entity's state (as it is presented to other entities) holds information about a wide range of aspects; we use the scheme "Attribute" to describe a piece of information(value) about a certain aspect (aspect).

```
┌─ Attribute ──────────────────
│ aspect : Aspect;
│ value   : Data;
└──────────────────────────────
```

For convenience, we can use the idiom (a:v) to denote the attribute

$\langle aspect \rightsquigarrow a, value \rightsquigarrow v \rangle$, i.e. the attribute about aspect a with value v

The model abstracts away from the way information is represented or typed, so there may be more than one attribute about the same aspect for a single entity; for example, one's state may include an attribute about "location" with the value "home"(*location:home*) and another attribute also about "location" with the value "kitchen" *(location: kitchen)*

The model does not prevent that one's state may include contradictory attributes (allowing for intentional misinformation by the user or the imperfect technology). For example, *John* could make available to *Anna* an attribute *(wishforwalk: yes)*, while at the same time he could make available to *Tom* the attribute *(wishforwalk: no)*. To exploit this one can populate the attribute space with a relationship that denotes contradicting attributes.

One's attributes and the entities that they are available to may change over time; a function type *AttributeProvider* is defined such that when an instance of it is invoked in a real situation, it returns an attribute and the set of entities that the generated (returned) attribute is made available to. Hence, an attribute provider may return different attributes available to different entities depending on the situation:

$$AttributeProvider ::= RealSituation \rightarrow (Attribute \times \mathbb{F}\ Enitity)$$

For an instance of *AttributeProvider* p, we can use the idiom p^r to denote *first* $p(r)$ and $p^r.e$ to denote *second* $p(r)$. Hence, p^r denotes the attribute that p returns at situation r, and $p^r.e$ denotes the set of entities that p^r is made available to.

Just like the original focus–nimbus model, nimbus represents a sub-space across which an entity makes its state available to others. Hence, for each entity i, we assume that *nimbus_i* includes all the entity's i attribute providers:

$$\forall i : Entity;\ nimbus_i : \mathbb{F}\ AttributeProvider$$

The above definitions can be used to answer the question "What is an entity exposing to other entities in a given situation?", i.e. we can define a function n_{ij} such that when applied to a real situation, it returns the attributes of i that are available to j:

$$\forall r : RealSituation;\ i, j : Enitity;\ n_{ij} : RealSituation \rightarrow \mathbb{F}\ Attribute$$
$$n_{ij}(r) = \{a : Attribute|\ (\exists\ p : AttributeProvider;\ p \in$$
$$nimbus_i \bullet (a = p^r) \wedge (j \in p^r.e))\}$$

In Fig. 3 we can see a schematic representation of the above definition. Figure 6.3 shows three attribute providers of entity i (*p1, p2, p3*) and their corresponding attributes in a situation r (i.e. *a1, a2, a3*).

Attribute provider *p2* makes attribute *a2* available to entity j; *p1* makes *a1* available to entities *j* and *k*; *p3* makes *a3* available to entity *k*. Consequently, the nimbus of entity i to j at this situation is $n^r_{ij}=\{a1,a2\}$ and the nimbus of entity i to k at this situation is $n^r_{ik}=\{a1,a3\}$.

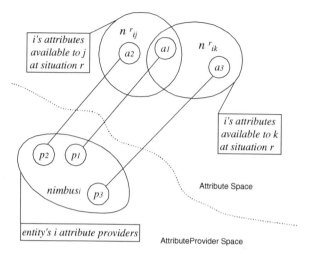

Fig. 6.3 The nimbus of entity i to entities j and k

6.3.3 Resources, Resource Providers and Focus

Previously we addressed the question "What is an entity exposing to other entities in a given situation?" by defining an entity's nimbus in terms of the attributes it makes available to other entities. However, the question "What is an entity aware of regarding other entities?" is twofold; not only do we need to know what is available for observation to an entity, but also do we need to know on what aspects an entity is focusing, and more particularly how the entity is planning to transform (render) the available attributes about an other entity to observable items.

Systemwise we assume that an entity has a limited set of resources to render the provided attributes regarding aspects of other entities. The scheme *Resource* describes an aspect of interest and a function that transforms the corresponding attributes to an observable item.

$$
\begin{array}{|l}
\hline
\textit{Resource} \\\\
\textit{aspect} : Aspect; \\
\textit{render} : \mathbb{F}\ Attribute \rightarrow ObservableItem; \\
\hline
\end{array}
$$

Apparently, an entity may assign more than one resource that renders the same aspect(s) of another entity. For example, *John* can render *Anna's wishForWalk* both by a lamp at home and an icon on his mobile phone.

One's resources may change depending on the situation; to incorporate this in the model a function type *ResourceProvider* is defined, which when applied to a real situation returns a resource and an entity that it is assigned to. Hence, a single resource provider may return different resources assigned to different entities depending on the situation:

$$ResourceProvider ::= RealSituation \rightarrow (Resource \times Entity)$$

For a *ResourceProvider* instance p we use p^r to denote *first* $p(r)$ and $p^r.e$ to denote *second* $p(r)$. Hence, p^r denotes the resource that p returns at the situation r, and $p^r.e$ denotes the entity that p^r is assigned to.

Likewise with nimbus, focus represents a sub-space within which an entity focuses its attention. To incorporate, we assume that for an entity i, *focus$_i$* includes the set of all entity's i resource providers.

$$\forall i : Entity;\ focus_i : \mathbb{F}\ ResourceProvider$$

With the above definitions we can now answer "On what is an entity focusing regarding other entities?", i.e. given focus$_i$ we define f_{ij} to return only those resources of entity i that focus on entity j:

$$\forall r : RealSituation;\ \forall i, j : Entity;\ f_{ij} : RealSituation \rightarrow \mathbb{F}Resource|$$

$$f_{ij}(r) = \{c : Resource | (\exists p : ResourceProvider;\ p \in focus_i \bullet (c = p^r) \wedge (j = p^r.e))\}$$

In Fig. 6.4 we can see a schematic interpretation of an entity's focus. On the bottom left of it we can notice three resource providers of entity's i focus (i.e. *p1 p2 p3*), and their corresponding resources in a situation r (i.e. *r1,r2,r3*).

The resource provider *p1* assigns the resource *r1* to display information from entity j; *p2* assigns *r2* to j; *p3* assigns *r3* to k. Consequently, the focus of entity i on j at this situation is $f^r_{ij} = \{r1,r2\}$ and the focus of entity i on k at this situation is $f^r_{ik} = \{r3\}$.

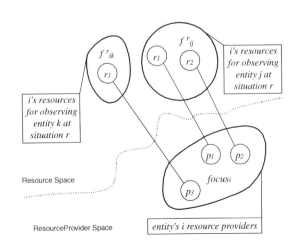

Fig. 6.4 Focus of entity i on entities j and k

6.3.4 Focus–Nimbus Negotiation and Awareness Systems

Earlier in the discussion of observable items, we introduced the awareness-characteristic function a_{ij}, which under a given situation r returns the set of observable by entity i items that present information regarding entity j:

$$\forall i, j : Entity; \ a_{ij} : RealSituation \rightarrow \mathbb{F} \ ObservableItem;$$

The set of observable items that are available to an entity characterize its awareness of other entities' situation and activities. However, the definition of a_{ij} above is weak, since it does not specify the relation between what is represented about i and how this is presented to j. Our interest then is to describe a_{ij} more strongly, in coordination with the original focus–nimbus model, as a functional composition of nimbus and focus.

Figure 6.5 shows the attributes that an entity "j" makes available to an entity "i" at a situation "r" (i.e. $a1$, $a2$, $a3$) through n^r_{ji}. On the top left we see their projection (A) on the *Aspect Space*, i.e. the aspects they refer to. For example, the attribute a_1 contains information about aspect Y, so its projection on the *aspect space* is Y.

We also notice the resources that i assigns for observing j at r (i.e. $r1, r2$) through f^r_{ij} and the resource projection (B) on the *Aspect Space*, i.e. the aspects that the resources are meant to render. For example, the resource r_2 is designated to render the aspect X, so its projection on the aspect space is X.

The intersection $A \cap B$ represents the aspects that i is designated to observe about j, and j is making available to i at the situation r. Consequently, the set of items that i can observe about j (a^r_{ij}) are the result of rendering those attributes of n^r_{ij}

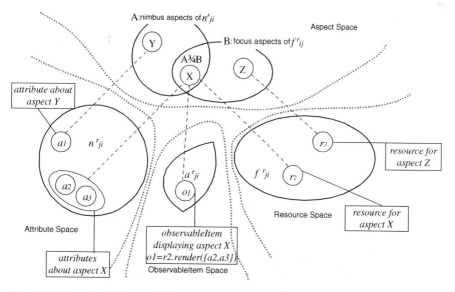

Fig. 6.5 Illustration of focus–nimbus negotiation and awareness that entity i has of entity j

that project on $A\cap B$ (i.e. *a2* and *a3*) using those corresponding resources of f^r_{ij} that project on $A\cap B$ (i.e. *r1*); therefore (see bottom of Fig. 6.3) a^r_{ij} includes the observable item $o1=r2.render(\{a2,a3\})$.

Based on the above insights, we can generalize the negotiation of the reciprocal foci and nimbi between two entities as follows:

$$a_{ij} ::= RealSituation \nrightarrow \mathbb{F}\ ObservableItem; \forall\ r : RealSituation\ ;$$

$$a_{ij}(r) = \{v : ObservableItem\ |\ (\forall\ c : Resource;\ c \in f^r_{ij} \bullet$$

$$v = c.render(\{u : Attribute\ |(u \in n^r_{ji}) \wedge (u.aspect = c.aspect)\}))\}$$

Hence, a_{ij} is a functional composition of n^r_{ji} and f^r_{ij}, which given a situation r, returns the observable items that are the result of rendering those attributes that entity j makes available to entity i (through n^r_{ji}), which in the same situation are focused by entity i (by examining the common aspects of the attributes in n^r_{ji} and the resources in f^r_{ij}) using the corresponding render functions.

The definitions introduced so far can be wrapped together in a scheme that describes an awareness system. The scheme defines the set of entities in a system, their nimbi and foci, as well as their reciprocal awareness information using the definitions we have introduced so far:

In the remaining sections we will be using the idioms *nimbus_i* for *nimbus(i)*, *focus_i* for *focus(i)*, n_{ij} for *n(i,j)*, f_{ij} for *f(i)*, a_{ij} for *a(i,j)*, n^r_{ij} for *n(i,j)(r)*, f^r_{ij} for *f(i,j)(r)* and a^r_{ij} for *a(i,j)(r)*.

AwarenessSystem ─────────────────────────────────────

enitities   : $\mathbb{F}$ *Entity*;

nimbus   : *Entity* $\nrightarrow$ $\mathbb{F}$ *AttributeProvider* ;

focus   : *Entity* $\nrightarrow$ $\mathbb{F}$ *ResourceProvider*;

n : $(Entitiy \times Entity) \nrightarrow (RealSituation \nrightarrow \mathbb{F}\ Attribute)$;

f : $(Entitiy \times Entity) \nrightarrow (RealSituation \nrightarrow \mathbb{F}\ Resource)$;

a : $(Entitiy \times Entity) \nrightarrow (RealSituation \nrightarrow \mathbb{F}\ ObservableItem)$;

───

dom nimbus=entities; *dom focus=entities*;

$\forall\ r$: *RealSituation*; i, j: *Entity*; $i,j \in$ *entities*;

$\forall\ u$: *Attribute*; c: *Resource*; v: *ObservableItem*

$r \mapsto u \in n_{ij} \Longleftrightarrow \exists\ p$: *AttributeProvider*; $p \in nimbus_i\ |(u=p^r) \wedge\ (j \in u.access)$

$r \mapsto c \in f_{ij} \Longleftrightarrow \exists\ p$: *ResourceProvider*; $p \in focus_i\ |\ c=p^r) \wedge (j = c.entity)$

$r \mapsto v \in a_{ij} \Longleftrightarrow \exists\ p$: *Resource*; $p \in f^r_{ij}\ |$

$\qquad v= p.render(\{u$:*Attribute* $|\ (u \in n^r_{ji}) \wedge (u.aspect=c.aspect)\}))\}$

6.3.5 Closing the Gap

In the model presented above, we addressed the question "What are the entities aware of regarding each other in a particular situation?" On the other hand, in the model definition we discuss notions such as observable items without accounting whether real-world entities (such as actors) actually do perceive them and therefore are physically (inherently) aware of them. It is interesting to address whether we can connect the notion of observable items, and the awareness-characteristic function a_{ij}, with the quantitative notion of modelling awareness with the original focus–nimbus model; i.e. to answer the question "how aware(physically) is a physical entity (e.g. an actor) of an observable-item".

For that we can consider that each *observableItem* has an inherent/physical nimbus, and each *entity(actor)* has an inherent focus. The lamp in the simple example introduced in Section 2.2 has an inherent nimbus that is defined by its physical position, its brightness, etc. Likewise *John* (as an actor) has an inherent (physical) focus that is defined also by his position, his posture, his eye gaze, etc. Apparently, the composition of an entity's inherent focus with an observable item's inherent nimbus defines how aware the entity is of the observable item itself. If we assume that a system has sufficient resources/capabilities to apply Rodden's focus–nimbus model in the *Entity–ObservableItem* relationship (i.e. we can define the focus–nimbus composition), then we can reason in detail about the information (observable items) that one is physically aware of.

Therefore we may think of a function n^+ that associates an *ObservableItem* with its inherent nimbus in any situation, a function f^+ that associates an *Entity* with its inherent focus in any situation, and an awareness quantifier function a^+:

$$n^+ : RealSituation \times ObservableItem \rightarrow InherentNimbus;$$

$$f^+ : RealSituation \times Entity \rightarrow InherentFocus;$$

$$a^+ InherentFocus \times InherentNimbus \rightarrow InherentAwareness$$

For an *entity* x and an *observableItem* u, the expression $a^+(f^+(r,x), n^+(r,u))$ quantifies the question "How aware is entity x of observable item u at situation r?" Assuming a predefined threshold h we can state that x is aware of u at situation r when its inherent awareness $a^+(f^+(r,x),n^+(r,u))$ is greater than the predefined threshold.

One may doubt the feasibility of computing functions n^+, f^+ and a^+ as they refer essentially to human perception and cognition. Yet, coming back to our simple scenario, we can imagine that *John* apart from focusing on *Anna* is also sharing other information with her or other entities. It could be, for example, that among others *John's* nimbus contains attributes about his location. Consequently, apart from other entities that have access to *John's location*, it could be that the system could also use this information to approximate *John's* physical focus and consequently detect whether he is aware of the *walk lamp* that indicates *Anna's* wish to walk (e.g. since he is sitting at a desk next to the lamp, the heuristic can be applied that he is likely to notice it).

Generalizing, one's physical focus may be approximated with varying degrees of success by knowing whether they are present in front of the computer or, even further, by monitoring their head pose or even their eye gaze. In other words, an entity's *nimbus* can be used to *approximate/define* its *inherent focus* allowing reasonable approximations of n^+, f^+ and a^+.

It is important to notice here that although we can model an entity being physically aware of an observable item, we cannot assume that the entity is also cognitively aware of the presented information, since we do not model the cognitive processes of awareness (e.g. *Anna's aware watch* may display *John's availability*, *Anna* may be physically aware of the displayed information, but still at the same time *Anna* may be unaware of *John's availability*). As noted, user cognition is outside the scope of the model presented here; such issues can be addressed by models such as the formalization of *performative interaction* (Dix et al., 2005), which enables, for example, the distinction among directly or indirectly perceived phenomena, or the model of Modica and Rustichini (1994), who formalize awareness by examining it in contrast with the notions of *unawareness, certainty* and *uncertainty*.

6.3.6 Example

In this section we will project the simple scenario introduced earlier on the model presented.

6.3.6.1 Anna's Nimbus

We can reflect on the nimbus of *Anna* in the scenario introduced earlier; *Anna* lets *John* know if she feels like walking by turning the switch on/off. In terms of the system, *Anna* makes available to *John* in any situation r an attribute a ($a \in n^r_{Anna,John}$) about her "wishforWalk"; *Anna's* nimbus contains an attribute provider that in any real situation returns the aforementioned attribute and adjusts the attribute's value according to the state of the switch:

$$sw\ 1 : AttributeProvider;\ sw\ 1 \in nimbus_{Anna} | \forall\ r : RealSituation;$$

$$(sw\ 1^r.aspect = wishforWalk) \land$$

$$(sw\ 1^r.value = if\ switchclosed(switch\ 1, r)\ then\ true\ else\ false) \land (sw\ 1^r.e = \{Anna\})$$

Thus, *sw1* is an attribute provider in *Anna's* nimbus, which when applied in a situation r returns an attribute (*sw1^r.aspect*: *sw1^r.value*) and an entity set (*sw1^r.e*) that includes *John*. The attribute's aspect is *wishforWalk* and its value is either *true* or *false* (depending on the state of *switch1*).

Now we can wrap up *Anna's* nimbus ($nimbus_{Anna}$)

$$nimbus_{Anna} = \{sw\ 1\}$$

Using the definition of n_{ij} we can verify that:

$$\forall\, r : RealSituation;\ n^r_{Anna,\ John} = \{sw\ 1^r\}$$

6.3.6.2 John's Focus

Continuing our example, imagine that "John uses a lamp to display Anna's wish for a walk and vice versa". A lamp *(resource)* is assigned to display Anna's *wishFor-Walk* aspect.

Systemwise, *John's* focus on *Anna* contains a resource r ($r \in f\ ^r_{John,Anna}$) that renders attributes about the aspect "wishforWalk". John's focus ($focus_{John}$) contains a resource provider that returns this resource and adjusts the resource's rendering (*illumination*) according to the attributes that the system provides:

$$wr\ 1 : ResourceProvider;\ wr\ 1 \in focus_{john} | \forall\, r : RealSituation;$$

$$(wr\ 1^r.aspect = wishForWalk) \wedge$$

$$(\forall s : \mathbb{F}\ Attribute;\ wr\ 1^r.render(s) =$$

$$if\ (\exists\, p : Attribute;\ p \in s | p.aspect = wishForWalk \wedge p.value = true)\ then$$

$$lightIllumination\ (lamp\ 1, 240\ V)\ else\ lightIllumination\ (lamp\ 1, 0\ V)) \wedge$$

$$(wr\ 1^r.e = Anna)$$

Thus, *wr1* is a *ResourceProvider that* returns a resource that renders attributes about *wishforWalk* either by turning on *lamp1* or by turning it off; $wr1.e$ denotes that the returned resource should be assigned to *Anna*. Consequently, *wr1* is a resource provider in *John's* focus, which when applied to a real situation r returns a resource that can render *Anna's wishforWalk* .

We can wrap up John's focus ($focus_{John}$):

$$focus_{John} = \{wr\ 1\}$$

We can apply the definition of f_{ij} to verify:

$$\forall\, r : RealSituation;\ f^r_{John,\ John} = \varnothing;\ f^r_{John,\ Anna} = \{wr\ 1^r\};$$

6.3.6.3 John's Awareness

Returning to our example, John's observable items about Anna's state are the result of rendering the value of Anna's *wishforWalk* as it is provided to John (i.e. $sw2^r$) using the resource that John assigned for this purpose (i.e. $wr1^r$). Conversely, Anna's observable items about John's state is the result of rendering the value of John's *wishforWalk* as it is provided to Anna (i.e. $sw1^r$) using the resource that Anna assigned for this purpose (i.e. $wr2^r$):

$$\forall r : RealSituation;$$
$$a^r_{John,Anna} = \{wr\ 1^r . render(\{sw\ 2^r\})\};\ a^r_{John,\ John} = \varnothing;$$

6.4 Communication Patterns

In this section we will present and analyse several communication aspects that can emerge within an awareness system using the model described above. We will use as a starting point a slightly more elaborate scenario that involves a few actors and an awareness system that they use as means of lightweight communication:

> John is using an awareness system to communicate with wife Anna and their 9-year-old daughter Doty, their daily activities. John is sharing with Anna and his mother his location, so that they have a feeling about him. On the other hand, at John's office, he is using a digital-frame that helps him stay aware of his family's situation. Moreover, John is able to see on the same display information about his colleagues' activities and his own tasks at hand, helping him to be more efficient at work…

6.4.1 *John's Nimbus and Plausible Deniability*

In the above context we can imagine that among other things "John is making available to Anna his location". Let us project this statement on the model: in terms of the system there exists a situation when (the entity that corresponds to) *John* makes available to (the entity that corresponds to) *Anna* some attributes about *John's* "location". Thus, there is some situation r where there exists (at least) an attribute in John's nimbus instance to Anna that holds information about the aspect "location", i.e.:

$$\exists r : RealSituation;\ a : Attribute;\ a \in n^r_{John,Anna} | a.aspect = \text{'}location\text{'}$$

Taking into account that the attributes are "generated" from attribute providers we can further state that

$$\exists r : RealSituation;\ p : AttributeProvider;\ p \in nimbus_{John}|$$
$$(Anna \in p^r.e) \wedge (p^r.aspect = \text{'}location\text{'})$$

Thus, p is an attribute provider in *John's* nimbus, which when applied in situation r returns an attribute *(location: p^r.value)* and an entity set (p^r.e) that includes *Anna*.

The exact value of the attribute(s) about John's location can vary both in detail and accuracy; for example, it could be *(location: home)*, *(location: away)*, *(location: car)*, *(location: work)*, or *(location: office)*, *(location: meeting-room)* and so on.

Likewise with *Anna*, we can imagine that *John* is also making available attributes about his location to his *mother*. However, in contrast to *Anna*, *John* is revealing less details to his *mother*; for example, at a certain situation *r*, *John's* nimbus to *Anna* contains the attribute *(location: meeting-room)*, while his nimbus to his *mother* contains the attribute *(location: work)*. This selective presentation of information about oneself can be for the purposes of self-presentation, politeness or simply privacy protection. In this case where information is presented at a diminished level of detail, we talk of "blurring". It is interesting to see how such patterns can be modelled.

Price (Benford et al., 1995) describes "blurring" as the ability to decrease the precision of one's location. In a wider context we can replace "location" with any aspect of one's nimbus. To account for the term "decrease" we define "blurring" in comparison to a reference entity. Hence we consider that an entity is *blurring* information about an aspect to another entity when the first is revealing *less information about this aspect* to the latter than a reference entity. The most typical example is when a video image from another person is blurred so that the identity of the individuals shown is not conveyed; see, for example, the use of filters by Hudson and Smith (1996).

Before proceeding to a formal definition, let us consider the phrase "less information about an aspect". This phrase implies that we need to take into account the term "information about an aspect". For that, we introduce a function *attributesAbout*, which when applied on a set of attributes and an aspect returns only those attributes that concern the specified aspect:

$$attributesAbout : \mathbb{F}\ Attribute\ \times\ Aspect\ \to\ \mathbb{F}\ Attribute$$
$$\forall\ s : \mathbb{F}\ Attribute;\ a : Aspect;\ attributesAbout(s, a)\ =$$
$$\{u : Attribute;\ u\ \in\ s\,|\,u.aspect = a\}$$

To evaluate the expression "less information" we consider that if an attribute set *s* is a subset of an attribute set *t*, then the set *s* contains less information than the set *t*. For example a set that includes an attribute about *location* with value *home* *(location: home)* contains less information than the set {*(location: home)*, *(location: bedroom)*} since the first set is a subset of the latter.

In our example, however, *John's* attributes about his location that are exposed to *Anna* is the set {*(location: meeting-room)*}, while to his *mother* it is the set {*(location: work)*}, and apparently the second is not directly a subset of the first. Nevertheless in our scenario domain we can assume that *(location: meeting-room)* implies the attribute *(location: work)*.

This insight can be expanded further more; for example, an attribute(*a1*) about aspect "activity" with a value "sleeping" implies an attribute(*a2*) about aspect "location" with a value "bed", and the latter may imply an attribute(*a3*) about "location" with value "home" and so on. More generally we can take into account implications from attribute tuples, triads, quads, or from any set of attributes. Based on the above remarks we can generalize ontological associations between attributes using a simple function:

$$impliedAttributes: \mathbb{F}\ Attribute\ \rightarrow\ \mathbb{F}\ Attribute\ ;$$

Apparently, the exact definition of the aforementioned function can be tailored to meet any application domain; on the other hand, such an ontology can be global, or entity specific, or even situation specific.

The exact definition of this function is out of scope; however, assuming its existence we can define $n^{*\,r}_{xy}$ to return all implied attributes of $n^{\,r}_{xy}$.

$$\forall r: RealSituation;\ n^{*r}_{ij} = \{a: Attribute|\ a \in$$
$$impliedAttributes\,(n^{r}_{ij})\}\}$$

Taking into account a simple attribute ontology like the one described earlier, we could now state that indeed the attribute set $\{(location:\ work)\}$ contains less information than the set $\{(location:\ meeting\text{-}room)\}$ since the latter implies the first. Consequently, we can formally define "blurring" by incorporating the ontological relationships of attributes:

$$-isBlurring - to- : RealSituation \rightarrow\ \mathbb{P}\,(Entity\ \times\ Aspect\times Entity)$$
$$let\,x,\ y: Entity;\ a: Aspect;\ r: RealSituation;$$
$$x\ isBlurring\ a\ to\ y\,(r)\ \Leftrightarrow\ (x, a, y)\ \in -isBlurring - to - (r)\ \Leftrightarrow$$
$$\exists z: Entity \mid attributesAbout(n^{*r}_{xy}, a)\ \subset attributesAbout(n^{*r}_{xz}, a)$$

i.e. an entity x is blurring information about an aspect a to y when all the attributes about a that are made available to y (explicitly or by implication) are a subset of the attributes about a that are made available to an entity z (explicitly or by implication). Note that the reference entity z can be any entity including x itself.

Similar to the definition of blurring, one can model other plausible deniability patterns, such as "deception" and "denial".

6.4.2 Placing John's Focus in his Nimbus and Social Translucency

Continuing our scenario, we can imagine that "John has on his desk at work a digital frame that shows to him the activities of other people; the frame has a couple of press-to-see buttons that are assigned to display information from different entities (e.g. Anna, Doty, Mother and so on). While, for example, he is pressing the first button, the system displays to him information about Anna's activities, or when no button is being pressed, the digital frame displays information about his to-do list at work."

Let us project initially *John's* focus on the model; systemwise there are situations where – the entity corresponding to – *John* employs a resource that renders *Anna's* attributes about, say, her "activity"; i.e.

$$\exists\, r:RealSituation;\ u:Resource;\ u\ \in\ f^r_{John,Anna}\,|a.aspect = \text{'}activity\text{'}$$

More precisely, taking into account that the resources are determined by resource providers, we can further state that there is a resource provider in his focus which under a situation r returns resources that are assigned to render *Anna's* activities.

$$\exists\, r:RealSituation;\ p:ResourceProvider;\ p\ \in\ focus_{John}$$
$$(p^r.e = Anna) \wedge (p^r.aspect = \text{'}activity'\text{)}$$

The same resource provider in other situations could return resources that are assigned on displaying his daughter's activities or his mother's activities or his to-do list and so on:

$$\exists\, p:ResourceProvider;\ r\,1, r2:RealSituation;\ p \in focus_{John}\,|$$
$$((p^{r1}.e = Anna) \wedge (p^{r1}.aspect = \text{'}activity'\text{))}\quad \wedge$$
$$((p^{r2}.e = Doty) \wedge (p^{r2}.aspect = \text{'}activity'\text{))}\quad \wedge$$
$$((p^{r2}.e = John) \wedge (p^{r2}.aspect = \text{'}to-do-list'\text{))}\quad \wedge$$
$$\cdots$$

An interesting pattern could emerge in the above situation; *John* could 'place' his focus in his "nimbus" towards *Anna*; in other words, he could expose to Anna attribute(s) that describe his *focus*, thus letting her adjust her behaviour accordingly (e.g. Anna could tell whether it is a nice moment to interrupt him by checking if he is currently focusing on her, or she could verify that John glanced at their daughter's activities and so on).

Such patterns are quite close to the notion of social translucency described by Erickson and Kellogg (2000) and Erickson et al. (2002). Social translucent systems make visible aspects of an actor to another in such a way that they also feedback the fact that the actors are aware of these aspects and in doing so make them accountable for their actions. We can summarize Erickson's notion in the statement "because I know that you know my situation, I adjust my behavior accordingly", and broaden this statement to "because I know that you know *mine or someone else's situation*, I adjust my behavior accordingly".

Based on the afor ementioned insights we can introduce the term external translucency using the statement "I am aware of your focus". Thus, "I am aware of what you are focusing on me (and possibly other entities)". This statement involves both "I focus on your focus" and "I *can* be aware of your focus". The first (I focus on your focus) signifies that some of my focus resources are assigned to display your focus. The second (I *can* be aware of your focus) signifies that your focus (e.g. the focus resources that you assigned to render information that I or others make available to you) is made available to me. Hence you allow me to observe how you are observing me (or other entities).

In more detail, the statement "I can be aware of your focus on me (or someone else)" is equivalent to the statement "you expose to me your focus on me (or someone else)" or that there exists an attribute included in your nimbus that indicates your focus on me (i.e. an attribute about the aspect "your focus on me/someone else"):

$$An\ entity\ y\ exposes\ to\ x\ its\ focus\ on\ z$$

$$\_exposesTo\_ItsFocusOn\_ : RealSituation \rightarrow \mathbb{F}\ (Entity\ \times\ Entity\ \times\ Entity)$$

$$\forall r: RealSituation;\ x,\ y,z: Entity;\ \bullet$$

$$y\ exposesTo\ x\ ItsFocusOn\ z\ \Leftrightarrow$$

$$(x,\ y,\ z)\ \in\ \_exposesTo\_ItsFocusOn\_(r)\ \Leftrightarrow$$

$$\exists u: Attribute;\ u\ \in\ n^r_{y,x}\ |\ u.aspect\ =\ 'focus\ y\ on\ z'\ \wedge$$

$$u.value\ =\ f^r_{yz}$$

Hence we consider that an entity y exposes to an entity x its focus on an entity z when there exists an attribute in y's nimbus to x about the aspect "focus of y on z" that has as value y's focus on z (f^r_{yz}).

In our example we could say that in some situation r, "John $exposesTo$ Anna $hisFocusOn$ Doty", i.e.

$$(John,\ Anna,\ Doty) \in\ \_exposeTo\_ItsFocusOn\_(r)\ \Leftrightarrow$$

$$\exists u: Attribute;\ u\ \in\ n^r_{John, Anna}|$$

$$(u.aspect\ =\ 'focus\ of\ John\ on\ Doty')\ \wedge\ (u.value\ =\ f^r_{John, Doty})$$

> Like physical entities (i.e. actors), agents can also employ social translucence. For example, a system could inform its users whether it is focusing on them or not, thus allowing them to protect their privacy.

The above concept can be expanded to further notions such as self-awareness (i.e. "I am aware of my nimbus"). In our scenario, for example, it could be that when *John* is not pressing any of the digital-frame buttons, the frame displays his nimbus (e.g. the kind of aspects he is making available to others or the exact attributes about his location that are exposed to his *boss* and so on).

6.4.3 Keeping Symmetry Among John's and his Colleague's Nimbi

Let us reflect on the following simple situation: "John decided to share with his colleagues at work his to-do list, so that he can attract their attention in cases that he needs help, without explicitly asking for it. However, to reduce the risk of people gossiping about him, John requested from the system to maintain symmetricity with his colleagues regarding the aspect to-do".

Based on the "to-do" attribute(s) that each of *John's* colleagues makes available to him, the system can decide whether his "to-do" attribute(s) should be exposed to them. Apparently, in this example, the system applies John's constraints in order to maintain his nimbus symmetrical to each of his colleague's nimbus.

More generally we can replicate nimbus symmetricity on the statement "What is provided to me (by you) is what is provided to you (by me)" or in more detail "The attribute aspects that I make available to you are the same with the attribute aspects you make available to me":

$$\_nimbus\,Symmetrical\_ : Real\,Situation \rightarrow \mathbb{F}\,(Entity \times Entity)|$$
$$\forall\,r: Real\,Situation; x, y: Entity; \bullet$$
$$x\,\textbf{nimbusSymmetrical}\,y \iff$$
$$(x, y) \in \_nimbus\,Symmetrical\_(r) \iff$$
$$attribute\,Aspects\,(n^r_{xy}) = attribute\,Aspects\,(n^r_{yx})$$

Where

$$attribute\,Aspects : \mathbb{F}\,Attribute \rightarrow \mathbb{F}\,Aspect$$
$$\forall\,s : \mathbb{F}\,Attribute\,;$$
$$attribute\,Aspects\,(s) = \{a : Aspect\,|(\forall u : Attribute; u \in s$$
$$\bullet a = u.aspect)\}$$

Thus, we call two entities nimbus symmetrical when their reciprocal nimbi contain attributes about the same aspects.

The above definition can be refined by taking into account the ontological associations of attributes introduced earlier through the function *implied-Atrtibutes*.

Apart from nimbus symmetry, we can consider this interesting characteristic of awareness systems in various levels such as "focus symmetry" (i.e. *What I am focusing on you is what you are focusing on*) or "awareness symmetry" (i.e. *What is displayed to me about you is what is displayed to you about me*), or "render symmetry" (i.e. *the way I render information about you is the way you display information about me*) and so on.

6.4.4 Making a Stranger Aware of Anna's Nimbus

Earlier in this chapter we discussed the ability to model the inherent (physical) awareness that entities maintain about the observable items surrounding them; consequently, we can assume a function *isPhysicallyAwareOf* that allows us to reason about entities' physical awareness of observable items in a given situation.

Imagine, for example, that *Tom*, a colleague of *John*, visits *John* at his office: In this situation, *Tom* would be physically aware of the observable items that are displayed at *John's* digital display. Despite that systemwise *Anna* is exposing only to *John* her activities, *Tom* in this case is also becoming potentially physically aware of *Anna's* activities due to the fact that his inherent(physical) *nimbus* is intersecting with the physical focus of *John's* observable item about *Anna's location* (i.e. the display of the digital frame). A system that would be able to approximate *Tom's* physical *focus* could easily apply constraints that would not allow him to become physically aware of *John's* observable items, protecting *John's* and *Anna's* privacy.

In other words, another important issue that is worth attention is the classification of intentionally/unintentionally sound versus inadvertent information sharing.

We consider that an entity x is inadvertently aware of an observable item u when x is physically aware of u, and u is one of the items that are generated through the system for x:

$$\_isIntentionallyAwareOf\_ : RealSituation \rightarrow (Entity \times ObservableItem)\bullet$$
$$\forall r : RealSituation;\ x : Entity;\ u; ObservableItem \bullet$$
$$x\ is IntentionallyAwareOf u\ (r)\ \Leftrightarrow\ (x, u) \in$$
$$\_isIntentionallyAwareOf\_(r)\ \Leftrightarrow$$
$$(x\ isPhysicallyAwareOf u\ (r)) \wedge (\exists\ y : Entity\ |\ u \in a^r_{xy})$$

Likewise one could classify that an entity x is inadvertently aware of an observable item u when x is physically aware of u, but u is not anyone of the observable items that are generated through the system for x.

In our example, given a well-defined function "*isPhysicallyAwareOf*", the system could detect that *Tom* is inadvertently aware of John's digital frame, and based on John's privacy boundaries, it could be turned of automatically.

6.5 Conclusion

This chapter presented a formal model of awareness that extends the focus–nimbus model, and especially the more abstract version of the model by Rodden (1996). Rodden uses focus and nimbus as the primitives of his model and discusses their relationship without detailing their content. In this chapter, we have described awareness in terms of entities, aspects, attributes and resources, making explicit the object of awareness, i.e. the relationship of the information an entity can potentially provide about itself to that actually observed by another entity. The extra level of detail enabled us to describe properties of awareness systems and communication patterns relevant for their social interaction with each other.

In this chapter we discussed social translucency and symmetry. Elsewhere (Metaxas and Markopoulos, 2007) we have discussed the notion of selective presentation of information about oneself for protecting one's privacy, e.g. by deception, blurring or hiding. The model lends precision to the definitions of these properties. For example, social translucency has been introduced in an eloquent essay by Erickson and Kellog (2000) and has been illustrated by numerous examples and with vignettes that give it a lot of face validity. Without an underlying model of awareness, social translucency and the other properties we discussed remain loosely defined, vague and difficult to compare to each other.

While we have paid attention to modelling information held and shared between the entities connected, we have also abstracted away from the propagation of awareness information as in Simone and Bandini (2002) and Fuchs et al. (1995). In this way we avoid focus on what are implementation concerns and focus on aspects more critical for the users of the system.

The precision used in the model is something we find useful for this analysis at a theoretical level. We do not suggest the use of formal models as a tool in the development of awareness systems. Nevertheless, as with the original focus–nimbus model, we expect that the model can provide the conceptual foundation for several applications. Indeed, we are now developing a platform for the creation of awareness systems that support the concepts of our model and the relations between them at an implementation level.

While we have spent some efforts at formality and precision, which are necessary for achieving a coherent and consistent model, we believe a lot can be gained by the informal use of abstract models. In discussing awareness systems it is interesting to illustrate how their components correspond to the elements of the model, i.e. how they can be seen as implementations of the model we presented. In doing this and in abstracting from the low-level interaction details, we can focus on how awareness is achieved and discuss awareness in terms important for characterizing the social interaction between communicating parties.

6.6 Glossary

Sets, relations, and functions

$\mathbb{P}\,X$	all subsets of X
$\mathbb{F}\,X$	all finite sets of X
$X \times Y$	Cartesian product of X and Y
$X \leftrightarrow Y$	binary relations between X and Y
$X \nrightarrow Y$	partial functions from X to Y
$X \rightarrow Y$	total functions from X to Y
$x \mapsto y$	a pair of elements, i.e. $x \mapsto y \mathrel{\hat{=}} (x, y)$
$x\,R\,y$	the relation $- R -$ holds between x, and y, i.e. $(x, y) \in -R-$
$-R-$	the relation R used as a set
$\langle a \rightsquigarrow x,\ b \rightsquigarrow y \dots\rangle$	a sequence of bindings used to describe an instance of the Scheme $[a : A\,;\, b : B....]$

Acknowledgments This work is supported by the European Community under the "Information Society Technologies" Programme, FP6, project ASTRA IST 29266.

References

Benford, S. and Fahlen, L. (1993). *A spatial model of interaction in large virtual environments*. In Proceedings of ECSCW'93, Milan, 1993, pp. 109–124.

Benford, S., Bowers, J., Fahlen, L., Mariani, J., and Rodden, T. (1995). *Supporting cooperative work in virtual environments*. The Computer Journal, 38(1).

Benford, S., Bullock, A., Cook, N., Harvey, P., Ingram, R., and Lee, O. (1993). *From rooms to cyberspace: models of interaction in large virtual computer spaces*. In Interacting with Computers, 5(2), pp. 217–237.

Blaine A.P., Karim A., Bashar N. (2005). *Keeping ubiquitous computing to yourself: A practical model for user control of privacy*. International Journal of Human–Computer Studies, 63(1–2), pp. 228–253.

Boyle, M. and Greenberg, S. (June 2005). *The language of privacy: Learning from video media space analysis and design*. ACM ToCHI, 12(2), pp. 328–370.

Dix, A., Sheridan, J., Reeves, S., Benford, S., and O'Malley, C. (2005). *Formalising performative interaction*. Proceedings of DSVIS'2005. (Newcastle, UK, 13–15 July 2005). Springer, LNCS 3941, pub. 2006. pp. 15–25.

Erickson, T. and Kellogg, W. (2000). *Social translucence: An approach to designing systems that Mesh with social processes*. In Transactions on Computer-Human Interaction. New York: ACM Press, 7(1), pp. 59–83.

Erickson, T., Halverson, C., Kellogg, W.A., Laff, M., and Wolf, T. (2002). *Social translucence: Designing social infrastructures that make collective activity visible*. Communications of the ACM, 45(4), (Apr. 2002), pp. 40–44.

Fuchs, L., Pankoke-Babatz, U., and Prinz, W. (1995). *Supporting cooperative awareness with local event mechanisms: The GroupDesk system*. In Proceedings of ECSCW'95, pp. 247–262.

Hong, J.I. and Landay, J.A. (2004). *An architecture for privacy- sensitive ubiquitous computing*. In Mobisys'04. Boston, MA., pp. 177–189.

Hudson, S.E., and Smith, I. (1996). *Techniques for addressing fundamental privacy and disruption tradeoffs in awareness support systems*. In Proceedings CSCW'96, ACM Press, pp. 248–257.

Iachello, G., Smith, I., Consolvo, S., Chen, M., and Abowd, G. (2005). *Developing privacy guidelines for social location disclosure applications and services*. Proceedings of the Symposium on Usable Privacy and Security (SOUPS 2005).

Metaxas, G. and Markopoulos P. (2007). *'Aware of what?' A formal model of awareness systems that extends the focus-nimbus model*. In the Proceedings of Engineering Interactive Systems 2007 EIS 2007, LNCS 4940, pp. 429–446.

Modica, S. and Rustichini, A. (1994). Awareness and Partitional Information Structures, Theory Dec. 37, pp. 107–124.

Rodden, T. (1996). *Populating the application: A model of awareness for cooperative applications*. In Proceedings of the ACM 1996 (CSCW'96), pp. 87–96.

Schmidt K. (2002). *The problem with 'Awareness' introductory remarks on 'Awareness in CSCW'* Computer Supported Collaborative Work, 11(34), pp. 285–298.

Simone, C. and Bandini, S. (2002). *Integrating awareness in cooperative applications through the reaction-diffusion metaphor*. Computer Supported Cooperative Work: The Journal of Collaborative Computing. Dordrecht: Kluwer Academic Publisher, 11(3–4), pp. 495–530.

Sohlenkamp, M., Fuchs, L., and Genau, A. (1997). *Awareness and cooperative work: the POLITeam approach*. Proceedings of HICSS 30, Jan. 9–11, Wailea, Hawaii, IEEE Computer Society Press, pp. 549–558.

Spivey, M. (1992). *The Z Notation*, 2nd ed., Hemel Hempstead, England: Prentice Hall International.

Chapter 7
Phatic Interactions: Being Aware and Feeling Connected

Frank Vetere, Jeremy Smith and Martin Gibbs

7.1 Introduction

Studies in awareness systems tend to focus on the informational aspects of interactions. This emphasis is warranted in systems that aim to support instrumental activities, such as collaboration and coordination (e.g. Begole and Tang, 2007) or messaging (e.g. Cheverst et al., 2007). Such activities usually involve the use of information, sometimes collected by sensors, about location, status and activity. However, when awareness systems have the core aim to maintain human relationships, the benefits may come not just from the sharing of awareness information per se, but more from the simple act of exchange.

These simple exchanges are very common and, although significant, are often unremarkable. For example, during an instant messaging exchange, an individual may comment about the changing weather; "The rain is clearing". This appears to be a trivial comment, but it may be alluding to something much more important. For example, George and Jan may have been arguing and Jan is attempting to re-kindle their relationship. The intentions and situational context of such exchanges are critical in understanding the significance of the interaction. Clearly words are not simply carriers of facts. This is no revelation for linguists and social theorists, but it is often neglected within the design practice of those involved in sociotechnical systems. Such systems are often regarded are conduits of fact-carrying information, rather than virtual places to gather and exchange tokens for social capital. In conveying information about status, location, activity, etc., the individual may in fact be attempting to establish rapport through increasing familiarity (Bickmore and Picard, 2005) to maintain an existing relationship (Fiske, 1990), maintain a mutual cognitive environment for the efficient conduct of communication (Zegarac and Clark, 1998), or keep communication channels open (Fiske, 1990). Information, then, is not only judged against traditional measures (e.g. accuracy, reliability, fidelity) but also by the degree to which it supports the maintenance of social relationships.

F. Vetere (✉)

Department of Information Systems, University of Melbourne, Australia
e-mail: f.vetere@unimelb.edu.au

P. Markopoulos et al. (eds.), *Awareness Systems*, Human-Computer Interaction Series,
DOI 10.1007/978-1-84882-477-5_7, © Springer-Verlag London Limited 2009

We argue that awareness systems are not best understood as systems for communicating information, and so should not be regarded as just another type of information system. The role and relative importance of information – as accurate representation of facts that are not self-evident or already known – requires some reassessed. For awareness systems, especially those in domestic and social settings, it is the motivation to build "ties of union" (Malinowski, 1949) over and above the exchange of information that often dominates the interaction. In these settings, where goals are less instrumental, where time is for consuming rather than for saving, and where qualities such as humour, play and rapport have a stronger role than accuracy, efficiency and effectiveness, we need new ways of thinking about awareness. In this chapter we argue that semiotic models of human communication can provide a theoretical bedrock that affords broader analysis of awareness. From this foundation we go on to discuss the concept of *phatic interactions* and explain how it can provide new ways to think about awareness and can generate interesting approaches to the design of awareness systems.

7.2 Human Communication

7.2.1 Approaching Communication

Human communication is an immensely broad multidisciplinary domain of study. It attempts to reconcile disparate concerns, ranging from effective presentation techniques to literary criticisms. Researchers of interactive systems have not typically drawn upon communication theories to any major extent; however, there are notable exceptions. These include the use of communication theories to model Human–Computer Interactions (Reynolds, 1998), Winograd's language/action approach (based on the work of Austin and Serle) to CSCW applications (Winograd, 1988), and the use of semiotic principles for multimedia (Purchase, 1999) and interface design (de Souza, 1993; Nadin, 1988; Pimenta and Faust, 1997; Prates et al., 1997).

There are two broad philosophical approaches to communication studies (Fiske, 1990). The first school adopts a process, or transmission, model. This model exploits the conduit metaphor (Reddy, 1993) of communication. The process approach is concerned with how senders encode messages, how receivers decode messages, and how transmitters use communication channels. It is concerned with the efficiency and accuracy of the transmission. According to this approach, a sender attempts to impart something or alter the behaviour or state of mind of the receiver. When this does not occur, or occurs at an unsatisfactory level, it is considered communication failure. The sender's intention, be it stated or unstated, conscious or unconscious, is paramount. The process approach has had a pervasive influence in communication research, and it underlies much of our everyday understanding of communication. Shannon and Weaver's (1949) model of communication and Lindsay and

Norman's (1972) model of Human Information Processing are typical of this approach.

The second approach is concerned with how messages (or texts or artefacts) interact with people in order to produce meaning. It is concerned with the production and exchange of meanings and the role of texts within a culture. The main method of study is semiotics (Nöth, 1990). Misunderstanding is not necessarily evidence of communication failure, as it is in the process school, but may result from a contextual (e.g. sociocultural) difference between the sender and receiver. The semiotic school sees the message as a collection of signs that are only meaningful through interactions with the receiver. The semiotic school shifts emphasis from the sender to the reader, and from the message to how it is read. Reading a message is considered just as important as producing the message. The semiotic approach places less emphasis on the process of communication and stresses the generation of meaning. Unlike process-model approaches, semiotic messages do not pass through linear steps or stages. One semiotic model of communication that is relevant to awareness systems is proposed by Roman Jakobson.

7.2.2 Jakobson's Model of Communication

Jakobson's (1981) model of communication bridges the gap between the process and the semiotic schools. Jakobson is concerned with both the meaning and the internal structure of the message. Jakobson's model (Fig. 7.1) consists of two layers; the "factors" that describes six elements of language use (shown in bold) and the "functions" that explain what humans do with the language when they use it (shown in italics).

The six factors build on the familiar process school model. An *addresser* sends a message to an *addressee*. The *message* has content and makes reference to a *context* that is something other than itself. The addresser and the addressee make *contact* via physical channels and psychological connections. A *code* provides the shared meaning by which the message is structured.

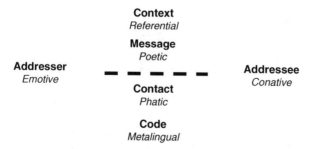

Fig. 7.1 Jakobson's model of communication. The factors are indicated in *bold* and the functions are in *italics*

Each factor has an associated function. The *emotive* function refers to the addresser's emotions, attitudes and intonations (including all the elements that make the message uniquely personal). The *referential* function refers to the role that communication plays in drawing addressee's attention to the shared environment or context. The *poetic* function refers the role that the form of the message plays in the communication, especially in artistic communication where messages are often formed with close attention to their aesthetic affect. The *metalingual* function refers to the use of language by which people confirm the use of the same codes. The *conative* function refers to the aspects of language that aim to create a certain response in or change the behaviour of the addressee.

Finally, the *phatic* function is concerned with the awareness that communication is possible, even when no message is exchanged. Within interaction design research, other communicative functions, especially those concerned with the informational content of the message, have been widely addressed. Even the conative function, which deals with the aspects of communication that aim to change behaviour, is at least partly addressed by captology (Fogg, 2002). However, the phatic function, which until recently has been mostly ignored in sociotechnical research, has a unique role in awareness systems.

7.2.3 The Phatic Function

The idea of phatic communication was first introduced by Malinowski (1949) as a "type of speech in which the ties of union are created by a mere exchange of words". It was later adopted by Jakobson (1981) into his model of communication. Phatic exchanges do not inform, and do not express any particular thought. They do, however, strengthen social bonds and establish the possibility of communication. Phatic communication occurs when, for example, comments are made about the weather ("nice day"), inquiries about health ("How do you do?") or affirmation of some obvious state of the world ("we won!"). The phatic function endeavours to keep channels of communication open and to maintain the physical and psychological contact between addresser and addressee. It is the use of communication signs for the maintenance of important social relationship confirming that communication is possible or in place.

The phatic function operates when messages are not intended to specifically provide information per se. The purpose of phatic interaction concerns the process of communication, not its substance. The purpose may be to prolong communication, to discontinue communication, to check whether the communication channel is operational ("Hello, can you hear me?"), to attract attention, or to confirm continued attention ("Are you listening?") (Jakobson, 1981). In saying "hello", there is no noise to overcome, no complex entropic message to send and the audience is generally receptive. In essence, there is no communication problem to solve. However, the phatic act of communication is not a waste of time or effort. Even though no new information is sent, the act ensures existing communication channels are kept open and usable. This message maintains and strengthens existing relationships in order to facilitate further communication. Participating in this form of phatic communication may not alter the relationship; however, not participating in it may tend to weaken it.

Jakobson suggests the phatic function is a primordial property of communication. The endeavour to start and sustain communication is the only communication function that is shared with animals (e.g. "talking" birds). It is also the first verbal function acquired by infants who are able to communicate before being able to send or receive informative messages (Jakobson, 1981). The act of phatic communication also occurs in other cultural and art forms. For instance, the refrain of many popular songs is highly predictable; yet by singing it our membership of a particular group or culture is reaffirmed.

Schneider (1988) took the notion of phatic communication further by coining two maxims of phatic discourse. Drawing on the literature and his own research, he proposed two maxims: *politesse* and *friendliness* to categorise phatic discourse into two groups; the first being concerned with avoiding offence, and the second being friendly. Politesse is the minimal observance of politeness in response to the pressures of social norms, and is associated with situations where strangers are forced into close proximity by circumstances such as elevators or bus stops and feel they have to fill a certain period of time (Schneider, 1988). The second maxim of phatic discourse, the friendliness maxim, is very different and is more concerned with establishing and maintaining social contact and according to Schneider (1988) is more evident in social gatherings among friends. Friendliness phatic discourse is orientated towards positive actions, such as saying something nice or creating "common ground" (Clark, 1996). As awareness systems seek more to maintain and strengthen relationships, (as opposed to avoiding unpleasant silences), the friendliness maxim of phatic communication is more relevant to awareness systems than the politesse maxim.

7.2.4 Phatic Awareness

For human–computer systems, the phatic function is relevant when the design is explicitly used to maintain user interest, to appeal, to entertain, to ensure users are sufficiently present in order to allow the technology to do its task (e.g. tolerating delays in online transactions by displaying a progress bar). Support for the phatic function does not explicitly concern the utility of the interaction, the usefulness of the information or the ease-of-use of the technology — though each will probably contribute. Support for the phatic function concerns the likelihood of a user maintaining an interaction with the technology, in spite of its usability and other instrumental purposes.

For human–human systems that are technologically mediated, of which awareness systems are a part, the phatic function sustains social connection and human awareness. In such sociotechnical systems, the phatic function is concerned with exchanges that serve to maintain channels for communication between people, that signal and acknowledge presence and awareness of another person, and that support and affirm relationships. They are primarily aimed at establishing and maintaining social bonds between individuals over and above the exchange of information and hence do not necessarily express any particular thought nor aim to exchange facts about the world. The efficient, accurate or effective transmission of information content is relatively unimportant. Rather, the focus is on maintaining the possibility for communication and signalling an awareness and readiness to communicate. This does not mean that phatic communications lack content or lack information. Rather, systems designed to support phatic communication are systems that do not necessarily require large amounts of information to convey significance and meaning.

Thus phatic communication in awareness systems can be thought of as communication that is low in information or data but is nevertheless high in significance and/or meaning. In everyday communication, this is often observed as "small-talk". Such exchanges are important and have been described as "crucial in holding a community or society together" (Fiske, 1990). Instead of conveying a message that is high in content, individuals may use light-weight exchanges for important social reasons. Regardless of the specific motivation, phatic awareness stresses the social motivation over and above the exchange of information.

Even though our discussions have focussed on the phatic function, it should be remembered that this is just one of six basic functions of communication (see Fig. 7.1). Exchanges across awareness technologies will naturally involve several of these six functions, working together to achieve a satisfying interaction. However, depending on the type of interaction, one or more of these functions are likely to dominate. Ironically, even though it is the phatic function that is most concerned with awareness, it is also least likely to be dominant in awareness systems. When designers focus on the informational aspects of awareness systems, other communicative functions, such as referential function (stressing representational issues) or the metalingual function (stressing appropriate use of language) are more likely to dominate their design. We argue that by addressing the phatic function directly and explicitly, we accentuate one of the core concerns of awareness systems. By asking "What phatic exchanges should the awareness system support?" instead of "What information should the awareness system convey?", we reorient our design focus to seriously consider the degree to which awareness systems contribute to a feeling of ongoing human connectedness.

7.3 Phatic Technologies

Technologies, whose dominant communicative function is phatic, can be broadly described as phatic technologies (Gibbs et al., 2005). We illustrate a few here.

Phatic interactions are often observed in technologies that are generally regarded as having instrumental purposes. For example, the frequent but short use of SMS, e-mail, telephone calls and letters often has a dominant phatic function (Licoppe and Smoreda, 2005). Couples use short phatic exchanges as tokens of affection, letting the other partner become aware they are in their thoughts. Licoppe and Smoreda (2005) propose that the management of social contacts occurs in two distinct modes. The first mode is a replacement for face-to-face contact or existing older technologies. The second mode is "connected presence as another form of mediated sociability", and refers to a particular use of technology as an additional socialisation tool. It is the repetition, rather than the content of these short messages that maintain the relationship tie and form a sense of connectedness. This mode of socialisation primarily consists of frequent short calls and messages, where the discursive content of the communication is less important than the act itself, and hence phatic in nature. This is in accordance with Thurlow (2003) who also found that a large component of SMS communication takes place on a phatic level, mainly through the use of humour.

Phatic interactions are observed in instant messaging (IM) conversations. Nardi, Whittaker and Bradner (2000) discuss the use of IM technologies to sustain social connections, negotiate availability and retain workplace context over a distance, beyond simple information exchange. They introduce the concept of *outeraction* as a set of communicative processes that socially extend to others, thereby enabling information exchange. These outeractions may occur through "awareness moments" that produce a feeling of connection with others. Nardi et al. suggest that IM can be used to create a sense of awareness of another, and that this awareness forms a social bond without exchanging any explicit information. Clearly, outeraction is the phatic function in another name. However where outeraction is considered outside the information exchange process, phatic interactions are included within Jacobon's communication model.

Phatic interactions are also discussed in research products and experimental technologies. For example, TACT (Hoffman et al., 2007), a low resolution tactile portable device, is used to connect physically distant couples. Individuals touch a square array of lights, creating patterns that occur on the others device in a synchronised manner. Serendipity is nurtured through a visual call through the device to make the other partner aware of their wish to communicate. Another experimental phatic technology is an interactive pillow (Schiphorst, et al., 2007) that is sensor-enhanced with a tactile surface and mediates physical communication over a distance. This pillow was developed "for establishing communication rather than precise communication acts". Other examples include the "Virtual Intimate Object" (Kaye, 2006) a single bit device between separated couples and the "Whereabouts Clock" (Brown et al., 2007) that supports familial reassurance and connectedness by providing approximate location details.

Researchers have used a phatic analysis to examine the role of new technologies in the support and encouragement of communication (Calvi, 2005). Calvi proposes a framework for sociability in online communities and stresses the important of phatic exchanges in her analysis. She argues that traditional measures such as usability, usefulness and utility need to be placed aside, or at least complimented, with measures of the social connectedness. Such measures were conducted in the ASTRA project (Romero et al., 2007), which was predominantly motivated to highlight "the personal effort" one makes as a token of affection or as a way to bond with another. ASTRA, an awareness system for connecting households and mobile family members, was evaluated against notions of connectedness though field tests and the Affective Benefits and Costs of communication questionnaire (ABC-Q). The researchers demonstrated measurable impact on the notion of connectedness, while controlling for potential costs of this communication, such as those relating to privacy.

7.4 Exploring Phatic Interactions

Our understanding of the importance of phatic interaction in human relationships has emerged from three studies we have conducted over recent years. These studies have explored various manifestations of phatic interactions and have sought to generate a richer understanding of how this concept can be mobilised with in the design of interactive systems. We present a very brief overview of each here.

7.4.1 Mediating Intimacy

The value placed on ongoing connectedness was observed in a study of personal and intimate communication between six established couples (Vetere et al., 2005). In this study, cultural probes, interviews and focus groups were used to document expressions of intimacy over 7 weeks.

Simple expressions of affection within notes, e-mails and mobile text messages were acknowledged as being important. For example, signing off an e-mail with the phrase "love you lots", a phrase that carries weight because it is used regularly, reciprocally, and though perhaps not exclusively it is insufficiently commonplace to be experienced as "our". Such exchanges may have seemed trivial to outsiders, but they were laden with emotional significance for the participants.

We found significance and meaning in what may appear, too easily to an outsider, as "idle chatter". The regular and frequent exchanges, that have little if any informational value, were key to the strength of the ongoing social binding. This finding shares much with the earlier work examining the retention and later reviewing of SMS messages that carry little instrumental value (Taylor and Harper, 2003).

The facility to chat idly, to "waste" time with someone you care for was a valuable expression of the care they shared for each other. The substance of their communication was not always important. It was the reassurance that they were connected, that a channel of communication was available to them, and that this somehow strengthened and nurtured the relationship. These phatic exchanges were genuinely valued.

Individuals clearly desired technologies that support and maintain social connections with friends, family and partners (Gibbs et al., 2005). A prototype, *SynchroMate*, was created to mediating intimacy through serendipitous exchanges within strong-tie relationships. The prototype was comprised of a small disc-shaped object that fitted in the palm of the hand and allowed communication between two individuals through short iconic "doodles". Serendipity was assisted through the fact that each individual knew the other was composing a "doodle" before the message arrived. We created another prototype, *Hug-over-a-distance* (Mueller et al., 2005) that attempted to mediate physical phatic exchanges through an inflatable vest, operating wirelessly over a computer network.

7.4.2 Intergenerational Play

In our second study we set out to understand how grandparents and their grandchildren interacted with each other and to uncover design opportunities for technologies to better support this intergenerational relationships. Our motivation was the growing perception that traditional notions of the family in general and grand-parenting in particular, are under strain. Families are becoming more nomadic, for reasons of both employment and lifestyle choice. Regardless of whether ageing occurs in the home or within supportive facilities, the extended family is increasingly distributed. In particular grandparents are becoming isolated from their children and grandchildren. Furthermore, the home is becoming a space in which work and family life coalesce. Changes to the nature of work, e.g. 24/7 availability, casualisation of workforce, significant travel to workplace, is blurring the distinction between work and family and squeezing opportunities for traditional family activities. This is particularly confronting for grandparents, who partly as a result of their children's complex work arrangements, have limited access to grandchildren. Opportunities to socialise and play with their grandchildren are severely curtailed because they are separated by distance (e.g. due to work commitments) or time (e.g. due to shift work routines).

Furthermore, sociable connection has been shown to improve the wellness of aged people helping them to remain living in their own homes thus reducing the cost to the residential care system. Other research (Evjemo et al., 2004) also shows that simple telephony is not sufficient support for the grandparent–grandchild relationship. A more personal, richer context, such as play activity, is required.

We studied the grand-parenting relationship through observing grandparents playing with their grandchildren in semi-formal play group settings. We also engaged six extended families over a period of 2 months in our research with the use of cultural probes. We found that grandchildren and grandparents engaged in a variety of playful activities with each other. These play activities did not necessarily involve engagement in formal rule-based game play. Rather, they were opportunistic and episodic and the participants often turned the various resources within the current environment to play activities. It involves a range of activities including teasing, storytelling, the exchanging of significant objects, as well as games. While playful, these intergenerational engagements also intertwined with a range of themes including imparting family history and culture, storytelling, sharing food, and creating familial notions of magic and science. However, in making sense of these activities, it became clear to us that much of what was occurring was relationship building, and what most valued was the interaction itself, over and above any information or exchange that occurred as part of the interaction. It was not uncommon for grandparents, and grandchildren (abettedly to a lesser extent), to express the enjoyment they received from having opportunities to engage with the other.

As result of our work with these families we developed the "Collage" (Ashkansy et al., 2007) a touch-screen based display that carries photographs and text messages created by a mobile device and sent via a GSM network to the display. The photographs and images are shared and public displayed within the home of both the grandparents and the grandchildren, thus creating a communal archive of familial interactions. The items are available to grandparent and grandchildren simultaneously for viewing and manipulating. When one person moves an item, the same item moves on the other screen. This had the effect of attracting the attention of others and facilitated playful interaction, as each party attempt to either arrange the items before the other, or disrupt the other's arrangement. We found that family members often engaged in this kind of simultaneous engagement with the images on the system. Some claimed to be able to know or guess who the other person playing with the system was based on their activities and responses.

7.4.3 Online Social Networks

As online social networks become widespread it is important to consider their particular and unique affordances, so that we can understand them in their current form and determine how we can better design for them in the future. Existing social models and theories, many of which are only empirically present within traditional "offline" communications, are now being challenged and shaped by the way individuals are interacting online through these new technologies.

In our third study, aiming to examine the presence and nature of online phatic communication, the activities of eight online social network users of Facebook (www.facebook.com) were closely examined for 2 weeks through a diary study, online observation and a follow-up interview. It was proposed that since phatic communication is a key component of traditional offline socialisation, these phatic exchanges should also be present within the social online social networking communities.

We found that phatic communication did indeed occur throughout the online social network and that it was manifested in various communicative methods. These methods included, comments, virtual gifts, personal messages and in particular *the poke*. The poke is an inbuilt function that was created by Facebook "without any specific purpose" (Facebook, 2007). When an individual pokes another person, a small unobtrusive note appears in the receivers profile indicating that they have been "poked" by the sender (Fig. 7.2). No other contextual information (date, time, motivation, etc.) is displayed apart from the sender's name. It was found that the poke was used in four ways: (i) to attract attention for interaction (i.e. making the recipient aware they wished to communicate); (ii) to initiate a new conversation; (iii) to play or have a game with someone; and (iv) to acknowledge someone's presence

Fig. 7.2 Facebook pokes

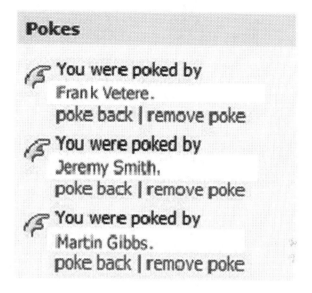

(e.g. "saying hi"). These four uses of the poke provide examples that illustrate an awareness system with "aesthetic communication appliances that exchange minimal or abstract information or convey simple meanings" (Markopoulos et al., 2007).

Online phatic communication broadly (not just via the poke) also seemed to fall into four distinct categories: (i) maintaining an existing relationship; (ii) initiating a conversation; (iii) developing a new relationship; and (iv) being polite and observing social norms.

Phatic communication was expressed in participant comments such as "keeping friends on the radar" and "keeping in touch". Participants explained even the small act of sending these short silly messages, jokes and comments was enough to let a friend be aware they were thinking of them, even though in the words of one participant "it's never really anything insightful". It seems that these short communicative phatic messages served a purpose in keeping individuals in touch and making others aware that they were in their thoughts.

Another use of phatic communication was to develop a new relationship with a new acquaintance. This was often to "break the ice" and determine if the other person was willing to engage in a more in-depth conversation or to see if they had a common interest. It also had the effect of letting the other individual become aware that the other was interested in communicating further with them. This was most often through "a poke" but also through the use of comments.

Similarly phatic communication was used to initiate conversation. The data showed that people would communicate phatically to make the recipient aware they were interested in initiating a conversation. For example, one participant explained "sometimes [a poke is] to see what response I get, so if they poke back then I might start talking to them" while another said "You might ask silly stuff like how you doing, but then after a while you don't want to ask them that question so you want to go on to more important stuff".

Much of the online communication was based around the motivation of letting another individual become aware to the fact that they were thinking about them in one way or another. In the words of one social network member "Sometimes it's something completely random and it doesn't make sense, but you just want to say 'hi and I'm here and I'm thinking about you' ". And in the words of another "I like knowing that he is thinking of me and it's nice that he is making an effort and it makes me smile. So when I get [a message] I know he's thinking of me and it makes me happy". These two examples reflect the phatic function in that they seek not to convey information but more to sustain a relationship. They enable individuals to communicate with another with the intent of making them aware that they are thinking of them. In this sense the online social networking service is being used as an awareness system to develop and sustain social relationships through the vehicle of phatic communication.

7.5 Conclusion

In this chapter we have reported on insights gained from our research examining how people use information and communication technologies as part of their domestic, non-working lives. We have found that people want and use technologies to help them maintain social connections with friends, family and partners. This has lead to the insight that a potentially fruitful, and certainly interesting, approach to the design of awareness technologies is one that emphasises, and prioritises, social connection over the transmission and reception of informational content. In to order describe and evoke an alternative way of thinking about the design of awareness systems that highlights this social connection aspect of technology, we have drawn on the notion of the phatic function of language. The phatic function in language is concerned with maintaining communicative connection. Phatic communication involves communication where the phatic function is dominant, which is not say that other linguistic functions are not also present in phatic communication. Phatic technologies are technologies that are designed and/or used to support phatic communication. The concept of phatic technology places social connection at the forefront of design and suggests a fresh and fertile emphasis for the design of awareness systems.

We believe awareness systems should not be regarded as just another type of information systems. Approaching awareness systems as information systems suggests these systems are conduits for the transfer of information. It places emphasis on the effective, efficient and accuracy of information transmission. Rather, our work has shown that these are not appropriate for understanding technology use by families, friends and partners. We argue that by placing explicit emphasis on the phatic function, we are able to highlight the core concern of awareness systems. By asking "What phatic exchanges should the awareness system support?" instead of "What information should the awareness system convey?" we reorient our design focus to seriously consider the extent to which awareness systems contribute to feelings of awareness and ongoing connectedness between people.

This chapter presents the idea of phatic communication as a way of reorientation discussions of awareness systems towards concerns about the maintenance of social connection and rapport rather than the exchange of information. Support for phatic acts ensure existing communication channels are kept open and usable and serve to maintain and strengthen existing relationships in order to facilitate further communication. A phatic analysis does not offer a prescriptive solution to the problems of awareness systems. However, it does provide a suggestive concept that allows designer, researcher and though-leaders to talk and think about these systems differently within the broader framework of a semiotic communication model.

References

Ashkansy, S., Benda, P. and Vetere, F. (2007). Happy coincidences in designing for social connectedness and play through opportunistic image capture. *In Proceedings of Designing User Experience (DUX) 2007.*

Begole J. and Tang J.C. (2007). Incorporating human and machine interpretation of unavailability and rhythm awareness into the design of collaborative applications. *Human–Computer Interaction*, 22, 7–45.

Bickmore, T. W., and Picard, R. W. (2005). Establishing and maintaining long-term human-computer relationships. *ACM Transactions on Computer-Human Interaction (TOCHI)*, 12(2), 293–327.

Brown, B., Taylor, A., Izadi, S., Sellen, A., Kaye, J., and Eardley, R. (2007). Locating Family Values: A Field Trial of the Whereabouts Clock. Ubicomp 2007: 354–371.

Calvi, L. (2005). Sociability with ubiquitous technologies: A view on phatic interactions. *In proceedings of SIGCHI.nl conference*, ACM Press.

Cheverst, K., Dix, A., Fitton, D., and Graham, C. (2007). Exploring awareness related messaging through two situated-display-based systems. *Human–Computer Interaction*, 22, 173–220.

Clark, H. H. (1996). Using Language. Cambridge, UK, Cambridge University Press.

de Souza, C. S. (1993). The semiotic engineering of user interface languages. International Journal of Man-Machine Studies, 39, 753–773.

Evjemo, B., Svendsen, G. B., Rinde, E., and Johnsen, J. A. K. (2004). Supporting the distributed family: The need for a conversational context. *Proceedings of the Third Nordic Conference on Human-Computer Interaction*, 309–312.

Facebook (2007). http://www.Facebook.com/help.php?page=20 accessed on 13 September, 2007.

Fogg, B. J. (2002). Persuasive Technology: Using Computers to Change What We Think and Do. San Fransisco, CA, Morgan Kaufmann.

Fiske, J. (1990). *Introduction to Communication Studies. New York, Routledge.*

Gibbs, M., Vetere, F., Howard, S. and Bunyan, M. (2005). SynchroMate: A phatic technology for mediating intimacy. *DUX: Conference on Designing for User eXperience*, San Francisco, CA (3–5 Nov).

Hoffmann, C., Jumpertz, S., and Marquet, B. (2007). On nurturing strong-tie distant relationships: from theory to prototype. *Conference on Human Factors in Computing Systems*. CHI '07, 2411–2416.

Jakobson, R. (1981). *Poetry of Grammar and Grammar of Poetry* (Vol. 3). The Hague, Mouton.

Kaye, J. (2006). I just clicked to say I love you: rich evaluations of minimal communication. *In CHI '06 Extended Abstracts on Human Factors in Computing Systems* (Montréal, Québec, Canada, April 22–27, 2006). CHI '06. ACM, New York, 363–368.

Licoppe, C. and Smoreda, Z. (2005). Are social networks technologically embedded? How networks are changing today with changes in communication technology. *Social Networks*, 27(4), 317–335.

Lindsay, P. H., and Norman, D. A. (1972). *Human Information Processing.* New York, Academic Press.

Malinowski, B. (1949). The problem of meaning in primitive languages. In C. K. Ogden and I. A. Richards (Eds.), *The Meaning of Meaning* (Tenth ed., pp. 296–336). London, Routledge and Kegan Paul Ltd (First ed., 1923).

Markopoulos, P., de Ruyter, B., and Mackay, W. (2007). Introduction to this special issue on awareness systems design. *Human–Computer Interaction*, 22, 1–6.

Mueller, F., Vetere, F., Gibbs, M., Kjeldskov, J., Pedell, S., and Howard, S. (2005). Hug Over a Distance CHI 2005 (Interactive Poster), Portland, Oregon USA (2–7 April), 1673–1676.

Nadin, M. (1988). Interface design: A semiotic paradigm. *Semiotica,* 69(3/4), 269–302.

Nardi, B. A., Whittaker, S., and Bradner, E. (2000). Interaction and outeraction: Instant messaging in action. *Proceedings of the 2000 ACM Conference on Computer Supported Cooperative Work*, 79–88.

Nöth, W. (1990). *Handbook of Semiotics.* Bloomingon and Indianapolis, Indiana University Press.

Oulasvirta, A., Petit, R., and Raento, M. (2007). Interpreting and acting on mobile awareness cues. *Human–Computer Interaction*, 22, 97–135.

Pimenta, M. S., and Faust, R. (1997). Eliciting interactive systems requirements in a language-centred user-designer collaboration: A semiotic approach. *ACM SIGCHI Bulletin*, 29(1), 61–65.

Prates, R. O., de Souza, C. S., and Garcia, A. C. B. (1997). A semiotic framework for multi-user interfaces. *ACM SIGCHI Bulletin*, 29(2), 28–39.

Purchase, H. (1999). A semiotic definition of multimedia communication. *Semiotica,* 123(3/4), 247–259.

Reddy, M. J. (1993). The conduit metaphor: A case of frame conflict in our language about language. In A. Ortony (Ed.), *Metaphor and Thought* (second ed., pp. 164–201). Cambridge, Cambridge University Press.

Reynolds, C. (1998). As we may communicate. *SIGCHI Bulletin*, 30(3), 40–44.

Romero, N., Markopoulos, P., Baren, J., Ruyter, B., IJsselsteijn, W., and Farshchian, B. (2007). Connecting the family with awareness systems. Personal Ubiquitous Computer, 11(4), (Apr. 2007), 299–312.

Schiphorst, T., Nack, F., KauwATjoe, M., de Bakker, S., Stock, Aroyo, L., Rosillio, A. P., Schut, H., and Jaffe, N. (2007). PillowTalk: Can we afford intimacy?. *In Proceedings of the 1st International Conference on Tangible and Embedded Interaction* (Baton Rouge, Louisiana, February 15–17, 2007). TEI '07. ACM, New York, 23–30.

Schneider, K. P. (1988). *Small Talk:* Analysing Phatic Discourse. Hitzeroth.

Shannon, C. E., and Weaver, W. (1949). *The Mathematical Theory of Communication*. Champaign, IL, University of Illinois Press.

Taylor, A. and Harper, R. (2003). The gift of the gab?: A design oriented sociology of young people's use of mobiles. *Computer Supported Cooperative Work*, 12(3), 267–296.

Thurlow, C. (2003). Generation Txt? The sociolinguistics of young people's text-messaging. *Discourse Analysis Online*, 1(1).

Vetere, F., Gibbs, M., Kjeldskov, J., Howard, S., Mueller, F., Pedell, S., Mecoles, K., and Bunyan, M. (2005). Mediating intimacy: Designing technologies to support strong-tie relationships. *CHI 2005*, Portland, Oregon USA (2–7 April).

Winograd, T. (1988). A language/action perspective on the design of cooperative work. *Human Computer Interaction*, 3, 3–30.

Zegarac, V., and Clark, B. (1998). Phatic Interpretations and phatic communication. *Linguistics,* 35, 24.

Chapter 8
Privacy Considerations in Awareness Systems: Designing with Privacy in Mind

Sameer Patil and Alfred Kobsa

8.1 Introduction

The earlier chapters of this book presented a conceptual understanding of awareness (Eggen and van Mensvoort, 2009, in this volume; Metaxas and Markopoulos, 2009, in this volume). A historical account (Rittenbruch and McEwan, 2009, in this volume) as well as descriptions of various implementations (see Part III) illustrate how various systems have attempted to foster greater awareness.

A common challenge faced by all awareness systems is the tension with an individual's desire for privacy (Hudson and Smith, 1996). Interaction between awareness and privacy is not limited to awareness systems but is a characteristic of everyday life. As Schwartz (1968) noted, "We are led to relinquish our private information and activities by the expediencies and reciprocities routinely called for in daily life. We all know, for example, that in order to employ others as resources it is necessary to reveal to them something of ourselves."

In the case of awareness systems, the benefits for the recipients of information typically come at the cost of the risks of reduced privacy for the individuals whose information is disseminated. Moreover, these systems require users to extend their existing practices regarding awareness and privacy, from the familiar physical domain to the newer digital domain. Situations that lack familiarity are known to be problematic for privacy management and may lead to privacy violations (Romero and Markopoulos, 2009, in this volume).

Privacy management in the digital domain poses precisely such difficulties. Certain characteristics of the digital domain differ substantially from the physical world, namely, high-speed transmission, potential persistence, and enhanced computation of information. The digital domain may also result in disembodiment (Health and Luff, 1991) (e.g., one may be represented only by a screen name). Disembodiment thwarts the ability to exploit the rich cues that are used readily in face-to-face interactions (e.g., posture, expressions, intonation). In addition,

S. Patil (✉)
Department of Informatics, University of California, Irvine CA, USA
e-mail: patil@uci.edu

P. Markopoulos et al. (eds.), *Awareness Systems*, Human-Computer Interaction Series, DOI 10.1007/978-1-84882-477-5_8, © Springer-Verlag London Limited 2009

dissociation of interaction (Bellotti, 1997) could occur when only the results of people's actions are shared while the actions themselves are not visible (e.g., a Wiki page with no version history available). Owing to these differences, the transformation of expectations and behaviors from the physical to the digital world is not always effective or even possible.

As a result, designers of awareness systems face the significant challenge of simultaneously satisfying users' awareness as well as privacy needs. Insufficient attention to either of these needs has the potential to undermine the usage of the system. When the users are unable to achieve appropriate levels of awareness and privacy without great effort, they may not exploit the system's potential fully. For instance, Lee et al. (1997) found that when privacy was desired, users of their Portholes video system preferred to turn their cameras off since fiddling with other privacy options, such as blurring the video, was too cumbersome. Similarly, Herbsleb et al. (2002) found it difficult to attain substantial usage of their chat system because its default settings were too private. The system imposed significant initial setup efforts on its users before it could provide any awareness benefits. Likewise, in our own research we found that users who were forced to use instant messaging (IM) due to organizational requirements often resorted to circumvention tactics. For instance, some set their status to "away" or "busy" even when they were not, or conversely, some changed their preferences so as to appear online even when they were away from their desks (Patil and Kobsa, 2004, 2005a). Such underuse or circumvention results in suboptimal use of awareness systems.

Focusing on awareness without paying sufficient attention to privacy aspects may also evoke strong user backlash. A recent example that involves the social networking site Facebook (http://www.facebook.com) is a poignant reminder. Facebook introduced a new awareness feature that automatically presented to each user an aggregation of every single activity of their friends. Tens of thousands of users were outraged because they felt that such automatic broadcast was a great violation of their privacy. The revolt ranged from online petitions and protest groups to threats of a boycott (Calore, 2006). This episode underscores that user opposition due to privacy concerns can translate into minimal use or even the abandonment of the system. If this happens, organizations stand to lose their investments in deployed awareness applications. Moreover, the companies that design and build these systems, as well as their customers, face the prospect of longer-term damage to their trust and credibility in the users' eyes (Adams, 1999; Adams and Sasse, 1999).

Thus, it is important for awareness systems to respect the privacy concerns of their users. This chapter analyzes theoretical and empirical work in order to aid designers in building privacy-sensitive awareness systems.

8.2 Privacy

The notion of privacy has recently received enormous attention both in the scientific literature and in the popular press. Figure 8.1 shows the number of non-fiction books

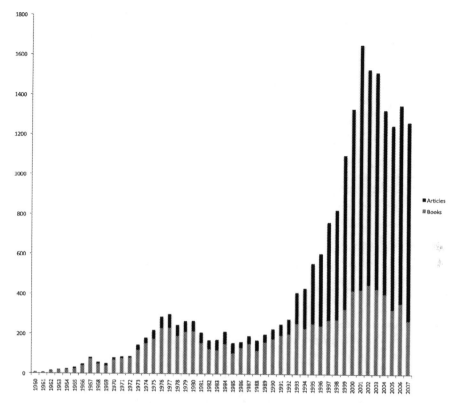

Fig. 8.1 WorldCat non-fiction books and articles with "privacy" in the title

and articles with "privacy" in their titles that have been published since 1960[1]. Of the about 21,000 publications, nearly two-thirds have been published in the past 10 years alone. This dramatic rise in privacy research productivity from the mid-1990s onward coincides with the advent of the World Wide Web and e-Commerce. The small peak in the 1970s corresponds with the global introduction of data processing into businesses and government administration. (Both of these changes engendered widespread privacy concerns, and led to privacy legislation in some parts of the world.) To some extent, the rapid increase of research articles as opposed to books mirrors the scientific disciplines in which privacy research takes place. While privacy research originated in the fields of law, psychology, sociology, communications, political science, architecture and urban design, it has since expanded into the computer and information sciences, organization and management research, economics, and the health sciences.

---

[1] The data were obtained through a search in WorldCat, the world's largest library network with 1.2 billion items from the catalogues of more than 10,000 libraries worldwide. WorldCat removes duplicates from the retrieval results.

The concept of privacy is so intricate that there is no universal definition of it. The difficulty of defining privacy stems from its highly situated (Suchman, 1987) and context-dependent nature. Even in the same situation, different individuals may have differing opinions and expectations regarding what privacy means to them (for example, Westin (1991) classified individuals as privacy fundamentalists, pragmatists, or unconcerned, based upon their stated privacy preferences). This context dependency and variability between individuals make dealing with privacy a difficult task. To quote Lederer et al. (2004):

> One possible reason why designing privacy-sensitive systems is so difficult is that, by refusing to render its meaning plain and knowable, privacy simply lives up to its name. Rather than exposing an unambiguous public representation for all to see and comprehend, it cloaks itself behind an assortment of meanings, presenting different interpretations to different people.

There are three main perspectives from which the notions of privacy are commonly described and analyzed. We discuss these in the following subsections (also see Table 8.1 for a summary).

Normative Perspective. Analyzed philosophically, privacy is an ethical concept (Negley, 1966; Johnson, 1985; Mason, 1986). Privacy is viewed as a "right" of individuals, and, thus, as a matter of "freedom". For example, Warren and Brandeis (1890) characterized privacy as "the freedom to be left alone." From this perspective, privacy is a civil liberty that needs to be protected through legal and political means. Traditionally, the focus of privacy protection has been on laws, contracts, and policies aimed at protecting the individual from large entities such as corporations and governments (Lessig, 1999). Increasingly, however, legislation is being extended to protect one's privacy from other individuals (for instance, laws against hacking, online stalking, and online voyeurism).

Social Perspective. From the social perspective, privacy has psychological and cultural roots (Westin, 1967; Schwartz, 1968). Privacy is "socially constructed" based on the behavior and the interactions of individuals as they

Table 8.1 Three perspectives regarding the concept of privacy

Perspective	Concept of privacy	Enacted by	Consequences of privacy violation
Normative	Right or freedom	Laws, contracts, policies	Civil and/or criminal penalties
Social	Socially constructed	Individual and collective everyday social action	Potential embarrassment or breakdown in relationship(s), etc.
Technical	Control over data and information	Automated and/or manual access control	Identity theft, unauthorized access, illegal use of information

conduct their day-to-day affairs. For instance, in Goffman's (1959) analysis "the expressive component of social life has been treated as a source of impressions given to or taken by others," where expression "has been treated in terms of the communicative role it plays during social interaction." This manifests itself in Rachels' (1975) claim that "privacy is necessary if we are to maintain the variety of social relationships with other people that we want to have." Thus, managing privacy allows us to manage social relationships. Altman (1975) described the process of privacy management as a "dialectic and dynamic boundary regulation process," conditioned by the expectations and experiences of the parties involved, and under continuous negotiation and refinement. Given the differences in norms, expectations, experiences, behaviors, and laws across cultures, it is no surprise that privacy manifests itself differently in different cultures (Westin, 1967; Milberg et al., 1995). Viewed socially, the notion of privacy evolves as external changes bring about changes in expectations and behavior, or as technology introduces new forms or means of interaction.

Technical Perspective. The technical perspective views privacy in terms of the functional characteristics of digital systems. Discussions from this perspective tend to investigate how ethical and social considerations could be operationalized. Privacy is thus treated as the desire for selective and adequate control over data and information, both incoming and outgoing. For example, Stone et al. (1983) describe privacy as the "ability of the individual to personally control information about oneself, whereas Samarajiva (1997) extends it to the "control of outflow of information that may be of strategic or aesthetic value to the person and control of inflow of information including initiation of contact." The issues under consideration include the capture, storage, ownership, usage, and access of personal data. For instance, the code of Fair Information Practices was developed from this perspective (US Department of Health Education and Welfare, 1973).

To summarize, the social perspective focuses on what practices relate to privacy, while the normative discussions look at whether a particular behavior is ethically (or legally) justified. The technical discourse is concerned with how the ethical and social understandings can be represented formally and implemented practically in an operational system. The three perspectives are not mutually exclusive but interdependent. Privacy laws may be enacted based on technical or social considerations, while social interactions may be altered due to changing laws and technology.

Having laid out the foundational understandings of privacy, we now proceed to discussing how awareness and privacy interact with each other.

8.3 Relationship Between Awareness and Privacy

Given that the concepts of awareness and privacy are both related to disclosure, it should not be surprising that the two interact with each other. This interaction between awareness and privacy is not new. Westin (1967) describes it as a balancing act:

Privacy is neither a self-sufficient state nor an end in itself, even for the hermit and the recluse. It is basically an instrument for achieving individual goals of self-realization. As such, it is only part of the individual's complex and shifting system of social needs, part of the way he adjusts his emotional mechanisms to the barrage of personal and social stimuli that he encounters in daily life. Individuals have needs for disclosure and companionship every bit as important as their needs for privacy. As ancient and modern philosophers agree, man is a social animal, a gregarious being whose need for affiliation marks his conduct in every society. Thus, at one hour a person may want lively companionship and group affili-ation; at another moment, the intimacy of family or close friends; at another the anonymity of the city street or the movie; at still other times, to be totally alone and unobserved. To be left in privacy when one wants companionship is as uncomfortable as the inability to have privacy when one craves it.

... All individuals are constantly engaged in an attempt to find sufficient privacy to serve their general social roles as well as their individual needs of the moment. Either too much or too little privacy can create imbalances which seriously jeopardize the individual's well-being.

In the context of awareness systems, the equilibrium corresponds to a reconcilia-tion of the benefits of awareness for improving effectiveness and efficiency, and the potential risks of reduced privacy.

In the physical setting of everyday life, individuals utilize the spatial and architec-tural features (e.g., a door) of the environment (Schwartz, 1968), the biological and cognitive features of humans (e.g., limitations of human memory; Westin, 1967), and the shared understanding of norms (Westin, 1967) to meet their awareness and privacy needs. Thus, situations in which one's familiarity with the aspects of day-to-day affairs breaks down (e.g., moving to a foreign country) have been observed to be problematic for privacy management.

Privacy is managed based on one's familiarity with these features and one's understanding of norms, acquired through daily life experiences. This, of course, does not imply that privacy violations could never occur in familiar everyday set-tings. In fact, privacy violations due to accidental disclosure are not uncommon (Schwartz, 1968). When a violation of privacy does occur, and is detected, indi-viduals typically engage in social negotiation until a commonly agreed upon (or comfortable) state of privacy is reached for everyone involved. For instance, Westin (1967) describes social practices such as covering one's face, averting others' eyes, or facing the wall. As Palen and Dourish (2003) point out, "[p]rivacy is understood to be under continuous negotiation and management, with the boundary that distin-guishes privacy and publicity refined according to circumstance."

Recent technological developments, such as those in Computer-Supported Col-laborative Work (CSCW), have introduced the digital domain as an additional arena in which awareness and privacy need to be reconciled (Agre and Rotenberg, 1997). The next subsection describes how the digital domain, due to its relative novelty and its unique characteristics, poses new challenges in this regard.

8.3.1 Digital Domain

We noted earlier that situations in which familiarity breaks down are problematic for privacy management, and could lead to privacy violations. Awareness systems create exactly such problems since they require users to extend their privacy management practices from the familiar physical domain to the relatively new digital domain.

Additionally, certain characteristics that distinguish the digital domain from the physical world are important from a privacy standpoint. Salient among these are:

Transmission. The ease, speed, and low cost with which data are transmitted in the digital domain are major reasons why it is attractive for fostering awareness. However, these advantages come at the expense of increased risk for unauthorized access through technical means such as hacking and network sniffing, and higher potential damages that may result from such attacks.

Persistence. Due to the availability of practically infinite storage capacity, the digital domain increases the temporal dimension of data indefinitely. In contrast, information about the vast majority of routine activities in the non-digital world could be trusted to be merely ephemeral. The digital "trails" of one's activities undermine "plausible deniability" (Nardi et al., 2000) of facts and actions that one may not want to admit to. It also separates information from the context in which it was generated (Dix, 1990). Moreover, the storage of personally identifiable information introduces legal issues of accountability, liability, etc. For example, a Chinese journalist was convicted of leaking state secrets based on records of his Internet activities provided by Yahoo! Inc. (Kahn, 2005).

Computing Power. Data in the digital form are amenable to the kinds of analysis that are almost impossible in a non-digital format. Additionally, computing power makes it possible to automate such analyses. For example, techniques like data mining, pattern detection, social network analysis, event notification, and visualization can be used for inference, prediction, profiling, surveillance, and much more.

Disembodiment and Dissociation. As mentioned earlier, interactions between individuals mediated by the digital domain can suffer from disembodiment (Heath and Luff, 1991) and dissociation (Bellotti, 1997). Disembodiment and dissociation hinder one's ability to present oneself as effectively to others as in a face-to-face setting and result in a breakdown of social and behavioral norms and practices. For example, Goffman (1959) describes how people present different appropriate "faces" in real life quite seamlessly. Yet, a direct operationalization of this metaphor in a digital system turned out to be unsuccessful (Lederer et al., 2003c). Moreover, disembodiment could force individuals to be explicit about certain information that is otherwise intuitive or implicit (Bellotti, 1997).

As a result of these distinctions, the digital domain can inhibit behaviors that may be fluid and seamless in the social realm. Thus, privacy runs into what Ackerman (2000) characterizes as the social–technical gap, i.e., "the divide between what we know we must support socially and what we can support technically." On the other hand, characteristics of the digital domain enable actions that may otherwise be impossible or prohibitively difficult to achieve socially. Lessig (1999) sums this up rather nicely:

> In the 1790s the technology was humans; now it is machines. Then the technology noticed only what was different; now it notices any transaction. Then the default was that search-able records were not collected; now the default is that all monitoring produces searchable records. These differences add up.

8.4 Relevant Research

Over the past few years, the importance of taking action on privacy issues engen-dered by awareness systems has gained attention. Research that tackles this problem falls along three major themes: users studies of specific awareness systems, design principles and guidelines derived from theoretical considerations, and privacy-enhancing technical solutions. We discuss each of these below.

8.4.1 User Studies

Initial findings related to privacy were primarily noted "on the side" in studies aimed at evaluating experiences with the awareness aspects of systems. Dourish (1993) characterizes privacy controls along a "social–technical continuum." On the social end of this continuum, social pressures and norms are relied upon to prevent system abuse, while on its technical end, technology prevents attempted misuse. Social con-trols are likely to work well within small and relatively well-knit communities only (Dourish, 1993; Ackerman et al., 1997). Even in such environments with high levels of interpersonal trust, social controls may result in very strong protective behaviors such as turning the system off or altering one's work habits (Mantei et al., 1991). In contrast, technical privacy protections raise the acceptance and adoption of a sys-tem by virtue of the fact that it increases users' trust that the system would protect privacy (Dourish, 1993). Later studies confirm that trust in a system is an important implicit factor in privacy assessments (Adams, 1999; Adams and Sasse, 1999; Patil and Lai, 2005).

Palen (1999) found that socio-technical mechanisms controlled privacy even in highly open network calendaring environments. Users managed privacy partly via technical access control, partly via the norm of reciprocity[2], partly via practices such as cryptic entries, omissions, defensive scheduling, and partly via social anonymity within the larger organizational context. Lee et al. (1997) suggest that the mere existence of mechanisms to address privacy needs is not enough; these mechanisms need to be lightweight. In other words, users desire mechanisms that allow them "to increase or decrease privacy, to inform other users of their new privacy state, and to provide immediate feedback of the change," in a way that "facilitates the tight

---

[2] Palen (1999) found that individuals with unusually restrictive, or unusually liberal, calendar access settings often had immediate colleagues with similar access configurations.

coupling between the means to change privacy and the means to obtain feedback that privacy is attained" (Lee et al., 1997). As Herbsleb et al. (2002) discovered, the lack of lightweight, low-burden privacy management mechanisms increased setup time. Moreover, Grinter and Palen (2002) illustrate (albeit with teenagers) that users adapt system capabilities to their own ends. Teens in their study made enterprising use of access permissions, profiles, status messages, and screen names to manage privacy. Additionally, Nardi et al. (2000) noticed that plausible deniability of physical presence was used frequently by IM users as a means for privacy management.

Recently, studies of awareness systems have started targeting privacy as the primary object of investigation. These studies have unveiled a number of factors that affect users privacy judgments. These include users relationship with the information recipient, the purpose and usage of requested information, the context, and the sensitivity of the content (Adams, 1999; Adams and Sasse, 1999; Lederer et al., 2003b; Patil and Kobsa, 2004; Consolvo et al., 2005; Olson et al., 2005). Lederer et al. (2003c) also showed that a-priori manual configuration of privacy preferences is better than automatic strategies, especially for information that users deem important.

Generic privacy attitudes and behaviors could also come into consideration in awareness systems. Therefore, it is instructive to look at a few privacy studies conducted in other contexts, such as e-Commerce. For instance, as mentioned above, Westin (1991) classified individuals into three cluster, privacy fundamentalists, pragmatists, and unconcerned. This distinction may also apply to privacy concerns in the context of awareness systems. Milberg et al. (1995) and Bellman et al. (2004) reported that privacy concern varies by country. At the same time, they mentioned that "secondary use" and "improper access" rank as the top two concerns across most nationalities. Cranor et al. (1999) listed anonymity and information sensitivity as important privacy-related factors for Internet users. Finally, Fox (2000) showed that users are often ignorant of the basic concepts underlying their digital domain activities and do not typically utilize the tools available for privacy protection.

8.4.2 Theories, Principles, and Guidelines

Privacy is recognized to be a nuanced and situated concept that escapes universal definition. The rich body of literature on privacy in the social sciences is testimony to its intricate connections with the broader social context (Dourish and Anderson, 2005). Owing to this complexity, technology designers have found it difficult to translate the privacy-related findings of the various user studies into concrete system design guidance. Researchers have tried to address this problem by framing the theoretical insights into privacy in forms that are more amenable to system designers. For instance, Boyle and Greenberg (2005) describe a vocabulary of privacy that permits designers to discuss privacy in an unambiguous manner. To suggest ways of thinking about privacy in socio-technical environments, Palen and Dourish (2003) outline a model of privacy that is based on the theory developed by social psychologist Irwin Altman (1975, 1977). It characterizes privacy as a process that regulates the boundaries of disclosure, identity, and temporality. This process is both dynamic (i.e., shaped by personal and collective experiences and expectations) and dialectic (i.e., under continuous boundary negotiation).

Researchers in the technology trenches distilled this general guidance on privacy into specific design principles and guidelines in order to enable better privacy management. Bellotti and Sellen (1993) propose a design framework based on feedback and control regarding information capture, construction, accessibility, and purpose. In essence, feedback mechanisms aim at providing users with information that helps them make privacy judgments, and control mechanisms empower them to take appropriate actions to manage privacy. In addition, Bellotti and Sellen (1993) provide 11 criteria for evaluating design solutions: trustworthiness, appropriate timing, perceptibility, unobtrusiveness, minimal intrusiveness, fail-safety, flexibility, low effort, meaningfulness, learnability, and low cost. Langheinrich (2001) draws upon Fair Information Practices (U.S. Department of Health Education and Welfare, 1973) in proposing that privacy-sensitive systems ought to notify the user appropriately, seek consent, provide choice, allow anonymity or pseudonymity, limit scope with proximity as well as locality, ensure adequate security, and implement appropriate information access. Iachello and Abowd (2005) add the principle of proportionality, "any application, system tool, or process should balance its utility with the rights to privacy of the involved individuals." In contrast, Lederer et al. (2004) outline five pitfalls: obscuring potential information flow, obscuring actual information flow, emphasizing configuration over action, lacking coarse-grained control, and inhibiting existing practice. Hong et al. (2004) further develop privacy risk models to analyze how well a system meets such principles or avoids the pitfalls. These risk models are a set of information sharing questions pertaining to the social and organizational context in which the system is situated, and the technology which is used to implement the system. Finally, to incorporate user perceptions, Adams and Sasse (1999) provide a privacy model based on the interacting concerns of information sensitivity, information receiver, and information usage.

8.4.3 Design Techniques

Incorporating the principles and guidelines into working systems continues to pose challenges for designers. Improving privacy management requires addressing multiple conflicting concerns simultaneously (Hudson and Smith, 1996), such as privacy vs. awareness, risks vs. benefits, control vs. overhead, and feedback vs. disruption. To complicate matters further, an acceptable solution to these trade-offs is highly dependent on the user as well as the context.

Several techniques have been proposed and explored for the implementation of such principles. These include the following:

- encryption (Diffie and Hellman, 1979);
- access control via preferences, policies, and roles (Edwards, 1996; Wickramasuriya et al., 2004);

- mechanisms to reduce the burden of preference specification such as lightweight interfaces (Lau et al., 1999), or grouping and templates (Olson et al., 2005; Patil and Lai, 2005);
- automatic or manual control of the granularity of disclosed information (Dourish and Bly, 1992; Lee et al., 1997; Palen, 1999; Consolvo et al., 2005);
- feedback via visualization (Gross et al., 2003), sound (Gaver et al., 1992), intelligent agents (Ackerman and Cranor, 1999), and contextual disclosure (Kobsa and Teltzrow, 2005);
- distortion of disclosed information (Boyle et al., 2000);
- support for anonymity (or pseudonymity) (Appelt, 1999);
- inference of appropriate awareness disclosure based on modeling (Begole et al., 2002).

Describing these techniques is beyond the scope of this chapter. The reader is referred to the cited works for details. In practice, no technique alone can satisfy all requirements and constraints. A typical awareness system would likely combine multiple privacy management approaches.

8.5 Positioning Awareness Systems

In order to choose the most relevant insights from prior work, we propose that a given awareness system be positioned in a space of three independent dimensions (see Fig. 8.2). We discuss these dimensions below.

8.5.1 Nature of Awareness Mechanisms

By their very nature, all awareness systems deal with capturing, storing, analyzing, disseminating, and/or displaying awareness information in some form. However,

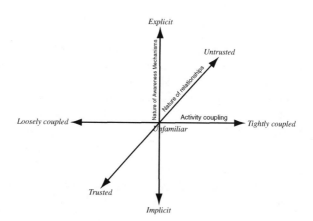

Fig. 8.2 Positioning awareness systems along privacy-relevant dimensions

there is a distinction to be made between systems that are built specifically for awareness purposes (e.g., Dourish and Bly, 1992; Appelt, 1999; Cadiz et al., 2000), and those that provide awareness implicitly by virtue of their use (Bellotti, 1996). For instance, the primary purpose of e-mail is to communicate the content of a message. Yet, by virtue of the timestamp, IP address, server names, and other header information, e-mail reveals additional information implicitly[3]. Thus, awareness systems can be characterized to lie along a continuum ranging from explicit to implicit awareness functionalities (see Fig. 8.2). For example, a system like instant messaging (IM) that provides communication mechanisms along with awareness (Nardi et al., 2000) could be positioned somewhere in the upper half.

Systems that deal with awareness information explicitly try to expose the benefits of awareness in a direct manner. As a result, they may also draw direct attention to the associated privacy issues. In contrast, when awareness is implicit or secondary to the function of a system, the primary attention of the user is on other aspects of the task carried out with the system (e.g., the user is much more likely to focus on the contents of an e-mail message rather than on the IP address from which the e-mail is being sent). Consequently, the privacy aspects remain invisible in such cases (Bellotti, 1996).

8.5.2 Activity Coupling

The user activities that awareness systems support lie along a continuum from loosely to tightly coupled (Olson and Teasley, 1996; Olson and Olson, 2000; Neale et al., 2004). For instance, the work of software developers working on two separate modules of the same program may be less tightly coupled than that of a developer and a tester working on the same module.

As Olson and Olson (2000) explained, tightly coupled activities typically require "frequent, complex communication among the group members, with short feedback loops and multiple streams of information." Therefore, when the work is tightly coupled, the awareness among collaborators of each other's activities is automatically improved as a side effect of more frequent and prolonged interactions. Given the shared (and often synchronous) focus on the same activity, awareness functionalities in these circumstances are mainly concerned with ensuring that the parties involved are aware of the focus and understanding of others (Dourish and Bly, 1992). On the other hand, when collaborative activities are loosely coupled, awareness is impoverished. In such cases, a variety of factors may affect awareness unfavorably. These include less frequent and asynchronous interaction between collaborators, less shared context, and the involvement of the collaborators in multiple simultaneous tasks and projects (Olson and Teasley, 1996; Pinelle and Gutwin,

---

[3] It is also important to note that researchers have been exploring systems that could be built on top of other systems to make implicit aspects of awareness more explicit (Fisher and Dourish, 2004; Froehlich and Dourish, 2004).

2003). Thus, the looser the coupling, the greater is the need for external support by awareness systems.

Similarly, privacy expectations in loosely coupled distributed activities can be expected to be greater than in the case of tightly coupled work. This may be caused by the same factors that engender impoverishment of awareness (i.e., less frequent and asynchronous interaction, less shared context, multi-tasking, etc.) Additionally, if the work is geographically distributed across different countries, different privacy attitudes and laws of different nationalities may need to be considered (Milberg et al., 1995; Bellman et al., 2004). In contrast, tightly coupled activities involve more focused (and often synchronous as well as colocated) interactions that allow one to monitor privacy closely.

8.5.3 *Nature of Relationships*

The nature of the relationships among various users of an awareness system forms the third dimension. These relationships can range from trusted and familiar (e.g., a colleague with whom one shares an office) to unfamiliar (but known, e.g., an employee in a different branch of the organization) to untrusted (e.g., a stranger who might read one's blog). The degree of familiarity with the individual with whom one interacts is important in shaping attitudes and behaviors. For instance, greater familiarity reduces the importance of static awareness information (Danis, 2000) because collaborators are likely to already know it or could ask for it directly (Lederer et al., 2003a). Lederer et al. (2003a) point out differences in privacy considerations when dealing with familiar as opposed to unfamiliar parties. While a great deal of research and legislation focuses on privacy protection from organizations and unknown people (e.g., governments, corporations, hackers, stalkers, marketers), the other side of the continuum has received lesser attention. Yet, this side – ranging from the trusted to the unfamiliar – is of greater importance when dealing with awareness systems.

8.6 Designing with Privacy in Mind

Designers can utilize the above work of others to tackle privacy issues in their own awareness systems. Yet, we believe that in order to improve the privacy sensitivity of awareness systems, a focus on privacy is needed right from the earliest conceptual phases of system development. As the term "awareness system" implies, the purpose of the system is to foster awareness. Hence, system designers have so far focused on providing awareness while privacy has only received secondary attention. We urge designers to treat privacy on an equal footing with awareness when building systems. The above-mentioned principle of proportionality (Iachello and Abowd, 2005) is a step in that direction. However, it deals mainly with a cost–benefit analysis of awareness and privacy to decide whether or not a system should be built at all. We take one step further and advocate that even after using this principle at the beginning of the design process to decide that an awareness system should be built, designers must continue to consider privacy at every subsequent step in the design cycle.

Two examples from our own research – one positive and one negative – illustrate why it is essential to keep privacy in mind at all stages of system development.

8.6.1 Workplace Awareness Application

We designed an awareness application called mySpace to support the collaborative work of knowledge workers who were located in the same building (Patil and Lai, 2005). The mySpace application is a browser-based interactive visualization of a user's physical workplace that provides dynamically updated information about people, places, and equipment. Recognizing that mySpace would lead to privacy concerns, we sought to empower the users to manage their privacy according to their own preferences. Our initial intuition (based on the experience with the organizational culture) was to allow users to specify one set of preferences for their immediate team, and another set for all others. Additionally, we wanted to make the operation of the system transparent for users all individual pieces of information to which mySpace had access. Yet, we feared that doing so would scare users into selecting more privacy-protective preferences, thereby undermining the awareness benefits.

Instead of proceeding to build the system as envisioned, we conducted a user study of an early prototype. To our surprise, we found that our intuition was not aligned with the users' desires. Users wanted to manage privacy at a finer grain by specifying preferences differently for multiple groups of contacts. Also, increased system transparency promoted trust in the system and seemed to reassure users that the system would honor their preferences. This resulted in increased awareness being provided to close, trusted groups of contacts. Studying how users deal with privacy aspects at the prototype stage allowed mySpace to be sensitive to the practices of its target population. It also spared the costs and difficulties of correcting privacy management mechanisms retroactively after deployment.

8.6.2 Instant Messaging Privacy Plugin

Our experiences gained from attempting to improve the privacy management in existing IM systems illustrate the weaknesses of the retrofitting approach. Based on several interviews and a survey of IM users (Patil and Kobsa, 2004, 2005b), we identified several avenues for improving IM privacy management. However, not having access to the servers of the commercial IM networks made the task of implementing our improvements challenging. We thus packaged our privacy management extensions as a plugin for the open source multiple-IM client GAIM (now Pidgin). The plugin is called PRISM (for PRivacy-Sensitive Messaging). The architecture of the enhanced IM system is shown in Fig. 8.3.

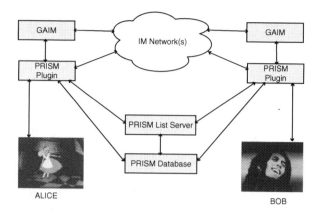

Fig. 8.3 System architecture for PRISM

As can be seen, it was necessary to maintain a separate server and a database in order to provide some of the privacy extensions. One enhancement that PRISM provides is to allow users to view the IM activities of others at a group level in order to facilitate a comparison with one's own activities. The database logs various IM actions of interest, such as when users log in, log off, or change their availability status. Since PRISM does not have access to the servers of the IM networks, such logging is essential for generating the visualizations of the activities. Ideally, the servers of the IM network would need to be extended to incorporate these functions.

More significantly, we often ran into limitations imposed by the specifics of the IM protocol(s). For instance, we aimed at empowering users to specify their privacy preferences differently for different groups of contacts. However, the IM protocol(s) lacked sufficient nuance to achieve this for all settings. For example, we were able to allow users to specify a different status for different groups but unable to provide a way to specify that only certain groups could view the length of time they were idle. Such deficiencies reflect inadequate attention to user privacy practices during the development of the IM protocol(s).

Finally, we aimed at building privacy enhancements that were generic such that they did not rely on the specifics of any single IM system. However, ensuring such common cross-IM experience is a challenging task because IM systems differ in the details of their protocols and of their server implementations. For example, some IM systems allow one to broadcast the length of the user's idle time, others do not; some IM systems allow multiple simultaneous logins, others do not. We found that catering to the lowest common denominator limits the extent to which the IM client can add, or improve upon, privacy management features. The only remaining option is to treat each protocol differently. This approach may confuse users because the privacy management experience and expectations are no longer uniform.

Overall, PRISM serves as a cautionary example and illustrates the challenges and difficulties that designers are likely to face when attempting to retrofit privacy enhancements rather than designing systems with privacy in mind right from the outset.

8.7 Conclusion

Handling user privacy appropriately is a significant challenge for awareness systems. Inadequate attention to privacy issues may be a barrier to their success. To build awareness systems that are sensitive to the privacy needs of their users, designers ought to pay attention to privacy at every stage of system design. In order to be effective in this task, designers need to be aware of the various ways in which privacy can be understood. They should also pay attention to the special characteristics of the digital domain that may affect privacy management. Fortunately, designers can draw upon a substantial body of insights regarding privacy in the research literature. Appropriate techniques need to be chosen based on a careful evaluation of the context of the work activities and the social relationships within which the awareness system under consideration operates. Designing awareness systems with privacy in mind has the potential to enhance privacy sensitivity significantly, and to empower users to satisfy their awareness as well as privacy needs optimally.

Acknowledgments   Some of the research described was supported by NSF grants nos. 0205724 and 0808783. We wish to acknowledge our collaborator Jennifer Lai. We also wish to thank the subjects who participated in our study on mySpace. Finally, we are grateful to Mihir Mahajan for commenting on various drafts of this chapter.

References

Ackerman, M.S.: The Intellectual Challenge of CSCW: The Gap Between Social Requirements and Technical Feasibility. Human–Computer Interaction **15**, 179–203 (2000)

Ackerman, M.S., Cranor, L.: Privacy Critics: UI Components to Safeguard Users' Privacy. In: CHI '99: CHI '99 Extended Abstracts on Human Factors in Computing Systems, pp. 258–259. ACM, New York, NY (1999). DOI http://doi.acm.org/10.1145/632716.632875

Ackerman, M.S., Starr, B., Hindus, D., Mainwaring, S.D.: Hanging on the 'Wire: A Field Study of an Audio-only Media Space. ACM Trans. Computer–Human Interaction **4**(1), 39–66 (1997). DOI http://doi.acm.org/10.1145/244754.244756

Adams, A.: Users' Perception of Privacy in Multimedia Communication. In: CHI '99: CHI '99 Extended Abstracts on Human Factors in Computing Systems, pp. 53–54. ACM, New York, NY (1999). DOI http://doi.acm.org/10.1145/632716.632752

Adams, A., Sasse, M.A.: Privacy Issues in Ubiquitous Multimedia Environments: Wake Sleeping Dogs, or Let Them Lie? In: Seventh IFIP Conference on Human–Computer Interaction INTERACT'99, pp. 214–221 (1999)

Agre, P.E., Rotenberg, M. (eds.): Technology and Privacy: The New Landscape. MIT Press, Cambridge, MA (1997)

Altman, I.: The Environment and Social Behavior: Privacy, Personal Space, Territory, Crowding. Brooks/Cole, Monterey, CA (1975)

Altman, I.: Privacy Regulation: Culturally Universal or Culturally Specific? Journal of Social Issues **3**(3), 66–84 (1977)

Appelt, W.: WWW Based Collaboration with the BSCW System. In: SOFSEM '99: Proceedings of the 26th Conference on Current Trends in Theory and Practice of Informatics on Theory and Practice of Informatics, pp. 66–78. Springer-Verlag, London, UK (1999)

Begole, J.B., Tang, J.C., Smith, R.B., Yankelovich, N.: Work Rhythms: Analyzing Visualizations of Awareness Histories of Distributed Groups. In: CSCW '02: Proceedings of the 2002 ACM Conference on Computer Supported Cooperative Work, pp. 334–343. ACM, New York, NY (2002). DOI http://doi.acm.org/10.1145/587078.587125

Bellman, S., Johnson, E., Kobrin, S., Lohse, G.: International Differences in Information Privacy Concerns: A Global Survey of Consumers. The Information Society **20**(5),
313–324 (2004)

Bellotti, V.: What You Don't Know Can Hurt You: Privacy in Collaborative Computing. In: HCI
'96: Proceedings of HCI on People and Computers XI, pp. 241–261. Springer-Verlag, London,
UK (1996)

Bellotti, V.: Design for Privacy in Multimedia Computing and Communications Environments. In:
P.E. Agre, M. Rotenberg (eds.) Technology and Privacy: The New Landscape, pp. 63–98. MIT
Press, Cambridge, MA (1997)

Bellotti, V., Sellen, A.: Design for Privacy in Ubiquitous Computing Environments. In: ECSCW
'93: Proceedings of the Third European Conference on Computer–Supported Cooperative
Work, pp. 77–92. Kluwer Academic Publishers, Norwell, MA (1993)

Boyle, M., Edwards, C., Greenberg, S.: The Effects of Filtered Video on Awareness
and Privacy. In: CSCW '00: Proceedings of the 2000 ACM Conference on Computer Supported Cooperative Work, pp. 1–10. ACM, New York, NY (2000). DOI
http://doi.acm.org/10.1145/358916.358935

Boyle, M., Greenberg, S.: The Language of Privacy: Learning from Video Media Space Analysis and Design. ACM Trans. Computer–Human Interaction **12**(2), 328–370 (2005). DOI
http://doi.acm.org/10.1145/1067860.1067868

Cadiz, J.J., Gupta, A., Grudin, J.: Using Web Annotations for Asynchronous Collaboration
Around Documents. In: CSCW '00: Proceedings of the 2000 ACM Conference on Computer Supported Cooperative Work, pp. 309–318. ACM, New York, NY (2000). DOI http://
doi.acm.org/10.1145/358916.359002

Calore, M.: Privacy Fears Shock Facebook. Wired News (2006). DOI http://www.wired.com/
science/ discoveries/news/2006/09/71739

Consolvo, S., Smith, I.E., Matthews, T., LaMarca, A., Tabert, J., Powledge, P.: Location Disclosure
to Social Relations: Why, When, & What People Want to Share. In: CHI '05: Proceedings of the
SIGCHI Conference on Human Factors in Computing Systems, pp. 81–90. ACM, New York,
NY (2005). DOI http://doi.acm.org/10.1145/1054972.1054985

Cranor, L.F., Reagle, J., Ackerman, M.S.: Beyond Concern: Understanding Net Users' Attitudes
About Online Privacy. AT&T Labs-Research Technical Report **TR 99.4.1** (1999)

Danis, C.M.: Extending the Concept of Awareness to Include Static and Dynamic
Person Information. SIGGROUP Bulletin **21**(3), 59–62 (2000). DOI http://doi.acm.org/
10.1145/605647.605657

Diffie, W., Hellman, M.E.: Privacy and Authentication: An Introduction to Cryptography. Proceedings of the IEEE **67**(3), 397–427 (March 1979)

Dix, A.J.: Information Processing, Context and Privacy. In: INTERACT '90: Proceedings of the
IFIP TC13 Third International Conference on Human–Computer Interaction, pp. 15–20. North-
Holland Publishing Co., Amsterdam, The Netherlands (1990)

Dourish, P.: Culture and Control in a Media Space. In: ECSCW '93: Proceedings of the Third European Conference on Computer-Supported Cooperative Work, pp. 125–137. Kluwer Academic
Publishers, Norwell, MA (1993)

Dourish, P., Anderson, K.: Privacy, Security... and Risk and Danger and Secrecy and Trust and
Identity and Morality and Power: Understanding Collective Information Practices. Institute
for Software Research (ISR) Technical Report, University of California, Irvine **UCI-ISR-05-1**
(2005)

Dourish, P., Bly, S.: Portholes: Supporting Awareness in a Distributed Work Group. In:
CHI '92: Proceedings of the SIGCHI Conference on Human Factors in Computing
Systems, pp. 541–547. ACM, New York, NY (1992). DOI http://doi.acm.org/10.1145/
142750.142982

Edwards, W.K.: Policies and Roles in Collaborative Applications. In: CSCW '96: Proceedings of
the 1996 ACM Conference on Computer Supported Cooperative Work, pp. 11–20. ACM, New
York, NY, USA (1996). DOI http://doi.acm.org/10.1145/240080.240175

Eggen, B., van Mensvoort, K.: Making Sense of What is Going Around. In: P. Markopoulos, B. de Ruyter, W. Mackay (eds.) Awareness Systems: Advances in Theory, Methodology and Design. Springer-Verlag, pp. xxx–xxx (2009)

Fisher, D., Dourish, P.: Social and Temporal Structures in Everyday Collaboration. In: CHI '04: Proceedings of the SIGCHI Conference on Human Factors in Computing Systems, pp. 551–558. ACM, New York, NY (2004). DOI http://doi.acm.org/10.1145/985692.985762

Fox, S.: Trust and Privacy Online: Why Americans Want to Rewrite the Rules. Pew Internet & American Life Project (2000)

Froehlich, J., Dourish, P.: Unifying Artifacts and Activities in a Visual Tool for Distributed Software Development Teams. In: ICSE '04: Proceedings of the 26th International Conference on Software Engineering, pp. 387–396. IEEE Computer Society, Washington, DC (2004)

Gaver, W., Moran, T., MacLean, A., Lüvstrand, L., Dourish, P., Carter, K., Buxton, W.: Realizing a Video Environment: EuroPARC's RAVE System. In: CHI '92: Proceedings of the SIGCHI Conference on Human Factors in Computing Systems, pp. 27–35. ACM, New York, NY (1992). DOI http://doi.acm.org/10.1145/142750.142754

Goffman, E.: The Presentation of Self in Everyday Life. Doubleday, Garden City, New York (1959)

Grinter, R.E., Palen, L.: Instant Messaging in Teen Life. In: CSCW '02: Proceedings of the 2002 ACM Conference on Computer Supported Cooperative Work, pp. 21–30. ACM, New York, NY (2002). DOI http://doi.acm.org/10.1145/587078.587082

Gross, T., Wirsam, W., Graether, W.: AwarenessMaps: Visualizing Awareness in Shared Workspaces. In: CHI '03: CHI '03 Extended Abstracts on Human Factors in Computing Systems, pp. 784–785. ACM, New York, NY (2003). DOI http://doi.acm.org/10.1145/765891.765990

Heath, C., Luff, P.: Disembodied Conduct: Communication Through Video in a Multi-Media Office Environment. In: CHI '91: Proceedings of the SIGCHI Conference on Human Factors in Computing Systems, pp. 99–103. ACM, New York, NY (1991). DOI http://doi.acm.org/10.1145/108844.108859

Herbsleb, J.D., Atkins, D.L., Boyer, D.G., Handel, M., Finholt, T.A.: Introducing Instant Messaging and Chat in the Workplace. In: CHI '02: Proceedings of the SIGCHI Conference on Human Factors in Computing Systems, pp. 171–178. ACM, New York, NY (2002). DOI http://doi.acm.org/10.1145/503376.503408

Hong, J.I., Ng, J.D., Lederer, S., Landay, J.A.: Privacy Risk Models for Designing Privacy-Sensitive Ubiquitous Computing Systems. In: DIS '04: Proceedings of the 2004 Conference on Designing Interactive Systems, pp. 91–100. ACM Press, New York, NY (2004). DOI http://doi.acm.org/10.1145/1013115.1013129

Hudson, S.E., Smith, I.: Techniques for Addressing Fundamental Privacy and Disruption Tradeoffs in Awareness Support Systems. In: CSCW '96: Proceedings of the 1996 ACM Conference on Computer Supported Cooperative Work, pp. 248–257. ACM, New York, NY (1996). DOI http://doi.acm.org/10.1145/240080.240295

Iachello, G., Abowd, G.D.: Privacy and Proportionality: Adapting LegalEvaluation Techniques to Inform Design in Ubiquitous Computing. In: CHI '05: Proceedings of the SIGCHI Conference on Human Factorsin Computing Systems, pp. 91–100. ACM Press, New York, NY (2005). DOI http://doi.acm.org/10.1145/1054972.1054986

Johnson, D.G.: Computers and Privacy. In: Computer Ethics. Prentice-Hall, Englewood Cliffs, NJ (1985)

Kahn, J.: Yahoo helped Chinese to Prosecute Journalist. International Herald Tribune (2005)

Kobsa, A., Teltzrow, M.: Contextualized Communication of Privacy Practices andPersonalization Benefits: Impacts on Users' Data Sharing and Purchase Behavior. In: D. Martin, A. Serjantov (eds.) Privacy Enhancing Technologies: Fourth International Workshop, PET 2004, LNCS 3424, pp. 329–343. Springer (2005). DOI http://dx.doi.org/10.1007/11423409˙21

Langheinrich, M.: Privacy by Design–Principles of Privacy-Aware Ubiquitous Systems. In: Ubi-Comp '01: Proceedings of the 3rd International Conference on Ubiquitous Computing, pp. 273–291. Springer-Verlag, London, UK (2001)

Lau, T., Etzioni, O., Weld, D.S.: Privacy Interfaces for Information Management. Communications of the ACM **42**(10), 88–94 (1999). DOI http://doi.acm.org/10.1145/317665.317680

Lederer, S., Hong, J., Dey, A.K., Landay, J.: Personal Privacy Through Understanding and Action: Five Pitfalls for Designers. Personal Ubiquitous Computing **8**(6), 440–454 (2004). DOI http://dx.doi.org/10.1007/s00779-004-0304-9

Lederer, S., Mankoff, J., Dey, A.K.: Towards a Deconstruction of the Privacy Space. In: Ubicomp 2003 Workshop on Ubicomp Communities: Privacy as Boundary Negotiation (2003a)

Lederer, S., Mankoff, J., Dey, A.K.: Who Wants to Know What When? Privacy Preference Determinants in Ubiquitous Computing. In: CHI '03: CHI '03 Extended Abstracts on Human Factors in Computing Systems, pp. 724–725. ACM, New York, NY (2003b). DOI http://doi.acm.org/10.1145/765891.765952

Lederer, S., Mankoff, J., Dey, A.K., Beckmann, C.: Managing Personal Information Disclosure in Ubiquitous Computing Environments. Technical Report, Computer Science Division, University of California, Berkeley **UCB-CSD-03-1257** (2003c)

Lee, A., Girgensohn, A., Schlueter, K.: NYNEX Portholes: Initial User Reactions and Redesign Implications. In: GROUP '97: Proceedings of the International ACM SIGGROUP Conference on Supporting Group Work, pp. 385–394. ACM, New York, NY (1997). DOI http://doi.acm.org/10.1145/266838.267359

Lessig, L.: Code and Other Laws of Cyberspace. Basic Books, Inc., New York, NY (1999)

Mantei, M.M., Baecker, R.M., Sellen, A.J., Buxton, W.A.S., Milligan, T., Wellman, B.: Experiences in the Use of a Media Space. In: CHI '91: Proceedings of the SIGCHI Conference on Human Factors in Computing Systems, pp. 203–208. ACM, New York, NY (1991). DOI http://doi.acm.org/10.1145/108844.108888

Mason, R.O.: Four Ethical Issues of the Information Age. MIS Quarterly **10**(1), 5–12 (1986)

Metaxas, G., Markopoulos, P.: Abstractions of Awareness. In: P. Markopoulos, B. de Ruyter, W. Mackay (eds.) Awareness Systems: Advances in Theory, Methodology and Design. Springer-Verlag, Berlin, pp. xxx–xxx (2009)

Milberg, S.J., Burke, S.J., Smith, H.J., Kallman, E.A.: Values, Personal Information Privacy, and Regulatory Approaches. Communications of the ACM **38**(12), 65–74 (1995). DOI http://doi.acm.org/10.1145/219663.219683

Nardi, B.A., Whittaker, S., Bradner, E.: Interaction and Outeraction: Instant Messaging in Action. In: CSCW '00: Proceedings of the 2000 ACM Conference on Computer Supported Cooperative Work, pp. 79–88. ACM, New York, NY (2000). DOI http://doi.acm.org/10.1145/358916.358975

Neale, D.C., Carroll, J.M., Rosson, M.B.: Evaluating Computer-Supported Cooperative Work: Models and Frameworks. In: CSCW '04: Proceedings of the 2004 ACM Conference on Computer Supported Cooperative Work, pp. 112–121. ACM, New York, NY (2004). DOI http://doi.acm.org/10.1145/1031607.1031626

Negley, G.: Philosophical Views on the Value of Privacy. Law and Contemporary Problems **31**(2), 319–325 (1966)

Olson, G.M., Olson, J.S.: Distance Matters. Human–Computer Interaction **15**(2/3), 139–178 (2000)

Olson, J.S., Grudin, J., Horvitz, E.: A Study of Preferences for Sharing and Privacy. In: CHI '05: CHI '05 Extended Abstracts on Human Factors in Computing Systems, pp. 1985–1988. ACM, New York, NY (2005). DOI http://doi.acm.org/10.1145/1056808.1057073

Olson, J.S., Teasley, S.: Groupware in the Wild: Lessons Learned from a Year of Virtual Collocation. In: CSCW '96: Proceedings of the 1996 ACM Conference on Computer Supported Cooperative Work, pp. 419–427. ACM, New York, NY (1996). DOI http://doi.acm.org/10.1145/240080.240353

Palen, L.: Social, Individual and Technological Issues for Groupware Calendar Systems. In: CHI '99: Proceedings of the SIGCHI Conference on Human Factors in Computing Systems, pp. 17–24. ACM, New York, NY (1999). DOI http://doi.acm.org/10.1145/302979.302982

Palen, L., Dourish, P.: Unpacking "Privacy" for a Networked World. In: CHI '03: Proceedings of the SIGCHI Conference on Human Factors in Computing Systems, pp. 129–136. ACM, New York, NY (2003). DOI http://doi.acm.org/10.1145/642611.642635

Patil, S., Kobsa, A.: Instant Messaging and Privacy. In: Proceedings of HCI 2004, pp. 85–88 (2004). DOI http://www.ics.uci.edu/kobsa/papers/2004-HCI-kobsa.pdf

Patil, S., Kobsa, A.: Privacy in Collaboration: Managing Impression. In: The First International Conference on Online Communities and Social Computing. ACM, New York, NY (2005a) DOI http://www.ics.uci.edu/~kobsa/papers/2005-ICOCSC-kobsa.pdf

Patil, S., Kobsa, A.: Uncovering Privacy Attitudes and Practices in Instant Messaging. In: GROUP '05: Proceedings of the 2005 International ACM SIGGROUP Conference on Supporting Group Work, pp. 109–112. ACM, New York, NY (2005b). DOI http://doi.acm.org/10.1145/1099203.1099220

Patil, S., Lai, J.: Who Gets to Know What When: Configuring Privacy Permissions in an Awareness Application. In: CHI '05: Proceedings of the SIGCHI Conference on Human Factors in Computing Systems, pp. 101–110. ACM, New York, NY (2005). DOI http://doi.acm.org/10.1145/1054972.1054987

Pinelle, D., Gutwin, C.: Designing for Loose Coupling in Mobile Groups. In: GROUP '03: Proceedings of the 2003 International ACM SIGGROUP Conference on Supporting Group Work, pp. 75–84. ACM, New York, NY (2003). DOI http://doi.acm.org/10.1145/958160.958173

Rachels, J.: Why Privacy Is Important. Philosophy and Public Affairs 4(4), 323–333 (1975)

Rittenbruch, M., McEwan, G.: An Historical Reflection of Awareness in Collaboration. In: P. Markopoulos, B. de Ruyter, W. Mackay (eds.) Awareness Systems: Advances in Theory, Methodology and Design. Springer-Verlag, Berlin, pp. xxx–xxx (2009)

Romero, N., Markopoulos, P.: Grounding Privacy with Awareness. In: P. Markopoulos, B. de Ruyter, W. Mackay (eds.) Awareness Systems: Advances in Theory, Methodology and Design. Springer-Verlag, Berlin, pp. xxx–xxx (2009)

Samarajiva, R.: Interactivity as Though Privacy Mattered. In: P.E. Agre, M. Rotenberg (eds.) Technology and Privacy: The New Landscape, pp. 277–309. MIT Press, Cambridge, MA (1997)

Schwartz, B.: The Social Psychology of Privacy. The American Journal of Sociology 73 (6), 741–752 (1968). DOI http://www.jstor.org/stable/2775779

Stone, E.F., Gueutal, H.G., Gardner, D.G., McClure, S.: A Field Experiment Comparing Information-Privacy Values, Beliefs, and Attitudes Across Several Types of Organizations. Journal of Applied Psychology 68(3), 459–468 (1983)

Suchman, L.A.: Plans and Situated Actions: The Problem of Human–Machine Communication. Cambridge University Press, New York, NY (1987)

U.S. Department of Health Education and Welfare: Records, Computers and the Rights of Citizens. Report of the Secretary's Advisory Committee on Automated Personal Data Systems **Publication No. 1700–00116** (1973)

Warren, S.D., Brandeis, L.D.: The Right to Privacy. Harvard Law Review 4(5), 193–220 (1890)

Westin, A.F.: Privacy and Freedom. Atheneum, New York (1967)

Westin, A.F.: Harris-Equifax Consumer Privacy Survey 1991 Equifax, Inc., Atlanta, GA (1991)

Wickramasuriya, J., Datt, M., Mehrotra, S., Venkatasubramanian, N.: Privacy Protecting Data Collection in Media Spaces. In: MULTIMEDIA '04: Proceedings of the 12th Annual ACM International Conference on Multimedia, pp. 48–55. ACM, New York, NY (2004). DOI http://doi.acm.org/ 10.1145/1027527.1027537

Chapter 9
Grounding Privacy with Awareness: A Social Approach to Describe Privacy Related Issues in Awareness Systems

Natalia Romero and Panos Markopoulos

9.1 Introduction

By their very nature, awareness systems bring about an increase in the level of communication between the individuals they connect. Sharing information regarding people's whereabouts and activities raises privacy concerns, potentially compromising their ability to control who receives what information about them, in what form and at what times. Such privacy concerns can be more pronounced in cases where such information is captured and disclosed automatically, which can lead to unintentional and undesirable disclosure of information (Belloti and Sellen, 1993; Markopoulos, 2005).

Researchers in the fields of computer-mediated communication and ubiquitous computing have been investigating interactive mechanisms that could help prevent undesirable self-disclosure and protect people's private information. For example, where video communication is used, a control to degrade the quality of video could be provided (Neustaedter et al., 2006; Zhao and Stasko, 1998); where recording takes place in a room, people inside could be informed about it; or when the context-sensing technology tracks the location of individuals in a building they could be given controls to turn this feature on or off. Such mechanisms can be valuable safeguards for tempering the potential of computing technologies to create and distribute records of one's activities that threaten one's privacy.

However, users of such technologies experience privacy needs primarily regarding their interpersonal privacy rather than about issues related to unwanted information disclosure (Palen and Dourish, 2003). Interpersonal privacy needs concern intentions to interact with others. People in their daily life constantly, and fluently, adjust their behaviour to address these needs, whether to initiate interactions with others or to respond to such intentions. Continuous and ubiquitous connectivity

N. Romero (✉)
Eindhoven University of Technology, The Netherlands

P. Markopoulos et al. (eds.), *Awareness Systems*, Human-Computer Interaction Series, DOI 10.1007/978-1-84882-477-5_9, © Springer-Verlag London Limited 2009

brings about the risk that individuals engage in technology-mediated interactions with others unintentionally and perhaps even unaware of it.

In this chapter, we adopt a social psychology perspective on the concept of privacy, examining how it is manifested in the context of interpersonal interactions. Following the definition of Irwin Altman (1975), we consider privacy as a dynamic and dialectic process, in which an individual experiences and exhibits a continually changing need to interact socially and share information regarding one's self with others. Privacy concerns in mediated settings amount to experiencing an undesirable level of communication such as too much or too little interaction, or interaction occurring at an inappropriate time.

According to Altman, the degree to which an individual engages in interaction with others represents the outcome of a border regulation process between this individual and his/her environment. Applying Altman's theory to the context of mediated communication results in several corollaries (Palen and Dourish, 2003): Privacy is a collaborative coordination process; coordination of privacy is manifested in the need to regulate potentially conflicting interpersonal borders; disclosure of information is necessary in order to manage these borders.

In light of the above, awareness systems can be seen as a platform for efficiently sharing information about oneself and for managing one's privacy borders. To this point the mechanisms by which users perform this process in a mediated setting are not sufficiently understood. This chapter introduces a theoretically motivated model that describes how users manage their privacy borders that is aimed at informing the design of relevant interactive mechanisms. While the mechanisms that we describe are quite general (since they derive from a general theory of interpersonal communication) our discussion and analysis focus on how people can negotiate reachability for communication in mediated settings. Following the privacy vocabulary by Boyle and Greenberg (2005), we target the notion of *solitude control,* i.e. how individuals reach out to communicate with others or maintain their privacy borders to avoid interaction with others.

Nardi et al. (2000) discuss social communicative processes surrounding media information exchange, which they call *outeraction.* Outeraction concerns communication that focuses on monitoring and ensuring progress of the overall communication rather than the content of the communication as such. Nardi et al. identify several types of outeraction in the use of instant messaging systems, such as negotiating availability, attaining connectedness, sustained intermittent conversations, managing progress of the communication and switching to other media. They argue that outeraction falls outside the scope of current communication theories, which mainly focus on the coordination of information exchange (see Chapters 9 and 20 of this volume for a related discussion). Particularly with regards to negotiating availability, Nardi et al. question a common assumption of these theories, which assumes that the recipient is present at the moment the initiator attempts to exchange information. Nardi et al. have illustrated how in practice this is not the case, as the initiator cannot guarantee that the recipient will always acknowledge his/her initiation attempt. Communicators develop strategies to manage tensions and possible conflicts surrounding the initiation of a communication. Nardi et al. go on to identify and describe the need for negotiation prior and outside the information exchange, though they do not describe the exact mechanisms and operations that are necessary to implement such negotiation. The work presented here aims to address this apparent shortcoming in our current understanding of interpersonal privacy, by identifying mechanisms through which communicators coordinate their availability and establish a shared understanding of their respective intentions to interact.

The following sections describe the nature of interpersonal privacy in the context of (technology) mediated interactions and introduce the Privacy Grounding Model (PGM) – a model that describes how communicating individuals collaborate in order to satisfy their respective privacy needs. A preliminary and summative description of PGM can be found in Romero and Markopoulos (2005). Since then the model has been refined, validated experimentally and used as the basis for designing interactive mechanisms for supporting interpersonal privacy regulation; see thesis by Romero (2008). Awareness systems in this context are seen as a tool and a resource for optimizing this dynamic process. We shall end with a discussion on the design of solutions for supporting the process of privacy grounding.

9.2 Interpersonal Privacy: A Social Approach

Typical scenarios describing interpersonal privacy embody situations of initiation and closing of conversations. Figures 9.1, 9.2 and 9.3 show extracts from actual logs of instant messaging activity by a small-distributed community. The extracts are shown in five columns featuring: the time when the interaction event happened, the type of event (typing text or change of status), the content, the sender (From) and recipient (To). These extracts illustrate the need of communicators to share representations regarding their intents for opening and closing borders for interaction. Communicators tell others about their desire to interact, announce their (un)availability for immediate interaction, indicate their desire to avoid interruptions, or to assess the urgency/importance of an interaction attempt.

Figure 9.1 presents three colleagues (P1, P2 and P3) connected to a common virtual "room" they created to coordinate the tasks of a project they are working on.

Time	Type	Content	From	To (room)
14:34:00	TYPING	Pause?	P2	Room 1
14:34:11	TYP2ING	Yeah!	P3	Room 1
14:34:58	TYPING	Come P1	P2	Room 1
14:35:10	STATUS	Away as a result of idle	P1	
14:35:12	TYPING	Nudge, nudge	P3	Room 1
14:35:58	STATUS	Available	P1	
14:36:02	TYPING	OK	P1	Room 1

Fig. 9.1 Negotiating others' availability: P2 wants to get the attention of members of Room 1. P3 uses explicit mechanisms (nudge, nudge) to get the attention of P1 despite her (automatic) away status. P1 implicitly informs (status generated by the system) that she is momentarily unavailable

Time	Meta content	Content	From	To (room)
15:41:21 TYPING		Have you finished the report?	P4	P5
15:41:53 TYPING		Mon [moment]	P5	P4
15:43:22 TYPING		Yah, it is ready to share	P5	P4

Fig. 9.2 Representing unavailability: P5 explicitly announces that he is not able to immediately react to P4's request

Time	Meta content	Content	From	To (room)
14:14:57 TYPING		The videos are ready!	P3	Room 1
14:15:00 TYPING		Who takes which?	P3	Room 1
14:15:16 STATUS		Log-off room	P3	Room 1
14:15:19 STATUS		Log-in room	P3	Room 1
14:15:29 TYPING		Here I'm back again!	P3	Room 1
14:15:59 TYPING		Hello?	P3	Room 1
14:16:02 TYPING		So	P1	Room 1
14:16:04 TYPING		So, which video to whom?	P3	Room 1

Fig. 9.3 Negotiating own availability: P3 tries to get others' attention using multiple instalments to represent the importance of her message

The extract shows how colleagues, P2 and P3, explicitly try to reach their colleague P1 despite the fact that she indicates that she is away with an automatic "away" status. This indication should normally be taken to imply that P1 is focusing on other activities.

Figure 9.2, illustrates a one-to-one conversation between P4 and P5, in which P5 uses a lightweight reaching mechanism (direct content-question, no preamble) while P4 has the need to explicitly notify his delay.

Figure 9.3 shows how P3 is in the common room trying to reach her team in multiple instalments till one member in the team "finally" reacts. In a period of 1 min P3 sends a sequence of four messages to disclose her need to communicate as well as her availability. Since there is no indication of any sort by other members of the team, P3 uses explicit signals in her last message ("hello?") to emphasize her intentions (urgency) to communicate, even though only a short time has elapsed.

Altman defines privacy from a social psychology perspective as "an interpersonal boundary process by which a person or a group regulates interaction with others..." (Altman 1975, p. 6) or as a "selective control of access to the self or to one's group..." (Altman, 1975, p. 18).

Figure 9.4 shows how this boundary regulation process results in desired and undesired states of interaction with the environment. An individual's borders towards his/her environment are shown as a line that is continuous when the borders are closed, preventing any interaction and dashed when the borders are open, allowing interaction to take place. An attempt by person (U) to initiate interaction with the environment (E) is represented by an arrow pointing from (U) to (E); similarly an arrow pointing from (E) to (U) illustrates that one or more people in the environment try to interact with this person.

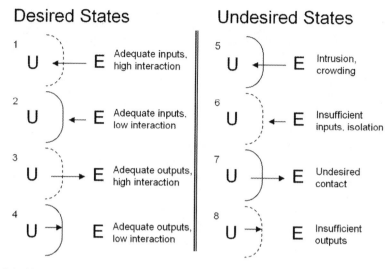

Fig. 9.4 Altman's model of privacy borders regulation. At the *left* four desired states of interaction between user (U) and environment (E); at the *right* four undesired states of interaction (adapted from Altman, 1975)

(1) Person (U) is open for interaction and accepts the request from the environment (E). Example: (U) opens the door and lets someone else (E) in.

(2) (U) seeks isolation closing her borders for interaction and succeeds in doing so, preventing (E) from interacting with her. Example: passers by (E) refrain from small-talk with (U).

(3) (U) seeks for interaction opening his/her borders to (E) achieving the desired interaction. Example: (U) calls (E) and establishes a conversation.

(4) (U) refrains from interacting with (E).

(5) (U) seeks isolation but fails to prevent (E)'s approach. Example: (E) barges in a closed door.

(6) (U) seeks interaction but inadvertently blocks of interactions originating from (E). Example: (U) invites (E) for communication, but (E) does not engage.

(7) (U) seeks isolation closing his/her borders but is unable to avoid interacting with (E). Example: (U) prefers to avoid (E), but feels obliged to call.

(8) (U) seeks to interact but does not succeed to do so. Example: (E) was not home when (U) called.

Altman's definition introduces the notion of a current and a desired state of interaction, mapping users' behaviours to the representation of their intentions to interact. Altman focuses on individuals and their attempt to implement their privacy preferences in relation to their environment. His model overlooks the fact that the environment comprises in actors with their own agenda seeking also to satisfy the privacy needs they are expecting.

Time	Meta content	Content	From	To (room)
11:16:36	STATUS	Extended away	P6	
11:16:41	TYPING	Fixed!!	P4	P6
11:16:49	TYPING	Great	P6	P4

Fig. 9.5 Privacy describes as a dynamic collaborative border regulation process. Despite the implicit border of P6 indicating unavailability, P4 coordinates his interaction with P6

Petronio (2002) extends the model of Altman considering privacy regulation as *a collaborative coordination process during which two actors reach an agreement regarding their intentions and expectations*. While Petronio puts forward this view and discusses extensively the nature and the existence of a rule-based coordination system that users develop, her theory does not describe by which process privacy borders and the corresponding privacy rules are formed. Her theory focuses on the outcome of privacy coordination and the nature of the privacy rules developed cooperatively, rather than the exact mechanisms by which the required coordination is achieved.

In this chapter we discuss how the Common Ground theory by Clark (1996) can fill this gap letting us describe the coordination by which communicators reach a commonly acceptable state of interaction.

For example, Fig. 9.5 shows an extract from the instant messaging logs described earlier, in which colleague P4 notifies P6 about something, despite that P6 is indicating being unavailable. Nevertheless, P6 reacts enthusiastically, apparently pleased with the intrusion. What according to Altman's scheme might be considered as an undesired state is actually welcomed by the receiver who adjusts her borders to this new situation.

Based on Altman's theory, Boyle and Greenberg (2005) developed a Privacy Vocabulary that describes the process of privacy regulation in terms of three interpersonal borders:

- *Solitude* represents the control of "interactional borders", the access to the self. Solitude mechanisms describe how individuals represent their privacy borders to reach a desired level of interaction (interpersonal distance) in a spectrum where failure is indicated by the extremes of crowding (others have granted too much access to the self) and isolation (one cannot interact with others).
- *Autonomy* represents the control of "self-definition borders" that determined one's behaviours while expressing one's identity. Autonomy mechanisms describe how individuals define the type of interaction they were willing to engage in, whether collaborative or individualistic. It addresses the control over one's own behaviour, whether to preserve it (one always does as one wishes) or constrain it (one adapts one's behaviour and appearance to conform to group expectations).
- *Confidentiality* represents the control of "informational borders", the access to personal information regarding aspects such as fidelity, amount and quality of the information disclosed. Confidentiality mechanisms describe how individuals adapt the presentation of the self, defining the quality of the interaction by

means of the level of disclosure of personal information. The control of access refers not only to restricting it but also to granting access to some information.

Each type of border control is manifested through a number of mechanisms people employ to regulate their privacy when connected through technology means, such as video, text, or voice. These three privacy controls are synergistic, meaning that encouraging aspects of one may empower aspects of the other two: one's availability disclosure might protect one's solitude by constraining others to initiate undesired interruption while at the same time it is likely to help them regulate their autonomy in an informed way. Similarly, the symbiosis of the three controls identifies autonomy as the power to enact privacy choices of solitude and confidentiality. Therefore solitude and confidentiality cannot be guaranteed if autonomy is not guaranteed and vice versa.

Boyle and Greenberg define a space to understand users' preferences regarding privacy borders control in mediated communication. The three identified border controls contribute to the description of users' needs regarding the coordination of interpersonal borders, however, the vocabulary represented the regulation of borders as primarily an individual activity rather than a collaborative one.

9.3 Common Ground Theory

The Common Ground theory (Clark, 1996) provides an extensive description of how people coordinate their face-to-face communication conjointly on the basis of a *contribution model* where individuals exchange presentations, meanings and understandings in order to communicate. All verbal communication activities are considered as joint actions where communicators contribute to the development of *common ground*. In this chapter, a syntactic distinction is made to represent a semantic difference between "Common Ground" as Clark's theory and "common ground" as contributions that both parties can consider as shared.

In Clark's theory *signalling* and *grounding* are relevant practices that describe communicators' contributions to coordinate each other's communication needs. Signalling and grounding represent the process in which the intentions to communicate become common ground, therefore intentions are shared and understood by everyone. Signalling represents communicators' actions to *signal* intentions; grounding represents the actions to reach shared understanding of such signalled intentions. Signalling and grounding are governed by the principle of *least collaborative effort* and *track-II signals* to indicate that people are motivated to do the least necessary and as lightweight as possible to reach common ground.

This section introduces some elements of the Common Ground theory (Clark, 1996) that are used in the development of our own model for signalling and grounding privacy in mediated communication. Readers wishing for a thorough exposition of Common Ground theory are referred to the excellent tutorial introduction by Monk (2003) or Clark's own extensive exposition of his theory (Clark, 1996).

9.3.1 Coordination of Communication Activities as a Collaborative Process

A basic premise in Common Ground theory is that any communication activity can be described as a collaborative coordination process where two or more entities engage in *joint activities*. The ultimate goal of joint activities is to reach agreement regarding the intentions and understandings individuals try to communicate. Even in situations that might be considered as adversarial, e.g. a debate or an argument, communicators can be seen as cooperating in order to make sense of each other. So while people might not be sharing motives and tasks and are not cooperating at the level of intentions and actions, they are considered to be collaborating to achieve a meaningful communication.

9.3.2 Contribution Pairs: Presenting and Understanding Intentions to Communicate

Joint activities are described by a sequence of *contribution pairs* consisting of *presentations* to signal intentions and *acceptances* to signal understandings of those intentions. In other words, in a contribution the initiator presents an utterance to express an *intention* and the recipient gives evidence of *understanding* of that presentation. Openings, turn-takings and closings are examples of such joint actions that are instrumental in coordinating face-to-face situations.

9.3.3 Lightweight Coordination Mechanisms: Track-II Signals

Clark emphasizes the distinction between two signalling tracks where communication occurs. *Track-I signals* relate to the content of communication, while *track-II signals* provide the means to coordinate the process of communication in track-I.

Coordinating the communication process involves a series of actions by communicators to ensure that signals in track-I are presented at a proper time and in a proper way. It is in track-II that the initiator asks for confirmation to initiate a conversation and the recipient provides evidence of understanding regarding the initiator's intent. For example, when communicating a reference number over the phone, the initiator might use multiple instalments to spell number by number, pausing in between and expecting that the recipient will repeat (for confirmation) each number as soon as it has been spelled. The pause and the implicitly requested confirmation constitute track-II signals.

Successful track-II signals are characterized as:

- *Brief* so track-II signals provide limited information and with few variations in the way they are presented.
- *Distinctive* from track-I signals meaning they are easily identified as process related rather than content related.

- *Background* letting track-I signals always be prominent.
- *Simultaneous* to track-I signals, implying that track-II signals are presented without interfering with representations of content.

9.3.4 Least Collaborative Effort: Developing and Using Common Ground Representations

Grounding is described as the process of developing new common ground or using existing representations of common ground. Clark identified three basic *common ground representations* that communicators can use as a shared basis to commonly agree on their intentions and understandings:

- *Conventions* represent any custom or practice that could be associated with the use of a communication protocol. They define the way communicators interact with each other, e.g. turn taking, acknowledging receipt and waiting for someone to finish.
- *Current representations* represent any external demonstration of track-I signals, which all communicators can see, such as pointing at, indicating and demonstrating.
- *Shared previous events* represent any information related to previous events that have been shared by all communicators.

Joint activities to develop common ground representations are ruled by the principle of *least collaborative effort*: communicators try to express no more than what they perceive as sufficient for advancing the current communication. Therefore developing common ground representations are meant to provide "evidence enough for current purposes" so people with a minimal collaborative effort contribute to establish a shared understanding of their communication needs.

9.4 The Privacy Grounding Model

The Privacy Grounding Model (PGM) combines elements of the theories of Common Ground (Clark, 1996) and the Privacy Vocabulary (Boyle and Greenberg, 2005) to provide a theoretical foundation of the social communicative aspects of interpersonal privacy coordination. PGM is aimed at identifying mechanisms that support interpersonal privacy coordination.

The model is structured in three levels of abstraction that connect theoretical concepts of coordination (*components*) with the description of their identified behaviours (*mechanisms* and *characterizations*) as illustrated in Fig. 9.6. The first three components (*collaboration*, *signalling* and *grounding*) represent the Common Ground elements introduced in PGM. The last component (*regulation*) represents the context (the base) in which the model is designed for – the regulation of privacy borders.

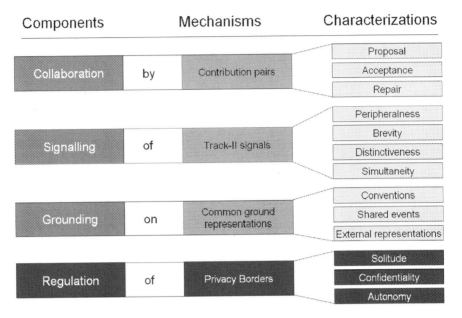

Fig. 9.6 The Privacy Grounding Model (PGM)

In the next sections, the model is described introducing each of its abstraction layers. The first layer identifies the components of *collaboration, signalling* and *grounding* in the *regulation* of privacy. The second layer delves into the mechanisms as the devices by which communicators operate each component to coordinate *privacy borders*. Finally, the third layer expands the characterizations of the model, which provide a comprehensive description of the mechanisms in the coordination process.

9.4.1 Components

At the highest level of abstraction, PGM combines three Common Ground components to describe interpersonal privacy coordination in the context of the *regulation* of privacy borders:

- *Collaboration* represents the dialectic aspect of privacy coordination: privacy coordination takes place through joint actions, in which actors conjointly contribute to the presentation and understanding of their privacy intentions.
- *Signalling* represents communicators' actions to signal their intentions to interact.
- *Grounding* represents the communicators' actions to reach common understanding of their signaled intentions.

At this level, the regulation of privacy is represented by the social activities that communicators engage in to develop coordination devices as grounded representa-

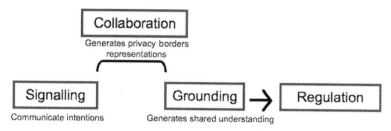

Fig. 9.7 The grounding of privacy: users generate privacy borders representations engaging in collaborative practices of signalling and grounding. This process results in the development of sufficient common ground for communicators to cooperatively regulate their privacy borders

tions of privacy borders. The process of grounding privacy implies that the development of coordination devices is dynamically achieved by the community and not by the system itself. In Fig. 9.7, the elements of collaboration, signalling and grounding are modelled to describe the social activities in the generation of coordination devices.

Members of a networked community *collaborate* by presenting their privacy borders through different channels available. For example, borders could be represented by information shared through video broadcast, in chat messages, or by users' online status. For opening or closing of privacy borders, the communicator should seek that others see and understand that representation. *Signalling* and *grounding* help people to make those representations become shared and mutually understood by others:

– By *signalling*, individuals communicate their intentions regarding interpersonal privacy of their borders' representations.
– *Grounding* helps individuals develop common ground that establishes a shared understanding over those privacy borders.

Table 9.1 shows one scenario of the privacy signalling and grounding process.

Table 9.1 Signalling and grounding scenario

Scenario	Signalling and grounding
Anne, a media space user, blurs her video image to represent her closed border for interaction	Anne is signalling borders
Pete sends a message to Anne: "you looked blurred!"	Pete is signalling borders
Anne signals the intentions of her blurred video with a message: "I need time to read"	Anne is grounding meaning
Pete reacts with a message "I hate reading"	Pete is grounding understanding
Anne signals a more explicit explanation "I am busy reading"	Anne is grounding meaning
Pete grounds Anne's intentions blurring his own video with a message "I am also reading". From now on they use blurring as a coordination device	Pete is grounding understanding => coordination device

9.4.2 Mechanisms

At the second level, PGM describes the social mechanisms associated with signalling and grounding in the regulation of privacy borders. These mechanisms support:

- Collaboration through pairs of presentations and reactions. To describe collaboration the model considers *contribution pairs* as the joint activity where both initiators and recipients collaboratively use pairs of presentations and reactions to represent privacy intentions and to communicate their understanding of those intentions, respectively. A coordination activity consists of at least one contribution pair, but it usually involves a sequence of contribution pairs where communicators present and react to privacy meanings and understandings until an agreement has been reached.

  > For example, Pete, an online user in a chat room, presents his availability for communication by selecting the representation of his online status to "available", but triggers no explicit reaction. Then he decides to use a more explicit representation "I am back", which triggers a reaction from Anne: "any news?" indicating her understanding of his availability. In this example, Pete used two contribution pairs to coordinate his intention to initiate conversation. First, he used an incidental presentation of his availability, which was coupled with an empty reaction from Anne that could be perceived as an omission or a rejection to Pete's intention or even as intentionally ignoring Pete's signal. Later, he used an explicit presentation of his availability, which was successfully coupled with an explicit reaction from Anne by which they could develop a shared understanding.

- Signalling of intentions through track-II instances. To describe signalling, the model refers to the *track-II signals*[1] that communicators use to represent their privacy needs when engaging in interaction with others. For example, Pete signals his intentions for interaction by updating his online status, changing his presence name in the buddy list or sending a chat message. Different signals represent different levels of effort to be produced and attended to.
- Grounding privacy intentions through common ground representations. To describe grounding, the model refers to the use of *common ground representations*, which contain the necessary shared knowledge for communicators to reach a common understanding of the meanings of their privacy representations. For example, social rules, shared experiences and shared representations of a situation, work as shared knowledge that establishes understanding of that situation and helps members of a community to behave in a socially acceptable manner.

---

[1] Other terms we use to represent track-II signals are: coordination signals, collateral signals or secondary signals.

9.4.3 Characterizations

At the third level, characterizations typify the social interaction space of contribution pairs, track-II signals and common ground representations for coordinating solitude, confidentiality and autonomy privacy borders. Characterizations reflect the choices made by communicators to develop collaboration, signalling and grounding mechanisms to coordinate privacy. The choices depend on the desired outcome and on the amount of effort communicators want to invest.

Table 9.2 maps the goals of each component and their mechanisms with the efforts and choices identified in the characterizations.

The choices as mentioned in Table 9.2 characterize individuals' effort to coordinate privacy regarding each component:

Table 9.2 Characterizations of PGM components

	Goal	Effort	Choices
Collaboration	Using contribution pairs to communicate privacy borders	Level of engagement to exchange contribution pairs	Presentations, reactions and repairs
Signalling	Using track-II signals to indicate intentions regarding privacy borders	Intentionality to communicate privacy intentions	Peripheralness, simultaneity, brevity and distinctiveness of the coordination signal
Grounding	Using common ground representations to achieve common understandings of privacy borders	Develop or use of common ground to achieve understanding	Conventions, previously shared events, external representations

- Collaboration choices are characterized by the use of *proposals* as presentations of intentions to initiate interaction, and *acceptances* or *repairs* as reactions to communicate agreement or to fix a previously produced presentation, respectively. Repairing a presentation implies modifying, adapting, or repairing the meanings of an existing presentation by adding a new presentation. For example, consecutive instalments could be used to repair a presentation by not only adding more detailed information but also by increasing the level of disruptiveness and emphasizing one's expectations for a reaction. The following chat scenario represents an example of Pete using repair:

> Pete says: Hi!
> Pete says: I'm back!
> Pete says: are you home?
> Pete says: do you have a minute?
> Pete says: just need a minute with you to coordinate tomorrow's meeting
> Anne says: Sure! Let's meet.

- Signalling choices are characterized by *brevity, distinctiveness, peripheralness* and *simultaneity*.

  To guarantee that presentations a nd reactions regarding privacy are understood correctly, communicators plan and adjust the effort that is assumed as necessary to successfully represent their coordination signals. Communicators assess whether they can rely on existing representations to contribute incidentally to the coordination process or if they need to signal their contributions intentionally:

  - *Incidental signalling* describes situations where the signal is produced implicitly as a side effect of an external action, meaning that the signal is incidentally produced, e.g. the automatic change of online status to "away".
  - *Intentional signalling* refers to situations where planned actions are executed to become signals; therefore the signals are deliberately and explicitly produced, like for example, sending a message " I am back".

  Whether communicators choose to use incidental or intentional signalling depends to a varying extent on the reaction of the communication partner. This reflects a strong coupling between the actions of signalling and grounding. Signalling is not only the means for creating/presenting a privacy representation but also the means of indicating progress in the grounding process.

  Typically in mediated settings, intentional track-II signals are less brief, less in the background, less simultaneous but more distinctive than incidental track-II signals. They are commonly used when implicit grounding effort (based on existing common ground representations) has failed.

- Grounding choices are represented by the three common ground representations of the Common Ground theory: conventions, shared events and external representations. Common ground representations in mediated communication may be any signal outside the main communication channel that serves track-I. In the example above, the action of blurring one's video could be used to provide a common ground representation of one's non-availability with the intention to keep others from initiating undesired interactions.

  To ensure that grounding is achieved, communicators assess whether they need to develop common ground and incur additional effort, or whether they can use existing common ground and therefore minimize the effort needed for grounding:

  - *Developing common ground* means that communicators consider existing common ground as insufficient to represent their privacy borders; therefore additional effort is required to achieve a common understanding of their representations.
  - *Using common ground* means that communicators assume that existing common ground is sufficient as a shared representation of their privacy borders. Communicators utilize existing representations as a shared basis for presenting and understanding their privacy borders.

9.5 Using PGM in Awareness Systems

Signalling and grounding are collaborative practices that contribute to the coordination of privacy by helping communicators to establish a mutual understanding of their privacy borders, even in cases when privacy borders are breached. For example, if Pete initiates communication with Anne even after she has blurred her video to represent unavailability, she could react to Pete's initiation by acknowledging her unavailability. Or the system could somehow highlight Anne's blurring effect to Pete, so he could make a better guess of Anne's unavailability status.

In mediated settings, the workload of manually signalling privacy intentions to different members of one's social network can be excessive. Automatic solutions can provide low-effort means of representing one's privacy borders, e.g. an automatically updated presence or availability status. However, such solutions usually come at the cost of increasing uncertainty whether a particular signal has been attended properly and understood correctly. The usual way to ensure a correct understanding of signals' intentions is to provide more detailed information, e.g. not only if one's phone is on, but also whether it is on silent or loud mode (see Chapter 10). The more detailed the signals, the more informed the entities can be and the better prepared to perform expected functions. But this extra information can further aggravate privacy concerns. In face-to-face social networks this dilemma finds a solution through collaborative coordination activities where the entities engage in joint actions to express signals and understandings till they reach a mutual understanding.

A limitation of mediated communication technologies is that most representations that could inform communicators about privacy needs are not always as readily available and low-effort as in face-to-face settings. For example, collocated communicators can ground a reaction using a "verbal" silence which meaning can be grounded on the basis of other lightweight signals such as body gestures (nodding, leaning forward, etc.) or physical actions (moving away, opening a book, etc.). These simultaneous signals become lightweight contributions to communicators' understanding of the intention of that silence. However, in mediated communication, a silence is more difficult and ambiguous to be presented along with other signals. The lack of collateral channels makes it difficult for a recipient to ground a reaction using a silence in a lightweight manner; and for the initiator to deduce in a lightweight manner the recipient's intention relating to such a silence.

The exposition of PGM above underlines the need for lightweight signalling and grounding mechanisms for communicating privacy borders The remainder of this section discusses how PGM helps describe how awareness systems and, more generally, mediated communication systems support the coordination of interpersonal privacy. The discussion focuses on availability management, in particular on how initiations of interactions can be supported in a lightweight manner.

Similar to face-to-face settings, in communication-mediated systems the implemented channels can be classified as content or outeraction channel depending on whether they are primarily supporting content exchange or the coordination process, respectively. Table 9.3 shows examples of content and outeraction channels for mediated settings.

Table 9.3 Examples of content and outeraction channels in mediated settings

Content channels	Outeraction channels
Text	Colour-coded visualization
Voice	Presence information (status/video)
Picture	Notification
Web links	Alerts

Incidental coordination represents contributions that require little effort, as existing common ground is assumed sufficient to communicate interaction needs. It is usually represented in outeraction channels where availability for communication can be deduced and even grounded with little effort. For example, users connected with a video link may notice each other's presence but, also, that they have taken notice of each other's presence without explicitly seeking to do so. Nevertheless, incidental contributions can also be manifested in a content channel where a track-I signal represents implicitly the intention to interact. For example in an instant messaging scenario, a person that initiates interaction by directly asking a work-related question considers it as grounded that the recipient will react to the message once they see it, given the knowledge of the way the medium works and conventions for its use by the community. These situations require substantial common ground between communicators.

Intentional coordination represents contributions that require additional effort to develop missing common ground. In content channels, communicators can communicate privacy needs explicitly but also with more effort, in a manner that guarantees others' attention and understanding. For example, if an "away" status notification in an outeraction channel is deemed as an insufficient representation, then a more explicit signal is needed to express (or disambiguate) privacy intentions, like a text message "I'm not able to attend messages, I'll get back to you after lunch". Using a content channel for developing intentional track-II signals implies a bigger effort both for producing as well as for attending the signal, since signals in content channels are not brief, nor simultaneous and nor in the background. The benefit is that they can be highly distinctive as representations of privacy intentions and therefore a sound basis for grounding and coordinating privacy needs. In outeraction channels, communicators can also produce intentional coordination signals but these are less distinctive than in content channels; they are however more lightweight, as these signals are characterized as brief, somewhat distinctive as coordination signals (based mostly on existent conventions), simultaneous (to any content signal) and in the background (they are mostly seen as notifications in the periphery).

Concluding, PGM identifies different coordination scenarios (incidental or intentional), which result in different choices for signalling and grounding mechanisms depending on the available content and outeraction channels. Subject to the success of the chosen mechanisms, transitions may occur from one scenario to another. For example, an initiation produced as an incidental coordination in the content channel may require an intentional coordination if there is a need to communicate more explicitly initiator's expectations for reactions.

9.5.1 Least Collaborative Effort and Track-II Characterizations

Common ground representations help minimize the collaborative effort required to develop a shared understanding of privacy borders. Such representations are shared basis, i.e. they are known by all the parties involved and their meanings are understood by everyone. Awareness systems can provide a low-effort source of privacy representations based on the awareness information they are constantly updating and broadcasting, such as availability status and presence information. However, in most cases such representations do not guarantee that they are shared basis. Users cannot readily assume that privacy border information has been shared unless a backchannel is available by which the receiving party can ground such representations.

In order to support the development of common ground on the basis of awareness representations, awareness systems should provide signalling and grounding mechanisms that allow users to produce sufficient signals so that such representations become shared basis for coordination. To minimize collaborative effort such signals should follow the four track-II characterizations described above. For example, simultaneity implies that mediated communication systems should provide at least two distinct channels: one for content (track-I) and another for coordination (track-II) signals. In the case that mediated application is restricted to provide only one channel for communication, mechanisms should be designed to enhance the distinctiveness of the track-II signal within this channel, e.g. provide outeraction signals that are perceptually distinct to content signals communicated in the same channel.

9.5.2 Intentionality, Channels and Ambiguity

To achieve privacy coordination, communicators seek to balance their needs for incidental and intentional coordination cooperatively and iteratively. They do so adapting to the channels available and to the effort they are willing to expend or request from others for developing a common ground. There are cases when communicators need to add/request additional effort in order to ensure a sufficient understanding of the privacy borders. In other situations, communicators put priority on achieving a lightweight coordination process.

In practice, this could be achieved by supporting each content channel with at least one outeraction channel that allows for intentional coordination (therefore increasing the chances for success) but without the costs of conducting that activity in the content channel. For example, representations of text messages (content channel) could be grounded using a (physical) button (outeraction channel) that produces track-II signals to achieve lightweight intentional grounding on the text representations. Pressing a dedicated physical button when a new message arrives at an inappropriate time could help the recipient ground that this message has been noticed and that it cannot be responded to immediately.

As discussed by Altman, the regulation of privacy borders is a process that incurs affective costs once a shared understanding is achieved, as one might have to adapt his/her privacy needs in order to reconcile with a situation that evolves against one's own desires. In the context of initiating communications, affective costs may refer to experiencing obligations to interact and communicate with others when this was not initially desired, expectations that may be unmet, loss of face relating to one being accountable for engagement, or not in a communication activity; see Romero et al. (2007) and Chapter 20 in this book for a discussion of related affective costs. Aoki and Woodruff (2006) have discussed the value of designing systems that leave room for ambiguity, allowing for plausible deniability when one is avoiding communication (see also Palen and Dourish, 2003), or more generally allowing individuals to equivocate. Accordingly privacy grounding mechanisms should preserve such ambiguity and no coerce users into disclosing more of their situation and intentions than is necessary.

9.6 Case Studies

We present three case studies where the PGM model is used to analyse privacy coordination practices relating to three different systems. Findings from the evaluation of these systems as presented by their originators in related publications are re-examined though the lens of the PGM model.

9.6.1 Push-to-Talk

Push-to-talk (PTT) was implemented as a half duplex audio communication medium based on cellular radio communication. Woodruff and Aoki (2003) report how the half duplex and lightweight nature of the communication gives rise to a sense of reduced interactional commitment. Test participants in their study, a group of college friends sharing a house, reported that they appreciate the immediate access to another person and the relatively low interactional demands of the conversation styles afforded. They reported benefits relating to reduced openings and closings, plausibility of delayed or omitted responses, reduced feedback and interleaved interaction.

In terms of PGM, PTT offers a single channel to represent interaction in which both track-I and track-II signals have to be communicated. The simplicity of the channel to open and close conversations supports users to develop a light protocol for initiating interactions. However, in situations of conflicting interests the system fails to provide any outeraction channels based on track-II signals to lightweight-develop a common understanding regarding availability for interaction.

The lack of support of lightweight intentional signalling by PTT can explain participants' preference to use PTT only with close friends, with whom the required common ground regarding privacy (interaction) is already in place. Participants' concern to use PTT with parents reflects their unavailability to control that interaction as desired: "if my dad had a radio [referring to PTT] ... I would just be in constant sorrow for all my days" (Woodruff and Aoki, 2003).

In summary, PTT lacks lightweight support to allow signalling and grounding privacy borders. It forces users to communicate and deploy contribution mechanisms in a single channel, thus increasing the interactional commitment of the whole process.

9.6.2 Media Spaces

The term *Media Space* refers to early communication systems providing sustained audiovisual links between people and places. This section analyzes a study reported by Dourish et al. (1996) regarding their personal experience of several years using the Portholes media space.

Portholes consists of an audio/video link connecting two office rooms sustaining the experience of a virtually shared office. The video link is supported by a camera pointing at any particular angle and a small video monitor displaying presence and availability. The audio link uses a microphone and headsets with a volume control. Users can decide by themselves whether to open or close the video or audio channels independently, using an on/off switch for each channel.

Dourish et al. conducted a long-term ethnographic study of Portholes. During this study, the following situation was observed: an online user received a phone call at her office and took her headset off without noticing that she left the audio connection to the system open. Consequently, other online users were able to overhear her phone conversation. The only alternative to stop overhearing was to disconnect from the system. In addition, online users did not have the means to signal to the unintended discloser what was happening. This example explains how a technological solution failed to support social mechanisms to coordinate sensitive situations, resulting in a socially awkward and embarrassing experience for its users.

Portholes supports two communication channels: audio representing a content channel and video representing an outeraction channel. Intentional and incidental signalling are then limited to audio and video channels, respectively. As a result, when one channel is turned off, the options for signalling and grounding privacy borders are limited. For example, without video, the audio channel cannot incidentally indicate when an audio signal was shared and accessed by its users, thus limiting the possibilities to use such signals as shared representations of privacy. Similarly, in a situation with a video-only presence, the system fails to offer signalling and grounding mechanisms to coordinate privacy.

In summary, signalling and grounding privacy borders are not sufficiently supported by the design of such a media space. The lack of support of track-II signals to signal and ground "the shared space" defined by the available audio and video representations does not support people to develop a common understanding of their behaviours in unfamiliar situations.

9.6.3 Reachability Management Systems

Reachability Management Systems (RMS) are technical solutions that offer automated availability control before establishing a direct communication channel

(Reichenbach et al., 1997). The general process of reachability negotiation works as follows: during the signalling phase of a call the caller transmits information about the nature and purpose of the communication request, the request is then evaluated and negotiated by the RMS; if the request fulfils the callee's conditions, the callee is personally contacted.

Reichenbach et al. (1997) address a particular tension in the design of reachability management systems: the need to protect callers' personal information while at the same time accounting for their intentions to communicate to callees. Their solution requires callers to provide the context and the urgency of a call without having to disclose their identity. Callees can react to such proposals by accepting it or requesting more information. Callers can use a variety of grounding representations to such as vouchers to convey urgency of requests or surety, an amount of money for accepting the call. Callees, on the other hand, can predefine different reactions to incoming proposals, such as requesting the identification or a surety from an unidentified caller. These solutions protect callees from engaging in undesired calls, by forcing callers to explicitly represent their intentions regarding the communication until an agreement is reached.

In terms of PGM, this system offers an intentional coordination channel that callers and callees use to distinctively coordinate a phone call before establishing the actual phone call (voice exchange). Such intentional signalling is lightweight as it is more in the background and brief compared to the alternative of answering the phone and finding out only later that it is not worth answering. Due to the context of use (mobile phone calls) it is questionable whether these coordination signals can be simultaneous to the actual exchange of information (the call) as they try to coordinate the initiation prior the actual call.

Summarizing, this system offers an intentional coordination channel for grounding intentions to interact before the intended contact is established. However, it can be argued that an unnecessary high effort is placed upon callers to formulate and present their initial proposal. The system does not guide callers regarding the feasibility of the options they set. Arguably, awareness of the callee would help callers make a better guess of what is the proper proposal to offer.

9.7 Discussion

9.7.1 PGM Use – A Social Analysis of Disclosure and Solitude Control

In the context of mediated communication, e.g. with messaging systems, media spaces or even modern social networking applications awareness information plays a dual role. On the one hand it provides the means for lightweight interaction, facilitating the content and the process of communication. The more information shared the more common ground can be developed and therefore the more efficient the coordination process becomes. But at the same time, too much information disclosure render people vulnerable to undesired states of interaction, which implies the needs for higher control of solitude.

Our exposition of PGM shows that apart from the obvious privacy concerns related to information sharing through awareness systems (and generally through modern communication media) this information sharing is an essential tool for interpersonal privacy control. Awareness systems can be instrumental in the process of privacy border coordination as they update their users regarding respective availability, presence and so on. The design of signalling and grounding mechanisms is a major challenge for the design of related communication technologies which should facilitate lightweight sharing of information while developing a sufficient understanding of awareness representations to become shared basis of privacy borders. Based on PGM we seek solutions that facilitate collaborative practices to contribute to the understanding of awareness representations; such solutions should support lightweight signalling and grounding mechanisms. The model also identifies the need to support incidental and intentional coordination, which implies the design of outeraction mechanisms that facilitate the use of track-II signals representing understandings of privacy borders.

9.7.2 PGM Contribution – Signalling and Grounding Privacy Intentions

The design framework by Bellotti and Sellen (1993) addresses privacy concerns of users applicable to the broader set of applications in mediated communication. An important aim of their work is to avoid situations where users are monitored without their knowledge, or that information about them is put to uses and accessed by parties they would not wish to. While important, such a consideration of privacy does not consider its dialectic nature, as it has been described by Altman. It captures some of the dynamic and context sensitive nature of people's privacy needs, but it does not acknowledge how individuals decide to open up or close privacy borders or how an individual's availability is the result of the interaction with other parties. Nor does it take into account the dynamic nature of social interaction with other parties, and that individuals may need to adapt privacy borders repeatedly during their interaction with others. For example, one's buddy list may show that this person is unavailable for communication but this user may appreciate an interruption given an appropriate justification by the approaching party. PGM addresses these issues by describing the mechanisms used by individuals to acknowledge the real meaning behind a signal.

Palen and Dourish (2003) provide a first conceptual framework to understand the impact of technology and privacy in HCI. They introduce the concept of *genres of disclosure* to explain that deliberate disclosure of awareness can limit accessibility. Genres of disclosure aim to set the expectations around technology and privacy representations producing the right social expectations, guiding the interpretability of actions, and considering the dynamics of technology and social practices. This framework provides a first understanding of interpersonal privacy concerns regarding technology, but does not help understand the process of communicating privacy intentions when disclosing awareness. PGM examines how signalling and grounding awareness information may provide the necessary *common ground* to help communicators coordinate their interpersonal privacy borders to initiate or close conversations.

Aoki and Woodruff (2005) suggest *ambiguity* as an important social resource in the design of communication applications which closely relate to our concept of grounding privacy. They look at the social difficulty of unexplained unresponsiveness and how that can be resolved by supporting interactional ambiguity. They propose an illustrative framework with ideas of what ambiguity could be in the design of related applications. One aspect of their framework that primarily interests us is the question of how to reduce responsiveness without causing social difficulties. They claim ambiguity plays a crucial role. PGM assumes that providing explanations to unresponsiveness seems to be crucial to participants who wish to acknowledge "a" story behind the unresponsiveness. Quoting from their discussion "the success of face-work is not its truth per se but that it is accepted by the participants." PGM emphasizes that any solitude control (such as a non-reaction) to be accepted needs to be grounded, but at the same time should respond to other interpersonal privacy control such as confidentiality or autonomy. Therefore grounding should occur on the basis of an ambiguity source of reasons, where individuals can explicitly refer to "any" reason in order to contribute to "a" sufficient understanding for the current coordination purposes.

9.8 Conclusions

This chapter has introduced the Privacy Grounding Model, an adaptation of Clark's Common Ground and the theory of privacy borders regulation from Altman. The model identifies the components of the Common Ground theory that address the aspect of collaborative coordination that could be generalized outside the context of conversation dialogue. The model contextualizes the theory of Common Ground to the regulation of privacy borders in the domain of mediated communication. Elsewhere we report on an empirical study to validate the model in terms of its ability to describe and explain instances of privacy negotiation observed in logs. The relevance of the model to the design of communication media is demonstrated by some case studies.

The discussion and the analysis in this chapter have focused on solitude control, leading to an understanding of how collaborative mechanisms can support or hinder privacy coordination. It leads us to suggest the addition of outeraction channels to support track-II signals that lightweight ground existing awareness representations to develop the sufficient common ground for privacy coordination.

Acknowledgments This research was supported by the FP6 FET programme, project ASTRA IST-2004-29266 and the IP project 27654 PASION.

References

Altman, I. (1975). *The Environment and Social Behaviour – Privacy, Personal Space, Territory, Crowding.* Monterey, CA, Wadsworth.

Aoki, P. M. and Woodruff, A. (2005). Making space for stories: ambiguity in the design of personal communication systems. In *Proceedings of the SIGCHI Conference on Human Factors in Computing Systems,* CHI '05. ACM, pp. 181–190.

Bellotti, V. and Sellen, A. (1993). Design for privacy in ubiquitous computing environments. In *Proceedings of the Third Conference on European Conference on Computer-Supported Cooperative Work,* ESCW '93, pp. 77–92.

Boyle, M. and Greenberg, S. (2005). The language of privacy: learning from video media space analysis and design. *ACM Transactions on Computer–Human Interaction (TOCHI),* vol. 12(2), pp. 328–370.

Clark, H. (1996). *Using Language.* New York, Cambridge University Press.

Dourish, P., Adler, A., Bellotti, V., and Henderson, A. (1996). Your place or mine? Learning from long-term use of audio–video communication. *Journal CSCW,* vol. 5(1), pp. 33–62.

Markopoulos, P. (2005). Designing ubiquitous computer human interaction: the case of the connected family. In Isomaki, H., Pirhonen, A., Roast, C. and Saariluoma, P. (Eds.) *Future Interaction Design.* London, Springer, pp. 125–150.

Monk, A. (2003). Common ground in electronically mediated communication: Clark's theory of language use. In Carroll, J. M. (Ed.)*HCI Models, Theories and Frameworks: Towards a Multidisciplinary Science.* San Francisco, CA, Morgan Kaufmann, pp. 265–289.

Nardi, B., Whittaker, S., and Bradner, E. (2000). Interaction and outeraction: instant messaging in action. In *Proceedings of the 2000 ACM Conference on Computer Supported Cooperative Work,* CSCW '00. ACM, pp. 79–88.

Neustaedter, C., Greenberg, S., and Boyle, M. (2006). Blur filtration fails to preserve privacy for home-based video conferencing. *ACM Transactions on Computer–Human Interaction,* vol. 13(1), pp. 1–36.

Palen, L. and Dourish, P. (2003). Unpacking "privacy" for a networked world. In *Proceedings of SIGCHI,* PP. 129–136.

Petronio, S. (2002). *Boundaries of Privacy: Dialectics of Disclosure.* Albany, State of University of New York Press.

Reichenbach, M., Damker, H., Federrath, H., and Rannenberg, K. (1997). Individual management of personal reachability in mobile communication. In *Proceedings of the IFIP TC11 SEC'97 on Information Security in Research and Business,* pp. 164–174.

Romero, N.A. (2008). Coordination of interpersonal privacy in mediated communication. PhD Thesis, Eindhoven University of Technology.

Romero, N. A. and Markopoulos, P. (2005). Common ground to analyze privacy negotiation in awareness systems. In *Human–Computer Interaction – INTERACT 2005.* Lecture Notes in Computer Science, Rome, Italy, Springer, pp. 1006–1009.

Romero, N., Markopoulos, P., Baren, J., Ruyter, B., IJsselsteijn, W., and Farshchian, B. (2007). Connecting the family with awareness systems. *Personal Ubiquitous Comput.* Vol. 11(4), pp. 299–312.

Woodruff, A. and Aoki, P. M. (2003). How push-to-talk makes talk less pushy. In *Proceedings of the 2003 International ACM SIGGROUP Conference on Supporting Group Work,* GROUP '03. ACM, pp. 170–179.

Zhao, Q. A. and Stasko, J. T. (1998). Evaluating image filtering based techniques in media space applications. In *Proceedings of the 1998 ACM Conference on Computer Supported Cooperative Work,* CSCW '98. ACM Press, pp. 11–18.

Chapter 10
Awareness Information with Speech and Sound

Anssi Kainulainen, Markku Turunen and Jaakko Hakulinen

10.1 Introduction

In modern work environments, people have many tasks, collaborate with other people and use various equipment and services. Staying aware of other people, processes and situations in work environments is important. We naturally use our hearing to maintain this awareness; hearing other people talk let us know they are present, sounds of people walking, typing, etc. help us stay aware of overall situation almost without conscious effort. Such awareness can also be supported by technology; information can be presented with varying levels of subtlety ranging from loud warning signals to subtle cues, such as the sound of a hard drive indicating activity in a computer. Creating a computer system that supports our awareness of coworkers and overall situation in the workplace can increase our productivity and make the workplace a more social and enjoyable place.

In this chapter, sound-based awareness support is discussed. Speech and various kinds of non-speech audio are considered and we describe how they differ from and complement each other, and how they can be used together to support awareness information. An example application, an ambient soundscape application providing background information in office environments (Kainulainen et al., 2006), is used to illustrate these aspects. Through some examples, we will consider how such systems could be evaluated. We end with a discussion on how historically separated fields of speech interaction and non-speech audio interaction could benefit from each other, and should merge to achieve a common goal.

But first, we start by defining the notion of "awareness systems", as used in this context. This includes the importance of awareness and shift of the focus of attention in the environments such systems are used in.

A. Kainulainen (✉)
Speech-based and Pervasive Interaction Group, TAUCHI, Department of Computer Sciences, University of Tampere, FIN-33014, Finland
e-mail: Anssi.Kainulainen@cs.uta.fi

P. Markopoulos et al. (eds.), *Awareness Systems*, Human-Computer Interaction Series, DOI 10.1007/978-1-84882-477-5_10, © Springer-Verlag London Limited 2009

10.1.1 Awareness Systems

Since there are numerous different types of awareness systems available (e.g. systems to support group awareness, peripheral awareness, information awareness and social awareness), the term "awareness system" has become very ambiguous (Brush, 2005). Dourish and Bellotti's (1992) classical definition of awareness as "understanding of the activities of others, which provides a context for your own activity", is too generic. A generalized breakdown of awareness systems is given by Dix et al. (2004, pp. 700), where the authors classified types of awareness related to "who is there," "what has happened," and "how did it happen." Brush also points out the importance of emphasizing the differences between "what" a system provides awareness of and "how" it does it. Her example of "task awareness" as a type of information to be provided contrasted to "peripheral awareness" as a mechanism for providing awareness explains this well.

In our definition, awareness systems are tools to achieve and maintain awareness information of people and services embedded in the environment.

Kraut et al. (1988) show how fairly simple computer applications could enable informal communication, even when physical proximity is not available anymore, as is common in modern separated work environments where collaboration can take place across continents. Media Spaces of Bly et al. (1993) was an implementation of sharing video stream between separate places, and they also noticed how even only the sounds carried in the video feed were enough to keep people aware about what was going on at the other location. Traditionally, awareness systems are applications which a user is explicitly interacting with on his personal desktop computer. In many such systems, awareness information is explicitly requested by the user when needed, or it is continuously displayed in its own windows of an application explicitly initiated by the user, so the user is able to look at it when needed. That could be described as "pulling" awareness information. When information technology becomes more and more ubiquitous and services are always present, there is quite much implicit interaction. For example, a collection of sensors provides data for presence awareness systems to feed this information to user without explicitly being requested. That could be described as "pushing" awareness information. With such systems, it is easy to provide too much information too often; an important aspect of "pushing" awareness information is avoiding information overload. This is why the information should be presented so that it does not require constant shift of the focus of attention from users.

10.1.2 Group Awareness

Dourish and Bellotti's (1992) definition for awareness includes a strong emphasis on social or group awareness, since it is the activities of other people that sets the basis for one's own actions. Kraut et al. (1988) explain how informal or "low cost" communication and interaction are vital to the work of individuals as well as to the groups they form.

You (2000) collects many definitions for awareness in the group work context, according to which:

- Awareness is knowledge of the state of the environment, environment being a temporally and spatially bound setting for people interacting within it.
- Awareness is dynamic, because the environment changes, and thus awareness needs to be kept up to date.
- Maintaining awareness is not the main target of tasks. It is necessary, but not enough. It enables smooth completion of tasks.

Endsley (1995)sees three main phases for becoming aware as *sensing, understanding* and *projecting*. Sensing means noticing a change in perceptual stimuli which is cognitively interpreted to be meaningfully different from previous stimuli. In addition to change, the state and properties of the environment, and dynamics of important factors are sensed. Understanding means collecting and combining the factors sensed in the first phase, and understanding their meaning in the light of current tasks and objectives. Projecting means predicting the future activities, state, and needs of the people within the environment, at least in a short time span. It is important to see that in this process, the role of computer applications is to mediate and provide information which people can use to create the answers themselves. The sensing, understanding and projecting processes are done by people, computer applications only need to provide cues and tools for them. This sets a certain style or role for interaction, related to the difference of "what" and "how" as previously pointed out by Brush.

It is difficult to decide what information is important in what context and for whom. You condenses the most common important computer-aided awareness support mechanisms to *abstraction, time dependence, aggregation, possibility of influence and personalization.*

Abstraction means deciding which level of detail and symbolicity information is presented in. Time dependence means the time span of awareness information to be presented, whether it includes past, present or (supposed) future. Aggregation means dividing and combining awareness information, whether it is presented as individual components and events, collected overviews, or as a continuous flow. Possibility of influence means who, how much and how can the awareness information and its viewpoint be influenced. It means whether the recipient can influence the source of information, the methods of gathering and presenting the information, or adapt it to better suit current needs and tasks. Personalization means whether the information is presented in an individually adapted form or for a larger group of people. Personalization can include the use of other mechanisms.

Sounds as a medium suits these mechanisms in different ways. As we will learn in Sects. 10.2, 10.3 and 10.4, sound is good for aggregating information on several levels of abstraction, including different time spans. Personalization is possible, but the public nature of sounds makes that more challenging, as it does with the possibility of individual influence. Due to these reasons, we will focus more on peripheral awareness support of multiple users, as opposed to individual interactive participation taking place in the focus of attention.

10.1.3 Attention Shift and Peripheral Awareness

Attentiveness means the direction and selectiveness of mental activity. In the process of knowing and becoming aware, attention shift is important. Shifting attention involves the utilization of the periphery of senses. Matthews et al. (2003) divide the level of attention into four categories: *preattention, inattention, divided attention* and *focused attention*. These categories represent a range from not affecting a person's consciousness at all, and affecting behaviour even without being conscious of the effect, to shared and full mental focus on an object. Attention shifts between all these categories can be involuntary or voluntary depending on stimuli or level of conscious effort. We shift our focus both intentionally, as parts of our actions, task planning, thoughts and feelings and automatically, as a reaction to the events, objects and people around us. This means we do not always need specially designed notifications or heightened levels of output, if our internal motivations make something worth attending to.

Many ambient intelligence awareness systems are based on the human ability to shift the focus of their attention, and the need for different levels of engagement in different phases and modes of work (Gaver, 1991). Sometimes the system needs to grab the attention of its users and focused interaction has to take place. Sometimes the system needs to stay in the background and not disturb, only occasionally offering subtle cues for the users to take action upon. Awareness systems utilizing the peripheral-sensing capabilities of humans can convey information of which people are aware, but have not focused their attention to (Wisneski et al., 1998). Inattention and divided attention can be used in calm ambient presentations. Inattention does not burden a person's cognitive capacity. This means that awareness support applications have to be unobtrusive and not demand attention unnecessarily with interruptions or low media quality (for example, low quality sound samples). To succeed in this, the presentation they use have to be consistent and continuous. In addition, since ambient intelligence environments often have more than one person present, the awareness needs of the individual and the awareness needs of the group of people might not be compatible; the level of obtrusiveness has to also match the social and task situation. Thus, the strategy of the least obtrusive awareness system could be a wise choice, at least in non-critical systems.

Because sounds can be heard without focusing our attention to them, they form a good medium for providing awareness information, both attention grabbing and peripheral. Sound can also convey information on various levels of abstraction and with different encodings and therefore it can be suited to many social situations. In the following, we discuss how speech and sounds can be used to achieve those aims.

10.2 Properties of Speech and Non-speech Audio

Speech and non-speech audios have several physical, acoustical and psychological qualities, which have a strong effect on how they can and should be used in awareness information presentation. A more detailed description of perceptual and acoustic properties of sounds outside the context of awareness support can be found from, e.g. a textbook by Rossing et al. (2002).

Speech and non-speech sounds are efficient and expressive, well suited for multimodal interaction, natural, public and omnidirectional. For example, speech has been shown to be the most efficient and important communication modality in many cases (Chapanis, 1975; Huang et al., 2001), and enables expression of information which may be hard with other modalities. It carries linguistic as well as emotional information. Sounds can also express information in multiple ways at the same time, e.g. through pitch, timbre, loudness, direction, duration, rhythm and melody.

Concrete sounds, i.e. recordings of naturally occurring sounds, are by definition natural in origin. They are efficient, because the meanings are already learned, and sometimes almost hardwired to create reactions and emotions. Animal warning cries, car horns and such create strong reactions without specific learning or interpretation of abstractions. Speech can also be a natural interface element (Kamm, 1994), because people are used to receiving awareness information in public places through, e.g. announcements in train stations. Speech also very effectively makes systems anthropomorphic; when people hear speech, they tend to build a picture of the person talking based on the voice and speaking style.

Sounds efficiently support multimodal interaction, since, for example vision and hearing are independent of each other. They can support each other in a common goal (Brewster, 2002), disambiguate each other (Oviatt et al., 2004), or otherwise enable concurrent multitasking. This is one of the clearest advantages when using sounds in pervasive awareness support systems, where users focus on some tasks and peripherally monitor others.

Sound is mostly a public medium, omnidirectional and surrounding in nature. It is not restricted into small areas, does not require orientation towards the sound source, and it can reach a large number of people simultaneously. For the same reasons, sound can capture attention faster than vision, regardless of previous orientation. Sound can stay in the periphery of our attention, which leaves more room for other more focused interaction, even with other sounds. For example, this is evident in the cocktail party effect; people can easily focus their attention to a single speaker or conversation even when there are many other people talking at equal volumes (Stifelman, 1994).

Sounds have their limitations, of which, e.g. Brewster (2002) mentions low precision, the difficulty of expressing absolute values, interdependence of value expressing elements, serial nature of information and irritability of sound feedback. Low precision refers to, e.g. relatively low human capability of sound direction sensing and relative frequency perception. Interdependence means the way certain sound parameters, e.g. perceived frequency and loudness, affect each other. When compared to non-speech audio, speech can present absolute values, such as numbers and relations.

Common to all audio output are serial nature, irritability and public nature. The serial nature of auditory information means that information is temporary, and has to be repeated for closer inspection. This also limits the amount of information that can be presented with speech. By irritability Brewster means sound pollution that occurs because of too strong loudness as well as of the omnidirectional and surrounding nature of sound, evident when, e.g., public announcements, commercials and background music of individual stores, mobile phones and personal music players all compete with your attention and present privacy challenges while you walk in a shopping centre. Schafer (1977, p. 88) speaks of schizophonia, or splitting sounds from their original contexts, when making sounds audible without the original sound source being present.

Next we will discuss how these properties of sounds can be used for interaction between people and computer applications.

10.3 Auditory Interaction Techniques

Sounds can be divided into several "archetypes" depending on the way they are traditionally used in interaction to present information. Speech, auditory icons, earcons, music, soundscapes and sonifications have different purposes and implications when used in awareness support, derived from the qualities discussed in the previous section.

In user interfaces, speech can be either prerecorded or synthesized. Prerecorded speech can be of excellent quality, and can contain intricate emotional information, especially when professional voice actors are used. It is also rather inflexible, because adjusting its acoustic properties or content is challenging and laborious. Using synthesized speech and natural language generation is a more flexible approach, but does not usually reach the same level of speech quality and realism are recorded speech. Some elements, such as emotional speech, are under research (Schröder, 2001), and the difference compared to recorded is small in the most advanced synthesizers available today.

Auditory icons are related to natural sounds which are familiar to users. They convey meaning which is derived from their origin rather than acoustic properties, and are therefore intuitive. Typical examples are sounds of animals, sirens, sounds related to closing and opening of things, etc. Sometimes their use is related to cultural conventions, since many sounds are found and understood only in certain areas and contexts. Auditory icons or "found sounds", need not to be abstract, and they can carry psychological and cultural meanings unlike abstract sounds. Because of their origin, they may also carry more acoustic information than needed, and be misleading. Because auditory icons are often recorded sound samples, their parameterization is limited. Several techniques have been presented to manipulate and synthesize auditory icons (Gaver, 1993).

Instead of conveying information on their origin like auditory icons, earcons represent information in their acoustic parameters. As earcons are usually not known to the users beforehand and they may be abstract, their use requires learning, but on the other hand they are free from the limitations the natural sounds often have and once learned, they can be easily recognized. Earcons have the advantage that they can be well controlled and structured (Brewster, 2002). They can be combinations of, e.g. melodies or changes in volume and timbre, which then form combined meanings like words in a sentence. They can also hierarchically inherit characteristics of other earcons, which gives another dimension for encoding information into acoustic properties of sound.

Elementary sounds can be used together to construct longer and more complex presentations, i.e. music and soundscapes. In addition to internal parameters of single notes, such as pitch and timbre, music has several structural parameters, such as rhythm, melodies and chords that can be used to convey information. Music can be used to represent graphical entities, such as diagrams (Alty and Rigas, 1998) or background monitoring of concurrent activities (Tran and Mynatt, 2000). It can also be used to provide a non-obtrusive, coherent aural environment which is also aesthetically pleasant. With the development of musical arts into different directions, especially with the emergence of electro-acoustic music, it is difficult or impossible to make distinction between what is commonly thought of as music and what is "just" sounds or noises.

Similar to music, individual sounds can be used to form soundscape compositions, i.e. auditory counterparts to visual portraits or models of landscapes (Schafer, 1977). Soundscapes consist of keynote sounds (e.g. background sound of waves or traffic), sound signals (e.g. discrete foreground sounds like horns and whistles) and sound marks (e.g. unique auditory landmarks), which all have different roles, behaviour and levels of obtrusiveness. Soundscape compositions can be used to encompass environments and create atmospheres and identities to locations, and tie different interaction elements together. The different roles of sounds can change in time and their relationships can be utilized to convey further information.

All in all, sounds can be very efficient in creating meaningful representations, for example, to give quick overviews for complex situations, or help in data mining. Sonification is a generic term used to refer to mapping between information and its auditory representation. According to Kramer et al. (1999), *sonification is the transformation of data relations into perceived relations in an acoustic signal for the purposes of facilitating communication or interpretation.* It should be noted that this does not define what techniques or elements (e.g. auditory icons, earcons) sonifications contain. Sonification is an auditory counterpart to the term visualization.

In practise, sonifications can be used as a way of presenting overviews on large data sets and a way to help exploring them (Hermann, 2002). In medical applications, sounds can be used to sonify, e.g. epileptic or otherwise pathological EEG features (Baier et al., 2006). Sonifications are also suitable for factory production controls (Gaver et al., 1991), or mission-critical applications, e.g. cockpit audio interfaces. Some of the sonifications can even be profoundly touching while presenting statistical data, as in Guernica (2006), which sonifies war and world population data (Potard, 2006). When using sound, there is only a thin red line between artistic and informational goals as well as methods (Vickers and Hogg, 2006).

Next we will discuss some of these techniques in relation to awareness systems.

10.4 Guidelines for Auditory Presentation Techniques

When using auditory icons, the most important usability factors for auditory icons, according to Mynatt (1994), are identifiability, conceptual mapping, physical parameters and user preference. In addition to those, soundscapes and musical presentations also require complex techniques for ensuring continuity and consistency of presentations. Conceptual mappings, compositional control, timing and transitions are very important areas of system design and development of peripheral soundscapes (Kainulainen et al., 2006).

This section collects different aspects of auditory presentation techniques, and presents guidelines on which purposes and how they should be used in awareness applications. We have categorized the basic forms of auditory presentation techniques, presented in the previous subsections, and here give guidelines on which applications and context they are suitable for, and what challenges and limitations they have. The aspects we discuss of, in regard to each of the techniques, are as follows:

- temporal aspects, i.e. seriality, continuity and speed;
- precision, i.e. amount and nature of data;
- peripherality, i.e. attention shift and multitasking;
- emotional aspects;
- publicity and privacy;
- naturalness and aesthetics;
- data mapping, i.e. interdependence of elements, cultural dependence and acoustic parameters;
- learning curve, i.e. intuitiveness and difficulty; and
- control techniques, i.e. parameter and composition control.

The following sections discuss each of these aspects in the context of different basic auditory presentation techniques.

10.4.1 Speech

Temporally, speech is always *serial*, which makes it a relatively slow output media. Thus, it is not good for applications, which need to present continuous data streams or large datasets, or require quick reactions. On the other hand, it is very *precise* for presenting absolute values, abstract concepts and other linguistic information, unlike other forms of audio. Speech is suitable for summarizations of that kind of data.

- Speech is mostly suitable for applications which require focused attention. Speech is not usually very *peripheral*, since it tends to grab our attention easier than other forms of audio.

- Speech is a *natural* form of input and recorded speech provides an excellent naturalness. Synthesized speech output, however, is challenged by language production and synthesis problems. Humans are very sensitive to speech quality, which may limit its *aesthetic* uses.
- Synthesized speech requires special *control techniques*, e.g. language creation and synthesis control. These may prove challenging in applications, where the application platform is technically less capable. Recorded speech, on the other hand, is straightforward to use even in low-end machines.
- *Emotionally*, speech can contain *rich vocal cues* through, e.g. intonation and choice of words. In speech synthesis systems, however, they are difficult to control with current technology. It is also important to notice that speech easily anthropomorphizes the application it is used in, which can be an advantage, e.g. when creating ties between users and applications is important.
- Speech is language dependent and not generic in that sense, which has to be taken into account when mapping information to speech presentation. Although its public nature makes it suitable for addressing large groups, for some applications, e.g. airports and other multicultural places, this can be a problem.
- The *learning curve* of speech interfaces is very quick, excluding early childhood and non-native speakers. This makes speech very suitable for sparsely used applications and even for helping to learn to understand other forms of presentation.

10.4.2 Auditory Icons

Temporally, auditory icons are *discrete events*, but can be used as elements of larger auditory displays which span over time. They can be used to present *relative* values.

- Auditory icons can be both *focal*, e.g. sirens and cries, or *peripheral*, e.g. when used as keynote sounds such as the humming of trees. Peripherality is strongly dependent on the rest of the soundscape and the state of the user.
- Since auditory icons are "found sounds", they can carry *strong emotional content* the original sound source itself contained, e.g. in a cry of a baby. This can be used to the advantage of the presentation because of the short learning curve, but it can be also difficult to avoid unintended meanings hidden in the acoustic properties of the original sound. For the same reasons, while being less public than speech, auditory icons are more public than earcons, since most people can derive some meaning from the sound source.
- Recorded sounds can be *natural*, since they often are sounds naturally occurring in some environment. Acoustic properties and acoustic ecology have to be considered, since most sounds have a context they naturally appear in, and it is easy to create dissonance, e.g. through unmatching echoic properties.
- Acoustic parameters of auditory icons are more difficult to manipulate compared to earcons. Information is linked more to *the origin of the sound* rather than the acoustic properties of the sound itself.

- Auditory icons are comparatively *quick to learn*, since naturally occurring sounds have some intuitive meaning. This means they are good for systems which users cannot practise to use much.
- Auditory icons are prerecorded discrete sound elements, which are relatively easy to play back even on limited systems, e.g. small embedded systems. Manipulating their acoustic properties dynamically often requires more complicated signal processing, which might require more computing power.

10.4.3 Earcons

Temporally, earcons are *discrete*, just like auditory icons. They can be used to present *relative* values, and also *hierarchical* information, which makes them ideal for presenting more complex and interrelated data.

- *Emotional references are harder to create* with earcons, compared to auditory icons, because of their abstract nature, but it is possible through using a musical approach, e.g. with melodies.
- Synthesized and abstract sounds might *not* be *found in nature*, but they can be as aesthetic as any other sound.
- Since earcons are symbolic, they usually need to be learned, which makes them *less public*. Naturally, a popular and common earcon, e.g. the notification sound of Windows XP user interface, can be understood by many people.
- Earcons *require learning*, depending on the complexity of the presentation and mappings used.
- Acoustic parameters of synthesized earcons can be *easily manipulated*, which makes mapping easier to design and implement.
- Controlling earcons is easy, since they require discreet playback capabilities, and the acoustic parameter control is not as complicated as with auditory icons.

10.4.4 Music

Temporally, music is usually composed of phrases longer than discrete sound icons. Even completely *continuous* music can be used in user interfaces. Music is often *hierarchical, layered* and conveys information on a wider band than earcons or auditory icons.

- Traditionally, music is often used in a *peripheral role*, e.g. as background music in user interfaces. This does not exclude more focal uses of music, e.g. as sonification. Music can be quite versatile when changing attention between the periphery and focus of awareness. Music can convey *rich emotional content*, but it is also tied to the context of use and the listener's personal experiences.

- Music is *less public* than speech, and because people are already used to hearing music from mobile devices, even less public than some auditory icons or earcons, depending on the content and design.
- Mapping information to music is often *culturally dependent*, since composition techniques and music theory are mostly tied to historical development. Despite this, a common *cultural frame of reference is already learned* because of the pervasiveness of music. Even people without specific education in music theory can recognize many musical techniques. Music can also be interpreted from a purely *aesthetic and intellectual* viewpoint, without ties to cultural references or personal experiences, just like, e.g. abstract art.
- Controlling musical presentations involves music and composition theory, which are complex fields of research in themselves. Many techniques have been developed for, e.g. controlling chords, rhythms, harmonics and so on. Continuous music presentation also requires transition techniques and other means for ensuring consistency.

10.4.5 Soundscapes

Temporally, soundscape compositions are usually *continuous* presentations. Soundscapes are good for monitoring changes and continuous data and large data sets in overviews. Because of this, soundscapes are also often peripheral.

- The publicity and privacy of a soundscape also depends on the style it follows. Musical and abstract soundscapes are less public than realistic soundscapes, although soundscapes that mimic natural soundscapes might not even be noticed by others in a suitable context. The same applies to the aesthetics of a soundscape; they can be pleasing and natural.
- Controlling soundscape presentations depends on the presentation style, but is usually similar to the complexity of musical control, at least in regard to controlling continuity and consistency.
- Next we will illustrate these guidelines in the light of some example auditory awareness systems.

10.5 Auditory Awareness Systems

Sound and awareness information work together well, as discussed and illustrated by many applications. However, the process of turning information maintained by a computer into a successful soundscape that helps users is not a trivial process. In addition to designing a successful soundscape, the system must also be implemented so that it can gather and process the information, transform it to the presentation and control the presentation as necessary. In this section, these issues are discussed with concrete examples. First, the structure of auditory awareness applications is presented and the main elements of auditory soundscapes are introduced. Finally, we present some well-known auditory awareness systems, including an auditory awareness application for office environments by Kainulainen et al. (2005), and its underlying generic auditory awareness system architecture (Kainulainen et al., 2006).

10.5.1 Structure of Auditory Awareness Applications

Figure 10.1 illustrates generic properties of the auditory awareness support application. The first phase is to collect data from various sources, such as implicit activity information from movement sensors and explicit information from personal computers (e.g. calendar applications). The second phase is the refinement of the information, for example by using rule-based or statistical reasoning to make higher level abstractions. In the third phase, the mapping between the awareness information and available auditory presentation methods is made. In the fourth phase, the resulting auditory presentation is sent to the audio engine to be played out.

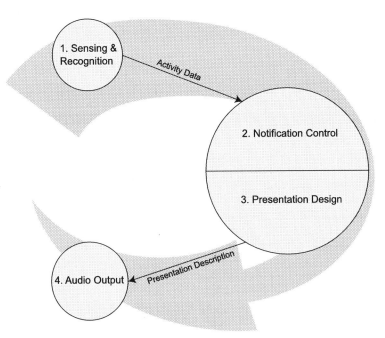

Fig. 10.1 The auditory awareness support process

Three most important areas of auditory soundscape design are information mapping, handling continuity and consistency, and composition control. Information can be mapped to concrete presentations in many ways. The continuity and consistency of a presentation affect its calmness and unobtrusiveness. There are many methods of defining and controlling whole compositions. We pay special attention to adaptivity and interactivity of the audio presentation. Next, we present the elementary elements of the presentation design.

10.5.1.1 Mapping Between Concepts and Presentations

Soundscapes are created by combining multiple individual sounds together, defining rules and variation for their qualities, behaviour and interaction. Changes in the soundscape, the objects moving in it and interacting with each other can easily be understood as a whole. In order to present meaningful information using audio we need to define the mapping between the information and its auditory presentation. The mapping can be as follows:

- A direct connection between a variable and a sound, where the change of the value of a variable causes a change in the sound or its qualities directly, as a continuous stream or as finite icons.
- Static, binary or dynamic, where static sounds can present atmospheric, default and unchanging information, binary sounds can present the presence of a person or other true/false information, and dynamic sounds can present information on processes and interaction.
- Hierarchically structured, where sounds can be related to multiple categories at the same time, for example to identity, presence and activity in a certain task categorization, determined by their melodies, tones and harmonies.
- Complete compositions or virtual constructs of objects, where the elements are viewed as individual objects with rules and patterns guiding their behaviour and their interaction.
- Linguistic connection, i.e. language is used to present the information. Presenting information with speech can be straightforward speaking of the required attributes, or it can include a sophisticated process of analyzing values and presenting them in some relative, summarized or otherwise more comprehensible form.

After a soundscape has been defined, it can be rendered much in the same way as three-dimensional graphics, continuously in real time. The interaction of individual elements generates the richness of the whole presentation. All this requires ways to bind different types of information to sound elements and compositional structures in different levels of abstraction, which can be dynamically edited in real time depending on input according to rules which dictate their behaviour.

10.5.1.2 Timing, Transitions, Continuity and Consistency

Awareness support systems usually aim at keeping the users consistently aware of relevant information. Because of this, the presentation can be continuous; users hear it all the time or at least very often. Because of this, the presentation must be unobtrusive so that it does not hinder users' concentration on their tasks. This requires consistent, continuous presentation with subtle transitions. It should be noted though, that in some cases, e.g. during critical notifications like fire alarms, smooth and seamless transitions are unwanted. Sensing the seams between sound sources and events can also provide important contextual information or meta-awareness (Chalmers and Galani, 2004).

In order to create consistent and continuous presentations, methods for timing and synchronization of sound elements are crucial. New sound elements and changes in the old elements have to be timed correctly to maintain consistent presentation. Changes in the information cause changes in the presentation, and these changing points, or transitions, have to be smooth and natural. The timing and handling of transitions require control system. Some relevant work has been done in the area of computer game music (Whitmore, 2003).

When a decision of a change in the presentation has been made, the transition from the previous state to the next has to be handled smoothly. A transition can be just silence between two consecutively played elements or their direct splicing, a crossfade or synchronized overlap of common rhythms, use of effects to ease the transition, or in the best case completely seamless. A seamless transition is difficult to achieve even in musical terms, let alone technically automated. In the most difficult case, music and the system that produces it have to be ready to make the transition at any moment. The bigger the change the more difficult it is to achieve seamlessly.

Technology-wise, transitions can be carried out by jumping in premarked points of the predefined composition, either within the same or to a different presentation. A collection of these decision points can form a decision tree (Land and MacConnell, 1994). Transitions can also be handled by making a layered presentation. A layered transition means adding and removing sounds or tracks from the composition in layers. A transition matrix can also be used to handle the transition between every possible track combination with especially composed transition-tracks. It is also possible to track the harmonies of a piece of music (Temperley, 1997) so that new instrument layers could begin in harmony with the previous ones. Chord maps (Mugglin, 2005) can be used to define even complicated rules after which certain chords can move into others.

Sometimes compositional elements start to repeat themselves, which might even become irritating. Alternative sound elements can be randomized according to certain rules. Generative music (Eno, 1996) is specialized in randomness and indeterminacy. Alternating and randomized elements might ease repetition, but gives rise to a possible recognition problem, so it would require closer design and study before being applied.

A soundscape application should have a control system for timing elements in the mixing phase, and handling different ways of making transitions from one information state to another. The system has to be extensible, since there is no way to predict all possible ways in which timing and transitioning can be performed.

10.5.1.3 Controlling Auditory Presentation Compositions

The larger the amount of information to be presented is, the more demanding is the task of controlling the sound presentation during application runtime. With more elaborate rules describing the presentation, the complexity of the application's functionality grows. Because of the growing complexity, it might become useful to separate application design between programmers and composers. The software component producing and controlling the sound presentation has to be flexible and versatile, and it has to offer a clear tool for designing presentations.

Even with the trend towards a continuous soundscape, it can still react to information flow in many ways. It can react to changes in the information to be presented directly in real time, with a delay or even by anticipating events. Direct reaction means real-time changes in the presentation, which could mean, for example, an instant notification of someone's arrival to work, regardless of the situation of the rest of the presentation. Real-time reactivity means concurrent operation of independent components. A delayed reaction means that the change is timed for the next moment it is aesthetically or psychologically appropriate. Anticipation means preparing to prearranged and known chains of events or statistically probable situations. By anticipating events the transition to a change in the sound presentation can be started before the change actually takes place.

One of the major challenges is to define how the software component which controls the sound presentation communicates with the rest of the system, what elements of the presentation can be changed, and how the system triggers these changes. Computer games and systems supporting them, e.g. LucasArts iMuse (Land and MacConnell, 1994), Microsoft Direct Music (Microsoft Corporation, 1998) and IXMF (Grigg, 2003), are good examples for these challenges, since they have used different kinds of triggers in setting off changes in their sound presentations for a long time already. Similar triggering techniques can be employed to react also to real-world situations. For this purpose, the sound presentation software component needs an open interface and a way to communicate back to different external information sources.

Control can also be achieved by using events and scripting to create a link between soundscapes and the underlying information sources. Scripting in this context means a way of building complex combinations and events from single rules and commands with a simple annotation mechanism or language. This need is clear when defining how the system should combine computer activity results, speaker recognition results and other information sources together and bind them into presentation elements. Technology-wise, scripting requires a language general enough, so that other soundscape control methods and components can be used, and events can be defined in a clear and easy way. This kind of scripting can be thought to be a parallel and somewhat overlapping way of defining a sound presentation to traditional musical composition. There are many kinds of scripting languages and notations, ranging from concurrent audio programming languages like

ChucK (Wang and Cook, 2003) to synthesis markup languages like SSML (Taylor and Isard, 1997).

An efficient soundscape control mechanism used in a large and complex presentation design task would require a common abstraction of specialty areas for application designers and composers to work together. The same mechanism has to provide means for direct, delayed and anticipated changes. An open interface to external information sources and a callback mechanism are required. Real-time reactivity and concurrently running components are required for some situations. A scripting language is needed to allow configurability and extensibility.

In conclusion, there is a strong need for tools of composition and dynamic control. The application should have an easy-to-use interface for iterative design and experimenting with different kinds of compositions. On the other hand, the application should have an efficient and flexible protocol for communicating with the information sources and other applications. These two extremes should come together in a dynamic and interactive manner. We have addressed these challenges by designing a new architecture for design and construction of auditory soundscapes (Kainulainen et al., 2006). This framework includes an easy to use markup and script language for the composers to define the presentations. At the same time, the markup language allows a clearly defined format for application designers to use while implementing the applications. The architecture has been used to implement an auditory awareness application for ubiquitous office environments. The application and the architecture are presented in the following section with other example applications.

10.5.2 Example Applications

Audio Aura (Mynatt et al., 1998) is one of the most well-known auditory awareness systems. It provides users serendipitous information, i.e. information that is not necessary for their actions but can be useful when perceived. The information is tied to physical locations and delivered via portable wireless headphones. The information includes status of e-mail mailbox, information about people's presence and general workgroup awareness, "group pulse".

Audio Aura utilizes three different types of audio discussed earlier; sound effects (auditory icons), music (short music segments; earcons), voice and a rich combination of these. The sound effect based soundscape consists of different sounds of beach; e.g. cries of seagulls. In this musical soundscape, changing melodies, pitch and rhythm convey information. The mappings are mostly simple, e.g. more notes mean more e-mail. The voice-based soundscape simply provides information with speech.

In the design of the sound effects for Audio Aura, sonic ecologies, i.e. semantic compatibility of different sounds has been considered. When all the sounds are related to beach, they fit each other and feel consistent. This way the soundscape should remain in periphery. The ecology has also been considered by Mauney and Walker (2004), who provide monitoring of stock market information with nature sounds such as birdcalls, insect songs, rain and thunder. They report learning is indeed necessary to understand a soundscape like this; during the initial listening users cannot comprehend the structure of the sonification but during the third listening the users could follow the structure. Natural sounds have also been used in the soundscapes of ambientROOM system (Wisneski et al., 1998) and by Kilander and Lönnqvist (2002) in their weakly intrusive ambient soundscape system.

Using music, not just earcons, requires a slightly different approach to control and composition. One example of music-based auditory awareness systems has been presented by Jung and Butz (2005; Butz and Jung, 2005). They play the musical soundscape from public speakers instead of private earphones. The music consists of a core part, which is always present, and optional tracks, such as additional instruments. Each user has an individual sound (e.g. an instrument, a melody, or a rhythmic pattern). These can be included into music at appropriate moments. Because of this, the sonification cannot react immediately, but must wait until an appropriate point in the composition is reached to play a particular sound. Because of the individual elements, users are usually aware of only their own notifications. They do not know what components belong to other users and therefore can consider them just parts of the music. This provides certain weak privacy to the public presentation and because of this invisibility the authors consider the auralization potent for such applications as museums and memorial places where traditional announcements are not appropriate. In addition to providing the presented information, Butz and Jung note that musical presentations can be used to provide emotional cues to provide certain mood.

10.5.3 A Speech-Based and Auditory Ubiquitous Office Environment

Next we present how awareness information is gathered and used in a ubiquitous office environment. The environment has been constructed using speech recognition, speech synthesis and speaker recognition technologies and multimodal information sources are used for tasks such as positioning of users. The environment is augmented with services such as interactive spoken guidance and system-supported speech-based messaging (Kainulainen et al., 2005). Here we focus on unobtrusive group awareness information.

In workplaces, such as offices, it is often important to avoid disturbing people and provide indirect ways of communication to increase awareness of the situation in the workplace, using unobtrusive methods. This enables direct communication to take place in a meaningful way, when it is appropriate. As presented in previous sections, speech and non-speech audios provide natural and efficient ways for such settings.

In the augmented office environment different ways of communication are used. Subtle indirect methods are used to lessen the information overload yet keep the information available to trigger more active interaction. A presence awareness application keeps people informed about each others' activities and presence with minimal cognitive load. When needed, an audio messaging application gives colleagues an informal ad hoc method of communicating between people and receiving news and other notifications from the environment. For visitors, the system offers route guidance services to keep them aware of the environment itself. In order to enable all of the ways of communication, the system needs to have information about the different applications running in the environment and the state of the environment. Next we present the enabling technologies and different applications in more detail.

10.5.3.1 Data Gathering

In order to provide awareness information, the system has to be aware of the objects and structures of the office space and the position of each user. The system contains a spatial object model to represent the environment (Prusi et al., 2005). Depending on the degree of detail this model consists of rooms, corridors and halls, or in more detail doors, windows, furniture and other less stable objects in the environment. The model of the environment is based on the description of objects, their attributes and relations between the components. The model concerning the shape and structure of the office serves all the applications of our environment, therefore it needs to cover structural information for route finding, descriptive vocabulary information for speech-based guidance as well as information concerning the interaction possibilities and input and output devices of each location.

Positioning of the users is a common problem in mobile and ubiquitous systems awareness systems. An easy way is to equip users with positioning devices, such as RFID sensors, but we wanted to avoid this, and instead we wanted to embed all technology in the environment. In an office context, reliable positioning of a user has to be done using several techniques and input channels together. The system recognizes people's movements using electro-mechanical film (EMFi) sensors placed on the floor. The positioning information produced by the sparsely placed EMFi sensors is not reliable enough as such for tracking individual people's movements. Combined with positioning information gathered from other input devices, such as activity daemons that monitor the usage of mouse, keyboard and application activity and speaker identification results at the interaction points, more precise knowledge of the locations of users is achieved.

10.5.3.2 Awareness Information

The system includes several methods to keep people aware of activities inside their environment in indirect ways. The system aims at bringing information calmly to the periphery of people's attention, in order to find less burdening ways to inform people (Weiser and Brown, 1997). Presence information is given in a transparent and unobtrusive manner using environmental audio, regarding to the activity data collected. Information is presented in the form of soundscapes that consist of thematically similar sounds, such as sounds of birds singing. This is similar to the approach taken in the Audio Aura system (see previous section).

The application collects presence and activity information by tracking how often people use their computers. Activity within a certain time frame (e.g. 5 min) is interpreted to be recent enough, and the location of the activity is interpreted as the location of the person. The activity and presence of each person of the work group is depicted by an appropriate sound, such as the singing of a bird. Sounds are mixed together dynamically depending on the situation and interleaved in layers in order to create a presentation as natural and calm as possible. The application mixes sounds dynamically together according to certain constraints. To avoid congestion at the busiest moments, only a certain amount of sounds are allowed to play simultaneously. Sounds are mixed to partially overlap, and a new sound can be introduced to the soundscape only when the previous sounds are at a suitably calm point, e.g. during pauses or low-energy points in birdcalls. In our installation, people's offices are all in a row along the same hallway, the seating order is used as the order of sounds. These rules make the soundscape seem like a moving glance around the environment. Playback is handled by highly directional EMFi loudspeakers placed in public places and personal offices. In early mornings and late evenings when only a few people are present, the soundscape resembles a quiet lakeside in the wilderness with just a few birdcalls echoing over the water. During active moments there are more birds creating a more active atmosphere. In addition to sounds of birds, we have also used actual walking sounds of users (Mäkelä et al., 2003).

In order to support group awareness in more direct ways, we have implemented a speech-based application to help people to communicate and receive messages while they are moving in the office environment. Messaging services are commonly used in group work for informal and ad hoc communications. Speech-based messaging contains vocal subtleties, emphases and emotions which cannot be conveyed in text-based communication (Sawhney and Schmandt, 1999). Spoken dialogue technologies can be used to support the communication between the users, and act as a partner in the conversation to bring in added value such as guiding the messages to correct locations. We have implemented a messaging system based on speech and speaker recognition, microphones and loudspeakers placed in corridors, halls and private offices. Microphones in offices are connected to the desktop computers of the group members and they act as triggers to the dialogue in addition to their primary use (Kainulainen et al., 2005).

Next, we present the underlying generic audio awareness architecture.

10.5.3.3 Audio Awareness Architecture

In order to facilitate development of auditory awareness applications we have developed a generic architecture for producing and controlling soundscapes. It implements the generic model presented in Fig. 10.1 and follows the design guidelines presented in Sect. 10.4. The architecture takes into account the special needs of pervasive computing environments, where the target audience moves around in space and from social situation to another, and where tasks and technological

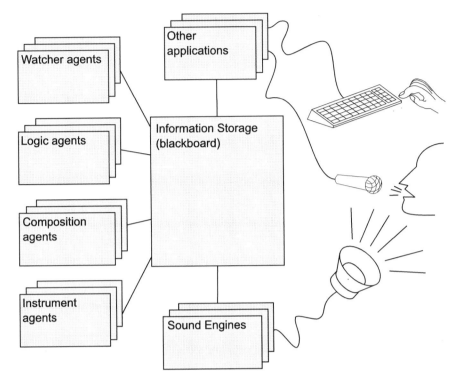

Fig. 10.2 The general structure of the audio awareness architecture

capabilities of the environment change. In addition, different users, such as users with special needs, are taken into account. For example, different versions of the same presentation can be easily created to suit the diminished capabilities of hearing impaired.

The general structure of the architecture is illustrated in Fig. 10.2. Technology-wise, the architecture is built on top of the Jaspis speech and pervasive computing application framework (Turunen et al., 2005). Since the architectural solutions presented here are built on top of the common underlying framework, the functionality is available also to other applications built on top of Jaspis. The structure and functionality is largely object-oriented, and it follows the agent–evaluator–manager principle. Managers form the basic blocks and handle the coordination of the applications: information gathering management, logic management, composition management, instrument management and such. The production and control of the sound presentation is decentralized to subtasks of different agents. The agents are compact, highly specialized and numerous software components, which enables easy reuse and extension of functionality. They handle small tasks and responsibilities and are dynamically chosen to suit the task at hand. Agents both inherit functionality and take advantage of configurability through scripting. Evaluators choose which agents to use at a specific moment, and thus handle the system level adaptation. This adaptivity is important in handling the changing presentations.

Awareness information and its auditory representation are stored in a shared system knowledge base, or Information Storage, on different abstraction levels. This kind of a blackboard is similar to Hearsay-II (Erman et al., 1980), which describes a classical way to present information in different levels of abstraction. All of the agents can modify the presentation according to their specifications and the situation. Flexible information flow is made possible by the central Information Storage, where information is available and modifiable to all agents.

The presentation created and controlled by the agents is produced by sound engines which parse the commands and requests given by the agents. The communication works both ways, so events in the presentation can trigger further activity of the agents, and thus even of other applications through the common architecture. The architecture supports distribution, which means that it is possible to run each agent and engine on separate platforms in different physical locations (Salonen et al., 2005). This answers to an essential requirement in ubiquitous computing environments, where hardware environments are distributed and diverse.

10.6 Summary and Discussion

This chapter presented how speech and non-speech audios could be used in awareness systems. The focus was on group and peripheral awareness systems in ubiquitous and mobile computing settings. We described how speech and non-speech audios are efficient, expressive, natural, omnidirectional and public media, and what limitations they have. Six common auditory interaction techniques were discussed, namely speech, auditory icons, earcons, music, soundscapes and sonifications. We presented guidelines for using these techniques in awareness systems depending on aspects ranging from psychoacoustics to implementation.

Example applications were presented, in the light of which we further discussed the issues presented in the guidelines. The general structure of auditory awareness applications as well as a generic system architecture was presented. Elements of awareness soundscapes and mappings between data and presentation were discussed. Auditory presentation control issues were discussed, especially ensuring continuity and consistency through timing and transitions.

10.6.1 Evaluation of Auditory Awareness Systems

Evaluation of auditory awareness applications, as presented in this chapter, can be considered from two perspectives. First, we can measure the quality of auditory presentations, and their elements, from different viewpoints using standard methods targeted for auditory and spoken user interfaces. For example, we recently used controlled listening experiment to measure how well test participants can recognize auditory public transport route descriptions in the evaluation (Kainulainen et al., 2007) of a mobile multimodal route guidance application TravelMan (Turunen et al., 2007). The main idea is to use soundscapes to support location awareness and navigation of people using public transportation. We conducted a test comparing three different auditory route descriptions (spoken, non-speech and combined) with 57 participants. Participants were divided in six groups for counterbalancing. Each auditory description design was presented as three recognition tasks of increasing difficulty. Each task consisted of one audio presentation followed by a multiple-choice task from four graphical presentations. Tasks were followed by an opinion questionnaire. In a nutshell, the test showed that auditory icons weakened the overall opinion of the presentations when used together with speech, but they were liked more than non-speech only presentations. On the other hand, the combined presentations were the most difficult to recognize. This gives rise to the question whether combining different kinds of sound is especially difficult. Recorded "natural" sounds together with synthesized speech, even with a relatively high-quality synthesis, might not fit in the same sound ecology easily. There have been similar results between recorded and synthesized speech (Gong and Lai, 2003), and even between different types of speech syntheses, which hint that moving from one type of sound to another is difficult. Speech and non-speech sounds could be seen as different modalities and combining them is not trivial.

In another controlled experiment we used recorded sounds of people walking as auditory icons that inform the presence of coworkers in office environments (Mäkelä et al., 2003). The main idea is to use walking sounds as a natural part of the overall sound ecology to provide non-obtrusive awareness information to coworkers. The aim of the controlled experiment was to evaluate the ability of people to identify the walking sounds of their coworkers based on their everyday experience. This was tested by playing recorded walking sounds to the subjects and asking their opinion on the identity of the walker. The experiment showed that without any training, simple recorded walking sounds were too hard to recognize. A teaching session improved the recognition rates significantly but such training is not a very desirable requirement. The careful design of walking sound based auditory icons could however help this problem. By supporting the impression people have about each other could make the sounds more distinguishable without losing benefits of prior knowledge.

The second approach focuses on long-term evaluation of auditory awareness application. Since the measuring of usefulness and acceptability of these applications takes time, typically weeks or months, we cannot use short-term evaluation methods such as controlled experiments. Here we suggest two particular methods: long-term pilot studies combined with novel subjective metrics applied from marketing. We have gained good experiences from the use of ecologically valid long-term pilot studies for speech interfaces (Turunen et al., 2006). In particular, we can use these methods to study how the attitude of users changes over the time. In our previous studies we have found great differences between controlled experiments, initial use of applications and established use of applications (Turunen et al., 2006). This can be combined with the use of novel subjective metrics to evaluate the appropriateness of our auditory awareness applications. In our previous research we have applied widely used service quality evaluation metrics for the evaluation of speech interfaces (Hartikainen et al., 2004). Here, we produce a subjective measure of the gap between expectations and perceptions in several quality dimensions. In this way, we can produce information that can be used in the iterative development of the awareness presentations. This can be a very useful tool to in addition to efficiency and user satisfaction-oriented paradigms. For example, the results could imply that it is more critical to concentrate on privacy than on pleasantness. Such results are vital for making auditory awareness applications more acceptable.

10.6.2 Complementary Speech and Non-Speech Audio

Our experiences with both spoken and non-speech audio interaction have brought forward a question on the still-continuing separation of the two styles of interaction. Traditionally, spoken interaction and sonification have been quite separate fields of study, and that separation tends to show in applications and research prototypes. Speech-user interfaces use auditory icons for prompting dialogue turns or music to indicate that the user needs to wait for the application to finish its processing. Sonifications have used speech synthesizers to output human-like vocalizations of data, even without using words (Hermann et al., 2006). Spoken words have been used as such or further processed to more resemble auditory icons than speech (Walker et al., 2006). Although there are such examples of utilizing the whole gamut between speech and non-speech audios, the theoretical background and enabling tools and techniques have not fully addressed the issue of complementary speech and non-speech audios.

The definition of sonification includes the word "communication", but examples of sonifications usually lack the communicational and interactive aspects of spoken dialogue research. On the other hand, speech technology often limits itself to linguistic approaches of human–human interaction, while people do not act similarly with computer applications as they do with humans (Turunen et al., 2005), and hybrid vocal/auditory behaviour could prove acceptable and more intuitive than single modality approaches. This hybrid approach would encompass everything from traditional spoken interaction, through natural and abstract vocalizations to iconic sounds, music and soundscapes in a manner that these auditory presentations would coexist in applications by definition. Auditory elements could emphasize and reference to each other, provide peripheral support, alternative output styles and means for smoothly changing between different levels of abstraction and subtlety.

Similarly, evaluation methods should reflect this widening of perspective. Traditionally separated and specialized evaluation approaches can be successfully reintroduced to serve a unified aim. Methods from fields as separate as, e.g. marketing, can bear fruit when applied as discussed previously.

The idea is not completely new, but scholarly boundaries are slow to change. Mynatt et al. (1998) addressed the issue when discussing different auditory ecologies in the Audio Aura. Voices, sound effects and music were seen as distinct ecologies, while a composite of all of them were seen as another ecology. Vickers and

Hogg (2006) discussed the same issue through presenting the abstract-concrete and informative-aesthetic axes of sonifications and music, and showing how much the different communities could benefit from each other.

We feel a wider theory is needed to address the acoustic, psychoacoustic and linguistic issues in a complementary manner. There are many commonalities already, but further work is required to tie them together and to develop, e.g. common tools for synthesis control and output.

References

Alty J and Rigas D (1998) Communicating Graphical Information to Blind Users Using Music: The Role of Context. Proceedings of CHI '98: Human Factors in Computing Systems, ACM Press, 574–581

Baier G, Hermann T, Sahle S and Stephani U (2006) Sonified Epileptic Rhythms. Proceedings of the 12th International Conference on Auditory Display (ICAD 2006)

Bly SA, Harrison SR and Irwin S (1993) Media Spaces: Bringing People Together in a Video, Audio, and Computing Environment. Communications of the ACM 36(1):28–46

Brewster SA (2002) NonSpeech Auditory Output. In: Jacko J and Sears A (eds.) The Human–Computer Interaction Handbook: Fundamentals, Evolving Technologies and Emerging Applications. Lawrence Erlbaum & AssociatesE, Mahwah, NJ

Brush AJ (2005) Terminology and Evaluation: Two Challenges for Awareness Systems Research. Position paper for CHI 2005 Workshop on Awareness Systems: Known Results, Theory, Concepts and Future Challenges

Butz A and Jung R (2005) Seamless User Notification in Ambient Soundscapes, Proceedings of the International Conference on Intelligent User Interfaces (IUI2005)

Chalmers M and Galani A (2004) Seamful Interweaving: Heterogeneity in the Theory and Design of Interactive Systems. Proceedings of the 5th Conference on Designing Interactive Systems: Processes, Practices, Methods, and Techniques

Chapanis A (1975) Interactive Human Communication. Scientific American, 232:36–42

Dix A, Finlay J, Abowd G and Beale R (2004) Human–Computer Interaction, 3rd edn. Pearson Education, Upper Saddle River, NJ

Dourish P and Bellotti V (1992) Awareness and Coordination in Shared Workspaces. Proceedings of the ACM CSCW Conference on Computer-Supported Cooperative Work, 107–114

Endsley M (1995) Measurement of Situation Awareness in Dynamic Systems. Human Factors 37(1):65–84

Eno B (1996) Generative Music. A Talk Delivered at the Imagination Conference, San Francisco, 8 June 1996. Published in: In Motion Magazine, 7 July 1996

Erman LD, Hayes-Roth F, Lesser VR and Reddy DR (1980) The Hearsay-II Speech-Understanding System: Integrating Knowledge to Resolve Uncertainty. ACM Computing Surveys (CSUR), 12(2):213–253

Gaver WW (1991) Sound Support for Collaboration. Proceedings of the Second European Conference on Computer-Supported Collaborative Work, 293–324

Gaver WW (1993) Synthesizing Auditory Icons. In: Ashlund S, Mullet K, Henderson A, Hollnagel E, White T (eds.) Proceedings of the ACM CHI 93 Human Factors in Computing Systems Conference. Amsterdam, The Netherlands, 228–235

Gaver WW, Smith RB and O'Shea T (1991) Effective Sounds in Complex Systems: The ARKola Simulation. Proceedings of CHI '91

Grigg C (2003) Preview: Interactive XMF – A Standardized Interchange File Format for Advanced Interactive Audio Content. 115th Audio Engineering Society Convention

Gong L and Lai J (2003) To Mix or Not to Mix Synthetic Speech and Human Speech? Contrasting Impact on Judge-Rated Task Performance Versus Self-Rated Performance and Attitudinal Responses. International Journal of Speech Technology, 6(2):123–131

Hartikainen M, Salonen E-P and Turunen M (2004) Subjective Evaluation of Spoken Dialogue Systems Using SERVQUAL Method. Proceedings of ICSLP 2004, 2273–2276

Hermann T (2002) Sonification for Exploratory Data Analysis. Ph.D. Thesis, Bielefeld University

Hermann T, Baier G, Stephani U and Ritter H (2006) Vocal Sonification of Pathologic EEG Features. Proceedings of the 12th International Conference on Auditory Display (ICAD 2006)

Huang X, Acero A and Hon H-W (2001) Spoken Language Processing – A Guide to Theory, Algorithm, and System Development. Prentice-Hall, Upper Saddle River, NJ

Jung R and Butz A (2005) Effectiveness of User Notification in Ambient Soundscapes. Proceedings of the workshop on Auditory Displays for Mobile Context-Aware Systems at Pervasive 2005

Kainulainen A, Turunen M, Hakulinen J, Salonen E-P, Prusi P and Helin L (2005) A Speech-Based and Auditory Ubiquitous Office Environment. Proceedings of 10th International Conference on Speech and Computer (SPECOM 2005), 231–234

Kainulainen A, Turunen M and Hakulinen J (2006) An Architecture for Presenting Auditory Awareness Information in Pervasive Computing Environments. Proceedings of the 12th International Conference on Auditory Display (ICAD 2006), 121–128

Kainulainen A, Turunen M and Hakulinen J (2007) Soundmarks in Spoken Route Guidance. Proceedings of the 13th International Conference of Auditory Display (ICAD 2007)

Kamm C (1994) User Interfaces for Voice Applications. In: Roe D and Wilpon J (eds.) Voice Communication Between Humans and Machines. National Academy Press, Washington, DC, 422–442

Kilander F and Lönnqvist P (2002) A Whisper in the Woods. Proceedings of the Eight International Conference on Auditory Display (ICAD 2002)

Kramer G, Walker B, Bonebright T, Cook P, Flowers J, Miner N; Neuhoff J, Bargar R, Barrass S, Berger J, Evreinov G, Fitch W, Gröhn M, Handel S, Kaper H, Levkowitz H, Lodha S, Shinn-Cunningham B, Simoni M and Tipei S (1999) The Sonification Report: Status of the Field and Research Agenda. Report Prepared for the National Science Foundation by Members of the International Community for Auditory Display. http://www.icad.org/node/400 Accessed 19 December 2007

Kraut R, Egido C and Galegher J (1988) Patterns of Contact and Communication in Scientific Research Collaboration. Proceedings of the 1988 ACM conference on Computer-Supported Cooperative Work, CSCW '88

Land MZ and MacConnell PN (1994) Method and Apparatus for Dynamically Composing Music and Sound Effects Using a Computer Entertainment System. U.S. Patent 5,315,057, 24 May 1994

Mäkelä K, Hakulinen J and Turunen M (2003) The Use of Walking Sounds in Supporting Awareness. Proceedings of ICAD 2003, 144–147

Matthews T, Rattenbury T, Carter S, Dey A and Mankoff J (2003) A Peripheral Display Toolkit. Intel Research Berkeley, Technical Report IRB-TR-03-018

Mauney BS and Walker BN (2004) Creating Functional and Livable Soundscapes for Peripheral Monitoring of Dynamic Data. Proceedings of the Tenth International Conference on Auditory Display ICAD2004

Microsoft Corporation (1998) Composing Music for Interactive Titles: An Overview of DirectMusic Producer. http://msdn.microsoft.com/library/default.asp?url=/library/en-us/dnmusic/html/interact.asp Accessed 3 June 2005

Mugglin S (2005) Music Theory for Songwriters. http://members.aol.com/chordmaps/ Accessed 3 June 2005

Mynatt ED (1994) Designing with Auditory Icons: How Well Do We Identify Auditory Cues? Proceedings of CHI'94

Mynatt ED, Back M, Want R, Bear M and Ellis JB (1998) Designing Audio Aura. Proceedings of the SIGCHI Conference on Human Factors in Computing Systems

Oviatt S, Coulston R and Lunsford R (2004) When Do We Interact Multimodally? Cognitive Load and Multimodal Communication Patterns. Proceedings of the Sixth International Conference on Multimodal Interfaces (ICMI 2004)

Potard G (2006) Guernica 2006: Sonification of 2000 Years of War and World Population Data. Proceedings of the 12th International Conference on Auditory Display (ICAD 2006)

Prusi P, Kainulainen A, Hakulinen J, Turunen M, Salonen E-P and Helin L (2005) Towards Generic Spatial Object Model and Route Guidance Grammar for Speech-Based Systems. Interspeech 2005

Rossing T, Moore F and Wheeler P (2002) The Science of Sound, 3rd edn. Addison Wesley, Reading, MA

Salonen E-P, Turunen M, Hakulinen J, Helin L, Prusi P and Kainulainen A (2005) Distributed Dialogue Management for Smart Terminal Devices. Proceedings of Interspeech 2005, 849–852

Sawhney N and Schmandt C (1999) Nomadic Radio: Scaleable and Contextual Notification for Wearable Audio Messaging. Proceedings of the ACM CHI 99 Human Factors in Computing Systems Conference, 96–103

Schafer RM (1977) The Soundscape – Our Sonic Environment and the Tuning of the World. Destiny Books, Vermont, USA

Schröder M (2001) Emotional Speech Synthesis: A Review. Proceedings of the 7th European Conference on Speech Communication and Technology, Eurospeech 2001

Stifelman LJ (1994) The Cocktail Party Effect in Auditory Interfaces: A Study of Simultaneous Presentation. MIT Media Laboratory Technical Report

Taylor P and Isard A (1997) SSML: A Speech Synthesis Markup Language. Speech Communications, 21(1–2):123–133

Temperley D (1997) An Algorithm for Harmonic Analysis. Music Perception, 15(1):31–68

Tran QT and Mynatt ED (2000) Music Monitor: Ambient Musical Data for the Home. Proceedings of the IFIP WG 9.3 International Conference on Home Oriented Informatics and Telematics (HOIT 2000), 173:85–92

Turunen M, Hakulinen J, Räihä K-J, Salonen E-P, Kainulainen A and Prusi P (2005) An Architecture and Applications for Speech-Based Accessibility Systems. IBM Systems Journal, Special Issue on Accessibility, 44(3)

Turunen M, Hurtig T, Hakulinen J, Virtanen A and Koskinen S (2006) Mobile Speech-based and Multimodal Public Transport Information Services. Proceedings of MobileHCI 2006 Workshop on Speech in Mobile and Pervasive Environments

Turune M, Hakulinen J, Kainulaine A, Melto A and Hurtig T (2007) Design of a Rich Multimodal Interface for Mobile Spoken Route Guidance. Proceedings of Interspeech 2007 – Eurospeech, 2193–2196

Vickers P and Hogg B (2006) Sonification Abstraite/Sonification Concrète: An 'Æsthetic Perspective Space' for Classifying Auditory Displays in the Ars Musica Domain. Proceedings of the 12th International Conference on Auditory Display (ICAD 2006)

Walker BN, Nance A and Lindsay J (2006) Spearcons: Speech-Based Earcons Improve Navigation Performance in Auditory Menus. Proceedings of the 12th International Conference on Auditory Display (ICAD 2006)

Wang G and Cook PR (2003) ChucK: A Concurrent, on-the-fly Audio Programming Language. Proceedings of the International Computer Music Conference (ICMC):219–226

Weiser M and Brown JS (1997) The coming age of calm technology. In: Denning PJ and Metcalfe RM (eds.) Beyond Calculation: The next fifty years of computing, Springer-Verlag, New York Inc.

Whitmore G (2003) Design with Music in Mind: A Guide to Adaptive Audio for Game Designers. Gamasutra.com, 29 May 2003. http://www.gamasutra.com/resource˙guide/ 20030528/whitmore˙pfv.htm Accessed 19 December 2007

Wisneski G, Ishii H, Dahley A, Gorbet M, Brave S, Ullmer B and Yarin P (1998) Ambient Displays: Turning Architectural Space into an Interface Between People and Digital Information. Proceedings of the First International Workshop on Cooperative Buildings (CoBuild '98)

You Y (2000) A Survey for the Study of Awareness in Co-Operative Systems. Proceedings of IRIS 23, Laboratorium for Interaction Technology, University of Trollhättan Uddevalla, Sweden

Part III
Applications

Chapter 11
Awareware: Narrowcasting Attributes for Selective Attention, Privacy, and Multipresence

Michael Cohen and Owen Noel Newton Fernando

11.1 Introduction

The domain of CSCW, computer-supported collaborative work, and DSC, distributed synchronous collaboration, spans real-time interactive multiuser systems, shared information spaces, and applications for telexistence and artificial reality, including collaborative virtual environments (CVEs) (Benford et al., 2001). As presence awareness systems emerge, it is important to develop appropriate interfaces and architectures for managing multimodal multiuser systems. Especially in consideration of the persistent connectivity enabled by affordable networked communication, shared distributed environments require generalized control of media streams, techniques to control source → sink transmissions in synchronous groupware, including teleconferences and chatspaces, online role-playing games, and virtual concerts.

There are two main techniques currently used for managing information in contemporary systems to address the problem of human information overload—proximity-based filtering, as used by many games and as formalized by the Benford et al. model described further, and explicit degree-of-interest (DoI) filtering, as seen in buddy lists of instant messaging (IM) systems or clan-based chat channels of massively multiplayer online role-playing games (MMORPGs).

Anticipating ubicomp-networked appliances and information spaces, we are exploring the integration of various multimodal (auditory, visual, haptic) I/O devices into mixed and virtual reality groupware suites. Such environments are characterized, in contrast to general multimedia systems, by the explicit notion of the position (location and orientation) of the perspective presented to respective users; often such vantage points are modeled by the standpoints and directions of icons in a virtual space. These icons might be more or less symbolic (abstract) or figurative (literal), but as representatives of human users, are therefore "avatars" (Benford et al., 1995). Avatars reify embodied virtuality, treating abstract presence as a user interface object.

M. Cohen (✉)
Spatial Media Group, University of Aizu, Japan
e-mail: mcohen@u-aizu.ac.jp

P. Markopoulos et al. (eds.), *Awareness Systems*, Human-Computer Interaction Series,
DOI 10.1007/978-1-84882-477-5˙11, © Springer-Verlag London Limited 2009

This chapter reviews the basic and extended notions of awareness and presence in virtual environments, explains the idea of multipresence, surveys related models of groupware awareness, and presents a formalization of narrowcasting, which ideas are deployed in two integrated interfaces, for workstations and mobile phones, considered as case studies.

11.1.1 Presence, Telepresence, and Copresence

Presence may be the most elementary component of virtual collaboration. It has been used broadly, but generally presence is the feeling of "being there," as disquietingly suggested by Fig. 11.1. Schroeder (2003) and Slater et al. (1996) define presence as "a state of consciousness, the (psychological) sense of being in the virtual environment." In the context of environment, presence describes the degree to which one feels a part of some virtual space — that the space exists and one is occupying it.

The term "telepresence" has been used in industry since scientists and engineers started to design and develop remote control systems and industrial robots. Generally, telepresence (Benford et al., 1998) allows users to experience a physical space through display and control interface elements connected to remote sensors and actuators.

"Notice anything different?"

Fig. 11.1   Metapresence. (© The New Yorker Collection 2006 Tom Cheney from cartoonbank.com. All rights reserved.)

"Copresence" (Sandhu et al., 1999) is a sociological concept that describes the way people interact with each other. Copresence is primarily used to refer to either telepresence (the sense of being together with other people in a remote physical environment) or virtual presence (the sense of being together with other people in a technology-generated environment).

The sense of copresence is different from the mode of copresence: whereas mode of copresence refers to one's spatiotemporal collocation with others, sense of copresence involves one's perceptions and feelings of being with others. One's sense of being with others is basically a psychological phenomenon, which may or may not correspond to the actual state of copresence. An individual, for example, can be made to feel that he or she is interacting with another human, even through the individual is in fact completely alone. Psychological states — such as mood, alertness, and prior experiences — affect one's sense of copresence, and environmental factors — such as temperature, light, sound, and smell — may also influence one's sense of being with others.

11.1.2 Awareness and Presence Awareness

The concept of "awareness" has been used in numerous ways in the Human–Computer Interaction (HCI) (Muller et al., 1997) and CSCW literature (Grudin, 1994). Awareness has been defined (Dourish and Bly, 1992) as "an understanding of the activities of others, which provides a context for [one's] own activity." This definition encompasses many kinds of displays of colleagues' actions in shared information spaces — such as whiteboards, alerts about people's status, access privileges to information, prior actions, and so on.

Presence awareness provides information like the location, identity, activities, and neighbors of someone. A wide range of distributed applications requires presence awareness (Christein and Schulthess, 2002; Velez et al., 2004; Donath and Viégas, 2002), including instant messaging (IM) systems, and groupware applications like chat, audio- or video-conferencing systems. Well-known current applications include messengers like those from AOL, Yahoo!, or MSN, as well as CSCW applications and virtual 3D communities like Active Worlds or Second Life. Currently, presence awareness is mostly used for IM systems to let users know when others, especially those on contact (or buddy) lists, are online and willing to accept messages. Presence-aware groupware applications are sensitive to the receptiveness of the respective participants. When a messaging system is part of an integrated communications platform, presence awareness can become more sophisticated. It can notify others when a user is online, willing to accept phone calls at home, or has a mobile phone turned on (Marmasse et al., 2004). A conferencing system might know that a session member is asleep, and not awaken him/her for non-urgent real-time voice chat. Users might even set presence messages so others trying to contact them will learn that they have gone out for a while and will return at a certain time.

11.1.3 Narrowcasting and Privacy

In analogy to uni-, multi-, and broadcasting, "narrowcasting" refers to the deliberate filtering of multiple duplex information streams, a model for rich CSCW and social networking. Narrowcasting systems extend broad- and multicasting groupware systems by allowing various information streams to be filtered, for privacy, security, and user interface optimization. The narrowcasting operations described in this chapter suggest an elegant infrastructure for such collaborative environments, an idiom and service for selective attention and presence awareness. For simple example, a user's voice might by default be shared with all others in a chatspace, but an appropriate interface would allow a secret to be shared with some select subset ("inner circle") of the session members.

Traditional mixing idioms for enabling and disabling various audio sources employ mute and solo functions which selectively disable or focus on respective source channels. As summarized in Table 11.1, which previews the case studies presented later in this chapter, sinks are defined as duals of sources in virtual spaces (Cohen, 2000), logical media stream receivers. Exocentric interfaces, which explicitly model not only sources, but also position and multiplicity of sinks, motivate the generalization of audio mixer commands mute & select (or cue or solo) to exclude and include, manifested for sinks as deafen & attend, a narrowing of stimuli by explicitly or implicity blocking out and/or concentrating on selected entities, as elaborated in Fig. 11.2.

Narrowcasting functions, which filter stimuli by explicitly blocking out and/or concentrating on selected entities, can be applied not only to other users' sources and sinks for privacy, but also to one's own, for selective attendance or presence. "Privacy" has two interpretations, as suggested in Fig. 11.3. The first association is that of avoiding "leaks" of confidential information, protecting secrets. But a second interpretation means "freedom from disturbance," in the sense of not being bothered by irrelevance or interruption. The distributed interfaces described in this chapter feature narrowcasting operations that manage privacy (Ackerman, 2004) in both senses by filtering duplex information flow.

The inclusion and exclusion narrowcasting commands for sources and sinks are like analogs of burning and dodging (shading) in photographic processing. The duality between source and sink operations is tight, and the semantics are identical: an object is inclusively enabled by default unless (a) it explicitly excluded (with mute [as in Fig. 11.4] or deafen) or (b) peers of the same self/non-self class are explicitly included (with select or attend) when the respective object is not.

That is, if any avatar has been selected, non-selected avatars are implicitly muted if their self-designation state is the same as a selected avatar. In the same manner, if any attended avatars are in a given space, non-attended avatars are implicitly deafened if they are in the same class (self or non-self) as an attended avatar.

These narrowcasting attributes are not mutually exclusive and their dimensions are orthogonal. Because a source or sink is active by default, invoking exclude and include operations simultaneously on an object results in its being disabled.

Table 11.1 Roles of $^s\mathrm{OU}_{\mathrm{Tput}}^{\mathrm{rce}}$ and $^s\mathrm{IN}_{\mathrm{put}}^{\mathrm{k}}$: iconic and figurative attributes of narrowcasting functions extend avatars to denote invoked filters

	Source	Sink
Function	Radiation/transmission	Reception
Level	Amplification	Sensitivity
Direction	OUTput	INput
Instance	speaker	Listener
Transducer	Loudspeaker	Microphone or dummy-head
Organ	Mouth	Ear
Tool	Megaphone, bullhorn	Ear trumpet
Exclude	`mute`	`deafen`
Inhibit in ι·Con	△	−△−
Inhibit self in Multiplicity		
reflexive	(thumb up)	(thumbs back)
Inhibit other in Multiplicity		
transitive	(thumb down)	(thumbs up)
Include	`select` (`solo` or `cue`)	`attend:` `confide` and `harken`
Assert target in ι·Con	$\overset{+}{\triangle}$	+△+
Assert target in Multiplicity		
explicit	(megaphone)	(ear trumpets)
Assertion side-effect in Multiplicity		
implicit	(translucent hand)	(translucent hands)

The general expression of activation is

$$\texttt{active}(x) = \neg\texttt{exclude}(x) \wedge (\exists\, y\, (\texttt{include}(y) \wedge (\texttt{self}(y) \Leftrightarrow \texttt{self}(x)))) \Rightarrow \texttt{include}(x). \quad (1)$$

So, for mute and select, the relation is

$$\texttt{active}(\text{source } x) = \neg\texttt{mute}(x) \wedge (\exists\, y\, (\texttt{select}(y) \wedge (\texttt{self}(y) \Leftrightarrow \texttt{self}(x)))) \Rightarrow \texttt{select}(x), \quad (2a)$$

mute explicitly turning off a source, and select disabling the collocated (same window/room/space) complement of the selection (in the spirit of "anything not mandatory is forbidden"). For deafen and attend, the relation is

$$\texttt{active}(\text{sink } x) = \neg\texttt{deafen}(x) \wedge (\exists\, y\, (\texttt{attend}(y) \wedge (\texttt{self}(y) \Leftrightarrow \texttt{self}(x)))) \Rightarrow \texttt{attend}(x). \quad (2b)$$

Fig. 11.2 Formalization of narrowcasting and selection functions in predicate calculus notation, where '¬' means "not," '∧' means conjunction (logical "and"), '∃' means "there exists," '⇔' means mutual implication (equivalence), and '⇒' means "implies"

For instance, a sink might be first attended, perhaps as a member of some non-singleton subset of a space's sinks, then later deafened, so that both attributes are simultaneously applied. As audibility is assumed to be a revocable privilege, such a seemingly conflicted attribute state disables the considered sink, whose audition would be restored upon resetting its deafen flag. Symmetrically, a source might be selected and then muted, akin to making a "short list" but relegated to backup.

11.1.4 Multiple Spaces

Non-immersive perspectives in virtual environments enable flexible paradigms of perception, especially in the context of frames-of-reference for conferencing and musical audition. In the model described in this chapter, users designate one or more avatars as "self," to establish correspondence between human pilots and virtual presence. Such exocentric interfaces, which explicitly include a representation of the subject as a "full citizen," allow users to perceive themselves "out of body," as well as the juxtaposition of multiple spaces.

Dix et al. (2005) described their experiences of spaces in the Equator project,[1] in particular the way in which multiple spaces, both virtual and physical, can coexist. People and objects may have locations in and relationships to both physical space and one or more virtual spaces, and these different spaces together interact to constitute overall system behavior and user experience.

The narrowcasting model mediates interactions between virtual and physical spaces to allow users to have presence in multiple places simultaneously. The workstation- and mobile-based interfaces described later in this chapter both support multiple spaces to enhance multipresence-enabled conferencing capabilities in CVEs.

---

[1] www.equator.ac.uk

Fig. 11.3 The price of privacy. (© The New Yorker Collection 1996 Sam Gross from cartoon-bank.com. All rights reserved.)

11.1.5 Multipresence, Anycasting, and Autofocus

A human is indivisible and a person cannot physically be in multiple places at once. However, a unique feature of the interfaces described here is the explicit ability of a user to delegate several representatives simultaneously, increasing *quantity* of presence (Cohen, 1998). Such multipresence enables us to overcome some

"With your kind permission, I've taken the liberty of putting Marvin on 'mute.'"

Fig. 11.4 Social narrowcasting. (© The New Yorker Collection 2008 J.B. Handelsman from cartoonbank.com. All rights reserved.)

fundamental constraints of this human condition. Our interfaces encourage multipresence (Christein and Schulthess, 2002), by supporting self-designated avatars in multiple places simultaneously — allowing, for example, a user to monitor several spaces at once, refining the granularity of control.

Multiple sources are useful in directing one's remarks to specific groups. Multiple sinks are useful for monitoring several places at once, especially in situations in which a common environment implies social inhibitions to rearranging shared sources like musical voices or conferees, as well as individual sessions in which spatial configuration of sources, like the arrangement of a concert orchestra, has mnemonic value.

An "anycast" is a transmission between a sender and one of possibly several receivers on a network. The term exists in contradistinction to "multicast,"

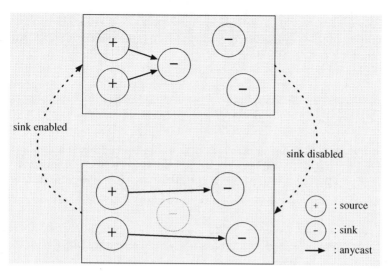

Fig. 11.5 Autofocused source → sink transmissions: if an intercepting auto-focused sink is deafened (or peers attended), remaining sinks adopt orphaned, anycasting, sources.

transmission between a sender and multiple receivers, and "unicast," transmission between a sender and a single receiver. An anycasting service uses some criteria to choose a "best" or single destination from a set of candidates. We apply the same idea, finding the best sink (the one for which the source is loudest) for each source using an "autofocus" technique, illustrated in Fig. 11.5 and described as follows.

In an audio interface that composites soundscapes from sinks' perspectives, the apparent paradoxes of multipresence, having avatars in multiple places or spaces simultaneously, are resolvable by such an autofocus feature, which uses reciprocity, logical exchangeability of source and sink, to project overlaid soundscapes and simulate the precedence effect to consolidate the audio display. If the sinks are distributed across separate conference rooms, each source is localized only with respect to the colocated sink. If multiple sinks share a single space, an autofocus algorithm is employed by anticipating "the rule of the first wavefront" (Vyas et al., 2007b; Haas, 1972; Blauert, 1997; Gilkey and Anderson, 1997), the tendency to perceive multiple identical simultaneous sources from different locations as a single fused source. Rather than adding and averaging the contribution of each source (DiPaola and Collins, 2002; Tolone et al., 2005) to possibly multiple sinks, our system localizes each source only with respect to its respective best sink, consolidating the display. Multipresence encourages the narrowcasting-articulated audition (for sinks) or address (for sources) of multiple others.

11.1.6 Multipresence Scenarios

Most user interfaces support clipboard operations, cut/copy/paste. Such clipboard operations, enabled by dynamic deletion and creation of avatars, can be used

for teleporting (cut & paste) and cloning (copy & paste) in CVEs, allowing avatars to convey narrowcasting attributes across multiple spaces in distributed
applications and heterogeneous sessions.

A simple teleconferencing configuration typically consists of several icons, representing distributed users, moving around a shared conference space. Multipresence systems allow users to fork themselves, effectively increasing their attendance
in virtual environments. For example, in a chatspace, a user might choose to designate two avatars as self, one to stand near an avatar corresponding to the user's
mate, and another, perhaps on the other side of the "room," to stand near an avatar
corresponding to the user's friend. Each of these avatars enjoys a local perspective,
a situation awareness encompassing where the respective conversationalists are relative to the (no longer unique) self-associated avatar, as manifested visually and
auditorily.

In a parallel virtual rock concert, for continued example, a listener might want
to pay close attention to both the drum and rhythm guitar, avoiding rearranging the
instruments around a singleton sink to maintain consistency with other attendees.
An active listener could fork his/her presence as self-designated avatars, locating
one avatar near the drum, and pasting another near the guitar. To focus on only
the previously described chatspace, the listener might attend his/her avatars in
it, so his/her other sinks in the virtual concert would be implicitly deafened. If
he/she wanted to direct his/her voice privately to friends in either space, he/she
might attend the friends' avatars, thereby implicitly deafening the others'.

11.2 Related Research

Gutwin and Greenberg (1998a,b) and Benford et al. (1994) provide contrastable
models of awareness issues in groupware. Gutwin et al.'s model attempts to identify the constituent information sources that communicate awareness and provide
a framework that can assist the evaluation and design of awareness capabilities in
groupware (Cockburn and Weir, 1999). Benford et al. derive a model for awareness and interaction in virtual environment which focuses on the information space
in mediating awareness. Each of these models is briefly described below. Benford
et al.'s model (which is also considered in the "Abstractions of Awareness" chapter
(Metaxas and Markopoulos, 2009)) is quite similar to our narrowcasting model,
so we review and compare it with the narrowcasting idioms more completely in
Section 11.4.

Gutwin et al.'s model is derived from a top-down decomposition of awareness
types, with particular emphasis on "workspace awareness," defined as awareness
of others that is mediated by, or closely related to, actions on or around a shared
workspace. This model identifies four types of awareness, which are specifically
applied to group work dynamics:

> *Informal Awareness* regards the sense of community among a group of col-
> leagues (Viégas and Donath, 1999; Vyas et al., 2007a).

Conversational Awareness regards backchannels of communication that contextualize interaction.

Structural Awareness regards the protocols and structures used to formalize collaboration.

Workspace Awareness regards the capabilities of the media of collaboration, "the awareness mediated by the workspace."

Benford et al.'s "spatial model of interaction" describes interaction based on metaphorically physical properties of space. The ability of a subject to perceive an object is affected by distance, direction, and possible obstructions. The key awareness abstractions in this model are "aura," "focus," and "nimbus":

Aura is the portion of space in which interaction is enabled and allowed.

Focus ("attention function") is the cumulative scope of regard. The more an object is within one's focus, the more aware one is of it.

Nimbus ("publicity function") is an object's projection, its extent of exposure. The more a subject is within one's nimbus, the more aware it is of one.

"Massive" (Greenhalgh and Benford, 1995) is a distributed virtual reality system providing facilities to support user interaction and cooperation via text, audio (Radenkovic et al., 2002), and graphics media, and interaction is controlled by these spatial models of interaction. The particular emphasis of Massive was on large-scale multiuser virtual environments, i.e., environments which might eventually support hundreds or thousands of simultaneous users. Aims of the Massive project (and its spatial model) were to provide rich forms of interaction which draw upon real-world behavior to make them useful and controllable in highly populated virtual worlds.

A third relevant model considers the form of the computing platform. With the spread of wireless communication and the desire to "travel light," collaboration across PCs and mobile devices (PDA, mobile phones, etc.) (Read and Maurer, 2003; Rashid et al., 2006; Papadopoulos, 2006; Raento and Qulasvirta, 2008) is a likely trend for future groupware applications. Velez et al. (2004) investigated performances and communication patterns when collaborators use unequal computer platforms for their collaboration. They explored whether people use the same type of platform (homogeneous) or different platforms (heterogeneous) for communication, mainly considering PCs (personal computers) vs. PDAs (personal data assistants) for heterogeneous platforms. Their findings suggest that limited device capabilities can affect who is actually in charge and attention must be paid to the types of representations used on the mobile platform, as poor representations may affect the collaboration relationship between communicating colleagues. They also observed a flexibility of approaches in the communication exchanges as subjects used the voice channel to work towards a viable exchange pattern that would help them solve the problems created by the platform differences. The integrated systems described in the following case studies can also be considered as a multiplatform approach to enhance performance and communication patterns when collaborators use heterogeneous computer platforms for their collaboration.

11.3 Awareware: Audio Windowing Narrowcasting Systems

Vision and audition are the two main human senses for obtaining information about the outside world and full CSCW applications need both modes (at least!). Visual windowing systems allow multiple and multiwindow applications to share display resources; audio windowing systems, in analogy to graphical windows, can bring order to a cacophony of multiple simultaneous sound sources. Audio windowing can be thought of as a frontend, or articulated user interface, to a system with a spatial sound backend (Cohen and Ludwig, 1991a,b; Cohen and Koizumi, 1998; Cohen, 2006). Using our audio windowing system, users will be able to control the spatialized audio (and other real-time media streams) of inevitable multiparty chatspaces, using the cocktail party effect (Aoki et al., 2003) as well as narrowcasting to make useful sense of the cacophony, as imagined by Fig. 11.4.

Audio windowing narrowcasting commands control superposition of soundscapes. Using the awareness parlance of Benford et al. (1994) an aura delimited by a graphical window is like a room, in which sink attributes affect focus and source attributes affect nimbus. On a logical level, sound sources and sinks are resources assigned to users. Shared virtual environments like chatspaces require generalized control of user-dependent media streams.

We present two case studies of "awareware," describing audio windowing interfaces for workstations and mobile devices (Fernando et al., 2006), both supporting multiple spaces (Dix et al., 2005) to enhance narrowcasting conferencing capabilities in CVEs: a workstation WIMP style (windows/icon/menu/pointer) GUI (graphical user interface), and a MIDlet (mobile information devices applet) for 2.5 and third generation mobile phones. The workstation- and mobile-based interfaces encourage use of multiple spaces, leveraging multipresence-enabled conferencing features. Dynamic deletion and creation of avatars controlled by clipboard operations enable teleporting (cut&paste) and cloning (copy&paste) avatars in distributed applications and heterogeneous sessions for both interfaces (Fernando et al., 2005), conveying narrowcasting attributes across multiple spaces.

11.3.1 "Multiplicity": Java3D Workstation-Platformed Multiperspective Interface

The workstation-based audio windowing narrowcasting system, named "Multiplicity" (with a nod to the eponymous movie (Raento and Oulasvirta, 2008)), developed with JSE and Java3D, runs on Mac OS X, Microsoft Windows, and Sun Solaris. An arbitrary number of avatars can be instantiated and associated with users at runtime. Attributes of narrowcasting functions extend the figurative avatars to denote the invoked filters. Multiplicity can display multiple perspectives from various standpoints, including exocentrically from various strategically placed cameras and egocentrically (both endocentric and tethered) with respect to a selected avatar, in hybrid visual configurations or stereographically.

11.3.1.1 Multiple Spaces

Multiple spaces are supported in Multiplicity via launching multiple instances of the application. An arbitrary number of applications can be run, corresponding, for example, to domestic, academic, professional, and musical spaces. Upon launching an instance of the application, a user provides a space name, upon which all the networked attributes of that space are based, including channel IDs, position parameters, and narrowcasting attributes. This approach allow users to seamlessly inhibit an arbitrary number of virtual spaces.

11.3.1.2 Visual Representation of Narrowcasting Operations

A human user can be represented in virtual space by one or more avatars. A figurative avatar in virtual space is naturally humanoid, including especially a head, since it not only embodies a center of consciousness, but also important communication organs: ears, mouth, and eyes. Exclude and include source and sink operations can be visually represented by attributes which can distinguish between operations reflexive, invoked by user associated with a respective avatar, and transitive, invoked by another user in the shared environment.

Figurative representations of narrowcasting operations suggest sender- and receiver-side filtering. For exclude operations, virtual hands cover avatars' ears and mouths, with orientation suggesting the nature of the blocking. Exclude audio operations mute and deafen are shown in Fig. 11.6. A source representing an avatar denotes mutedness with an virtual hand clapped over its mouth, oriented differently (thumb up or down) depending on whether the source was muted by its owner (or one of its owners) or another, unassociated user. Hands clapped over the ears

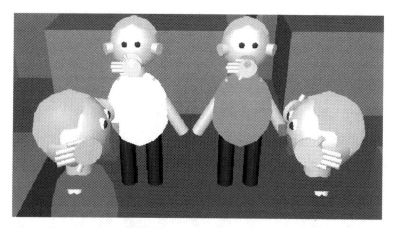

Fig. 11.6 Exclude narrowcasting operations in Multiplicity: in this example, avatars in the center rear are muted, by self (*thumb up*) and other (*thumb down*), respectively, while *left*- and *right*-most (in the *front*) avatars are deafened, by self (*thumbs down*) and other (*thumbs up*), respectively.

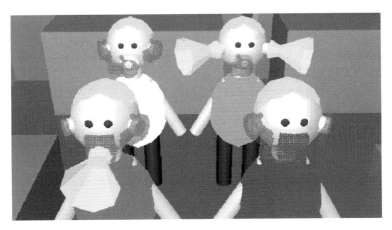

Fig. 11.7 Include narrowcasting operations in Multiplicity: the avatar in the *front left* is `selected`, so its complement (comprising all the other avatars) is `muted` (denoted by the translucent hands before the mouths), and the avatar in the *back right* is `attended`, so its complement is `deafened` (denoted by translucent hands before the mouth).

are also oriented differently depending on the agent of deafness, thumbs down in the case of reflexive invocation by a user desiring quiet, and thumbs up to denote other-imposed deafness, invoked by another desiring secrecy.

For include operations, `select` and `attend` attributes are denoted by characteristic features, as shown in Fig. 11.7. A megaphone appears in front of `selected` avatars' mouths, and ear trumpets straddle `attended` avatars' ears. If any avatar has been `selected`, non-`selected` avatars of the same `self`/non-`self` class are implicitly `muted`. In the same manner, if any `attended` avatars exist in a given space, non-`attended` avatars are implicitly `deafened`. Translucent hands represent these effects, implicit `mute` represented by a translucent hand clapped over the mouth, and implicit `deafen` represented by translucent hands clapped over the ears. Such narrowcasting attributes are conveyed by avatars even as they move or replicate (via the clipboard) to other spaces, as illustrated by Fig. 11.8.

11.3.1.3 Visual Representation of Autofocus Operations

In the absence of an autofocus function, a multipresent user associated with multiple sinks might hear each source from several locations, each a manifestation of its respective displacement from each sink. An autofocus function discovers a unique, most sensitive sink for each source by compiling narrowcasting attributes from each source to each sink, and then choosing the respectively closest active ones. (Sink sensitivities depend upon distances from the sources, which are assumed to be omnidirectional.) The position of each source's best sink is denoted by flying animated arrows, as shown in Fig. 11.9.

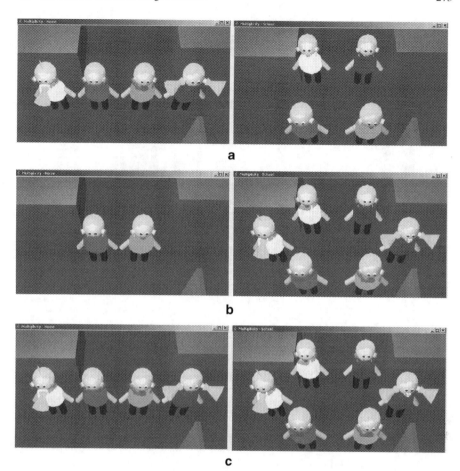

a

b

c

Fig. 11.8 Teleporting and cloning across Home and School instances of Multiplicity. **(a)** Before clipboard operations (both instances of Multiplicity run in the same login on a computer share the session clipboard): Avatar #0 (*left*) is selected and #3 (*right*) is attended in the Home space, so their complements are implicitly muted and deafened, respectively. (No narrowcasting attributes are yet applied to avatars in the School space.) **(b)** After teleporting (cut/paste) operations: Avatars #0 and #3 have been cut from the Home space (along with their narrowcasting attributes, including selfness) and pasted into the School space, as avatars #4 (*midground left*) and #5 (*midground right*). Newly pasted avatar #4 is selected and #5 is attended, so their complements are again implicitly muted and deafened, respectively. **(c)** After cloning (copy/paste) operations: Avatars #0 and #3 have been copied in the Home space (along with their narrowcasting attributes) and pasted into the School space. Newly pasted avatar #4 is selected and #5 is attended, so their complements are once again implicitly muted and deafened.

Fig. 11.9 Autofocus visualization in Multiplicity: Anycasting source → sink vectors are visualized by arrows, flying from each source to its respective "best sink." (The user's sinks, designated as `self`, have stars rotating above their heads.)

11.3.2 "ι·Con": (iαppli DoJa) Mobile Device-Platformed Dynamic Map

A mobile-based audio windowing system, named "ι·Con," developed with Java ME (Micro Edition) and DoJa (DoCoMo Java), runs on (NTT DoCoMo) iαppli mobile phones. Featuring selectable icons with one rotational and two translational degrees of freedom, the "2.5D" dynamic map interface is used to control position, sensitivity, and audibility of avatars in a groupware session. Its isosceles triangle icons are representations of symbolic heads in an orthographic projection, including narrowcasting attributes. The interface also has musical and vibrational cues to signal mode changes and successful transmission/reception (which feedback is important in wireless communication, as it is much less deterministic than wireline systems).

11.3.2.1 Multiple Spaces

Multiple spaces are supported directly within the mobile-based interface (there being no symmetric multitasking on the mobile phone operating system), integrated with other applications through a servent (server/client hybrid) HTTP↔TCP/IP gateway. Area-division multiplexing of the graphical display is used for the mobile interface to display multiple spaces. In consideration of the small screen display of mobile devices, the mobile interface currently supports only two virtual rooms ("Home" and "School"), but a general multiwindowing system would allow an arbitrary number of spaces.

11.3.2.2 Visual Representation of Narrowcasting Operations

Symbolic representations of narrowcasting operations were developed for mobile interface by flattening figurative 3D avatars to 2.5D icons, as seen in Fig. 11.10. In the ι·Con application, narrowcasting attributes' graphical displays are triply encoded — by position (before the "mouth" for mute and select, straddling the "ears" for deafen and attend), symbol ('+' for include and '−' for exclude), and color (green for assert and red, yellow, and orange for inhibit — by self, other, and implicitly, respectively).

Fig. 11.10 Narrowcasting attributes on mobile graphical display (a) In the Home space, avatar #0 is attended, so its complement (comprising all the other avatars) is deafened; and avatar #3 is selected, so its complement is implicitly muted. In the School space, avatars #0 and #2 are respectively muted and deafened by self while avatars #1 and #3 are respectively muted and deafened by others. (b) In the Home space, #0 is simultaneously attended and selected and also selected for rotation (as indicated by its "halo"), while in the School space, #0 is simultaneously attended and deafened.

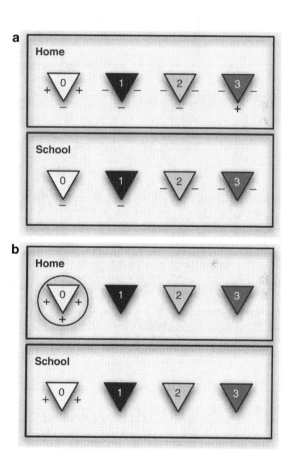

11.3.2.3 Visual Representation of Autofocus Operations

The autofocus function described earlier (in Section 11.1.5 and Fig. 11.9) is also applied to the ι·Con interface, which discovers the best sink for each source (the one for which the source is loudest). A disk is drawn above each source, colored the same as the respective best sink. In the simple case, when narrowcasting attributes

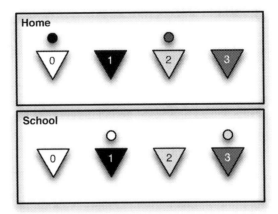

Fig. 11.11 Autofocus visualization in *ι*·Con: Home's #1 and #3 and School's #0 and #2 are self-designated icons, and therefore candidates for "best sink." In the Home space, #0's and #2's best sinks are #1 and #3, respectively — a circle the same color as #1 is drawn above source #0 while a circle colored the same as #3 is drawn above source #2. In the School space, #1's and #3's best sinks are #0 and #2 — a circle the same color as #0 is drawn above source #1, while a circle colored the same as #2 is drawn above source #3.

are not applied, the *ι*·Con interface discovers the best sink for each source considering only distance, as shown in Fig. 11.11.

When narrowcasting attributes are applied to icons in this mobile interface, the best sink for each source depends on the those attributes as well as designation (select or non-self) of the icons. For example, when a user selects a self-designated avatar, other self-designated avatars are implicitly muted. In the same manner, when a user selects a non-self-designated avatar, other non-self-designated avatars are implicitly muted. Depending on the situation, users can change the determination of the best sink for each source using narrowcasting attributes, as shown in Fig. 11.12(a).

11.4 Narrowcasting Attributes for Presence Awareness

The configurations described by Benford et al. are re-presented in an original taxonomy (Fernando et al. 2006) shown in Table 11.2. There are many ways of mapping those situations into arrangements supported by the narrowcasting idioms described in this chapter. For instance, direct analogies between nimbus and source "visibility" (audibility, etc.) and between focus and sink attention allows the equivalences illustrated by Table 11.3 as include narrowcasting operations (attend/select), and Table 11.4 as exclude narrowcasting operations (deafen/mute). A subject focuses attention on an object as a sink focuses on a source. An object attracts attention from a subject as the autofocus function causes an "anycasting" source to discover a best sink. For example, if a source is muted, either by its owner or the other participant, its nimbus excludes the other avatar. For instance, one might hold

Fig. 11.12 Narrowcasting attributes are applied to self and non-self avatars and autofocus behavior displayed in different situations. Home #0 and #3 and School #0 and #3 are self-designated avatars (a) In the Home space, self-designated avatars are deafened (#0) and selected (#3), causing #0 to be implicitly muted. In the School space, non-self-designated avatars are deafened (#1) and selected (#2), causing #1 to be implicity muted. (b) In the Home space, self-designated avatars are deafened (#0) and muted (#3). In the School space, non-self-designated avatars are deafened (#1) and muted (#2).

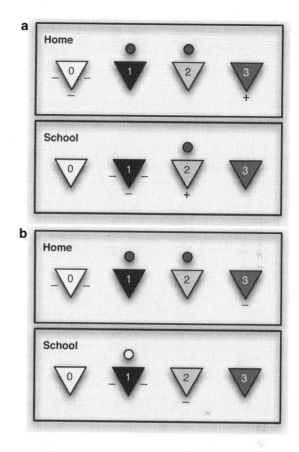

their hand over their mouthpiece (microphone) or push a "Hold" button (like that in audio chatspaces) of a phone handset to block the transmission or use a "sneeze" button to freeze a video stream.

As a narrowcasting interface is designed for more than two participants, there are differences between, for instance, selecting a source and muting its compliment. Tables 11.3 and 11.4 show a coarse projection of a much more complicated space. Neither do Tables 11.2, 11.3, and 11.4 distinguish between narrowcasting attributes invoked by oneself vs. by another. That is, capability can be determined by combined narrowcasting attributes, independent of agent, but in context such distinctions are very important. A cannot hear B if B is muted by A or by B himself, but there is a big difference socially, especially in presence of a third actor C, who could hear B muted transitively by A or others (besides C) but not reflexively (by B). If all the attributes invoked by one's self vs. by another only for Table 11.4 are considered, there are many possible situations, some of them symmetric. For example, if A mutes himself, nobody can hear A (except A), so it does not matter if A is also muted by B. To complete the taxonomy, Table 11.5 crosses attend and mute, and Table 11.6 crosses attend and mute.

Table 11.2 Modes of mutual awareness (Benford et al.)

		B focused on A		B not focused on A	
		A ∈ B's nimbus	A ∉ B's nimbus	A ∈ B's nimbus	A ∉ B's nimbus
A focused on B	B ∈ A's nimbus	10. Fully reciprocal mutual awareness	9. Withdrawal	7. Monitoring	5. Ignoring
	B ∉ A's nimbus	(9.)	8. Mutual minimal awareness	6. Eavesdropping	4. Minimal asymmetrical awareness
A not focused on B	B ∈ A's nimbus	(7.)	(6.)	3. Mutual overhearing	2. Overhearing / distraction
	B ∉ A's nimbus	(5.)	(4.)	(2.)	1. No mutualawareness

Circles depict the nimbus projected by an object, and arrows depict the direction of the subject's focus. Because of symmetry, the relation is basically reducible to a triangular matrix, with analogous transposition reflected across the main diagonal.

Table 11.3 Include narrowcasting modes for mutual awareness (attend and select)

		B attended		B not attended	
		B selected by A	B not selected by A	B selected by A	B not selected by A
A attended	A selected by B	10. Fully reciprocal mutual awareness	9. Asymmetric reciprocal mutual awareness	7. Asymmetric reciprocal mutual awareness	5. Asymmetric awareness
	A not selected by B	(9.)	8. Mutual overhearing	6. Lurking, asymmetric awareness	4. Minimal asymmetric awareness
A not attended	A selected by B	(7.)	(6.)	3. Symmetric awareness	2. Minimal asymmetric awareness
	A not selected by B	(5.)	(4.)	(2.)	1. Minimal mutual awareness

Table 11.4 Exclude narrowcasting modes for mutual awareness (deafen and mute)

| | | B not deafened | | B deafened | |
		B not muted	B muted	B not muted	B muted
A not deafened	A not muted	10. Minimal mutual awareness	9. Censor, withdrawal	7. Monitoring	5. Isolate
	A muted	(9.)	3. Null symmetric awareness	6. Eavesdropping	4. Null asymmetric awareness
A deafened	A not muted	(7.)	(6.)	8. Null symmetric awareness	2. Null asymmetric awareness
	A muted	(5.)	(4.)	(2.)	1. No mutual awareness

Table 11.5 Corresponding narrowcasting modes for mutual awareness (attend and mute)

| | | B attended | | B not attended | |
		B not muted	B muted	B not muted	B muted
A attended	A not muted	10. Fully reciprocal mutual awareness	9. Withdrawal	7. Monitoring	5. Ignoring
	A muted	(9.)	8. Mutual minimal awareness	6. Eavesdropping	4. Minimal asymmetrical awareness
A not attended	A not muted	(7.)	(6.)	3. Mutual overhearing	2. Overhearing / distraction
	A muted	(5.)	(4.)	(2.)	1. No mutual awareness

The +s at the ears, straddling the iconic heads, denote explicitly enabled sinks, and −s before the mouths denote disabled sources.

Table 11.6 Corresponding narrowcasting modes for mutual awareness (deafen and select).

		B not deafened		B deafened	
		B selected by A	B not selected by A	B selected by A	B not selected by A
A not deafened	A selected by B	10. Fully reciprocal mutual awareness	(7.)	(9.)	(5.)
	A not selected by B	7. Monitoring	3. Mutual overhearing	6. Eavesdropping	(2.)
A deafened	A selected by B	9. Withdrawal	(6.)	8. Mutual minimal awareness	(4.)
	A not selected by B	5. Ignoring	2. Overhearing/distraction	4. Minimal asymmetrical awareness	1. No mutual awareness

The $-$s at the ears, straddling the iconic heads, denote disabled sinks, and +s before the mouths denote enabled sources.

11.5 Future Research

11.5.1 Role-Based Issues

Roles are a powerful concept for facilitating distributed systems management and enforcing access control (Read and Maures, 2003; Park et al., 2001; Kern et al., 2002; Subramanya and Yi, 2005). The basic idea of role-based collaboration is that a collaborative system that can designate explicitly what objects users can access with which specific rights, and can also designate which users they can manage or communicate with, they can then accomplish their jobs meaningfully and efficiently.

Should a student be allowed to deafen a teacher, or a teenager be allowed to mute a parent? The models described in this chapter ignore such higher order considerations, like visibility of applied attributes. The interfaces described are transparent: any attributes invoked by any participant are revealed to the other users in the session. Such "perfect information" (from game study, in which all actors have access to all information) begs the question: If A mutes B, should B always be aware of it? Depending on the conditions, such transparency could be appropriate or not. A parent might insist upon the ability to override a teenager's "ignore" command: "How dare you mute me?" Such role-based issues are subtle and sociological and are the subject of ongoing consideration.

11.5.2 Next-Generation Mobile Phones

4G Mobile services (Kobylarz, 2004) will include network (Huber, 2004) technology integration, SDR (software-defined radio), and advanced multimedia (Slater and Steed, 2002) mobile communications (IPv6, high-resolution video transmission digital broadcasting, security, etc.) including 3D VR-style interfaces. The catchphrase for 4G is ABC: "always best connected," suggesting the possibility of persistent sessions, as imagined by Fig. 11.13.

11.5.3 Convergence

Besides wireline-connected workstation-based interfaces, narrowcasting might find an even more fertile platform in mobile devices (Hazas et al., 2004). The "4-play" convergence of telephony, television/video, Internet, and wireless is driving a proliferation of new devices and services. Mobile terminals, almost as intimate as clothing, are a kind of wearable computer, and a diversity of ever-next-generation functionalities and form factors for smartphones is emerging, including mobile stereotelephony, inspired by cyberspatial audio (Cohen et al., 1999) and augmented audio models. Meanwhile, location-based services — along with seamless handoff, FMC (fixed-mobile convergence), and heterogeneous roaming via MIMO (multiple

"I have to hang up now. You just walked through the door."

Fig. 11.13 "Always best connected" yields practically persistent sessions. © The New Yorker Collection 2000 William Haefeli from `cartoonbank.com`. All rights reserved.)

input/multiple output) smart antennas leading to software-defined radio (SDR) and cognitive radio — leverage geolocation and portable GPS/GIS.

11.5.4 "Polite Calling" for Social Gracefulness

Advanced sensing — including optical systems, position trackers, and motion sensors in mobile phones — encourages ubicomp (ubiquitous computing) and ambient intelligence, including an indirect awareness of user status and availability, "presence," which, along with explicit status settings by a user, enable "polite calling" that is respectful of the accessibility of a callee, including distractedness or preoccupation, sleep, social context, etc. Agents delegated on behalf of a caller and callee could negotiate an appropriate interruption, based upon caller insistence and callee receptiveness, including dropping down to voice- or video-mail, or ringing through a "don't disturb" in the case of emergencies.

Such filters will also increase the number of welcome calls, since callers will no longer have to self-censor, secure in the knowledge that a callee is appropriately shielded. (For simple example, one now hesitates to call even intimate friends and relations in the middle of the night for fear of waking them up, but if it was assumed that everyone had a gateway for active call screening that knew about their sleeping, then one could call spontaneously, hoping that the callee was receptive, but confident that if they were not that "the machine" would intercept and not bother the sleeping callee for non-urgent matters.)

Like some proposed measures to deal with telemarketers' SPIT (spam over IP telephony) and SPIM (spam over instant messaging), perhaps some negotiations would force the caller to electronically post a financial surety or bond of indemnification into escrow, which the callee could keep if the call is deemed a nuisance or not sufficiently important.

The distinction will blur between "calling" someone to establish a circuit, and "calling to" someone to get their attention. Articulated models of privacy like narrowcasting will allow users to distribute their attention, availability, and virtual presence. Multipresence and persistent channels, encouraged by ABC (always best connected) networks, will extend the way people communicate.

11.6 Conclusion

The basic goal of the research described in this chapter is to develop idioms for selective attention, privacy, and presence: narrowcasting for groupware applications, whether the interface is via workstation or a nomadic device like a mobile phone. We described deployment a multiplatform implementation of multipresence-enabled narrowcasting functions, including autofocus determination for both workstations and mobile devices. The workstation application features a multiperspective interface, including logical separation of eyes and ears (virtual camera and stereo microphones), exploiting the "phantom source" feature we developed. The mobile interface features equivalent exocentric narrowcasting commands, displayed and controlled in a manner appropriate for the unique form factor of the contemporary mobile phone. The platform-agnostic deployment of the audio narrowcasting idioms — including deafen, mute, select, and attend — encourages modernization of office- and mobile-based conferencing, leveraging session integration across coextensive spaces and anticipating multipresence enabled by higher bandwidth and more durable or even persistent mobile connectivity. One will have presence in many different places as well as ability to shift attention back and forth. For instance, one's family members, schoolmates, friends, etc. will have virtual copresence and one can virtually go back and forth among different spaces.

Normally, what one sees is tightly aligned with what one hears, since the eyes and ears are "concentric," locked together as they are in one's head, but users can fork themselves through designation of multiple avatars, compositing phantom sources via the superposition of multiple sinks' soundscapes. For instance, one might "fork presence" in virtual rooms corresponding to home (chatspace), school (teleconference), and music (virtual concert). Activity or information in a space might cause the user to focus on that particular soundscape, using narrowcasting functions (Pentland, 2005). As suggested by Fig. 11.14, being anywhere is

"Sorry, I can't—I have to be everywhere."

Fig. 11.14 Divine ubiquity. (© The New Yorker Collection 2003 Bruce Eric Kaplan from cartoonbank.com. All rights reserved.)

better than being everywhere, since it is selective; multipresence is distilled ubiquity, narrowcasting-enabled audition (for sinks) or address (for sources) of multiple objects of regard. This research can be considered an extension of presence technology (Tsingos, 2004), and anticipates deployment of such narrowcasting protocols into session protocols like SIP/SIMPLE (Johnston, 2004; Boyer et al., 2002; Alam et al., 2007a, b, 2009) or the internet infrastructure (routers, etc.) itself.

References

Ackerman, M.S.: Privacy in pervasive environments: Next generation labeling protocols. Personal Ubiquitous Comput. 8(6), 430–439 (2004). DOI http://dx.doi.org/10.1007/s00779-004-0305-8

Alam, M.S., Cohen, M., Ahmed, A.: Articulated narrowcasting for privacy and awareness in multimedia conferencing systems and design for implementation within a framework. JVRB: J. Virtual Reality Broadcasting 4(9) (2007a)

Alam, M.S., Cohen, M., Ahmed, A.: Narrowcasting—Controlling media policy in multimedia conferencing. In: Proceedings of IEEE CCNC: 4th Consumer Communications and Networking Conference, pp. 110–115. Las Vegas (2007b)

Alam, S., Cohen, M., Ashir, A., Villegas, J.: Narrowcasting in SIP: Articulated privacy control. In: A. Syed, M. Ilyas (eds.) SIP Handbook: Services, Technologies, and Security of Session Initiation Protocol, chap. 14, pp. 323–345. Taylor & Francis (2009)

Aoki, P.M., Romaine, M., Szymanski, M.H., Thornton, J.D., Wilson, D., Woodruff, A.: The Mad Hatter's Cocktail Party: A social mobile audio space supporting multiple simultaneous conversations. In: Proceedings of CHI: ACM Conference on Computer–Human Interaction, pp. 425–432. Ft. Lauderdale (2003)

Benford, S., Bowers, J., Fahlén, L.E., Greenhalgh, C., Snowdon, D.: User embodiment in collaborative virtual environments. In: Proceedings of CHI: SIGCHI Conference on Human factors in computing systems, pp. 242–249. ACM Press/Addison-Wesley Publishing Co., Denver (1995). ISBN 0-201-84705-1

Benford, S., Bowers, J., Fahlén, L.E., Mariani, J.A., Rodden, T.: Supporting cooperative work in virtual environments. Comput. J. **37**(8), 653–668 (1994)

Benford, S., Greenhalgh, C., Reynard, G., Brown, C., Koleva, B.: Understanding and constructing shared spaces with mixed-reality boundaries. ACM Trans. Comput. Hum. Interact. **5**(3), 185–223 (1998). DOI http://doi.acm.org/10.1145/292834.292836

Benford, S., Greenhalgh, C., Rodden, T., Pycock, J.: Collaborative virtual environments. Commun. ACM **44**(7), 79–85 (2001). DOI http://doi.acm.org/10.1145/379300.379322

Blauert, J.: Spatial Hearing: The Psychophysics of Human Sound Localization, revised edn. MIT Press (1997). ISBN 0-262-02413-6

Boyer, D., Ginsberg, A., Goud, V., Handel, M.: Presence awareness for future telecommunication systems. In: A. Pakštas, R. Komiya (eds.) Virtual Reality Technologies for Future Telecommunications Systems, chap. 4, pp. 31–44. Wiley, West Sussex, England (2002). ISBN 0-470-84886-3

Christein, H., Schulthess, P.: A general purpose model for presence awareness. In: Proceedings of Fourth International Conference on Distributed Communities on the Web pp. 24–34. Sydney (2002)

Cockburn, A., Weir, P.: An investigation of groupware support for collaborative awareness through distortion-oriented views. IJHCI: Int. J. Hum. Comput. Interact. 11(3), 231–255 (1999)

Cohen, M.: Quantity of presence: Beyond person, number, and pronouns. In: T.L. Kunii, A. Luciani (eds.) Cyberworlds, chap. 19, pp. 289–308. Springer-Verlag, Tokyo (1998). ISBN 4-431-70207-5; www.u-aizu.ac.jp/~mcohen/welcome/publications/QuantityOfPresence.pdf

Cohen, M.: Exclude and include for audio sources and sinks: Analogs of mute ... solo are deafen & attend. Presence: Teleoperat. Virt. Environ. **9**(1), 84–96 (2000). ISSN 1054-7460; www.u-aizu.ac.jp/~mcohen/welcome/publications/ie1.pdf

Cohen, M.: Articulated modeling of distributed privacy: Transitive closure of composition of narrowcasting and multipresence. In: Proceedings of CIT: Sixth International Conference on Computer and Information Technology. Seoul (2006)

Cohen, M., Herder, J., Martens, W.L.: Cyberspatial audio technology. J. Acous. Soc. Jap. (English) **20**(6), 389–395 (1999). ISSN 0388-2861; www.u-aizu.ac.jp/~mcohen/welcome/publications/JASJ-reviewE.pdf

Cohen, M., Koizumi, N.: Virtual gain for audio windows. Presence: Teleoperat. Virt. Environ. **7**(1), 53–66 (1998). ISSN 1054-7460

Cohen, M., Ludwig, L.F.: Multidimensional audio window management. IJMMS: J. Person Comput. Interact. **34**(3), 319–336 (1991a). Special Issue on Computer Supported Cooperative Work and Groupware. ISSN 0020-7373

Cohen, M., Ludwig, L.F.: Multidimensional audio window management. In: S. Greenberg (ed.) Computer Supported Cooperative Work and Groupware, chap. 10, pp. 193–210. Academic Press, London (1991b). ISBN 0-12-299220-2

DiPaola, S., Collins, D.: A 3D Virtual environment for social telepresence. In: Proceedings of Western Computer Graphics Symposium Vernon, BC, Canada (2002)

Dix, A., Friday, A., Koleva, B., Rodden, T., Muller, H., Randell, C., Steed, A.: Managing multiple spaces. In: P. Turner, E. Davenport (eds.) Spaces, Spatiality and Technology, *The Computer Supported Cooperative Work Series*, vol. 5. Springer (2005). ISBN 1-4020-3272-2

Donath, J.S., Viégas, F.B.: Chat circles series: Explorations in designing abstract graphical communication interfaces. In: Proceedings of DIS, Conference on Designing Interactive Systems pp. 359–369. London, England (2002)

Dourish, P., Bly, S.: Portholes: Supporting awareness in a distributed work group. In: Proceedings of CHI'92: Human Factors in Computing Systems, pp. 541–547. Addison-Wesley (1992)

Fernando, O.N.N., Adachi, K., Duminduwardena, U., Kawaguchi, M., Cohen, M.: Audio Narrowcasting and Privacy for Multipresent Avatars on Workstations and Mobile Phones. IEICE Trans. Inform. Syst. **E89-D**(1), 73–87 (2006). ietisy.oxfordjournals.org /cgi/content/refs/E89-D/1/73, ISSN 0916-8532

Fernando, O.N.N., Saito, G., Duminduwardena, U., Tanno, Y., Cohen, M.: Cloning and teleporting avatars across workstations and mobile devices in collaborative virtual environments: Clipboard operations for virtual reality. In: Proceedings of ICIA'05: International Conference on Information and Automation. Colombo, Sri Lanka (2005). www.ent.mrt.ac.lk/ iml/ICIA2005/Papers/JP001CRC.pdf

Gilkey, R.H., Anderson, T.R. (eds.): Binaural and Spatial Hearing in Real and Virtual Environments. Lawrence Erlbaum Associates, Mahway, NJ (1997). ISBN 0-8058-1654-2

Greenhalgh, C., Benford, S.: Massive: A collaborative virtual environment for teleconferencing. ACM Trans. Comput.–Hum. Interact. **2**(3), 239–261 (1995)

Grudin, J.: Computer-supported cooperative work: History and focus. (IEEE) Computer **27**(5), 19–26 (1994). DOI http://doi.ieeecomputersociety.org/10.1109/2.291294

Gutwin, C., Greenberg, S.: Design for individuals, design for groups: Tradeoffs between power and workspace awareness. In: Proceedings of CSCW: ACM Conference on Computer supported cooperative work, pp. 207–216. ACM Press, Seattle (1998a). ISBN 1-58113-009-0

Gutwin, C., Greenberg, S.: Effects of awareness support on groupware usability. In: Proceedings of CHI: SIGCHI Conference on Human Factors in Computing Systems, pp. 511–518. ACM Press/Addison-Wesley Publishing Co., Los Angeles (1998b). ISBN 0-201-30987-4

Haas, H.: The influence of a single echo on the audibility of speech. J. Aud. Eng. Soc. **20**, 146–159 (1972)

Hazas, M., Scott, J., Krumm, J.: Location-aware computing comes of age. IEEE Comput. Magaz. **37**(2), 95–97 (2004)

Huber, J.F.: Mobile next-generation networks. (IEEE) MultiMedia **11**(1), 72–83 (2004). DOI http://doi.ieeecomputersociety.org/10.1109/MMUL.2004.1261110

Johnston, A.B.: SIP: Understanding the Session Initiation Protocol. Artech House, London (2004). ISBN 1580531687

Kern, A., Kuhlmann, M., Schaad, A., Moffett, J.: Observations on the role life-cycle in the context of enterprise security management. In: Proceedings of SACMAT'02: 7th ACM Symposium on Access Control Models and Technologies, pp. 43–51. ACM Press, Monterey, CA (2002). ISBN 1-58113-496-7

Kobylarz, T.J.: Beyond 3G: Compound wireless services. (IEEE) Computer **37**(9), 23–28 (2004). DOI http://doi.ieeecomputersociety.org/10.1109/MC.2004.120

Marmasse, N., Schmandt, C., Spectre, D.: Watchme: Communication and awareness between members of a closely-knit group. In: N. Davies, E.D. Mynatt, I. Siio (eds.) Ubicomp, *Lecture Notes in Computer Science*, vol. 3205, pp. 214–231. Springer (2004)

Metaxas, G., Markopoulos, P.: Abstractions of awareness. In: P. Markopoulos, B. de Ruyter, W. Mackay (eds.) Awareness Systems: Advances in theory, methodology and design, chap. 6. Springer (2009). Human Computer Interaction

Muller, M.J., Wharton, C., McIver Jr., W.J., Laux, L.: Toward an HCI research and practice agenda based on human needs and social responsibility. In: Proceedings of CHI: SIGCHI Conference on Human Factors in Computing Systems, pp. 155–161. ACM Press, New York (1997). DOI http://doi.acm.org/10.1145/258549.258640

Papadopoulos, C.: Improving awareness in mobile cscw. IEEE Trans. Mobile Comput. **5**(10), 1331–1346 (2006)

Park, J.S., Sandhu, R., Ahn, G.J.: Role-based access control on the web. ACM Trans. Inf. Syst. Sec. **4**(1), 37–71 (2001). DOI http://doi.acm.org/10.1145/383775.383777

Pentland, A.S.: Socially aware computation and communication. (IEEE) Computer **38**(3), 33–40 (2005). DOI http://dx.doi.org/10.1109/MC.2005.104

Radenkovic, M., Greenhalgh, C., Benford, S.: Deployment issues for multi-user caudio support in CVEs. In: Proceedings of ACM Symposium on Virtual Reality Software andTechnology, pp. 179–185. ACM Press, Hong Kong (2002). DOI http://doi.acm.org/10.1145/585740.585770

Raento, M., Oulasvirta, A.: Designing for privacy and self-presentation in social awareness. PUC: Personal and Ubiquitous Computing **12**(7), 527–542 (2008)

Ramis, H., Miller, C.: Multiplicity (1996). Columbia Pictures Corp.

Rashid, O., Mullins, I., Coulton, P., Edwards, R.: Extending cyberspace: Location based games using cellular phones. Comput. Entertain. **4**(1), 4 (2006). DOI http://doi.acm.org/10.1145/1111293.1111302

Read, K., Maurer, F.: Developing mobile wireless applications. (IEEE) Internet Comput. **07**(1), 81–86 (2003). DOI http://doi.ieeecomputersociety.org/10.1109/MIC.2003.1167345

Sandhu, R., Bhamidipati, V., Munawer, Q.: The ARBAC97 model for role-based administration of roles. ACM Trans. Inf. Syst. Secur. **2**(1), 105–135 (1999). DOI http://doi.acm.org/10.1145/300830.300839

Schroeder, R.: Beyond presence and copresence: A phenomenological account of experiences in shared virtual environments. In: Proc. Presence. Aalborg, Denmark (2003)

Slater, M., Linakis, V., Usoh, M., Kooper, R.: Immersion, presence, and performance in virtual environments: An experiment using tri-dimensional chess. In: M. Green (ed.) VRST: ACM Virtual Reality Software and Technology, pp. 163–172 (1996). ISBN 0-89791-825-8

Slater, M., Steed, A.: Meeting people virtually: Experiments in shared virtual environments. In: R. Schroeder (ed.) The Social Life of Avatars: Presence and Interaction in Shared Virtual Environments, pp. 146–171. Springer, London (2002)

Subramanya, S.R., Yi, B.K.: User-controlled, multimedia-enhanced communication using prior knowledge and experience. (IEEE) MultiMedia **12**(2), 90–95 (2005). DOI http://dx.doi.org/10.1109/MMUL.2005.40

Tolone, W., Ahn, G.J., Pai, T., Hong, S.P.: Access control in collaborative systems. ACM Comput. Surv. **37**(1), 29–41 (2005). DOI http://doi.acm.org/10.1145/1057977.1057979

Tsingos, N.: Perceptual audio rendering of complex virtual environments. In: Proceedings of ACM Siggraph 2004, pp. 249–258. San Diego (2004)

Vaughan-Nichols, S.J.: Presence technology: More than just instant messaging. (IEEE) Computer **36**(10), 11–13 (2003). ISSN 0018-9162

Velez, M., Tremaine, M.M., Sarcevic, A., Dorohonceanu, B., Krebs, A., Marsic, I.: "Who's in charge here?" Communicating across unequal computer platforms. ACM Trans. Comput. Hum. Interact. **11**(4), 407–444 (2004). DOI http://doi.acm.org/10.1145/1035575.1035579

Viégas, F.B., Donath, J.S.: Chat circles. In: Proceedings of CHI: ACM Conference on Computer–Human Interaction, pp. 9–16. Pittsburgh (1999). ISBN 0-201-48559-1; www.media.mit.edu/~fviegas/chat_circles.pdf

Vyas, D., van de Watering, M.R., Eliëns, A., van der Veer, G.C.: Being social work: Designing for playfully mediated social awareness in work environments. In: A. Venkatesh, T. Gonzalves, A. Monk, K. Buckner (eds.) Home Informatics and Telematics: ICT for the Next Billion. Springer (2007a). Vol. 241; IFIP: International Federation for Information Processing; ISBN 978-0-387-73696-9

Vyas, D., van de Watering, M.R., Eliëns, A., van der Veer, G.C.: Engineering social awareness in work environments. In: Universal Access in Human–Computer Interaction: Proceedings of 12th Int. Conference on Human–Computer Interaction, pp. 254–263. Beijing (2007b). LNCS 4555; ISBN 978-3-540-73280-8

Wallach, H., Newman, E.B., Rosenzweig, M.R.: The precedence effect in sound localization. Am. J. Psychol. **57**, 315–336 (1949)

Chapter 12
Emotinet: A Framework for the Development of Social Awareness Systems

Jesús Ibáñez, Oscar Serrano, and David García

Abstract This chapter describes Emotinet, a flexible and extensible framework for the development of social awareness systems. Emotinet was initially designed and developed to facilitate our explorations on how to augment a person's work environment with information which enables his/her to feel the presence of intimate companions. The vehicle we deem to be appropriate for this situation is indirect communication. The presence we intend is based on the activities of these intimate people. A first social awareness system has already been developed by using Emotinet. This system is also described in this chapter. In short, with a certain periodicity the user is presented, on a peripheral user interface (windows desktop or digital picture frame), with a new collage composed of pictures indirectly triggered by their loved ones. In particular the pictures are triggered by the text they write and read, while working on their PCs.

12.1 Introduction

In recent years we have been interested in indirect information in order to augment digital spaces. In this sense, for instance, we designed and developed Musimage (see Fig. 12.1), a novel visual interface which displays pictures according to the songs being played at the time (Garcia, 2005). Music triggers recollections. By listening to a particular song, we remember events and feelings we had while listening to that song in the past. Our original idea was to design a user interface that, on the one hand, accompanies the user in this recollection process, and on the other hand, is able to "illustrate" the song. By using the interface, the user selects the songs to be played, but the pictures are chosen automatically. For each song to be played, the system selects a set of pictures, according to various criteria corresponding to certain features of the song (namely lyrics and year). In this way the sequence of pictures is

J. Ibáñez (✉)
Department of Technology, University Pompeu Fabra, Barcelona, Spain
e-mail: jesus.ibanez@upf.edu

P. Markopoulos et al. (eds.), *Awareness Systems*, Human-Computer Interaction Series, DOI 10.1007/978-1-84882-477-5_12, © Springer-Verlag London 2009

Fig. 12.1 Snapshot of Musimage

induced by user's actions (selection of songs), and the pictures themselves constitute indirect information about the user's actions.

We then shifted toward the exploration of this kind of indirect information as a means of reinforcing the feeling of being accompanied in social awareness systems. Rather than transmitting information captured directly from remote people (or directly triggered by them), we wanted to work with information which is indirectly influenced by their actions. Thus, we designed and developed a proof of concept, which is described in Ibáñez et al. (2006).

After that, as we wanted to explore these ideas through new applications, we decided to design a flexible and extensible software (Emotinet) which facilitates the development of this kind of social awareness system. In general, software support for building applications can be classified as libraries, frameworks, toolkits, or infrastructures. A library is a generalized set of related algorithms. Frameworks provide a basic structure for a certain class of applications. Toolkits build on frameworks by also offering a large number of reusable components for common functionality. Finally, an infrastructure is a well-established, pervasive, reliable, and publicly accessible set of technologies that acts as a foundation for other systems.

Emotinet can be seen as a framework as it provides a basic structure for social awareness applications. The design of Emotinet follows the plug-in philosophy. Thus, new plug-ins can be added, for instance to collect information from new sources and to show information on new devices. The current version of Emotinet offers a few reusable components for common functionalities and more components are currently being added. In this sense, Emotinet is growing toward a toolkit as more and more components are added.

More concretely, Emotinet provides several things: an API to facilitate the addition of both new plug-ins for capturing information about a user's activities and situation, and new plug-ins to show information about a user's activities and situation; managers for both kinds of plug-in; the control of compatibility between provider and consumer plug-ins in terms of nature and type of information; and a manager of the user's contacts and the information available from their related plug-ins. The basic architecture of Emotinet is based on the widget approach and the communication level is built upon a preexistent infrastructure (XMPP).

A first social awareness system, Coll(int)age, has already been developed by using Emotinet. In short, with a certain periodicity the user is presented, on a peripheral user interface (windows desktop or digital picture frame), with a new collage composed of pictures indirectly triggered by their loved ones. In particular the pictures are triggered by the text they write and read, while working on their PCs.

Both Emotinet and Coll(int)age are described in this chapter. The structure of the chapter begins with a review of related work. Following this we present the design of Emotinet. We also detail the first social awareness system developed over Emotinet, Coll(int)age. Finally we provide the conclusions and future work.

12.2 Related Work

In this section we will be looking at peripheral displays and awareness systems. First, we chose to concentrate on the displays that draw the attention of the user on the periphery. Public information is mostly exposed in that way and falls under this category, such as clocks, posters, and windows. Computationally enhanced variations of this category are classified as a peripheral display. An initial example would be a "dangling string" attached to a motor (Weiser and Brown, 1996), which were created together by an artist and a technologist. Depending on network load, the string spun around at different speeds.

Peripheral displays do not demand the user's full, and they can be classified in two categories: ambient and alerting. Ambient displays do not distract people from their main task and allow at the same time to perceive different data. Alerting displays use more direct means to attract people's attention. However, it is difficult to be clear-cut about this distinction. Many alerting displays include an ambient component when they are not actively alerting the user. Whereas an ambient display may at times alert a user about something. The user interface of our application, Coll(int)age, is a peripheral display, more specifically, an ambient display.

We can observe a current trend which explores symbolic representations (Pedersen, 1998) of captured activity data rather than just showing full video and audio. Symbolism uses an intermediate means to present anew the events, and understanding the symbolic representations forces people to interpret it. In our case, the activities of loved ones and their symbolic representations do not have a direct link. In our system the pictures are collected from the Internet, based on a textual simplification of the user's activity. Thus, we can rather speak of indirect information than of symbolic representation.

In recent years lot of effort has gone into designing peripheral displays. Some of them employ projectors (Youll and Spiegel, 1999; Rodenstein, 1999), while others are embedded in augmented objects (Wisneski et al., 1998; Prante et al., 2003) or in an architectural space (Antifakos and Schiele, 2003; Marti and Seetharam, 2001).

We must, however, insist on our particular interest in using screens for peripheral displays. To mention a few of the famous ones, we list here InfoCanvas (Miller and Stasko, 2002), Informative Art (Holmquist and Skog, 2003), SideShow (Cadiz et al., 2002) and What's Happening (Zhao and Stasko, 2002).

In InfoCanvas and Informative Art information is deployed as an abstract representation. InfoCanvas displays eye-pleasing scenes such as a cartoon-like beach landscape where elements convey information: the color of a woman's bathing suit may represent current traffic conditions or the altitude of a bird may indicate a particular stock's activity. Informative Art, on the other hand, mimics famous paintings, subtly changing certain elements of the composition to convey awareness information. For instance, the composition of a Piet Mondrian painting is borrowed to indicate the current weather in six different cities.

Literal, iconic representation of information has been explored with SideShow (Cadiz et al., 2002) and What's Happening (Zhao and Stasko, 2002). Sideshow allows the user to have regularly updated peripheral awareness of information from accessible web sites or databases. Visually the Sideshow interface works via a sidebar on one's primary display that cannot be covered by other applications. The sidebar is filled with a variety of items called "tickets", each of which contains a small summary of information. For example, the ticket pointing to one's Outlook calendar shows how long one has until the next meeting, as well as the first few words from the meeting title. If users decide they want to find out more information about a particular item, they can move their mouse over a ticket and an extended window appears. Coll(int)age, like Sideshow, aims to achieve peripheral awareness. However, while Sideshow objective was to improve working environments by facilitating coordination among coworkers, our application has a different aim, i.e., exploring the use of indirect information as a way of reinforcing the feeling of being accompanied by our loved ones. Thus we can consider Coll(int)age and Sideshow complementary.

What's Happening (WH hereinafter) is a set of two systems designed to help promote awareness of activities in a local community. The first tool is the WH Communication-Bar, a small footprint on a person's computer display which is designed to remain visible. The system shows short "blurbs" of automatically collected local content such as official announcements and community events, as well as external ones such as news reports and weather forecasts. The second tool is the WH Screen-Saver that shows graphics and text excerpts from pages on web sites in the community. Thus, WH is aimed at providing local information (in particular announcements, discussions, and information from the web pages of the community members) which helps people to be in touch with each other. Coll(int)age, as WH, utilizes pictures in a peripheral display. However, while WH employs pictures from the web pages of the community members (explicit information showing static states), our system uses collages composed by pictures collected from the Internet according to the current activity of our loved ones (indirect information showing dynamic states).

Both WH and Sideshow can be classified as *awareness systems*, which according to Markopoulos et al. (2005b) can be defined as systems whose purpose is to help connected individuals or groups to maintain a peripheral awareness of the activities and the situation of each other. Awareness systems is a fructiferous ground for new research, and further interesting systems have been proposed, in the last years, for both workplaces (Dourish and Bly, 1992; Jancke et al., 2000) and social/family life (Hindus et al., 2001; Markopoulos et al., 2003, 2004; Dey and de Guzman, 2006). The purpose of framework Emotinet, described here, is to facilitate the construction of this kind of awareness systems.

12.3 Emotinet

Social awareness systems are systems whose purpose is to help connected individuals or groups to maintain a peripheral awareness of the activities and the situation of each other (Markopoulos et al., 2005b). Thus, generally speaking, a social awareness system, which allows a user X to be aware of the activities of a user Y, can be decomposed in three basic components: a module which captures data/information about Y's activities and situation, a module which shows this data/information in a way and place that allows X to be aware of it, and a communication layer which connects both modules. Of course, this is a simplification as each of these components can be a sophisticated system composed in turn of several elements (for instance a user's contacts manager).

From our point of view, a framework for social awareness should provide a reusable basic structure for social awareness applications which facilitates the construction of this kind of system. Moreover, it should include an example (a particular social awareness system) showing the functioning of the framework. Furthermore, ideally it should be open and extensible, so that as programmers create new components for their applications, these components can be easily employed by other programmers for other applications.

More concretely, the reusable basic structure for social awareness applications provided by the framework should include mechanisms to facilitate the addition of new modules to capture information about a user's activities and situation; a way to manage that kind of modules and the information provided by them; mechanisms to facilitate the addition of new modules to show information about a user's activities and situation; a way to manage these kinds of modules; mechanisms to clearly specify the nature and type of the information provided and consumed by modules to capture and modules to express information, respectively; a way to manage and assure compatibility between provider and consumer modules in terms of nature and type of information; a way to manage the user's contacts (and the information available from their related modules); and a communication layer to connect both kinds of modules.

There are no formal studies on architectures for social awareness platforms. Architectures for context awareness platforms, on the contrary, have been widely studied and discussed in the past, and we believe that some lessons can be learnt from these discussions. From our point of view, social awareness systems can be built by using both a context awareness architecture and an adequate communication layer. Actually, the component of a social awareness system which captures the activities and situation of a user is, from our perspective, a particular kind of context awareness system.

A system is said to be context-aware when it, in some way, adapts or reacts to changes in context. In turn, context is defined by Dey (2001) as "any information that can be used to characterize the situation of an *entity*, where an entity is a person, place, or object that is considered relevant to the interaction between a user and an application, including the user and the application themselves." In this sense, a social awareness system can be seen as a particular kind of context awareness system where (1) the entity whose situation is characterized is a person and (2) the action carried out by the system is informing other people about the characterized situation.

Among others, three main approaches have been proposed for context awareness architectures: (1) the widget approach (Salber et al., 1999), adapted from the architecture of graphical user interfaces; (2) the service infrastructure approach (Hong and Landay, 2001), a pervasive middleware model in which much of the work of collecting and processing context information can be decoupled from the application itself; and (3) the blackboard approach (Winograd, 2001), which has been used widely in various artificial intelligence applications.

All the three approaches have advantages and disadvantages. The widget approach is the most efficient of them and allows for the finest control. However, the general problems of this approach are that a system with widgets is compiled together and it is not robust to component failures. We chose the widget approach as the basic architecture for Emotinet and made a decision to avoid the drawbacks of this approach. In particular, we decided to employ the OSGi (Open Services Gateway initiative) technology to build the widget architecture. The OSGi technology is a dynamic module system for Java, which allows adding new modules (widgets or plug-ins) even while the system is running. Moreover, an OSGi system is tolerant to failures of components. Emotinet follows the widget approach, building the communication level upon a preexistent infrastructure (XMPP).

The widget approach was firstly proposed in the Context Toolkit (Salber et al., 1999), which separates the context acquisition process from the delivery and use of context by using three types of abstraction: widgets (components that provide applications with access to context sensed from their operating environments); servers (used to collect the entire context about a particular entity, such as a person); and interpreters (responsible for implementing the interpretation of context information, transforming between different representation formats or merging different context information to provide new representations).

12.3.1 Architecture

As to the distributed infrastructure of the prototype, we considered three different approaches: the multi-agent system approach, the Peer-to-Peer (P2P) networks, and the instant messaging infrastructures. Note that instant messaging systems can be considered as a particular kind of P2P applications. However, they are frequently considered as an approach on its own and particular protocols have been designed for these systems.

In general, designing the application as a multi-agent system facilitates the separation of different functionalities into different components (agents). It also facilitates the addition of new agents providing new functionalities. We already designed and developed a multi-agent system in Garcia (2005), on top of the JADE (Java Agent DEvelopment Framework) platform (Bellifemine et al., 2007). The multiagent approach proved to be useful and extensible in that case. It was really appropriate for that application. However, the kind of framework we describe in this chapter fits even better than the P2P philosophy. Moreover, the P2P approach and technologies seem to be more mature. In fact, the past years have seen a revolution in the P2P research community with the introduction of structured P2P overlay networks, which offer an efficient, scalable, fault-resilient, and self-organizing substrate for building distributed applications. Thus, after evaluating the state of the art in P2P systems, we decided to base the first prototype of Emotinet on Dermi (Decentralized Event Remote Method Invocation) (Pairot et al., 2004), which is inspired by several applications that have emerged as a result of these structured P2P substrates. Dermi is a completely decentralized event-based object middleware built on top of a structured P2P overlay. Its primary objective is to provide developers the necessary abstractions to develop wide-area-scale distributed applications. Dermi uses a P2P publish-subscribe event system and offers several services to the application layer: P2P call abstractions, a decentralized way to locate objects, and a distributed interception service.

However, even though Dermi is a cutting-edge technology with a great potential, it is not yet very extended. In fact, even older and more established open P2P technologies (like JXTA) are not very extended nor well supported. In this sense, the infrastructures for instant messaging have certain advantages. They are widely extended and better supported. Jabber is particularly interesting. It is a set of streaming XML protocols and technologies that enable any two entities on the Internet to exchange messages, presence, and other structured information in close to real time. The Jabber protocols are free, open, public, and easily understandable. Moreover, the Internet Engineering Task Force (IETF) has formalized the core XML streaming protocols as an approved instant messaging and presence technology under the name of XMPP, and the XMPP specifications have been published as RFC 3920 and RFC 3921. Jabber technologies are very stable. Hundreds of developers are working on Jabber technologies. There are tens of thousands of Jabber servers running on the Internet today and about 10 million people use Jabber (apart from 56 million users of Google Talk, which uses these protocols as well). The current version of Emotinet

is built upon Jabber/XMPP. This allows users to employ their own previous account
in Emotinet and to keep their old lists of contacts.

Figure 12.2 shows the overall architecture of Emotinet, which has been completely developed in Java. Next we describe the main modules of the core architecture. The *contact manager* is the module which manages the user's list of contacts
(controls the presence of contacts, notifications of change of state, etc.) and the own
user's state (registers the user in the network of contacts, controls the status, etc.).
The contact manager also controls the communication between the user and his/her

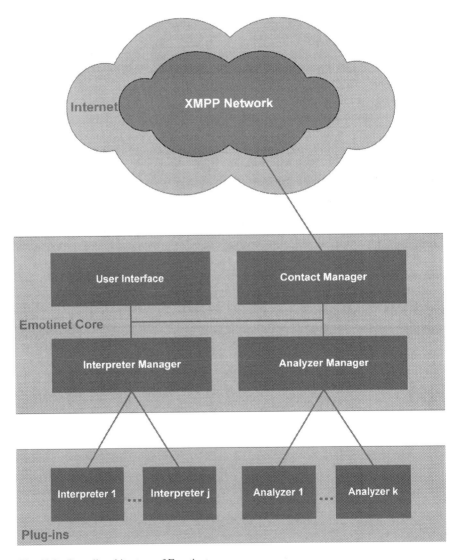

Fig. 12.2 Overall architecture of Emotinet

contacts. It encapsulates the logic of the communication protocols (sending and reception of data). The contact manager module has been designed to decouple the system from concrete implementations of contact controllers. It is even able to work with various controllers simultaneously. Our concrete contact controller has been developed as a XMPP client by employing the open source Smack library (Ignite realtime).

As we pointed out earlier, Emotinet is extensible. In particular, it can be extended through the addition of two kinds of plug-ins: analyzers and interpreters. An *analyzer* is a plug-in that extracts (or captures) information from specific sources. Then, it formats and filters the information according to particular rules. Finally, the analyzer adds some meta-data to the information which is then prepared to be sent to another contact. An *interpreter* is a plug-in that takes as input the information provided by other contacts and translates it into a new representation (according to particular rules) and eventually shows it on a concrete display. Thus, for instance, an analyzer could capture the text a user X is reading on his/her PC, filter and format the text according to particular criteria (reducing the text to a vector of words, for example), and add some meta-data to it (indicating the time frame, for example). Then, this information could be sent to another contact, the user Y. An interpreter on the PC of the user Y could take this information, translate it into a visual abstract representation and show it on a graphical window.

The *analyzer manager* is the module which manages the analyzers employed by the system. It provides mechanisms to work (jointly or individually) with the active analyzers, controlling them and solving the exceptions triggered by them. The analyzer manager is also responsible for selecting, collecting, and grouping the information generated by the analyzers, when a specific request (sent by a user's contact) is received.

The *interpreter manager* is the module responsible for delivering the information receipt from the user's contacts to the appropriate active interpreters. Each interpreter can be associated to several particular contacts. Two or more interpreters can share a contact (that is, they can be associated to a same contact simultaneously) whether they obtain from him the same or different kind of data. The interpreter manager deals also with the resolution of compatibility between contacts and interpreters. Each contact specifies the kinds of data which it is able to provide. Furthermore, each interpreter specifies the kinds of data which it requires. Thus, the interpreter manager can determine if a particular contact is compatible with a concrete interpreter.

The kinds of data that the analyzers provide and the interpreters require are specified at two different levels: structural and semantic. At the *semantic level*, the meaning category of the data is specified according to a shared vocabulary (a very simple ontology). At the *structural level*, the physical representation of the data is specified, including both the type of atomic elements of data (for example, integer, float, and string) and its grouping structure (for example, vector, set, and matrix). Thus, for instance, a contact could specify that it is able to provide lists of string (structural level) representing the topics of the songs listened by its user (semantic level).

By using the Emotinet framework, new social awareness systems can be created by developing the required interpreter and analyzer plug-ins (if they are not already available) according to the Emotinet API. The developer should also declare, in a particular XML format, the nature and type of information produced or consumed by his/her plug-ins, so that Emotinet can check compatibility among plug-ins. In order to run the social awareness system, once the plug-ins are created, the Emotinet framework should be installed on the computers of the involved users. The new developed interpreter and analyzer plug-ins must be added to Emotinet, by just moving them to the plug-ins folder (this can be done even while the Emotinet is running).

12.3.2 The User Interface

The user interface has been internationalized, following the i18n recommendations (W3C). Thus, the interface is available in several languages. Figure 12.3 shows the interface in three of the available languages, particularly English, Spanish, and Catalan. From the user interface, the user can check the compatibility between his/her contacts and interpreters. For each contact, the compatible interpreters are shown. Thus, the user can select/deselect per contact the interpreters he/she wants to connect/unconnect to that contact. Moreover, from the user interface, the user can also specify the analyzers (from his/her repertoire of analyzers) that he/she wants to make available to his/her contacts. Furthermore, the plug-ins installed in the system

Fig. 12.3 The user interface in English, Spanish, and Catalan

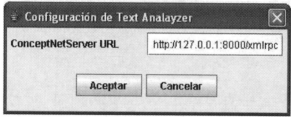

Fig. 12.4 The plug-ins can be configured from the user interface

(both analyzers and interpreters) can also be configured from the user interface (see Fig. 12.4), through the flexible mechanisms that it provides. In addition, the user interface allows the user to carry out typical actions like login/logout, management of his/her list of contacts, etc.

12.4 The First Application

This section describes Coll(int)age, the first social awareness system developed by using Emotinet. This application is aimed at augmenting a person's work environment with information which enables his/her to feel the presence of intimate companions. The vehicle we deem to be appropriate for this situation is indirect, continuous, and peripheral communication. The presence we intend is based on the activities of these intimate people. In short, with a certain periodicity the user is presented, on a peripheral user interface (windows desktop or digital picture frame), with a new collage composed of pictures indirectly triggered by their loved ones. In particular the pictures are triggered by the text they write and read, while working on their PCs.

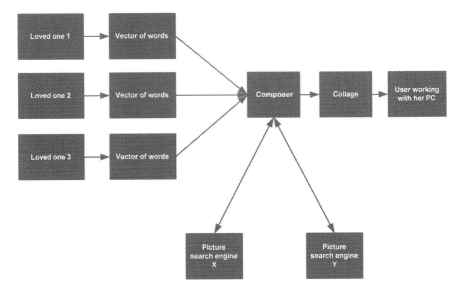

Fig. 12.5 A simple scenario

Figure 12.5 illustrates the overall process through a simple scenario where a user wishes to feel the presence of three loved ones. With a certain periodicity, a vector of words is automatically constructed from the data collected, during that period, in the PC of each of these three loved ones. These vectors of words reflect the topic and mood induced from the users' activity during that period. The vectors corresponding to the three loved ones are collected and employed as keywords to search for pictures in picture search engines on the Internet. An automatic composer creates a new collage using the recently retrieved pictures. The collage is then presented to the user on a peripheral user interface (the windows desktop in this case).

Coll(int)age includes two plug-ins: (1) an analyzer for text/activity processing which reduces the text read and written by the user during a particular period to a vector of words and (2) an interpreter for constructing collages of pictures from a set of vectors of words.

The next subsection illustrates the overall functioning of Coll(int)age through a practical case with real data. Following this, the design principles of the system are introduced. Then, two subsections describe the plug-in for text/activity processing and the plug-in for constructing collages.

12.4.1 Example of Use

In this section, we show the overall functioning of the system through a practical case with real data. Sam is a user who wants to keep in touch with his four best

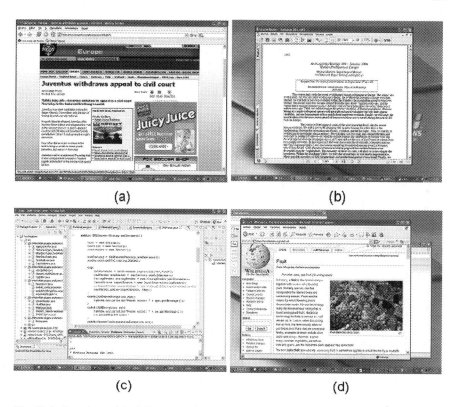

Fig. 12.6   Snapshots of the PC screens of Ana, Peter, Bob and Tom

friends (Ana, Peter, Bob, and Tom). All of them are users of Emotinet. Sam selects these four contacts from the user interface, in order to be presented with a collage (on the desktop of his PC) which allows him to feel the presence of his friends.

In the meantime Ana is reading the web page shown in Fig. 12.6a, which contains news about the Juventus football club. The Emotinet system working on her PC generates the XML structure displayed in Fig. 12.7a, which is then reduced to the following vector of words: ["aim", "arbitration", "juventus", "club", "next level", "not", "better", "italian", "withdraw its appeal"]. By using these words, pictures are retrieved from the Internet and the collage shown in Fig. 12.8a is constructed.

Peter is reading the pdf document shown in Fig. 12.6b, which is a paper about human prehistory in Europe. The Emotinet system working on his PC generates the XML structure displayed in Fig. 12.7b, which is then reduced to the following vector of words: ["find", "modern human", "we", "human evolution", "neanderthal", "anthropology", "region", "teach", "washington dc"]. By using these words, pictures are retrieved from the Internet and the collage shown in Fig. 12.8b is constructed.

304 J. Ibáñez et al.

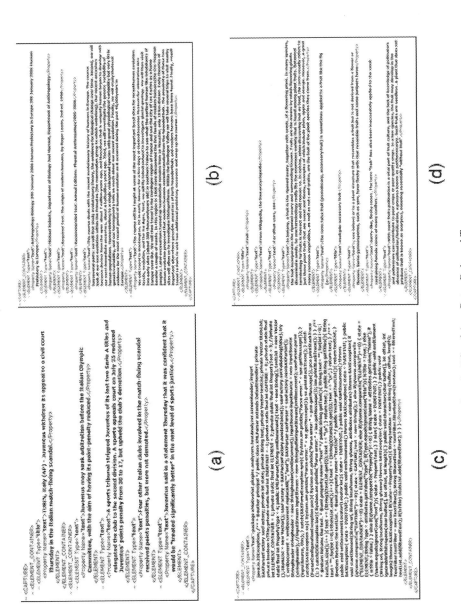

Fig. 12.7 XML structures generated from the data captured on the PCs of Ana, Peter, Bob, and Tom

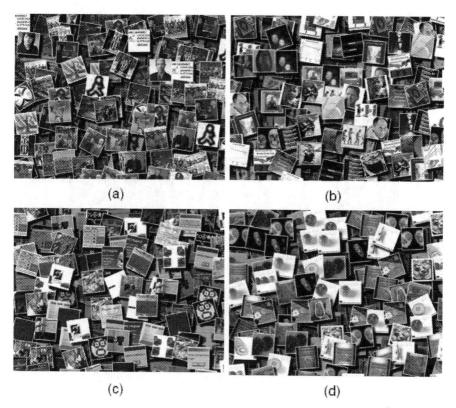

(a) (b)

(c) (d)

Fig. 12.8 Collages composed from the vectors of words generated on the PCs of Ana, Peter, Bob, and Tom

Bob is programming a Java application by using the Eclipse IDE, as shown in Fig. 12.6c. The Emotinet system working on his PC generates the XML structure displayed in Fig. 12.7c, which is then reduced to the following vector of words: ["try", "system", "err", "getmessage", "println parse error", "printstack-trace", "author", "saxfactory", "io"]. By using these words, pictures are retrieved from the Internet and the collage shown in Fig. 12.8c is constructed.

Tom is reading the web page shown in Fig. 12.6d, which is an entry about fruit in the Wikipedia. The Emotinet system working on his PC generates the XML structure displayed in Fig. 12.7d, which is then reduced to the following vector of words: ["fruit", "seed", "see", "many species", "absence", "cuisine", "ovary", "flowering plant", "fertilization", "resemble fruit"]. By using these words, pictures are retrieved from the Internet and the collage shown in Fig. 12.8d is constructed.

Finally, from the four constructed partial collages, the global collage shown in Fig. 12.9 is generated and presented to Sam on his PC desktop.

Fig. 12.9 Final collage presented to Sam

12.4.2 Design Principles

Coll(int)age has been designed taking three main principles into account: transparency (from the user's point of view), indirection of data (before it is presented to users), and peripheral display of the presentation.

If we want the system to be utilized by users, it should be as easy to use as possible. Ideally, it should be "transparent" for users. In fact, users of Coll(int)age are not required to do any special action for the system to work. That is, Coll(int)age does not require the user to annotate media, nor the user is asked to provide periodical feedback, etc. The user only has to select the loved ones he/she wants to feel the presence of, by selecting them from his/her list of contacts. Since that moment, the functioning of the system is automatic and transparent for the user.

We think that a way to avoid the problem of privacy is through the indirection of information. Rather than transmitting information directly captured from remote people (or directly triggered by them), we can work with information which is indirectly influenced by their actions. In this sense, Coll(int)age does not show data directly captured from remote people (text read or written by them), but information indirectly triggered by that data. In fact, two levels of indirection are applied: (1) the texts read or written by the users are translated into vectors of words which, even though are intended to reflect the overall topics of the texts, may not be included in the original texts; and (2) these vectors of words are translated into collages of pictures which are collected from the Internet (not from the users' PC) by employing picture search engines and using keywords from the previously generated vectors of words. Thus, the information eventually displayed (collages of pictures) has been generated by indirecting the original information collected from the PCs of the loved ones.

The kind of communication we intend to promote through the use of Coll(int)age is continuous, so that the user is able to feel the presence of his/her loved ones continuously. More concretely, the user is continuously presented with information triggered by his/her loved ones. This approach, to be effective, requires the information to be presented on a peripheral display. Otherwise, it would be pretty distracting for the user and he/she could not pay attention to his/her tasks. In this sense, Coll(int)age has been designed to use peripheral displays (in particular, the Windows desktop and a digital picture frame).

12.4.3 Text Processing

The analyzer for text/activity processing is composed of two modules: the text extractor and the text analyzer. The *text extractor* is the module that analyzes the activity of the user and extracts text when it is adequate. In particular, it extracts text that the user is (probably) reading or writing. The process of text extraction starts when the following preconditions are fulfilled: (1) the user types some keys or moves the mouse; (2) the active window keeps active during a certain time frame; and (3) the last extraction was carried out a certain time ago. In the current implementation of the text extractor, the text written and read by the user is captured by employing the MSAA (Microsoft Active Accessibility) technology (Microsoft). By using MSAA, our plug-in is able to extract text from any user interface which implements the Active Accessibility service (for instance, Internet Explorer, Firefox, Acrobat Reader, Notepad, and Eclipse).

The *text analyzer* is the other module of the analyzer plug-in for text/activity processing. It is aimed to assign topics to the text previously extracted by the text extractor. It employs ConceptNet (Liu and Singh, 2004) as a tool to extract the topic and mood from the text captured on the PCs of the loved ones. ConceptNet is a semantic resource that is structurally similar to WordNet, but whose scope of contents is general world knowledge. ConceptNet is generated automatically from the English sentences of the Open Mind Common Sense (OMCS) corpus (Singh et al., 2002), and it is integrated with the MontyLingua engine for natural language processing (Liu, 2003). ConceptNet supports various contextual commonsense-reasoning tasks. In particular, the *topic-gisting* and *affect sensing* functionalities are employed by the Emotinet plug-in for text analysis.

12.4.4 Collage Composer

The collage composer is an interpreter plug-in which receives as input a set of vectors of words, and constructs as output a collage of pictures which somehow reflects the vectors of words. The collage is then presented on a particular user interface.

More concretely, the plug-in collects pictures by using several picture search engines on the Internet (Flickr, Yahoo, etc.) and utilizing as keywords some

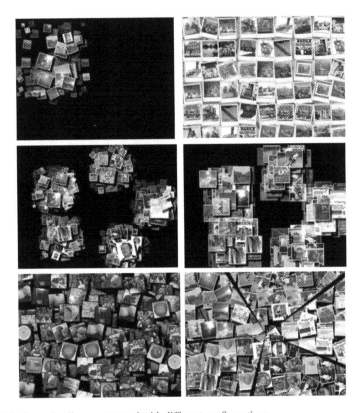

Fig. 12.10 Several collages generated with different configurations

combinations of words from the vectors of words that the plug-in receives as input. After that, the plug-in constructs a collage with the retrieved pictures. This functionality has been developed in Python, using the Python Imaging Library (Lundh, 2005). The current implementation of the plug-in allows the user to configure the kind of collage he/she would like to be presented with. Figure 12.10 shows several collages generated with different configurations, including different techniques for grouping pictures, different spatial distributions, and different parameters of design of individual pictures (like the thickness and color of the frame of the picture or the angle the picture is rotated by). Finally, once the collage is constructed, it is presented on the appropriate user interface (windows desktop or digital picture frame).

12.5 Conclusions and Future Work

This chapter has described the design of Emotinet, a flexible and extensible framework for the development of social awareness systems. Emotinet was initially conceived to facilitate our explorations on how to augment a person's work environment with information which enables him/her to feel the presence of intimate companions. The vehicle we deem to be appropriate for this situation is indirect communication. The presence we intend is based on the activities of these intimate people. However, Emotinet has been designed as a more general, flexible, and extensible framework which facilitates the development of social awareness system in general. In fact, the design of Emotinet follows the plug-in philosophy. Thus, new plug-ins can be easily added, for new functionalities.

The chapter has also detailed the design and functioning of Coll(int)age, the first social awareness system developed by using Emotinet. In short, with a certain periodicity the user is presented, on a peripheral user interface (windows desktop or digital picture frame), with a new collage composed of pictures indirectly triggered by their loved ones. In particular the pictures are triggered by the text they write and read, while working on their PCs. The functioning of the system is transparent for users (that is to say, it does not require them to carry out any special actions such as annotating media or interacting with a specific device).

We really think that Emotinet is a useful and intuitive framework for developing social awareness systems. Therefore, we encourage other researchers and programmers to use it for developing their own applications. We also encourage them to extend Emotinet with new plug-ins providing new functionalities. In fact, our future work include the addition of new plug-ins, like analyzers for both mouse activity and keyboard activity, and interpreters for composition of abstract representation of data.

On the other hand, Coll(int)age (and therefore Emotinet) has already been intensively employed by a few users during the last few months. The functioning of the system has been successful and quite stable. However, further study is necessary in order to infer relevant conclusions. Although the evaluation of awareness systems is not simple, effort has been made to define mechanisms to evaluate this kind of systems, as both the ABC (Affective Benefits in Communication) questionnaire (vanBaren et al., 2003) and the IPO-SPQ (IPO Social Presence Questionnaire) (de Greef and Ijsselsteijn, 2001). Moreover, interesting studies with users have been already reported (de Greef and Ijsselsteijn, 2001; Markopoulos et al., 2005a, 2004) in literature. We are basing our user study on these questionnaires.

Acknowledgments   We would frankly like to thank Leticia Lipp for generously proofreading. This work has been partially funded by the European Union IST program through the project "ICING: Intelligent Cities for the Next Generation".

References

Antifakos, S., Schiele, B.: LaughingLily: Using a flower as a real world information display. In: UbiComp. Seattle, Washington (2003)

Bellifemine, F.L., Caire, G., Greenwood, D.: Developing multi-agent systems with JADE. Wiley Series in Agent Technology. John Wiley & Sons Ltd, New York, NY (2007)

Cadiz, J.J., Venoliaa, G.D., Jancke, G., Gupta, A.: Designing and deploying an information awareness interface. In: CSCW, pp. 314–323 (2002)

Dey, A.K.: Understanding and using context. Personal and Ubiquitous Computing **5**(1), 4–7 (2001). DOI http://dx.doi.org/10.1007/s007790170019

Dey, A.K., de Guzman, E.: From awareness to connectedness: The design and deployment of presence displays. In: CHI '06: Proceedings of the SIGCHI conference on human factors in computing systems, pp. 899–908. ACM Press, New York, NY (2006). DOI http://doi.acm.org/10.1145/1124772.1124905

Dourish, P., Bly, S.: Portholes: Supporting awareness in a distributed work group. In: CHI '92: Proceedings of the SIGCHI conference on human factors in computing systems, pp. 541–547. ACM Press, New York, NY (1992). DOI http://doi.acm.org/10.1145/142750.142982

Garcia, D.: Multi-agent system for automatic presentation of multimedia elements depending on the context. Master's thesis, University Pompeu Fabra, Barcelona, Spain (2005)

de Greef, P., IJsselsteijn, W.A.: Social presence in a home tele-application. CyberPsychology and Behavior **4**, 307–315 (2001)

Hindus, D., Mainwaring, S.D., Leduc, N., Hagström, A.E., Bayley, O.: Casablanca: designing social communication devices for the home. In: CHI '01: Proceedings of the SIGCHI conference on human factors in computing systems, pp. 325–332. ACM Press, New York, NY (2001). DOI http://doi.acm.org/10.1145/365024.383749

Holmquist, L.E., Skog, T.: Informative art: Information visualization in everyday environments. In: 13st international conference on computer graphics and interactive techniques in Australasia and South East Asia, pp. 229–235. Melbourne, Australia (2003)

Hong, J.I., Landay, J.A.: An infrastructure approach to context-aware computing. Human-Computer Interaction **16**(2, 3 and 4), 287–303 (2001)

Ibáñez, J., García, D., Serrano, O., Blat, J., Navarro, R.: Towards affective collages of presences. In: Ubiquitous intelligence and computing (UIC), *Lecture Notes in Computer Science*, vol. 4159, pp. 1154–1163. Springer, Wuhan, China (2006)

Ignite realtime: Smack API (Simple and Powerful Java client API for XMPP). Available at http://www.igniterealtime.org/projects/smack/

Jancke, G., Grudin, J., Gupta, A.: Presenting to local and remote audiences: Design and use of the telep system. In: CHI '00: Proceedings of the SIGCHI conference on human factors in computing systems, pp. 384–391. ACM Press, New York, NY (2000). DOI http://doi.acm.org/10.1145/332040.332461

Liu, H.: Montylingua v1.3.1, toolkit and api. 2003. Available from http://web.media.mit.edu/hugo/montylingua/

Liu, H., Singh, P.: Conceptnet: A practical commonsense reasoning toolkit. BT Technology Journal **22**(4), 211–226 (2004)

Lundh, F.: Python imaging library handbook (2005). Available from http://www.pythonware.com/library/pil/handbook/index.htm

Markopoulos, P., IJsselsteijn, W., Huijnen, C., Romijn, O., Philopoulos, A.: Being there – concepts, effects and measurements of user presence in synthetic environments, chap. Supporting social presence through asynchronous awareness systems, pp. 261–278. IOS Press, Amsterdam (2003)

Markopoulos, P., IJsselsteijn, W., Huijnenb, C., de Ruyter, B.: Sharing experiences through awareness systems in the home. Interacting with Computers **17**(5), 506–521 (2005a)

Markopoulos, P., Romero, N., van Baren, J., IJsselsteijn, W., de Ruyter, B., Farshchian, B.: Keeping in touch with the family: Home and away with the astra awareness system. In: CHI '04: CHI '04 extended abstracts on human factors in computing systems, pp. 1351–1354. ACM Press, New York, NY (2004). DOI http://doi.acm.org/10.1145/985921.986062

Markopoulos, P., de Ruyter, B., Mackay, W.E.: Awareness systems: Known results, theory, concepts and future challenges. In: CHI '05: CHI '05 extended abstracts on human factors in computing systems, pp. 2128–2129. ACM Press, New York, NY (2005b). DOI http://doi.acm.org/10.1145/1056808.1057121

Marti, S., Seetharam, D.: Weathertank: Interface for non-literate communities and ambient visualization tool. MIT Media Lab (2001)

Microsoft: Microsoft active accessibility. Available at http://msdn.microsoft.com/library/en-us/msaa/msaastart 9w2t.asp

Miller, T., Stasko, J.: Artistically conveying peripheral information with the infocanvas. Technical Report GIT-GVU-02-11, Graphics, Visualization, and Usability Center, Georgia Institute of Technology, Atlanta, GA (2002)

Pairot, C., Garcia, P., Skarmeta, A.F.G.: Dermi: A new distributed hash table-based middleware framework. IEEE Internet Computing 8(3), 74–84 (2004)

Pedersen, E.R.: People presence or room activity supporting peripheral awareness over distance. In: Conference on human factors in computing systems, pp. 283–284. Los Angeles, CA (1998)

Prante, T., Rcker, C., Streitz, N., Stenzel, R., Magerkurth, C., van Alphen, D., Plewe, D.: Hello.wall – beyond ambient displays. In: UbiComp. Seattle, Washington (2003)

Rodenstein, R.: Employing the periphery: The window as interface. In: CHI. ACM Press, New York, NY (1999)

Salber, D., Dey, A.K., Abowd, G.D.: The context toolkit: aiding the development of context-enabled applications. In: CHI '99: Proceedings of the SIGCHI conference on human factors in computing systems, pp. 434–441. ACM Press, New York, NY (1999). DOI http://doi.acm.org/10.1145/302979.303126

Singh, P., Lin, T., Mueller, E.T., Lim, G., Perkins, T., Zhu, W.L.: Open mind commonsense: Knowledge acquisition from the general public. In: First international conference on ontologies, databases, and applications of semantics for large scale information systems, Lecture Notes in Computer Science, vol. 2519. Springer, Berlin (2002)

vanBaren, J., IJsselsteijn, W.A., Romero, N., Markopoulos, P., de Ruyter, B.: Affective benefits in communication: The development and field-testing of a new questionnaire measure. In: PRESENCE 2003, 6th annual international workshop on presence. Aalborg, Denmark (2003)

W3C: The W3C Internationalization (I18n) Activity . Available at http://www.w3.org/International/

Weiser, M., Brown, J.S.: Designing calm technology. PowerGrid Journal 1(1) (1996)

Winograd, T.: Architectures for context. Human–Computer Interaction 16(2, 3 and 4), 401–419 (2001)

Wisneski, C., Ishii, H., Dahley, A.: Ambient displays: Turning architectural space into an interface between people and digital information. In: First international workshop on cooperative buildings (CoBuild).Springer, Berlin (1998)

Youll, J., Spiegel, D.: Ambient dayplanner: A tangible interface for public and private appointment calendars. MIT Media Lab (1999)

Zhao, Q.A., Stasko, J.T.: What's happening?: Promoting community awareness through opportunistic, peripheral interfaces. In: Working conference on advanced visual interfaces (AVI), pp. 69–74. Trento, Italy (2002)

Chapter 13
Conversational Awareness in Text-Based Computer Mediated Communication

Minh Hong Tran, Yun Yang and Gitesh K. Raikundalia

Abstract Text-based computer-mediated communication (TxtCMC) supports an instant exchange of messages among geographically distributed people. TxtCMC, such as Instant Messaging and chat tools, has increasingly become widespread and popular at home and at work. Supporting conversational awareness is an important aspect of TxtCMC. Conversational awareness provides a user with information about the presence and activity of others, and therefore helps to establish a context for the user's own activity. Unfortunately, current interface design of TxtCMC provides inadequate support for conversational awareness, especially in support for awareness of *turn-taking, conversational context* and *multiple concurrent conversations*. This research aims to address these three issues by (1) conducting an empirical study to identify the user need for conversational awareness and (2) designing an interface to support this type of awareness. This chapter presents two innovative prototypes, namely *Relaxed Instant Messenger* (RIM) and *Conversational Dock* (Con-Dock). RIM integrates a sequential interface with an adaptive threaded interface to support awareness of turn-taking and conversational context. ConDock adopts a focus + context visualisation technique to support awareness of multiple conversations. The evaluations of the two prototypes show that they meet their design objectives and were found useful in enhancing group communication.

13.1 Introduction

Text-based computer-mediated communication (referred to as TxtCMC henceforth) supports an instant exchange of messages between people. TxtCMC has increasingly become a popular communication means at home and at work (Isaacs et al., 2002; Muller et al., 2003; Nardi et al., 2000; O'Neill and Martin, 2003). TxtCMC aids online conversation by allowing simultaneous participation and helping users to be more focussed on the task at hand (Walther, 1996).

M.H. Tran (✉)

Faculty of Information and Communication Technologies, Swinburne University of Technology, P.O. Box 218 Hawthorn, Victoria 3122, Australia

e-mail: mtran@ict.swin.edu.au

P. Markopoulos et al. (eds.), *Awareness Systems*, Human-Computer Interaction Series, DOI 10.1007/978-1-84882-477-5_13, © Springer-Verlag London Limited 2009

TxtCMC is somewhat akin to face-to-face spoken conversations in the sense that messages are often relatively short, quick and even incomplete (Dix et al., 2004, McDaniel et al., 1996; Smith et al., 2000). However, TxtCMC differs from face-to-face conversations because TxtCMC users are distributed over distance. Users are able to pick up only a limited set of visual and non-visual cues of conversation partners. As a result, inadequate awareness information about the context of group conversation is provided to users (Segerstad and Ljungstrand, 2002; Tran et al., 2005). Research shows that TxtCMC is often found inefficient and takes more time for users to reach final agreement when making their decision based on group discussion (Farnham et al., 2000; Hiltz et al., 1986; Walther, 1996). Users found it more difficult to keep track of each other's presence and conversational activity.

One of the approaches to improve the effectiveness of TxtCMC is to design an interface that can provide sufficient support for awareness information (Farnham et al., 2000; Walther, 1996). Babble (Erickson et al., 1999) conveys information about users' presence and the level of their activity in a conversation. Babble also provides "social proxies" to show users' level of engagement in a conversation. Farnham et al. (2000) present Lead Line that supports awareness of conversational context by attaching scripting to regular text chat. Smith et al.'s study of Threaded Chat (Smith et al., 2000) shows the use of a threaded interface in organising related turns in conversation to facilitate turn-taking. Rittenbruch, Mansfield and Viller (published in this book) investigate the use of intentional enrichment to enhance awareness support. The researchers' study of AnyBiff shows that supporting direct intentional disclosure is useful in sharing awareness information about group activity. The goal of this research is to investigate an interface design that can enhance conversational awareness support in TxCMC.

In the remainder of this chapter, we first review previous research into awareness in TxtCMC. Section 13.3 presents an empirical study that was conducted to advance our understanding of awareness and to set out design requirements. Section 13.4 presents the design and evaluation of two prototypes, named *Relaxed Instant Messenger* (RIM) and *Conversation Dock* (ConDock). We then conclude the chapter with a discussion reflecting our experience in developing RIM and ConDock and outline possible directions for future research.

13.2 Review of Awareness Support

This section reviews related research on four major categories of awareness, including presence awareness, emotional awareness, identity awareness and conversational awareness.

13.2.1 Presence Awareness

Presence awareness refers to knowledge of the availability of other people in a user's contact list, who are often referred to as "buddies". Supporting presence awareness is one of the most fundamental and important features in TxtCMC. This support helps users decide if and when to move into conversations (Nardi et al., 2000). At a rudimentary level, presence awareness informs users if their buddies are online or offline, as implemented in all popular TxtCMC systems, including AIM (http://www.aim.com/), MSN Messenger (http://messenger.msn.com/), Yahoo Messenger (http://messenger.yahoo.com/), Gaim (http://gaim.sourceforge.net/), Trillian (http://www.ceruleanstudios.com/) and Jabber (http://www.jabber.org/).

At a higher level, TxtCMC incorporates many other mechanisms for presence awareness such as sound alerts and live video to inform users when buddies come online and go offline. Hubbub (Isaacs et al., 2002) uses auditory cues to support presence awareness; whenever buddies go online, their "sound IDs" are played at the user site. IMVis (IMVis et al., 2002) and Chat Circles (Viegas and Donath, 1999) explore alternative metaphors to represent presence awareness. IMVis develops a 3D tunnel to show available buddies around the outside edge of the tunnel, and less available buddies closer to the vanishing point of the tunnel. Chat Circles represent users as coloured circles. The circles expand as a new message arrives, and become blurry after a period of idleness. In addition, TxtCMC users can set presence statuses such as "On the phone" and "Stepped out" to inform buddies of their availability. Moreover, other TxtCMC clients, such as Activity Meter (Isaacs et al., 2002) and Chat Circles, even provide the level of users' activities.

When TxtCMC becomes part of an integrated communication platform, more sophisticated support for presence awareness is required. For example, as the mobility factor is added, a new degree of presence awareness is introduced. Hubbub shows if users are online and also indicates whether they logged in from their PCs or their PDAs. MOST (Cheverst et al., 1999) and WebWho (Ljungstrand and Segerstad, 2000) provide awareness of both virtual and physical presence.

13.2.2 Emotional Awareness

Emotions are a social need and play an important role in human communication. Both a person's own affective state and perception of the affective states of others influence the process and outcome of a conversation (Damasio, 1994). There has been a growing interest in providing expressive representation of emotions in TxtCMC (Garcia et al., 1999). At the most basic level, TxtCMC users convey their emotional state like happiness, anger or sadness by using punctuations and acronyms, such as ":-)" for a smiling face, ";-)" for a winking face and "LOL" for laughing out loud (Dix et al. 2004). Smale and Greenberg's study of IM (Smale and Greenberg, 2005) shows that people use an editable display name field to indicate their emotional state. Advancing from that, TxtCMC applications have integrated those punctuations with animated graphical emoticons, such as "Audibles" in Yahoo Messenger (http://messenger.yahoo.com/) and "Winks" in MSN Messenger (http://messenger.msn.com/), to reflect the affective state of a sender and the illocutionary force of the messages. Conductive Chat (DiMicco et al., 2002) even explores a new way to convey emotions by incorporating people's skin conductivity levels into a conversation.

13.2.3 Identity Awareness

Enabling users to develop and sustain their own identities is one of the key issues in online communities (Preece, 2000). Identities of TxtCMC users can be developed in many ways, ranging from a rudimentary form of using different text colours to more sophisticated forms such as unique nicknames, customised avatars, unique sound IDs, and so on. A single person might use TxtCMC for different purposes (e.g. personal and business) under different identities. Handel and Herbsleb (2002) show that people in the workplace often participate in many different groups. Hence, there is a need for supporting multiple identities in TxtCMC. In the current design of TxtCMC, *one username* carries *one virtual identity*. This one-to-one model is used by the four most popular TxtCMC systems including AOL, ICQ, MSN and Yahoo. Users carry multiple identities by registering usernames with one or many networks, but there is weak coherence between those identities.

13.2.4 Conversational Awareness

Conversational awareness involves people's knowledge of a conversation that includes information about the *content* and *context* of a conversation. This section discusses conversational awareness in the three aspects of turn-taking, conversational context and multiple conversations.

13.2.4.1 Awareness of Turn-Taking

Turn-taking is one of the fundamental processes of human conversations (Dix et al., 2004). In face-to-face communication, turn-taking is supported by a suite of fine-grained back channels such as body language, eye contact, voice intonation, facial expression, and so on. Unfortunately, those fine-grained back channels are difficult to find in TxtCMC due to the distributed nature of the communication means.

Various solutions to support awareness of turn-taking in TxtCMC have been developed. The simplest solution is that conversants explicitly offer the floor to other people by asking direct questions such as "What do you think, Bob?". However, this solution is limited as it does not suit the conversational style of TxtCMC in which exchanged messages are short and instant (Dix et al., 2004). As a result, other alternatives have been studied. For example, TxtCMC tools provide awareness cues such as the textual "who is typing" indicator in messengers of MSN, Yahoo and Trillian, the visual "focusing" and "not-focusing" cues used in Hubbub (Isaacs et al., 2002), and the auditory typing cues used in Babble (Erickson et al., 1999). Yet, effective support for organising turn-taking rules and resolving floor control conflicts is still very limited (Cech and Condon, 2004).

Threaded Chat (Smith et al., 2000) adopts the threaded model that has been widely implemented in discussion boards to support turns and replies in chat conversations. However, the threaded model suffers several usability problems such as difficulty in navigation and difficulty in providing the focal point of a conversation, as discussed in Smith et al. (2000). Herring (1999) studied the coherence of messages in chat. The study found that users often define non-standard adaptive practices to manage turn-taking in TxtCMC, such as "%" indicates the end of the message but no floor offered. Herring also found that fragmentation of TxtCMC is advantageous in providing an opportunity for sparking social conversation.

13.2.4.2 Awareness of Conversational Context

The richness of face-to-face conversations is obtained naturally by people's implicit understanding of situational information, or *context*. However, this knowledge about a conversation is not easy to acquire when people communicate via TxtCMC.

Commonly, TxtCMC applications help users stay aware of conversational context by displaying a *quasi-shared* window—a window containing messages sent by all participants in a conversation. A quasi-shared window displays local messages instantly and remote messages in order of their arrivals at a central server. Consequently, the order of messages can be different from one user's screen to another. Despite this inconsistency, a quasi-shared window is useful in providing TxtCMC users with some degree of shared understanding of the flow of messages. Other systems, such as Chat Spaces (Geyer et al., 2004), Thread Arcs (Kerr, 2003) and Lead Line (Farnham et al., 2000), have investigated alternative interfaces to support conversational context.

Additionally, conveying information about users' activities, such as if they are typing, talking or focusing/not focusing on a conversation window, helps maintain awareness of the context of a conversation. Chat Circles uses the cadence of size of coloured circles on a user's screen to show the flow of conversations. Babble uses a graphical representation called "social proxies" to show the activity that people carry out with the application. Social proxies provide users with an intuitive sense of context in conversations. Some other applications, such as Gaim and Trillian, even notify local users when remote users close conversation windows, and display a timeout flag if a conversation is inactive for too long.

13.2.4.3 Awareness of Multiple Conversations

In the literature, very little research examines support for awareness of multiple conversations. This form of awareness refers to a user's awareness of ongoing conversations in which the user is engaged. To the best of our knowledge, using "tabs" to organise multiple conversations is the only support that TxtCMC applications, such as Gaim and Trillian, provide to assist users in managing multiple conversations. We refer to this technique as "tabbed conversations". Grouping conversations into tabs within a single frame saves screen estate: instead of displaying many windows, tabbed conversations only require as much screen estate as one single window alone.

In addition, tabbed conversations provide visual indicators (e.g. a coloured flash) to inform users of new messages at a particular conversation.

The disadvantage of tabbed conversations is that the technique requires users to switch between tabs in order to read new messages at an inactive tab. Although switching tabs is a simple task, the problem lies in the fact that it forces users to leave a conversation in which they are currently engaged. While the tabbed conversation technique is useful in presenting the local context of a particular message, it provides limited information about the global context of multiple conversations.

13.3 User Needs and Requirements Analysis

To advance our understanding of conversational awareness, we conducted a comprehensive empirical study of TxtCMC. The study involved an online survey and face-to-face interviews. In this section, we first report the results of the study with respect to support for conversational awareness, and then present a set of design requirements that are derived from the study.

13.3.1 Empirical User Study

The online survey consisted of demographic multiple choice questions, a 7-point Likert scale disagree/agree questionnaire and open-ended questions. A total of 149 participants, including 48 females (32%) and 111 males (68%), took part in the survey. The participants were students from several Australian universities. All of the participants were regular users of TxtCMC.

After the survey was completed, we conducted further informal face-to-face individual interviews with six participants including two females and four males, who were selected from the survey respondents. The interviews were unstructured, using open-ended questions and follow-up questions based on participants' responses. The questions focused on participants' current use of TxtCMC applications and problems that they often had with the applications.

In this section, we present findings in relation to three categories of conversational awareness, including awareness of turn-taking, awareness of conversational context and awareness of multiple conversations. Note that at many points during the discussion, various aspects of conversational awareness interweave one another. Hence, the reader might realise that findings reported in one category can also be part of another category.

Awareness of turn-taking: Many awareness cues provided in a one-to-one conversation are either missing or become significantly less effective in a group conversation. For example, a "who is typing" cue is missing in group chat especially when more than one person is typing at the same time. This leads to many problems in maintaining turn-taking and resolving floor control conflicts. "I rarely use group conference but I once chatted with four friends and it was very difficult. . . because they were talking about many things at the same time. It was hard to follow", commented one respondent (Tran et al., 2005).

Awareness of conversational context: The study shows that there is a need for providing better support for awareness of conversational context in TxtCMC. Participants responded that they often wanted to refer to earlier messages of the same conversation (mean = 4.9; std. dev. = 1.58) yet TxtCMC provide limited support for this. Users often have to copy the messages to which they want to refer from the quasi-shared window and paste them to a new message. This issue is similar to *deictic reference*, a problem of referring to objects using gestures and eye gazes (Dix et al., 2004). Another issue related to the support for awareness of conversational context is the ability to link related messages. The participants found this matter rather manageable in a one-to-one conversation, but it becomes significantly problematic in a group conversation where branching turns often occur (Tran et al., 2005).

Awareness of multiple conversations: The majority of the respondents (92%) had chatted one-to-one with two or more people simultaneously. More than half of them had chatted with more than three people at the same time. In addition, five out of the six interviewed participants responded that at one time or another they had typed into a window that was not the one intended, especially when they had multiple conversations happening at the same time. Such a mistake may occur because of weak support for managing multiple conversations. One respondent commented that "My biggest problem when chatting with more than one person is maintaining a presence in each conversation, so conversations should be arranged easily. For example, I would really appreciate if it [conversation] could lock into a corner and then perhaps another chat window could be stacked beneath it or beside it so that I can understand what's going on".

13.3.2 Design Requirements

Based on the findings from the empirical study, we derive a set of three design requirements to enhance support for conversational awareness.

(R1) Activity cues: It often occurs in a conversation that more than one user types messages concurrently. While typing messages, users also check periodically whether other people are typing messages too. Thus, textual and visual cues are used to provide awareness information about people who are typing in a conversation. These cues can handle the situation where multiple users are typing at the same time. Furthermore, the textual and visual cues should provide awareness information about users' currently composed messages.

(R2) Message coherence: One aspect of managing turn-taking in TxtCMC is turn disruption. Adjacent pairs of messages are interrupted by irrelevant messages and intervene with one another. So far, this phenomenon has been the rule rather than the exception in TxtCMC (Herring, 1999). One of the users' adaptive practices to address turn disruption is to back track messages. That is, when users have problems in understanding a new message, they back track earlier messages posted in

the quasi-shared conversation window to gain a better understanding of the context of new messages. To enhance awareness of turn-taking, an interface needs to allow users to quickly and conveniently recognise adjacent pairs of messages. Providing adequate support for adjacent pairs helps resolve the back message tracking behaviour.

Another characteristic of an online conversation is that it often involves multiple topics. In some cases topics are related, but in many cases they are discrete. As a conversation is evolving, unintended topics emerge. Topics emerge as they relate to various aspects of the task at hand and to social interaction. Due to the cardinality of topics, topic branching is more problematic and more difficult to manage in task-related group conversation. Therefore, TxtCMC tools should assist users in managing and keeping track of messages from different topics.

(R3) Multiple conversations: It is common that users interact with several peers simultaneously. Our empirical study calls attention to the fact that support for awareness of multiple conversations is an important issue, but it has not been supported sufficiently by current TxtCMC tools. An alternative interface design is required to help users manage multiple conversations. In particular, the interface allows users to stay aware of the arrival of new messages as well as switching conveniently between conversations.

13.4 Mechanisms Supporting Conversational Awareness

From abovesaid design requirements, we developed two novel prototypes, namely *Relaxed Instant Messenger* (RIM) and *Conversation Dock* (ConDock). RIM supports conversational awareness by providing activity cues (R1) and enhancing message coherence (R2). ConDock facilitates awareness of multiple conversations (R3). This section presents user interfaces and evaluations of RIM and ConDock.

13.4.1 Relaxed Instant Messenger (RIM)

RIM combines the sequential interface model with the threaded model to improve support for conversational awareness. This mixed interface model has shown its potential in the design of e-mail systems (Kerr, 2003; Rohall et al., 2001; Venolia and Neustaedter, 2003) and chat tools (Geyer et al., 2004). The interface of RIM consists of four main panels: *Tree Canvas, Message Canvas, Chat Area* and *Buddy List* (Fig. 13.1).

Tree Canvas (A): The threaded interface that displays messages in a tree-based layout. Messages in each thread are displayed in chronological order. Users are able to create sub-threads and rearrange an order of messages (e.g. moving messages from one thread to another). Tree Canvas also includes Topic List that displays top-level threads of a conversation (i.e. referred to as "topics") and the number of messages inside each topic. Topic List highlights an active thread which is the thread containing the user's most current message.

Message Canvas (B): The sequential interface that shows messages in chronological order. A coloured icon is displayed in front of each message to indicate the

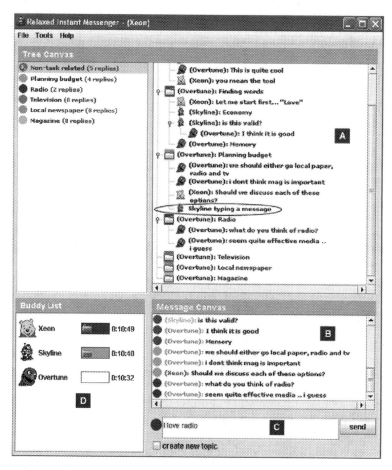

Fig. 13.1 Relaxed Instant Messenger (RIM)

thread to which a message belongs. Message Canvas also allows users to locate corresponding positions of messages on Tree Canvas. When users click on a message on Message Canvas, the message's corresponding position on Tree Canvas is highlighted.

Chat Area (C): A textbox field in which users can enter their messages. Chat Area includes a coloured icon that is used to indicate a parent thread containing a message being composed. We developed *Utterance Rule-based Principle* (URP) that allows assigning new messages to appropriate threads in a semi-automatic manner. URP defines two rules:

[Rule 1]: A user's new message is allocated at the same level and under the same thread (i.e., the same topic) with the user's last message.

[Rule 2]: A user changes topics by highlighting a desirable topic on Thread Canvas.

When the "create new topic" box is checked, a message composed in Chat Area is considered as a top-level thread (i.e. a new topic is created).

Buddy List (D): A list that shows information about users' presence and their conversational activities (e.g. users' names, online status, avatars and typing activities). Buddy List also provides a *visual* cue of "Who are typing" to indicate that *multiple* users are composing messages simultaneously.

13.4.1.1 RIM Support for Conversational Awareness

RIM supports two aspects of conversational awareness, including awareness of turn-taking and awareness of conversational context.

Support for turn-taking: RIM provides support for awareness of turn-taking in three ways. First, RIM provides activity cues of "Who are typing" to show that users are composing messages. These cues are able to show *multiple* users typing messages simultaneously. As seen in Fig. 13.1D, two users—Xeon and Skyline—are composing new messages at different threads. Second, when users compose messages in Tree Canvas, a textual cue of "Who are typing" is displayed at the nodes where new messages are being edited. For example, Fig. 13.1A illustrates an example of a textual cue showing "Skyline typing a message". This also helps users control turn-taking in conversation. Third, RIM codes topics in different colours. Messages of each topic are coded in the same colour as the topic. Coloured dots displayed in front of messages are designed to help users easily identify topics to which messages belong. In addition, visual "Who are typing" cues are coloured to indicate topics to which new messages belong. This helps remote users determine the thread containing a new message even before the message is sent. In other words, these visual cues convey information about users' conversational intention, such as "Who are typing" and "Where new messages go".

Support for conversational context: RIM enhances support for awareness of conversational context by allowing users to form a structured conversation and tailor the layout of a conversation. Users are able to create threads and post messages directly to a specific thread. In other words, related messages can be visually grouped in the same thread, so this supports message coherence pairs. Furthermore, a new top-level thread (i.e. a topic) can be created that assists users in managing messages from different topics. In addition, the depiction of coloured dots conveys the global context of threads, the most frequently discussed thread, and so on.

13.4.1.2 Evaluation of RIM

The evaluation of RIM involved 21 participants, including 12 females and 9 males. The participants were Australian university students and had used TxtCMC tools (e.g. IM and chat) for more than 2 years. They had never worked together in a team before the experiment. The participants were allocated to seven groups of three.[1] Each group participated in a two-hour experiment and was asked to perform four

---

[1] RIM aims to support synchronous discussion of a small group, thus we used groups of three people.

problem-solving tasks using two different TxtCMC tools. A maximum time that the participants were given to finish each task was twenty minutes. Problem-solving scenarios were selected as the experimental tasks because they represent a typical group conversation in which people discuss different alternatives and agree on a final solution.

The two TxtCMC tools used in the experiment were Gaim (http://gaim. sourceforge.net/) and RIM. Gaim is an open-source TxtCMC tool that implements multiple messaging protocols of MSN, AOL, Yahoo, etc. The user interface of Gaim is an example of a conventional TxtCMC tool. One of the experimental goals was to compare participants' performance using a conventional TxtCMC tool and RIM. To minimise the learning effect, an order of tasks using Gaim and RIM was counterbalanced. Logged conversations and interviews were used to compare Gaim with RIM and to analyse the effect of RIM on participant's performance.

Logged Variables

Table 13.1 shows the means of logged variables, including completion time, the number of turns and the number of words in each turn.

Completion Time: Completion time was significantly shorter using RIM rather than Gaim (see Table 13.1).

Structure of Conversations: Two aspects of a conversation were examined, including the number of turns in a conversation and the number of words in a turn. The number of turns of a RIM conversation is significantly less than that of a Gaim conversation. It could be possibly argued that users of RIM took longer turns than when they used Gaim. However, the analysis showed that there is no significant difference between the number of words in a turn when RIM and Gaim were used. To understand why fewer turns were taken in a RIM conversation, we analysed the nature of turns in the logged conversations. We classified turns into two groups: *non-task* turns and *task-related* turns. Non-task turns are not directly related to the task at hand. They are often social messages (e.g. "hello", "how are you", or "Can you increase your font, it is a bit small"). Task-related turns are relevant to the task (e.g. "The cost of magazine is too high, we should reconsider", or "I doubt the effectiveness of TV, given its expensive cost").

The analysis showed that there is no significant difference between the numbers of non-task turns of a Gaim conversation and a RIM conversation, but a RIM conversation involves significantly fewer task-related turns than a Gaim conversation (see Table 13.2).

Table 13.1 Measurement of logged variables

	Mean (std. dev.)		Test significance
	RIM	Gaim	
Completion time	993.2 (17.7)	1184.3 (21.4)	$t(13) = 14.71; p < 0.001$
Number of turns	149.4 (16.3)	220.5 (22.5)	$t(13) = 12.07; p < 0.001$
Number of words	7.2 (3.1)	6.9 (2.1)	$t(1572) = 8.16; p = 0.214$

Table 13.2 Analysis of non-task turns and task-related turns

	Mean (std. dev.)		Test significance
	RIM	Gaim	
Number of non-task turns	18.7 (2.6)	22.1 (5.1)	$t(13) = 7.43; p = 0.381$
Number of task-related turns	130.7 (19.3)	198.4 (23.7)	$t(13) = 11.54; p < 0.001$

Furthermore, by analysing the content of logged conversations, we realised that RIM conversations were more coherent than those of Gaim, in the sense that it seemed easier for users of RIM to organise and realise related turns. Particularly, RIM conversations involved fewer repeated turns and clarifying questions than Gaim conversations. The above comparisons of completion time and the structure of conversations between RIM and Gaim showed that RIM was used more efficiently than Gaim in supporting the tasks.

Specifically for RIM conversations, we also measured variables related to the number of topics and the depth of the threaded interface. The number of topics is measured based on the number of top-level threads. The depth of the threaded interface refers to the number of levels that are nested under the top-level threads. A top-level thread is denoted as "level 1", and the level increases every time a child node is created. From these two variables, we calculate the centre of the threaded interface. The centre indicates the level at which most messages are located. The centre is calculated based on the total number of messages at each level.

The measurement of these three variables is useful in extending our understanding of how RIM was used in supporting group discussion. Table 13.3 shows the measurement of RIM conversations. On average, participants created five top-level threads in a conversation (mean = 5.33). The centre of a tree shows that most of the messages were posted at one level below the main thread (mean = 2.23). The depth of a message tree is around 3 (mean = 3.17). Often, participants created sub-nodes to answer, question and comment on other participants' messages. This interactive behaviour is very difficult to support using the sequential interface solely.

Testing Utterance-based Rule Principle (URP): We hypothesised that participants would use Chat Area, which implements URP, more often than interacting directly with Tree Canvas. The following hypothesis was tested:

H: "Chat Area is used more often than Tree Canvas by users to compose new messages"

Table 13. 3 Structure of the threaded interface of RIM

	Minimum	Maximum	Mean	Std. dev.
Number of branches	3	8	5.33	1.63
Centre of a tree	1	5	2.23	0.02
Depth of a tree	2	4	3.17	0.75

Table 13.4 *t*-Test comparison of the numbers of messages via Chat Area and Tree Canvas

Tasks	Results of a *t*-test comparison
Task 1	$t(20) = 16.52, p < 0.001$
Task 2	$t(20) = 6.91, p < 0.001$

A one-tailed *t*-test was used to test H by comparing the mean of the number of times that participants used Chat Area and Tree Canvas to post messages. The comparison showed that Chat Area was used more often than Tree Canvas by participants when composing messages, as seen in Table 13.4.

The logged data show that participants often clicked on Tree Canvas when they posted direct questions and answers to other participants' messages, and when they changed to another topic. As Chat Area was used by participants as a primary method of posting messages, the user test clearly showed that URP has been useful in automatically posting new messages to correct threads.

In addition, we measured the percentage of errors occurring in RIM conversations, referred to as "thread errors", to verify the correctness of URP. We considered a thread error as an occurrence when a message is typed in Chat Area and placed at a tree node that was not the one intended (e.g. a message was posted in an incorrect topic or at a wrong level). Figure 13.2 shows error rates that occurred in RIM. On average, error rates were 4 and 5% in Task 1 and Task 2, respectively.

By analysing the logged data, we found that these thread errors occurred when users wanted to change threads. In such situations, users were supposed to specify new threads explicitly (e.g. by double clicking on Tree Canvas), however, they still used Chat Area to post messages. Consequently, new messages were located in their current threads instead of new threads that users intended. When thread errors occurred, users had either ignored them and posted the next message in the right threads, or actually corrected themselves by creating duplicates of the misplaced messages at the actual targeted threads.

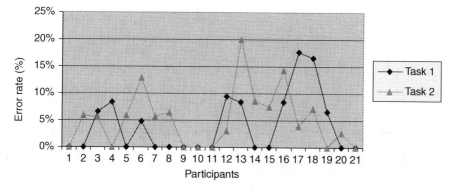

Fig. 13.2 Error rates (%) of URP

Observational Analysis

In addition to quantitative analysis, an observational analysis of users' behaviour in the study showed several interesting insights. In what follows, we discuss observational findings related to participants' behaviour in maintaining conversational awareness.

When RIM was used, participants' turn-taking behaviour was different from when Gaim was used. First, participants changed their turn-taking behaviour based on the presence of multiple textual and visual "Who are typing" cues. Participants used these cues to decide whether they should start composing messages. For example, if a person who posted a question continued typing another follow-up message of the same topic (i.e. identified by the same colour), other people often delayed their responses until that person finished posting the follow-up message. In this sense, the multiple textual and visual cues were used to convey users' conversational intentions. The way that participants used these cues was different from an explicit turn-taking mechanism in face-to-face interaction. In RIM conversations, participants composed messages simultaneously and in most cases they did not offer the floor explicitly. However, participants used the cues to interpret the other people's conversational intentions and adjusted their conversational activity appropriately. Furthermore, participants often performed multiple activities simultaneously. For example, participants glanced at the textual and visual typing cues while composing messages. If a new message arrived, participants also attended to them even if they were in the middle of composing their messages. Participants took part in simultaneous activities and adjusted those activities based on their perception of other people's conversational activities. Second, it is known that TxtCMC encourages simultaneous contribution. This leads to disrupted adjacency if users' simultaneous messages are unrelated (i.e. topic branching). With textual and visual "Who is typing" cues, RIM provides more feedback of other users' messages. We rarely observed from the experiment that three participants typed messages of three different topics simultaneously. It was often that when a participant realised that the other two participants were typing messages, if their messages belonged to different topics (e.g. different colours), the participant then waited for the others to complete posting messages. As a result, it points to the fact that the number of turns of RIM conversation was significantly less than the Gaim conversation (Table 13.1). Nevertheless, overall this manner of controlling turns makes RIM conversations more manageable.

We realised two phenomena in relation to RIM support for conversational context. First, as mentioned above, questioning and answering often occurred in the experiment. Participants used RIM to post questions or answers directly to other people's posts. Even though in many cases other people's posts were posted several messages earlier and interrupted by irrelevant messages. Furthermore, using the threaded interface, participants were able to specify directly a message to which they wanted to post a follow-up message. Second, using colours to code messages of the same topic was also observed to be useful. In the sequential interface, the message-history window provides users with the global context of the conversation. Yet users are required to scan through messages in the history window. In RIM, by looking at coloured icons, participants could quickly gain the global context of what was being discussed. For example, the list of the same coloured icons meant that a group was currently discussing the same topic. If an icon was inserted in the middle of the list of different-coloured icons, this icon was visually distinguished. We observed that when RIM was used, participants often scrolled up and down the history window. Participants commented that they often scrolled up and down the screen to observe the distribution of coloured icons, which informed them of how a conversation was evolving.

13.4.2 Conversation Dock (ConDock)

ConDock adopts a focus + context visualisation technique, called a fish-eye view (Furnas, 1986; Greenberg et al., 1996), to support awareness of multiple conversations. ConDock was implemented as a plug-in for MSN Messenger (http://messenger.msn.com/).

The interface of ConDock includes a single window containing all conversations in which a local user is engaged. In this window, conversations are visualised in a miniature view as seen in Fig. 13.3a. Users are able to navigate through

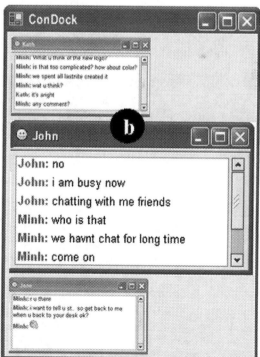

Fig. 13.3 Conversion Dock (ConDock): (**a**) normal view and (**b**) magnified view

conversations by moving a mouse over the miniature views. As a user moves the mouse over a particular conversation, the miniature view of that conversation is enlarged whilst miniature views of other conversations are resized appropriately (Fig. 13.3b). This creates a visual effect like fish-eye views. If users want to post messages to a particular conversation, they can drag the miniature view out of ConDock and interact with the window as normal. When users minimise a conversation window, it is then placed back into ConDock instead of on the task bar.

13.4.2.1 ConDock Supports Awareness of Multiple Conversations

ConDock includes visual cues to support presence awareness of new messages. When a new message arrives at a particular conversation in ConDock, the window containing that conversation is flashing, and a new message is highlighted in another colour. The window stops flashing and the colour changes to the default colour after a user attends to the conversation by moving a mouse over the window.

ConDock provides the global context of all conversations in which a local user is engaged. In addition, ConDock allows users to see a detailed view of each individual conversation if required.

13.4.2.2 Evaluation of ConDock

A field trial was conducted to evaluate ConDock. The goals of the evaluation were to test the usefulness of ConDock in helping users manage multiple conversations, to extend our understanding of how users handle multiple conversations and to identify the strengths and weaknesses of the design.

Eight participants, including five males and three females, were recruited for the field trial of ConDock. The participants were university students in their twenties. All of them had used MSN Messenger for more than 1 year on a daily basis. Participants used ConDock for a period of 3 weeks at home. They were asked to run ConDock whenever they engaged in more than one conversation with their buddies. At the end of each week, participants were asked to complete a 7-point Likert scale questionnaire. At the end of the third week, we arranged time to meet participants face-to-face in an informal interview to ask them about their experience with ConDock as well as perceiving their comments on how ConDock could be improved. During the 3-week trial, each participant was asked to keep a digital diary which is a Microsoft Word document that recorded their positive and negative comments on ConDock. The diary also contained screenshots of ConDock to illustrate scenarios in which ConDock was found or not found useful in supporting participants' conversations.

ConDock Supports Awareness of Multiple Conversations

The usefulness of ConDock in aiding users to manage multiple conversations was evaluated based on participants' responses to the 7-point Likert scale questionnaire and their comments in the interviews. Overall, ConDock was found useful in helping users manage their conversations (mean = 4.87; std. dev. = 1.33). In general, participants' feedback showed that placing all conversations within a single window frame and allowing an accessible way of reading new messages is the most valuable feature of ConDock. As commented by participants:

> "I like how conversations are stacked at one place. And it is fairly easy to move from one conversation to another",
> "It is convenient that I just need to move the mouse over ConDock to read messages... without having to switch continually between windows."

Interaction Style in ConDock

In the 7-point Likert scale questionnaire, participants were also asked to rate the design and implementation of fish-eye views and window drag in ConDock. First, regarding a fish-eye view, there were conflicting streams of participants' feedback on the adoption of a fish-eye view and on the actual implementation of a fish-eye view in ConDock. On the one hand, participants liked an interesting concept of a fish-eye view (mean = 4.96; std. dev. = 1.04). On the other hand, they were not satisfied with the current implementation of fish-eye views in ConDock (mean = 2.79; std. dev. = 1.10). The main reason for these opposing responses was because the fish-eye view currently implemented in ConDock is too sensitive to mouse movement, and it was flickering as the focal point of the fish-eye view changes, as addressed in the discussion section. However, this shortcoming can be fixed with better implementation.

13.5 Discussion and Conclusions

This section compares awareness support of current TxtCMC tools and our prototypes (i.e. RIM and ConDock). Here, we also present design lessons learnt from the empirical study and the development of the prototypes.

13.5.1 Comparison of Awareness Support

We have introduced new awareness features that are implemented in RIM and ConDock. Table 13.5 compares awareness support provided by current TxtCMC and our prototypes.

13.5.2 Lessons from Developing Awareness Support

Supporting conversational awareness in TxtCMC is a two-facet issue, involving both *social* and *technical* challenges. Social challenges involve an understanding of people's social interactions (e.g. policies and purposes), while technical challenges are

Table 13.5 Comparison of support for conversational awareness

Conversational awareness	Current TxtCMC	Our prototypes
Turn-taking	• Single "Who is typing" cue in a group conversation • Where is a person typing (a node in a thread)	• RIM shows multiple "Who is typing" cues in group conversation • RIM uses colours to indicate "Where a new message goes" (i.e. which thread)
Conversational context	• Quasi-shared window • Grouping turns in threads • Scenery background images	• RIM group-related messages into threads • RIM uses a top-level thread to represent each topic of a conversation
Multiple conversations	• Tabbed conversations	• ConDock uses the fish-eye view to support awareness of multiple conversations by showing both a global view and a detailed view

concerned with developing technology that fulfils the social needs of users and with designing usable interfaces.

The social and technical challenges to research on awareness in TxtCMC also result from the fact that TxtCMC has been used for social and/or work-related interaction. TxtCMC is well known as a lightweight communication tool that facilitates people's social interaction. However, in recent years, it has shown a great potential to support work-related activities. These two different contexts of use affect the social needs of users and how TxtCMC tools should be designed. For example, when TxtCMC is used for social purposes, it can involve large groups and people's interaction can be ad hoc (e.g. how they meet together and form a group) whereas most work groups are small and usually planned in advance. Our empirical study has identified many themes with regard to the support for social conversations such as emotional awareness and multiple identities. However, in the organisational context, other aspects of awareness (e.g. structural awareness of a conversation and awareness of turn-taking) become more important because such awareness support has an impact on the effectiveness of users' tasks.

13.5.3 Conclusions

The empirical study, involving an online survey and interviews, contributed to our understanding of conversational awareness and its current support in TxtCMC. Based on the findings from the empirical study, we designed two innovative prototypes, including *Relaxed Instant Messenger* (RIM) and *Conversation Dock*

(ConDock). RIM combines the threaded interface and the sequential interface to enhance awareness of turn-taking and awareness of conversational context. Con-Dock utilises a focus+context visualisation technique to support users' awareness of multiple conversations. The evaluations showed positive feedback on RIM and ConDock, and that the prototypes met their design goals. RIM was found useful in supporting group conversation, in comparison to a conventional TxtCMC tool. ConDock was found useful in helping users control and navigate through multiple conversations. The evaluations also show a number of research issues and design challenges that need to be further addressed.

References

AOL's Instant Messenger. http://www.aim.com/

Cech, C. G. and Condon, S. L., "Temporal Properties of Turn-Taking and Turn-Packaging in Synchronous Computer-Mediated Communication", *Proceedings of the 37th Hawaii International Conference on System Sciences HICSS'04*, Big Island, Hawaii: IEEE Computer Society Press, pp. 107–116, 2004.

Cerulean Studios. http://www.ceruleanstudios.com/

Cheverst, K., Davies, N., Mitchell, K., and Blair, G. S., "The Support of Mobile-Awareness in Collaborative Groupware", *Personal Technologies Journal*, 3, 33–42, 1999.

Damasio, A. R. *Descarte's Error: Emotion, Reason, and the Human Brain*, New York: Gosset Putnam Press, 1994.

DiMicco, J. M., Lakshmipathy, V., and Fiore, A. T., "Conductive Chat: Instant Messaging with a Skin Conductivity Channel", *Poster Presentation, Conference on Computer Supported Cooperative Work CSCW'02*, New Orleans, LA: ACM Press, 2002.

Dix, A. J., Finlay, J., Abowd, G. D., and Beale, R. *Human-Computer Interaction*, Harlow, England: Pearson, Prentice Hall, 2004.

Erickson, T., Smith, D. N., Kellogg, W. A., Laff, M., Richards, J. T., and Bradner, E., "Socially Translucent Systems: Social Proxies, Persistent Conversation, and the Design of 'Babble'", *Proceedings of the SIGCHI Conference on Human Factors in Computing Systems CHI'99*, Pittsburgh, PA: ACM Press, pp. 72–79, 1999.

Farnham, S., Chesley, H. R., McGhee, D. E., Kawal, R., and Landau, J., "Structured Online Interactions: Improving the Decision-Making of Small Discussion Groups", *Proceedings of the ACM Conference on Computer Supported Cooperative Work CSCW'00*, Philadelphia, PA: ACM Press, pp. 299–308, 2000.

Furnas, G. W., "Generalized Fisheye Views", *Proceedings of the SIGCHI Conference on Human Factors in Computing Systems CHI'86*, Boston, MA: ACM Press, pp. 16–23, 1986.

Gaim. http://gaim.sourceforge.net/

Garcia, O., Favela, J., and Machorro, R., "Emotional Awareness in Collaborative Systems", *Proceedings of the Fifth International Workshop on Groupware CRIWG'99*, Cancun, Mexico: IEEE Computer Society Press, pp. 296–303, 1999.

Geyer, W., Witt, A. J., Wilcox, E., Muller, M., Kerr, B., Brownholtz, B., and Millen, D. R., "Chat Spaces", *Proceedings of the 2004 Conference on Designing Interactive Systems DIS'04*, Cambridge, MA: ACM Press, pp. 333–336, 2004.

Greenberg, S., Gutwin, C., and Cockburn, A., "Using Distortion-Oriented Displays to Support Workspace Awareness", *People and Computer XI (Proceedings of the HCI'96)*, Imperial College, London: Springer-Verlag, pp. 229–314, 1996.

Handel, M. and Herbsleb, J. D., "What Is Chat Doing in the Workplace?", *Proceedings of the 2002 ACM Conference on Computer Supported Cooperative Work CSCW'02*, New Orleans, LA: ACM Press, pp. 1–10, 2002.

Herring, S. C., "Interactional Coherence in CMC", *Proceedings of the 32nd Annual Hawaii International Conference on System Sciences HICSS'99*, Maui: IEEE Computer Society Press, pp. 20–22, 1999.

Hiltz, S., Johnson, K., and Turoff, M., "Experiments in Group Decision Making: Communication Process and Outcome in Face-to-Face Versus Computerized Conferences", *Human Communication Research*, 13, 225–252, 1986.

IMVis: Instant Messenger Visualization Neustaedter, C., Greenberg, S., and Carpendale, S., *Video Proceedings of the ACM Conference on Computer Supported Cooperative Work CSCW'02*, ACM Press, 2002.

Isaacs, E., Walendowski, A., and Ranganthan, D., "Hubbub: A Sound-Enhanced Mobile Instant Messenger That Supports Awareness and Opportunistic Interactions", *Proceedings of the SIGCHI Conference on Human Factors in Computing Systems CHI'02*, Minneapolis, MN: ACM Press, pp. 179–186, 2002.

Isaacs, E., Walendowski, A., Whittaker, S., Schiano, D. J., and Kamm, C., "The Character, Functions, and Styles of Instant Messaging in the Workplace", *Proceedings of the 2002 ACM Conference on Computer Supported Cooperative Work CSCW'02*, New Orleans, LA, USA: ACM Press, pp. 11–20, 2002.

Jabber. http://www.jabber.org/

Kerr, B., "Thread Arcs: An Email Thread Visualization", *IBM Research Report RC22951 (W0310-175)*, 2003.

Ljungstrand, P. and Segerstad, Y. H., "Awareness of Presence, Instant Messaging and WebWho", *ACM SIGGROUP Bulletin*, 21, 21–27, 2000.

McDaniel, S. E., Olson, G. M., and Magee, J. C., "Identifying and Analyzing Multiple Threads in Computer-Mediated and Face-to-Face Conversations", *Proceedings of the 1996 ACM Conference on Computer Supported Cooperative Work CSCW'96*, Boston, MA: ACM Press, pp. 39–47, 1996.

MSN Messenger. http://messenger.msn.com/

Muller, M. J., Raven, M. E., Kogan, S., Millen, D. R., and Carey, K., "Introducing Chat into Business Organizations: Toward an Instant Messaging Maturity Model", *Proceedings of the 2003 International ACM SIGGROUP Conference on Supporting Group Work GROUP'03*, Sanibel Island, FL: ACM Press, pp. 50–57, 2003.

Nardi, B. A., Whittaker, S., and Bradner, E., "Interaction and Outeraction: Instant Messaging in Action", *Proceedings of the 2000 ACM Conference on Computer Supported Cooperative Work CSCW'00*, Philadelphia, PA: ACM Press, pp. 79–88, 2000.

O'Neill, J. and Martin, D., "Text Chat in Action", *Proceedings of the 2003 International ACM SIGGROUP Conference on Supporting Group Work GROUP'03*, Sanibel Island, FL: ACM Press, pp. 40–49, 2003.

Preece, J. J. *Online Communities: Designing Usability, Supporting Sociability*, Chichester, UK: John Wiley & Sons, 2000.

Rohall, S. L., Gruen, D., Moody, P., and Kellerman, S., "Email Visualizations to Aid Communications", *Late-Breaking Hot Topics Proceedings of the IEEE Symposium on Information Visualization*, IEEE, pp. 12–15, 2001.

Segerstad, Y. H. A. and Ljungstrand, P., "Instant Messaging With WebWho", *International Journal of Human-Computer Studies*, 56, 147–171, 2002.

Smale, S. and Greenberg, S., "Broadcasting Information Via Display Names in Instant Messaging", *Proceedings of the Conference on Supporting Group Work GROUP'05*, Sanibel Island, FL: ACM Press, pp. 89–98, 2005.

Smith, M., Cadiz, J. J., and Burkhalter, B., "Conversation Trees and Threaded Chats", *Proceedings of the 2000 ACM Conference on Computer Supported Cooperative Work CSCW'00*, Philadelphia, PA: ACM Press, pp. 97–105, 2000.

Tran, M. H., Yang, Y., and Raikundalia, G. K., "Supporting Awareness in Instant Messaging: An Empirical Study and Mechanism Design", *Proceedings of the Australian Conference on Computer Human Interaction OzCHI'05*, Canberra, Australia: ACM Press, ISBN number: 1-59593-222-4, 2005.

Venolia, G. and Neustaedter, C., "Understanding Sequence and Reply Relationships Within Email Conversations: A Mixed-Model Visualization", *Proceedings of the SIGCHI Conference on Human Factors in Computing Systems CHI'03,* Ft. Lauderdale, FL: ACM Press, pp. 361–368, 2003.

Viegas, F. B. and Donath, J. S., "Chat Circles", *Proceedings of the SIGCHI Conference on Human Factors in Computing Systems,* Pittsburgh, PA: ACM Press, pp. 9–16, 1999.

Walther, J. B., "Computer-Mediated Communication: Impersonal, Interpersonal, and Hyperpersonal Interaction", *Communication Research,* 23, 3–43, 1996.

Yahoo. http://messenger.yahoo.com/

Chapter 14
Fostering Social Engagement and Self-Efficacy in Later Life: Studies with Ubiquitous Computing

Margaret E. Morris, Jay Lundell, Terry Dishongh and Brad Needham

Abstract This chapter describes a multiyear project with a team of social scientists and engineers at Intel focused on emerging technologies and successful aging. Theories of behavioral change are linked to the capabilities of emerging technologies for capturing and reflecting variability in activity and health status. The technologies described in this chapter reflect an attempt to integrate psychological theory and ethnographic research with ubiquitous computing. Ethnographic research that we conducted at the outset of this project consistently underscored the value of social engagement for successful aging. It also pointed out the significant social barriers encountered by many older adults. These barriers – which include changes in lifestyle, mobility, and cognitive functioning – are compounded by a perceived inability to change isolating circumstances. To address these social needs and barriers, we developed a set of prototypes involving sensor networks and feedback displays. This chapter describes the social health technologies that we developed, reactions of the older adults and family caregivers who participated in in-home trials, and implications for future development. We also describe the need for tools to encourage self-awareness and self-efficacy for a broad range of health concerns.

14.1 Introduction

Social engagement is increasingly recognized as a critical element of health within social science and medicine. Longitudinal studies have demonstrated the protective and therapeutic value of social engagement for illnesses ranging from the common cold to dementia (Berkman et al., 2000; Fratiglioni et al., 2000; Sarason et al., 1998). Recent research has extended the analysis of social networks on health from cognitive aging to cross generational concerns such as obesity

M.E. Morris (✉)
Digital Health Group, Intel Corporation
e-mail: margaret.morris@intel.com

P. Markopoulos et al. (eds.), *Awareness Systems*, Human-Computer Interaction Series, DOI 10.1007/978-1-84882-477-5_14, © Springer-Verlag London Limited 2009

(e.g., Tamburlini et al., 2007). Recent research, widely covered in the popular press, has extended this analysis of social networks from cognitive aging to cross generational public health concerns such as obesity (e.g., Tamburlini et al., 2007). An extensive ethnographic study of aging, conducted by an interdisciplinary team at Intel, underscored the value of social capital for successful aging (Morris et al., 2003). One man's statement, "I'm a rich man, I have three daughters," conveyed the dependence of life satisfaction on interrelatedness. Our research focused on cognitive aging and the role of social engagement in preventing the onset and progression of dementia. The value of social engagement for cognitive functioning and other aspects of health appears to stem from emotional and instrumental support, the continuation of meaningful life activities, and the feeling of having a positive impact on others. The cognitive stimulation inherent in social interaction is probably also at play in the prevention of dementia: the mental orchestration required to plan an interaction may not be so different from that involved in puzzle solving or tasks involving executive functioning that are undertaken to preserve cognitive health. Moreover, social interaction often goes hand in hand with other cognitively stimulating activities: conversation, perspective shifting, critical questioning, planning events for the future, and physical activity. The following sections describe barriers to social engagement that emerged from our ethnographic research and opportunities to facilitate satisfying interaction.

Significant barriers to social engagement exist for many older adults. Retirement, the death of a spouse, and a diminishing network of surviving peers radically decrease social opportunities. Vision impairments and other physical problems that limit mobility and driving can leave people virtually locked in their homes. Some participants in our ethnography described themselves as "shut-ins." Others compared later life to a deserted island. Elders expressed a longing for the spontaneous contact and occasions for making new friends that they enjoyed in earlier stages of life. Many lost contact with an already diminishing peer group after relocating to live with or near their children. Dissonant feelings about losing contact with friends were sometimes resolved by reorienting energy around families. This focusing of social energy on children and grandchildren may be more compelling than contact with distant friends or recently made acquaintances (Frederickson and Carstensen, 1990), but we observed significant downsides of this reliance on family for social contact: Elders often felt lonely and powerless with regard to initiating interactions, and the daughter or son with the most caregiving responsibility often experienced burnout and frustration.

Cognitive changes may present the strongest barrier to communication for older adults. Some cognitive abilities persist and strengthen throughout life, but normative decreases in processing speed make it hard for many elders to participate in rapidly moving conversations. Alzheimer's disease, estimated to afflict approximately 50% of people over the age of 85, brings about far more severe communication challenges. Difficulty in identifying people, recalling previous conversations, and recalling other socially relevant information add awkwardness and anxiety to interactions (Morris et al., 2003). Our participants expressed anguish when unable to recall a name and embarrassment as they stood apart from a conversation they simply could not follow. "I don't say anything ... I'll ask her (my wife) about it after," explained one man. In addition to memory and planning, domains such as spatial orientation, motor control, and judgment are frequently affected in dementia. As a result, spouses often become 24-hour caregivers; they too lose social contact and are therefore at increased risk for a range of health problems.

Cognitive changes threaten social identity. The inability to communicate confidently and clearly is especially problematic with regard to a critical aspect of social engagement – the feeling of influencing and helping others. We observed painful identity threats, for example, a man who was asked to stop teaching because he repeatedly lost focus during lectures, another whose perceptual and motor impairments prevent him from making repairs to a house that he designed and built, and a woman who now struggles for a week to plan the type of family dinners that she used to execute on the spur of the moment. These shifts were sometimes denied for long periods of time, either by the elder or by their families, who did not welcome the change in responsibilities. There are endless examples of these role losses, and they are experienced across gender, race, and socioeconomic lines. Shame about these role losses, the fear of burdening others, and the ongoing stigma associated with dementia push these individuals even further away from social support.

A perceived inability to change social circumstances was expressed by many participants in our ethnography of cognitive aging. The statement of one man in his eighties, "Loneliness is part of old age and there ain't a damn thing you can do about it," exemplifies this hopelessness. The belief that there is nothing one can do to increase contact perpetuates isolation. Such cycles of pain and perceived loss of control, described as "learned helplessness" by psychologist Martin Seligman (Seligman and Seligman, 1989), can seriously impair mental and physical health. Seligman's research on attributional style – our quick inferences about causality in everyday life – suggests that it would be more adaptive for individuals to perceive isolation as a temporary and changeable situation rather than a permanent condition. Attuning to the variability in negative states is also a component of mindfulness practices. Awareness of variability has been encouraged in the treatment of extreme physical pain (e.g., in burn units) and depression but not yet in the way we address isolation.

14.2 Tools for Social Self-Efficacy

Self-efficacy, a confidence in one's ability to bring about change, is a productive lens for health technology innovation. Albert Bandura (1977) demonstrated self-efficacy as a critical dimension of psychological development, well-being, and professional success. Those with a high degree of self-efficacy are more likely to take risks to pursue goals and more likely to feel that they have succeeded. Social self-efficacy is the belief that one can effectively negotiate interpersonal situations and develop positive relationships. The predominantly negative societal attitudes about aging in the West may undermine social self-efficacy in later life. The elderly are defined largely in terms of impairments, and cast into understimulating environments and roles with limited influence. Consequently, older adults themselves may focus less on their accumulation of wisdom than on cognitive limitations, such as memory loss or delayed information processing, and therefore suffer further insecurity about their ability to effectively connect with others.

Self-efficacy principles align with capabilities of ubiquitous computing. The four strategies outlined by Bandura for increasing self-efficacy – mastering a goal, observing success by similar people, being reminded of one's strengths and abilities by others, and inferring readiness to achieve a goal on the basis of one's physical and emotional states – are supportable by sensing and feedback technologies. Wearable and environmental sensors offer increasingly meaningful data about activities and health states in the contexts of daily life. And, ambient displays, whether on a computer, television, watch, phone, or clothing, can present these data in terms of instructions and motivating feedback. To support self-efficacy, displays should present role modeling visualizations, trending of one's own behaviors and abilities, and feedback to increase awareness of one's emotional and physical states.

Fostering self-awareness of behavioral, cognitive, and emotional patterns related to social interaction was the goal of the current project. To foster this self-awareness and ultimately encourage social interaction, feedback displays need to highlight variability and opportunities for change. This general principle of illustrating variability is central to biofeedback, which has helped patients become more aware of and able to control muscle contractions related to pain. Historically practiced in clinical or laboratory settings, biofeedback is slowly migrating into everyday life: for example, games have been developed to help kids with diabetes understand glucose dynamics (Kumar et al., 2004). Behavioral feedback is similarly shifting outside the clinic: for example, digital photography has been studied to help diabetic patients and dieters reflect on the physiological effects of their food selections (Frost and Smith, 2003). These and other examples present contextually rich data and invite individuals to reflect on the biological and behavioral relationships and invite experimentation with new health strategies.

The next step is to broaden the focus of dynamic feedback from physical to social and emotional conditions. To date, innovative feedback has focused on biological metrics (e.g., blood glucose) and some simple behavioral indices (e.g., steps per day) to motivate diet and exercise changes. Little has been developed to help people track the factors associated with interpersonal and mood changes. Concept feedback studies have revealed interest among many people in tracking multivariate mind–body relationships over time (Beaudin et al., 2006). To facilitate behavioral change, such feedback systems need to be highly personalized and tailored to an individual's short- and long-term goals. The displays also need to be sufficiently compelling – aesthetically and psychologically – to override resistance to self-examination and difficult behavioral change. Given the protective effects of social engagement, it makes sense to explore creative monitoring and feedback tools to help people overcome isolation as a starting point for emotional health feedback systems.

14.3 Prototypes Developed to Foster Social Engagement

We developed a prototype system to motivate social engagement. Our goals were to help people see dynamics in their behaviors, highlight others' availability, and provide contextual prompts to facilitate conversation. The central component of the platform was a social network feedback display continuously updated with sensor and self-reported data. Two additional prototypes were presence lamps that provided information about others' availability and contextual cues to facilitate phone interactions. In the spirit of fostering self-efficacy, all of the displays were reflective and suggestive rather than prescriptive. This approach was also informed by the clinical practice of motivational interviewing, in which change is invited by presenting personalized health information. The displays mirrored current social state and behavioral trends but did not direct the elder to take any specific action, such as making a phone call. Explicit social directives were avoided because we were making inferences from experimental sensors about loneliness – a complex and fairly sensitive topic. The chances of specific instructions seeming inappropriate at any particular moment were significant. Another reason we avoided directives, or related features such as autodial of friends and family, is that these instructions could remove important opportunities for stimulation and self-efficacy. The executive functioning skills of planning and coordinating may be central in why social interaction is protective against dementia.

The goals of fostering social self-efficacy guided concept development and design. These systems were intended primarily to empower elders with information about themselves and other people and invite reciprocal exchange. To avoid stigmatizing elders with objects that looked like "assistive technologies," we tried to use existing objects in the home, familiar interfaces, and visually appealing representations of health states. This approach departs from the exclusive focus on monitoring in most sensor-based health technologies for older adults.

Next we explain the three guidelines for fostering self-efficacy and describe the social health prototype that aligns with each guideline.

14.3.1 Guideline 1: Depict Loneliness as a Temporary Drop in Social Activity Rather Than a Permanent Condition

The theories of learned optimism and self-efficacy suggest that people will feel more in control of their social situation if they perceive their social activity levels as dynamic or variable. The quote referenced above from one participant, "Loneliness is a part of old age and there ain't a damn thing you can do about it," represents the kind of helplessness that we wanted to shift by illustrating variability. This man described social engagement as something that he had completely lost and could not bring about on his own. Ideally, he would recognize the situational challenges he faces, such as not being able to drive by himself at night, understand his own patterns of isolation, and develop time-based strategies to compensate for these barriers.

Ethnographic research conducted for this project suggested that social engagement and feelings of isolation vary not only over the lifespan but also across relatively short periods of time. Gerontological studies point to changes over the lifespan, with a pruning of relationships in later life (Frederickson and Carstensen, 1990). We too encountered people who were very socially active in midlife but who became reclusive following retirement, the death of a spouse, illness, and relocation toward their family caregivers but away from their friends. This movement toward isolation in later life among people who were previously social has been implicated as a major risk factor for dementia and has raised the question of whether social withdrawal is an early indicator of dementia (Saczynski et al., 2006). We also observed micropatterns that have not been explored in traditional gerontology: Repeated interviews with the same participants showed variability in isolation over very short time periods. One woman who was content during the week dreaded the loneliness she experienced on the weekends, a time she felt neglected by her family. Another woman, active and content during the day, despised the evening hours, describing her retirement community as "a morgue after 7 p.m."

Visualization of social patterns could raise self-awareness and help people develop tailored strategies to improve social engagement. Microvariability in social behaviors and feelings of loneliness can be gathered through sensor measures. An early example of this measurement is Choudhury's "sociometer," which patterned social roles and conversational turn-taking from captured speech signals (Choudhury and Basu, 2005). These sensor-based methods are complemented by experience sampling methods in which individuals are frequently prompted to describe social interaction and social satisfaction, typically on a handheld device.

14.3.1.1 Prototype 1: Social Network Displays

We created dynamic social network visualizations to provide older adults with a real-time mirror of their contact with family and friends. The displays (see Figs. 14.1 and 14.2) showed how much time the elder was spending with people in the network, based on sensors and an online journal. Different modalities of the displays showed trends of social activity and aggregations of the data by person (e.g., how much time an elder spent with specific friends or family members over time). This display was an exploration of how social networks could be applied to motivate behavioral change (Morris, 2005). Traditionally, social network analysis has been used to analyze organizational dynamics and flows of information. This type of analysis identifies the centrality and clusters of individuals as well as the density of the links that connect them. The modeling of personal communication is radically changing the nature of professional and personal communication. Interesting representations are explored in research by Donath (2002) and Fisher and Dourish (2004), and online offerings such as the "Circle of Friends" application on Facebook.

The social network visualizations we developed were intended not just to capture an individual's contact list but to describe social states and motivate social engagement. We wanted to convey information in a way that would empower elders to ini-

Fig. 14.1 The solar model of social activity. The elder, positioned at the center of the display, is surrounded by planetary representations of friends and family. Movement toward and away from the elder is generated by sensor data

Fig. 14.2 Social activity displays: (**a**) solar display, (**b**) line graph and (**c**) bar graph show variability to promote social self-efficacy

tiate interaction and help their caregivers become more effective social liaisons. The social network visualizations were placed in the homes of both elders and their primary caregivers. The primary caregiver, typically an adult daughter, could monitor her own contact with the elder as well as that of other family members and friends. We expected the display would prompt contact for some caregivers, and that for others it would invite a strategy for redistributing contact and responsibilities among a larger set of friends and family.

A solar system visualization was selected to represent social activity because it is a vital symbol of relatedness. The solar system has an intrinsic structure, but like social interconnectivity, it is always in movement. It is emotionally resonant and visually appealing to people across age, race, gender, and educational and socioeconomic lines. It is a metaphor that we thought would invite attachment and identification, two critical components for adoption. We wanted a visual metaphor that elders would see as a positive self-reflection and that friends and family, should they see it, would also want to be part of.

The older adult is represented as the sun, positioned in the center of the display. The goal was to present compelling opportunities for elders to draw others into the centers of their worlds. Family and friends rotate around them as planets; their proximity to the sun –updated hourly – was determined by the extent and modality of their contact and their emotional significance to the elder. The planets' inward movement reflected and was intended to reinforce the success of the elderly person's social efforts. The solar display shows current social state and a historical trace: a line between each person's initial and current level of contact with the elderly person at the center.

Friends and family could see themselves in the display and monitor how much time they and others were spending with the elder. We thought that for some, the desire to appear on the display and to move in toward a central position in the display might motivate contact. We wanted these other family members to view the display in their caregiving capacity and also to reflect on their own lives (Fig. 14.1).

To preserve confidentiality and limit stigma, minimal information is conveyed to the casual viewer; details such as names and photos of contacts appear only when a particular planet is selected. Users could toggle between the solar display and several other views, including a line graph (a longitudinal indication of the elder's aggregate contact with everyone in the social network) and a bar graph (showing levels of contact with each person on a given day). Figure 14.2 depicts these three image modalities; a text summary of social activity was also included.

14.3.2 Guideline 2: Provide Windows into Others' Availability

Many elders we interviewed dreaded the idea of burdening their children or other people. Fears of imposing at an inconvenient time often stopped them from making calls. This avoidance, and underlying fear of rejection, often overrode their desire for contact. Analogous dilemmas came from their children, who wanted to feel "in touch" but did not always have time for a long conversation. The children of elders especially wanted the reassurance that their parents were okay and were going about their normal routines.

Cues about others' availability might lower elders' fears of rejection and provide confidence that a phone call or visit would be well received. For their children, indications that their parents are awake and going about their daily activities may provide a piece of mind. Such cues about another's availability can be inferred from sensors or other location-awareness systems. Our work in this area was inspired by the "presence lamp" developed at Interval research (Hindus et al., 2001).

14.3.2.1 Prototype 2: Presence Lamp

We developed a bidirectional presence lamp, linked to sensors and actuators, to provide elders with visibility into the availability of their children and to give children

Fig. 14.3 Presence lamps provide lightweight indicators of wellness and allow elders and their children to signal their availability to one another

a sense of their parents' routines. The caregivers' lamp was activated by a sensor in the elder's home; it switched on whenever the elder sat in his or her typical chair (Fig. 14.3). The elder's lamp switched on when the caregiver pressed a key fob; this was a way of saying "I'm home now," or "It's a good time to call if you want to." Informally we referred to this as "okayness checking" – a lightweight, approximate indicator of someone's state.

14.3.3 Guideline 3: Provide Cues to Foster Mastery of Social Situations

Self-consciousness about memory loss is one of the factors that push elders into isolation. Forgetting names and other critical information creates awkward and painful social interactions. Some described rehearsal strategies such as practicing names while looking at a wall of family photos before a wedding or other gathering, but the critical need, not always aided by this preparation, was for helpful hints at the moment of an encounter. Many relied on a spouse to whisper names or information relayed in recent conversations. The shame and awkwardness related to memory loss may be one of the early reasons that people with dementia shy away from answering the phone or initiating calls. Given that phones are a critical tie to the outside world and inherently smart about participants, they are a logical site for social prompts. Some extremely complex systems have been developed for social prompting, such as Starner's eyewear (Starner et al., 1997), but even simple prompts may have benefit if they are offered at the right moment.

14.3.3.1 Prototype 3: Context ID

We developed an enhanced caller ID application called "Context ID" to facilitate phone conversations. The Context ID prototype displayed an image of the caller, his or her relationship to the elder, and the date of last contact. Calls from the care-

Fig. 14.4 Context ID. Just-in-time cues of the caller's name, face, relationship, and last contact are provided to ease anxiety about recognizing people and starting conversation

giver/study partner were also annotated with highlights of the last interaction, which were pulled from the caregiver's online journal. Incoming calls were matched to a database of names and numbers collected during interviews at the beginning of the study. The visual prompts appeared when the phone rang and remained on the display throughout the call (Fig. 14.4).

These three displays were part of a platform that included wireless sensors: a phone sensor board linked with a caller ID service, mote radios to relay sensor data to an in-home laptop server, and a laptop for social heath displays. The laptop also contained an online journal that we developed for elders to report their social interactions.

14.4 Participant Reactions

We gathered feedback about these systems during a 3-month in-home field study with six pairs of elderly people and their primary caregivers. We conducted case-study evaluations. In an introductory phase, the elder's social activity was measured by an online journal and a sensor platform. During the second half of the study, we continued this sensor and self-report measurement but added the three social health displays described above: the solar-based social network, the presence lamp, and context ID. We interviewed participants at key junctures in the study (specifically during intake, end of baseline, and end of intervention). Following are some emergent themes from these interviews related to self-efficacy and social engagement.

Display preferences: In keeping with self-efficacy theories, people preferred the displays that helped them succeed in their social and familial roles. Most elders preferred the solar display and chose it as their default display instead of either the line graph or the bar chart. They appreciated its circularity and movement and reported using it as a game-like stimulus for family conversation. In contrast, several caregivers expressed a preference for the line graph; one woman explained, "The solar display tells me more about how much other people are interacting with my mom, but the line graph is what really tells me what she's doing." There was a general dislike of text adaptation of the visual displays. Historical views, trends that required several clicks to activate, were used more by caregivers than elders. These reactions underscore the importance of representing data according to the goals of particular audiences. In general, people seem to like seeing themselves literally at the center of things or having the data depiction centered on their needs and aspirations.

Interest in variability: Elders and caregivers were surprised by the ups and downs in their social activity levels as depicted in the displays. They expressed interest in spotting downward trends early on and intervening to avoid isolation and depression.

Awareness of social needs: Displays drew elders' attention to deficits not only in the amount of social contact but also in the members of their networks. For most, this meant an awareness of inadequate peer contact. By the end of the study, several had made shifts in increasing contact with friends: One elderly woman formed a list of old friends with whom she was going to reconnect, another started intensifying interactions with acquaintances, and another became significantly more socially involved in her retirement community.

Dialogue facilitation: The social displays and lamp sparked discussion about communication patterns with family and friends. As one caregiver explained, the displays provided a shared visual reference and permission to discuss sensitive issues, particularly her mother's lack of peer relationships and passivity in family interaction.

Enthusiasm for Journaling: Enthusiasm for the online journal increased markedly when the three displays were introduced. Participants had used the journal for 6 weeks during the baseline phase of the study and were asked to continue using it once the three displays were introduced. The online social journal was designed as a validation of sensor data, but people typically viewed it as a therapeutic tool. The ability to select photos of social contacts was particularly appealing. For some, mastering the journal built confidence; and anticipating the journaling seems to have motivated social interaction. Increased acceptance of journaling when it is coupled with feedback supports the model of embedded assessment and indicates directions for health technologies to increase self-efficacy.

Mastery of Technology: Participants surprised us and themselves with their ability to use the prototypes. Because the elders of the participant dyads were born before 1938, we expected them to have little experience with computers. To reduce the interface complexity, the keyboard and the track pad of the elder's laptop were covered with an opaque plastic board. Contrary to our expectations, several had significant experience with computing applications. All of the participants, even those without this familiarity, were able to use the interfaces for monitoring and feedback. This use provided a sense of accomplishment. Those with more technical experience rejected the simplicity of the prototype. One participant removed the plastic cover from the keyboard to play games embedded in the operating system and three complained that the limited interface prevented them from email and online chatting. These observations point to the danger of simplified interfaces, which may limit beneficial activities and stigmatize users. They also indicate opportunities for adaptive systems, which expand features based on an individual's use patterns.

Caregiver awareness: The displays also appeared to help adult children become more aware of their roles – be they overburdened or under-active caregivers – and modulate their activity accordingly. Some children who were not terribly active in their parents' care have painful insights after repeated exposure to dips in their parents' social graphs or seeing themselves at the outskirts of the solar display.

Reassurance and lightweight communication: The lamp and displays gave additional information to caregivers who were content with their level of involvement but who wanted additional reassurance about their parent's well-being. Sometimes the lamps prompted a call but other times the presence signals provided people with a feeling of connectedness and intimacy, independently of whether phone calls were made at this time. As one woman said, the lamp "just gave me a warm feeling about her."

Caregiver validation: The displays were most helpful for those adult children who were very actively involved as caregivers. They appreciated the validation of their caregiving activities, and some wanted to share the displays to spark other relatives' involvement. In fact, most caregivers shared the displays with siblings and enjoyed a playful competition about who could be the closest planet (i.e., the best child). Family members made a point of checking their position in the elder's social network when visiting either the elderly relative or the primary caregiver. Some even conducted informal tests to see how much contact would make a perceptible difference in the display. Any system failures in registering phone calls or visits from these relatives elicited strong complaints.

Caregiver self-reflection: Ultimately, the displays sparked new insight among some participants about the significant time and energy they devote to caregiving. One woman explained that seeing her central position in her mom's network made her realize how many areas of her own life she had been neglecting. Consequently, she initiated several strategies to bring other people into her mom's daily life and started scheduling time for her own hobbies and interests. Another woman, who at the beginning of the study insisted that her father was entirely self-sufficient and that she was "by no means a caregiver," began to see how much she was doing for him: "I now realize that I kind of am a caregiver and I feel okay about pushing him to see other people." This perceptual shift was validating: she felt more confident that she played a valuable family role and more energetic about helping her father maintain outside social ties.

14.5 Future Directions

Extensions of this research primarily involve mobility and more elaborate feedback to facilitate social engagement. There was a clear desire among elders and caregivers for systems that worked outside the home and that were accessible to a larger family or social network. Mobile systems should ideally be able to sense contact in all the places it occurs and provide contextually appropriate feedback. For an older man, a mobile display might show behavioral feedback to motivate him to start an interaction, cues about forgotten names during or just before an interaction, and an indicator of when his daughter or someone else is available to talk (see Fig. 14.5). Another direction that emerged from this research is the creation of tools that help adults in midlife address their own health concerns while staying in better touch with parents. Such feedback for midlife adults could include feedback on emotional and physical health states or time management systems. Several caregivers expressed an interest in something like the solar display that reflected their progress on various activities and goals – one woman wanted to see progress on her reading and how much time she was spending with her husband. Such feedback could converge with caregiving features tested in this study (Fig. 14.6). If such life-optimization applications were adopted in midlife, there is greater likelihood that they could meaningfully assist in early detection and prevention of disease. For, in addition to providing immediate value propositions for health improvement or caregiving, they could help establish personal baselines and show meaningful patterns of change. Emerging technologies can reach vast numbers of people and offer feedback that could enhance self-efficacy with regard to mental and physical health. A project called Mobile Heart Health (Morris and Guilak, 2009) has begun to explore the use of mobile technologies for self-awareness and emotional regulation.

The promises of technology to foster social engagement and self-efficacy have strengthened dramatically in years since the research described in this chapter was

Fig. 14.5 Mobile applications for availability signaling and remote caregiving

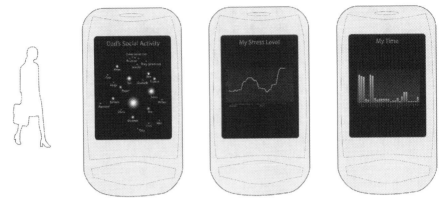

Fig. 14.6 Mobile applications for remote caregiving and self-reflection

started. To start, communication technologies such as WiMAX and 700 MHz radio spectrums provide far more pervasive connectivity. WiMAX removes constraints associated with sparse Wi-Fi or poor wired access. The adoption of the 700 MHz spectrum by Google and Microsoft is paving new ground for ubiquitous computing (Kaplan, 2008). Also on the horizon are low-power Wi-Fi radios integrated into embedded systems for sensors and simple information displays. Home health applications of these Wi-Fi solutions have recently been demonstrated by Healthsense (Fuhr, 2008).

Social self-efficacy will be supported by these ubiquitous technologies as well as new interaction models. Tools such as Facebook have normalized social networking across generations. The mobile versions of these applications, e.g. such as those for the Apple iPhone, allow for very frequent updating of geographical and social context. Many elements of context will be captured seamlessly, and other behavioral documentation will require less effort from users than in the past. These tools will permit rich self-reflection and allow people to view the daily activities of others in their social networks with little restriction (Merrit, 2008). Ideally these tools will evolve to encourage people to share select types of information with the relevant clusters of people in their networks.

Acknowledgments We thank current and former colleagues at Intel, particularly Jason Cassezza, Kevin Rhodes, Stefanie Danhope-smith, Brooke Foucault, Tim Brooke, Dominic D'Andrea, and Eric Dishman.

References

Bandura, A. (1977). Self-efficacy: Toward a unifying theory of behavioral change. *Psychological Review*, 84:191–215.

Beaudin, J.S., Intille, S.S., and Morris, M.E. (2006). To track or not to track: User reaction to concepts in longitudinal health monitoring. *Journal of Medical Internet Research*, 8(4):29.

Berkman, L.F., Glass, T., Brissette, I., and Seeman, T.E. (2000). From social integration to health: Durkheim in the new millennium. *Social Science & Medicine*, 51:843–857.

Choudhury, T., and Basu, S. (2005). Modeling conversational dynamics as a mixed memory Markov process. In *Advances of Neural Information Processing Systems 17 (NIPS 2004)*, Vancouver, BC: MIT Press.

Donath, J. (2002). A semantic approach to visualizing on-line conversations. *Communications of the ACM*, 45:45–49.

Fisher, D., and Dourish, P. (2004). Social and temporal structures in everyday collaboration. *Proceedings of CHI'04*, pp. 551–558.

Fratiglioni, L., Wang, H., Ericsson, K., Maytan, M., and Bengt, W. (2000). Influence of social network on occurrence of dementia: A community-based longitudinal study. *The Lancet*, 355:1315–1319.

Frederickson, B.L., and Carstensen, L.L. (1990). Choosing social partners: How old age and anticipated endings might make people more selective. *Psychology and Aging*, 5:335–347.

Frost, J., and Smith, B.K. (2003). Visualizing health: Imagery in diabetes education. *Proceedings of the 2003 Conference on Designing for User Experiences*, June 06–07, San Francisco, CA

Fuhr, B. (2008). Healthsense press release 2008.

Hindus, D., Mainwaring, S.D., Leduc, N., Hagström, A.E., and Bayley, O. (2001). Casablanca: Designing social communication devices for the home. In *Proceedings of the SIGCHI Conference on Human Factors in Computing Systems* (Seattle, Washington). CHI'01. New York, NY: ACM Press, pp. 325–332.

Kaplan, P. (2008). Google can bid in wireless auction: Regulators. *Rueters News Service*, http://www.reuters.com/article/businessNews/idUSN1447941620080114

Kumar, V.S. et al. (2004). The DAILY Trial: A wireless portable system to improve adherence and glycemic control in youth with diabetes. *Diabetes Technology and Therapeutics*, 6:445–453.

Merrit, R. (2008). Beyond the iPhone, *EE Times*, August 11, 2008.

Morris, M., Lundell, J., Dishman, E., and Needham, B. (2003). New perspectives on ubiquitous computing from ethnographic studies on cognitive decline. *Proceedings of Ubiquitous Computing (UbiComp 03)*, A.K. Dey, A. Schmidt, and J.F. McCarthy, eds., Springer-Verlag, pp. 227–242.

Morris, M. (2005). Social networks as health feedback displays. *IEEE Internet Computing*, 9:29–37.

Morris, M. (2007). Technologies for heart and mind: New directions in embedded assessment. *Intel Technology Journal*, 11:1. http://www.intel.com/technology/itj/2007/v11i1/7-heart-mind/1-abstract.htm

Morris, M., and Guilak, F. (2009). Mobile Heart Health. *IEEE Pervasive Computing*, 8(2):57–61.

Saczynski, J.S., Pfeifer, L.A., Masaki, K., Korf, E.S.C., Laurin, D., White, L., and Launer, L.J. (2006). The effect of social engagement on incident dementia: The Honolulu-Asia Aging study. *American Journal of Epidemiology*, 163(5):433–440, March 1.

Sarason, I.G., Sarason, B.R., and Perce, G.R. (1998). Social support, personality and health. *Topics in Health Psychology*. New York: John Wiley & Sons, pp. 245–256.

Seligman, M.E., and Seligman, M.E.P. (1989). Explanatory style: Predicting depression, achievement, and health. *Brief Therapy Approaches to Treating Anxiety and Depression*, M.D. Yapko, ed., New York: Brunner/Mazel, pp. 5–32.

Starner, T., Mann, S., Rhodes, B., Levine, J., Healey, J., Kirsch, D., Picard, R., and Pentland, A. (1997). Augmented reality through wearable computing. *In Presence*, 6(4):386–398, Winter.

Tamburlini, G., Cattaneo, A., Knecht, S., Reinholz, J., Kenning, P., Rosén, M., Christakis, N.A., and Fowler, J.H. (2007). The spread of obesity in a social network. *New England Journal of Medicine*, 357:1866–1868.

Chapter 15
Awareness of Daily Life Activities

Georgios Metaxas, Barbaros Metin, Jutta Schneider, Panos Markopoulos and Boris de Ruyter

15.1 Introduction

The well-publicized aging of Western societies has prompted a growing interest into technologies that support awareness in cross-generational families. The idea of supporting continual and partly automated flow of information between seniors living alone and their social intimates has been gaining ground among researchers but even among industries. It is anticipated that such an information flow can help bridge geographical distance, discrepant lifestyles, and daily routines, potentially providing peace of mind to both parties and feelings of being connected.

An early influential project that explored this possibility was the Casablanca (Hindus et al., 2001) project. The design concepts this project developed are still current today, including electronic notice boards shared between households, using decorative objects (e.g., a lampshade) to provide friends or family with an indication of an individual's presence, etc.

The Aroma project (Reuben et al., 1990) let users stay in touch by adding to everyday means of communication (such as telephone and e-mail) with a shared media space. The media space was organized as a pair of windows on different workstations, each displaying abstract visual and auditory effects, all together reflecting the state of affairs at the remote site. The visual effects were represented as an abstract, dynamic painting in which the dynamics reflect the changes in the combined auditory and the visual state of the remote site.

Astra (Markopoulos et al., 2004) examined how sharing photographs and brief handwritten notes or sketches can support cross-household communication, enhancing the connectedness experienced by the communication actors and an exploration of intentional communication for the extended family that was shown to enhance feelings of connectedness and to prompt direct communications.

Projects such as Intel's CareNet (Consolvo et al., 2004) and Honeywell's I.L.S.A (Haigh et al., 2004) have examined the use of similar systems for supporting aging

G. Metaxas (✉)
Eindhoven University of Technology, the Netherlands
e-mail: margaret.morris@intel.com

P. Markopoulos et al. (eds.), *Awareness Systems*, Human-Computer Interaction Series, DOI 10.1007/978-1-84882-477-5_15, © Springer-Verlag London Limited 2009

in place; they focus on providing professional care-givers information about elder's medication, nutrition, falls, etc. A related light-weight communication-oriented concept was the Digital-Family-Portrait (DFP) (SCL-90-R, 1994); DFP was designed to provide peace of mind to adult children regarding a lone parent living at a distance. DFP presents graphically the activity level of the senior and other contextual information at their location (e.g., weather). This system constituted a significant advance over earlier such systems as it was deployed and tested in the field, whereas earlier systems (e.g., Mynatt et al., 2001) only tested briefly in the lab or activity sensing were simulated by Wizard of Oz techniques (for example, CareNet (Consolvo et al., 2004) relied on telephone interviews with participants to feed the display with awareness information). Recent projects such as SharedLife (Wahlster et al., 2006) explore the possibilities of extracting and encoding "personal memories" using contextual information and sensor input either for personal use or for sharing among individuals.

Looking at current research prototypes of awareness systems connecting households, it is noteworthy that they are still semantically impoverished with little progress made toward system interpretation of awareness information. The Inter-living project (Hutchinson et al., 2003) explored several communication appliances to connect family members, whereas interesting concepts were produced and the project has accomplished long-term field deployment (6 months), the information communicated does not involve any system interpretation. The Digital-Family-Portrait mentioned above (SCL-90-R, 1994) only goes so far as visualizing an aggregation of sensor firings over the day rather than attempting a more meaningful interpretation of this data. An important reason for this is that it is difficult to obtain reliable interpretations of user activity and to prevent false alarms. This does not represent only a technical challenge; improvements in technology may improve the quality of the data obtained but the inherent design challenge remains of basing awareness on potentially flawed inferences regarding human activity.

In the present study, we examine the feasibility of providing semantically rich interpretations of sensor activity and applying the concept of "seamful design" (Chalmers et al., 2004) in order to support users who are exposed to the imperfections of the sensing technology. We examine the use of narrative information to disambiguate graphical status presentations of awareness information, in line with Gershon et al. who argue that images are susceptible to uncertainties and require some declarative statements for clarification (Gershon and Page, 2001).

The study reported in this chapter explored the feasibility of automatically generating a detailed journal of daily activities, and through several iterations of design and evaluations explored how such information can be usefully presented. This iterative process lead to the conception and the design of the *Daily Activities Diarist*, a wireless Activity-of-Daily-Life (ADL)-journal from data collected through a wireless sensor network installed at the home of seniors. Two field trials were conducted with the Daily Activities Diarist lasting 2 weeks each. In each case, the household of an elderly person living alone was connected to that of their adult children. The field trials provide an initial assessment of whether awareness of such information is valued by the elderly and their children.

In the remainder of this chapter we sketch out the user studies that lead to the design of our awareness system, we explain the motivation behind its design, and summarize its implementation briefly. Finally, we describe two trials that we run for 2 weeks each and outline future work.

15.2 User Studies

By its nature awareness can be seen as the flip side of privacy (Boyle and Greenberg, 2005), requiring the capture and disclosure of information about an individual. Continuous presentation of awareness information about one's social intimates can lead to an information overflow (Khan et al., 2006) or at least to regular disruption of the receiver of this information. These trade-offs were investigated by a user study that involved interviews, focus group sessions, and questionnaires with both seniors and social intimates.

15.2.1 User Profiles

In this chapter the term "Senior adults" refers to people over the age of 65, retired, that have children, and do not suffer from any serious illness. Our target group of senior adults mostly approximates Healthy hermits (Moschis, 1996), i.e., senior individuals remaining in relatively good health yet somewhat withdrawn socially. Healthy hermits have experienced at least one life-changing event such as the death of a spouse. They do not like their isolation or that they are expected to act like old people. Adults who are 85 years old constitute the upper age limit of this population, as they tend to become frailer and have more health problems after that age. The senior adults targeted live alone. However, they have a good and close relationship with their children. They communicate with each other on a regular basis.

The second target group consists of "intimate socials" (or social intimates) of the senior adults, such as sons and/or daughters (Neustaedter et al., 2005; Pedersen and Sokoler, 1997). This group consists of people in the age of 45–60 years old who have a close personal relationship with their parents, but live a certain distance away from them (e.g., at a different city), and mostly have a different life rhythm than their parents.

15.2.2 Interviews

Interviews were conducted with seniors ($N = 4$, 69–85 years old) and intimate socials ($N = 3$, 54–57) to realize their attitudes and patterns of communication. Staying up-to-date with events in the other's life, communicating their own experiences, exchanging practical information, showing interest, reinforcing the relationship, and giving or receiving emotional support were reported as the main reasons of communication by both groups. Elderly are more interested in everyday happenings in the lives of their social intimates; the latter want to know more about general activities of the elderly in the day and if they have any needs and/or problems.

The interviews revealed that seniors fear to bother or to annoy their children when they contact them too often or too long. On the other hand they feel checked up on by daily phone calls from their children. They do not want to share bad moods and feelings with their social intimates.

The intimate socials reported wanting to know how their parents feel, i.e., what their moods are. It is also important for them to know where they are (in or out the house), and if they are asleep or not. All in all they would like to get a general impression of their daily activities.

In both groups it was apparent that women more often mediate social and emotional contacts. Elderly men are more likely to initiate contact only if they have a clear and practical purpose in mind, such as a question they want to ask. The above-mentioned findings are consistent with earlier studies, such as Mahoney and Barthel (1965) and Melenhorst et al. (2001), the NESTOR-LSN survey (Dykstra and Knipscheer, 1995) and the Digital-Family-Portraits project (Mynatt et al., 2001).

15.2.3 Focus Groups

To confront the target groups with the notion of awareness systems and to evaluate our initial concept designs two focus group sessions were held; one with senior adults ($N = 6$, 75–86) at the "Wilgenhof" elderly home and one with intimate socials ($N = 5$, 45–54) at the Philips High Tech Campus.

More specifically a collection of nine related design concepts were presented to both groups and used as a discussion basis in the focus group sessions (Fig. 15.1 shows two of the mockups we used as a prompt to examine a scenario). The mockups were presented as paper prototypes through a mechanical frame that allowed flipping between the various drawings. This helped simulate the dynamic behavior of the system, showing the transaction between different awareness information at different moments in the day. It is worth mentioning that all the examples used in focus group sessions were based on an analogy with a real-world window. For example, Fig. 15.1, displays a greeting scenario where a social intimate is seeing through the window her parent greeting when the day starts.

Fig. 15.1 Two of the prompts used in the focus group sessions

Both groups were quite positive about prospective system attributes such as its unobtrusiveness. Interestingly the main concerns about privacy arose at the social-intimate side, who did not wish to compromise the privacy of their elderly relative, while a typical response given by elderly was "Anyhow, we know everything about each other". Social intimates expressed an interest in being aware of the physical status on the other side (e.g., sleeping, eating), critical events such as rapid decline of the parent's health. They were also interested in knowing the feelings and moods of their parents; however, seniors were reluctant regarding the communication of negative feelings.

15.2.4 Questionnaires

Rather than taking a technology centric perspective of in surveying the acceptance of communicating different kinds of information that are possible to sense automatically, we aimed to understand privacy issues and user preferences regarding awareness information without reference to the way this information can be captured. A questionnaire was assembled based on various inventories of activities-of-daily-life (ADL) to examine what kind of activities the seniors ($N = 10$, avg. age 81) want (or don't mind) to share on one hand, and what their social intimates ($N = 15$, avg. age 45) want to be informed about on the other.

The questionnaire was compiled from different published inventories such as the "Activities of daily life list" (Mahoney and Barthel, 1965), the "Instrumental activities of daily life" (Lawton and Brody, 1969), and the "Advanced activities of daily life" (Rowan and Mynatt, 2005). These inventories provide comprehensive lists of activities at minute-level detail initially intended for profiling the level of self-efficacy of an individual. By asking subjects to indicate the degree to which they would like their social intimates to be aware of the activities listed, we get a comprehensive understanding of their need to share awareness information. The activities that were more of interest for our design were

- Day-to-day maintenance activities, such as feeding, sleeping, personal hygiene, and dressing.
- Instrumental activities, such as shopping, calling, cooking, doing the laundry, and using the phone.
- Daily life concern activities, which arise out of individual abilities and interests, such as social activities.

The format of these questions is illustrated in Fig. 15.2. Each questionnaire included 49 such items. The outcome dictated that home presence/absence, bed occupation, visiting friends/having visitors, followed by other activities like having a walk, cooking, shopping, etc. could be shared from the senior side to the social-intimate side without jeopardizing their privacy. Another interesting finding was that the senior adults overall wanted to share good moods and feelings ($N \geq 9$) but not negative ones ($N \leq 3$).

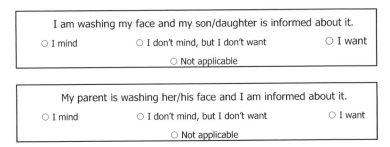

Fig. 15.2 Example question from the questionnaire for the elderly (*top*), and for the social intimates (*bottom*)

15.3 Prototype Design and Implementation

15.3.1 Conceptual Design

Based on the user studies described and more specifically on the senior adults' activities that could be shared with their intimate socials without putting privacy at risk, we chose activities such as walking, sleeping, having visitors, cooking and eating, to populate an auto-generated ADL-journal. Due to the stated preference of elderly to keep negative feelings private, we discarded from this journal moods and feelings. Apart from the synchronous exchange of real-time activity data, the conceptual design was supplied with a history of logged activity data to bridge the different life paces of the user groups.

Further to the graphical display of activities, we decided also to use a narrative presentation with more detailed feedback and reasoning about the displayed activities. The narrative feedback was chosen to address the problems that may rise from false alarms and user-misinterpretations, when graphical information visualization is invoked. Our goal was to minimize these problems by providing semantic cues and explanatory statements using narration as a complement to graphical visualization of the extracted activities.

In order to maintain peripheral-awareness and light-weight interaction with the end-users (i.e., the social intimates), the features of the ADL-journal were presented through an "interactive dynamic poster", assembling the following goals:

- Major changes in the poster can be identified from a long distance using icons (see Fig. 15.3); therefore, social intimates can maintain a peripheral awareness of the elderly activities at the other side.

Fig. 15.3 Graphical presentations of "away", "at home", "in bed", "at the kitchen", and "with visitors"

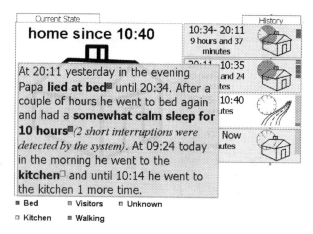

At 20:11 yesterday in the evening Papa **lied at bed** until 20:34. After a couple of hours he went to bed again and had a **somewhat calm sleep for 10 hours** *(2 short interruptions were detected by the system)*. At 09:24 today in the morning he went to the **kitchen** and until 10:14 he went to the kitchen 1 more time.

Fig. 15.4 Screen shot of subject's A1 *Daily Activities Diarist*, showing all three levels of detail presented to users

- Distance is an element of interaction; the closer the user gets to the poster/display, the more detailed information she can get. More detailed information is offered as a historical list on the right column of the display (see Fig. 15.4)
- When the poster/display is within reach-of-hands, the user can directly invoke a detailed narrative explaining the system status and activity journal created (Fig. 15.4). In this way social intimates can acquire more information about the system's reasoning regarding the displayed activities.

15.3.2 Architectural Overview

In Fig. 15.5 we see an overview of the system architecture. The sensor network at the elderly side collects raw data that are pulled from the ADL-State Extractor. The ADL-State Extractor abstracts in software terms the sensors and interprets the collected signals to predefined ADL-states. These states are time-stamped and pushed to the ADL-State Database Host where they are stored in a database for later process. When it is needed (e.g., on request or on specific intervals), the ADL-Semantics Extractor pulls the corresponding states from the database, filters, and transforms them to an ADL-journal that is described in a XML-semantics file. Depending on the configuration, the XML data are pushed to or pulled by the Presentation Server, which does the final transformation to HTML code. The location of Presentation Server is resolved from a Point-to-Point Server that redirects the Client requests to the resolved URL.

15.3.3 Wireless Sensor Network and ADL-State-Extraction

A wireless sensor network was used to collect data from the elderly homes. Presence at home, mobility, sleep, and other activities are extracted using the raw data

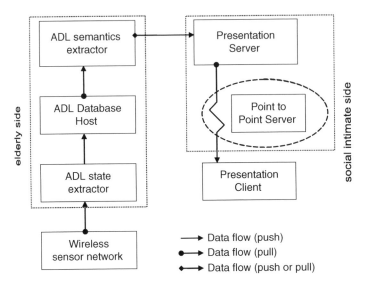

Fig. 15.5 Overview of the prototype architecture, its components, and their location in the current experimental configuration

collected from this first layer. The wireless sensors are abstracted in software terms by ADL-State-Extractors, which transform the collected raw data to ADL-states.

The Sensor network is responsible for all the collected data that are fed in to the system. Presence at home, activity, sleep, and other activities should be extracted by using the data collected from this first layer. The implementation of this layer was based on Crossbow wireless sensors. These are small programmable wireless-communication motes that can be connected to a variety of sensors. The Crossbow motes are equipped with TinyOS, an open-source operating system designed for wireless embedded sensor networks.

With the aforementioned framework the Crossbow motes were programmed to support some basic functionality that initiates the activity extraction at the ADL-State extractor side.

15.3.4 Presence and Mobility Detection

A subject's presence or absence detection is done using the Crossbow MICA2dot wireless coin-size mote (Fig. 15.6). The mote is placed in the subject's key fold.

Fig. 15.6 From *left* to *right*: mica2dot mote, key-fold with mica2dot, and mica2 mote

When the subject is present at home, any signal from the sensor can be detected from the sensor and interpreted as presence, and vice versa when a subject is absent.

In order to detect the mobility of a subject, an accelerometer sensor is added to the mote. When the subject is away the accelerometer records the subject's activity. The activity data can be interpreted later by the system, when the subject is back at home.

In order to make possible the above and to maintain low power consumption, the MICA2dot is programmed to transmit its state every 10 s. Additionally, every 30 s it gets 1 s of high sampling acceleration data. When the energy of the 1 s acceleration samples is higher than a predefined "walking" threshold, the 30 s interval is marked as high activity and vice versa.

On the ADL-state extraction side, the sensor is abstracted in software terms, and the collected data are transformed to presence/absence states. The high- and low-activity counters are compared with the latest known values in order to calculate the subject's mobility while the subject was away. Furthermore, some filters were introduced to overcome problems with lost messages. For example, although the system expects a signal from the sensor every 10 s, the subject is considered to be away only if no signal is received for more than a minute.

15.3.5 Kitchen Activity Detection

Activity in the kitchen and other rooms was identified by monitoring the light condition of cupboards. For example, by monitoring light emittance inside a refrigerator we can tell when the door was opened. The combination of these events from various sources, like cupboards and refrigerators, is used to extract information regarding activity in the kitchen (and possibly other rooms).

For the above purpose we equipped MICA2 motes (Fig. 15.7, left) with photosensors and programmed the motes to measure light emittance every 2 s. If the measured light exceeds a "cupboard open" threshold, the sensor sends a signal to the system. To avoid battery drain, the sensors are programmed not to transmit more than once per minute.

On the ADL-state-extraction side, a collection of these motes is abstracted in software, and the collected data are transformed to kitchen activity data. A sequence of "open cupboards" is interpreted as high kitchen activity with the corresponding duration and intensity.

Fig. 15.7 Placing a wireless mote with a photo sensor in a cupboard (*left*), an illustration of a pressure-pad used for bed-activity detection (*right*)

15.3.6 Bed/Chair/Visitors Activity Detection

A combination of a MICA2 mote and a pressure-pad (Fig. 15.7, right) is used to detect whether a subject is lying on a bed or sitting on a chair. The MICA2 is programmed to make a measurement of the pressure-pad's analog output every 10 s, and the measured value is then transmitted to the system.

On start-up, the ADL-state-extraction component makes the assumption that initially the subject is not lying. Therefore the first readings are used to calculate a "lying" threshold. The same assumption is done when the subject is away, making possible to adapt the "lying" threshold to the changing physical condition of the pressure-pad. A sensor-reading higher than the "lying" threshold is translated as a "bed-active" state and vice versa. Time delay filters are used to overcome lost signals from the MICA2 mote similar to the presence detection.

Furthermore, on the ADL-state-extraction side, a collection of these motes can be used to detect the presence of visitors (e.g., when more than one chair's state is active, the system turns on the "visitors" state).

15.3.7 ADL-Semantics Extractor and State Database Host

The states that are extracted from the ADL-state-extraction components are stored in a database at the ADL-State Database Host as a sequence of states. This sequence, however, may contain logical errors or reliability errors that cannot be addressed from the previous layer (ADL-state-extraction). For example, a pressure-pad could turn on before presence is detected due to network traffic or the presence sensor may not be detected at some intervals due to poor network signal resulting in a series of falsely alternating present/absent states.

The ADL-semantics extractor is a software component that is aimed at resolving these issues, by further processing the extracted state-data, and transforms the later to a nested XML ADL-journal. The XML formatted journal allows flexibility on the final rendering and enables a higher level of semantic analysis.

15.3.8 Presentation Server

The Presentation Server makes the final analysis and rendering of the XML semantics to HTML. The tree structure of the XML ADL-journal is transformed using XSL to an HTML document that presents the argumentation regarding the presented activities in order to avoid misunderstandings and to give access to more detailed information. For example, when the duration of a "bed" state is less than 3 hours the interpretation is "nap" or when a "bed" state is interrupted more than three times the interpretation is "disrupted sleep", and so on.

The HTML document contains explanations like "At 23:30 yesterday in the evening John went to bed and had a somewhat disrupted sleep until 07:45 today in

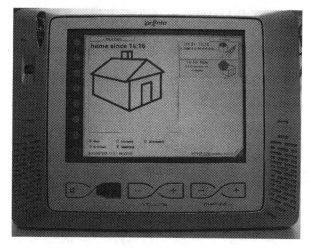

Fig. 15.8 Daily Activities Diarist displayed on a Philips iPronto device, showing the current state (*left*) and the history (*right*)

the morning. Then (at 08:20) he went to the kitchen for half an hour". Furthermore, the system explains its argumentation on user request (e.g., "somewhat disrupted sleep" expands to "two interruptions were detected by the system at 1:45 and at 4:30...."). In Figs. 15.4 and 15.8 one can notice an actual instance from a subject's ADL-journal with a narrative explanation of some extracted activities.

15.4 Evaluation

Two field trials were conducted each involving two households that of a senior participant and that of their social intimates. Each trial lasted 2 weeks. Our aim was to explore the overall experience of living with such a system, patterns of usage to the extent allowed by the duration of the study and affective benefits and costs incurred.

15.4.1 Participants

Family A included a male senior (80) (subject A1), his son (44) (subject A2), daughter-in-law (43) (subject A3), and their two children. The senior A1 is in good health but uses a so-called "walker" when going out. Therefore, trips on his-own are restricted to, e.g., getting the newspaper or visits to neighbors. However, he is still an active person.

Family B included a female senior (85) (subject B1), her daughter (57) (B2), and her son-in-law (57) (B3). The senior B1 is in good health and although she also uses a "walker" to go out, she is still very mobile.

15.4.2 Apparatus and Maintenance

The system was installed in the home of the senior participants. Both apartments were similar in size and layout (small bedroom, living room, kitchen, hallway, and bathroom). In their children's homes two Philips iPronto devices (originally intended as "smart remote controls") were used to display the ADL-journals (Fig. 15.9).

In the end of the first week batteries were changed as scheduled, and then the system was left to run for 7 more days. Interviews with each participant were conducted at the end of the second week. We also used standardized questionnaires to measure social connectedness using the ABC questionnaire (Wahlster et al., 2006) and well-being through the subjective complaints questionnaire (van Baren et al., 2003). Given the small sample size these were not intended for quantitative analysis but to prepare larger scale trial and to see if any interesting variations in connectedness/well-being could be indicated by our participants.

Fig. 15.9 Presentation Client (iPronto) at participant's B2/B3 living room

15.4.3 Results

Social intimates at both trials found the given information in the story telling function sufficiently explanatory, although they did not all use it equally often – "The story telling function was very explanatory, the information which I needed was all provided" – subject A2. Subjects A2 and A3 consulted the narrative regularly (e.g., after waking up and after work). The other subjects were not that interested in acquiring in-depth information so frequently.

Participants, A2 and A3, had to get accustomed to the system the first day but as early as the second day they started relying upon it. Participant A2 used the system to check whether his father was at home or not before calling him, sometimes he checked what he had been doing during the day, if he was sleeping, etc. Some of the information they were interested in was not supported by the system's configuration – "I would like to know if my father is within 'de Akkers', or outside 'de Akkers' or if he is at another place, such as the supermarket" – subject A2. However, the information provided was experienced overall by participant A2 and A3 as sufficient and appreciated as meaningful.

In contrast, during the second trial technical problems lead to different reactions by participants B2, B3 who found no value in the information provided: "I did not really trust the system, it malfunctioned a lot, and I had to reset it quite a few times." – subject B2. Also, they did not feel comfortable with the unidirectional nature of the system fearing that it compromised their parents' privacy – "My mother (in law) should be able to make contact through the system when she wants." – Subject B3, "The system makes me feel as a spy, and it makes her feel as being spied" – subject B2. An erroneous system operation caused subject B2 to be unnecessarily alarmed regarding her mother; also the constant flow of information on her mother's activities made her nervous. She did not however react by immediately calling or visiting her – "Yesterday the system showed that my mother was out at night, and this kept us awake all night. However, we were hesitant to disturb her." – subject B2. Both participants thought the system should be made more obtrusive for alerting to critical or life-threatening events.

The participants noted that they prefer to be informed if sensors or other system parts not obvious to them malfunction, e.g., when batteries drain or when the network is down. This could prevent them from misinterpretations caused by system failures.

From their side, seniors expressed no complaints about the sensors installed in their homes, claiming that they were oblivious to them. Perhaps surprisingly, none of the seniors felt their privacy was invaded. "No privacy issues... it is my son" – subject A1. This however should not be assumed as sufficient evidence that no privacy issues arise; a longer term trial would be more likely to uncover situations where privacy could be compromised or for both parties to better appreciate the privacy risks involved.

An unexpected positive finding (provisional given our small sample) was the reduction of agoraphobia of both participating seniors as measured by post-trial questionnaires. Both seniors reported going out more often than usual; this may be attributed to the safety they felt knowing that their children are aware of their activities.

15.5 Conclusion

Journaling ADLs and displaying them as peripheral social awareness cues can potentially help elderly and their social intimates to be connected. We have argued that a narrative presentation of awareness information that provides rich semantic feedback regarding the system reasoning offers practical advantages over impressionistic graphical presentations of the instantaneous status of the elderly. Clearly a larger empirical basis is needed, but it has to be noted that the difference between these displays is more reliably appreciated by test participants during actual rather use of the system in the field, rather than lab-based evaluations.

Running longer term field trials of such systems poses significant challenges, as is evident from current state of the art. Longer term field trials of communication systems rely on capture and communication of raw audio–video data or text/graphical input by users. For example, the Interliving project involved field trials of several months of their communication appliances. On the other hand, the technical and social challenges of installing sensor-based awareness systems at the homes of participants result in a long set-up phase to get the system reliable and a comparatively shorter term deployment and actual use of the system. For example, Mynatt et al. report actual use of their DFP system by one subject for 1 week after a set-up period of about a year.

Clearly, sensor-based awareness systems need to become more robust and easily configurable, so that deployment is faster at many different households. In order to enable longer term user trials with larger sets of participants, we are currently re-engineering the Daily Activities Diarist to support end-user configurability of the information flow between the connected households. This is necessary to adapt to the different social and physical contexts of the participants' homes and to allow them to provide personalized descriptions of locations and activities that are meaningful to them and their social intimates.

Awareness systems even when aiming for peace of mind have a safety critical nature; the affective costs of an occasional malfunction can outweigh their benefits as they can unsettle relatives mistakenly. The need to portray the seams of the system, as argued recently by Chalmers et al. (2004), can be an appropriate design approach in order to avoid false alarms and to provide more meaningful explanations. For example, an other step toward seamful design would be to use network-health and battery-status metrics when reporting activities in order to insert into the narrative confidence qualifications, e.g., "your parent is probably outside", or "Papa might had a disturbed sleep" where "probably" and "might" can be expanded at the request of the user to an explanation about the sensor-network health and battery-status on demand.

References

Boyle, M., and Greenberg, S., The language of privacy: Learning from video media space analysis and design. ACM ToCHI (June 2005), 12(2), 328–370.

Chalmers, M., and Galani, A., Seamful interweaving: Heterogeneity in the theory and design of interactive systems. Proceedings of DIS 2004, New York: ACM Press (2004), 243–252.

Consolvo, S., Roessler, P., and Shelton, B.E. The CareNet display: Lessons learned from an in-home evaluation of an ambient display. Proceedings of Ubi Comp 2004, Heidelberg: Springer (2004), 22–29.

Dykstra, P.A., and Knipscheer, P.M. The availability and intergenerational structure of family relationships. In: C.P.M. Knipscheer, J. de Jong Gierveld, T.G. Tilburg, and P.A. Dykstra (eds.). Living arrangements and social networks of older adults, Amsterdam: VU University Press (1995), 37–58.

Gershon, N., and Page, W. What storytelling can do for information visualization. Commun ACM (2001), 44(8), 31–37.

Haigh, H.Z., Kiff, L.M., Myers, J., Guralnik, V., Kirschbaum, K., Phelps, J., Plocher, T., and Toms, D. The Independent LifeStyle Assistant™ (I.L.S.A.): Lessons learned. Proceedings of AAAI, San Jose, CA (2004), 852–857.

Hindus, D., Mainwaring, S.D., Leduc, N., Hagström, A.E., and Bayley, O. Casablanca: Designing social communication devices for the home. Proceedings of CHI 2001, New York: ACM Press (2001), 325–332.

Hutchinson, H., Mackay, W., Westerlund, B., Bederson, B.B., Druin, A., Plaisant, C., Beaudoin-Lafon, M., Conversy, S., Evans, H., Hansen, H., Roussel, N., Eiderbäck, B., Lindquist, S., and Sundblad, Y. Technology probes: Inspiring design for and with families, Proceedings of CHI 2003. CHI Lett (2003), 5(1), 17–24.

Khan, J.V., Markopoulos, P., Mota, S.A., IJsselsteijn, W.A., and de Ruyter, B. Intra-family communication needs; how can awareness systems provide support? Conference: 2nd International Conference on Intelligent Environments (IE06), New York: ACM Press (2006), 84–89.

Lawton, M.P., and Brody, E.M., Assessment of older people: Self-maintaining and instrumental activities of daily living. Gerontologist (1969), 9, 179–186.

Mahoney, F.I., and Barthel, D.W. Functional evaluation: The barthel index. Maryland State Med J (1965), 14, 61–66.

Markopoulos, P., Romero, N., Baren, J.v., IJsselsteijn, W., de Ruyter, B., and Farshchian, B. Keeping in touch with the family: Home and away with the ASTRA awareness system. Proceedings of CHI 2004, New York: ACM Press (2004)

Melenhorst, A.S., Rogers, W.A., and Caylor, E. The use of communication technologies by older adults: Exploring the benefits from the users' perspective. Proceedings of the HFES, Santa Monica, CA: Human Factors and Ergonomics Society (2001), 221–225.

Moschis, G.P. "Life stages of the mature market". Am Demogr (September, 1996), 18, 44–50.

Mynatt, E.D., Rowan, J., Jacobs, A. and Craighill, S. Digital family portraits: Supporting peace of mind for extended family members. Proceedings of CHI 2001, New York: ACM Press (2001), 333–340.

Neustaedter, C., Elliot, K. and Greenberg, S. Understanding interpersonal awareness in the home. ACM CHI 2005 workshop on awareness systems, New York: ACM Press (2005).

Pedersen, E.R., and Sokoler, T. AROMA: Abstract representation of presence supporting mutual awareness. Proceedings of ACM SIGHI conference on human factors in computing systems, New York: ACM Press (1997), 234–241.

Reuben, D.B., Laliberte, L., Hiris, J., and Mor, V. A hierarchical exercise scale to measure at the Advanced Activities of Daily Living (AADL) level. J Am Geriatr Soc (1990), 38, 855–861.

Rowan, J., and Mynatt, E.D. Digital family portrait field trial: Support for aging in place. Proceedings of CHI 2005, New York: ACM Press (2005), 521–530.

SCL-90-R: Symptom Checklist-90-R. Administration, scoring and procedures manual LR derogatis. Minneapolis, MN: National Computer Systems, Inc. (1994).

van Baren, J., IJsselsteijn, W.A., Romero, N., Markopoulos, P., and de Ruyter, B. Affective benefits in communication: The development and field-testing of a new questionnaire measure. PRESENCE 2003, Aalborg, Denmark, October (2003).

Wahlster, W., Kroner, A., and Heckmann, D. SharedLife: Towards selective sharing of augmented personal memories. In O. Stock, M. Schaerf (eds.): Reasoning, action and interaction in AI theories and systems. Essays Dedicated to Luigia Carlucci Aiello, Berlin, Heidelberg: Springer (2006), LNAI 4155, 327–342.

Chapter 16
Design and Evaluation of Intentionally Enriched Awareness

Markus Rittenbruch, Tim Mansfield, and Stephen Viller

Abstract   In this chapter we introduce and explore the notion of "intentionally enriched awareness". Intentional enrichment refers to the process of actively engaging users in the awareness process by enabling them to express intentions. We initially look at the phenomenon if sharing intentional information in related collaborative systems. We then explore the concept of intentional enrichment through designing and evaluating the AnyBiff system which allows users to freely create, share and use a variety of biff applications. Biffs are simple representation of predefined activities. Users can select biffs to indicate that they are engaged in an activity. We summarise the results of a trial which allowed us to gain insights into the potential of the AnyBiff prototype and the underlying biff concept to implement intentionally enriched awareness. Our findings show that intentional disclosure mechanisms in the form of biffs were successfully used in a variety of contexts. Users actively engaged in the design of a large variety of biffs and explored many different uses of the concept. The study revealed a whole host of issues with regard to intentionally enriched awareness which give valuable insight into the conception and design of future applications in this area.

16.1 Introduction

Awareness concepts in HCI increasingly utilise the notion of *context awareness*. The move towards context emphasises the need for a richer set of awareness information that goes beyond the traditional 5 W-questions[1] which are a defining characteristic of early awareness mechanisms. A number of systems have implemented context representation, notably *placeless documents* (Dourish et al. 1999) and *event*

M. Rittenbruch (✉)
NICTA and HxI Initiative, Locked Bag 9013, Alexandria NSW 1435, Australia
e-mail: markus.rittenbruch@nicta.com.au

[1] Where, when, who, what and how.

P. Markopoulos et al. (eds.), *Awareness Systems*, Human-Computer Interaction Series,
DOI 10.1007/978-1-84882-477-5_16, © Springer-Verlag London Limited 2009

notification infrastructure (Prinz and Gross 2004). Additional contextual information can lead to a richer description of activities and situations in awareness systems. However, additional information also poses additional challenges and questions for the design of awareness mechanisms. How can we gather additional information that will help users to contextualise their actions? How can additional information reflect people's intentions and context? How can additional information help receivers to effectively select information that is relevant to them?

In this chapter we will introduce and explore the notion of "intentionally enriched awareness". Intentionally enriched awareness is based on the idea of enabling users to be actively involved in the process of providing awareness information. If users are enabled to provide additional contextual information they can add meaning to seemingly disjoint activities. For instance, people generally know why they are editing documents, in which work context particular changes are made, whether the edits are rushed or thorough and so on. However, few awareness mechanisms allow users to leverage this knowledge as part of the awareness process. Practically, intentional enrichment of information could be achieved by a variety of means ranging from annotation, through setting status messages that indicate activities, to the selection of pre-defined or dynamically evolving context descriptions. The objective of the model of intentionally enriched awareness that we discuss here is to provide a structured approach to think about how this information can be harnessed and integrated into the awareness process.

For the following discussion we will employ a simple actor–receiver model that is common for many event-based awareness mechanisms (Lövstrand, 1991; Fuchs et al., 1996). The actor is the source of the awareness information while the receiver is the person potentially interested in some of the information.[2] We refer to the process of actors providing information about their intentions, circumstances and context as "intentional disclosure". One of the main challenges posed by this approach is that being involved in the process of gathering awareness information creates additional workload for actors, potentially leading to a disparity between work and benefit (Grudin, 1994). However, there are many examples of intentional enrichment outside awareness systems. For instance, annotating changes in a word document, aggregating and individualising information in blogs, tagging URLs and media with freely defined categories in social bookmarking services like del.icio.us[3] and photo sharing sites like flickr,[4] setting the status information on an instant messaging client to define availability or location, and so on. All of these activities require a certain effort, yet people constantly engage in them because the perceived benefit at least equals the workload. The challenge for designing intentionally enriched awareness

---

[2] A number of terminologies have been suggested to describe the roles of actors and perceivers, e.g. sender–receiver, actor–observer, informer–informant all of which define the balance between the two roles in slightly different ways. We will continue to use the terms 'actor' and 'perceiver' for the remainder of this chapter.

[3] http://del.icio.us

[4] http://flickr.com

systems is to provide awareness tools that enable the enrichment of information, yet reduce the effort that is required in doing so.

While mechanisms that allow actors to contribute contextual information exist, very few are integral parts of awareness systems. We have previously proposed a framework (Atmosphere) that enables intentionally enriched context awareness and provides mechanisms on different scales of effort (Rittenbruch, 2002). In this chapter we will define a model of intentionally enriched awareness that is based on the Atmosphere model. We will furthermore describe the design, implementation and evaluation of the AnyBiff system which implements one particular aspect of intentional awareness. AnyBiff is a generic activity announcement tool that lets users share intentions to engage in activities and social context with relative ease. The concept extends the notions which were implemented in the CoffeeBiff application which originated at the Distributed Systems Technology Centre (DSTC) (Fitzpatrick et al., 1999).

16.1.1 Chapter Structure

We will explore the concept of intentionally enriched awareness from a number of angles. Initially we will look at existing awareness research and motivate intentional enrichment as a necessary enhancement to existing awareness concepts (Section 16.2.1). Following this we will define the notion of intentionally enriched awareness (Section 16.2.3) which is based on our earlier work in this area (Rittenbruch, 2002). We will then briefly summarise common practices of intentional disclosure in a number of different areas (Section 16.3). Following this we will summarise findings from a previous implementation and evaluation of an intentionally enriched awareness service (Rittenbruch et al., 2007). The AnyBiff system is a generic implementation of the biff concept described by Fitzpatrick et al. (1999) allowing users to freely create, share and use a variety of activity and status indicators. The field trial and evaluation of AnyBiff provide valuable insights into the design of intentionally enriched awareness services as well as the applicability of the underlying model. We will reflect on those findings and discuss design implications.

16.2 Intentionally Enriched Awareness

16.2.1 Motivation

The necessity for intentionally enriched awareness is motivated by two arguments. The first argument analyses the role of intentional activities by looking at the roles of actors in existing awareness models. The second argument is based on Heath et al.'s observation that actors in distributed work settings deliberately try to gain the attention of their colleagues and skillfully gauge the level of obtrusiveness needed to do so (Heath et al., 2002), and Schmidt's critique of passive awareness which builds on these results (Schmidt, 2002).

16.2.2 The Passive Actor

When Fuchs et al. introduced their event distribution model in 1996, awareness models were considerably simpler than today (Fuchs et al., 1996). The model introduced an actor and a perceiver[5] connected by an event pipeline.[6] Events based on the actor's actions were automatically gathered and sent to a database, called the event-history. The receiver would access the database to gain access to the event information that he was interested in. There were several filters that allowed the flow of information to be restricted. On the actor's side there was an individual privacy filter that allowed actors to set privacy policies for the events gathered about them. A global filter would allow for the filtering of general conditions, e.g. in order to comply with organisational policies. On the perceiver's side an individual interest filter allowed the perceivers to subscribe only to those events they were interested in. Despite its simplicity the pipeline model remains a valid approach that describes the underlying mechanism of many event-based awareness services.

What is striking is that the role of the actor is one of the few aspects that have not been addressed in more detail over the years. While the receiver has an increasing amount of control over which awareness information is received and how it is received, the actor does not contribute additional information other than being the target of an automated gathering process. This is even more surprising in the light of the fact that the actor has detailed knowledge about the activities he performs, including information about his intentions and the context within which activities take place; information that is either hard or impossible to deduce from automatically gathered events.

Our notion of awareness introduces the possibility that the actor can choose to externalise internal processes (intentions, reasons, etc.) and inform others of actions which cannot be directly sensed by the computer. We do not want to be misunderstood as criticising event-based awareness concepts per se. The gathering and distribution of awareness events is a necessary requirement for any awareness service that does not rely solely on a direct audio or video connection. Our emphasis lies on enrichment. Intentional enrichment does not replace awareness information. It allows internal motives to become part of the information gathered by an awareness system.

16.2.2.1 Awareness and Deliberation

The next question to consider is whether intentional enrichment can be part of the process of how co-workers become aware of each other or whether it is simply a form of communication. The latter position is being emphasised by the notion of

---

[5]A number of terminologies have been suggested to describe the role of the actor and perceiver, e.g. sender–receiver, actor–observer, informer–informant all of them defining the balance between the two roles in slightly different ways. We will continue to use the terms 'actor' and 'perceiver' for the remainder of this chapter.

[6]Implemented by a notification service.

"passive awareness" (Dourish and Bly, 1992). Dourish later defined awareness as being a passive process: "The passive nature of information is important. Information arises directly out of each person's activity, rather than having to be managed explicitly" (1997). Schmidt critiques this notion of awareness as being too restrictive in order to understand the complex interaction between actors in awareness processes:

> But the notion of 'passive awareness' (...) is problematic in its own right, in that it mystifies what we need to understand: the practices through which actors align and integrate their distributed but interdependent activities. As if an actor's passive awareness of the state of the cooperative effort is the inscrutable effect of merely "being there" the result of some kind of osmosis... (Schmidt, 2002).

Schmidt continues with an analysis of Heath and Luff's work on awareness in collaborative workplace settings (Heath and Luff, 1991; Heath et al., 2002). He explores the notion that actors deliberately direct the attention of their colleagues in order to coordinate activities or emphasise aspects of their work. In doing so actors often choose a level of obtrusiveness that is appropriate to the situation (Schmidt, 2002). This skilled behaviour is in stark contrast to an understanding of awareness that does not include the active participation of actors. By acknowledging these work routines Schmidt extends the notion of awareness:

> (...) because of the fine-grained repertoire of modalities of monitoring and displaying, ranging from sometimes quite inconspicuous to something dramatically obtrusive, no clear distinction exists between, on the one hand, the coordinative practices of monitoring and displaying, normally referred to under the labels of 'mutual awareness' and 'peripheral awareness', and, on the other hand, the practices of directing attention or interfering for other purposes. In fact, by somehow displaying his or her actions, the actor is always, in some way and to some degree, intending some effect on the activities of colleagues. The distinction is not categorical but merely one of degrees and modes of obtrusiveness (Schmidt, 2002).

Schmidt's argument further supports the notion the actor can fulfil an active role in an awareness process.

16.2.3 A Model of Intentionally Enriched Awareness

We have argued that intentionally disclosed information can be an invaluable resource for facilitating awareness between users. A number of questions remain: Which techniques can be used to facilitate the process of intentional disclosure? What type of information can be supported? and How can the effort involved in this process be reduced? We will seek to answer these questions by describing a model of intentionally enriched awareness which incorporates different concepts to facilitate information disclosure.

We will initially take a look at the Atmosphere model (Rittenbruch, 2002), which is one of the foundations of our current model. We will then reflect on the relationship between disclosure and effort and introduce different disclosure mechanisms.

16.2.3.1 Atmosphere

The model of intentionally enriched awareness is conceptually based on our earlier work on contextual awareness (Rittenbruch, 2002). The Atmosphere framework was concerned with representing a richer set of context information, centred around the questions "Why has this happened?" and "In which context did this happen?". The framework introduced two classes of interaction techniques which allowed actors to provide contextual information with different levels of effort. "Active methods" allowed for a direct provision of contextual information, while "structural methods" used shared representations of context to allow users to assign work activities to contexts. These methods were implemented using two concepts "contextors" and "spheres". Contextors were pre-defined shared representations of user actions. Users would indicate certain activities by selecting the appropriate set of contextors. Spheres were a hierarchical representation of a particular working context. Similar to shared workspaces, documents could be associated with particular spheres. Spheres also contained sets of contextors to represent actions within a particular context. The sphere concepts comprised a variety of more detailed concepts, including a differentiation between private and group spheres, different type of sphere trees, as well as concepts to represent relationships between spheres.

Several of these concepts are used in a modified form in our model of intentionally enriched awareness. The AnyBiff prototype described in the context of this chapter can be seen as an implementation of the contextor concept. A simplified version of spheres is used to model indirect disclosure (see Section 16.2.3.3). While the Atmosphere work was focused on the conceptual representation of context information in awareness models, the model of intentionally enriched awareness takes a broader look at the issues underlying intentional disclosure of information.

16.2.3.2 Effort and Disclosure

We have previously introduced a model that links the effort of disclosing information to the richness of the disclosed information (Rittenbruch et al., 2007). A high level of detail, e.g. the detailed description of an activity, in general requires a high level of communicational effort on behalf of the actor. An activity like ticking a box in a shared spreadsheet in comparison requires considerable less effort but at the same time is likely to be more constrained in its meaning.

The act of disclosing information can be represented on a scale of involvement and effort. On the low end on the scale the actor is not involved at all. No information is disclosed, but the actor's actions within collaborative systems are automatically represented as events (see Fig. 16.1, no disclosure). This approach is commonly found in event-based awareness systems, like AREA (Fuchs 1999). On the high end of the scale the actor is very involved in the process of expressing intentions, for instance being engaged in a direct communicational act with a perceiver explaining a certain activity (see Fig. 16.1, explanation). While the actor is able to portray a high level of intentional detail, the communicational effort to do so is likely to be very high and no support to reduce this effort is offered. Explanatory activities

	Low	Engagement		High
Concept	No disclosure	Indirect disclosure	Direct disclosure	Explanation
Effect	No effort	Little effort	Some effort	High effort
Applied concept	Event-based awareness mechanism	Workspaces, Locales	Annotation, biff concept	Communication tools
Implementation	e.g. GroupDesk	e.g. Placeless documents, Orbit	e.g. CoffeeBiff, AnyBiff	e.g. Instant messaging, Phone

Intentionally enriched awareness

Fig. 16.1 Intentionally enriched awareness

commonly require the actor to use additional tools like e-mail to communicate intentions. Intentionally enriched awareness is situated between those two extremes (see Fig. 16.1).

16.2.3.3 Disclosure Mechanisms

In order to support actors to express contextual information we introduce two basic concepts, *direct disclosure* and *indirect disclosure*. Direct disclosure requires an immediate action by an actor in order to disclose information. Indirect disclosure allows actors to indicate the general context of their work rather than an immediate action. The following figure shoes how direct and indirect disclosure are situated on a scale of effort.

Direct disclosure is implemented by providing pre-defined indicators which allow users to indicate imminent or current activities (Rittenbruch, 2002) (see Fig. 16.1, direct disclosure). Direct disclosure is characterised by three main aspects. First, it requires immediate user action in order to disclose information. Unlike indirect disclosure where intentions can be inferred from a given context, direct disclosure is an immediate act through which users express their intentions to other users. Second, direct disclosure is characterised by a low level of communicative effort. Disclosing information should only involve a small number of interactions, like clicking a button or selecting a menu item. Thus, the concept differs from explanations which require a significant communicative effort. Third and finally, direct disclosure mechanisms need to account for a large variety of information that users need to express. They therefore need to be highly flexible and tailorable.

Indirect disclosure in comparison does not require an immediate action on behalf of the actor to indicate a particular activity. We previously discussed the aspect of relating an activity to a particular context as part of the Atmosphere framework (see Fig. 16.1, indirect disclosure). Indirect disclosure allows actors to pre-define and arrange commonly used contexts. Information can be disclosed with relatively low effort by choosing the appropriate context representations for streams of activities (Rittenbruch, 2002). For example, the Orbit system (Mansfield et al., 1997a) and "placeless documents" (Dourish et al., 1999) both partially implement this aspect of awareness.

16.3 Related Work

In this section we will look at a number of examples of systems which allow for intentional disclosure of information. We will look at two sets of systems. The first set of systems and practices is based on the explicit disclosure of information and is closely related to the concept of direct disclosure. Within this set we discuss four groups of systems: First, we will explore how instant messaging clients and related systems can be used to share personal information, including information about current activities. Second, we will briefly touch upon creating awareness through posting messages to ambient displays. Third, we will look at the practice of "today" messages and systems that build on that notion. And last, we will look at concepts that are very similar to the AnyBiff system which we implement here, including other implementations of biffs and an affective computing interface which shares emotional state.

The second set of systems which represents aspects of a user's context are more relevant for the concept of indirect disclosure. We will look at the practice of tagging and systems that implement shared workspaces in this context.

16.3.1 Sharing Status

The potential of instant messaging to support informal interaction and awareness is becoming increasingly well understood (Nardi et al., 2000; Herbsleb et al., 2002; Isaacs et al., 2002; Voida et al., 2002). Instant messaging clients support awareness about the presence and availability through "buddy lists" (Rittenbruch and McEwan, 2008, in this book). An increasing number of instant messaging clients also provide the option to show status messages to other users. Status messages can either be pre-defined messages concerned with availability (e.g. available, busy, away)[7] or custom status messages[8] which allow users to define messages freely.

Status messages have become a focus of research as they allow users to relay awareness information which extend the original focus on availability. Smale and Greenberg (2005) have investigated how instant messaging clients are used to broadcast personal information to other members of a group. Their initial study showed how people used "display name" fields as makeshift status messages as the client used in their study did not support custom status messages. They identified a rich set of communication practices used to communicate different aspects of a person's work or personal context to others. The main use of status messages was to indicate current activities, emotional state, location and personal comments and opinions. The study also revealed that status messages were occasionally used to broadcast information to the group.

---

[7]Found in the original version of ICQ (http://www.icq.com).

[8]Example, in Apple iChat (http://www.apple.com/macosx/features/ichat/).

Another related system that is used to share activities with peers is Twitter. [9] Twitter asks a single question, "What are you doing today?". The information that people provide is forwarded to the list of peers who have subscribed to the feed that a person creates, usually via SMS messages. While currently no research exists on this system it makes an excellent example for how status messages can be used outside IM clients.

16.3.2 Displaying Messages

A number of authors have explored the effects of displaying freeform messages on ambient displays to create awareness (e.g. Greenberg and Rounding, 2001; Dey and De Guzman, 2006; Cheverst et al., 2007). This idea has recently gained traction in the context of domestic environments (e.g. Saslis-Lagoudakis et al., 2006). While the particular mode of notification has no immediate impact on our notion of intentional enrichment we are interested in the question how users are encouraged to create messages. The ASTRA system (Romero et al., 2007) is interesting in this context as it encouraged the use of the system through a ToTell list, a set of items that would trigger social and emotional communication.

16.3.3 Today Messages

Brush and Borning (2005) reported on the use of "today" messages in their lab. Group members would send daily free form e-mails titled "today" to their work group outlining activities and any other information they choose to disclose. The practice originated within a group of software engineers who used "today" messages as part of their software development process. The authors of the study hypothesised that this simple process can lead to a low conceptual load for users in comparison to more involved formal reporting. The use of "today" messages by six different groups was studied. The results show that most users perceive the effort involved in reading and writing "today" messages as low; however, some users would perceive the lack of a format as unproductive. The content of "today" messages varied between individuals and groups. Some groups included critique into their messages, while other groups included more personal information. The authors found that a determining factor for the success of "today messages" is the participation rate of group leaders. The authors suggested a couple of technical implications. First, subscriptions should be flexible and not bound to a mailing list so users can subscribe to those today messages they are interested in. Second, "today" messages should promote reciprocity; users should be able to determine who is reading their messages.

---

[9]http://twitter.com; There are a number of systems that provide similar functionality, e.g. Jaiku (http://www.jaiku.com) or facebook status updates (http://www.facebook.com).

The idea of "today" messages has been applied in Smale and Greenberg's "Transient Life" system (Smale and Greenberg, 2006). Transient Life is a sidebar which supports users in gathering transient information on the fly. The information gets collected and is sent out in the form of a "today" message by user request. The type of information gathered by Transient Life includes, lists of activities, to-do's, emotional status and photos.

16.3.4 Single-Click Sharing

Single-click interfaces like CoffeeBiff (Fitzpatrick et al., 1999) are closely related to the concept of direct disclosure. We will briefly look at the development of the biff concept in context.

16.3.4.1 A History of Biff

In October 1980 BSD 4.0, a Unix variant was released to the world. It included a tiny command line program called "biff" named after a dog owned by one of the students, Heidi Stettner (Salus, 1994). The program monitored the user's mailbox and, when mail arrived, either wrote a message to the terminal or simply rang the terminal bell to notify the user.

In February 1986 the X Window System, a graphical windowing system developed at MIT was released including a small graphical program called "xbiff" which duplicated biff's essential function but graphically using a small image of an American-style mailbox to notify the user (see Fig. 16.2, left picture).

In May 1997 Elvin, a distributed notification system developed at DSTC Pty Ltd was released (Segall and Arnold, 1997). One of the first client programs for Elvin was "xebiff" which used the Elvin infrastructure to monitor the user's mailbox. A student working with the Elvin project was very fond of a multi-player videogame called "xpilot" and was always keen to find partners to play with. He adapted the xebiff program to make "xpilotbiff" – using the xpilot icon in place of the mailbox.

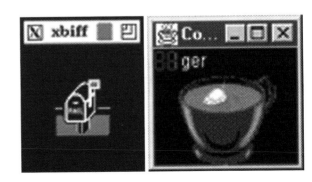

Fig. 16.2 The xbiff and CoffeeBiff interface

Players signalled their desire to start a game by clicking on their icon, which caused all the other potential players' icons to change state, signalling that someone was in the game and ready to play.

Shortly after that, a second simple adaptation was developed to signal intent to visit the coffee room. This program, "xcoffeebiff", incorporated several novel features. By clicking on the program's coffee cup icon, all users' corresponding icons changed state, displayed a scrolling username display showing the names of everyone who had clicked and incremented a counter so users could see at a glance how many people were heading for coffee (Fitzpatrick et al., 1999). Figure 16.2 (right picture) shows a screenshot of CoffeeBiff, a version of xcoffeebiff running on PCs. The biff has been activated by one user. The name of the user who activated the biff, "Geraldine", is scrolling across the username display.

This sequence of related tools introduces concepts that are each important to AnyBiff. First, the notion of a simple indicator of a state change, unobtrusively within the user's field of view. Second, the notions of tying the simple notifier to an agreed action or state and indicating intent to participate by clicking. Third, augmenting the simple display to indicate which people have signalled their intent.

16.3.5 Sharing of Structure

The second approach is based on the implicit sharing of intentional information. Artefacts are arranged and categorised through hierarchical or non-hierarchical structures which link them to a particular work or personal context. We will look at shared workspaces and the practice of tagging in this context.

16.3.5.1 Shared Workspaces

The shared workspace metaphor has been a common metaphor for the design of groupware systems for around 15 years. The term is used widely ranging from concepts that imitate shared physical workspaces (Ishii, 1990; Ishii and Arita, 1991), over shared media spaces (Bly et al., 1993), to shared data repositories that contain additional functionality to support collaboration. A number of systems that support awareness incorporate the latter notion of shared workspaces, e.g. DIVA (Sohlenkamp and Chwelos, 1994), GroupDesk (Fuchs et al. 1995), BSCW (Bentley et al., 1995), TeamRooms (Roseman and Greenberg, 1996) and Orbit (Mansfield et al., 1997b) to name just a few (see Rittenbruch and McEwan, 2008 for a comprehensive summary).

We are interested in shared workspaces as a means to structure information and share this structure with other users. Shared workspaces also go beyond just sharing information by typically providing congruent views of that information to all participants to enable them to share a common context.

Orbit (Mansfield et al., 1997b) teased apart these two ideas using the "Site and Means" and "Individual View" concepts from Fitzpatrick's (2003) Locales Framework. Orbit provided shared collections of data called "zones" that provide a shared space in which collaboration can occur but allowed multiple shared "views" into those zones. By using the same view on a zone participants could maintain congruent views when needed and shift to different views to support a different level of involvement and interest. Orbit allowed participants to have views into multiple zones at the same time.

16.3.5.2 Tagging

Tagging (Marlow et al., 2006) is a very different approach to contextualise information. It describes the practice of attaching keywords to postings of photos[10] or other content and URLs. Tags are freely formed and do not adhere to pre-defined categories. Tags allow users to discover related posts or content that has been identified by the same keyword(s). Thus tags form a loosely structured, user-defined categorisation space often referred to as folksonomy. The process of tagging does not necessarily need to be undertaken with the explicit intention of sharing content or categories. Golder and Huberman (2006) found that a considerable amount of tagging on the social bookmarking site del.icio.us is done for personal use. However, they point out that due to the fact that sharing sites which use tags are generally public, other users can browse content and tags and receive "recommendations" even if they were unintentional.

16.3.5.3 Disclosure in Social Networking

A whole range of other disclosure practices, which are centred around the notion of social software, aim at the disclosure of personal information to peers in social networks. This includes the disclosure of personal information in profiles (Boyd and Heer, 2006), the public articulation of self (or "fake-self") on social networking sites (Boyd, 2004) and the public disclosure of social networks (Donath and Boyd, 2004). While these practices are interesting they focus more on the creation of social network than the support for group collaboration and are beyond the scope of this chapter.

16.3.6 Discussion

How are these approaches related to intentionally enriched awareness? We will look at three groups of systems that relate to direct disclosure (sharing status, "today" messages and single click sharing) and one group of systems that relate to indirect disclosure.

16.3.6.1 Systems Related to Direct Disclosure

Systems that share status are a good example for how intentionally disclosed information is used to create a sense of awareness. However, the system we described

---

[10]Example, flickr (http://www.flickr.com).

differs from biffs in a number of important aspects. First, IM status messages, Twitter and systems that allow users to post messages to ambient displays provide information in a relatively unstructured manner. While this allows for flexibility and creativity which is desirable for informal awareness it also creates ambiguity and requires additional effort. In comparison biff interfaces are limited to a particular type of information (e.g. "drinking coffee") but are very unambiguous and require minimal effort to express an intention. In addition there is an important difference concerning the user interface metaphor behind IM clients and biffs. IM clients are user-centric, while biffs are activity-centric. The focus on a particular activity allows users to determine very quickly how many people are engaged an activity (e.g. 10 people are having coffee). To extract the same information from differing IM status messages will in general be a more involved and time-consuming activity.

The structure of today messages relies on conventions between users although templates could be used for a more structured approach. While today messages allow users to express a rich set of information it is time-consuming when compared to the simple indication of an activity in a biff. On our scale of effort it is closer to the concept of explanation than to direct disclosure. In addition to the aspect of effort required there is a temporal aspect involved. Today messages allow users to explain what they have done rather than allowing them to indicate what they are doing right now.

16.3.6.2 Systems Related to Indirect Disclosure

The systems discussed here, shared workspaces and tagging systems, differ in a number of ways. Shared workspaces in general are more structured, while the use of tags allows for flexibility. However, shared workspaces, tags and spheres, which are our implementation of indirect disclosure, are quite different on another level. Shared workspaces are tightly coupled with artefact. Awareness on activities in shared workspaces in general is awareness on modifications of artefacts. Tags are normally not used in an awareness context; however, they can indicate that a piece of information or an artefact belong to certain categories or a loosely defined context. Spheres in comparison are situated between shared workspaces and tags and use user-defined representations of context. They are not focused on artefacts, they rather indicate a periods of activities in a user defined context (Rittenbruch, 2002).[11]

16.4 The AnyBiff System

AnyBiff is a prototypical implementation of a direct disclosure mechanism. It is a generic tool that allows users to generate, share and use a multitude of activity indicators, referred to as "biffs". Single biffs are conceptually similar to CoffeeBiff

---

[11] The detailed discussion of spheres is beyond the scope of this chapter. Please see Rittenbruch (2002) for more detail on the concept.

(Fitzpatrick et al., 1999). The AnyBiff user interface consists of a multitude of vertically aligned biffs which are freely chosen and combined by the user. Users can define the set of biffs they are using by either subscribing to existing biffs or creating new biffs in order to share them with others. Anybiff exhibits the three characteristics of a direct disclosure mechanism. Users directly indicate activities by clicking on biffs which indicate certain activities. The interaction with biffs requires few interactions and is low effort. And finally, the AnyBiff concept is highly generic and allows for the creation of any type of biff that a user might require.

16.4.1 AnyBiff Design

AnyBiff is characterised by a combination of vertically aligned biffs, which can be freely created and combined by users.

16.4.1.1 Interface Elements

Figure 16.3 depicts an example AnyBiff interface. The user "Jane" has subscribed to two biffs "Lunch" and "Meeting". The lunch biff has been activated by two users, "Bob" and "Jane".

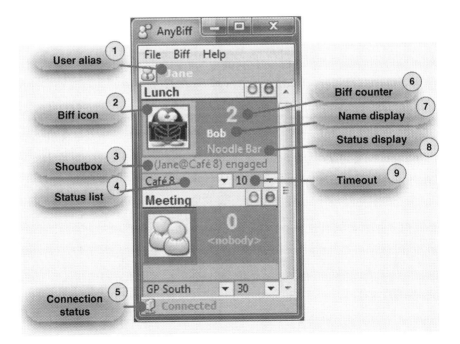

Fig. 16.3 AnyBiff interface

An icon (1) signifies a certain activity and makes it easy to visually distinguish biffs. Clicking on the icon activates a biff; clicking a second time deactivates it. The biffs serve as input as well as output interface. A counter (6) indicates the number of users that are engaged in each biff. The username of each active user will flash in a name display (7) indicating which users are engaged. In addition, the status that each user selected when engaging a biff is displayed in the status display area (8). Users can specify a timeout (9). A biff activation will expire after the time specified in the timeout has elapsed. For each activation of a biff users can select a status from the status list (4). A fixed set of statuses is pre-defined by the creator of a biff. In addition users can add custom status messages. Each biff has a shoutbox (3), which is a little tickertape style communication tool attached to each biff. Users can send and receive messages which are seen by all subscribers of the same biff. There is some minimal functionality that allows users to delete single or all messages from the scroller. Users are furthermore free to choose a user alias (1).

Each biff has two optional display modes: minimised and maximised. In maximised mode users can access all the interface features described above. In minimised mode, the display is limited to a small icon, the biff counter and the name display. Users who wish to change the status, the timeout or want to use the shoutbox need to change to maximised mode.

AnyBiff needs to be online in order to connect to the notification service and AnyBiff server. A connectivity indicator (5) shows the current connection status.

16.4.1.2 Biff Creation

Biffs are created using a Wizard. The wizard lets a user choose a name, a description and an icon for a biff. On a second screen the user can define a list of status messages for a biff. All biffs that are created are sent to the server and automatically shared with all other users of the system. There is no notion of a private biff. The existence of new biffs is indicated with an indicator icon at the user interface. New biffs are furthermore highlighted in the list of biffs from which users subscribe to or unsubscribe from biffs.

16.4.1.3 Biff Subscription

Users can select biffs from a list which is kept up-to-date on the server. The list shows the name, description and icon of each biff as well as the number and names of the current subscribers.

16.4.1.4 Notification Mechanisms

The main output for biff notifications are biffs themselves. They show all the relevant information including the number of active users, their user names and their status per biff. In addition users could choose to use sound notification to be aware of activities if the AnyBiff main window was hidden. The AnyBiff client furthermore

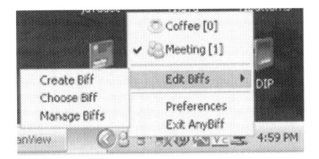

Fig. 16.4 System tray representation of AnyBiff (PC version)

integrated with the operating system it was running on. The PC version had a representation on the system tray allowing users to control and administer biffs (see Fig. 16.4). The Mac OS version integrated with the Mac specific IM application iChat. Selecting a biff would set the iChat status accordingly, e.g. selecting the Lunch biff with the status "Noodle bar" would result in a "not available" in iChat with the status line "Lunch (Noodle bar)". The different forms of integration with the operating system on PCs and Macs were caused by platform-dependent inconsistencies of the implementation framework we used.

16.4.1.5 AnyBiff Architecture

AnyBiff is based on a client server architecture. Elvin (Fitzpatrick et al., 1999), a pure notification service, is used as communication layer. Clients communicate biff selection events and shoutbox messages directly through Elvin. The client is written in Java to assure platform independence. The server consists of a biff, a status and a subscription service. The biff service administers all existing biffs within the system and propagates creation, deletion and modification events to all clients. The status services keep a persistent snapshot of the current status of all biffs. If a client connects it is provided with the current statuses of all biff it is subscribed to. The subscription service manages subscription numbers for each biff. All usage, subscription and biff modification events were logged in a database as part of the trial release of the software. Elvin was chosen in favour of language-specific communication options like Java RPC or Java JINI technology in order to allow for an easy extension of the concept with a variety of clients written in different languages.

16.5 AnyBiff Evaluation

The following section summarises some of the results gained from our evaluation of AnyBiff. See Rittenbruch et al. (2007) for a detailed list of results.

16.5.1 Methodology

AnyBiff was introduced to two research organisations. The Australasian CRC for Interaction Design (ACID) is a Cooperative Research Centre (CRC) funded by the Australian government. ACID's core activities are research, development and commercialisation in the field of the creative industries. ACID currently has 180 members including academics from participating organisations, industry participants, research assistants, post-graduate students and a small number of full-time staff. The organisation is distributed across Australia and New Zealand. The Interaction Design Research Division (IDRD) at the University of Queensland is a research group in the School of Information Technology and Electrical Engineering (ITEE) at the University of Queensland (UQ). The IDRD consists of 10 academic staff and 20 postgraduate students who are distributed over 2 campuses.

We used different AnyBiff servers and different notification services allowing us to research the use within these organisations independently from each other. The deployment of AnyBiff allowed us to evaluate its use and to address a range of research questions regarding the biff concept as well as the underlying concepts of intentionally enriched awareness in general and direct disclosure in particular. With regard to AnyBiff we were interested in how users would conceive and conceptualise the generalisation of the biff concept. In particular we were interested to observe the evolution of the mutual awareness environment that users would create by using AnyBiff. Which biffs would users create? Which biffs would become popular? Which groups of users would share biffs?

The study is based on 15 semi-structured interviews with ACID and IDRD members. We interviewed a cross section of ACID and IDRD members, including academics, postgraduate students, research assistants and administrative staff. The interviews lasted between 20 and 30 min and were semi-structured to allow for a consistent focus on a range of topic areas while leaving enough flexibility to explore particular topics in more detail. An interview guide was used to ensure that relevant topic areas were covered.

The study resulted in a rich set of qualitative data which was analysed using a number of methods. Relevant aspects from each interview were identified and aggregated using affinity diagramming. The affinity diagramming resulted in a number of topic areas that represent common themes found throughout the interviews. The data were also analysed according to the categories provided by the interview guide. Results gained from this method allowed us to see trends within particular topic areas.

In addition the usage of AnyBiff was logged at the server over the period of the trial. We gathered data on the use of biffs, on the creation deletion and modification of biffs and last on the subscription of biffs. The data gained from logging were analysed for a number of factors, including the most used biffs, the most subscribed biffs, the assignment of biffs to users and usage trends. Users were also encouraged to leave e-mail feedback on usage and conceptual issues throughout the trial. The data gathered from e-mail feedback consisted mostly of descriptions of particular interface issues. All names that appear in quotes throughout this chapter have been altered to assure the anonymity of users.

16.5.2 Findings

The results are structured into four major subsections: AnyBiff usage, conceptual issues, biff-specific usage and GUI problems. *AnyBiff usage* refers to the use of the system as a whole and classifies the biffs that users created throughout the trial. This subsection largely relies on the analysis of system logs. The remaining sections are based on the analysis of the interviews we conducted. The *Conceptual issues* section outlines fundamental issues, relating to the usage of an intentionally enriched awareness service that became apparent during our study. The *Biff-specific usage* section summarises usage behaviour and issues that were found to be a direct result of the interaction with the biff concept, e.g. how users gauged the scope of biffs, how the biff concepts were utilised to achieve different outcomes by different users, etc. Last but not least, the *GUI problems* section summarises problems with the AnyBiff GUI. While the analysis of GUI problems were not the main focus of the study, they helped us to understand which problems were of a conceptual nature, and which ones could be attributed to implementational shortcomings.

16.5.2.1 AnyBiff Usage

AnyBiff was used by a total of 38 users at ACID and 16 users at the IDRD. About 13 ACID users created a total of 26 biffs during the trial period, while 8 IDRD users created a total of 13 biffs. A small number of users participated in both trials and created similar or identical biffs for the IDRD and the ACID system. In the context of this analysis, these biffs are counted as separate entities as they were used by different user populations.

Biff Classification

The most commonly used biffs were categorised into a number of groups in order to discern different types and approaches of biffs. The classifications include the two default biffs *Coffee* and *Meeting,* which were part of the standard installation. The classifications do not account for all biffs as some biffs were merely created by users to test and understand the concept of biffs. Figure 16.5 lists the names and descriptions of biffs (as generated by the biff creator), as well as information about which trial the biff was used in (ACID or IDRD). A number of the biffs will be discussed in more detail in subsequent sections. Biffs were categorised into six distinct groups: *location and activity indicator, activity inducement biffs, in-between awareness, biff concept evolution, fun biffs* and a category *other* to account for biffs that did not fit into the former categories.

The difference between activity indicator and activity inducement biffs may be a fine line. While both indicate engagement with certain activities, the second

Name	Description	Trial
Location and activity indicators		
Biffs that indicated activities and / or locations. Biffs that indicated activities often specified potential locations as biff statuses. Conversely, biffs that specified locations usually listed activities in their status lists.		
The following biffs indicated engagement in activities		
Thesis	Do you know where your thesis is right now?	IDRD
Procrastination	Working but open to chat	ACID, IDRD
Doing that work thing		ACID
Meeting	Are you in a meeting?	(default) ACID, IDRD
The following biffs indicated location in relation to a work activity		
Working at my desk		ACID
Working at home	Avoiding interruptions, but still happy to be contacted	ACID
ACID media lab	The dungeon	ACID
Activity inducement biffs		
Biffs that were used to initiate and coordinate (often social) activities with other users		
Coffee	Engage in an important social activity	(default) ACID, IDRD
Lunch	Want to have lunch, going soon, open on discussion where to go	ACID, IDRD
HackySack	Anyone interested in a game of hack?	IDRD
Choc run	Off to find some chocolate	IDRD
At the pub	At the local – join us for a drink	ACID
In-between awareness		
Biffs utilising AnyBiff's ability to sustain a notification status if a user has gone offline		
On the road	About to head between locations	ACID, IDRD
Home	Going home or at home	IDRD
Away	Far from home	IDRD
Going home now	Ciao	ACID

Fig. 16.5 Classification of biffs

category comprises biffs that are to be understood as a joining in activity (often social), while biffs in the first category are predominantly used to indicate a certain status, such as availability or location. This distinction, however, is not strict, as the pure indication of a status can lead to engagement in social activities, e.g. in the case of the biff: *Procrastination – Working but open to chat*. The question whether biff notifications are perceived as inducements or statements is discussed in detail in section "Conceptual issues – Inducement or statement?" All other categories are discussed in detail in section "Biff-specific usage".

Biff Usage

Figure 16.6 summarises subscription and usage numbers of the most popular biffs. Usage numbers differed from the subscription numbers.

The usage behaviour reported during the interview reflected the usage figures identified by the server log analysis. Biffs were most commonly used either with the intention to initiate a social activity (mainly coffee and lunch breaks) or to indicate availability or unavailability due to participation in an activity (e.g. meetings, thesis writing). Participants who issued biff notifications were equally interested in receiving notifications about ongoing activities, including social activities as well as the location and availability of other participants.

Biff	Subscriptions	Biff	Usage
Most commonly subscribed biffs		**Most commonly used biffs**	
ACID		ACID	
Meeting	38 subscriptions	Working at my desk	51 uses
Coffee	37 subscriptions	Doing that work thing	42 uses
Avoiding mutants	9 subscriptions	Coffee	41 uses
Lunch	6 subscriptions	Avoiding mutants	26 uses
Doing that work thing	5 subscriptions	Meeting	25 uses
Working at home	5 subscriptions	ACID media lab	12 uses
Procrastination	5 subscriptions		
IDRD		IDRD	
Coffee	16 subscriptions	Coffee	83 uses
Meeting	16 subscriptions	Lunch	49 uses
Lunch	16 subscriptions	Meeting	44 uses
IDRD	10 subscriptions	Thesis	23 uses
On the road	7 subscriptions	Jackhammer	14 uses
		Radio silence	12 uses

Fig. 16.6 Biff subscription and usage

16.5.2.2 Conceptual Issues

Throughout our study we identified a number of fundamental issues regarding the usage of an intentionally enriched awareness service. These issues are of a conceptual nature and relate to the underlying model of intentionally enriched awareness rather than the design of the AnyBiff prototype itself.

Trade-Off Between Notification and Communication

While participants appreciated the ability to indicate intent with relative ease, they also reflected on tradeoffs between intentional notifications and communication. For instance, a number of participants appreciated the fact that coordinating activities with colleagues using biff notifications were more efficient when compared to using instant messaging for the same task. However, many participants considered it important to have chat capabilities available in addition to AnyBiff, should they require to negotiate joint activities further.

IM and chat tools were widespread and popular amongst our user population. However, a number of users complained about the potential disruptiveness of this communication approach. Those users saw AnyBiff as an alternative to quickly announce intent. AnyBiff was occasionally used in situations where users were co-located. Despite the fact that their colleagues were close they chose to use AnyBiff to indicate social activities in an unobtrusive manner in order not to interrupt their colleagues.

Inducement or Statement?

The activation of biffs can be interpreted in two fundamentally different ways. On the one hand, a notification can be understood as an invitation that announces that a certain activity is about to commence and that fellow users are invited to participate in this activity. On the other hand, it can also be interpreted as a statement that a consensus has been reached and indicates that people are already engaged in the activity. For example, seeing that four people have engaged the lunch biff can mean two things. Either these people are trying to coordinate a lunch meeting and are waiting for others to join them or they have already left for lunch. We refer to the first type of usage as *inducement* and the second type of usage as *statement*.

The reason for this potential ambiguity lies in the conceptual design of biffs. A biff does not provide facilities that will allow the user to distinguish an inducement from a statement. Designers faced with this issue can travel two different paths: They can either increase the complexity of the concept by adding additional categories. These might only be valid for a subclass of biffs. Alternatively, the designer can keep the concept simple, and instead let the users create solutions utilising existing biff facilities. Since our aim was to explore the concept behind biffs, our design rationale was to choose the second option and then observe how users would deal with this ambiguity. Our study revealed that users developed three different approaches to address this problem. First, users utilised the shoutbox to negotiate further details on joint activities. Second, special biffs were created that indicated specific induction activities. Finally, the differentiation of status messages was used to indicate whether an activity was an inducement or a statement.

A number of users suggested the creation of biffs that would be readily perceived as inducement rather than statement biffs. Participants suggested the creation of a *Ready for Coffee* or *Coffee Cravings* biff, as well as replacing the Lunch biff with a *Hungry* biff. Surprisingly, in none of these cases did users actually create any of these alternatives. A likely explanation is that the biffs in question *Lunch* and *Coffee* were amongst the most popular biffs in the system.

Some users utilised biff statuses in order to differentiate between inducement and statement. The creator of the HackySack biff added two statuses that reflected this distinction: *Hack?* and *Hack!*. *Hack?* is an invitation and question to see whether anybody is interested in a game of HackySack. *Hack!* is the announcement that people have left to play HackySack.

16.5.2.3 Biff-Specific Usage

The following section summarises results regarding usage behaviour and issues that were found to be a direct result of the interaction with the biff concept.

Persistence and In-Between Awareness

Another aspect of biff usage is the fact that biff notifications are persistent. A notification is terminated only if a user deselects a biff or deliberately turns off AnyBiff. If the user just disconnects her laptop for instance to move to another location the notifications she issued remain active till they expire. Our participants created a whole range of different biffs[12] to exploit this behaviour.

The *On the road* biff was used to indicate whether somebody was travelling from point A to point B. The *Home* and *Going Home Now* biffs were a functional subset of the former biff and indicated whether people were on their way home from work. The *Away* biff indicated longer term unavailability due to conference travel or vacation.

Biff Concept Evolution

Participants created a range of biffs that showed new and unexpected uses of the biff concept. The appearance of these biffs is congruent with the concept of evolving use of groupware (Andriessen et al., 2003). Users will adapt tools to their needs even if the use was not intended by the designers. We will look at the *Radio silence* which extended the anticipated use of AnyBiff.

The *Radio silence* biff contained the following description: *Busy beyond belief, I'm going incommunicado till I get some work done.* The biff was created to clearly indicate that a user was not to be disturbed, while at the same time allowing a small window of connectivity for urgent matters. The creation of this biff can be seen as an effort to establish a coherent away status throughout the group. Existing *not available* statuses that users used in IM client were often ambiguous and did not give indications under which circumstances users could be contacted or not.

---

[12]These biffs are documented in the *in-between awareness* category in Fig. 16.7.

Localised Critical Mass Issues

The fact that AnyBiff is a generic tool combined a variety of different groups and interests led to the occurrence of an interesting variation on the critical mass issue commonly found in groupware (Grudin, 1994). We identified two localised versions of this issue. First, activities that users observe within a certain biff do not necessarily relate to their social group and can therefore be less relevant to them. Second, the critical mass issue does not only apply to AnyBiff as an application as a whole but even more so to every single biff. While some biffs became very popular, others were abandoned quickly or just dwindled away. However, unlike a failed introduction of a groupware application due to general critical mass issues, the phenomenon of critical mass per biff can be seen as part of a natural selection process of biffs. Users generate ideas and offer them up to a community and some get accepted while others are not popular enough. Another difference is that biffs do not necessarily need large user numbers to be successful. A biff can be useful to a small group of two or three people if it fulfils a specific purpose for the group.

Scope of Biffs

There are two aspects of scope with regard to biffs. The first aspect is concerned with the question of how general or specific a biff should be. Is it better to generate very specific biffs allowing for a precise expression of intent to a selected group of people, or is it better to create more general biffs that potentially address more than one activity and are likely to engage more users but are less precise? The second aspect is concerned with the interplay between biffs. Should users use one biff to indicate an activity, another biff with a different status or even multiple biffs?

It is apparent that there is a trade-off between very specific biffs on the one hand and very generic biffs on the other hand. The advantage of generic biffs is that with a minimal amount of subscriptions users can receive a maximum amount of information. Deploying generic biffs is also likely to help overcome biff-specific critical mass issues. In comparison biffs that specify more specific activities allow for a more individualised and tailored approach to both the representation of activities as well as the subscription to specific activities. Our results indicate that generic biffs were particularly useful when user numbers were low. As soon as user numbers increased, then differentiation and more specific biffs become more relevant.

Regarding the question of how users chose which biff to use, the results are less clear. Using a generic tool like AnyBiff that allows users to create any sort of biff can naturally lead to ambiguities. One of our participants reflected on this issue: "It's interesting the different types of biff that people make and the different ways that people think about it and the ways you wrap your head around it: 'Do I use that biff or do I use another biff with a different status?', that kind of granularity problem." However, in practice we observed little conflict resulting from intersecting biffs. Users were more likely to use already existing popular biffs to express their intent rather than using more obscure and less popular biffs for the same purpose. We did not observe that a biff become more popular than an intersecting biff. A longitudinal study might be necessary to gain further insight into this subject.

16.6 Design Implications

We will summarise our findings and discuss design implications centred around three key points. *Potential and challenges of intentional disclosure* summarises results from the log analysis as well as sections "localized critical mass" and "integration with social routines". *The space between awareness and communication* summarises results from sections "Trade-off between communication and notification" and "Persistence and in-between awareness" and last *Genericity, ambiguity and evolution* summarises results from sections "Induction or statement?", "Scope of biffs" and "Biff concept evolution".

16.6.1 Potential and Challenges of Intentional Disclosure

Our findings show that intentional disclosure mechanisms in the form of biffs were successfully used in two different fields of application (ACID and IDRD). Users actively engaged in the design of a large variety of biffs and explored many different uses of the concept which revealed a range of underlying issues. Challenges remain in a number of areas. With regard to the user interface, the issue of screen real estate indicates that the current implementation of AnyBiff is conceptually limited to a small number of biffs. Users on average subscribed to 3–6 biffs at a time. Interface mechanisms that would allow active biffs to be represented in the foreground while hiding inactive biffs could increase the number of biffs users can display. However, the number of biffs that a user population can sustain is limited, as we have seen in the "localised critical mass issue".

With regard to the further design of intentionally enriched awareness services different interfaces that display information with a smaller footprint need to be explored. A worthwhile approach could be the integration with IM applications allowing for a combination of different styles of interaction. Integration with an existing IM application that includes a representation of personal availability could also be instrumental in facilitating the adoption of the concept of direct disclosure to a wider user community.

16.6.2 The Space Between Awareness and Communication

Intentional notifications exist in an interesting space between event-driven awareness notifications and communication. The act of disclosing intentional information can be seen as a limited communication act. It does not require users to interact with peers beyond the initial notification. This has advantages and disadvantages. On the one hand, intentional notifications can be very efficient in quickly coordinating joint activities, especially if they build on existing routines. On the other hand, the limitations of this type of notification make it difficult to negotiate more complex situations and require supplementation with additional chat tools or verbal interaction.

Users were well aware of the trade-off between communication and notification. We observed that they used AnyBiff to their advantage where it offered enhanced capabilities over chat tools. AnyBiff was often used in situations that did not warrant direct communication. It was also commonly used even in co-located situations in an effort not to disrupt colleagues. The "in-between awareness" class of biffs showed that users capitalised on AnyBiff's ability to create persistent notifications.

With regard to the design of groupware, AnyBiff offers a unique form of user interaction that has not yet been explored in detail. The constant switch between announcement style communication and chat in order to address the varying complexities of coordinating activities further supports our hypothesis that an integration of intentional disclosure tools with chat tools like IM could be beneficial to users.

16.6.3 Genericity, Ambiguity and Evolution

Our study highlighted two kinds of ambiguities that are systemic to the biff concept. First, the question whether a biff activation is to be understood as an inducement or a statement. And second the question of the scope of a biff and whether to choose a more general or specific scope when designing biffs.

Genericity can lead to ambiguity. Generic and tailorable tools allow users to adapt software to their specific needs. The use of tailorable software in distributed settings is fraught with a range of complex challenges, e.g. Morch, 1994; Stiemerling et al., 1999. However, our study showed that AnyBiff was used despite its ambiguities. The potential weakness brought on by the concept's genericity turned out to be also one of its strength. The system evolved with its usage. Biffs were part of a natural lifecycle. Popular biffs often gained further popularity and were modified to accommodate new user populations. Unpopular biffs became marginalised and survived only if they fulfilled a very specific need for a small group of people. Biffs that explored new ideas were constantly generated and exposed to the critical eye of fellow users. The biffs summarised in the class "Biff concept evolution" show the inventiveness of our users and their willingness to explore the biff concept. While the phenomenon is by no means exclusive to AnyBiff and has been described in the context of evolutionary use of groupware (Andriessen et al., 2003) it shows that systems that offer users the opportunity to express intent can evolve and adapt to different environments. Designers of awareness systems are encouraged to take those lessons into account and allow users to express individual aspects of awareness in addition to providing standard awareness information.

Further work is needed to determine the implications of the long-term use of intentional awareness mechanisms. We expect the issue of ambiguity to intensify if the user population grows beyond its current size. Designers wishing to integrate intentionally enriched awareness into their systems might well decide to restrict, to some extent, the genericity in favour of a more standardised approach. Different notions of direct disclosure, for instance different classes for inducement or statement, or a clear indication of the scope of direct disclosure could be introduced but come at the cost of loosing flexibility. Designers will have to choose the appropriate level of genericity based on the needs of their users and the intended field of application.

16.7 Summary and Conclusions

In this chapter we have explored the notion of intentionally enriched awareness by implementing and evaluating the AnyBiff system which allowed users to create, share and use different types of biffs. Biffs are simple widgets that allow users to announce their intention to engage in a pre-defined activity (e.g. "having coffee").

We have shown that a generalised biff concept can be an effective means to mediate different notions of announcing the engagement in shared activities within small workgroups. Our participants created a wide range of biff applications, some of which even challenge the original assumptions of the biff concept as shown in the *Biff concept evolution* class of biffs.

On a conceptual level our findings show that intentionally enriched awareness can be achieved through the implementation of a direct disclosure mechanism. The design and evaluation of AnyBiff has helped us to identify a whole range of additional challenges to our awareness model. Among those, two conceptual issues are of particular relevance: *induction or statement* and *trade-off between communication and notification*. Those challenges are located at different ends of the scale in our model of intentionally enriched awareness. We believe that our concept of direct disclosure can be logically extended in two different directions. One direction is to move direct disclosure towards communication and explanation, accounting for the *trade-off between communication and notification*. An example for such an extension is the combination of intentional disclosure mechanisms and instant messaging. The other direction, which relates to *induction or statement,* signifies a move towards indirect disclosure and uses a more structural approach to represent activity and context. The identified challenges leave ample room for further exploration of the concept of intentionally enriched awareness.

References

Andriessen JHE, Hettinga M, Wulf V (2003) Introduction to special issue on evolving use of groupware. Comput Support Coop Work 12(4): 367–380

Bentley R, Horstmann T, Sikkel K et al. (1995) Supporting collaborative information sharing with the World-Wide Web: The BSCW Shared Workspace system. In: Proceedings of the 4th International World Wide Web Conference (WWW'95). Darmstadt, Germany: 63–74

Bly S, Harrison S, Irwin S (1993) Media spaces: Bringing people together in a video, audio, and computing environment. Commun ACM 3(1): 28–47

Boyd D, Heer J (2006) Profiles as conversation: Networked identity performance on friendster. In: Proceedings of the 39th Annual Hawaii International Conference on System Sciences (HICSS '06). Washington, DC: IEEE Computer Society

Boyd DM (2004) Friendster and publicly articulated social networking. In: Proceedings of the Conference on Human Factors in Computing Systems (CHI '04), Extended Abstracts. New York: ACM Press

Brush AJB, Borning A (2005) 'Today' messages: Lightweight support for small group awareness via email. In: Proceedings of the 38th Annual Hawaii International Conference on System Sciences (HICSS '05). Big Island, HI: IEEE Computer Society: 10

Cheverst K, Dix A, Fitton D et al. (2007) Exploring awareness related messaging through two situated-display-based systems. Hum Comput Interact 22(1&2): 173–220

Dey AK, De Guzman ES (2006) From awareness to connectedness: The design and deployment of presence displays. In: Proceedings of the Conference on Human Factors in Computing Systems (CHI '06). New York: ACM Press: 899–908

Donath J, boyd d (2004) Public displays of connection. BT Technol J 22(4): 71–82

Dourish P (1997) Extending Awareness Beyond Synchronous Collaboration. http://www.dourish. com/publications/chi97-awareness.html. Accessed 2008/09/15

Dourish P, Bly S (1992) Portholes: Supporting Awareness in a Distributed Work Group. Monterey, CA: ACM Press. 541–547

Dourish P, Lamping J, Rodden T (1999) Building bridges: Customisation and mutual intelligibility in shared category management. In: Proceedings of the Conference on Supporting Group Work (GROUP '99). New York: ACM Press: 11–20

Fitzpatrick G (2003) The Locales Framework: Understanding and Designing for Wicked Problems. Dordrecht, Boston, London: Kluwer Academic Publishers

Fitzpatrick G, Mansfield T, Kaplan S et al. (1999) Augmenting the workaday world with elvin. In: Proceedings of the Sixth European Conference on Computer-Supported Cooperative Work (ECSCW '99). Dordrecht, The Netherlands: Kluwer Academic Publishers: 431–450

Fuchs L (1999) AREA: A cross-application notification service for groupware. In: Proceedings of the Sixth European Conference on Computer Supported Cooperative Work (ECSCW'99). Dordrecht, The Netherlands: Kluwer Academic: 61–80

Fuchs L, Pankoke-Babatz U, Prinz W (1995) Supporting cooperative awareness with local event mechanism: The group desk system. In: Proceedings of the Fourth European Conference on Computer Supported Cooperative Work (ECSCW'95). Dordrecht, The Netherlands: Kluwer Academic Publishers: 247–262

Fuchs L, Sohlenkamp M, Genau A et al. (1996) Tranzparenz in kooperativen Prozessen: Der Ereigisdienst in POLITeam. In: Proceedings of the Deutsche Computer Supported Cooperative Work (DCSCW '96). Dortmund, Germany: 3–16

Golder S, Huberman BA (2006) Usage patterns of collaborative tagging systems. J Inf Sci 32(2): 198–208

Greenberg S, Rounding M (2001) The notification collage: Posting information to public and personal displays. In: Proceedings of the Conference on Human Factors in Computing Systems (CHI '01). New York: ACM Press: 514–521

Grudin J (1994) Groupware and social dynamics: Eight challenges for developers. Commun ACM 37(1): 92–105

Heath C, Luff P (1991) Collaborative activity and technological design: Task coordination in London underground control rooms. In: Proceedings of the Second European Conference on Computer-Supported Cooperative Work (ECSCW '91). Dordrecht, The Netherlands: Kluwer Academic Publishers: 65–80

Heath C, Svensson MS, Hindmarsh J et al. (2002) Configuring awareness. Comput Support Coop Work 11(3–4): 317–347

Herbsleb JD, Atkins DL, Boyer DG et al. (2002) Introducing instant messaging and chat in the workplace. In: Proceedings of the Conference on Human Factors in Computing Systems (CHI '02). New York: ACM Press: 171–178

Isaacs E, Walendowski A, Whittaker S et al. (2002) The character, functions, and styles of instant messaging in the workplace. In: Proceedings of the Conference on Computer Supported Cooperative Work (CSWC '02). New York: ACM Press: 11–20

Ishii H (1990) Teamworkstation: Towards a seamless shared workspace. In: Proceedings of the Conference on Computer Supported Cooperative Work (CSCW'90). New York: ACM Press: 13–26

Ishii H, Arita K (1991) ClearFace: Translucent multiuser interface for teamworkstation. In: Proceedings of the Second European Conference on Computer-Supported Cooperative Work (ECSCW '91). New York: ACM Press: 163–174

Lövstrand L (1991) Being selectively aware with the khronika system. In: Proceedings of the Conference on European Computer Supported Cooperative Work (ECSCW'91). Dordrecht, The Netherlands: Kluwer Academic Publishers: 265–277

Mansfield T, Kaplan S, Fitzpatrick G et al. (1997a) Evolving orbit: A progress report on building locales. In: Proceedings of the Conference on Supporting Group Work (Group '97). New York: ACM Press: 241–250

Mansfield T, Kaplan S, Phelps T et al. (1997b) Orbit – supporting social worlds. In: Proceedings of the Fifth European Conference on Computer Supported Cooperative Work (ECSCW' 97). Dordrecht, The Netherlands: Kluwer Academic Publishers: 13–14

Marlow C, Naaman M, Boyd D et al. (2006) HT06, tagging paper, taxonomy, Flickr, academic article, to read. In: Proceedings of the Seventeenth Conference on Hypertext and Hypermedia (HT '06). New York: ACM Press: 31–40

Morch AI (1994) Designing for radical tailorability: Coupling artifact and rationale. Knowl -Based Syst 7(4): 253–64

Nardi BA, Whittaker S, Bradner E (2000) Interaction and outeraction: Instant messaging in action. In: Proceedings of the Conference on Computer Supported Cooperative Work (CSCW '00). New York: ACM Press: 79–88

Prinz W, Gross T (2004) Modelling shared contexts in cooperative environments: Concept, implementation and evaluation. Comput Support Coop Work 13(3–4): 283–303

Rittenbruch M (2002) Atmosphere: A framework for contextual awareness. Int J Hum Comput Interact 14(2): 159–180

Rittenbruch M, McEwan G (2008) An historical reflection of awareness in collaboration. In: Markopoulos P et al. (eds) Awareness Systems: Advances in Theory, Methodology and Design. London, Berlin, Heidelberg: Springer Verlag

Rittenbruch M, Viller S, Mansfield T (2007) Announcing activity: Design and evaluation of an intentionally enriched awareness service. Hum Comput Interact (HCI) 22(1&2): 137–171

Romero N, Markopoulos P, Van Baren J et al. (2007) Connecting the family with awareness systems. Pers Ubiquitous Comput 11(4): 299–312

Roseman M, Greenberg S (1996) TeamRooms: Network places for collaboration. In: Proceedings of the Conference on Computer Supported Cooperative Work (CSCW '96). New York: ACM Press: 325–333

Salus PH (1994) A Quarter Century of UNIX. Addison-Wesely: Boston.

Saslis-Lagoudakis G, Cheverst K, Dix A et al. (2006) Hermes@Home: Supporting awareness and intimacy between distant family members. In: Proceedings of the Australasian Computer-Human Interaction Conference (OzCHI '06). New York: ACM Press: 23–30

Schmidt K (2002) The problem with 'awareness'. Comput Support Coop Work 11(3–4): 285–298

Segall B, Arnold D (1997) Elvin has left the building: A publish/subscribe notification service with quenching. In: Proceedings of the Australian UNIX and Open Systems User Group Conf. (AUUG '97). 243–255

Smale S, Greenberg S (2005) Broadcasting information via display names in instant messaging. In: Proceedings of the Conference on Supporting Group Work (GROUP'05). New York: ACM Press: 89–98

Smale S, Greenberg S (2006) Transient life: Collecting and sharing personal information. In: Proceedings of the Australasian Computer–Human Interaction Conference (OzCHI '06). New York: ACM Press: 31–38

Sohlenkamp M, Chwelos G (1994) Integrating communication, cooperation, and awareness: The DIVA virtual office environment. In: Proceedings of the Conference on Computer Supported Cooperative Work (CSCW '94). New York: ACM Press: 331–342

Stiemerling O, Hinken R, Cremers AB (1999) Distributed component-based tailorability for CSCW applications. In: Proceedings of the Fourth International Symposium on Autonomous Decentralized Systems (ISADS '99). Tokyo, Japan: IEEE Computer Society: 345–352

Voida A, Newstetter WC, Mynatt ED (2002) When conventions collide: The tensions of instant messaging attributed. In: Proceedings of the Conference on Human Factors in Computing Systems (CHI '02). New York: ACM Press: 187–194

Chapter 17
Situatedness of Awareness Information: Impact on the Design and Usage of Awareness Systems

Keith Cheverst, Alan Dix, Dan Fitton, Connor Graham, and Mark Rouncefield

17.1 Introduction

This chapter focuses on our exploration of awareness-related messaging by users of a situated display-based messaging system. The system, known as Hermes, was initially deployed outside offices in the Computing Department at Lancaster University (see Cheverst et al., 2003a,b) and a significant portion of its use related to awareness, e.g. a member of staff posting a message on her door Hermes display accounting for her absence or indicating her future presence. A second version of the Hermes system has recently been across 40 offices in the Computing Department's new home, a building called Infolab 21.

The first version of the Hermes system ran for approximately 27 months until a move of building in June 2004. The number of door display owners during this period was 12 (although only ten units were ever deployed at one time). Owners included lecturers, research assistants, PhD students and administrative staff. The approximate number of messages posted by owners during this time was 5500.

In terms of functionality, the primary purpose of Hermes was to enable support for coordination both among staff and between staff and students. For example, on one occasion a lecturer and owner of a door display, in order to let visitors know his anticipated future presence, "texted" to his door display the message:

On bus – in shortly.

In developing Hermes, we were particularly interested in exploring whether some of the traditional methods for supporting coordination through sharing personal information, such as sticking a post-it note outside one's office door, could be achieved with a digital equivalent that might provide different or enhanced properties and affordances and encourage or encompass different patterns of use, such as remote interaction.

K. Cheverst (✉)
Department of Computing, Infolab, Lancaster University, UK
e-mail: kc@comp.lancs.ac.uk

P. Markopoulos et al. (eds.), *Awareness Systems*, Human-Computer Interaction Series, DOI 10.1007/978-1-84882-477-5_17, © Springer-Verlag London Limited 2009

Fig. 17.1 The Hermes deployments: (**a**) displays outside offices in the initial deployment and (**b**) latest version of a Hermes display in the current deployment

A view along one of the Computing Department's corridors showing three of the deployed Hermes door displays appears in Fig. 17.1a. Figure 17.1b shows the latest version of the Hermes display outside an office in the Infolab building.

As always with this kind of work there is a tension between the particular nature of the deployment contexts and the desire to generalize the results to enable future design. In this chapter, we have largely utilized qualitative analysis informed by some more quantitative measures derived from raw data. This approach reflects the fact that we would not expect to see the same numerical patterns of usage to repeat themselves, but rather that we expect themes that emerged during their use to recur in future deployments in new situations. In our quantitative analysis we have used a sample of the logs (300 messages for Hermes) which we believe is suitably representative given the level of precision we require – namely that we wish to uncover broad classes of behaviour, not to theorize concerning precise frequency of occurrence. In our qualitative analysis we have relied partly on our own enculturation gained through personal experience of the settings and partly through broad shared understandings of "what is going on" at the settings.

The remainder of this chapter is structured as follows. The next three subsections discuss our understandings of terms crucial to this chapter, namely: *Situated Displays*, *Place*, *Situatedness* in general, *Awareness* and the interrelationship between these terms. The final part of this introduction discusses previous research related to the support of awareness by situated display-based systems. Following the introduction we present a detailed description of the Hermes system and the usages and themes (relating to awareness) that emerged from its long-term use. In the third section we present issues that designers need to consider when designing for systems such as Hermes and this chapter closes by presenting some concluding remarks.

17.1.1 *Situated Displays and the Importance of Place*

Research into *situated displays* belongs in both the *Computer Supported Cooperative Work* (CSCW) and *Ubiquitous Computing* (see Weiser, 1991) fields and has received considerable interest in recent years due, in part, to the widespread availability of cheap and reliable display devices (across a range of sizes), wireless communications and various sensing devices. From a technical perspective, the availability of these technologies enables deployments to occur at a relatively low financial cost. Furthermore, the widespread adoption of personal communication devices such as mobile phones provides an additional avenue to support interaction with situated displays.

It is in the use (novel and otherwise) of situated displays to support group work that we focus upon in this chapter. In examining this use we acknowledge that this use sometimes extends beyond the intentions of the designer(s) and that significant understanding is required in order to avoid inappropriate deployments. Indeed, fundamental to this notion of *situated* is the notion of *place* which Harrison and Dourish (1996:69) define as

> a space which is invested with understandings of behavioural appropriateness, cultural expectations, and so forth.

Thus the notion of place encompasses not only the physical aspects of the environment and the constraints these impose on behaviour (such as group activity) but also what actions and patterns of behaviour are expected there and the particular routines that have developed there over time.

17.1.2 *Dimensions of Situatedness*

While the displays on which messages appear are situated, the messages themselves can also be considered as situated – not simply due to inheriting context from the placement of the displays but from a number of other dimensions. Consider, for example, the common *"out for lunch"* message appearing on a Hermes door display. If this message appears on an owner's door display then the placement of the message clearly associates the message with the particular owner. Furthermore, both the placement and the fact that the message is not addressed to a particular person implies that the message is deliberately being broadcast to any person passing by the owner's office (only a subset of who is likely to be particularly interested in this piece of information).

The location also has potential cultural significance, for example, some cultures have more relaxed lunch periods.

While placement is clearly an important dimension another significant dimension "situating" the message is that of time. Consider, for example, the implications of the message being viewed on a Friday at 10 a.m., at 12.30.p.m. and at 2 p.m. At 10 a.m. a visitor to the door might simply assume that the office owner has not reset the message on her door display. At 12.30 p.m., the visitor might assume that the message is accurate and that the visitor might be away for some time. At 2.30 p.m., the visitor might also assume the message to be accurate but might hold some doubts and might also anticipate the imminent return of the message owner.

Of course, shared knowledge of rhythms and routines and the anticipated audience of messages also have significant impact. It may be common knowledge to those in the department that on a Friday the office owner typically has an extended lunch break starting around 1 p.m. – knowing that this is common knowledge the owner may consider the simple form of message sufficient. However, if the owner anticipated a possible visit by someone from outside the department then she may choose to provide more information.

Such a message may also have particular significance in the context of messages placed in the immediate past and what may be expected in the future. If the message was preceded by an earlier message, such as

Around all day,

then her potential availability later in the day is more assured than if no earlier message had been left and no such assurance had been made. In addition, the message is also situated in its immediate surroundings. For example, the message could have a different meaning if it is placed next to an open door compared to the same message placed next to a closed door with a light visibly switched on in the room.

17.1.3 Definitions of Awareness

Awareness is a common term in HCI and CSCW but has many different meanings. Often this is left unstated but a few authors have attempted to articulate more precisely what constitutes awareness. Schmidt and Simone (2000) distinguish four levels/kinds of awareness:

(a) Perception of the field of work
(b) Inferences from that to enable indirect perception of activities of others
(c) Direct perception of "bodily conduct" of others which includes

   (c.i) their focus of attention and also
   (c.ii) overheard conversations, etc.

(d) overhearings of other participants' explicit acts to coordinate their awareness with each other.

Dix distinguishes three kinds of awareness in the context of a CSCW framework (see Fig. 17.2 and Dix, 1997):

 (i) Who is there – who is around and their availability,
 (ii) What has happened – what things have altered or been changed in the shared environment,
(iii) How did it happen – what were and are the things that people did to make things the way they are.

Schmidt and Simone's (a) category corresponds roughly to Dix's (ii) category and relates to the current state of the work environment. Schmidt and Simone's (b) and (c.i) correspond to Dix's (iii) the way in which things are or have happened. Note all of these are related to the work environment and the things in it, in the vocabulary of Dix's CSCW Framework they are focused on the *Artefacts of Work*.

Fig. 17.2 Awareness in the CSCW framework (Dix, 1997): P – participants in collaboration, A – shared artefacts of work

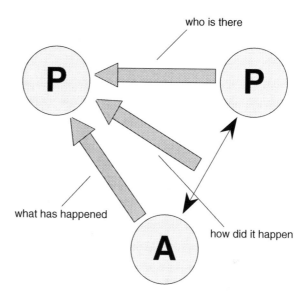

In contrast, Schmidt and Simone's (c.ii) and (d) and Dix's (i) are about the people in the situation directly, not so much their effects on other things. Virtually all the awareness information reported in the literature related to situated displays seems to be in these people categories, and we shall see in Section 17.3.2 that this is also the case with Hermes. However, because of their situated dimension, the issue of location is often central. Dix's CSCW Framework is focused around the relationship between people and artefacts and Schmidt and Simone's analysis has the same underlying assumption. In contrast, the awareness we will find in this chapter is about the relationship between people and place: who is (or is not) where and why.

Schmidt and Simone (2000:5) also point out two other critical dimensions of awareness: level of attention and reflexivity. On the former they note that awareness is used to include phenomena:

from peripheral awareness to focused attention.

Most of the awareness mechanisms for situated (especially office) displays seem to be more explicit: visitors reading calendars, etc. However, the location of displays can also make it possible (or not) for passers-by to notice (or become aware without consciously noticing) the general activity of others.

The issue of reflexivity is central to situated displays. Schmidt and Simone (2000) discuss the way in which participants orient themselves to expose their activities to others and hence make their actions intelligible [c.i] by others. This orientation may be very explicit or more subtle (and possibly unconscious). For example, it is possible to explicitly leave a note on an office door saying:

in the building, but not in my office

however, one of the authors will instead simply lock his door, but leave the light on which, because the walls are glass, more subtly gives the same message. In all the published studies of situated and office displays we know about, awareness information is explicitly supplied and often also codified *"in office"*, *"away"*, etc. We shall see in many examples how, when given a suitably rich medium, the supplier crafts this awareness information on situated displays beyond simple codified responses. Schmidt and Simone point out that this reflexivity in awareness is also played out by the recipients of awareness cues as they orient themselves to make their reception apparent. However, the nature of most public displays means that this is uncommon.

As we have noted, awareness information on situated displays is often (naturally) related to location (or activity as a proxy for location). A simple awareness message such as a post-it note saying *"out of office"* posted on an office door may carry several simultaneous meanings:

- Position: what I am doing / where I am
- Negation: what I am not doing / where I am not
- Explanation: why I am not doing it / why I am not somewhere

Often, only the first of these is explicit in the message but others may be implicit. In the case of the *"out for lunch"* post-it note, it says

- Position: I am eating lunch (explicit)
- Negation: I am not in my office (implicit)
- Explanation: I am not in my office because I am eating lunch

Of course, to someone who knows the person posting the message *"out for lunch"* may mean that the reader can guess where the "lunch" is. Also the awareness often has a temporal as well as spatial connotation; *"out for lunch"* carries an implication "not in my office now, but likely to be after lunch time".

17.1.4 Situated Displays and Awareness

Foundational research into the issues arising from the use of situated displays to support awareness and cooperation between work colleagues was carried out through the deployment and long-term evaluation of the Portholes shared video space. The Portholes system was a joint effort between the Systems Science Lab at Xerox PARC (based in Palo Alto) and Rank Xerox EuroPARC (based in Cambridge) carried out in the early 1990s in order to study the potential for supporting coordination between work colleagues through peripheral awareness (Dourish and Bly, 1992) and to explore the control/privacy issues that naturally arise from the deployment of such a system (Dourish, 1993).

Significant work in this area has also been conducted by O'Hara and colleagues. For example, the RoomWizard system (O'Hara et al., 2003) comprises an installation of PDA-sized display appliances situated outside of meeting rooms, providing the functionality to book a meeting room (locally and via the web) and check if a meeting room is available. Ethnographic techniques were used to investigate "meeting practices" before the installation of RoomWizard, and again during the deployment and use of the system. This enabled the identification and investigation of a set of issues arising from this use, e.g. unexpected functions such as enabling peripheral awareness and navigation. O'Hara and colleagues (2003:71) also note that complex usage patterns built up around what was effectively a very simple appliance:

> Whilst the RoomWizard at first appears to be a simple electronic duplicate of a room reservation system, it is far more complex than this in use.

Another significant piece of work by O'Hara is the Txtboard system (O'Hara et al., 2005) which again takes the form of a small display, in this case designed to be mounted on a wall in a home environment. TxtBoard incorporated a mobile phone to allow the reception of SMS messages which once received were displayed using all the available screen area. A study describing the use of TxtBoard by a family over a 2-month period revealed several aspects of use, most notably, the importance of the placement of the displays. O'Hara and colleagues (2005:1708) conclude that part of the success of TxtBoard was its simplicity:

> Nevertheless, TxtBoard succeeded in large part because it offered a minimal addition to the home: that is to say, that in offering so little, it made a difference that was worthwhile. In sum, this study of TxtBoard shows that less can be more.

This notion of simplicity and offering users a "lightweight" means for interaction is an insight that resonates strongly with our experiences of the Hermes deployment.

Another example of work on situated displays that (at least in part) support notions of awareness is McCarthy's work on the "OutCast" system/service (McCarthy et al., 2001). This provided (McCarthy et al., 2001:338):

> information about the owner that is intended for others to view.

The OutCast system used a relatively large touch-screen display, which would be embedded in a cubicle (office) wall and connected to a computer situated inside the owner's office. The OutCast system could be configured by its owner to display a range of content, including information to support general awareness, e.g. public calendar entries captured from the owner's "Outlook" calendar or location information obtained from the owner's infrared badge.

Work at Carnegie Mellon University explored how office doors can be augmented with computer generated displays, in order to support the functions of "aesthetic display" and "interruption gateway" (Nichols et al., 2002:1). In terms of display technology, the system actually projects an image onto a window in the office door from a projector located in the office. This approach produces a relatively large image which is viewable on the public side of the office door. The information projected onto the office door is of three main types: virtual notes, digital art (such as web pages, personalized graphics, etc.) and awareness information. The presentation of awareness information utilizes a system called "StatusLight" which utilizes a simple traffic-light metaphor in order to enable users located in the office to stipulate their interruptability. Investigations into the observed usage of the system was cited as planned future work (Nichols et al., 2002).

Research exploring the ways in which situated digital displays can be used to support and foster small communities has been carried out by Greenberg and colleagues through work on the Notification Collage (NC) system (Greenberg and Rounding, 2001). This groupware system, developed and evaluated by a small research group at the University of Calgary, enables distributed and co-located colleagues to post media elements (e.g. live video feeds from desktop webcams or activity indicators) into either a public space (a large display in an open area such as a common room) or a private setting (e.g. a workstation display – typically on a secondary display). According to Greenberg and Rounding (2001:1):

> User experiences show that NC becomes a rich resource for awareness and collaboration. Community members indicate their presence to others by posting live video. They regularly act on this information by engaging in text and video conversations.

Greenberg and Rounding also describe the obdurate problem of managing appropriate privacy and distraction when supporting awareness in a system such as NC – such observations echo the insights described by Hudson and Smith (1996) who describe the joint trade-offs between supporting an awareness of the activities of others and privacy and between awareness and potential disturbance.

While the results of the above work make clear contributions to the "situatedness of awareness information" no one single system captures the combination of aspects that has motivated the Hermes deployment. In particular, this combination includes the placement of awareness information via some form of digital display at the entrance to a person's office (as with the Outcast system and the work by Nichols and colleagues) and the longitudinal deployment and evaluation of the system (as with Portholes deployment and the work of O'Hara and colleagues on the RoomWizard and TxtBoard systems, although the 2-month deployment carried out for this latter system might be considered too short for a longitudinal study in which enough time is required for evolving usage patterns to occur). Furthermore, a key motivation behind Hermes was to follow an approach whereby the system would evolve over time to encompass requests from users for different ways of interacting with the system, e.g. different methods for setting messages on their Hermes display.

17.2 Awareness in the Hermes System

The Hermes office door display system was deployed in the Computing Department of Lancaster University. The first Hermes unit was installed outside an office in April 2002 and additional units were installed over a 9-month period. The Hermes system ran for nearly 27 months and is currently being re-engineered for deployment in a new department building. Hermes door displays took the form of PDAs in a metal casing (see Fig. 17.3) which effectively turned the devices into information appliances by removing access to the PDA's buttons and (consequently) applications other than the Hermes software.

Fig. 17.3 A close-up of a
Hermes display showing an
owner's textual message

When developing the Hermes system we were very much interested in the
"place" (immediately adjacent to office doors) where these units would be deployed,
this being a place that possesses both private (in terms of it being a location closely
associated with the owner) and public (in terms of it facing onto a public corridor)
elements.

It should be noted that the examples described in this section occur within the
context of other mechanisms for communicating awareness, such as e-mail and even
an office door. Nichols and colleagues make a relevant comment about the nature of
office doors in Nichols et al. (2002:1):

> Office doors are more than entrances to rooms, they are entrances to a person's time and
> attention. People can mediate access to themselves by choosing whether to leave their door
> open or closed when they are in their office. Doors also serve as a medium for communi-
> cation, where people can broadcast individual messages to passersby, or accept messages
> from others who stopped by when the door was closed.

Nichols and colleagues illustrate how office doors themselves, even without a
glass window, can support the notion of "social translucence" (Erickson and Kellog,
2000). When first discussing this concept, in the context of

> designing systems that support communication and collaboration among large groups of
> people over computer networks,

Erickson and Kellog consider:

> ... what properties of the physical world support graceful human–human communication
> in face to face situations, and argue that it is possible to design digital systems that support
> coherent behavior by making participants and their activities visible to one another. We call
> such systems "socially translucent systems" and suggest that they have three characteristics
> – visibility, awareness, and accountability – which enable people to draw upon their social
> experience and expertise to structure their interactions with one another.

While supplementing the existing physical properties of the deployment domain that may be used by an owner to make her *"activities visible to one another"* (e.g. by leaving her office door ajar) the Hermes system works in a way that grants the user control to craft the way in which she expresses awareness-related messages on her Hermes display and, for example, account for her absence from the office.

17.2.1 Evolution of the Hermes System

The Hermes system evolved in a series of phases through its deployment. Initially only two units were deployed on the offices of system developers (two of the authors) but over time (and as the reliability of the system increased) further units were deployed. The phased development was used to respond to comments made by users (obtained through both questionnaires, semi-structured interviews and informal conversations in the workplace) such as requests for additional methods of interacting with the system. For example, one owner made an explicit request to be able to set messages via MSN Messenger (see the section on "The Importance of Fitting in with Existing Routines" below for more details).

Although hardware costs limited the number of displays to ten that could actually be deployed, during the deployment period a total of 12 owners made use of the system (four of these being authors of this chapter). It is difficult to give precise figures for what might be considered a "minimum" number of deployments (in terms of actual displays) for a study of this kind; however, we felt that fewer than ten displays (which approximated to one in five offices in the department) would have meant that individual displays would have been perceived as overly isolated by those in the department. Furthermore, where possible we deployed displays across adjacent offices in order to encourage a perception of "normality" and "ubiquity" with respect to the displays in the hope that this would again help stimulate a more natural usage of the system over time.

Although substantial efforts were made to improve the reliability of the system, some users encountered a significantly lower level of reliability than others. For example, one owner (a secretary) had a door display located in an area of intermittent wireless connectivity. Consequently, she encountered several failures when attempting to use her door display to share awareness information and (not surprisingly) she eventually lost confidence in the system. For other door display owners, the number of encountered failures were less and the usage of the system more significant.

Other door display owners coped well with a small number of failures and found the Hermes system a valuable part of their daily patterns. One owner (a lecturer in this case) who used the system to display between five and ten messages a day (the majority relating to awareness/presence information – see Section 17.2.4) made the following comment:

> I guess it's public spirited, it's trying to help people to be aware of what I'm doing and being able to find me more easily, or work out whether I'm available, or when I'll be back or something.

Another owner (a secretary) commented that she liked the fact that the system helped other people to find her when she was away from the office. This secretary was a previous user of a message whirler (a cardboard disk mounted on her door that could be rotated to reveal appropriate awareness information, such as "Photocopying") and that she abandoned using the whirler after receiving her own Hermes display (although the whirler remained stuck to her door).

The Hermes system was dismantled in July 2004 and a small number of working prototypes of a new version of Hermes (Hermes 2) were deployed in the new department building in May 2006. A full deployment across two corridors and 40 offices was completed in December 2007. From the user's perspective, one significant change from the original Hermes system is the use of a larger 7 in. widescreen display; this larger screen was chosen by the majority of door display owners from the original Hermes system during a "show case" study in which a variety of display options (based on high fidelity prototypes) were presented to previous owners, see Fitton et al. (2005) for more details.

In common with many such technology deployments, the users included the developers themselves and their close colleagues. This obviously runs the risk that users were "being helpful" to the researchers and that usage does not reflect true deployment. While this undoubtedly had some effect we do not believe this seriously diminishes the reliability of our own results. First these "being helpful" effects do not last long. It is common in reports of experimental technology deployments to see usage levels that rapidly peak followed by rapid decline to disuse. Instead we saw usage that, while sometimes sporadic reflecting personal circumstances, was relatively uniform in the long term, suggesting that the system was being used for its own sake. Second, users varied widely in their patterns of use and in particular were not shy to disregard or discontinue the use of features that did not fit their personal work patterns. Third, the system was to some extent "mission critical" (in the sense that an owner may use her door display as the sole means to communicate an important timely message to a colleague, e.g. the need to postpone a meeting at her office) and hence users (in this example both the owner and the colleague expecting the original meeting time) were not forgiving if a door display failed to display certain messages in a timely manner. This included the authors themselves, one of whom never used the ability to send messages to his display via SMS because of an early "bad experience". So, we feel that the worst potential dangers of being too close to the users were avoided. On the positive side, the personal knowledge of the users and their context and habits made the analysis of (often idiosyncratic) messages in the system logs, far more tractable than it would have been for strangers.

17.2.2 Typical Scenarios of Use

In terms of functionality, one of the primary purposes of Hermes was to support general coordination between lecturers, secretaries/technical support staff and students. For example, it was envisioned that a lecturer and owner of a door display,

so that students coming to her office would know to wait, might "text" to her door
display a message such as:

Stuck in traffic jam – will be 30 min late at least.

With Hermes, we were particularly interested in exploring whether some of the
traditional methods for sharing personal information, e.g. sticking a post-it note outside one's office door, could be achieved with a digital equivalent that might provide
different or enhanced properties and affordances and encourage or encompass different patterns of use, such as remote interaction. In effect, we were interested in the
extent to which the system would support coordination between colleagues through
the provision of awareness information.

The system architecture of the Hermes system is shown in Fig. 17.4. This figure
illustrates how the door displays were connected to a central server via a wireless
802.11 network. The central server was responsible for running the Hermes application and for storing the messages set by owners and those entered by visitors to the
door displays (such visitors could use an attached stylus to scribble a message on
the display's touch screen). The server was also responsible for accessing a database
storing owner preferences and for log storage (including the storing of fine grained
GUI actions by the user in addition to all messages). Figure 17.4 also illustrates the
various ways in which an owner of a door display could set a message, i.e. by texting using their mobile phone, through a web browser interface, via e-mail, through
an MSN messenger client or by using the touch sensitive screen on the door display
itself.

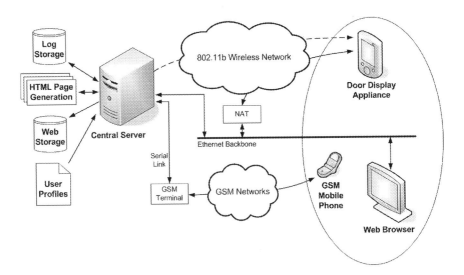

Fig. 17.4 The systems architecture of the original Hermes system

17.2.3 Analysis of Usage Logs

An analysis of a sample log of 300 messages (captured over a 5-month period commencing on November 2003 from all owners who set a message during that period) was carried out by three of the authors (all of whom were owners of door display units). This period of usage was chosen because by November 2003 Hermes owners had been using the system for many months and so it could be assumed that usage patterns had started to stabilize. Furthermore, the 5-month period represented a continuous period of usage during which no major modifications were made to the system and during which the system did not suffer any significant periods of down time – by November 2003 early reliability problems had been rectified.

This analysis revealed that approximately 80% of the total number of messages appearing in the log related in some way to the notion of supporting awareness, relating in particular to the notion of presence. A sample of the Hermes log file from this period including tags identifying how owner's set messages shared context in one of the three categories: *Activity*, *Temporal* and *Location* is shown in Fig. 17.5. Analysis relating to these three specific categories is presented in detail in Cheverst et al. (2003b).

Of the 300 messages analysed, 48 were either test messages or edits, the latter being messages that represented basic corrections/clarifications of a preceding message that took place within 3 minutes of the initial message being set. For example, in the log sample being used, the following message was set by a lecturer to appear on his door display:

away @ Cheltenham getting Honorary fellowship Wed & Thurs, back in on Friday.

However, within 3 min the lecturer changed his displayed message to:

away @ Cheltenham getting Honorary fellowship (am I getting that old!) Wed & Thurs, back in on Friday.

```
===============================
User Name: xxx
Time: 20:35
Date: 11/03/03
Message Type: TEMPOROARY TEXTUAL
Message: Away at COTREX workshop. Back Monday (probably no email in the meantime!
Context: TEMPORAL ACTIVITY
===============================
User Name: yyy
Time: 12:23
Date: 13/03/03
Message Type: TEMPOROARY TEXTUAL
Message: At COTREX mtg in Ambleside Thur pm + all day Fri
Context: TEMPORAL LOCATION ACTIVITY
===============================
User Name: zzz
Time: 12:33
Date: 15/03/03
Message Type: TEMPOROARY TEXTUAL
Message: meeting in Paris Monday, back in Tuesday 18ᵗʰ March
Context: TEMPORAL LOCATION ACTIVITY
===============================
```

Fig. 17.5 Sample of the tagged Hermes usage log

In the remainder of this chapter, we refer to the set of 252 messages as being "valid" messages.

17.2.4 Emergent Usages and Themes Relating to Awareness

This section presents a qualitative analysis of the usages and themes that arose from observing how the deployed system was used by the various door display owners in ways relevant to notions of awareness.

To obtain feedback from door display owners a variety of "formal" methods were used (in addition to chance conversations with owners at the drinks dispenser, etc.) including the use of questionnaires and semi-structured interviews.

Questions explored a variety of pertinent issues such as user expertise, context sharing, dependability and trust. One example question being:

> When not in my office I find it more acceptable to share information about my activity (e.g. gone to lunch) rather than my location (e.g. gone to lunch at the Venue).

Users were asked to respond between "strongly agree" and "strongly disagree" and were also given space in the questionnaire to provide any comments raised by the question.

The Hermes system was also very much "lived" by the investigators in the Computing Department at Lancaster – four of the authors owned door displays. Thus the themes below not only emerge from the analysis of logged message and responses to questionnaire items and interview questions but also from the subjective, personal and shared experience of living with the system.

17.2.4.1 Maintaining a Sense of Presence/Reason for Absence

One common use for messages set on Hermes door displays was to provide a sense of presence when away from the office. One typical example being:

> Working at home today – reviewing papers.

Another common use for messages was to provide an indication of why the person is not in their office, but in a way that they can be contacted if necessary, e.g. a popular message left by secretaries was simply:

> Photocopying.

Similarly, other staff would leave messages such as:

> Lecturing.

Of the 252 valid messages 229 (91%) of the messages related to the provision of presence information and of these, 172 messages (75%) provided information regarding the owners location or activity.

Through the semi-structured interviews we discussed with door display owners their reasons for deciding upon what was an appropriate level of information to share on their display. One secretary made the following comment when asked whether she had considered leaving additional information (e.g. location) to her (frequently used) *"gone for lunch"* message:

> It's not something that I've even thought of before, just 'gone for lunch' I think is enough information, I've never even considered saying where I'm going for lunch... I don't do it so nobody can find me, it's just gone for lunch, that's it!

A different secretary commented how she strongly preferred to share information about her activity (in this case gone for lunch) and expressed concerns about people coming to see her when at lunch outside of the department, stating:

> ...people only need to know that I am not available in my office, not necessarily where I am.

When asked to expand upon this issue of 'how much information is enough' one secretary commented on how her messages were *"well chosen"* and that:

> ...if someone knew I was at the photocopier they would know where I was and be able to estimate how long I might be.

A lecturer also commented how he found it more acceptable to share information about his activity rather than this location, primarily to protect his privacy, but he was interested in sharing different granularity of information under different circumstances:

> ...you don't want them tracking you down while you're down at X or gone for lunch. Whereas if it was someone who had some urgent problem that they wanted sorted out then you might be a little less upset if they turned up at X saying "I've got this immediate emergency, can you help?"

17.2.4.2 Establishing Mood and Personal Situation

As well as saying where a person is or what the person is doing, users also used the system to express how they were feeling. We found that 26 (10%) of the 252 valid messages could clearly be related to this category. Examples included purely textual messages, but also pictures and drawings. Figure 17.6 shows a message that both includes textual description of personal situation *"here but busy"* and also a sketch with significant emotional impact. A further example in which humor is clearly evident in the owner's message appears in Fig. 17.8.

Fig. 17.6 A message from a door display owner artistically expressing his mood

17.2.4.3 The "I'm Not Here but I Should Be" Awareness Message

One common use of the system was to display a message of the form:

I'm not here but I should be.

Of the valid messages analysed, there were four SMS-based messages all of which related to this category. One example of such a message left by one of the department's lecturers is:

in q at post office.

During interview, the lecturer who sent this message described it as follows:

I've definitely used it when I've had people coming to meet me here and I've been stuck, I was definitely stuck at the post office queuing once, I've been stuck on the bus, all sorts of places, and I've texted in and said I'm going to run late, and I've used that 3 or 4 times I guess.

17.2.4.4 Privacy, Control, Accuracy and Placement Issues

The location of a display is one of the key dimensions when considering the situatedness of a message. We were interested in exploring the extent to which owners wanted the visibility of their messages to be constrained to their door displays. In order to explore this issue we asked owners (as part of a closing semi-structured interview) to comment on their agreement with the following statement:

I would be happy for anyone to view the message on my doorplate remotely over the web.

One of the owners was not sure, seven of the owners disagreed (one strongly) citing security concerns and four owners agreed. Note that there was no significant relationship between the profession of the owner and their response to this question. For example, three of the four secretaries that were owners of door displays responded with disagree (one strongly) while the other secretary responded with agree.

Two of the owners that agreed described how they would alter their messages to make them vaguer while one display owner described how she would make her messages more accurate as people may be travelling long distances across campus to visit her office (the accuracy issue is discussed further in Section 17.3.3). One of the owners that disagreed commented on the privacy implications of making his messages widely accessible, his comments clearly imply that the placement of his door display reduced his privacy concerns as it restricted access to his messages to a specific community:

There is a community associated with my doorplate, you know people have to be able to get to my doorplate, and that probably makes them one of the staff or colleagues, and that affects what information I could put on there and I don't want burglar Bill with his web browser to go – oh look he's in such-and-such I'll go and burgle his house now.

17.2.4.5 The Importance of Fitting in with Existing Routines

The importance of fitting in with existing routines/patterns of behaviour is one of the most important issues to have arisen through both informal conversation and interviews with Hermes door display owners.

When designing and developing Hermes it was important to identify and support a set of interaction methods that fitted in with the users' existing tools and routines. For example, one owner, John, found the existing mechanisms available for setting messages inconvenient. However, he was a regular user of MSN Messenger and would often use this for providing awareness information to colleagues. He requested that Hermes be extended to enable him to set messages on his door display using his MSN Messenger client and the system was modified to support this interaction method. Subsequently, this owner rated the MSN Messenger integration as his favorite feature of Hermes. In fact, quantitative analysis of use showed that his average daily usage increased significantly following the deployment of this feature. When expressing why he thought this was the case, he made it clear that the interaction method was not only very easy and simple for him to use but also fitted well with his existing routines:

> It wants to be something you don't have to go out of your way to do.

John has two offices at the University, one in the Computing Department and one in a different department. John described how:

> ...what I would typically be doing is coming into computing at about 9 a.m. in the morning that's where I'd use Hermes just to change the status for the previous day to say that I'm in here. What I'm doing at the moment is tending to work in computing in the morning, spend a couple of hours here depending on the workload, and then I'll move across to X [the other department]. I'll typically update the status when I'm on my way out. Depending on what the workload is I may come back [to computing] at some time in the afternoon, so that way Hermes is really useful for me – I use it as an indicator of when I'm here and when I'm there.

Other comments from owners described how the system had become part of their routine. For example, one lecturer commented:

> I would update Hermes to say I'm working from home – it's part of my working routine.

Another owner (a secretary in this case) had a habit of sending messages to the departmental e-mail list, with a typical message being:

> Away Friday p.m. back Mon.

In order to leverage upon this existing pattern of use we enabled her to set messages on her door display via an e-mail message – this meant that she did not need to drastically change an existing routine but rather simply had to include the appropriate Hermes e-mail address in the "cc" field of the e-mail message. Other patterns of behaviour were also supported based on owner's evolved usage of the system. One significant example of this was support for default and temporary messages. The rationale for this feature is explained fully in Cheverst et al. (2003a). Described

Fig. 17.7 The Hermes
interface for enabling owners
to quickly set a temporary via
their own door display unit

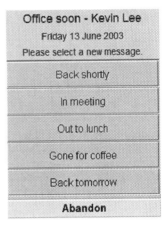

briefly, it enabled the owner of a door display to set both a default image (e.g. a cartoon strip) and a temporary message (e.g. *"gone for coffee"*). If a temporary message was set then this would occlude the default image but could be easily removed by tapping on the screen. Furthermore, following feedback that owners would often only think to set a message when leaving the office (thus seeing the office door display would act as a visual cue reminding the owner to leave a message) the system was modified to enable owners to set a temporary message by touching a button displayed on the door display itself. As can be seen in Fig. 17.7, each button would represent one of a set of pre-defined messages but the owner could opt to change any of these from the set of system defaults if she wished to do so.

17.2.4.6 Appropriated (or Unintended by the Designer) Use

The system was designed to enable owners to provide awareness information and one of the affordances of the digital medium was that we could, in effect, restrict messages appearing on the door display to be only those set by the owner. As mentioned above, one feature included in the system was designed to enable an owner to set a message on his or her door display by tapping on the screen to reveal a set of predefined messages (a screenshot illustrating of a typical set of messages is shown in Fig. 17.7) and then tapping again to select the desired message.

One example of appropriated use (meant here as use not explicitly intended by the designer) is demonstrated by one owner commenting that colleagues would occasionally update his door display if he forgot to do so, an unintentional feature afforded by the trading-off of security for ease of use:

> I use it to say out to lunch, and it's quite interesting that the guys, if I don't, as I always set it to out to lunch as I walk out the door, if I forget, they set it to out to lunch for me, which I think it is quite nice.

17.3 Design Considerations

In this section, we discuss design considerations based on our experiences with the Hermes system. One of the main themes to have arisen from our exploration of awareness issues relating to Hermes is the strong personal context given to awareness messages by the *situatedness* of the displays. The issue of what counts as *appropriate* accuracy when supporting awareness in these systems was another important theme. Still another theme that emerged concerns Hermes' connection to other communication technologies and how users rapidly adapted their use of the messaging technologies to fit in with existing communication routines and practices. These practices included the expression of mood and feelings: for example Hermes was used to express being busy (see Fig. 17.6).

17.3.1 The Situatedness of Displays

The implication of the *situatedness* of the displays is a central theme emerging from this work. As Mitchell (2005:9) eloquently states:

> Literary theorists sometimes speak of text as if it were disembodied, but of course it isn't; it always shows up attached to particular physical objects, in particular spatial contexts, and those contexts-like the contexts of speech-furnish essential components of the meaning.

The situatedness of Hermes displays provided significant context to the awareness type messages left by the sender of the message. For example, the fact that an office is empty gives significant context to the message "Out to Lunch". In this case, given the office is only occupied by one person, the identity of the message is clear and the message naturally provides an explanation for the empty office. The digital affordances of the Hermes door display meant that owners could take steps to ensure that awareness-based messages, e.g. *"gone for coffee"* were very secure but, where this impacted upon ease-of-use, security was not considered to be a priority. Indeed, this lack of security led to an interesting appropriation of the system in which some colleagues would set the "temporary" message of a door display owner on his/her behalf. Another factor that arose with Hermes was the differing opinions held by staff regarding whether information on their door displays should or should not only be accessible from the door display itself.

From this discussion we can identify several contextual factors:

- *Identity of message sender*: in the case of Hermes, the door display owner.
- *Identity of message recipient*: in the case of Hermes a visitor or passer-by at the door. Note that where the identity is not a single individual then additional names or abbreviations need to be given, however, even then the situatedness supplies sufficient context that these can be short or implicit. In many cases the identification of "anyone in this location" seems to be sufficient.

- *Work ecology and spatial layout*: in the case of Hermes the fact that someone coming to see the office owner must necessarily come to the door, forces attention.

As with the last example, all of the above impact on:

- *Security and privacy*: in the case of Hermes the acceptability of the short "one touch" messages that could in principle be set by anyone, but in practice only by "authorized" people (owner and colleagues).

17.3.2 Situatedness and Types of Awareness

Earlier in the chapter we discussed several kinds of personal awareness messages:

- *Position*: what I am doing/where I am.
- *Negation*: what I am not doing/where I am not.
- *Explanation*: why I am not doing it/why I am not somewhere

Examples of all of these have been found in Hermes:

- *What I am doing...* In Hermes, examples include an *"out for lunch"* or *"Lecturing"* message left on a Hermes door display.
- *What I am not doing...* Examples might include a Hermes owner leaving the message: *"Fred I'm at WW for lunch"* or *"in Q at post office"*.
- *Why I am not doing it...* Examples might include a Hermes owner leaving the message: *"Working at Home today reviewing papers"*.

Given these three categories it is then interesting to observe that the notion of situatedness seems to interact strongly with them. The way the message is situated (in time, for example) has something to say about the person sending a message and the intended audience of the message.

17.3.2.1 Awareness Messages of the Form: What I Am Doing...

In the first category above the location context provided by the situatedness of the display and the *"out for lunch"* message becomes a just-in-time explanation of why the person is not in their office. As such, the message makes stronger sense when displayed outside the empty office (something which is apparent to a visitor to the office) rather than, for example, on the secretaries home page. With this context the message effectively becomes:

> To anyone expecting to find me here in my office... The reason that I am not here is BECAUSE I am having lunch somewhere else.

The message is relevant to both those with an appointment and those that have visited her office on the off chance of finding the secretary in. Interestingly, this message was often left by a secretary who would have a "packed" lunch and eat it in her office but would (quite reasonably) not wish to be disturbed during that time.

This message would still have significant value if, for example, the message was available over the web because it could be used to reflect the fact that the secretary could not be reached by her office phone at that time.

17.3.2.2 Awareness Messages of the Form: What I Am Not Doing

In the second category the location context provided by the situatedness of the display and the *"Fred I'm at WW for lunch"* message again becomes a just-in-time explanation of why the person is not in their office but this time the audience is primarily Fred (but the message is of course there for others to see who may be trying to meet the lecturer) – with this context the message effectively becomes:

> To Fred... sorry I am not able to meet you now in my office BECAUSE I am at the WW having lunch, come and find me?

The lecturer concerned verified the meaning captured in this particular message during a conversation held with one of the authors within a few weeks of the message being set.

Similarly, the *"in Q at post office"* message becomes:

> To those expecting to find me here... sorry I am not able to meet you now in my office BECAUSE I am in Q at post office.

17.3.2.3 Awareness Messages of the Form: Why I Am Not Doing It...

In the third category the location context provided by the situatedness of the display and the *"Working at Home today reviewing papers"* message effectively becomes

> To those expecting to find me working here in my office (or expecting to find evidence of me being here today, light on etc.) I am not here BECAUSE I am Working at Home reviewing papers.

17.3.2.4 Relations to Broader Frameworks

Earlier, we noted that the majority of messages relate to *person and place* and so fit poorly into both the Dix (1997) framework and the Schmidt and Simone (2000) four awareness levels, both of which are focused on the relationship between people and work. The focus on the majority of the situated display messages are about availability and location: where, when and why people are or are not in particular places and how to contact them, that is the majority of messages are about articulation work (Schmidt and Bannon, 1992) – the coordination and organization that surrounds cooperative activities.

This is partly due to the short length of messages in Hermes – there are better media to talk about work (e-mail, face to face). Instead, these systems are used to talk about the processes (getting in the same place at the same time or at least getting in contact by other means) that enable you work and to talk about work. Instant messaging (IM), while also allowing protracted conversations, shares this short message length and in Nardi et al. (2000) study of IM, they found a similar focus on what they termed *outeraction*:

> The communications outside information exchange but supporting it.

The situatedness of the display also influences its relation to the artefacts of work. In the case of Hermes the display is outside the office, not in the place of work, but in some sense referring to it. In the Dix 1997 framework it is as if the Hermes displays sits right outside of the triangle … or at least the place where the triangle "happens". That is, by the combination of placement, purpose and functionality, these displays suit themselves to articulation work, to coordination about the potential for "doing" work. In contrast other situated displays are designed to be intimately part of "doing" work, for example an electronic whiteboard or shared projected desktop.

Situatedness also influences the audience. For Hermes, the fact that it is a person "at your door" gives them a certain role; in terms of collaborative activity they are likely to be or wish to become engaged in some form of communication or collaboration. For the visitor, they know who the recipient is (the door owner), and so can be directed to the work at hand, but for the door owner, while the recipient/reader is likely to be someone involved in some collaborative activity, it is not always clear which one. In some cases the message is explicitly addressed to an expected visitor, although even then it is effectively "overheard" by other visitors (Schmidt and Simone's level (c.ii)) involved in other collaborative activities. During our analysis of logs, we have seen examples of the rich way in which Hermes owners craft their message so as to convey different "messages" to different visitors – undoubtedly *"Marillion!"* meant something as a message to particular visitors, but for others it simply meant *"not here"*.

It appears that the general models of awareness need refinement to account for both articulation work, the fact that individuals are involved in multiple simultaneous collaborations and the need to consider "outsider" audiences.

17.3.3 Accuracy and Deliberate Imprecision Relating to Awareness

The trade-off between awareness of the activities of others and privacy (and between awareness and potential disturbance) is discussed in Hudson and Smith (1996). With Hermes, owners had control (expressiveness) over the level of preciseness with which they provide others with awareness information. For example, one Hermes owner (a lecturer) requested that their Hermes messages be automatically annotated with a time stamp while other owners did not want this to happen automatically. Our approach here was to enable the owner to specify preference for this particular activity. This issue is particularly interesting given that one of the potentials of digital technology over paper-based approaches (such as Post-It notes) is that given computational capabilities the information provided by the digital form could be highly accurate. For example, as mentioned earlier, a message initially set as *"gone for 5 min"* could be made to automatically count down. However, this would not reflect the actual imprecision associated with what is generally intended when leaving such a message.

In the case of Hermes, exploring the views of owners regarding the difference in precision of awareness messages revealed that they would feel happy having displayed on their door display compared to the information being viewable on a web page. In general, Hermes users commented that they would provide less precise information if it was to be available on the web – one can imagine that the message *"gone to the toilet"* makes sense at an office, but not on a web page (do I want my lavatorial habits web-mine-able?).

So imprecision can certainly be used to protect privacy, e.g. *"gone for lunch"* as opposed to *"gone to Joe's cafe"*. The importance of supporting imprecision in awareness systems has been studied previously. For example, work on the Audio Aura system (Mynatt et al., 1998) played a sound outside a colleague's office such that the volume of the sound varied according to the duration that the colleague has been away from her office. This approach was deliberately chosen because the imprecision would allay the privacy concerns of colleagues using the system. Similarly, the importance of an abstract (e.g. less accurate) representation of personal context was the focus of the Aroma System (Pedersen and Sokoler, 1997). This work considered how the applied degradation to a signal (e.g. an audio or video feed to a person's current location) could be used in order to control whether

more or less interpretive efforts are required by the reader of the abstraction

and so help protect a user's privacy in a system supporting awareness of colleagues. It is important to note that the Hermes system provided the user with significant control over the precision of information presented but at the cost of increased effort on behalf of the user to express the level of precision required.

17.3.4 Awareness and Support for Communication

The Hermes system supported coordination and cooperation through making awareness information visible and consequently can be considered as part of the cooperative arrangement (Martin et al., 2004) of the workplace. Within the Hermes logs we observed clear examples of messages that can be categorized as *Making others aware of a blocked communication channel*, e.g.

Away at CORTEX workshop. Back Monday (probably no e-mail in the meantime!)

Although such messages accounted for less than 1% of the messages analysed, one can argue that when the owner of a door display is away from his/her office there is effectively a blocked communication channel, i.e. the unavailability of the owner for face-to-face communication. As mentioned earlier the majority of Hermes messages were communicating presence-related information, effectively pointing out this blocked communication channel.

Fig. 17.8 Picture posted on a
Hermes display illustrating an
example of setting up
availability via another
channel

Following this, it was not surprising to find that a reasonably significant number of messages (9 of the 252 valid messages analysed) related to a category of *Setting up availability via another channel*. Figure 17.8 shows one (slightly ironic) message (in this case a picture) displayed on the door display of a lecturer's office.

Further discussion regarding these latter two categories can be found in Cheverst et al. (2007).

17.4 Concluding Remarks

In this chapter we have explored the situatedness of awareness information through a study of awareness-related messaging by users of a situated display-based messaging system called Hermes. The Hermes system was, to a large extent, designed to enable an "owner" to asynchronously send messages (using a variety of methods) to a digital display situated directly outside his or her office for the benefit of visitors to that office. The owner in this case would either be remote (i.e. not in their office) when sending a message (e.g. via a mobile phone or web page) or co-located with the display (e.g., when scribbling an *"out for lunch"* type message). In effect, the point of receipt of awareness is the display location and its interpretation is highly contextualized.

17.4.1 Summary of Design Considerations

While not presenting design guidelines, our experience of the Hermes system leads us to suggest that designers consider the following questions and associated issues:

Who can send messages to the display and should access to mechanisms for sending messages be shared?

In Hermes it was ostensibly the owner but the *leave message at door* facility (illustrated in Fig. 17.7) did effectively provide shared access and, as described above, enabled appropriation to take place. In Hermes, a large amount of personalization was supported which afforded high levels of control to the owner of a door display.

How public/private is the place where the messages will be displayed and who are the potential audience/receivers of this information?

This leads on to questions of how salient messages should appear in the public setting. For example, in the case of Hermes the overall design of the screen was such that it would not be overly salient to passers-by who were not visiting a particular office.

Regarding the creation of messages, what level of expressivity should be supported?

In Hermes users could choose along a spectrum from highly expressive scribbled messages (Fig. 17.6), uploaded photographs (Fig. 17.8) to prescribed (and very quick to select) short messages, e.g. *"gone for coffee"* (Fig. 17.7). The effort required by the user is also related to this issue of expressivity. The level of expressivity supported also relates to the extent to which users can direct a message to a particular individual or group and the extent to which they can control the precision of the information. Such control is crucial if notions of plausible deniability are to be supported. The importance of this has been recognized by other researchers and Lederer et al. (2004) include the need for social nuance including plausible deniability as their fifth potential pitfall for privacy in interactive systems.

How much context (for example the time when a message was sent) should appear with a given awareness message?

Some owners stated that they did not want their messages automatically timestamped. There is a growing literature in issues of user appropriation, but relatively little explicit design guidance. In the case of Hermes many aspects are deliberately not interpreted by the system (text, hand drawn notes, images) and it is precisely this, combined with the implied audience and context of these situated displays, that allows users to create their own nuanced interpretations.

References

Cheverst, K., Fitton, D., and Dix, A. (2003a). "Exploring the evolution of office door displays". In K. O'Hara, M. Perry, E. Churchill, and D. Russell (Eds.), *Public and situated displays: Social and interactional aspects of shared display technologies* (pp. 141–169). Dordrecht, The Netherlands: Kluwer Academic.

Cheverst, K., Dix, A., Fitton, D., and Rouncefield, M. (2003b). "Out to Lunch": Exploring the sharing of personal context through office door displays. *Proceedings of International Conference of the Australian Computer–Human Interaction Special Interest Group (OzCHI'03)*, Brisbane, Australia.

Cheverst, K., Dix, A., Fitton, D. Graham, C., and Rouncefield, M. (2007). "Exploring awareness related messaging through two situated display based systems", in Special Issue of *Human–Computer Interaction*, 22 (1–2), 173–220.

Dix, A. (1997). "Challenges for cooperative work on the web: An analytical approach". *Computer-Supported Cooperative Work: The Journal of Collaborative Computing*, 6, 135–156.

Dourish, P. (1993). "Culture and control in a media space". *Proceedings of European Computer-Supported Cooperative Work Conference (ECSCW'93)*. Dordrecht, The Netherlands: Kluwer Academic.

Dourish, P., and Bly, S. (1992). "Portholes: Supporting awareness in a distributed work group". *Proceedings of Conference on Human Factors in Computing Systems (CHI '92)*. New York: ACM.

Erickson, T., and Kellogg, W. A. (2000). "Social translucence: An approach to designing systems that support social processes". A *CMTransactions on Computer–Human Interaction*, 7, 59–83.

Fitton, D., Cheverst, K., Kray, C., Dix, A., Rouncefield, M., and Saslis-Lagoudakis, G. (2005). "Rapid prototyping and user centred design of interactive display based systems". *IEEE Pervasive Computing on Rapid Prototyping for Ubiquitous Computing*, 4 (4), 58–66.

Greenberg, S., and Rounding, M. (2001). "The notification collage: Posting information to public and personal displays". *Proceedings of Conference on Human Factors in Computing Systems (CHI 2001)*. Seattle, Washington. New York: ACM.

Harrison, S., and Dourish, P. (1996). "Re-place-ing space: The roles of place and space in collaborative systems". *Proceedings of Conference on Computer Supported Cooperative Work (CSCW '96)*. Boston, MA: ACM.

Hudson, S., and Smith, I. (1996). "Techniques for addressing fundamental privacy and disruption tradeoffs in awareness support systems". *Proceedings of Conference on Computer Supported Cooperative Work (CSCW '96)*. Boston, MA: ACM Press.

Lederer, S., Hong, I., Dey, K., and Landay, A. (2004). "Personal privacy through understanding and action: Five pitfalls for designers". *Personal Ubiquitous Computing*, 8, 440–454.

Martin, D., Rouncefield, M., and Sommerville, I. (2004). "Patterns of cooperative interaction: Linking ethnomethodology and design". *ACM Transactions on Computer–Human Interaction (ToCHI)*. New York: ACM.

McCarthy, J. F., Costa, T. J., and Liongosari, E. S. (2001). "UNICAST, OUTCAST & GROUPCAST: Three steps toward ubiquitous peripheral displays". *Proceedings of UbiComp 2001, Lecture Notes in Computer Science*. Berlin, Germany: Springer-Verlag.

Mitchell, W. J. (2005). *Placing words: Symbols, space, and the city*. Cambridge, MA: MIT Press.

Mynatt, E. D., Back, M., Want, R., Baer, M., and Ellis, J. B. (1998). "Designing audio aura". *Proceedings of Conference on Human Factors in Computing Systems (CHI '98)*. New York: ACM.

Nardi, B., Whittaker, S., and Bradner, E. (2000). "Interaction and outeraction: Instant messaging in action". *Proceedings of the Conference on Computer Supported Cooperative Work (CSCW 2000)*. Philadelphia, PA: ACM.

Nichols, J., Wobbrock, J., Gergle, D., and Forlizzi, J. (2002). "Mediator and medium: Doors as interruption gateways and aesthetic displays". *Proceedings of DIS2002*. New York: ACM.

O'Hara, K., Harper, R., Unger, A., Wilkes, J., Sharpe, B., and Jansen, M. (2005). "Txtboard: From text-to-person to text-to-home". *Proceedings of Conference on Human Factors in Computing Systems (CHI 2005)*. New York: ACM.

O'Hara, K., Perry, M., and Lewis, S. (2003). "Social coordination around a situated display appliance". *Proceedings of Conference on Human Factors in Computing Systems (CHI 2003)*. New York: ACM.

Pedersen, E. R., and Sokoler, T. (1997). "AROMA: Abstract representation of presence supporting mutual awareness". *Proceedings of the Conference on Human factors in computing systems (CHI '97)*. New York: ACM.

Schmidt, K., and Bannon, L. (1992). "Taking CSCW seriously: Supporting articulation work". *Computer Supported Cooperative Work (CSCW): An International Journal*, 1 (1–2), 7–40.

Schmidt, K., and Simone, C. (2000). "Mind the gap! Towards a unified view of CSCW". *Proceedings of COOP2000, 4th International Conference on the Design of Cooperative Systems*. Sophia Antipolis, France: NRIA.

Weiser, M. (1991). "The computer for the 21st century". *Scientific American*, 265, 94–104.

Part IV
Evaluating Awareness Systems

Chapter 18
Supporting Family Awareness with the Whereabouts Clock

Abigail Sellen, Alex S. Taylor, Joseph 'Jofish' Kaye, Barry Brown, and Shahram Izadi

Abstract We report the results of a field trial of a situated awareness device for families called the "Whereabouts Clock". The Clock displays the location of family members using cellphone data as one of four privacy-preserving, deliberately coarse-grained categories (HOME, WORK, SCHOOL or ELSEWHERE). The results show that awareness of others through the Clock supports not only family communication and coordination but also more emotive aspects of family life such as reassurance, connectedness, identity and social touch. We discuss how the term "awareness" means many things in practice and highlight the importance of designing not just for family activities, but in order to support the emotional, social and even moral aspects of family life.

18.1 Introduction

Research is increasingly drawing attention to the fact that designing technologies for the home is and should be a very different kind of undertaking from designing for the workplace. Work within the field of Human–Computer Interaction shows how the relationships, roles and activities of people within the home differ strongly from those in the workplace (e.g. Hutchinson et al., 2003; O'Brien and Rodden, 1997; Plaisant et al., 2006; Taylor and Swan, 2005). Other studies highlight the fact that the value of information technology in the home must be thought of more broadly and quite differently from technology in the workplace, such as in a more open-ended, less task-focused way (e.g. Gaver et al., 2006; Sellen et al., 2006b). This means not only that some office-based technologies may be simply inappropriate in a home environment but also that there may be unexpected difficulties when transferring such technologies across domains. For example, transferring networking technology from the office to the home has uncovered a host of

A. Sellen (✉)
Microsoft Research, 7 JJ Thomson Ave., Cambridge, UK, CB3 OFB
e-mail: asellen@microsoft.com

P. Markopoulos et al. (eds.), *Awareness Systems*, Human-Computer Interaction Series, DOI 10.1007/978-1-84882-477-5_18, © Springer-Verlag London Limited 2009

novel difficulties and problems (Sheehan and Edwards, 2007). In addition, because relationships amongst individuals in the home are significantly different from relationships in the workplace, notions of privacy, security and identity are also fundamentally different in the two contexts. For example, the meanings of "privacy" in the home, particularly in the context of adolescent children, are richly interwoven with other issues such as the expression of identity in a family setting (March and Fleuriot, 2006).

One implication of this is that awareness systems too, with their early roots in workplace domains, should be conceptualized and developed differently for home settings. There have been, of course, in recent times, many interesting research projects which have begun to examine and build awareness systems for the home. Many have explored lightweight and inventive ways of connecting extended family members across households. Such projects include concepts which involve transmitting quite abstract kinds of data through simple tactile gestures (Hindus et al., 2001; Hutchinson et al., 2003; Strong and Gaver, 1996) or through messaging (Hutchinson et al., 2003; Romero et al., 2007). Others have looked at the use of simple movement sensors within the home to connect elderly people with their distributed families (Consolvo et al., 2004; Mynatt et al., 2001). Common to these systems is that they aim to help bind friends and family together remotely and help people who are geographically separated feel more connected. Such systems also tend to involve ambient, situated devices that are interacted with in a peripheral way within the home environment.

The work reported here takes a somewhat different tack in focusing on how household members might connect with their *own* homes through an awareness device. Additionally, we focus on the use of location information of family members outside the house as a way to do so. Using this approach, we aim to deepen our understanding of the potential of technology to provide awareness of location and how this is transformed and used within the domestic environment. Thus one goal of this research is to build on previous work in awareness systems to further define what supporting awareness might mean for home life and to open up new kinds of technical possibilities as a result.

However, the results of this research also have implications more generally for ubiquitous computing or "Ubicomp" (Weiser, 1991). The use of location data in developing location-based services and devices is of course an extremely active area of research within the Ubicomp community. Here, the technical problems involved in tracking individuals and devices have generated a rich body of research (e.g. Anderson and Muller, 2006; Chen et al., 2006), as has the potential for new applications based on an awareness of one's own and others' geographical position (e.g. Brown et al., 2005; Harper et al., 1992; Romero et al., 2007). Studies of these systems have generated a range of issues for design, in particular how location awareness can conflict with privacy needs (e.g. Consolvo et al., 2005; Iachello et al., 2005). In studying how a different kind of location-based system, namely one situated in the home, is used, we additionally hope to offer a new perspective on the kinds of issues that Ubicomp has become concerned with. For more details of this discussion, see Brown et al. (2007).

The research we report in this chapter focuses on a device called the "Whereabouts Clock" (from here on referred to as "the Clock" or "the WAC"). The WAC is distinct in some sense in that it blurs the boundaries between awareness systems in the home and tracking applications. Specifically, we deliberately designed the WAC to offer *less* functionality than many existing tracking systems – communicating location with less accuracy than existing systems (such as GPS systems) and displaying information only within the home environment. In this sense, the WAC was more like a low-bandwidth awareness system than a tracking system. Further, similar to many of the home awareness systems we have discussed, the WAC was also designed as a situated device, to be attended to at a glance and in the periphery of attention within the home environment.

We present results from a field trial of the Clock with five families (26 users) over a total period of 6 months. As we will show, awareness, at least as demonstrated through the Clock, was not really about communicating geographical location or even activity. Rather it was about displaying information to support what families *already know* about each other and already share. More specifically, the value of the Clock came as much from the reassurance that knowing things are as one expects them to be as it did from dealing with exceptions or changing plans. This, we argue, is part and parcel of family life. Part of the "work" of being a family is to know what goes on and to know how things are. With the WAC, families were able to use location information to demonstrate their care for and attention to each other.

Drawing on this we argue that the design of awareness systems needs to take into account what awareness might mean in a family context. This study shows that awareness is a multi-faceted concept, playing into many important aspects of family life. It also shows how location awareness, as part of family life, is an emotional and moral affair as much as it is a tool for coordination or practicality. This opens up new technological possibilities for supporting home and family life.

18.2 Related Work

This work draws on the substantial body of research in the social sciences that investigates home and family life. Broadly, our ideas have been influenced by research that takes seriously the "work" put into the social organization of the family home. The underlying basis of this position is that family homes are not magically ordered places but rather places that take work to craft and sustain. Time, and often thought and care, is put into tidying, cleaning, feeding, planning, coordinating and generally ordering the household and its inhabitants so that it comes to feel like a home, at least to those who live there (e.g. Cowan, 1983; DeVault, 1994; Martin, 1984; Wood and Beck, 1994). Even a family's forms of talk – their negotiations, arguments, teasings, displays of affections and so on – play into this "doing" of family and home (Aronsson, 2006). Key here is the idea that the home's order is not always intentionally worked on. In a prosaic fashion, it is the everyday domestic chores, routines and so on that give shape to a home or, more specifically, the home as an idea or ideal (Douglas, 1991). Home is thus actively produced, a practical accomplishment of the ordinary and taken-for-granted doings and comings and goings of its members – their rituals and rhythms, if you will (Gubrium, 1988; Highmore, 2004).

As we have suggested, the presented work can be similarly located in research within the Human–Computer Interaction and UbiComp literature that has gradually sought to examine home and family life in detail. To list just a few examples, there is relatively early work on social communication practices in the home (Hindus et al., 2001) and similarly focused research from Crabtree and Rodden (2004) in which they examine domestic communication routines. Grinter and colleagues (2005) have tended to concentrate on, in the main, the practicalities of technology adoption and use in the home, but their studies of home networks do reveal how family members can understand and orient themselves towards technology in different ways. Recently, a small trend has emerged in studying aspects of home life that are culturally specific (e.g. Bell and Dourish, 2007; Woodruff et al., 2007). Although distinct in many ways, what this range of work has in common and what we broadly aim to incorporate in this chapter is a careful consideration of how technology plays into the social organization of the home, how, in short, it can both shape and be shaped by the social context it is situated in.

With regard to the underlying design of the technology, the WAC sits at the cross-section of location-based services and situated displays. As well as a longstanding research topic, there are now a number of commercial location-based services available in the marketplace, many of which provide a variety of ways of monitoring children and friends. For example, many cellphone service providers and operators are now leveraging location information as value-added services for their customers. Sprint's FINDME and Helio's Buddy Beacon (Hamilton, 2007) allow people to locate other cellphone users in the same network cell. Other social networking systems, such as Dodgeball (www.dodgeball.com), use text messaging to help people locate friends who are geographically nearby without relying on operator support. Some of these systems have a fringe following of dedicated users, but most are far from widespread. Many factors have impacted the broad adoption of these systems, including privacy concerns, technical issues, lack of a user base and more general usability issues with the technology.

Location and user tracking are also prevalent areas of research in the Ubicomp and mobile computing literature. An early example was the Active Badge system, originally concerned with the ways in which the capture of real-time location information could support life within office buildings (Harper et al., 1992). More recently, with advances in wireless networks, many different kinds of applications have been developed, but more centred on the consumer than on the office or the mobile worker. Some use location as a way of delivering context-sensitive information to tourists and shoppers (Brown et al., 2005). Others are more properly called "tracking applications" in that they focus on the delivery of location information itself. Popular applications here include ways of supporting gaming, friendship and family (Smith et al., 2005). Further, because of the potentially sinister connotations of "tracking" or "monitoring", much of this research is preoccupied with aspects of privacy (Iachello et al., 2005). Common to all of these applications is that location information is typically delivered to the same hand-held devices that generate that information (such as to cellphones or PDAs).

In contrast, the situated display literature reports an altogether different set of concerns, many of which have to do with the use of large displays designed to support community, whether it be in corporate life or urban settings (O'Hara et al., 2003). A few have explored ways of presenting information about location, but these do not normally relate to real-time data, confining themselves instead to calendar-based information, where, for example, grandparents are offered views of events affecting their grandchildren (Mynatt et al., 2001).

The separation of these two literatures can be linked to the different affordances being leveraged in each case: for the location-based services literature, it tends to be about the production and display of accurate information "on the hoof", where having that information in hand is paramount. For the situated display literature, the topic is how the persistent and "at-a-glance" display of information provides benefits in locations where the information is public or shared and is stable through time. In this research, the WAC brings these two sets of concerns together by combining the use of situated displays that afford persistent, at-a-glance access to information with the dynamic, real-time production of that information.

18.3 Designing a Location Awareness System for the Family

The idea of a clock displaying location rather than time is one that fans of Harry Potter will instantly recognize. In J.K. Rowling's books, the "Weasley" family has a magic clock with hands for each member of the family indicating their location or state. Partly inspired by this vision, we became convinced that designing a situated device with clock-like properties had some compelling affordances that helped to turn a "tracking" system into something more akin to a situated awareness device. The clock metaphor thus guided many of the major design decisions:

First, we wanted the WAC to be a situated display designed to be located in a place in the home (like the kitchen) where it becomes part of the routine of family life, much as a clock does. We wanted the interface to let families see information "at a glance"; that is, without time spent turning the device on or changing the settings to view its status. This meant that the WAC's display would be "always on", persisting in the periphery of vision in the way that information on a clock persists.

Again, as with a clock, we wanted the WAC to broadcast information to anyone in sight of the device (as opposed to a watch, for example, which is a personal device). However, although we wanted such information to be "publicly available" within the house, we decided that it should not be viewed remotely. This decision was one of our attempts to deal with the privacy issues that plague location-based systems and meant that only people entitled to be in the home would be able to see the device. This would act as a crude, yet very straightforward, form of access control, which we thought would help to allay families' concerns about privacy (even though, as we discuss later, this concern was perhaps overplayed in our design).

Lastly, we wanted the WAC to display only coarse-grained information (i.e. it shows only that a family member is at "home", at "work", at "school" or in an unlabelled region meaning "out" or "elsewhere"). We reasoned that for much of family life, precise location is not necessary: planning a meal, knowing someone is on their way home or being reassured a child is at school can be done with a relatively crude indication of location. Precise information might also be more intrusive of people's privacy. While this aspect is not necessarily clock-like, we felt it to be an important aspect of its design. The WAC in a sense gives as *little* information about location as possible, rather than striving for accuracy or richness in what it communicates.

In developing the WAC, we iterated through a number of different interfaces and physical forms in order to produce a prototype that families would be drawn to and want to have in their homes. An important step was an internal trial with an early version of the Clock that we tested with our own work group (Sellen et al., 2006). Another key step was to take early versions of the Clock home to try out over extended periods of time in our own households. As a result of this early testing, we made many refinements both to the underlying technology and to the design. However, the essential nature of its design, including the use of the clock metaphor, remained unchanged.

Figure 18.1 shows the final design of the WAC. The Clock itself is displayed on a tablet PC with touch input encased in a box made to look similar to that of a mantelpiece clock. The tablet is wirelessly connected via a GSM modem to a cellular network. In addition, a small physical "flap" hides softkeys for controlling both the volume of the Clock's chimes and the brightness of the display; a moving "pendulum" also showing signal strength. The Clock interface presents an animated representation of family location where members of the household are represented by icons linked to the location of their cellphones. Because we wanted engagement with the device to require minimal effort on the part of users from day to day, users have only to switch on their cellphones and the bespoke application starts running. When this happens, each user's icon appears bright and animated (appearing to "float" within each zone). If a user switches off either the application or the phone, their icon fades and becomes static. The WAC uses GSM cell ID available on cellphones to provide the location data. In this version, participants used Windows Mobile Smartphones running a custom client application (usually in addition to their own phones).

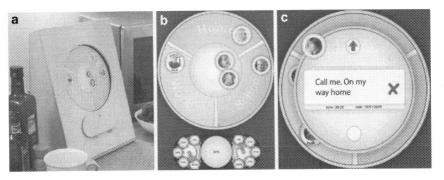

Fig. 18.1 Whereabouts Clock in its case (**a**), the interface (**b**), close-up of message window (**c**)

When at home, work or school, users need to first register or label these zones on their phones through a simple menu in the phone application. Upon registration, the Smartphone application records the underlying cell tower IDs within the proximity for that particular zone. Whenever the phone is switched on, the application continually scans for cell towers in range and maps the ID with strongest match onto a registered zone (indicating it as "out" if no zone has been registered for that ID). Updates are sent via SMS to the WAC display whenever the application determines that a person has moved from one registered zone to another. When this occurs, the Clock chimes to draw the attention to the move. After registering or labelling certain key locations using the phone as one of the three named zones, there is no further need to interact with the application. However, users were told that if they wanted they could change at any time what places they had set for the three different labels of "home", "work" and "school". For example, they could re-register any place as "school".

A final feature of the Clock was the ability for family members to send text messages from their cellphones to the Clock at home, a feature we added as a result of our initial trials. When a new text message arrives, the first couple of words rotate around the icon of the person who sent it and its arrival is signalled by the sound of a cuckoo clock. People at home can then touch the icon, and a window appears showing the whole message, time it was sent and labelled location from which it was sent. With this window open, users can also look back at past messages and delete unwanted ones. As a final part of the design, to include family members without cellphones (such as small children), we added icons which could be moved by hand and which played random animations and sounds when touched.

18.4 Trial Method

Our approach was to deploy the Clock into only a few households and observe its use over an extended period of time in order to see how households might adapt to and appropriate this new technology. We installed the Clock in five family homes for a period of at least 1 month with each family. Two of the families were particularly enthusiastic about the technology, so we left the Clocks with them for 2 months. In total, we ended up studying 26 family members with use ranging anywhere from 4 to 9 weeks. Households were selected from the local Cambridge area in which at least three members of the family owned cellphones and which had established practice of "texting" (or sending SMS messages) via their cellphones to each other. The households we selected cut across socioeconomic class and were idiosyncratic in many respects:

- **Household A** consisted of two parents with two boys, aged 11 and 13, and a lodger in his twenties. All had cellphones. The mother worked at a local school in Cambridge. The father, a vicar, lived 3 days a week in his parish vicarage in north London (an hour's drive away), but the main family home was in Cambridge.

The youngest son was in boarding school during the week in Cambridge, coming home only on weekends. The other son attended the local secondary school. The Clock was installed in the Cambridge house.

- **Household B** consisted of two parents with two boys aged 11 and 18 and one daughter aged 17, all living at home. The mother worked in teaching support and part-time for a local charity, and the father worked as an aerospace manager, having a long commute to and from work. The children were all at school. All three, but particularly the eldest two, were very active and relatively independent from the rest of the family.
- **Household C** consisted of two parents (a nurse and an IT consultant) and four children, a young boy aged 9, an older boy aged 12 (who lived with his mother outside the home we studied), a daughter aged 15 and a daughter aged 17, who had just started university in a different town, but who came home outside term time.
- **Household D** was a family of five: two parents, two daughters and one son (aged 13 and 15 years and 10 months, respectively). The father worked full-time in technical support at a small company and the mother part-time from home, welding parts onto circuit boards. Compared to the rest of the households, this family had the most unvaried routine. The daughters attended a nearby school and reported no extracurricular activities. The mother spent most weekdays at home looking after her young son and housekeeping.
- **Household E** consisted of two retired parents and one 18-year-old son living at home. Two WAC-enabled phones were also given to this family's 22-year-old daughter and her boyfriend, who lived together several miles away. The father spent much of his time at home, while the mother walked the household dog several miles each day and spent time gardening, either at home or in a garden allotment some distance from the house. The son was in the last year of high school and also worked part-time. The daughter worked locally and would visit several times a week after work and before returning to her boyfriend's. The boyfriend worked in a city 1 h away by train and often returned home late.

On the first visit to the households, the WAC was installed and family members were shown how to use it. In addition, they were provided with an instruction and trouble-shooting sheet. Data were gathered through a series of interviews at approximately 1 week intervals, which we scheduled with as many members of each family present as possible. On these visits, the families were asked questions about how they had used the Clock, how they felt about being tracked and whether they had sent text messages to the Clock. In addition, printouts of the sent messages provided a focus for further discussion. Questions were also directed at how, if at all, the Clock and messaging facility interleaved with household activities and routines. In the final interview, we asked all family members to imagine different possibilities for a whereabouts device, seeking comments and criticisms and directions for novel design ideas. All interviews were audio taped for later review and the interviews transcribed.

18.5 Results

The results of the trial can be viewed in a number of different ways. On the one hand, if this had been simply a test of a new prototype technology, the results were encouraging. Generally, we found each household made substantial use of the Clock, although family members did at times forget to carry their extra cellphones with them or to keep them charged. On average, participants' phones were tracked on 72% of trial days, ranging from a minimum of 47% to a maximum of 80% of trial days. In addition, each family member sent on average 1.6 messages per week to the Clock during the trial. However, perhaps a better testament to the use of the Clock was some families' distress at losing the Clock at the end of the trial. As one family put it: "We're going to miss it" – the Clock had become an almost integral part of their routines.

Having said that, the technology was not always as robust and reliable as we hoped – in particular, sometimes family members were seen to move in and out of different zones due to technical problems. As we will discuss later, these problems sometimes caused needless anxiety. The families also commented on various ways in which the design of the Clock could have been improved. For example, there was general agreement on how useful it would be to be able to send messages back *from* the Clock to individual people. This is a design feature which we could easily incorporate into future versions of the Clock.

Overall, however, the Clock proved to be a much more valued and compelling technology for the trial families than we had anticipated. Therefore, if we had been purely in the business of trying to develop a new product, we would have a strong case to make for pursuing this basic concept, albeit with the need to improve the robustness of the technology and to tweak the design.

But the lessons from this trial run deeper than this. In particular, by looking at the various ways in which the Clock was used and the reasons why it was valued, we can start to unpack the concept of "awareness" for families, at least in the ways that the Clock enabled it. As we will discuss in this section, awareness of other family members' movements supported not only *coordination* but also a set of values more emotive in nature. Awareness was also intimately connected to feelings of *reassurance, connectedness* and *togetherness* for these families. Aspects of *identity* and *social touch* came into play as well. All of these issues highlighted by the Clock, as we will argue, cause us to be more precise about what we mean by awareness and what aspects of family life are really at stake when we design such devices.

18.5.1 Unpacking Awareness in a Family Context

18.5.1.1 Coordination and Communication

The focus of most work on awareness emanating from workplace domains has been to support coordination and communication within the context of collaborative tasks. By conveying information about activity to one another, users can work more collaboratively, for example, when working remotely with one another (Dourish and

Bellotti, 1992) or when planning and coordinating activities (Nardi et al., 2000). Because of this, we fully expected the WAC to be used in the coordination and management of family activities. Indeed household members spoke of the ways in which they could better plan activities such as preparing meals by being able to see when someone was on their way home. In one case, a father reported how the WAC had informed him of his wife's early return home when he had expected her to miss dinner. This allowed him to offer an affectionate gesture by having dinner ready for her when she walked in the door. Households also made a number of references to what Household E called "put-the-kettle-on" movements on the Clock. Here, household members leaving a region or moving into HOME on the Clock (before they had physically arrived) would prompt those at home to put the kettle on for tea. Important here was an awareness of the household's rhythms: movements were "read" in different ways depending on the time of day and knowledge of the household routines. Trisha, the mother in Household E, captured this in describing an example of Clock use related to her son, Jon:

> A few times Jon has not left a message and around about quarter to six-ish I've seen his photo move up to HOME and I've thought "ooh, Jon is coming home," and I've had a cup of tea ready for him before he's even walked in the house.

Significantly, with the coarse granularity of position that the Clock communicated (not least to mention the underlying positioning algorithm), we noted that nearly all these readings of the Clock were "fail safe" – in that if they were wrong, the cost would be very low (such as a kettle boiled in vain). However, the messaging feature of the Clock was often used in coordination tasks when more precise information might be needed or in order for someone to account for their location on the Clock. Messages such as: "Just at the train station. X"; "In a meeting 4 next few hours"; "M11 accident, taking back roads" and "Jus walkin down road now. Sum1 stick kettle on;-p" fell squarely in this category. The last of the messages above also illustrates that not only could people reading the Clock use this information to plan activities but also those sending messages home could try to direct other people's activities more explicitly. Thus with the messaging, we saw a number of "calls to action" such as "Mum phone"; "Shopping done help please" and "Time for bed".

Inasmuch as activities such as making tea, making a meal or helping with shopping can be thought of as "collaborative tasks", the Clock functioned in a way that one might expect it to do so in a work environment. Here awareness of others' activities helped with issues such as the timing and planning of activities, and in doing so, could be seen to help some of events in the household to run more smoothly. However, the next four categories of use are more interesting in that they are not about tasks and also because they were talked about as more significant.

18.5.1.2 Reassurance

While coordination is perhaps the most obvious use of an awareness technology, the Clock was distinctive in that the most remarked upon benefit was the *reassurance* it provided for family members, and further emphasizes the differences between technologies for the workplace and for the home. Families regularly described, in both explicit and implicit ways, the Clock as reassuring:

> So I just come in and you know, "yep, everybody's in the right place. All's right with the world", you know, just at a glance... It's just umm, it is just nice. It's not checking up on people. It's just a nice little reassurance. Everyone's where they should be and everything's right, or at least their phones are in the right place [laughs]. I mean, you know, you can take these things too far... but you're not using it as a security device like that.

The WAC invoked not simply a reassurance of family members being at the right place at the right time, but also an overriding sense that everything was *going to routine*, that *all was well*. As expressed above there is a sense "that everything's right" in looking at the Clock and seeing that everyone is where they should be. Rachel, the mother in Household C, expressed, evocatively, something similar in talking about her eldest daughter away at university:

> When you can't visualize where your offspring are, you have this ridiculous sense of anxiety that's just bubbling very quietly. [...] I think in some way the Clock helps me think "yes, they've definitely got there, and they're definitely there now, and they're on their way home".

The Clock, then, appears to put Rachel at ease, providing reassurance of her distant daughter's whereabouts. Again, it was not that the Clock did this by providing precise geographical coordinates. As Rachel put it, the Clock was simply an additional tool for visualizing – a means of gleaning just enough information, as it were. Something we had not expected was how the Clock's chimes also played into this sense of reassurance. The Clock would be glanced at or approached when it chimed to see who it was that had moved and where they had moved from and to. Indeed, families spoke of being drawn almost compulsively to the Clock because of the chimes it made – parents who spent large portions of their days at home felt particularly strongly about the chimes. Meg, for instance, chose to place the Clock in her living room so that she could easily glance over to it whenever it chimed:

> There's just some sort of thing where you've got to see what – you know, it makes that noise that someone's moved and you just have to look. I don't know why. You just have to look.

Whatever be the underlying motivations, it appears reassurance came from being able to see the family as active and from seeing a family's movements to be in keeping with known-about routines. The coarseness of the location *works*, so to speak, because the ways of seeing or reading the Clock are deeply enmeshed with what family members already know and indeed have rights to know. What we see through the use of the Clock is that family members are able to intuit a state of affairs using relatively crude types of information. It is unclear in the design of the Clock whether more details or a higher level of accuracy in location would have provided a greater degree of reassurance. This led us to reflect on the fact that location is not purely a set of geographical coordinates; it is not valued for how precise those coordinates can be, but rather how location fits into the "family geography" of where the family is or more particularly, where the family *should be*.

18.5.1.3 Connectedness and Togetherness

Tied closely to the sense of reassurance associated with the Clock was another salient theme that emerged from our interviews, that of *connectedness* and *togetherness*. Much of this aspect of awareness clearly came from the graphical representation of each family member and the fact that the family was shown to "be together" at least in the sense of sharing the same display, when much of the time they were, in reality, not in the same place.

Whilst having the Clock, family members spoke of how it helped them to feel connected to those out of the house. In Meg's glances at the Clock (noted above), for example, she gained a sense of what other family members were "up to" and, in turn, gained a sense of connection with them. For Trisha (mother in Household E), the persistently displayed information also provided a way of feeling connected to those who were out. In her words, "It just keeps you that little bit closer all the while."

Other households adopted a more purposeful approach to using the Clock as a means of connection. For Household A, distributed across three different "homes", the mother, Jo, expressed a particular sense of how the Clock allowed her to feel connected to her family even when they were apart. She talked about how seeing the family members together on the Clock presented everybody being in the same place even when they were not – a virtual sense of everybody together. The Clock explicitly connected family members who while at homes in different parts of the country were still connected with what Jo saw as their *real* home.

This fleeting yet emotive aspect of the Clock was reiterated time and again in our interviews. In a fashion reminiscent of displayed family photos, the Clock provided a recurrent visual reminder of a family's togetherness. Indeed, the temporal rhythms that the Clock visualized brought out these moments of togetherness – particularly at poignant times such as dinner time. As Dan, the father in Household C put it, seeing everybody "nestling" together at the top of the Clock each night (even though some of his children were in different homes) gave him a strong sense of family unity.

One issue was that the reverse was also true in that it could instil moments of anxiety and separation from family members. Householders reported feeling worried when others in the household appeared where they should not be or were moving when they should be in one place. These feelings were elevated when, on occasion, the positioning algorithm would find itself on an edge and "flutter" between two different locations.

18.5.1.4 Expressing Identity

So far we have noted important ways in which household members came to see or "read" the WAC. We also found participants giving thought to how they were represented on the Clock to others – in other words, how they *expressed their identity* to others. This aspect of the Clock's use emphasizes how awareness is not just about the interpretation of data as a viewer or a receiver of information, but it is also about one's accountability to others. In other words, awareness is, in some sense, a two-way street.

For example, common was the way in which households appropriated the Clock's three location labels, HOME, WORK and SCHOOL, to control how they were seen and to suit their particular needs. Household E (where neither parent worked) presented perhaps the most extreme example of this. All but the son, Jon, labelled places in unexpected ways; the daughter assigned both her boyfriend's house and family house as HOME, and the local train station, where she picked her boyfriend up after work, as SCHOOL. The mother, who was not working, used SCHOOL to refer to her walking the dog (registering several spots along her usual walk as SCHOOL). She also used WORK to refer to gardening either in the garden attached to the house or in the family's garden allotment some distance from their home. While at home, the retired father would regularly use his cellphone to register himself as either at WORK or HOME depending on what he was doing.

Striking, here, was the ease with which they incorporated these inflexible labels into their household routines. We gave only minimal instructions to families on how to assign different geographical locations to the three available labels. Even so, all but one of the households used the labels to designate something else, or assigned multiple geographical locations to one label, and did so with no apparent problems or need for technical assistance. These adaptations were often based on subtle use of geographical location. Registering two different gardens as the single label WORK and an activity (dog walking) rather than a distinct place to SCHOOL seemed, if anything, a somewhat playful use of the Clock for Household E's mother, Trisha (a self-professed technophobe). It was also dealt with in stride by the rest of the family who knew what these labels meant and had no difficulty knowing where she was or what she was doing. Arguably, it was the coarseness of detail on the Clock that prevented the complexity from being overwhelming. It would seem the detail was sufficient to allow for a rough idea of location to be simply deduced. As several of our participants reported, if more detail was required, other channels of communication were available, such as a text message to the Clock or a phone call.

Indeed, some family members went as far as to use their reported location as a way of identifying their activities and expressing them to others. The father in Household E, Ted, moved himself on the Clock between WORK and HOME – re-registering his location each time he moved from using his computer to watching television – not unlike the use of availability messages in Instant Messaging. However, it also actively asserted a sense of social position or what might be termed, rather grandly, *identity*. Ted, if you like, was demonstrably composing his position vis-à-vis his family. This marking of social position in the home parallels the practice of *broadcasting identity* we have written about previously (Sellen et al., 2006). But it also shows how awareness systems can be as much a way of allowing people to express themselves, as they can be a way for people to interpret the actions of others.

18.5.1.5 Social Touch

A final recurring use of the Clock worth noting amongst the households relates to what we have in the past referred to as "social touch", where technology is used as a channel through which family members express affection for one another (Sellen et al., 2006). In this way, family members *demonstrate* their awareness of others and in doing so display the ties that bind them together.

Many of the examples of coordination we have described have strong elements of social touch, such as having a cup of tea or a meal ready for someone when they come through the door. However, this showed itself most explicitly in the messages family members sent to the WAC. There were obvious examples such as "Good morning all;-p" and "Nite nite every1. Cold nite here. B careful on the roads 2moro." In other cases, messages would be sent for some other purpose but would incorporate an element of social touch, a flourish, if you like, denoting one's thought for others. A particularly nice example of this was sent by Peter, the lodger staying at Household A. His message is to one of the family's young sons: "Harry, there's some hot chocolate in my cupboard if you'd like some. Hope you're not feeling too poorly, Peter". Peter is clearly making a thoughtful gesture in offering his hot chocolate to Harry. Interesting for us is his use of the Clock to do so. As with the "fail safe" use of the Clock for coordination, it appears such messages are not critical and have no immediate function. Instead, they simply add a distinct feel to a family and the relationships its members have with one another. From this perspective, it is worth noting that some of the households were far more emotionally demonstrative in their messaging on the Clock. Households A and E, for example, routinely sent messages appearing to supplement the "all is OK" status suggested by the display of people's whereabouts. On occasion, then, we saw the messaging via the Clock, perhaps unsurprisingly, weaves its way into family relations, playing its part in the emotional repartee between family members; as with so many practical things in the home, the Clock came to offer a resource for playing out its social organization.

18.5.2 Privacy

A final important aspect of the results has to do with privacy and the attitudes that the trial families expressed in response to this issue. Any tracking or location-based application inevitably raises a number of concerns with regard to potential of invasion of people's privacy. In part, this is due to the increasing ways in which our lives are tracked electronically and considerable public worry about how such information could be abused (Iachello et al., 2005). Privacy measures thus have featured prominently in location awareness prototypes. In the design of the WAC, we sought to address these concerns through both the fixed single location of the Clock, at home, and the limited coarse-grained information it shared.

At the very least, privacy concerns did not seem to inhibit the family's usage of the Clock. Indeed, despite repeated questioning, none of the families reported being concerned about a loss of privacy. In part, participants' comments led us to believe that the coarse-grained resolution of the tracking information helped considerably. One teenager put it this way:

Yeah, so a lot of my friends have said "So your parents are checking up on you" like. I said nah this is not that. It's not accurate enough. It doesn't tell you exactly where I am so I can go places and they won't know where I am.

But further than this, our repeated questioning around privacy was met with puzzlement by the families. As they explained, the Clock displayed information that they already shared. Thus the WAC was not seen as intruding any further into what they already knew or needed to know. Even questions about access to the Clock from outside the home failed to provoke worries about privacy. When asked about losing a phone that could display the Clock's information, Kris phrases this point well:

Well you get over don't you? It's the same thing as losing your phone anyway. And anyway, would it really matter? They don't know who it is, they don't know what "home" means, they don't, you know it doesn't bear any relation to anybody else that doesn't know.

It was only when we suggested radically more open designs – such as sharing location information with everybody on the Internet ("like MySpace" as one family put it) – that we could get families to object. As for the possibility of hackers, or malicious access to the tracking information provided by the WAC, again it was pointed out to us that the level of detail the Clock provided was only something that really made sense to those who knew a household's routines, namely close family and friends.

While not to downplay the tensions and pressures of family life, the reactions we received around privacy reflect the fact that family life is built significantly around shared awareness, without which much of the everyday coordination of the family (eating, driving children around, sharing costs and so on) would be impossible. As Martin (1984) describes so astutely, the knowledge and the control of a household's comings and goings are concerns continually being brokered, but, nevertheless, the very idea of home is built upon knowing and controlling just such matters. While it is possible that the families we studied were atypical, or indeed that the trial failed to encompass events where violations of privacy did arise, it could also be that privacy is more of a concern for us as researchers than it is of practical concern to families.

18.6 Awareness and Family Life

The results of this trial do two things: on the one hand, they highlight aspects of awareness that in many ways go beyond the concept as originally defined and explored in workplace contexts. This builds on and complements existing work on awareness systems in home contexts. On the other hand, the Clock and the way in which awareness played out within the family context offer us a lens through which we can begin to better understand what families are about. Despite its relatively primitive technical features, the practices we saw involving the Clock highlighted particular aspects of a family's routines and how the monitoring and the accountability of these routines are important elements in a family's ongoing sense of itself.

In technical terms, it should be evident that the version of the WAC we deployed incorporated a very basic capacity to support location awareness. The Clock's reliance on cell towers to locate users (or more specifically their phones) meant its accuracy was limited at best, and often not something to be rigidly relied on. The Clock's interface, with its coarse-grained representation of people's whereabouts, added a further degree of ambiguity. Indeed, by providing only two bits of information, as we described earlier, its resolution was crude.

Mindful of these technical limitations, we were struck by how our study's participating families readily incorporated the Clock into their routines. As we have noted, our early expectation was that the Clock would offer households a means of "seeing" and subsequently acting on exceptions to routines: when someone was not where they should be, was late to school or home and so on. Instead, the Clock was quickly incorporated into broader household patterns; householders would glance towards it in their routine movements around their homes and during their regular comings and goings. As indicated above, a casual reassurance was had from almost all of the household's parents by looking at the Clock at particular times of day and, sometimes, orienting their movements around the Clock's chimes. A form of being aware of family members' whereabouts seeped into and on occasion transformed the daily routines of our participating homes.

In considering this incorporation of the WAC into household routines, we came to see the Clock as providing more than merely location awareness. The families did not seem to be simply checking on where, geographically, any one person was in their glances towards the Clock. It seemed they were also locating family members with respect to their household rhythms. For example, when family members looked at the Clock to see another's whereabouts, they in a sense "read" what this meant about the recipient, taking into account what they knew and understood about that family member's context.

In one example reported to us, the mother of Household A, Jo, cycled home after work over a bridge that crossed a local river. This area she had previously labelled as SCHOOL as this was the regular site where she practiced rowing. SCHOOL was therefore known by the family to mean "Mum is rowing". Yet as she cycled home that night, the brief appearance of her on the Clock as being in the region of SCHOOL was not interpreted by the rest of the family as rowing, but rather as where in particular she was on her route home from work.

Awareness through the Clock thus fed into, if you like, a sense of being aware, of knowing family members' whereabouts in terms of not just where but also for what, when, with whom and so on. In a recent paper at UbiComp 2007, we used the phrase *location-in-interaction* to distinguish the simple physical location of people from how location is worked up as a category in social interaction (Brown et al., 2007). A similar distinction can be made in reflecting on awareness vis-à-vis the clock. We saw different forms of awareness made manifest through the WAC, which were not dictated by a specific attribute like physical or geographical location. Rather, awareness was worked up through family members actively interleaving the many and sometimes competing traces or threads of their everyday routines. Awareness was a *mental geography*, so to speak, of a home's members and their rhythms. In other words, the WAC reflected and supported an awareness of a "geography" that was not so much physical as it was in the collective "minds" of each family.

It is this last point that returns us to the issue that we began this chapter with: trying to understand awareness in terms of its importance for people in particular places (in this case, families in homes). From what we saw of the WAC in our study, it appears that the Clock was incorporated into an awareness of what it is to be a family, of the expectations its members have and of the ideas they have of how to coordinate, connect, express identity and ultimately reassure each other through these acts. Indeed, the Clock appeared to play into all of the things that family members undertake anyway as a matter of course. This is why Kris, when asked whether it would be problematic if she lost her phone, merely shrugged it off. If a stranger were to find it, it would not be a problem as "they don't know what 'home' means, they don't, you know, it doesn't bear any relation to anybody else that doesn't know." In short, the WAC provided for a form of awareness that emerges through one being in a household and coming to know how location, time and routines interleave in unique and distinctly meaningful ways.

18.7 Implications

Finally, it is interesting at this point to reflect on the early history of the topic of awareness within Human–Computer Interaction and to examine how far we have come. Dourish and Bellotti provided one of the earliest papers on the topic (Dourish and Bellotti, 1992), coming strictly from a work-oriented perspective and highlighting the importance of awareness as a topic in developing and designing collaborative work tools. For them, awareness was "an understanding of the activities of others, which provides a context for your own activity." This definition was, at the time, a succinct way of describing the concept, and the paper was influential in calling attention to aspects of awareness that need to be supported in order to successfully enable the accomplishment of group work. Much of the research that followed in that decade and beyond assumed a similar, task-focused approach.

Since that time, as HCI has made forays outside the of the work context and into domains such as the home, what we see is that the concept of awareness begins to take on a variety of different meanings. This research and other projects concerning more with the inter-connection of family and friends begins to reveal awareness as a richer and more diverse topic. The trial we report in this chapter, for example, has shown that awareness is an important concept above and beyond the accomplishment of shared tasks. Furthermore, it shows that awareness is more than simply supporting the mutual understanding of the activities of other people. Rather, when we begin to consider and explore aspects of awareness within the context of family life, it begins to emerge under many different guises and in many different roles. Awareness is not an abstract category but rather a lived process of relationship to others that is experienced by family members.

This manifests itself in the ways in which the WAC was used for processes of coordination and communication of short-term family activities: putting the kettle on for a homecoming family member or using the messaging function to arrange a pickup at the railway station. In some ways, these collaborative tasks of "doing family" resemble activities found in the workplace, and the families' use of the WAC bears resemblance to the uses of awareness technologies that others have observed in the workplace.

However, one important implication of this work is that awareness as is played out in family life may be more about the confirmation of what families already know about one another than it is about conveying or imparting information that is not known. Reassurance, we found, was key to why the Clock was valued in the families we studied. Thus, unlike a groupware tool where the sharing of the moment-by-moment communication of activities can help a group work towards a goal, with the WAC, what can be gleaned in a moment (or a glance) is instantly interpreted with respect to a wealth of intimate knowledge about how things ought to be.

A second implication of this study is that awareness in family context is bound up with the demonstration and display of a family's emotional connectedness with one another. Here, the WAC was used not always as an indication of family members' various locations but as a symbolic representation and reminder of their togetherness in a conceptual if not a physical sense. Awareness in this way takes on a new meaning. The graphical representation of each person in the family sharing a single display reinforced ideal notions of the family as a unit, impinging itself and drawing attention to itself visually. Likewise, the examples of parents who liked to see that all their children were "home", even if those homes were distinct geographical places, give us a new twist on awareness. It highlighted families' feelings of togetherness, showing how awareness can be just as much about emotional ties as it is about information. This is bolstered by the many examples of social touch: the WAC gave families new ways to show their affection for one another and also *to be seen* to be showing their affection. Awareness in this sense is about doing something demonstrable and visible to all the family and can provide insight into what it means for a family to consider themselves to be a family and the ways in which that sense of identity is made visible.

Third, the ways in which the Clock was used by family members to express something about themselves and account for themselves also show that awareness is not simply about how these displays are "read". Equally, they are about how people "write" to them. In other words, there were many examples of how different families appropriated the labels of the Clock to indicate to others something about their normal routines. Furthermore, family members showed their sensitivity to this by sending text messages to justify, reassure or otherwise make themselves accountable for actions which were out of the ordinary, which indicated something new about their status and so on.

Finally, there are important implications about privacy that this work helps to explicate. Whilst "tracking" has negative connotations and conjures up visions of abuse (or at the very least, intrusion), in the context of family life it takes on a different meaning. Here, tracking or location awareness finds its place within a broader context of awareness as being right and proper aspects of home life. It is right and proper for parents to know and care about where their children are, just as it is right and proper for children to be accountable for their actions. While there will always be tensions within the family as to what those accountabilities should be and where one draws the line, it is clear that the boundaries within a family unit are fundamentally different from those in working life, or even amongst friends. What we can therefore generalise from past studies of awareness in work domains with regard to privacy controls or guidelines is therefore questionable. The trade-off between awareness and privacy within family and home life needs to be understood on its own terms.

18.8 Conclusions

In this chapter we have focused on how a particular technology – the Whereabouts Clock – was integrated into family life. An extensive trial with the Clock in five households uncovered how it supported not just coordination and awareness, as commonly associated with location awareness systems, but rather reassurance, connectedness, expression of identity and social touch. These were not so much functional benefits as they were emotive ones– a feeling, as one of our participants put it, that "all is right with the world". The WAC supported these values without generating privacy concerns. It did this, in part, because of the coarse-grained information it communicated – an example of "less is more", offering enough functionality to fit with users' practices but not more than they needed or were comfortable with.

More generally, we have argued that the use of the Clock helps to elucidate aspects of awareness which go beyond and present a more diverse perspective on what awareness might mean and how technology can support it. We extend approaches that have been understood as "location-based computing" and "situated displays" by uncovering and emphasizing the ways in which families use and make sense of the WAC as part of being a family. In particular, we have shown that the complexities of family life are such that supporting it will involve technology embedded as much in the moral, emotional and caring aspects of family life as in the functional or technical. It is here we see the most interesting set of new challenges.

Beyond this, the results of this analysis, we hope, have offered a way of understanding what families and households are about. In this sense the Clock and its deployment have given us an excuse to examine a handful of households in some detail and to reflect on the practices that bind them together and make them tick. As such, we hope to have shown how situated awareness devices, such as the WAC, can serve as probes to help uncover and elucidate aspects of family life that are at once intuitively familiar and yet profoundly rich and complex.

Acknowledgements We are indebted to the families who gave generously of their time for this study. We are also grateful to Rachel Eardley for designing the Whereabouts Clock and to Richard Harper and Ken Wood for their valuable commentary and advice on an earlier version of this chapter.

References

Anderson, I. and Muller, H. (2006). Qualitative positioning for pervasive environments. *Third International Conference on Mobile Computing and Ubiquitous Networking (ICMU 2006)*, London, UK, 10–18.

Aronsson, K. (2006). Commentary 1. Doing family: An interactive accomplishment. *Text & Talk, 26*(4/5), 619–626.

Bell, G. and Dourish, P. (2007). Back to the shed: Gendered visions of technology and domesticity. *Personal Ubiquitous Computing, 11*(5), 373–381.

Brown, B., Chalmers, M., Bell, M., Macoll, I. and Hall, M. (2005). Sharing the square: Collaborative leisure on the city streets. *Proceedings of the 9th European Conference on Computer Supported Cooperative Work (ECSCW '05)*. Kluwer, Dordrecht, 427–429.

Brown, B., Taylor, A., Izadi, S., Sellen, A., Kaye, J. 'J.' and Eardley, R. (2007). Locating family values: A field trial of the Whereabouts Clock. *Proceedings of the 9th Int'l Conference on Ubiquitous Computing (UbiComp 2007)*. Insbruck, Austria, 354–371.

Chen, M., Sohn, T., Chmelev, D., Haehnel, D., Hightower, J., Hughes, J. and LaMarca, A., Potter, F., Smith, I., and Varshavsky, A. (2006). Practical metropolitan-scale positioning for GSM phones. *Proceedings of the 8th International Conference on Ubiquitous Computing (Ubicomp 2006)*, 225–242.

Consolvo, S., Smith, I., Matthews, T., LaMarca, A., Tabert, J. and Powledge, P. (2005). Location disclosure to social relations: Why, when, and what people want to share. *Proceedings of the SIGCHI Conference on Human Factors in Computing Systems (CHI '05)*. ACM Press, New York, NY, 81–90.

Consolvo, S., Roessler, P. and Shelton, B. E. (2004). The CareNet display: Lessons learned from an in-home evaluation of an ambient display. *Proceedings of the 6th Int'l Conference on Ubiquitous Computing (UbiComp '04)*. ACM Press, New York, NY, 1–17.

Cowan, R. S. (1983). *More Work for Mother: The Ironies of Household Technology from the Open Hearth to the Microwave*. Basic Books, New York.

Crabtree, A. and Rodden, T. (2004). Domestic routines and design for the home. *Journal of CSCW, 13*(2), 191–220.

DeVault, M. L. (1994). *Feeding the Family: The Social Organization of Caring as Gendered Work*. University of Chicago Press, Chicago.

Douglas, M. (1991). The idea of a home: A kind of space. *Social Research, 58*(1), 288–307.

Dourish, P. and Bellotti, V. (1992). Awareness and coordination in shared workspaces. *Proceedings of the 1992 ACM Conference on Computer-Supported Cooperative Work, (CSCW '92)*. ACM Press, New York, NY, 107–114.

Gaver, W., Bowers, J., Boucher, A., Law, A., Pennington, S. and Villar, N. (2006). The History Tablecloth: Illuminating domestic activity. *Proceedings of DIS 2006*. University Park, PA.

Grinter, R. E., Edwards, W. K., Newman, M. W. and Ducheneaut, N. (2005). The work to make the home network work. *Proceedings of the 9th European Conference on Computer Supported Cooperative Work (ECSCW '05)*. ACM Press, New York, NY, 469–488.

Gubrium, J. (1988). The family as project. *Sociological Review, 36*, 273–296.

Hamilton, A. (2007). A wireless street fight. *TIME Magazine, February 15th 2007*, New York.

Harper, R., Lamming, M. and Newman, W. (1992). Locating systems at work: Implications for the development of Active Badge applications. *Interacting with Computers, 4*(3), 343–363.

Hindus, D., Mainwaring, S. D., Leduc, N., Hagström, A. E. and Bayley, O. (2001). Casablanca: Designing social communication devices for the home. *Proceedings of the SIGCHI Conference on Human Factors in Computing Systems (CHI '01)*. ACM Press, New York, NY, 325–332.

Highmore, B. (2004). Homework: Routine, social aesthetics, and the ambiguity of everyday life. *Cultural Studies, 18*(2–3), 306–327.

Hutchinson, H., Mackay, W., Westerlund, B., Bederson, B., Druin, A., Plaisant, C., Beaudouin-Lafon, M., Conversy, S., Evans, H., Hansen, H., Roussel, N. and Eiderback, B. (2003). Technology probes: Inspiring design for and with families. *Proceedings of the SIGCHI Conference on Human Factors in Computing Systems (CHI '03)*. ACM Press, New York, NY, 17–24.

Iachello, G., Smith, I., Consolvo, S., Chen, M. and Abowd, G.(2005). Developing privacy guidelines for social location disclosure applications and services. *Proceedings of the 2005 Symposium on Usable Privacy and Security (SOUPS '05)*. ACM Press, New York, NY.

March, W. and Fleuriot, C. (2006). Girls, technology and privacy: "Is my mother listening?". *Proceedings of the SIGCHI Conference on Human Factors in Computing Systems (CHI '06)*. ACM Press, New York, NY.

Martin, B. (1984). Mother wouldn't like it!: Housework as magic. *Theory, Culture & Society, 2*(2), 19–35.

Mynatt, E., Rowan, J., Jacobs, A. and Craighill, S. (2001). Digital family portraits: Supporting peace of mind for extended family members. *Proceedings of the SIGCHI Conference on Human Factors in Computing Systems (CHI '01)*. ACM Press, New York, NY.

Nardi, B. A., Whittaker, S. and Bradner, E. (2000). Interaction and outeraction: Instant messaging in action. *Proceedings of the 2000 ACM Conference on Computer-Supported Cooperative Work, (CSCW '00)*. ACM Press, New York, NY, 78–88.

O'Brien, J. and Rodden, T. (1997). Interactive systems in domestic environments. *Proceedings of DIS '97*, ACM, New York, NY, 247–259.

O'Hara, K., Perry, M., Churchill, E. and Russell, D. (Eds.) (2003). *Public and situated displays: Social and interactional aspects of shared display technologies*. Springer, New York, NY.

Plaisant, C., Clamage, A., Hutchinson, H. B., Bederson, B. B. and Druin, A. (September 2006). Shared family calendars: Promoting symmetry and accessibility. *ACM Transactions on Computer–Human Interaction, 13*(3), 313–346.

Romero, N., Markopoulos, P., Baren, J., Ruyter, B., Ijsselsteijn, W. and Farshchian, B. (2007). Connecting the family with awareness systems. *Personal Ubiquitous Computing, 11*(4), 299–312.

Sellen, A., Eardley, R., Izadi, S. and Harper, R. (2006a). The Whereabouts Clock: Early testing of a situated awareness device. *Proceedings of the SIGCHI Conference on Human Factors in Computing Systems (CHI '06)*. ACM Press, New York, NY.

Sellen, A., Harper, R., Eardley, R., Izadi, S., Regan, T., Taylor, A. S., Wood, K. R. (2006b). HomeNote: Supporting situated messaging in the home. *Proceedings of the 2006 ACM Conference on Computer-Supported Cooperative Work, (CSCW '06)*. ACM Press, New York, NY, 383–392.

Sheehan, E. and Edwards, W. K. (2007). Home networking and HCI: What hath god wrought? In *Proceedings of the SIGCHI Conference on Human Factors in Computing Systems (CHI '07)*. ACM Press, New York, NY, 547–556.

Smith, I. E., Consolvo, S., LaMarca, A., Hightower, J. and Scott, J. (2005). Social disclosure of place: From location technology to communication practices. *Proceedings of the 3rd International Conference on Pervasive Computing (Pervasive'05), Munich, Germany*, 134–151.

Strong, R. and Gaver, B. (1996). Feather, scent and shaker: Supporting simple intimacy. In *Videos, Proceedings of the 1996 ACM Conference on Computer-Supported Cooperative Work, (CSCW' 96)*. ACM Press, New York, NY, 29–30.

Taylor, A. S. and Swan, L. (2005). Artful systems in the home. *Proceedings of the SIGCHI Conference on Human Factors in Computing Systems (CHI '05)*. ACM Press, New York, NY, 641–650.

Weiser, M. (1991). The computer for the 21st century. *Scientific American, 265*(3), 94–104.

Wood, D. and Beck, R. J. (1994). *Home rules*. The Johns Hopkins University Press, Baltimore, MD.

Woodruff, A., Augustin, S. and Foucault, B. (2007). Sabbath day home automation: "It's like mixing technology and religion". *Proceedings of the SIGCHI Conference on Human Factors in Computing Systems (CHI '07)*. ACM Press, New York, NY, 527–536.

Chapter 19
Evaluating Peripheral Displays

Tara Matthews, Gary Hsieh, and Jennifer Mankoff

Abstract Although peripheral displays have been a domain of inquiry for over a decade now, evaluation criteria and techniques for this area are still being created. Peripheral display evaluation is an acknowledged challenge in a field setting. This chapter first describes models and methods that have been tailored specifically to evaluating peripheral displays (measuring how well they achieve their goals). Then, we present evaluation criteria used in past evaluations of peripheral displays, ranging from issues such as learnability to distraction. After explaining how these criteria have been assessed in the past, we present a case study evaluation of two e-mail peripheral displays that demonstrates the pros and cons of various evaluation techniques.

19.1 Introduction

Although peripheral displays have been a domain of inquiry for over a decade now (Gaver et al., 1991; Weiser and Brown, 1996), evaluation criteria and techniques for this area are still being created. Peripheral display evaluation is an acknowledged challenge in a field setting (Carter et al., 2008; Mankoff et al., 2003). A user interface is a peripheral display if it is peripherally used (i.e., being used while multitasking and with low cognitive effort or interruption) (Matthews et al., 2007). Because peripheral use is important, criteria for peripheral display evaluation include awareness and distraction, which traditional desktop evaluation techniques do not emphasize. Gathering data about awareness and distraction is challenging. Awareness is difficult to evaluate because interactions with a peripheral display are often brief and changes in behavior may be small and unnoticeable. Distraction is difficult to measure without further distracting users. Various studies have explored how to gather data about peripheral displays in ways that take their unique usage constraints into consideration.

T. Matthews (✉)

IBM Research, Almaden Research Center, 650 Harry Road, San Jose, CA 95123, USA

e-mail: tlmatthe@us.ibm.com

P. Markopoulos et al. (eds.), *Awareness Systems*, Human-Computer Interaction Series,
DOI 10.1007/978-1-84882-477-5_19, © Springer-Verlag London Limited 2009

This chapter describes models and methods that have been tailored specifically to evaluating peripheral displays (measuring how well they achieve their goals). Then, we present evaluation criteria used in past evaluations of peripheral displays, ranging from issues such as learnability to distraction. After explaining how these criteria have been assessed in the past, we present a case study evaluation of two e-mail peripheral displays that demonstrates the pros and cons of various evaluation techniques.

19.2 Specialized Frameworks and Methods

Two evaluation frameworks (Matthews et al., 2007; McCrickard et al., 2003b) and two methods (Mankoff et al., 2003; Shami et al., 2005) have been created specifically for peripheral displays. The frameworks provide criteria that should be considered in peripheral display design and evaluation. The methods attempt to standardize questions that evaluators ask about their displays to gather data about important criteria. These frameworks and methods are discussed further in the next section to support our discussion of evaluation criteria.

19.2.1 Models

McCrickard et al. (2003b) present a design model for classifying different types of notification systems, and their definition of notification system includes peripheral displays. User goals are modeled based on the interruption, reaction, and comprehension caused by a system. The model can be used to suggest useful empirical and analytical evaluation metrics for tailoring usability evaluation methods. In particular, designers select target levels of *interruption*, *reaction*, and *comprehension* for their display and then evaluate it using these as criteria. They argue that key characteristics of a peripheral display evaluation are to (1) provide a realistic usage experience and (2) probe the use of the display according to trade-offs among interruption, reaction, and comprehension. As an example, McCrickard et al. present a survey they created for the Scope (Van Dantzich et al., 2002) with questions about the display's target level for each criterion.

Matthews et al. present an activity theory framework for evaluating peripheral displays (Matthews et al., 2007). As part of this framework, they discuss a set of evaluation criteria based on a literature survey, interviews with peripheral display creators, and an activity theory analysis of peripheral display use. The criteria are *appeal* (a user's qualitative enjoyment of a display), *awareness* (the amount of information shown by the display that people are able to register and use), *distraction* (the amount of attention the display attracts away from a user's primary action), *learnability* (the amount of time and effort required for users to operationalize their use of a peripheral display), and *effects of breakdowns* (how apparent breakdowns are to users and how easily users can recover from them). Given these criteria, the authors discuss peripheral display evaluation relative to design dimensions derived as part of the activity theory framework: scope (the number of activities supported), classes of activities supported (primary, secondary, or pending), and criticality (from low to high importance). Criteria will vary in importance and the practicality of evaluation methods will vary depending on a display's position along each design dimension. In general, as scope increases, so does the challenge of evaluating all criteria. When supporting primary and pending activities, displays tend to support a stable set of actions, making lab experiments more tenable. On the other hand, when supporting secondary activities, displays could be used in a variety of contexts, which may vary and change, making realistic usage difficult to simulate and necessitating an extended deployment. Finally, the criticality of information displayed changes the importance of evaluation criteria (e.g., for displays with *high criticality*, *awareness* is more important, while *aesthetics* are less important).

19.2.2 Methods

Two holistic methods tailored for peripheral displays attempt to standardize data gathering at early stages of peripheral display development. Shami et al. (2005) present context of use evaluation of peripheral displays (CUEPD), an evaluation method that relies on active user participation and emphasizes the experience of using peripheral displays. CUEPD captures the context of use through user scenario building, enactment, and reflection. Designers can use CUEPD when they have a working prototype to improve future designs. This new method attempts to increase realism in an in-lab experiment with scenarios collaboratively created by the designer and the user. It also provides guidance for evaluation criteria by suggesting survey question categories: noticeability, comprehension, relevance, division of attention, and engagement.

Mankoff et al. (2003) extended Neilsen's heuristic evaluation method by modifying the set of heuristics, based on a survey of ambient display designers, to reflect ambient display design goals. This modified method is meant for use in the early stages of design, suggesting usability goals to designers as they iterate. The ambient heuristics imply certain qualities of a usable ambient display that could lead to criteria for ambient display evaluation (e.g., the "peripherality of the display" heuristic implies that obtrusiveness is a metric).

Next we discuss common criteria used in peripheral display evaluations, and how the IRC model, the activity theory framework, the CUEPD, and the ambient heuristics relate. We also discuss specific examples of methods used in past studies to evaluate each criterion.

19.3 Evaluation Criteria

As mentioned in the Introduction, evaluation criteria represent a concrete way of measuring goals such as usability or low attention demand. Traditional graphical user interfaces tend to require focal attention to accomplish a set of predefined tasks.

Criteria for evaluating these interfaces are well established and many of them, such as user learnability, error visibility, usefulness, and user satisfaction, have been evaluated for peripheral displays as well. However, peripheral displays require a new set of criteria related to *attention issues* that are not usually measured in traditional interfaces. Peripheral displays tend not to be the focus of user attention, they are always used while multitasking, and there often is not a well-defined task being performed with them. In the following subsections we discuss two broad categories of criteria that are important in peripheral display evaluations: *traditional usability* criteria and criteria related to *attention issues*. We present past evaluations of peripheral displays that demonstrate the value of measuring both sets of criteria and how to effectively gather data about them.

19.3.1 Traditional Usability Criteria

The usability literature has developed a rich set of criteria for evaluating graphical user interfaces. Some of the most common usability criteria drawn from various Human–Computer Interaction and graphical user interface usability texts include the following (definitions below are from a survey of these usability texts; Seffah et al., 2006):

- *effectiveness*: the capability of the application to enable users to achieve specified tasks with accuracy and completeness (Booth, 1989; Brinck et al., 2002; Guillemette, 1995; ISO-9241-1, 1998; Shackel, 1991)
- *efficiency*: the capability of the application to enable users to expend appropriate amounts of resources in relation to the effectiveness achieved in a specific use context (Brinck et al., 2002; Constantine and Lockwood, 1999; Dumas and Redish, 1993; Hix and Hartson, 1993; ISO-9241-11, 1998; Nielsen, 1993; Preece et al., 1994; Schneiderman and Plaisant, 2004)
- *learnability*: the ease with which features needed for achieving particular goals can be mastered (Booth, 1989; Brinck et al., 2002; Constantine and Lockwood, 1999; Hix and Hartson, 1993; Nielsen, 1993; Preece et al., 1994; Schneiderman and Plaisant, 2004; Shackel, 1991)
- *memorability*: the degree to which the application's use can be remembered over time (Brinck et al., 2002; Constantine and Lockwood, 1999; Hix and Hartson, 1993; Nielsen, 1993; Schneiderman and Plaisant, 2004)
- *flexibility*: the degree to which the application can be tailored to suit a user's needs or preferences (Preece et al., 1994; Shackel, 1991)
- *errors*: the degree to which errors are avoidable, visible, and easy to recover from (Brinck et al., 2002; Constantine and Lockwood, 1999; Nielsen, 1993; Schneiderman and Plaisant, 2004)
- *usefulness*: the degree to which the application enables users to solve real problems in an acceptable way (Booth, 1989)
- *user satisfaction*: subjective responses from users about their feelings when using the application (Booth, 1989; Brinck et al., 2002; Constantine and Lockwood, 1999; Hix and Hartson, 1993; ISO-9241-11, 1998; Nielsen, 1993; Preece et al., 1994; Schneiderman and Plaisant, 2004; Shackel, 1991)

A number of these usability criteria are particularly important for peripheral displays. In this section, we highlight the traditional user interface criteria that have also frequently been evaluated for peripheral displays and the metrics used to gather data about them. These include *learnability, error visibility, usefulness,* and *user satisfaction*.

19.3.1.1 Learnability

Learnability is the amount of time and effort required for users to operationalize their use of a peripheral display (Matthews et al., 2007). Operationalize means *to accomplish a skilled level of use*, such that minimal attention is needed to use the display. Operational use is accomplished through extensive learning. If peripheral display designers can ease the learning process, their displays will be *used peripherally* more quickly (Matthews et al., 2007).

Van Dantzich et al. examined the learning process of simple, somewhat arbitrary visuals to convey a host of task information (e-mail, calendar, to dos, alerts) (Van Dantzich et al., 2002). This was important to their evaluation because the visuals chosen were not inherently meaningful or representative of the information they conveyed. They found that users learned to interpret the display in about an hour and enjoyed using the display. InfoCanvas is another display that uses nonintuitive information-to-visual mappings (Stasko et al., 2005). Creators asked users midway through a 1-month field study if they had learned to interpret the display without looking at a reminder sheet – all but one participant had. In an in-lab evaluation of IC2Hear, a sound awareness display for the deaf, participants were asked to rate how easy each display was to learn (Ho-Ching et al., 2003).

Other past peripheral display evaluation literature have focused on the design qualities that enable quick or easy operationalization, rather than on the user's learning process. For example, the ambient heuristics call for a "consistent and intuitive mapping," so that users spend less effort learning the mappings. The CUEPD survey asks if the user was able to understand information just by glancing at it, another indicator that information was easy to learn. Other evaluations have measured whether or not users *learned* to interpret a display (Skog et al., 2003), but not how long it took them or how challenging it was to learn.

It is important to evaluate that the learning process matches user expectations to bolster adoption. For example, an evaluation of sound displays for the deaf revealed that users disliked visualizations they thought were difficult to learn (Matthews et al., 2006c).

19.3.1.2 Error Visibility and Recovery

Error visibility refers to how apparent errors or breakdowns are to users and how easily users can recover from them. The visibility of errors is particularly important for peripheral displays because their updates tend to be subtle, infrequent, and not necessarily feedback based (i.e., the user often does not control the input and the display is not always reacting to the user's actions). Thus, users may not even notice breakdowns on a peripheral display.

Error visibility is often measured inadvertently when a display unexpectedly breaks down during an evaluation or deployment. Though not always considered before evaluations, errors can cause major problems for peripheral display users and evaluators. For example, in a field study we present later in this chapter, an e-mail peripheral display was not displaying anything for half a day before users noticed. This resulted in missing data for evaluators and less e-mail awareness for users. To avoid problems like this, the ambient heuristics state that "error prevention" is an important design consideration, since "users should be able to distinguish between an inactive display and a broken display" (Mankoff et al., 2003). Also, criteria from Matthews et al. include evaluating the "effects of breakdowns" (Matthews et al., 2007). We highlight the importance of considering this challenging aspect of peripheral display design, since it is often overlooked by designers and evaluators.

19.3.1.3 Usefulness

Usefulness is the degree to which the display provides value to the user. A common goal of peripheral displays is to convey information in a subtle, nondistracting way. However, a subtle display mechanism is at odds with conveying very important information; thus peripheral displays tend to show information of lower importance. The result is that compelling applications of peripheral displays are difficult to create. This is particularly problematic when peripheral displays share screen space with important task-related windows.

The ambient heuristics encourage designs that include "useful and relevant information." The CUEPD survey asks users about whether the display provides relevant, needed information (Shami et al., 2005). A number of studies have evaluated the usefulness of a display after participants had used it for a period of time. In a field study of the Sideshow display, Cadiz et al. (2002) asked users in surveys about usefulness and whether it was "worth giving up screen space to run Sideshow." Consolvo et al. (2004) found in a field study of the CareNet display (which provides adult children with awareness of their elderly parent's activities and environment) that it was useful to participants, having a positive impact on the elders' care. In a longitudinal field study of InfoCanvas, Stasko et al. emphasized the usefulness as a criterion, asking users several questions about it (Stasko et al., 2005). In general, usefulness tends to be measured using survey or interview feedback from participants who have used the display.

19.3.1.4 User Satisfaction

User satisfaction refers to a user's qualitative happiness or unhappiness with a display. All other criteria feed into a user's overall feelings about a display, hence this criteria is greatly affected by a user's priorities (i.e., which other criteria are most important to him or her) and is a general overview of a display's success.

Matthews et al. argue that user *appeal* is an important criterion. The CUEPD survey asks about a user's enjoyment using the display (Shami et al., 2005). Many peripheral display evaluations have asked about user satisfaction, such as "novelty and fun" and "summary impressions" (Stasko et al., 2005). In general, user satisfaction is typically measured through qualitative reports, such as surveys and interviews, following realistic usage.

Aesthetics is a design factor that can affect user satisfaction and has been prevalently discussed in peripheral display literature. A number of peripheral displays have emphasized aesthetics over intuitive designs (Dahley et al., 1998; Pedersen and Sokoler, 1997; Redström et al., 2000; Skog et al., 2003; Stasko et al., 2005). For these displays, it is important to evaluate aesthetic appeal to users. Accordingly, the ambient heuristics suggest the importance of an "aesthetic and pleasing design" and a "match between design of ambient display and environment" (Mankoff et al., 2003). Also, the CUEPD survey suggests gathering user feedback on the display's attractiveness (Shami et al., 2005).

19.3.2 Criteria Related to Attention Issues

Because peripheral displays are often used outside of a user's attentional focus, while multitasking, and in a nontask-driven manner, they require a new set of criteria related to *attention issues* that are not traditionally measured. A growing body of peripheral display evaluation literature has focused on two attention issues in particular: *awareness* and *distraction*. We discuss these issues in this section, along with examples of how they were measured in evaluations.

19.3.2.1 Awareness

Awareness refers to the amount of information shown by a display that people are able to register and use. It is a common criterion in most peripheral display evaluations. Past methods attempt to standardize questions about awareness. The CUEPD survey asks if users were "able to understand the information in the display" (Shami et al., 2005). The ambient heuristics prescribe that "useful and relevant information" is visible (Mankoff et al., 2003). The IRC model emphasizes questions about *reaction* and *comprehension*, which are similar to awareness (e.g., asking about a user's "overall sense of information") (McCrickard et al., 2003b). The activity theory framework also includes *awareness* as a criterion (Matthews et al., 2007).

Gaver et al. observed users as they monitor the status of a cola manufacturing process through the use of peripheral audio sounds (Gaver et al., 1991). Their observations and user reports both provided information about awareness in comparison to not using the sounds. More recent evaluations have asked users to specifically report on their awareness of displayed information, typically using Likert scales. For example, Mamykina et al. asked questions about attention (Mamykina et al., 2003), Mynatt et al. about the use of the periphery (Mynatt et al., 1998), Zhang et al. asked about awareness (Zhang et al., 2005), and Cadiz et al. asked about staying "aware of information that's critical for me to keep track of" (Cadiz et al., 2002). Consolvo et al. found through interviews following a field deployment that the CareNet display had a positive impact on elders' care and the caregivers' awareness of workload distributions.

Empirical evaluations have attempted to measure awareness through behavioral change. Arroyo and Selker asked participants to react to certain changes in a peripheral display and measured their level of awareness through their reaction speed (Arroyo and Selker, 2003). Dabbish and Kraut compared the timing of the messages sent by an "asker" to a "helper" for two different displays showing the helper's level of busyness (Dabbish and Kraut, 2004). In a task that involved using a peripheral display to manage multiple tasks, Matthews et al. gathered data about awareness using several metrics: the number of task switches, how quickly users resumed pending tasks when relevant information arrived, and the accuracy of task switches (e.g., did a user switch to e-mail when a spam message arrived?) (Matthews et al., 2006b). Ho-Ching et al. measured awareness of sound information by asking lab study participants to identify sounds as they were displayed (Ho-Ching et al., 2003).

19.3.2.2 Distraction

Distraction refers to the amount of attention a display attracts away from a user's primary task. It is another very common criterion measured in peripheral display evaluations. The ambient heuristics prescribe that a display "should be unobtrusive and remain so unless it requires the user's attention" and users "should notice an ambient display because of a change in the data it is presenting and not because its design clashes with its environment" (Mankoff et al., 2003). The CUEPD survey asks several questions about distraction (e.g., did the user notice the display? and was the user able to adequately focus on their primary task) (Shami et al., 2005). *Interruption* in the IRC model describes the event that causes a user to switch their focal attention to the notification, causing distraction from a primary task (McCrickard et al., 2003b). Finally, the activity theory framework discusses *distraction* as an important criterion (Matthews et al., 2007).

Distraction is often measured in lab studies in terms of directly observable properties of user behavior, such as changes in performance on a primary task (Arroyo and Selker, 2003; Ho-Ching et al., 2003; Matthews et al., 2006a), focal attention shifts to a secondary display (measured with eye tracking) (Dabbish and Kraut, 2004), and how often or how quickly a user switches to tasks about which the peripheral display conveys information (Matthews et al., 2006b). However, in some instances, users have been asked to report levels of distraction themselves, using Likert scale questions (Cadiz et al., 2002; McCrickard et al., 2003b; Zhang et al., 2005). This particularly makes sense in the field, where it is difficult to know exactly what the user's primary task is or to identify the cause of a change in performance on that task.

19.3.3 A Note About Design Mechanisms and Summary

In this section we have discussed criteria and methods for evaluating peripheral displays. Researchers also suggest various design mechanisms to accomplish many of the criteria discussed in this chapter. These include abstraction (Matthews et al., 2006b; Pedersen and Sokoler, 1997), glanceability (Matthews et al., 2006a; Van Dantzich et al., 2002), user customization (Stasko et al., 2005), sufficient information design, easy transition to more in-depth information (Mankoff et al., 2003), consistent visuals (Matthews et al., 2005; Van Dantzich et al., 2002), and many more. For example, glanceable visuals enable users to be more aware of information on a peripheral display with less distraction, which leads to greater user satisfaction (Matthews et al., 2006b).

In summary of this section, we first described models and methods that have been tailored specifically for peripheral displays. The models provide criteria that should be considered in peripheral display design and evaluation. The methods attempt to standardize questions that evaluators ask about their displays to gather data about important criteria. Next, we discussed two broad categories of criteria that are important in peripheral display evaluations: *traditional usability* criteria and criteria related to *attention issues*. We presented past evaluations of peripheral displays that demonstrate both the value of measuring these criteria and how to effectively gather data about them. In the next section, we present a case study evaluation of two e-mail peripheral displays that demonstrate the pros and cons of various evaluation techniques for evaluating some of these common criteria.

19.4 Case Study: Two E-Mail Display Evaluations

Here we present an example peripheral display evaluation process, intended to demonstrate the pros and cons of several in-lab and field evaluation techniques for gathering data about *awareness, distraction, learnability, error visibility, usefulness*, and *user satisfaction*. We start by describing the evaluated e-mail peripheral displays, which convey information about new e-mail messages (a graphical Ticker and a physical, colored Orb). We then discuss the formative and summative evaluation techniques used to evaluate and improve the displays. The evaluations gather data about the criteria mentioned previously, highlighting their importance for understanding the impact of a peripheral display. Finally, we compare the data yielded by the different evaluation techniques and discuss their pros and cons when applied to peripheral displays.

19.4.1 Display Designs to Improve E-Mail Awareness

Our studies focus on the e-mail domain, which can benefit greatly from peripheral displays. People are often distracted by e-mail, which can harm their productivity (Czerwinski et al., 2004). At the same time, e-mail is an important work tool that often requires regular monitoring. Knowing whether a new e-mail is important enough to interrupt the current task or can be ignored could significantly improve a user's ability to maintain task flow and resume tasks at opportune times (Matthews et al., 2006b). A past study showed that knowing which group a sender belongs to (e.g., coworker or family) is an important factor in deciding when to read a message (Dabbish et al., 2005). Our displays show e-mail sender group information in a glanceable way, to help users quickly and easily maintain awareness of new e-mail.

(a)   (b)

Fig. 19.1 The Ticker and Orb displays. (a) The Ticker, shown in a magnified callout, is located just above the windows taskbar. (b) The Orb is the pink globe to the right of the monitor

Our displays focused on the needs of administrative assistants managing e-mail since they receive many messages a day. We interviewed 10 administrative assistants, who indicated that they check e-mail frequently and often felt obligated to check who each new e-mail was from immediately upon notification, even though the new message might be spam or of little importance. Knowing which new messages are important could improve the overall productivity of the administrative assistants.

Peripheral displays may be a good solution for this problem. They could allow the assistants to focus on other tasks, while quickly and easily maintaining an awareness of their e-mail inboxes. To test this hypothesis, we developed two different peripheral displays for showing information about arriving e-mail. Our displays monitored a person's IMAP account for e-mail from up to five sets of e-mail addresses, each associated with a name or a nickname. We used two preexisting displays and modified them to display information about e-mail arrivals. The first display was a Ticker, a common type of on-screen display that shows scrolling text (shown in Fig. 19.1a). We chose a Ticker because they are common (many news channels use Tickers to show headlines, for example) and have been studied in the past (e.g., Maglio and Campbell, 2000; McCrickard et al., 2003a; Parsowith et al., 1998). The second was a commercial display called the Ambient Orb – a physical, frosted orb that sits on the user's desk and changes color in response to some input (see Fig. 19.1b). The Orb nicely complements the graphical, text-based Ticker, displaying information off the desktop and more abstractly (i.e., with color rather than a textual name and subject).

19.4.2 Formative Evaluation: Heuristic Evaluation

Formative evaluation is typically conducted during the design stage or early in the development stage. Fewer participants are typically needed than summative evaluations, since quick, iterative design cycles are valuable. Unfortunately, formative evaluation techniques used for traditional interfaces have focus primarily on the usability of graphical user interfaces intended for use in focal tasks. Therefore, most of them would not be able to provide feedback regarding awareness and distraction – two important criteria for evaluating peripheral displays. For this case study, a heuristic evaluation designed specifically for peripheral displays was used (Mankoff et al., 2003).

We conducted a heuristic evaluation of two versions of both the Ticker and the Orb with six graduate students who are all knowledgeable about peripheral display design. The evaluators were given a list of heuristics specifically designed for peripheral displays and asked to evaluate all four displays using the heuristic evaluation method, as described in Mankoff et al. (2003). In particular, evaluators were given descriptions and images of the displays in two scenarios. First was a notification version of each display that would change only when a new e-mail arrived from any of up to five people. Second was an ambient version that would constantly cycle through information about the current e-mails pending from each of up to five people. Evaluators were asked to indicate which version of each display they preferred.

19.4.2.1 Results

Five out of the six evaluators preferred the notification versions of the two displays. The notification versions were favored for two reasons: (1) there was a clear notification when a new e-mail arrived and (2) it was believed to be less distracting than the ambient version (which constantly cycled between information regarding the five people). Minimizing distraction was very important to our evaluators, who also suggested that we reduce the amount of animation, flickering, blinking, and other distracting aspects of the displays.

One evaluators suggested that we display the name or the nickname of the person who sent the e-mail, instead of the e-mail account from where the e-mail was sent, because knowing the sender is typically more important than knowing the specific e-mail address used. Nicknames enabled us to provide additional features, such as associating multiple e-mail addresses with one group nickname.

For the Ticker, some evaluators suggested we add an option to re-read an e-mail's subject if the user happened to miss it. In response, we enabled users to see the newest e-mail's subject line at any time by clicking on the Ticker.

19.4.2.2 Design Iteration

Based on our heuristic analysis, our final display designs were as follows:

- **Orb**. For the Orb, the user associated a color with each set of addresses. Most of the time, the Orb showed a shade of cyan indicating the number of unread e-mails from up to five people or (groups of people) combined, with lighter shades (increased brightness) indicating more unread e-mails. When an e-mail from a chosen person arrived, the Orb would transition to the color associated with that person for 10 s and then transition back into the cyan scale with a brighter shade

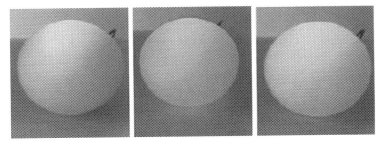

Fig. 19.2 Orb (*top*) and Ticker (***bottom***) sequence shown illustrates (**a**) a display with no unread e-mails, (**b**) the display showing the arrival of a new e-mail from Ashley, titled "Let's meet for lunch.", and (**c**) the display showing one unread e-mail

because of the new, unread message. Figure 19.2 (top) shows this sequence: the Orb transitions to red indicate a new message from Ashley has arrived and then transitions to a brighter cyan indicate there is one additional unread message in the inbox. When an e-mail from one of these people is read, the Orb shows a dimmer shade of cyan.

- **Ticker.** For the Ticker, the user associated a name with each set of addresses. Most of the time, the Ticker is not scrolling and displays only the summary text: the total number of unread e-mails from each of the five people or groups, with no animation. For example, it might read "unread: 3 John: 1 James: 2 Nancy: 0 Nora: 0 Ashley: 0." When an e-mail arrived from one of those people, the Ticker would begin to scroll at 7 characters per second, showing the name of the sender group and the subject of the new e-mail. Then it would revert to the summary text view (see the bottom of Fig. 19.2 for an example). Messages were shown for 25 s. When the Ticker was displaying summary text, users could click on a name to see message information.

19.4.3 Summative Evaluation

Summative evaluations are typically conducted when a display is fully functional. Because there is no consensus about the best approach for evaluating peripheral displays, we performed a series of different evaluations that included most of the techniques we found in previous work. For clarity and for the purpose of comparing different techniques, we split this section into a discussion of techniques we used in the lab and techniques we used in the field. After presenting the details of how each experiment was run, we summarize the techniques used to measure each of the criteria (see Tables 19.1 and 19.2). In the lab, we used a dual-task experiment and self-reports to evaluate the levels of awareness and distraction the displays caused. In our field study, we gathered self-report measures of awareness, distraction, learnability, error visibility, usefulness and user satisfaction via questionnaires and interviews and an objective measure of awareness (performance on knowledge questions about the peripheral display contents).

Table 19.1 Techniques used to measure awareness (Aw), distraction (D), error visibility (E), learnability (L), usefulness (U) and user satisfaction (S) in our lab study

	Aw	D	E	L	U	S
System log (primary task speed)		X				
System log (primary task accuracy)		X				
Knowledge questions	X					
Self-reports	X					

Table 19.2 Techniques used to measure awareness (Aw), distraction (D), error visibility (E), learnability (L), usefulness (U), and user satisfaction (S) in our field study

	Aw	D	E	L	U	S
Pre- and post-questionnaires	X	X	X	X	X	X
Interviews	X	X	X	X	X	X
ESM pop-ups (self-reports)	X	X				
ESM pop-ups (knowledge questions)	X					
System log (behavioral change)	X					

19.4.3.1 Lab Study

In this section, we first discuss the dual-task experiment setup and then describe in detail how each criterion was measured in this setup. Awareness was measured with knowledge questions and self-reports, while distraction was measured by system logs, focusing on performance changes in the primary task resulting from display use (see a summary of techniques used in Table 19.1).

Our lab study was a dual-task experiment. The primary task was to sort e-mail messages by saving them or removing them from a fake inbox that contained 1500 messages. The secondary task was to monitor the peripheral display. We chose our primary and secondary tasks such that the peripheral display would help to support the primary task. This helped to create a situation where the participant had a motive for monitoring the secondary display, while allowing us to reduce the extent to which we explicitly drew the user's attention to it. We chose to maximize realistic use by not interrupting the user at the time of a new update, but the trade-off was that users may not have recalled information when asked later.

We used a between-subjects design, with half the subjects using the Orb (Orb condition) and the other half using the Ticker (Ticker condition). We ran a total of 26 participants, divided equally between conditions. The participants were all college students between the ages of 18 and 23 and all of them had used e-mail before. The Orb was placed to the right of the monitor, within 50° of the user's focal vision. The Ticker was located across the entire bottom of the screen and took up 3% of the monitor's height.

The study was designed to represent a real-world situation where the participants needed to remove spam from their inbox. Participants were told to assume the role of a CEO of a major corporation. To make the study realistic, the CEO received three types of e-mail messages: junk mail (majority of the e-mails), important work-related messages from three of his/her employees (Robert Chang, Lisa Brown, and James Lewis) and social messages from 10 close friends who were famous celebrities (e.g., Arnold Schwarzenegger). Easily recognizable celebrity names were used to make it easier for the participants to recall the names of the friends. To ensure that participants could remember the employees' names, they were trained until they could pass a simple memory test. We considered allowing the participants to customize the employees' names for the study; however, we decided to use pre-set names to strengthen the control and reduce variability. The peripheral displays informed the user about messages from the three employees. Three employees, as opposed to the maximum five that the display supports, were used to decrease the challenge of memorizing the names. Participants were asked to save all e-mail from any of the three employees or from any of the 10 celebrities and to remove e-mail otherwise. Fifteen new e-mail messages arrived at predetermined, nonuniform intervals during the study. E-mail messages were sorted from least to most recent, so new arrivals were visible only on the peripheral display and not in the primary task inbox.

Participants performed the primary task for 3 min, allowing us to gather some baseline data. Then we started the peripheral display and gathered data for another 12 min. Participants were asked to remember as much information as possible from the peripheral display, as they would be given a quiz on the information later.

At the end of 12 min, we asked each participant a series of questions relating to the evaluation criteria. First, we asked each participant to self-report on awareness, answering questions such as "How often did you look at the display?" and "How much attention did you pay to the peripheral display?" Second, we asked objective questions that tested how much information a participant had retained from the displays, such as: "How many new e-mails did you receive from James?" and "From whom did you receive the most e-mails during the first half of the study?" There were a total of five knowledge questions. By asking general self-report questions before specific content questions, we hoped to minimize the impact that one type of question would have on answers to the next.

Like previous dual-task lab studies, we gathered data about distraction by measuring primary task accuracy and speed. We compared the 3 min of baseline performance data to the 12 min of dual-task performance. Accuracy was measured as the change in the percentage of correctly sorted e-mails, while speed was measured as the change in speed of sorting.

19.4.3.2 Field Study

In this section, we start by discussing the A–B–A' field study setup and then describe in detail the five different techniques used in the field and which criteria each technique allowed us to measure. Questionnaires and interviews were used to measure all of the six criteria. Experience-sampled self-report questions were used for both awareness and distraction, and experience-sampled knowledge questions and system logs were used to measure the level of awareness only (see a summary of techniques used in Table 19.2).

Our field study utilized an A–B–A' format, where there was a week-long baseline, two weeks with the displays present, and an additional baseline week. This structure allowed us to obtain and compare measurements before, during, and after participants had used our displays. We conducted a brief interview with each of our field study participants after he or she had used his/her display for a week during phase B to better understand display-use patterns. At the end of the display usage period (phase B), we conducted a more detailed interview with each participant and also asked each participant to complete a questionnaire.

Our field study included four participants, two using the Ticker and two using the Orb. Participants were all administrators in a department at our university. Participants were chosen based on their need to closely monitor e-mail from a small number of people and their having jobs that included a significant amount of time spent using other desktop applications. All of the participants customized the display to show new messages from five people of importance to them (no participants chose to create groups of e-mail senders).

We used an experience sampling method (ESM) during phase B. This technique was very challenging to design, raising many issues: when should we ask questions, how should we administer questions, what kinds of questions should we ask, and what questions would help us determine if participants were aware of displayed information. If experience sampling were not designed correctly, participants could get extremely frustrated with the study and/or not provide any useful feedback.

Since our users were in front of a computer most of the day, we decided to ask the ESM questions using pop-up windows. Six sets of questions were asked at random times during the day. We tried to keep questions simple to save the user time. We asked them to select a number on a Likert scale (1–5), rather than asking for a textual answer to each question. A participant could respond to the questions, or ignore the pop-up window, in which case it would disappear in 1 min. We used a low-resolution webcam to take a snapshot of the environment when the pop-ups appeared to provide additional context information (e.g., was the participant at his/her desk, meeting with someone, and not present). During a pilot of the field study, we were surprised to discover that users would use their e-mail browser to help them answer our questions. For this reason, we instructed users not to use their desktop e-mail reader to find the answers to questions.

We structured the pop-up process as follows: Preceding the appearance of the pop-up window, we shut down the Orb display by turning it black, and we shut down the Ticker display by turning it white and removing all text. Next, to reduce the chance that users retained an after image of the display, we showed many different colors (this also functioned as an attention-getting mechanism). Next, we asked distractor questions to help clear working memory, such as "What is the current temperature in the office?" Following this, we asked awareness questions, such as "How often did you look at the display?" and "How much attention did you pay to the peripheral display?" Next, participants were asked how distracting the display had been. Finally, participants were asked six knowledge questions to test how much information they had retained over time from the display. Examples of specific knowledge questions that we asked the participants included "How many new emails did you receive from *person A* during the past 15 min?" and "Who did you receive the most emails from during the past 15 min?"

Throughout the peripheral display usage period, we logged e-mail activities related to the e-mail sender groups being monitored with our display. Specifically, we logged when an e-mail from one of the five selected e-mail sender groups was added, read, or deleted. We did not log any e-mail subject lines for privacy reasons; therefore, our data only indicate whether or not a message was added/read/deleted and not which message it was.

19.4.3.3 Results

In presenting our results, we focus on measurable differences between displays and between techniques, across each of the evaluation criteria.

Awareness

Awareness was measured using self-reports and knowledge questions in both the lab and the field. In the field, we also measured it with a post-usage questionnaire, interviews, and behavioral change (i.e., logged e-mail response time). The results for awareness are summarized in Table 19.3. In general, performance differences in the field could not be tested for significance because we had only two subjects in each condition. Instead we report average accuracy on ESM questions for all four users while the displays were deployed.

In the lab, we found that the Ticker led to better recall of the information being displayed than the Orb ($M_{\text{Ticker}} = 3.2$, $M_{\text{Orb}} = 1.9$, $t(24) = -2.19$, $p = 0.038$). The average self-reported awareness of 2.9 ($\sigma = 0.9$) was the same for both displays.

In the field, we learned from self-reports (on a Likert scale of 1–5) that both displays enabled good awareness of e-mail arrivals ($M = 3.75$), but not of unread messages ($M = 1.75$). Interestingly, one of the four users (a Ticker user) reported that the display was effective for providing a summary of unread messages (rating the display 4 out of 5) and moderately effective for providing an awareness of new message arrivals (rating the display 3 out of 5).

The source of this disagreement in ratings was further clarified by our interviews. The three participants who rated the displays *high* on awareness of e-mail arrivals and *low* on awareness of unread e-mails (two Orb users and one Ticker user) told us that they checked their e-mail inbox almost immediately after each notification. Therefore, the number of unread messages remained at 0 most of the time. Orb users commented that color intensity (which represented the change in the number of unread messages) was difficult to perceive. The Ticker user commented that the status bar blended in too well with the background. She stopped noticing it after a few days of use. The last participant, who rated the displays *high* on awareness of unread e-mails and moderately high on awareness of e-mail arrivals, reported that notifications about newly arrived messages on her Ticker were too subtle. Unlike the others, she kept track of e-mails solely by looking at the status line indicating the number of unread e-mails from each address being monitored.

Table 19.3 Summary of awareness measures and results

	Results
Lab knowledge questions	Ticker enabled better accuracy. $M_{\text{Ticker}} = 3.2$, $M_{\text{Orb}} = 1.9$, $t(24) = -2.19$, $p = 0.038$
Lab self-reports	Difference not significant: same rating
Field pre- and post-questionnaires	

Good awareness of e-mail arrivals (3.75), but not of unread messages (1.75). Red is Orb and green is Ticker

Field interviews	Three users depended on the displays for notifications of new arrivals; one monitored the number of unread messages
Field ESM pop-ups (self-reports)	Difference not significant
Field ESM pop-ups (knowledge questions)	Difference not significant
Field system log (behavioral change)	

No difference between displays; mean time to open e-mail is significantly lower for both displays during use, than before ($F(67) = 6.71$ $p = 0.012$) or after ($F(67) = 6.39$ $p = 0.014$)

Our second measure of awareness in the field was knowledge questions about how many e-mails had actually arrived. However, a flaw in our study design resulted in limited data. Because we asked about only the last 15 min, in most cases no e-mails from any of the five people of interest had arrived, even though e-mail from other senders may have arrived. For example, among Orb users, there were only 11 cases where someone of interest had sent e-mail in the last 15 min. For the small number of cases available to compare, there was no difference in performance between Orb and Ticker users.

Our last measure of awareness in the field came from the system log. We recorded how long it took from when a message arrived until a participant opened it. This analysis included only messages from any of the five preselected people shown by the displays. Since our participants checked their e-mails fairly often, for our analysis, we excluded any e-mail that took more than 5 min to open, interpreting that as an indication that the participant was unavailable. The *time to open* metric was analyzed using a repeated measure mixed-model analysis of variance, with periods (A–B–A') and participants. Participants, nested within display type, were modeled as random effects. Mean *time to open* was not significantly different between displays ($F(3)<0.001$ $p = 0.994$); however, there was a difference between period A and B and B and A' ($M_A = 171, M_B = 108, M_{A'} = 168, F(67) = 6.71$ $p = 0.012$, and $F(67) = 6.39$ $p = 0.014$, respectively). This indicates that the presence of the displays increased the speed with which participants opened an e-mail after it arrived and thus that the presence of the displays increased awareness.

Distraction

In the lab, data about distraction were measured via changes in speed and accuracy, and with self-reports. In the field, distraction was measured with self-reports and interviews. The results for distraction are summarized in Table 19.4.

We found no statistically significant differences in distraction in the lab when comparing between baseline data and data from when the displays were in use. The second and third minutes of the study, during which time no displays were present, were used as the baseline (the first minute exhibited learning effects). Though not statistically significant, the average speed *decreased* slightly (by 7%) for the Ticker and *remained about the same* for the Orb. Accuracy, in turn, *increased* slightly (by 9%) for the Ticker and *remained about the same* for the Orb. We defined speed as (number of e-mails sorted)/(time in seconds). We calculated accuracy using the ratio of correct e-mails sorted to total e-mails sorted.

Table 19.4 Summary of distraction measures and results

	Results
Lab system log (primary task speed)	Difference not significant: Ticker speed decreased slightly
Lab system log (primary task accuracy)	Difference not significant: Ticker accuracy increased slightly
Field pre- and post-questionnaires	Three users reported they were not distracted at all; one Ticker user reported being somewhat distracting
Field interviews	Three users thought their displays were not distracting; one wanted it to be more distracting. Interviews revealed that the displays reduced the extent to which e-mail arrival distracted users by providing quick awareness of important versus unimportant messages
Field ESM pop-ups (self-reports)	Difference not significant, all rated display to be not distracting

In self-reports, participants in the lab reported being slightly distracted by both displays ($M_{\text{Ticker}} = 2.38$, $M_{\text{Orb}} = 2.31$). In the field, both participants using the Orb reported not being distracted at all, as did one Ticker user. In fact, during our interviews, one participant actually requested that we make the display *more* distracting. She explained that she had grown accustomed to being interrupted by the nature of her job and that she needed something flashier than simple scrolling to capture her attention. The other Ticker user rated the display slightly distracting.

Our interviews of field study participants also revealed an unexpected side effect of our displays. Two participants reported that without the peripheral display, they would check e-mail every time their e-mail program notified them of a new arrival. However, with the peripheral display, they tended to ignore their e-mail program's notifications. This meant that they were not task switching every time a piece of spam or other unimportant e-mail arrived. Thus, the peripheral display reduced distraction as a *secondary* effect.

Learnability, Error Visibility, Usefulness, and User Satisfaction

Field study participants were given a list of peripheral display heuristics (the same heuristics we used in our formative heuristic evaluation, see Fig. 19.3) and asked to rank how well the display matched each heuristic using a Likert Scale. Some of these heuristics measure learnability, error visibility, usefulness, and user satisfaction. The participants were also given a separate set of questions to collect information regarding overall use.

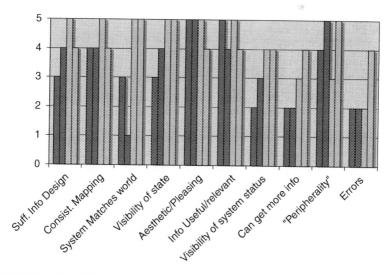

Fig. 19.3 Orb (*top*) and Ticker (*bottom*) sequence shown illustrates (**a**) a dim cyan display with no unread e-mails, (**b**) the display turning bright red, showing the arrival of a new e-mail from Ashley, titled "Let's meet for lunch.", and (**c**) the display turning a brighter shade of cyan than before the new message had arrived

Learnability. In general, our participants rated the displays highly for being easy to understand and having consistent and intuitive mappings.

Error Visibility. For both displays, the worst rating given was on "error prevention and user control," with ratings of 2, 2 (Orb) and 2, 4 (Ticker). These low ratings were caused by the fact that our system crashed whenever the users' IMAP service went down (this happened twice during the deployment, and additionally, one Orb went down two other times due to unrelated problems). The displays did not alert users of their breakdowns, and it took as long as half a day for a problem to be noticed, both because participants were not always at their desks (e.g., over lunch) and because they did not always receive e-mail from the five people being monitored frequently. There was one flaw with the Ticker that was not present in the Orb: other computer applications could occlude it.

Usefulness. Both displays rated very highly on "relevance and usefulness of the information." On our questionnaire, two participants (1 Orb and 1 Ticker) found the displays to be very useful (4 out of 5), while the other two somewhat useful (3 out of 5). Despite our participants' positive comments about our displays, we wanted to know if their success was due solely to the fact that they only notified users about certain messages from e-mail senders or if there were other aspects of their design that users liked. We asked users if they would still prefer our displays if standard e-mail notification solutions (e.g., pop-up windows provided by Outlook) could filter e-mails. Orb participants said they would still use the Orb due to its high visibility throughout their offices. Among the Ticker users, one responded that the pop-up and Ticker would essentially be the same, whereas another participant responded that she would have preferred the pop-up because it would show all the information in a single view rather than scrolling to reveal the information.

User satisfaction. While the Orb provided a more abstract representation of unread e-mail information than did the Ticker, and was rated lower on the "match between system and real-world" heuristic, users enjoyed using both displays and rated them very highly on "aesthetics and pleasing design."

During their interviews, the Orb participants seemed more excited about their displays than were the Ticker participants. One reason was that they appreciated the Orb's aesthetics. Another reason was the benefit of the Orb's visibility. It could convey information even when they were not working on the computer. Participants using the Orb could be walking around and talking to people and still notice color changes on the Orb. In our interviews, one Orb user commented that she enjoyed noticing the Orb changing color: "When you sit at a computer all day reading email, anything to jazz it up . . . like oh, she emailed me! . . .just makes it more interesting."

Two of our participants were curious if we planned to make our displays into a commercial product, as they would be interested in using it. Another participant asked us to conduct a much longer study with her so that she could continue using the Orb. As she put it, "I have become attached (to the display)."

19.4.3.4 Discussion

This case study highlights the importance of evaluating peripheral displays using multiple methods to gather data about the six evaluation criteria: awareness, distraction, learnability, error visibility, usefulness, and user satisfaction. In particular, multiple methods provided either redundant information or in some cases, one method filled in missing data from other methods (e.g., while lab study results did not lead to significant differences in distraction measures, interview results revealed that users found the displays reducing their distraction caused by e-mail). Gathering data about the six evaluation criteria enabled us to understand more completely the affect of our displays on users.

Discussion of Heuristic Versus Summative Evaluations

In many ways, it is incorrect to compare a heuristic evaluation with summative evaluation techniques. First, there is no clear point of comparison; we used the techniques at two different stages of the display development. Second, the purposes of the evaluations are different. A heuristic evaluation does not replace a summative evaluation, but rather it is an inexpensive evaluation technique that provides initial design feedback for quick iterations. However, we can still examine the results of the heuristic evaluation and gain a sense of what kinds of problems it was unable to uncover about peripheral displays.

The heuristic evaluation was unable to suggest a correct level of distraction. It resulted in a general suggestion to minimize the amount of animation, flickering, blinking, but it was not clear what types of updates would appropriately balance distraction and awareness. This is illustrated by the fact that one field study participant wanted the updates to be more distracting to bolster her awareness.

Another set of problems discovered from the field study that was not apparent from our heuristic evaluation relates to the error visibility and recovery criterion. In our field evaluation, we found that the displays did not provide feedback regarding breakdowns. While heuristic evaluators could have foreseen such potential problems, since the list of heuristics does include an "error prevention and user control" heuristic, it is hard to predict those problems without seeing the actual system and without using it as a peripheral display. This denotes a shortcoming with using heuristic evaluation and suggests a potential area of improvement in heuristic evaluation procedures to accommodate for these types of problems.

Discussion of Lab Versus Field Evaluations

Lab studies are designed to test specific aspect of peripheral displays in a controlled setting. To evaluate awareness caused by peripheral displays, correct responses to knowledge questions and self-reports can be measured. To evaluate distraction caused by peripheral displays, accuracy and speed on the primary task and self-reports can be used. Had the lab study generated significant results, it would have been capable of providing concrete feedback comparing the awareness and distraction of the displays, which is both hard and costly to do in the field. It is challenging to reach significant results in the field because of a multitude of uncontrolled environmental factors. However, having more users might have helped in our case.

The only conclusive evidence from our lab study was that the Orb users had lower awareness than the Ticker users. This finding contradicts our findings in the field regarding awareness. While low participant numbers prevent us from finding significant differences, our interviews do suggest that Orb users were just as capable as Ticker users of noticing incoming messages. It is not clear what caused this discrepancy. We speculate it may have been related to learnability: the orb may have taken longer to learn and so it did not perform well until it had been used for a longer period of time in the field study.

Discussion of Field Techniques

Our use of redundant measures in our field study enabled better triangulation of data, which led to a deeper understanding of our displays' usage. For example, ESM pop-ups provided a general sense that the displays did not support awareness of the number of unread e-mails well, but our final questionnaire helped us refine this result by showing that the displays were better at conveying information about e-mail arrival than about the number of unread messages. Interviews provided clarifying information: most of our users did not use the displays to monitor the number of unread e-mails because that number was almost always zero. None of these measures alone would have given nearly as complete a picture of how the displays performed.

How well did the methods we employed in the field study perform individually? Pre- and post-study questionnaires and interviews were comparable techniques used to collect qualitative feedback regarding overall use. They allowed us to explore the reasons for the answers participants gave us in more depth and better understand the impact of awareness and distraction in our displays on overall usability. ESM self-reports supplemented the questionnaires and interviews by surveying the participants in situ. While the ESM self-reports could potentially provide more realistic results, they interrupt participants. The system log measure of awareness allowed us to obtain statistically significant results regarding behavioral change, but it would not act well as a stand-alone measure because it does not explain why the behavior changed. The least successful of the techniques was our objective knowledge questions measuring awareness. We believe our knowledge questions were unsuccessful due to the problems described above with not timing them to be administered after new messages had arrived. If used correctly, knowledge questions could still be potentially very useful for gathering data about user awareness.

Based on our experiences, we recommend an A–B–A' format for peripheral display field evaluations, though the length of each segment could change depending on factors specific to the experiment being run. For example, the length of the A–B–A' phases could be adjusted based on issues such as expected adoption and learning curves. The A–B–A' format would allow for the evaluators to notice behavioral changes, as we did in this study with system logs.

When using experience sampling to evaluate peripheral displays, we believe that evaluators will have to make decisions about sampling frequency and question contents that are specific to their display's usage context. However, we recommend not requiring answers of participants, to reduce the burden if they are busy. We also learned that using pop-up windows for experience sampling can be effective. Though pop-ups are commonly perceived as annoying, most of our participants did not find them irritating except when they were extremely busy. In fact, all of our participants stated that they would not mind participating again in a similar study. The one participant who found the pop-ups to be extremely annoying mentioned that they were at least designed in a way that "it is like a friendly thing that you'd kind of want to interact with."

The field techniques presented in this case study have limitations. In particular, the evaluation was designed for people primarily using a desktop computer. For public displays which may be viewed in various contexts (e.g., while mobile), administering ESM questions is a problem. A potential solution is to ask users questions through their mobile devices as they walk past a display. Although the complexity of evaluation increases for off-the-desktop displays, we believe that ESM is a valuable technique for gathering data about awareness and distraction in the field.

19.4.4 Open Questions

Because realism is important to peripheral display evaluation, it is important to improve our ability to gather empirical data in the most realistic settings possible. The field study presented as part of our case study begins to address this need by demonstrating the effectiveness of experience sampling methods for gathering quantitative data about peripheral displays in situ. However, it remains an open question how to improve our ability to gather quantitative data in the field. Another open question is how to minimize attention that is unrealistically drawn to a display by an evaluation, something that makes existing field methods, such as experience sampling questionnaires and diaries, difficult to use.

19.5 Conclusion

Peripheral display evaluation is challenging, especially since it requires that criteria related to *attention* be examined in addition to more traditional usability criteria. Attentional criteria include *awareness* and *distraction*, which are difficult to measure due to their often unobservable nature and to the disruption caused by common evaluation techniques. To address these challenges, two evaluation frameworks (Matthews et al., 2007; McCrickard et al., 2003b) and two methods (Mankoff et al., 2003; Shami et al., 2005) have been created specifically for peripheral displays. The frameworks provide criteria that should be considered in peripheral display design and evaluation. The methods attempt to standardize questions that evaluators ask about their displays to gather data about important criteria. In addition, a growing body of peripheral display evaluation literature has highlighted a number of evaluation criteria: *awareness, distraction, learnability, error visibility, usefulness,* and *user satisfaction.*

We presented a case study evaluation of two e-mail peripheral displays both to demonstrate the use of various evaluation techniques for evaluating these common criteria and to highlight some pros and cons of various evaluation techniques. In the case study, we showed that heuristic evaluation and lab studies can provide important insights about the peripheral displays in a cost-effective manner. However, without actual field use, it is hard to predict the effects of the errors and to determine the right balance between awareness and distraction. In terms of techniques used in the field, questionnaire and interviews provided the most information, enabling us to explore our findings in depth. While the other field techniques tested (ESM and log analysis) can potentially be very useful, it is imperative to make slight modifications to customize them for the specific displays being evaluated (e.g., for ESM, question content and sampling frequency need to be determined).

References

Arroyo E, Selker T (2003) Arbitrating multimodal outputs: Using ambient displays as interruptions. *Proceedings of 10th International Conference on Human–Computer Interaction (HCI International)*, 591–595. Lawrence Erlbaum Associates, Crete, Greece.

Booth, P. (1989). *An Introduction to Human–Computer Interaction*. Lawrence Erlbaum Associates, London.

Brinck T, Gergle D, Wood SD (2002) *Designing Web Sites that Work: Usability for the Web*. Morgan Kaufmann, San Francisco.

Cadiz JJ, Venolia G, Jancke G, Gupta A (2002) Designing and deploying an information awareness interface. *Proceedings of the ACM Conference on Computer Supported Cooperative Work (CSCW)*, 314–323. ACM Press, New York.

Carter S, Mankoff J, Klemmer S, Matthews T (2008) Exiting the cleanroom: On ecological validity and ubiquitous computing. *Human–Computer Interaction Journal 23*(1):47–99.

Consolvo S, Roessler P, Shelton BE (2004) The CareNet Display: Lessons learned from an in home evaluation of an ambient display. *Proceedings of the 6th International Conference on Ubiquitous Computing (UbiComp)*, 1–17. Springer, Berlin.

Constantine LL, Lockwood LAD (1999) *Software for Use: A Practical Guide to the Models and Methods of Usage-Centred Design*. Addison-Wesley, New York.

Czerwinski M, Horvitz E, Wilhite S (2004) A diary study of task switching and interruptions. *Proceedings of the SIGCHI Conference on Human Factors in Computing Systems (CHI)*, 175–182. ACM Press, New York.

Dabbish L, Kraut RE (2004) Controlling interruptions: Awareness displays and social motivation for coordination. *Proceedings of the 2004 ACM Conference on Computer Supported Cooperative Work (CSCW)*. ACM Press, New York.

Dabbish L, Kraut RE, Fussell S, Kiesler S (2005) Understanding email use: Predicting action on a message. *Proceedings of the SIGCHI Conference on Human Factors in Computing Systems (CHI)*, 691–700. ACM Press, New York.

Dahley A, Wisneski C, Ishii H (1998) Water lamp and pinwheels: Ambient projection of digital information into architectural space. *Extended Abstracts of the SIGCHI Conference on Human Factors in Computing Systems (CHI)*, 269–270. ACM Press, New York.

Dumas JS, Redish JC (1993) *A Practical Guide to Usability Testing*. Ablex Publishing Co, Norwood, NJ.

Gaver WW, Smith RB, O'shea T (1991) Effective sounds in complex systems: the ARKOLA simulation. *Proceedings of the SIGCHI Conference on Human Factors in Computing Systems (CHI)*, 85–90. ACM Press, New York.

Guillemette RA (1995) The evaluation of usability in interactive information systems. In Carey JM (ed.), *Human Factors in Information Systems: Emerging Theoretical Bases* (207–221). Ablex Publishing Co, Norwood, NJ.

Hix D, Hartson HR (1993) *Developing User Interfaces: Ensuring Usability Through Product & Process.* John Wiley, New York.

Ho-Ching FW-L, Mankoff J, Landay JA (2003) Can you see what I hear? The design and evaluation of a peripheral sound display for the deaf. *Proceedings of the SIGCHI Conference on Human Factors in Computing Systems (CHI)*, 161–168. ACM Press, New York.

Iso-9241-11 International Standards Organization (1998) *Guidance on Usability.* (Report ISO 9241-11).

Maglio PP, Campbell CS (2000) Tradeoffs in displaying peripheral information. *Proceedings of the SIGCHI Conference on Human Factors in Computing Systems (CHI)*, 241–248. ACM Press, New York.

Mamykina L, Mynatt E, Terry M (2003) Time aura: Interfaces for pacing. *Proceedings of the SIGCHI Conference on Human Factors in Computing Systems (CHI)*, 144–151. ACM Press, New York.

Mankoff J, Dey AK, Hsieh G, Kientz J, Lederer S, Ames M (2003) Heuristic evaluation of ambient displays. *Proceedings of the SIGCHI Conference on Human Factors in Computing Systems (CHI)*, 169–176. ACM Press, New York.

Matthews T, Blais D, Shick A, Mankoff J, Forlizzi J, Rohrbach S, Klatzky R (2006a) *Evaluating Glanceable Visuals for Multitasking.* (Technical Report EECS-2006-173). U.C. Berkeley.

Matthews T, Czerwinski M, Robertson G, Tan D (2006b) Clipping Lists and Change Borders: Improving multitasking efficiency with peripheral information design. *Proceedings of the SIGCHI Conference on Human Factors in Computing Systems (CHI)*, 989–998. ACM Press, New York.

Matthews T, Fong J, Ho-Ching FW, Mankoff J (2006c) Evaluating non-speech sound visualizations for the deaf. *Behaviour & Information Technology*, 25(4):333–351.

Matthews T, Forlizzi J, Rohrbach S (2005) *Designing Glanceable Peripheral Displays.* EECS-2006-113. U.C. Berkeley.

Matthews T, Rattenbury T, Carter S (2007) Defining, designing, and evaluating peripheral displays: An analysis using activity theory. *Human–Computer Interaction Journal*, 22(1):221–261.

McCrickard DS, Catrambone R, Chewar CM, Stasko JT (2003a) Establishing tradeoffs that leverage attention for utility: Empirically evaluating information display in notification systems. *International Journal of Human–Computer Studies*, 8(5):547–582.

McCrickard DS, Chewar CM, Somervell JP, Ndiwalana A (2003b) A model for notification systems evaluation – Assessing user goals for multitasking activity. *ACM Transactions on Computer-Human Interaction*, 10(4):312–338.

Mynatt ED, Back M, Want R, Baer M, Ellis JB (1998) Designing audio aura. *Proceedings of the SIGCHI Conference on Human Factors in Computing Systems (CHI)*, 566–573. ACM Press, New York.

Nielsen J (1993) *Usability Engineering.* Academic Press, London.

Parsowith S, Fitzpatrick G, Kaplan S, Segall B, Boot J (1998) Tickertape: Notification and communication in a single line. *Proceedings of the Third Asian Pacific Computer and Human interaction (APCHI)*, 139–144. IEEE Computer Society.

Pedersen ER, Sokoler T (1997) AROMA: Abstract representation of presence supporting mutual awareness. *Proceedings of the SIGCHI Conference on Human Factors in Computing Systems (CHI)*, 51–58. ACM Press, New York.

Preece J, Rogers Y, Sharp H, Benyon D, Holland S, Carey T (1994) *Human Computer Interaction.* Addison-Wesley, Wokingham.

Redström J, Skog T, Hallnäs L (2000) Informative art: Using amplified artworks as information displays. *Proceedings of the Conference on Designing Augmented Reality Environments (DARE)*, 103–114. ACM Press, New York.

Schneiderman B, Plaisant C (2004) *Designing the User Interface.* Addison-Wesley, Reading, MA.

Seffah A, Donyaee M, Kline RB, Padda HK (2006). Usability measurements and metrics: A consolidated model. *Software Qual Journal*, 14:159–178.

Shackel B (1991) Usability—Context, framework, definition, design and evaluation. In Shackel B, Richardson S (eds.), *Human Factors for Informatics Usability* (21–38). University Press, Cambridge.

Shami NS, Leshed G, Klein D (2005) Context of use evaluation of peripheral displays. *Proceedings of the Tenth IFIP TC13 International Conference on Human Computer Interaction (INTERACT)*, 579–587. Springer, Berlin.

Skog T, Ljungblad S, Holmquist LE (2003) Between aesthetics and utility: Designing ambient information visualizations. *IEEE Symposium on Information Visualization (INFOVIS)*, 233–240. IEEE Computer Society, Seattle, WA.

Stasko J, Mccolgin D, Miller T, Plaue C, Pousman Z (2005) *Evaluating the InfoCanvas Peripheral Awareness System: A Longitudinal, In Situ Study.* (Technical Report GIT-GVU-05-08). Georgia Institute of Technology, Atlanta, GA.

Van Dantzich M, Robbins D, Horvitz E, Czerwinski M (2002) Scope: Providing awareness of multiple notifications at a glance. *Proceedings of the Working Conference on Advanced Visual Interfaces (AVI)*. ACM Press, New York.

Weiser M, Brown JS (1996) Designing calm technology. *PowerGrid Journal*, 1(1).

Zhang L, Tu N, Vronay D (2005) Info-Lotus: A peripheral visualization for email notification. *Extended Abstracts of the SIGCHI Conference on Human Factors in Computing Systems (CHI)*, 1901–1904. ACM Press, New York.

Chapter 20
Measuring Affective Benefits and Costs of Mediated Awareness: Development and Validation of the ABC-Questionnaire

Wijnand IJsselsteijn, Joy van Baren, Panos Markopoulos, Natalia Romero and Boris de Ruyter

20.1 Introduction

The interactions and relationships we have with other people form an essential social network that supports us and adds meaning to our lives. This well-known fact is illustrated by the massive success of communication media such as e-mail, mobile telephony, and text messaging and the massive adoption of social networking applications such as Facebook and Twitter.

This basic insight can be traced back to the days of Aristotle, or even earlier. Maslov's theory of human needs, formulated in the 1950s, illustrates that social interaction is essential to satisfying human needs at several levels, in particular needs for belonging, love, and esteem, although even at the more basic levels of physiological and safety needs, communication and coordination is essential to mental and physical well-being, and ultimately survival (see, e.g., House et al. 1988).

Reflecting this sentiment, Schutz (1966)describes three basic human needs in his interpersonal needs theory: inclusion, control, and affection. Inclusion refers to the need for the company and recognition of others, to 'establish and maintain a feeling of mutual interest with other people' (p. 18). It allows one to feel significant and worthwhile. Control refers to the need to feel a competent, responsible person and to establish a feeling of mutual respect for the competence and responsibleness of others. Affection is the need to form emotionally close relationships with other human beings, to establish and maintain a feeling of mutual affection, to love and be loved.

Baumeister and Leary (1995) argue in their belongingness hypothesis that 'human beings have a pervasive drive to form and maintain at least a minimum quantity of lasting, positive, and significant interpersonal relationships.' They stress that this drive cannot be satisfied by frequent interactions with strangers but, rather,

W. IJsselsteijn (✉)

Eindhoven University of Technology, Department of Industrial Engineering & Innovation Sciences, Den Dolech 2, 5612 AZ Eindhoven, Eindhoven, The Netherlands
e-mail: W.A.IJsselsteijn@tue.nl

P. Markopoulos et al. (eds.), *Awareness Systems*, Human-Computer Interaction Series, DOI 10.1007/978-1-84882-477-5_20, © Springer-Verlag London Limited 2009

it requires a context of stable, affective relationships. In other words, we are motivated by a profound need to cultivate relationships with other people in order to feel worthwhile and understood, and to express feelings such as friendship and love. The forming, maintaining, and enhancing of such relationships is one of the most powerful drives for humans to engage in communication.

Traditionally, this need has been addressed in the most natural way, which is face-to-face. We have meetings, either by chance or pre-arranged, in which we exchange information about our lives, engage in casual chat or share emotions. Communication technology affords mediated interactions, which broaden our communication horizon significantly. Our changing lifestyles, including families dispersing over larger areas, elderly living alone, and increased business travel, further underline the need for effective mediated communication. However, convenient as it may be when time or distance limits the opportunities for face-to-face meetings, there are severe doubts as to whether mediated communication can afford the same affective characteristics as face-to-face communication.

Many of our current communication systems were initially designed for industrial settings, and therefore primarily support the exchange of functional information. The Internet, for instance, was developed for communication between professionals (researchers and programmers in the United States Defense Department), but has now become a household technology which is used more often for interpersonal communication than for information or entertainment purposes (Kraut et al., 1998).

As Kuwabara et al. (2002) point out, an important distinction can be drawn between content-oriented communication and connectedness-oriented communication (a notion akin to phatic interactions described in Chapter 7). Whereas the former is focused on the exchange of information, the latter is aimed at maintaining relationships and fostering a sense of connectedness. For this latter goal, the knowledge that someone has thought of you and made the effort to communicate with you is often more important than the actual content of the message.

An increasing set of communication media explicitly designed to support connectedness-oriented communication. Popular examples include media and social networking applications like those mentioned above and an emerging class of systems supporting social awareness between family or friends. Well-known research prototypes include GeorgiaTech's Digital Family Portrait (Mynatt et al., 2001), Intel's related CareNet display (Consolvo et al., 2004), Presence Displays by Dey and De Guzman (2006), as well as the ASTRA prototype (Markopoulos et al., 2004; Romero et al., 2007). In this volume, systems of this ilk are the Emotinet of Chapter 12, the Diarist system of Chapter 15, and the Whereabouts clock of Chapter 18, or the social feedback displays of Chapter 14.

It is only recently that empirical research has begun documenting whether such systems can deliver the affective benefits their creators and proponents anticipate. A reason for this scarcity of results it that to date, only in a few occasions researchers have attempted to deployed and evaluated awareness systems for non-work-related purposes. As a result, little is known about the affective benefits that such systems deliver to their users. In fact, this is true for most traditional communication media; these have been extensively studied but related investigations typically do not address the affective outcomes of communication. For example, do people think about each other more after sending or receiving an e-mail? Do they feel more involved in each other's lives if they use instant messaging on a regular basis? Do they feel connected with each other while talking through the telephone, and how long does this feeling linger on after the conversation has been ended? Until now, there has been a lack of research instruments allowing us to answer these and related questions.

In this chapter, we describe the development and validation of a measurement instrument that is sensitive to measuring affective benefits and costs of communication. In the next section we explain the concept of social presence and its relevance to communication media. Subsequently, we introduce the concept of connectedness as a way to address some of the limitations inherent in the social presence concept. We then proceed to describe the development of our questionnaire measure assessing affective costs and benefits of communication, also known as the ABC-Questionnaire. Finally, we will relate the results of two studies in which the questionnaire was applied, in order to draw conclusions about its sensitivity, reliability, and validity.

20.1.1 Social Presence and Media Richness

Traditional assessments of communication media have often focused on social presence measurement. In their pioneering work, Short et al. (1976) conceptualize social presence as a way to analyze mediated communications. Their central hypothesis is that communication media vary in their degree of social presence and that these variations are important in determining the way individuals interact through the medium. For example, they hypothesize that users will choose a medium to accommodate the level of social presence which is desired based on the purpose of the interaction.

Media capacity theories, such as social presence theory and media richness theory (Daft and Lengel, 1984), are based on the premise that media have different capacities to carry interpersonal communicative cues. Theorists place the array of audio–visual communication media available to us today along a continuum ranging from face-to-face interaction at the richer, more social end and written communication at the less rich, less social end. Richer media are traditionally considered to be those that enable the transmission and display of nonverbal communicative cues. In face-to-face communication, the nonverbal channels are continuously attended to and communicate information that is primarily affective in quality and connected with personal relationships.

More recently, Biocca et al. (2003) have made significant advances in developing a more comprehensive theory of social presence. In line with most other definitions, they define social presence as a 'sense of being with another in a mediated environment.' They continue their shorthand definition by stating that 'social presence is the moment-to-moment awareness of co-presence of a mediated body and the sense of accessibility of the other being's psychological, emotional, and intentional states.' Importantly, they distinguish three distinct levels of social presence. Level one is the perceptual level – primarily the detection and awareness of the co-presence of the other's mediated body. The second, or subjective, level entails the sense that the user has of the awareness of the other, and the level of accessibility to the other's attentional engagement, emotional state, comprehension, and behavioral interaction. The third level is a dynamic, intersubjective level. It is comprised of the user's sense of the other's sense of social presence of them, i.e., the perceived symmetry of social presence. These theoretical concepts have been translated into a questionnaire measure, known as the Networked Minds Measure of Social Presence.

Social presence has been a widely applied metric in assessing for instance the effects of video communication (e.g., Freeman et al., 2003), avatar realism (e.g., Nowak and Biocca, 2003), computers as social actors (e.g., Lee and Nass, 2003), collaborative virtual environments (e.g., Xu et al., 2002), and other instances relevant to current communication media.

20.1.2 Social Connectedness

Returning to awareness systems, their aim is often simply to help people to stay in touch, i.e., to be reassured about the well-being of others, to let others share your experiences, or to let someone know you are thinking of him/her. Such systems fit into the category of connectedness-oriented communication as defined by Kuwabara et al. (2002), since the informational content of the message can be of secondary importance to the emotional, relational content that is being transmitted. What is important to note here is that the concept of social presence may not be the most appropriate and certainly not the only applicable metric. In effect, when considering the theoretical framework outlined by Biocca et al. (2003), discussed previously, the most basic level of perceptual awareness is almost absent in many current instances of awareness systems. From a media richness point of view, awareness systems can be very poor, and social presence measured along richness dimensions will be low. Yet the sense of social connectedness, the feeling of being in touch with the other, can be strong and the experience highly appealing.

A similar point can be made for more traditional media such as postcards. Postcards are highly valued by both the sender and the receiver, because they are perceived as very personal and have an appealing surprise effect. They are almost like a small present, which can be kept as a permanent reminder of the person who sent it. Another example of a 'lean,' low realism communication medium is SMS, which has been a huge and unanticipated success in interpersonal mediated communication for social purposes. It would be quite difficult to defend that the emotional impact of postcards and SMS can be attributed to feelings of social presence that they would evoke in their users. Both media are asynchronous and text-based, which places them at the low end of the media richness continuum.

Summarizing, it appears that social presence, though highly relevant for a number of media interfaces that emulate face-to-face communication, is insufficient for characterizing the full spectrum of feelings and experiences associated with mediated communication, and thus new concepts and methods are needed. This wider perspective is adopted by Liechti and Ichikawa (1999), who developed the notion of 'affective awareness,' defined as a 'general sense of being in touch with one's friends and family.' However, the exact nature of this feeling, how to achieve it, and how to assess it remain unexplored to date.

In line with van Bel et al. (2008), we define social connectedness as a positive emotional appraisal of the quality (level of intimacy) and quantity (network size) of interactions within ongoing social relationships. There are two main aspects of connectedness that significantly distinguish the concept from social presence. First, whereas social presence is a perceptual illusion which is directly caused by (and therefore temporally bound to) mediated contacts, connectedness is an emotional experience which is only indirectly influenced by the actual moment of a contact. Second, social presence arises when two or more users of a medium perceive that they are really together, in each other's physical vicinity, sharing the same space; in short, when they have the illusion that the communication medium has disappeared. This illusion ends immediately when the moment of contact has ended. Connectedness is of an entirely different nature: the crucial aspects here are mutual feelings of emotional involvement, thinking about each other, and staying in touch. These feelings, though they are fostered by contacts, do not necessarily disappear after a contact is ended, but may linger on in the background more or less permanently. In short, connectedness is the subjective appreciation of the social–emotional distance within one's intimate social network.

After an extensive review of the available literature, we found the aspects described above lacking from current media assessment methods. This prompted us to develop a new measurement instrument: a questionnaire addressing the affective costs and benefits of communication. Although at present, various authors have noted the importance of affective aspects in communication (e.g., Liechti and Ichikawa, 1999; Mynatt et al., 2001; Hindus et al., 2001; Kuwabara et al., 2002; Hutchinson et al., 2003), there has been little attempt at developing reliable and valid tools that allow measurement of such aspects in a quantifiable way. This limits systematic progress in the field, as it will be very difficult to compare competing design alternatives or even existing systems to each other in an objective way. Although we certainly recognize the value of qualitative methods in exploring unfamiliar or complex behaviors (and make extensive use of such methods ourselves), we also feel that a properly validated quantitative measurement tool provides a valuable and necessary operationalization. Such a tool allows for a significant disambiguation of the construct under study, limiting the role of subjective interpretation on the part of the experimenter, and enabling a comparison of results between different systems and studies.

20.2 Construction of the ABC-Questionnaire

20.2.1 Initial Development of the ABC-Q

A difficulty we initially encountered in the development of a questionnaire measure was a lack of relevant and commonly accepted literature that could underpin the process of generating items. To produce alternative starting points, we conducted a brainstorm session with five people working in the area of awareness systems and communication research. Original input to this brainstorm was existing literature on awareness, the results of an e-mail questionnaire about connectedness (Van Lanen, 2003), and a requirements study carried out in the context of the ASTRA project (reported in Romero et al., 2003). Each participant generated a number of aspects that he or she thought the questionnaire should address. These aspects were consequently grouped in an affinity diagram, which is a tool for organizing large amounts of information, in order to identify main themes. The resulting 10 main themes were Privacy, Obligations, Expectations, Effort, Thinking about each other, Situational awareness, Staying in touch, Sharing experiences, Recognition, and Group attraction. We identified two main dimensions: the first four themes can be seen as Costs of communication, whereas the latter six relate to Benefits. We named the questionnaire the Affective Benefits and Costs in Communication Questionnaire (ABC-Q).

For each theme except Group Attraction, a scale consisting of six questions was generated based on the brainstorm results. For group attraction, we found an existing questionnaire (Evans and Jarvis, 1986), from which we took the six items that were most appropriate to our situation, and incorporated them in our questionnaire. All items have a seven-point scale, which runs from 'strongly agree' to 'strongly disagree.'

The first version of the ABC-Q was reviewed by two experts on questionnaire design. They were asked to check whether items were understandable and had face validity, meaning that they appeared to measure the intended concept. On their advice, two items were removed from the questionnaire because they were unsuitable, and the wording of five items was slightly changed to make them clearer.

A pilot test was conducted to gather data for the item selection. Twenty participants (students and employees of Eindhoven University of Technology) completed the questionnaire, which now contained 58 items, regarding their communication with family members in the preceding week. The goal was to reduce the number of items to 40, i.e., four per scale. Criteria to remove items were as follows:

- The item did not contribute sufficiently to the scale (low/negative item-total correlation).
- Cronbach's alpha would improve when the item was removed.
- An item did not discriminate (low variance and/or extreme mean).

The reliability of the Effort scale turned out to be very low. A closer look at the inter-item correlations suggested that this scale was multidimensional. A short

Table 20.1 Reliability of the first version of the ABC-Q (40 items)

Scale	Alpha
ABC-Q	**.86**
Costs	**.64**
Obligations	.41
Expectations	.73
(Threats to) privacy	.76
Benefits	**.88**
Thinking about each other	.70
Situational awareness	.84
Sharing experiences	.81
Staying in touch	.58
Recognition	.72
Group attraction	.84

interview with several respondents confirmed that effort is a complex concept; it can be positive in one situation and negative in another. This observation was confirmed by the results of the requirements study, in which participants reported different types of effort. In the initial development of the ABC-Q we chose to remove the Effort scale from the questionnaire and address the concept using interviews. We will, however, return to the concepts of process and personal effort in our treatment of the revised version of the ABC-Q.

The internal consistency of the other scales ranged from sufficient ($\alpha = .41$) to good ($\alpha = .84$). The questionnaire as a whole showed an excellent internal consistency ($\alpha = .86$). Alpha values of all subscales, the two dimensions, and the whole questionnaire can be found in Table 20.1.

20.2.2 Validation Study

The ABC-Q was first applied in a field test conducted in the context of the ASTRA project. In this project, a prototypical awareness system was developed to help distributed family members to stay in touch with each other by sharing moments of their daily life in the form of pictures, drawings, and short text messages (Markopoulos, et al., 2004; Romero et al., 2007). The field test aimed to evaluate how people experienced the usage of this system in their daily life. This study offered an excellent opportunity to investigate whether the newly developed ABC-Q would yield sensible and stable results.

Two families, both distributed over two separate households, took part in the field test. In total, 13 people participated, consisting of 7 adults, 4 teenagers, and 2 children. The children were too young to complete the questionnaires, therefore questionnaire data were gathered from 11 participants.

A repeated measures design was used, consisting of two phases that lasted 1 week each. In the first week, communication between two related households using existing communication means was studied. In the second week, the ASTRA system was introduced in both households. In both the first and the second week, group interviews were conducted. Participants also kept a diary and completed two questionnaires: the IPO-SPQ measuring social presence (de Greef and IJsselsteijn, 2001), and the original, 40 item version of the ABC-Q. In this chapter, only results which are relevant for the evaluation of the ABC-Q will be discussed. For a more extensive description of results, see Romero et al. (2007).

The mean scores for all scales of the ABC-Q are shown in Fig. 20.1. The Wilcoxon test was used to test for significant differences between scores. The results show that the first three scales, relating to Costs, do not differ significantly between the first and the second week. The scales related to Benefits, however, show some marked differences. Participants thought about each other more often in the second week, when they were using the ASTRA system ($Z = -2.67$, $p = .008$). Also, their awareness of the situation of their family members was much higher ($Z = -2.31$, $p = .021$). Participants indicated they felt more connected to each other in the second week ($Z = -2.02$, $p = .043$). They also felt they were sharing more experiences with each other ($Z = -2.38$, $p = .011$). The level of group attraction was higher in the second week ($Z = -2.23$, $p = .026$). Recognition, finally, was slightly higher in the second week but this difference was not significant.

These results are in line with the hypothesized advantages of awareness systems, and as such also provide a basis for construct validity of the ABC-Q. As a further procedure to test the validity of the ABC-Q, we gathered qualitative interview data after the field test was finished. Participants reported that they felt more in touch with each other in the second week. They thought about each other more often,

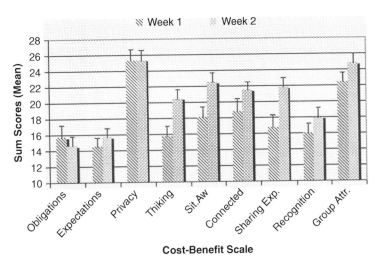

Fig. 20.1 Mean scores on the ABC-Q in the first and the second week of the field test. (Note: For all scales, the minimum score is 4 and the maximum score is 28)

were more aware of what their family members were doing, and could share more of their own experiences. Many remarks were made that support this. Some illustrative quotations:

> There was more involvement, more curiosity. I was thinking about them much more than usual.
> You become more conscious of what your family members are doing, and you also become curious.
> It is so good to see what they are doing. I always want to stay in touch, but I normally don't have the time. Now it is easier.
> It was fantastic to keep them up-to-date.

We see that there is a considerable agreement between these qualitative data and quantitative data as obtained by the ABC-Q, where affective benefits in week 2 were significantly higher than affective benefits in week 1 (with the exception of Recognition, which was non-significant), without any significant increase in affective costs from week 1 to week 2. The qualitative results from both diaries and interviews thus provide some evidence for convergent validity of the ABC-Q.

20.2.3 Extending the Questionnaire

Although the ABC-Q proved to be valuable and promising instrument, we felt that it still had certain conceptual shortcomings.

First of all, the concept of effort, which was originally omitted because of its ambiguity, was disambiguated and re-incorporated in the questionnaire. We added a 'process effort' scale in the costs dimension, and a 'personal effort' scale in the benefits dimension. Process effort is an investment on the part of the sender which is not appreciated as a meaningful effort on the part of the receiver. Personal effort, on the other hand, is seen and appreciated by the receiver as a meaningful part of the communication. For example, when sending a postcard, the effort of selecting a nice card and writing a personal message on the back will likely be appreciated. On the other hand, the effort associated with buying a stamp, or looking for a pen to write with, are unlikely to be appreciated by the receiver. By adding these different types of effort to both sides of the equation, we feel we have found a way of overcoming the limitation of the early ABC-Q of not including any items on effort due to the ambiguous nature of this concept.

Furthermore, each scale was extended with reciprocal items, addressing the user's perception of the feelings of his/her communication partner(s). For example, the item 'I feel involved in the other person's life' was matched by the item '(I think that) the other person feels involved in my life.' A similar approach was advocated by Biocca et al. (2003) in developing their Networked Minds Social Presence Questionnaire. Reciprocity is a fundamental element of awareness, as it is not merely our own feelings toward our communication partners, but also our assessment of how well we are appreciated, loved and recognized by others that drives our affective assessment of communication, very much in line with the interpersonal

Table 20.2 Reliability of the extended version of the ABC-Q (60 items)

Scale	Alpha
ABC-Q	**.96**
Costs	**.87**
Obligations	.75
Expectations	.88
(Threats to) privacy	.77
Process effort	.65
Benefits	**.96**
Personal effort	.79
Thinking about each other	.80
Sharing experiences	.86
Staying in touch	.85
Recognition	.92
Group attraction	.91

needs theory (Schutz, 1966) and the need to belong (Baumeister and Leary, 1995), as discussed in the Introduction.

Finally, the scales Situational awareness, and Sharing experiences were merged into one scale. This was done because the content of the items was very similar and a high correlation between these two scales indicated that they measured the same construct.

After these changes, the questionnaire contained 10 scales, consisting of eight items each; four items about the user's own feelings, and four items about the user's perception of the feelings of his/her communication partner. Since 80 items makes quite a lengthy questionnaire, we decided to try to reduce the number of items to a maximum of 60.

A pilot study was carried out in order to inform the item selection. Twenty-three participants (students and employees of Eindhoven University of Technology) completed the questionnaire regarding their communication with family members in the preceding week by e-mail, mobile phone, or SMS. Criteria to remove items were identical to those described in the previous section.

The internal consistency of all scales of the new version, after reducing the number of items to 60, ranged from satisfactory ($\alpha = .65$) to excellent ($\alpha = .92$). The new version of the ABC-Q showed higher alpha values for all subscales than the original version. The questionnaire as a whole showed an excellent internal consistency ($\alpha = .96$). Alpha values of all subscales, the two dimensions, and the whole questionnaire can be found in Table 20.2.

20.3 Conclusions

Although the ABC-Q is a measure that is still being refined, the results obtained thus far imply that the ABC-Q already is a useful measure. The initial pilot testing during the development phase has shown that the ABC-Q is a reliable measure, showing excellent internal consistency. In the field test, the ABC-Q proved to be sensitive to changes in condition (in our case, the introduction of the ASTRA Assessment system) in line with hypothesized effects, thereby providing first evidence for its construct validity. Moreover, the correspondence between the ABC-Q scores and the interviews is striking and encouraging, providing a basis for convergent validity of the measure.

The ABC-Q and its scoring guidelines are included as an Appendix to this chapter. An electronic copy of the formatted questionnaire can be obtained from the first author.

Acknowledgments   The development of the ABC-Q has been supported by the European Commission through the FP5 FET ASTRA Assessment Project (IST-2001-39270), and the FP6 FET ASTRA STREP (IST-2004-29266). The initial development of the ABC-Q has been previously presented at the 6th Annual International Workshop on Presence (PRESENCE 2003; van Baren et al., 2003) and at the 3rd Workshop on Social Intelligence Design (SID 2004; van Baren et al., 2004).

Appendix: The ABC-Questionnaire

Introductory Instructions

On the following pages you will be asked questions about you experiences regarding communication with your [target group, e.g., family members] using [medium, e.g., mobile phone].

There are no right or wrong answers; we are interested in your personal opinions and experiences. Do not think about questions for a long time, but try to rely on your first reaction.

Some questions ask you about the experiences of your [target group]. We are interested in your view on their feelings and experiences, so it is no problem if you are not sure about this. Just try to give the answer that you think is most suitable.

The Questionnaire

The ABC items are presented below in mixed order. Agreement with the statements presented should be scored on a Likert scale, e.g., from 1 (Strongly Disagree) to 7 (Strongly Agree).

1. I feel obliged to contact the other.
2. After a contact the other keeps thinking about me for a long time.
3. I find it difficult to infer from a contact how the other is doing.
4. I feel that the contacts with the other take a lot of time.
5. The contacts keep the other informed about important events in my life.
6. The other feels part of a group because of the contacts.
7. The other finds it difficult to stay in touch with me through this medium.

8. I try to make a contact feel special for the other.
9. If I contact the other, I expect him/her to respond.
10. The other experiences the contacts as an invasion of his/her privacy.
11. The other knows what I feel during a contact.
12. The other can easily avoid a contact if s/he wants to.
13. The contacts keep me informed about important events in the other's life.
14. I find it easy to keep to myself those things that I don't want to share.
15. I expect the other to contact me regularly.
16. The other hardly invests energy in the contacts.
17. During the day I regularly think back to a contact with the other.
18. The contacts make me feel involved in what is happening in our group.
19. The other finds it important that a contact feels valuable for me.
20. This medium helps me to keep contact with the other.
21. The other is disappointed if I don't contact him/her for a long time.
22. I find it difficult to share experiences with the other through this medium.
23. The contacts make the other feel a sense of unity in our group.
24. Through our contacts, the other learns more about me than I would like him/her to know.
25. The other puts effort into making a contact nice for me.
26. The contacts make me feel involved in the other's life.
27. The other could do some more effort to contact me.
28. Because of the contacts the other can identify with me.
29. If the other contacts me, I feel that I should respond.
30. Aside from our contacts, the other hardly thinks about me.
31. I feel part of a group because of the contacts.
32. The other expects me to contact him/her regularly.
33. I put effort into making a contact nice for the other.
34. Aside from our contacts, I hardly think about the other
35. The other finds it easy to keep to him/herself those things that s/he doesn't want to share.
36. I know what the other feels during a contact.
37. Because of the contacts the other knows how I am doing.
38. I hardly invest energy in the contacts.
39. The contacts make the other feel involved in my life.
40. The other feels obliged to contact me.
41. I am disappointed if the other doesn't contact me for a long time.
42. The other tries to make a contact feel special for me.
43. The other finds it difficult to share experiences with me through this medium.
44. The contacts make me feel a sense of unity in our group.
45. After a contact I keep thinking about the other for a long time.
46. The other feels that the contacts with me take a lot of time.
47. I find it difficult to stay in touch with the other through this medium.
48. Through our contacts, I learn more about the other than s/he would like me to know.

49. Because of the contacts I can identify with the other.
50. If I contact the other, s/he feels that s/he should respond.
51. If the other contacts me, s/he expects me to respond.
52. The contacts make the other person feel involved in what is happening in our group.
53. I experience the contacts as an invasion of my privacy.
54. The other finds it difficult to infer from a contact how I am doing.
55. I find it important that a contact feels valuable for the other.
56. During the day the other regularly thinks back to a contact with me.
57. I could do some more effort to contact the other.
58. I can easily avoid a contact if I want to.
59. Because of the contacts I know how the other is doing.
60. This medium helps the other to keep contact with me.

Scoring Instructions

The ABC-Q (Affective Benefits and Costs in Communication – Questionnaire) consists of 10 scales, which can be grouped into two main dimensions: Benefits of Communication and Costs of Communication. Each scale includes six items, three of which address the respondent's own feelings, and three of which address the respondent's perception of the feelings of his/her communication partner(s).

Total scores for each scale can be calculated by adding the responses of the six items in that scale. Therefore, each scale has a maximum value of 42 and a minimum value of 6.

It is also possible to calculate subscales for the respondent's own feelings and the respondent's perception of the feelings of his/her communication partner(s), if this is meaningful in the context of the study.

Most scales contain both indicative and contra-indicative items. Therefore, the following items should be recoded: 3, 7, 12, 14, 16, 22, 27, 30, 34, 35, 38, 43, 47, 54, 57, 58.

Recoding means that the responses to an item should be 'mirrored,' which can be done by replacing response 1 with response 7, 2 with 6, 3 with 5, 5 with 3, 6 with 2, and 7 with 1.

Below, an overview is given of the dimensions, scales, and subscales of the ABC-Q.

Benefits of Communication

Personal Effort
    Respondent's own feelings: 8, 33, 55
    Perception of other's feelings: 19, 25, 42
Thinking about each other
    Respondent's own feelings: 17, 34, 45
    Perception of other's feelings: 2, 30, 56

Sharing Experiences
   Respondent's own feelings: 13, 22, 59
   Perception of other's feelings: 5, 37, 43
Staying in Touch
   Respondent's own feelings: 20, 26, 47
   Perception of other's feelings: 7, 39, 60
Recognition
   Respondent's own feelings: 3, 36, 49
   Perception of other's feelings: 11, 28, 54
Group Attraction
   Respondent's own feelings: 18, 31, 44
   Perception of other's feelings: 6, 23, 52

Cost of Communication

Obligations
   Respondent's own feelings: 1, 29, 58
   Perception of other's feelings: 12, 40, 50
Expectations
   Respondent's own feelings: 9, 15, 41
   Perception of other's feelings: 21, 32, 51
Invasion of Privacy
   Respondent's own feelings: 14, 24, 53
   Perception of other's feelings: 10, 35, 48
Process Effort
   Respondent's own feelings: 4, 38, 57
   Perception of other's feelings: 16, 27, 46

References

Baumeister, R.F., and Leary, M.R. (1995). The need to belong: Desire for interpersonal attachments as a fundamental human motivation. Psychological Bulletin, 117, 497–529.

Biocca, F., Harms, C., and Burgoon, J. (2003). Toward a more robust theory and measure of social presence: review and suggested criteria. Presence: Teleoperators and Virtual Environments, 12, 456–480.

Consolvo, S., Roessler, P., and Shelton, B.E. (2004). The CareNet display: Lessons learned from an in home evaluation of an ambient display. In: Davies, N. et al. (Eds.), Proceedings of UbiComp 2004, LNCS 3205, Nottingham: Springer, 1–17.

Daft, R.L., and Lengel, R.H. (1984). Information richness: A new approach to managerial behavior and organizational design. In: Cummings, L.L., and Staw, B.M. (Eds.), Research in organizational behavior 6, Homewood, IL: JAI Press, 191–233.

de Greef, P. and IJsselsteijn, W.A. (2001). Social presence in a home tele-application. CyberPsychology and Behavior, 4, 307–315.

Dey, A.K., and De Guzman, E.S. (2006). From awareness to connectedness: The design and deployment of presence displays. Proceedings of CHI 2006, New York: ACM Press, 899–908.

Evans, N., and Jarvis, P. (1986). The group attitude scale. Small Group Behavior, 17, 203–216.

Freeman, J., Lessiter, J., Schreer, O., and Kauff, P. (2003). Evaluation of the VIRTUE video-conference system using the ITC-sense of presence inventory. Proceedings of Presence 2003, Aalborg, Denmark.

Hindus, D., Mainwaring, S.D., Leduc, N., Hagström, A.E., and Bayley, O. (2001). Casablanca: Designing social communication devices for the home. Proceedings CHI, 325–332.

House, J.S., Landis, K.R., and Umberson, D. (1988). Social relationships and health. Science, 241, 540–545.

Hutchinson, H., Mackay, W., Westerlund, B., Bederson, B.B., Druin, A., Plaisant, C., Beaudoin-Lafon, M., Conversy, S., Evans, H., Hansen, H., Roussel, N., Eiderbäck, B., Lindquist, S., and Sundblad, Y. Technology probes: Inspiring design for and with families. Proceedings of CHI 2003, New York: ACM Press, 17–24.

Kraut, R., Mukhopadhyay, T., Szczypula, J., Kiesler, S., and Scherlis, W. (1998). Communication and information: Alternative uses of the Internet in households. Proceedings of CHI 1998, New York: ACM Press, 368–383.

Kuwabara, K., Watanabe, T., Ohguro, T., Itoh, Y., and Maeda, Y. (2002). Connectedness oriented communication: Fostering a sense of connectedness to augment social relationships. IPSJ Journal, 43, 3270–3279.

Lee, K.M., and Nass, C. (2003). Designing social presence of social actors in human computer interaction. In *Proceedings of the SIGCHI Conference on Human Factors in Computing Systems* (Ft. Lauderdale, Florida, USA, April 05-10, 2003). CHI '03. ACM, New York, NY, 289–296. DOI=http://doi.acm.org/10.1145/642611.642662.

Liechti, O., and Ichikawa, T. (1999). A digital photography framework supporting social interaction and affective awareness in home communication. Proceedings of the International Workshop on Handheld and Ubiquitous Computing 1999, London, UK, 186–192.

Markopoulos, P., Romero, N., van Baren, J., IJsselsteijn W.A., de Ruyter, B, and Farshchian, B (2004). Keeping in touch with the family: Home and away with the ASTRA awareness system. CHI Extended Abstracts 2004, New York: ACM Press, 1351–1354.

Mynatt, E.D., Rowan, J., Jacobs, A., and Craighill, S. (2001). Digital family portraits supporting peace of mind for extended family members, Proceedings of CHI 2001, CHI Letters 3(1), 333–340.

Nowak, K.L., and Biocca, F. (2003). The effect of the agency and anthropomorphism on users' sense of telepresence, copresence, and social presence in virtual environments. Presence: Tele-operators and Virtual Environments, 12, 2–35.

Romero, N., van Baren, J., Markopoulos, P., de Ruyter, B., and IJsselsteijn, W. (2003). Addressing interpersonal communication needs through ubiquitous connectivity: Home and away. In: Aarts, E., Collier, R., van Loenen, E., and de Ruyter, B. (Eds.), Ambient Intelligence. First European Symposium, EUSAI 2003, Lecture Notes in Computer Science, vol. 2875, New York: Springer Verlag, 419–429.

Romero, N., Markopoulos, P., van Baren, J., de Ruyter, B., IJsselsteijn, W.A., and Farchian, B. (2007). Connecting the family with awareness systems. Personal and Ubiquitous Computing 10(4), 299–312.

Schutz, W.C. (1966). *The interpersonal underworld.* Palo Alto, CA: Science & Behavior Book.

Short, J., Williams, E., and Christie, B. (1976). The Social Psychology of Telecommunications. John Wiley, London.

van Baren, J., IJsselsteijn, W.A., Markopoulos, P., Romero, N., de Ruyter, B. (2004). Measuring Affective Benefits and Costs of Awareness Systems Supporting Intimate Social Networks. In: Nijholt, A., and Nishida, T. (Eds.), Proceedings of 3rd workshop on social intelligence design. CTIT Workshop Proceedings Series WP04-02, 13–19.

van Baren, J., IJsselsteijn, W.A., Romero, N., Markopoulos, P., and de Ruyter, B. (2003). Affective Benefits in Communication: The development and field-testing of a new questionnaire measure. PRESENCE 2003, 6th Annual International Workshop on Presence, Aalborg, Denmark, 6–8 October 2003.

Van Bel, D. IJsselsteijn, W.A., and de Kort, Y.A.W. (2008). Interpersonal connectedness: Conceptualization and directions for a measurement instrument. CHI'08 Extended Abstracts, ACM 978-1-60558-012-8/08/04.

van Lanen, F. (2003). Staying in touch over distance: An exploration of the concept of connectedness. Unpublished Masters Thesis. Eindhoven University of Technology.

Xu, L.Q., Lei, B., and Hendriks, E. (2002). Vision for a 3-D visualisation and telepresence collaborative working environment. BT Technology Journal, 20(1), 64–74.

Index

Printed in the United States
By Bookmasters